"This b[illegible] [illegible]markable a[illegible]ent and [illegible] be the [illegible]e volume on modern African history for some [illegible] to come."

—International Affairs

"A number of introductions to African history aimed at the undergraduate and general reader have appeared in recent years. Reid's text stands out among these as an invaluable teaching-tool due to its concise but appealing tone, its clear style, and its sensitive treatment of Africa's often tumultuous past and contested present-day experiences. This is an excellent introduction to Africa for the student reader."

—History

"This is a comprehensive, appealing and highly-accessible history of modern Africa which portrays the continent's turbulent past and contested present in all its variety and complexity. Its combination of sound scholarship, clear writing and humane understanding make it an important contribution to understanding of recent African history."

—Bill Nasson, University of Cape Town

"This is the book for which I have been waiting. The author has done all of us a great service in providing such an effective teaching tool."

—Richard Waller, Bucknell University

A History of Modern Africa

Concise History of the Modern World

Covering the major regions of the world, each history in this series provides a vigorous interpretation of its region's past in the modern age. Informed by the latest scholarship, but assuming no prior knowledge, each author presents developments within a clear analytic framework. Unusually, the histories acknowledge the limitations of their own generalizations. Authors are encouraged to balance perspectives from the broad historical landscape with discussion of particular features of the past that may or may not conform to the larger impression. The aim is to provide a lively explanation of the transformations of the modern period and the interplay between long-term change and "defining moments" of history.

Published

A History of Modern Latin America
Teresa A. Meade

Forthcoming

A History of Modern East Asia
Charles Armstrong

Chosen Nation: A History of the American People since 1886
Maurice Isserman

Europe since 1815
Albert Lindemann

A History of Russia since 1700
Rex Wade

A History of Modern Africa
1800 to the Present

THIRD EDITION

Richard J. Reid

WILEY Blackwell

This edition first published 2020

Edition History
John Wiley & Sons Ltd (2e, 2012); Blackwell Publishing Ltd (1e, 2009)

Registered Office
John Wiley & Sons, Inc., 111 River Street, Hoboken, NJ 07030, USA

Editorial Office
John Wiley & Sons, Inc., 111 River Street, Hoboken, NJ 07030, USA

For details of our global editorial offices, customer services, and more information about Wiley products visit us at www.wiley.com.

Wiley also publishes its books in a variety of electronic formats and by print-on-demand. Some content that appears in standard print versions of this book may not be available in other formats.

Library of Congress Cataloging-in-Publication Data

Names: Reid, Richard J. (Richard James), author.
Title: A history of modern Africa : 1800 to the present / Richard J. Reid.
Description: Third edition. | Hoboken : Wiley, 2019. | Series: Concise history of the modern world | Includes index. |
Identifiers: LCCN 2019014831 (print) | LCCN 2019015533 (ebook) | ISBN 9781119381952 (Adobe PDF) | ISBN 9781119381778 (ePub) | ISBN 9781119381921 (pbk.)
Subjects: LCSH: Africa–History. | Africa–Historiography. | Africa–Colonization–History. | Decolonization–Africa–History. | Slave trade–History–Colonies.
Classification: LCC DT20 (ebook) | LCC DT20 .R45 2019 (print) | DDC 960.3–dc23
LC record available at https://lccn.loc.gov/2019014831

Cover image: © Robert Muckley / Getty Images
Cover design by Wiley

Set in 10/13pt Photina by SPi Global, Pondicherry, India
Printed and bound in Singapore by Markono Print Media Pte Ltd

10 9 8 7 6 5 4 3 2 1

Still for Anna and May, and now also for Thea.

Contents

List of Maps

List of Plates

Acknowledgments

Events can be relied upon to leave the historian looking either prescient or foolish. Either way, the best that can be done is what has been attempted here: to bring the narrative up to date, and to highlight, by expanding the references, the key scholarly trends, and at least some of the key literature. Once again, my thanks go to those fellow travelers who, responding to Wiley's request, anonymously provided feedback on the previous edition; to my own friends and colleagues who offered constructive comments, including on behalf of their own students; and to the editorial team at Wiley for proposing a new edition and supporting its completion. I have become even more painfully aware of the inherent weaknesses of a general history, but I am even more convinced, in an ever-changing world, of the need to attempt one. And the failings in this text remain, of course, my own.

Acknowledgments for the Second Edition

I am now more keenly aware than ever before what a vulnerable creation is a general history, especially one that runs to the present. Thanks go to Wiley-Blackwell for the opportunity to perform some reconstructive surgery. I am also grateful to both published reviewers and providers of less formal feedback on the first edition for their suggestions and comments. As ever, the flaws are mine.

Acknowledgments for the First Edition

Whatever merits this book has are in large part thanks to the many people who have educated, inspired, and assisted the author in a myriad of ways over a number of years. These are too many to list in full here. But I should like to record my gratitude to just a few of them. Christopher Wheeler, now at Oxford University Press, suggested the book while he was still at Blackwell, and I am very grateful to him for the opportunity; Tessa Harvey and Gillian Kane at Wiley-Blackwell have been a pleasure to work with. Heartfelt thanks go to Richard Waller and an anonymous reviewer for their comments on an earlier draft. Murray Last, Robin Law, John McCracken, and Andrew Roberts have taught me more than they realize. Friends and colleagues at the University of Asmara in Eritrea and at Durham University and the School of Oriental and African Studies in the UK provided environments conducive to conceptualization and writing. Friends in eastern Africa have been both inspirational and questioning. Any remaining inadequacies are my responsibility.

1 Introduction

Understanding the Contours of Africa's Past

The stories of entire continents cannot adequately be told in single-volume histories. It is a matter of debate, indeed, why individual (or groups of) historians actually do what they do, and even more so, what it is that they aim to achieve. But in a volume such as this, the aim is – indeed, can only be – to grasp key ideas and apply them broadly; to appreciate thematic coherence while equally recognizing discord in this regard; to identify overall processes while paying due attention to the individuals and whirlpools that make up the great flow of human history. It is a sad but inevitable truth that in writing wide-ranging survey histories of peoples – even where, as in this one, the timeframe is carefully capped – the number of individual lives which are mentioned is infinitesimal, *vis-à-vis* the millions of lives which are actually lived. Yet above all the aim in a book like this is to do justice to Africa and Africans. If this is even approached, then the author can be, if not content, then at least somewhat relieved.

This book is concerned with the past two centuries, a timeframe that is not simply a matter of organizational convenience: rather, the central idea is that Africa's twentieth century cannot be understood in isolation from its nineteenth century and that transformative processes – political, social, and economic – span the entire period under examination and are distinctive to it.[1] We return to this later. More broadly, it is important, at the outset, to elucidate some of the core themes which run through the narrative, whether explicitly or implicitly. The continent remained underpopulated until the second half of the twentieth century, and thus, a host of states and societies were concerned first and foremost with the maximization of numbers.[2] As a result, African ideologies were frequently centered around the celebration of fertility, and myths of creation around the carving of civilization out of wilderness, and its subsequent defence against Nature. Fertility and reproductive capacity were sought through

A History of Modern Africa: 1800 to the Present, Third Edition. Richard J. Reid.

polygamy; control of people – frequently through the practice of slavery, for example – was more significant as a feature of social organization than control of land, which was plentiful, with a handful of important exceptions, as we shall see. Thus, for example, West African history is characterized by frequently violent competition for women because women underpinned male status, worked land, and produced children who would do likewise. Across the continent more generally, intergenerational conflict among men over women was common. Marriage was very much a public rather than a private affair, involving alliances between lineages; the distribution of women represented sociopolitical arrangements. Of course the status of women themselves varied greatly across the continent, ranging from low and exploited, to respected, influential, and economically independent.[3]

One of the major challenges for ruling elites across the continent – in the nineteenth century as in more recent decades – was the construction of permanent systems of governance by which large numbers of people might be controlled. Underpopulated regions in particular were often characterized by the instability of the polity and by the failure of would-be state-builders to extend their control beyond the "natural" limits imposed by demography and geography. In underpopulated areas, discontented people might rebel against the existing order – forming an "armed frontier" which might march on the center, or otherwise consume it – but they might just as easily migrate beyond the reach of that order, in so doing often causing its very downfall.[4] This constant cycle of violent fission and fusion drove much political and social change in Africa, and it was an increasingly violent process in the nineteenth century with the emergence of new polities and social systems. Territorial states with ambitions beyond the immediate community had to overcome the problem of how to ensure loyalty across a wider area and how to create supra-provincial identities. The problem is exemplified by the situation in the West African savannah, where states and empires have historically been confronted with localism and segmentation. The savannah was characterized by countless local communities, groups of villages which formed miniature states, known as *kafu*; the *kafu* symbolized the localism of African politics, and empire-builders had both to construct their polities around them, and to dominate them through military force and control of wealth.[5] Again, this was as true in the colonial and post-colonial eras as it was in the nineteenth century. Throughout the book, then, we are concerned with the emergence of identities, local, regional, even continental, over time, and the dynamics involved in the shaping of those identities.

In understanding the continent's history over the past two centuries, moreover, due emphasis needs to be placed on the *longue durée* as well as on dramatic change; there has been much continuity as well as upheaval between the eighteenth and the twenty-first centuries, and in many respects colonialism – the focus of the bulk of Africanist scholarship in recent decades[6] – constituted a mere "moment" in time, with a variable impact across the continent. Firstly, Africa's nineteenth century was a period of violent reformation, of political destruction and reconstruction, and the effects of this prolonged transformation continued to be felt deep into the twentieth century and beyond, especially during, and in the wake of, decolonization. Secondly, these internal processes of change need to be understood at least partly against the backdrop of emerging patterns of external economic relations – in essence, between Africa and the northern Atlantic economies – in the course of the nineteenth century. In many respects, colonial rule was only the latest manifestation of a Westernized commercial system – fundamentally disadvantageous, in terms of modern ideas about development, to African producers, though not necessarily to the elites who governed them – which long pre-dated it. Colonialism, then, was clearly significant in its own terms, as will be demonstrated in the course of the story which follows. Arguably, it had the greatest impact through the manner of its departure, in the sense that it left much of the continent ill-equipped to deal with the challenges of independence. But colonial rule must be contextualized: with regard to internal political development, it was in many respects co-opted into ongoing African processes of change, while in terms of external economy it represented only the latest stage of a system which had been a long time in the making. What came after it – the era of the "post-colony" and the "new" international order – must be understood in terms of what preceded it. What is certainly clear is that colonial rule was in many ways as African as it was European, and cannot be understood as some great unilateral imposition: Africans shaped their own societies in the age of foreign rule much more effectively than any colonial official or European government could, even in the face of – and to a large extent in response to – an aggressively extractive external economic system.

Social, political, and economic change, moreover – as with every other human community – was represented in African art and material culture. This is not a subject to which this volume has been able to devote much space, unfortunately; nonetheless, suffice to observe here that aesthetic endeavors often provide vital clues to African political as well as culture life. Art was a mediation between the living and the dead, and thus often underpinned political power, as well as attempting to ensure agricultural prosperity; sculptures represented – as with story-telling – social and political commentary and critique. Belief in the supernatural and the afterlife shaped Egyptian art and architecture, as it did along much of the Nile valley, notably in Nubia; Christianity spurred artistic achievement in the Ethiopian highlands, and Islam did the same along the east African coast and across the western African savannah.[7] African craftsmen – working in terracotta, gold, copper, brass, bronze, wood, and stone – told stories of the formation of kingship, the struggle against Nature, and the quest for fecundity; they produced material cultures which were both aesthetically pleasing and had sociopolitical utility, as they projected ideas about group cohesion or reinforced hierarchy. The spread of artistic styles, moreover, was the result both of political upheaval – population movement on the back of the slave trade, for example, or of widespread conflict – and commercial interaction. Traders brought culture as well as commodities, and networks of artistic exchange opened up in the precolonial era just as trading systems did. Africans borrowed from one another and adapted styles accordingly; and so too did external influence come to have an important impact on local art forms? Islamic input, again, is evident in Swahili architecture, notably,[8] and later European colonialism influenced the form which African artistic expression took in certain areas.[9]

Indeed, another of the core issues that arises in a study of Africa in the nineteenth and twentieth centuries is the continent's relationship with the rest of the world in general, and of course Europe in particular. It is important that we appreciate, from the outset, the degree to which Africa has been judged, or measured, by the "outside world"; this has happened to a remarkable degree and continues to happen in much the same way, both subliminally and more consciously, down to the present day.[10] Clearly, important external influences have been brought to bear on African cultural, economic, and political development. Islam was the most important such influence before the nineteenth century, first coming to the continent through Egypt and the Red Sea, from whence it spread across the Maghreb, as well as traveling up the Nile valley into northern and central Sudan; it would become established in the Horn, too, in the Somali plains and the Ogaden. From northern Africa, it would move via trade routes into the Sudanic belt and across West Africa, where it remains the dominant faith today. In sub-Saharan East Africa, too, Islam was a critical component of Swahili civilization. Overall, Islam would shape African culture and society, linking swathes of the continent to a dynamic and expanding Muslim world. The coming of Islam also involved the emergence of a long-distance slave trade, across the Sahara and linking the continent to the Middle East, the Arabian peninsula, and the Indian Ocean.[11] European influence, arguably, was much less than that of Islam before the nineteenth century, certainly in terms of direct cultural and political change: missionary activity, for example, beginning with the Portuguese in the fifteenth and sixteenth centuries, had limited success, and white settlement was negligible outside the Dutch colony at the southern Cape. Europe was largely restricted to trading posts and forts on the coast. Europeans did, however, introduce new crops to Africa from the Americas, and cassava, maize, groundnuts, and tobacco became central to many African agricultural economies.[12] Europe's greatest impact on the continent prior to about 1800 came through the Atlantic slave trade, which began in the early sixteenth century and reached its height in the seventeenth and eighteenth. Initially, it was dominated by the Portuguese, but later, they were edged out by the Dutch, the Danes, the French, and the British, who transported millions of Africans – the precise figure is a matter of contention – to the Americas.

Yet these were no unilateral impositions; they were, rather, complex, and multifaceted interactions, involving mutual borrowing and adaptation. The influence of ancient (pre-Christian) Egyptian – and, by extension, upper Nile valley – culture and civilization on the Hellenistic world is undeniable, for example, despite European attempts to sever Egypt from the rest of Africa through much of the nineteenth and twentieth centuries.[13] Later, the Islam that came to Africa was adapted to local needs and conditions, and the global faith would be greatly enriched through its Africanization; and Europe itself – in ways which we perhaps do not yet fully appreciate – would be fundamentally changed by its relationship with Africa, in economic, cultural, and perhaps political terms, during the era of the Atlantic slave trade. At the same time, moreover, by placing too much emphasis on the supposed "external," we not only run the risk of oversimplifying processes of historical interaction but we also risk losing sight of the key notion of *internal dynamics*. And these internal dynamics include the force of "people power"; processes of social formation; economic ingenuity and innovation; cultural and political creativity; the playing out of revolution – and, indeed, the reverse of the same coin, the establishment and broader acceptance of a given status quo. Kings are "bad," sometimes, and sometimes internal structures do not work; at other times "external" things are "good" and are adopted. This is true throughout history, and of all peoples and cultures; above all, of course, change is ongoing and experiential. It is also important to remember, even as we seek to identify the ways in which Africa has been objectified by the outside world, that history itself objectifies: the very discipline of the study of the past is an exercise in objectification. We need to keep this in mind when at times we rely on historical studies which have themselves been dependent upon "objectifying" European sources, especially for the nineteenth century.

Above all, emphasis should be placed on the importance of the nineteenth and twentieth centuries as a cogent timeframe for close examination, and one which encompassed clear lines of continuity as well as dramatic change. In many respects, the nineteenth century constituted something of a "golden age" of African political, economic, and cultural creativity; but it was also an extremely violent era, as "golden ages" often are, and the violence itself was routinely misunderstood at the time and has continued to be since. Colonialism, again – enormously significant though its impact was in certain key respects – was in many ways absorbed into *African* patterns of change, while the postcolonial era has borne witness to the resurgence of unfinished business, much of it dating to the pre-1900 age. All this, meanwhile, must be understood against the backdrop of a global economy several centuries in the making and increasingly inimical to Africa's own development. It is critical to stress the importance of Africa's *longue durée*, as otherwise particular patches of the continent's history – not least the most recent past, often viewed in curiously ahistorical isolation – simply will not make sense, and are certainly vulnerable to misapprehension.

A Brief History of the Study of Africa

African history as an academic discipline is relatively young. As recently as the early 1960s, an Oxford scholar could famously dismiss the continent's past as "the unrewarding gyrations of barbarous tribes"[14]; but even as he did so, new approaches to the study of African history were being developed. What we mean here, of course, is the application of an intellectual "modernity" to Africa; needless to say, Africans have long understood the histories of their own societies on their own terms. Since the middle of the twentieth century, however, European historical methodology in the Greco-Roman tradition has been utilized, for better or for worse, in the attempt to reconstruct the African past. In the 1950s and 1960s, professional historians and social scientists in a range of other disciplines, many of them based at African universities – Ibadan in Nigeria, the University of Ghana, Dar es Salaam in Tanzania – began to treat African history as a field for serious study; and it is no coincidence that this took place when most of Africa itself was gaining independence from European colonial rule.[15] With newly rediscovered sovereignty came new interest in Africa's deeper past: history, indeed, was seen as an essential part of the nation-building process. The past, of course, has long been used – or, more commonly, abused – by politicians, guerrillas, statesmen, and would-be builders of nations of every hue, and in Africa, as elsewhere, these would become less enthusiastic and more cynical about history as time went on. But the "nationalist history" of the 1960s launched a vigorous new academic discipline which continues to challenge racist, Eurocentric assumptions about the world and to reconstruct and interpret the historical journeys of the myriad of peoples and communities that make up the vast region we know today as "Africa."

Historians of Africa have made use of a range of sources.[16] The identification of usable sources was particularly important for the precolonial past, as few societies – with the exception of the Arabic north and the Ethiopian highlands – left behind written records. Archeology was used to chart material and cultural change over the longer term, while linguistic change and spread could also be employed in discerning social, economic, and political metamorphosis. Historians have also had to make use of the written sources of foreigners, beginning with those of the Arabic-speaking travelers and traders from the Middle Ages onward, and after the sixteenth century those of European missionaries, traders, and explorers; in the twentieth century, extensive use of a vast array of colonial records has supported new avenues of historical research. Yet scholars have also been able to utilize the recorded indigenous oral histories and traditions which are the heart of all communities[17] and the testimonies which have been recorded in the course of the twentieth century. Clearly, each of these types of source has its limitations as well as its contribution to make. Studies of archeology and language generally permit the historian to glimpse only very approximate timescales and only very broad patterns of change; the written words of foreigners are riddled with the cultural and social prejudices and misunderstanding characteristics of outsiders, though some are more problematic and insensitive than others. Indigenous oral histories themselves were prone to change and distortion over time, and as a general rule favored the authors' particular lineage as well as reflecting current political circumstances. Nonetheless, used with caution, these sources have proved invaluable, and their utilization in the 1950s and 1960s reflected a new respect for (and indeed empathy with) Africa's past.

Why had there been no attempt to reconstruct Africa's past systematically before this time? The answer, hopefully, can be found at various junctures in the course of this book. But suffice to say here that by the beginning of the twentieth century, by which time most of the continent had been brought under European colonial rule, there existed a firm belief that Africa did not *have* a history. This "truth" persisted through much of the colonial period: Africans were perceived as "primitive," "savage," and lacking in political, cultural, and technological sophistication. Europeans in this period possessed a deeply rooted belief in the superiority of their own civilization, and vast swathes of the non-European world, Africa included, were regarded as "inferior" on numerous levels. Concepts of inferiority were vital in that they justified colonial rule itself; and thus Africans were depicted as lacking history, a benighted people without a past, and with no future either, unless "rescued" by Europe from the fate assigned them by biology. Moreover, most African societies, outside the Islamic zone and the Ethiopian highlands, were nonliterate, and Europeans argued that a people without writing, without documentation, could not possibly have a history. Africa's "history," according to this view, began only when Europe introduced literacy to African elites – for most, only after the 1880s and 1890s. As for literate Muslims and Abyssinians (Ethiopians), these were slightly higher up the scale of civilization, but not much: their barbarity was inherent, and their written languages are merely expressions of semi-civilization.[18]

Not only were these ideas worked into the narratives of colonial power but they also shaped Europe's perceptions of Africa's precolonial past. Where evidence did exist of "civilization" – the state of Great Zimbabwe north of the Limpopo, for example, or the monarchical states of eastern and northeastern Africa – Europeans decided either that Africans were not ultimately responsible for it or that the particular peoples involved were not actually *African* in any case. External, usually lighter-skinned, influences must have created such cultures: thus were the marvellous stone buildings of Great Zimbabwe the handiwork of a mysterious, vanishing white race, and "Ethiopians" possessed of Caucasian ancestry.[19] In South Africa, racist presumptions of this kind had profound political consequences: twentieth-century *apartheid*, notably, rested in part on the conviction that white settlers had discovered an "empty land" in the seventeenth century, a land given to them by God, and inhabited by a few "blacks" who were in any case not too far above animals in the grand scheme of things.[20] These ideas were influential through much of the twentieth century, and during that time, Africa was represented largely through European cultural prisms. One of the key challenges for students of modern African history is to consider in what ways – if at all – this has changed in our own era.

It is not easy to ascertain exactly where these perceptions originated – their roots lie deep in Europe's own historical development – but there can be little doubt that the growth of the Atlantic slave trade was accompanied by the rise of European racism toward Africa. Between the fifteenth and the nineteenth centuries, Africans came to be seen as "natural" slaves, the products of undeveloped societies and cultures, and "blackness" thus became associated in the "Western" mind with servitude and savagery.[21] We will deal with some of these issues in greater detail in the early part of the book, but it is worth noting here that in the course of the eighteenth century, there emerged in Europe a public debate around the slave trade, a debate which would have a profound influence on perceptions of Africa and which in some ways continues to resonate today. One group was opposed to the slave trade, the abolitionists, and another defended it, the apologists, but they shared certain basic assumptions about African society itself. The apologists argued that because Africa was a savage and backward place, a kind of "living hell," the slave trade was a form of blessed release, taking Africans from their cursed environments and landing them in the Americas, a new beginning. Moreover, they argued, Africa produced slaves in any case, through endemic warfare; there was nothing to be done to stop this.[22] The abolitionist position was that because Africa was a savage and backward place, it was in need of European intervention which would introduce to it what became known as the "three Cs" – Christianity, Commerce, and Civilization.[23] The slave trade caused violence and suffering; Africans must be saved, from slave traders as well as from themselves. The two groups had in common a belief in African backwardness, their differences a matter of emphasis. It was the abolitionist position which prevailed, in terms of both tangible outcome – the slave trade was indeed "abolished," Denmark and Britain leading the way – and ethos, in that their view of Africa prevailed through the nineteenth century. By the end of the century, the argument held sway that only through European rule would Africa ever develop – economically, politically, and culturally. Africans were children who could only be helped by European parental guidance.[24] This, at least, would become the public justification behind colonial rule.

It was an ethos, as we have observed, that would only be seriously challenged in the middle decades of the twentieth century, during the twilight of colonialism and the dawn of African independence. The struggle for the present – the achievement of national sovereignty, stability, prosperity – also became the struggle for the past, as Africans and a new generation of Western scholars sought to overturn an array of cultural and historical distortions. The struggle continues, despite the inevitable sloughs of cynicism and the occasional blind alley. At the present time, when Africa apparently staggers from one crisis to the next along its postcolonial path, and people in the "developed" world seek "solutions" in much the same way as their eighteenth- and nineteenth-century predecessors did, the deeper history of the continent has never been more relevant. Unfortunately, "presentism" is dominant: despite some doubtless honorable intentions, Africa is too often treated ahistorically by policymakers and humanitarians, who frequently ignore, or have little interest in, the full force of Africa's history. Nonetheless, in an era of civil conflict, famine and drought, economic underdevelopment and mismanagement, corruption and political oppression, the search for Africa's way forward must begin in its past.

Land

Africa is the second largest continent in the world and encompasses enormous diversity in terms of geography and climate from the Mediterranean to the Cape of Good Hope.[25] Clearly, this natural diversity cannot be separated from the history of the continent's inhabitants: environment and human history are indelibly intertwined, and nowhere is this more demonstrable than in Africa, where disease and poor, thin soils have obstructed the growth of human settlement in many regions. The history of Africans is in large part the struggle to adapt to hostile environments. Arguably, the single most important disease in African history, for example, has been trypanosomiasis, or "sleeping sickness," spread by the tsetse fly and prevalent in forested and woodland areas. Its influence was particularly keenly felt in societies which relied heavily on animals, for example those employing horses and cattle across the Sudanic belt. Outbreaks of sleeping sickness, which often occurred when bush or vegetation encroached on formerly cleared areas, were attacks on society itself, while the prevalence of the tsetse fly in forested areas was a major influence on state-formation: horses, for example, could not be used in this environment.[26] It is important to consider these disease dynamics in understanding social and economic change.

Physically, Africa has a strikingly regular coastline, with relatively few natural harbors in the form of deep bays and peninsulas; along other stretches of coast, maritime activity is inhibited by sandbars. This has meant that Africans have not had the same opportunity as Europeans and Asians for maritime travel or exploration; with the exception of the coastal Mediterranean peoples, Africans have had frequent and intense contact with other continents only in comparatively recent times. This is not to suggest, again, that African society did not absorb external influences when these presented themselves, but rather that until the eighteenth and nineteenth centuries, African development was relatively self-contained; combined with difficult terrain and a low level of transport technology, this meant that African civilization was in some important respects essentially insular in development and outlook.

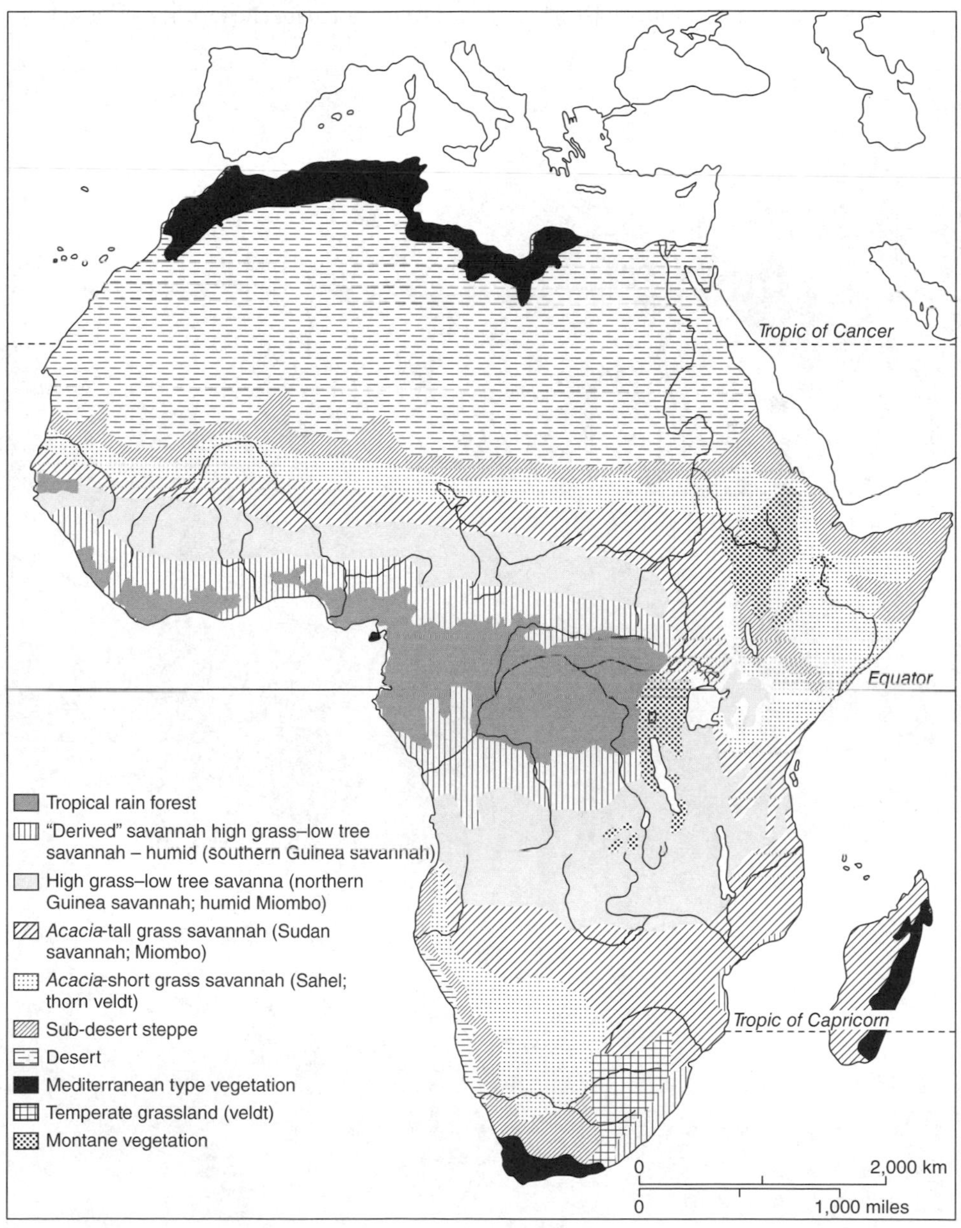

Main vegetation zones of Africa. Source: From M. Crowder (ed.), *Cambridge History of Africa*. Vol. 8: *c.1940–c.1975* (Cambridge, 1984), p. 194, Map 5; © 1984 by Cambridge University Press. Reprinted with permission from Cambridge University Press.

We can divide the continent's physical geography into eight approximate zones. First, we have the northern coastal lands of the Mediterranean: similar in climate to southern Europe, though usually warmer and drier, this zone is a coastal belt, varying in width, encompassing the northwestern part of the continent – the "Maghreb" (literally "the west" in Arabic) – where the belt is at its widest and covers the northern parts of modern Morocco, Algeria, and Tunisia. Mediterranean and Atlantic winds across the Atlas Mountains in Morocco and Algeria generate moisture, and the area is noted for the fertility of its soil.

Physical Africa. Source: From J. Iliffe, *Africans: The History of a Continent* (Cambridge, 1995), p. 2, Map 1. © 1995 by Cambridge University Press. Reprinted with permission from Cambridge University Press.

South of the Mediterranean coastal belt, the Sahara desert, the largest in the world, constitutes our second region. In the prehistoric era, the region appears to have had adequate rainfall and may have supported a substantial population; but for reasons which are not yet entirely clear – possibly because of a tilt in the earth's axis some 12,000 years ago – this vast area began to dry up (a process known as "desiccation"), and for many centuries, it has been uninhabited outside the oases which are scattered across it. However, the great desert should not simply be seen as an obstacle, severing contact between northern and sub-Saharan Africa, an assumption which is often made. Trans-Saharan communication was difficult, but oases (and camels) played a critical role in facilitating long-distance caravan routes, routes which have existed since antiquity, permitting contact between the peoples of the Maghreb and those of sub-Saharan western Africa. Nor is this zone completely lacking in arable land: as in the Atlas region, the mountains of the Hoggar, Tibesti, and Air generate enough moisture to facilitate agriculture.

Our next zone, adjacent to the Sahara, is the Nile valley. The river Nile is central to understanding the physicality of northeastern Africa. It is formed from two distinct rivers – the Blue Nile rising in the Ethiopian highlands, the White Nile issuing from Lake Victoria in East Africa – which meet at modern Khartoum, from whence the great river winds its way through the desert to the Mediterranean. Annual rains in the Ethiopian highlands and in interlacustrine East Africa cause the Nile to overflow, and as the river subsides, a rich, fertile mud is deposited, which has been carried from the upland slopes. Thus, a narrow strip exists on either side of the Nile, which contains some of the richest cultivable land in the world: it can support dense populations and has given rise to some of the oldest and most complex civilizations in the world, while also providing a link between Africans north and south of the Sahara.

Next, south of the Sahara in the west, desert gradually gives way to vegetation made possible by the warm equatorial winds which blow from the Atlantic. The "sudanic belt" is savannah, stretching across the continent. The term "sudan" was applied to this region by the Arabs of northern Africa and basically means "land of the blacks"; they also applied the word "sahel," meaning "shore," to the zone where the desert gives way to savannah. In other words, the desert was like a sea, and the beginning of the vegetation zone was its coast. The belt of increasing vegetation between the Sahara and the lush coastal forests is broken by a series of rivers which have had an enormous influence on the human history of the region. The Niger rises in the Futa Jallon range of Upper Guinea and loops north virtually into the Sahara before turning south into modern Nigeria where it links up with the Benue, another great river which rises in the mountains of Cameroon. The river then flows into the Atlantic through a maze of creeks and smaller rivers, the Niger delta. As with the Nile, rains in the Futa Jallon mountains cause the Niger to overflow its banks on its northward path; the resulting fertility means that the central Niger valley can support a relatively dense population and has been the scene of some of West Africa's most ancient and powerful kingdoms. The Senegal plays a similar role further west. To the east, Lake Chad, fed by rivers rising in Cameroon, also provides opportunities for agriculture and modifies the southern Saharan climate. Our next region, the west-central rainforest, lies to the south of the vast savannah region: this covers most of the West African coast, with the exception of the "Benin gap," stretching inland to varying distances and ultimately links up with the great forests of the central African basin to form one of the world's largest tropical forests.

The highlands of Ethiopia, our sixth region, is covered largely by volcanic material which breaks down to give a rich, deep soil; it is this soil which is carried north by the Nile and forms the basis of Egypt's fertility. Rain falls abundantly, and the cool uplands provide a favorable climate. The fertile highland area is a natural center of civilization; between it and the sea is the plain of Somalia, connected to Djibouti and coastal Eritrea, which is dry and torrid and incapable of sustaining a large settled population, instead being home predominantly to nomadic herdsmen.

Further south, the seventh zone, we have the vast plateau of east-central Africa which has its highest point in the Ruwenzori Mountains which form a kind of "spine" in the center of the continent. To the west of these mountains is the great Congo river system and rainforest, noted previously, but to the south, this gives way to savannah and the Shaba plateau where the river Zambezi rises. To the east of the Ruwenzoris lies the Great Lakes region of East Africa, the main ones being Victoria, Tanganyika, and Malawi, though there are many others. Much of the plateau land of east and central Africa is hot and dry, covered by tree scrub and difficult to cultivate, but there are important exceptions. The cool and fertile Kenyan highlands contain excellent farming country; the slopes of Kilimanjaro on the Kenyan–Tanzanian border, and the Shire highlands in modern Malawi have similar advantages; and the region between Lakes Victoria, Kyoga, and Kivu – modern Uganda, Rwanda, and Burundi – has abundant rainfall; and the resulting fertility has facilitated political sophistication.

Finally, in southern Africa, the vast plateau continues, separated from the ocean by a coastal strip. Southern Africa is also dry, open savannah country, covered by grass, bush, or thorn scrub; the winter months (June–August) can be cold. The region is free from malaria and the tsetse fly, which plague society further north. It is ideal for cattle-keeping, but cannot in general support densely populated agricultural societies; a partial exception to this can be found in the southeast, in the area around modern KwaZulu Natal.

People

This diversity of environment facilitated the emergence of distinct languages and cultures. Physical distinctions, too, evolved according to particular environments, which placed different demands on human societies in terms of survival and reproduction, and reflected processes of adaptation to those environments and climates, and responses to different patterns of nutrition. Thus, for example, there were the Khoisan in southern Africa, Afro-Mediterranean groups in the north, and Negroid peoples across the forests of western, central, and eastern Africa. Such physical distinctions were often erroneously referred to in terms of "race" in the nineteenth and twentieth centuries; further, Europeans (and in some areas, at the local level, Africans themselves) often used physical types to denote the degrees of "backwardness" of a given people, or the level of "civilization" they had achieved, whether in economic, political, or cultural terms. "Lighter-skinned" peoples, for example, were often held by Europeans to have brought more sophisticated technologies and political systems to a given area.[27] In fact, physical difference – for example in skin pigmentation – has nothing to do with "race." Biologically, there is only one human race, and groups sharing particular gene pools are properly referred to as "populations."

Physical diversification was attended by linguistic multiplicity, and research in this area in recent decades has revealed that continental Africa can be divided into four distinct language families, a family being defined as a group of closely related dialects developing from a common ancestor known as the "proto-language."[28] One of the largest families is known as Afro-Asiatic, encompassing much of the northern half of the continent as well as western Asia. Afro-Asiatic comprises many of the languages of Ethiopia, Eritrea, and the surrounding area, Berber in north Africa, and Hausa in the west; it also includes Hebrew and, rather more relevantly for Africa in recent centuries, Arabic. The Niger–Congo family, with its root in West Africa, embraces much of the southern half of the continent; one of the most important single offshoots is Bantu, and Bantu languages are now spoken across much of tropical Africa.[29] Nilo-Saharan languages are scattered across the Sahara, and some are spoken by other Negroid populations outside the Niger–Congo family, but they are mainly concentrated in the zone between Lake Chad and the Nile. Finally, Khoisan, perhaps the oldest of all the continent's language groupings, is associated with the pastoralists and nomadic hunter-gatherers of southern Africa, notably in the area of the Kalahari. Its distinctive "click" sound, however, is also heard in small pockets in Kenya and Tanzania. In very general terms, Afro-Asiatic, Niger–Congo, and Nilo-Saharan are associated with the spread of settled agriculture, albeit often combined with the keeping of livestock; and the growth and increasing dominance of these languages over a long period of time – millennia in some areas – may reflect improved access to food, relative population growth, and thus the marginalization of Khoisan speakers.

Africa's story over the past two millennia is essentially that of population migration, integration, and subdivision. In northern Africa, for example, Arab migration – out of the Arabian peninsula, into Egypt, and over subsequent centuries across the Maghreb and into the Nile valley – had begun soon after the rise of Islam itself in the seventh century. In the Maghreb, the process of "Arabization" is associated with the migration of Arab pastoral nomads, the Bedouin, between the tenth and thirteenth centuries. Those following the coast were known as the Banu Hilal, while those pushing inland were the Banu Sulaym. Their movement was attended by some degree of destruction and dislocation of extant agricultural communities; but they also carried with them Arabic language and culture, as well as Islam, and they gradually absorbed Berber communities. This period, indeed, saw the transformation of North Africa into part of the Arabic-speaking world.[30] Arabs crept slowly up the Nile valley, too; in particular, Islamization across the region was boosted by the southward migration of Arab pastoral nomad clans in the fourteenth century. Thereafter, Arabs moved into the central African interior, across Darfur and toward Lake Chad; but the process, while it brought Islam into these areas, was also characterized by intermarriage and social and cultural integration, and formerly mobile Arab communities became increasingly sedentary and "Africanized." In this way, older communities mutated, and new societies and cultures were formed.[31]

Similar processes can be identified in sub-Saharan Africa and are especially associated with the gradual migration of the Bantu-speakers from the area of the modern Nigeria–Cameroon border into eastern, central, and eventually southern Africa. Prior to the Bantu expansion, these regions were occupied largely by Khoisan speakers or speakers of languages related to Khoisan; as we have noted, these are still in evidence at the southern end of the continent. Over a long period of time, the peoples of the eastern Sudanic belt (for example the region of the upper Nile) diverged from those to the west in terms of economic systems: while eastern Sudanic peoples became nomadic and/or pastoralist, western African peoples became predominantly agricultural, developing sedentary lifestyles, although there were exceptions, notably the Fulani, many of whom remained nomadic and interacted with northern African groups. Agricultural West Africans developed larger and denser populations than in pastoral or nomadic regions, and the expansion of the Bantu was in part related to improving agricultural techniques and iron-working technology. The expansion seems to have begun around or shortly after 3000 BCE, by which time settled agriculture had reached the Bantu homeland, and it lasted for the next three millennia or more. Some groups, known as "North Bantu," began to move eastward along the fringes of the great equatorial forest, from Cameroon toward the Great Lakes; among these communities there then developed proto-East Bantu and proto-West Bantu. The West Bantu moved south into the central Congo basin by the middle of the first millennium BC and into the woodlands of Angola, while others broke off eastward toward Lake Tanganyika and the Zambezi; the East Bantu, by about 800 BCE, had reached lacustrine Africa, and Bantu-speakers were entering southern-central Africa – the area of present-day Malawi, Zambia, and Zimbabwe – in the early centuries CE. Current thinking suggests that this was *not* a "mass" migration but was rather piecemeal and localized, achieved by a multitude of shuffling advances stretched over many centuries.[32] But the net result was that Bantu-speakers colonized swathes of sub-Saharan Africa and can in many ways be considered the true pioneers of this vast region, opening it up to settled agriculture. It was a continent-wide population movement which involved complex interaction and exchange between migrating peoples and indigenous populations; above all, settled populations and food-producing communities laid the foundations for regionally distinct societies and cultures, leading in turn to larger populations and spurring further technological advances. The Bantu also contributed their manpower to the populations of the central and northern Americas as a result of the Atlantic slave trade, in which they were both protagonists and victims.

Complex material civilization, according to a standard historical view, is largely dependent upon urbanization, economic specialization, and social stratification, all of which require relatively dense populations; as we have noted, these were often lacking across the continent. There was, however, considerable diversity in respect of political structure and availability and use of forms of technology; there were important technological differences between Africa north and south of the Sahara, for example. Northern

Africa, as well as the Ethiopian Highlands, was technologically relatively advanced in so far that use was made of the plough, which increased the area of land under cultivation; south of the Sahara, however, the hoe was the main implement of cultivation, which only allows for a relatively small area of land to be cultivated at any given time.[33] The hoe, of course, was fit for purpose: in many parts of sub-Saharan Africa, the thin soils were not suited to plough cultivation, which tends to destroy weak soils and brings about soil erosion, and so the hoe was entirely appropriate to the ecological systems in which it was employed. It remains true that the hoe did not facilitate the volume of production which the plough did further north; but colonial officials, for example, frequently misunderstood the skill involved in its use, for sub-Saharan African farmers produced a wide variety of crops, both for subsistence and for commerce. Another major difference between the regions either side of the Sahara was in terms of transport, for while north Africans used the wheel, this was entirely absent in sub-Saharan Africa; in large part its use was prohibited by difficult terrain, and by the lack of pack animals to pull wheeled transport in tsetse-infected areas. Compared to other parts of the world, therefore, technological and commercial development took a particular form, and opportunities in these spheres were limited in some areas. Camels and horses could be employed in desert and savannah; but in woodland and forest, the bulk of transportation was on the head, which meant that heavier items of low value were scarcely worth carrying and that the most important items of long-distance trade were small and high-value, such as gold and ivory; slaves, of course, are self-transporting.

Lower productivity was also related to demography. As we have noted, Africa had a markedly low population density and large parts of it were underpopulated; thus, unlike in western Europe or southern Asia, for example, the scarce resource was not land but labor, and the control of people rather than land was the key to the growth of large, centralized social structures, and the means by which wealth and power might be acquired. African agricultural systems were often rotational in nature, and agriculture was extensive rather than intensive. With population growth inhibited, cultures and ideologies were developed around the core concept of fertility, and social structures, underpinned by such ideologies, were built around polygamy and slavery. Both involved the control of production and reproduction. Children themselves meant labor and the continuity of the community; the concept of kinship, whether real or invented, was critical, and in its absence, coercion was essential. In general, there were relatively few "landless people" compelled to work for low pay for an elite that owned great tracts of land, a phenomenon which would only appear during the colonial era with the displacement of entire populations to make way for white settlement, for example. Placed in this context, of course, the export of people via long-distance slave trades – whether across the Atlantic, the Sahara, or the Red Sea and Indian Ocean – was particularly destructive.

Finally, Africans built societies and political structures of staggering diversity and complexity across the continent. Europeans tended to categorize African political units as "tribes," a profoundly problematic term dealt with in later chapters; suffice to say here that it only has validity or utility in particular contexts and is largely a twentieth-century construct. In reality, African societies ranged from the nomadic to the centralized and territorial, from the transhumant pastoralist to the sedentary agricultural practice. Many societies were organized roughly around the idea of the clan, involving the concepts of kinship and genealogical descent; sometimes, again, these were imagined rather than actual. But it is dangerous to generalize, and many states and societies were formed around allegiance to outstanding individual leaders, or groups with particular political, technological, or spiritual talents, unconnected with kinship. Many were territorial, with sovereignty resting on spatial definition; sometimes even this was portable, however, especially in land-rich regions. The period of colonial rule altered to some extent the capacity of Africans to effect change, in different ways and at different times; but change, again, in the nineteenth as in the twentieth century, was continuous and continues apace in the twenty-first.

Notes

1 In that sense the analysis owes much to recent scholarship on "the modern": see for example C.A. Bayly, *The Birth of the Modern World, 1780–1914* (Malden MA, 2004).

2 For an excellent introduction, see John Iliffe, *Africans: The History of a Continent*, 2nd ed. (Cambridge, 2007), 1–5.

3 Iris Berger & E. Frances White, *Women in Sub-Saharan Africa: Restoring Women to History* (Bloomington & Indianapolis IN, 1999); Kathleen Sheldon, *African Women: Early History to the 21st Century* (Bloomington IN, 2017).

4 Igor Kopytoff (ed.), *The African Frontier: The Reproduction of Traditional African Societies* (Bloomington & Indianapolis IN, 1987).

5 Iliffe, *Africans*, 71–2. The process is dramatically conveyed in the oral epics of the region: see Bamba Suso & Banna Kanute, *Sunjata: Gambian Versions of the Mande Epic* (London, 1974/1999).

6 Richard J. Reid, "Past and Presentism: the "precolonial" and the foreshortening of African history," *Journal of African History*, 52:2 (2011).

7 Werner Gillon, *A Short History of African Art* (London, 1984); Tom Phillips (ed.), *Africa: The Art of a Continent* (London, 1995); Sam Fogg, *Ethiopian Art* (London, 2001).

8 Gillon, *Short History*, 330–33.

9 Sidney Littlefield Kasfir, *African Art and the Colonial Encounter* (Bloomington IN, 2007).

10 Philip D. Curtin, *The Image of Africa: British Ideas and Action, 1780–1850*, 2 vols (Madison WI, 1964); T.C. McCaskie, "Cultural encounters: Britain and Africa in the nineteenth century," in Andrew Porter (ed.), *The Oxford History of the British Empire: Vol III: The Nineteenth Century* (Oxford, 1999); Richard J. Reid, "Horror, Hubris and Humanity: the international engagement with Africa, 1914–2014," *International Affairs*, 90:1 (2014).

11 Nehemia Levtzion & Randall L. Pouwels, "Patterns of islamization and varieties of religious experience among muslims of Africa," in Nehemia Levtzion & Randall L. Pouwels (eds.), *The History of Islam in Africa* (Athens OH, 2000).

12 See for example James C. McCann, *Maize and Grace: Africa's Encounter with a New World Crop* (Cambridge MA, 2005).

13 The classic thesis is Martin Bernal, *Black Athena: The Afroasiatic Roots of Classical Civilization. Vol I: The Fabrication of Ancient Greece 1787–1987* (New Brunswick NJ, 1987); *Black Athena: The Afroasiatic Roots of Classical Civilisation. Vol II: The Archaeological and Documentary Evidence* (New Brunswick NJ, 1990). But see also Mary Lefkowitz, *Not Out of Africa: How Afrocentrism Became an Excuse to Teach Myth as History* (New York, 1996).

14 Quoted in A.G. Hopkins, *An Economic History of West Africa* (Harlow, 1973), 32.
15 For example, see Toyin Falola, *Nationalism and African Intellectuals* (Rochester NY, 2001), especially Part 3. For a contemporary and celebrated exposition, T.O. Ranger (ed.), *Emerging Themes in African History* (Nairobi, 1968).
16 See the journal *History in Africa: a journal of method*, established in 1974; and John Edward Philips (ed.), *Writing African History* (Rochester NY, 2005).
17 Jan Vansina, *Oral Tradition as History* (London, 1985).
18 E.S. Atenio-Adhiambo, "From African historiographies to an African philosophy of history," in Toyin Falola & Christian Jennings (eds.), *Africanizing Knowledge: African Studies Across the Disciplines* (New Brunswick NJ, 2002), 15–17; Joseph Miller (ed.), *The African Past Speaks: Essays on Oral Tradition and History* (Hamden CT, 1980).
19 Graham Connah, *African Civilizations: Precolonial Cities and States in Tropical Africa. An Archaeological Perspective* (Cambridge, 1987), 183; John Sorenson, *Imagining Ethiopia: Struggles for History and Identity in the Horn of Africa* (New Brunswick NJ, 1993), 21–37.
20 The idea is movingly conveyed in Rian Malan, *My Traitor's Heart* (London, 1991).
21 Curtin, *The Image of Africa*; and see the pioneering work of V.Y.Mudimbe, *notably The Invention of Africa: Gnosis, Philosophy, and the Order of Knowledge* (London, 1988), and *The Idea of Africa* (London, 1994).
22 For example, Archibald Dalzel, *The History of Dahomy, an Inland Kingdom of Africa* (London, 1793).
23 Mia Carter & Barbara Harlow, "The mission: christianity, civilisation and commerce," in Barbara Harlow & Mia Carter (eds.), *Archives of Empire, Vol II: The Scramble for Africa* (Durham & London, 2003), 243–5.
24 It is the fundamental idea behind Frederick Lugard, *The Dual Mandate in British Tropical Africa* (Edinburgh & London, 1922).
25 One of the best introductions is Jocelyn Murray (ed.), *Cultural Atlas of Africa* (New York, 1998).
26 The classic study is J. Ford, *The Role of the Trypanosomiases in African Ecology* (Oxford, 1971).
27 John Hanning Speke, *Journal of the Discovery of the Source of the Nile* (Edinburgh & London, 1863); C.G.Seligman, *Races of Africa* (London, 1966).
28 Joseph Greenberg, *The Languages of Africa* (Bloomington IN, 1963), and subsequent revised editions.
29 Derek Nurse & Gerard Philippson (eds.), *The Bantu Languages* (New York, 2003).
30 Humphrey Fisher, "The eastern Maghrib and the Central Sudan", in Roland Oliver (ed.), *The Cambridge History of Africa, Vol. 3, from c.1050–c.1600* (Cambridge, 1977).
31 P.M. Holt & M.W. Daly, *A History of the Sudan: From the Coming of Islam to the Present Day* (London, 2000), chap. 1 & 2.
32 See for example Jan Vansina, "New linguistic evidence and 'the bantu expansion'," *Journal of African History*, 36:2 (1995); Christopher Ehret, "Bantu expansions: re-envisioning a central problem of early African history," *International Journal of African Historical Studies*, 34:1 (2001).
33 Jack Goody, *Technology, Tradition and the State in Africa* (London, 1971).

Part I Polity, Society, and Economy: Ingenuity and Violence in the Nineteenth Century

Several broad themes are crucial to understanding much of Africa's nineteenth-century development, including the expansion of global commerce, the rapidly changing shape of African political structures, transformations in social structures and social relations, and – binding these together – the changing patterns of warfare. Violence in nineteenth-century Africa was both destructive and constructive; a military revolution, which took different forms across the continent, both drove and was in turn driven by rapid political, economic, and social change. The dynamism and creativity of the century between the 1790s and the 1890s need to be understood in order to fully appreciate the distinctive patterns of the twentieth century.

Long-distance and overseas trade changed the very nature of society and polity, presenting opportunities for the accumulation of wealth, which did not necessarily exist in rather simpler agricultural systems of local production and exchange. Global commerce brought about social mobility, both upward and downward, and this in turn involved shifts in the balance of political power. At the same time, the distribution of "luxury" or prestige goods by ruling elites was one of the most important means of securing political support in the nineteenth century: in Dahomey, the elaborate "annual customs" involved the distribution of such goods to the king's followers, and in Buganda, there existed a similar patronage and distribution system at the kingdom's political center. Imported goods, of course, had practical utility: political and commercial elites nearer the coast used foreign imports in exchange for horses further north, for example, as among the Yoruba. Commercial power, in other words, could be converted into military or political power. Those able to accumulate wealth in this way were also in a position to buy people – and in much of Africa, "power" was directly linked to the number of people either owned or over whom influence was exercised. Commercial power

A History of Modern Africa: 1800 to the Present, Third Edition. Richard J. Reid.

brought with it the power to expand one's following, the power to buy slaves, wives, or both – female slaves playing a particularly important role in the perpetuation of households and political establishments. The wealth derived from trade, therefore, could be transformed directly into political power, and this brought about dramatic transformations in terms of social mobility.

These themes are common across the continent; in other respects, however, there was a marked contrast in the experiences of West and East Africa. Fundamentally, in East Africa, the slave trade was expanding in the nineteenth century as it was declining in West Africa. In West Africa, the slave trade had facilitated – indeed had depended upon – the rise of hierarchical, political–military complexes, dominated by elites able to monopolize the import–export trade through their control of slaving and slave-trading. War was an economic as well as a political activity, representing an investment on the part of the state which – while not without risk, in terms of defeat and heavy casualties – could bring considerable returns and which ensured the dominance of extant elites. The nineteenth century saw this thrown into flux, following the abolition of the slave trade by most of the key European participants between the 1800s and the 1830s. A number of states continued to trade in slaves "illegally" until the 1860s; but these kinds of elites were increasingly undermined by the gradual decline of the commerce in human beings – and in some areas it was *very* gradual – and the rise of the so-called "legitimate" commerce in raw materials and agricultural produce; they lost significant political and economic privileges as they lost control of both trade and markets, and smaller producers could now compete with the "big men" as both groups moved into agricultural production. In some areas, however, although ruling elites found their positions weakened, they could use their political power to compensate for the dilution of their economic bases. In 1862 in Old Calabar, in the Niger Delta, for example, trade in small amounts of palm oil was prohibited by the chiefs, in an attempt to retain at least an oligopoly; and in mid-nineteenth century Dahomey, heavy taxes were imposed on the sale of palm oil.

Social change also resulted from the increased use of slaves within Atlantic African states and communities, itself the direct consequence of the expansion in agricultural production. In general, prices for slaves fell through the nineteenth century, making it easier for ordinary producers to acquire slaves; they were employed in farming, for transporting goods, as military followers, sometimes even as junior traders. There is some evidence to suggest that the treatment and general well-being of slaves deteriorated with the rise of "legitimate" commerce, owing to the comparative cheapness of slaves and the ability of their owners to work them harder than previously. Yet there were also opportunities for slaves: some responded violently to misuse, and indeed ever greater numbers of slaves in the economy gave them greater collective strength. Perhaps more importantly, however, the commercial changes of the nineteenth century meant that slaves themselves might accumulate wealth, buy their freedom, and build up political authority of their own.

On the other side of the continent, there was, rather, a tendency toward military rule, the direct result of the expanding slave and ivory trades. Warfare was the main source of slaves, involving the rise of warrior chiefs who gathered captives, built highly personalized armies, and created personal power. Commercial expansion in East Africa led to centralized authority, which was itself often rooted in the import of firearms and a range of prestige commodities. Heightened insecurity and increased levels of violence, together with the opportunities presented by commercial and military adventure, led to a breakdown in older forms of social structure, changing political forms, and in some areas the emergence of new identities – for example, across central and northern Tanzania – or the strengthening of existing identities and political structures, as in Buganda and in the Ethiopian highlands.

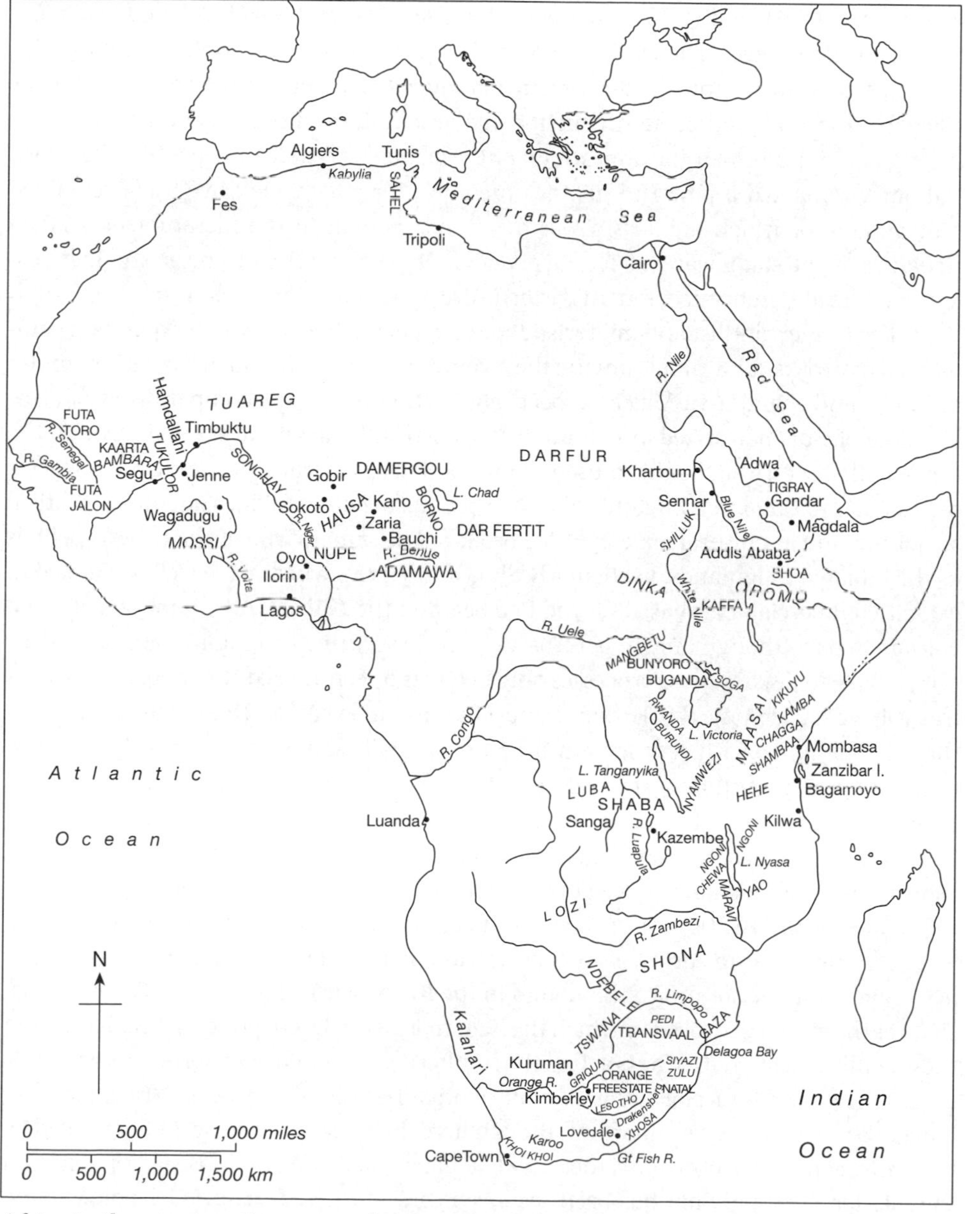

Africa in the nineteenth century: key peoples and places.

On both sides of the continent, the relationship between new commercial and political patterns and warfare was an intimate one. Much nineteenth-century African violence was concerned with the struggle to control trade and to gain access to its supposed benefits, among which was the firearm. The nineteenth century witnessed the rise of mercantilism – the linking of economic and political power – within many African societies, and the clearest manifestation of mercantilism was the use of war as an instrument of policy. Violent conflict certainly attended many of the changes taking place across the continent. When the Yoruba empire of Oyo, formerly a major slave-exporting state, collapsed in the 1820s and 1830s, it heralded the onset of several decades of conflict among the Yoruba themselves. The Yoruba competed for access to trade, as well as fighting with Muslim forces further north; the violence produced significant numbers of slaves for "illegal" export, a phenomenon which would at length prompt British intervention in the region, in the form of the annexation of the lagoon city-state of Lagos. Further west, Dahomey remained a powerful military presence, for which the slave trade remained crucial, and for which militarism was a core component in the hierarchical political structure of the state; war was a critical activity in the exercise of power and had profound cultural significance, too. In eastern Africa, dynamic and expansionist – if often short-lived – mercantilist and militaristic states appeared in response to expanding commercial networks, for example among the Nyamwezi and the Kimbu in the 1870s, under Mirambo and Nyungu-ya-Mawe, respectively. Further north, the comparatively ancient kingdom of Buganda seized its commercial opportunities aggressively, and through the nineteenth century, it sought to use military power as a means to commercial hegemony; similar to Dahomey, Buganda also incorporated a potent militarism into its political structures and its cultural makeup more broadly. The same is true of the *habesha* polities of the Ethiopian highlands, particularly Shoa and Tigray, which were well positioned to exploit commercial axes based on the Red Sea and the Gulf of Aden, and which used warfare in part (though only in part) as a means to securing economic dominance. Nor is it possible to discuss these processes only in terms of centralized statehood: in the central Rift Valley, among the Turkana and Maasai, for example, there was a tendency through the nineteenth century toward more specialized military leadership and new forms of age regimentation – though here, trade was marginal compared to the struggle for local resources, notably pastureland, often prompted by climatic change.

In Southern Africa, too, political and economic change was violent in the nineteenth century, as the Zulu state emerged from the several decades of conflict among the Ngoni to become, by the 1820s, one of the most successful military empires in the region, and indeed in sub-Saharan Africa as a whole. It was based on a ruthlessly efficient system of age regimentation, not unlike that found in the Rift Valley of East Africa. The repercussions of the military revolution which the Zulu represented were profound: refugees from these conflicts scattered as far north as the southern shore of Lake Victoria, to where they carried new models of political and military organization. In southern Africa, too, ever longer distance trade was important, though here the regional scene was complicated by the growing presence of white settlers, both at Cape Colony and in the Boer "republics" in the interior, creating what has been seen as a three-cornered struggle for political and economic space between the British, the Boers, and Africans themselves.

Each of these polities, of course, had distinctive cultural approaches to conflict, different means of military organization and leadership, and different objectives in the use of war as an extension of policy. The permanent armies of the Zulu, or of the pastoral societies of the Rift Valley, were relatively rare, with most states and societies relying on part-time militias called up in time of need (or desire). Buganda had no permanent professional army, but it did have a profound military culture and ethos; Mirambo's state relied on *ruga ruga*, young men equipped with guns, ambition, and a drive for commercial gain, their emotions heightened by the consumption of a local narcotic. Many of these societies, indeed, relied increasingly on the import of firearms, although the real impact of guns on warfare was variable across the continent; the states of coastal West Africa accumulated large numbers of them, as did those of the East African interior. In Ethiopia, successive emperors – Tewodros, Yohannes, and Menelik – were able to acquire quantities of modern or almost-modern weapons. Firearms were also the symbols of commercial, social, and political success, while also facilitating war itself; but again regional differences need to be acknowledged. In many parts of West Africa, guns were effectively adopted and utilized over time and through experience, and this was true in Ethiopia, too; but in Buganda, where guns were introduced only in the second half of the nineteenth century, they actually served to weaken the army's performance, owing to a lack of training and a misguided emphasis on the symbolic value of the weapon rather than the tangible contribution it might make. Across the continent, indeed, guns were often substandard, unreliable, and even dangerous; this placed African societies at a great disadvantage in the face of European encroachment in the closing years of the nineteenth century.

The history of African polity, society, and economy in the nineteenth century, then, is to a considerable degree concerned with the struggle to reformulate political and economic structures, with war frequently playing a major role as an instrument of policy. Expansionist centers clashed with armed frontiers, and new political and military cultures resulted, some of which were consolidating, despite the enormous flux around them, on the eve of the European partition of Africa. Much of this change was linked to the opportunities presented by overseas commerce, and this was true of the small trading states of the Niger Delta as it was of the centralized mercantilist kingdoms of the Ganda and the Zulu. For western, southern, and eastern Africa, ultimately, European imperialism was itself related to commercial and political developments within those regions. As we shall see, the belief that African society was inherently unstable meant that trade would be protected, if necessary through the forceful suppression of disorder and occupation of territory. Europeans saw internal disorder, strife, and warfare as impediments to commerce, while the slave trade continued "illegally" well into the nineteenth century; even those rulers who *did* maintain order would come to be seen as dangerous and unstable potentates who had to be removed in order to secure the operation of trade. We will return to these themes in Part III.

2 Western Transitions

Slave Trade and "Legitimate" Commerce in Atlantic Africa

One of the key themes in the history of Africa in the nineteenth century concerns the changing patterns of international trade.[1] It is important to note at the outset that Africans' experience of trade was by no means uniform across the continent but that there was, rather, considerable regional diversity, from the regions of coastal West Africa that were comparatively commercially developed, with a long history of involvement in global trade, to swathes of the eastern and central African interior which in the course of the nineteenth century were only beginning to experience long-distance commerce and its wide-ranging implications. Looking at sub-Saharan Africa as a whole, however, it is possible to make some preliminary statements on the manner in which international trade had a profound impact on African political, economic, and social development, influencing both political structures and social formation. It is also true that, at least in terms of the commercial relationship between Africa and Europe, the early nineteenth century in many ways marks the beginning of Africa's modern economic history. The very nature of this relationship, and of the patterns of trade themselves, led ultimately to the European partition of the continent in the final decades of the century: commercial and other economic interests were a powerful motive behind the "scramble" for Africa, as we shall see later in the book.

Africa had been, of course, part of a global economy for several centuries prior to 1800. The trans-Saharan trade had linked swathes of West Africa to the Mediterranean and Europe, via North Africa which since antiquity had been an integral part of the Mediterranean commercial basin,[2] while on the other side of the continent, the Indian Ocean had formed an enormous arena of commercial interaction which linked the eastern African Swahili coast with western and central Asia.[3] Most dramatically, of course, the slave trade from the fifteenth century onwards – and particularly the transatlantic

A History of Modern Africa: 1800 to the Present, Third Edition. Richard J. Reid.

system from the middle of the sixteenth century – had tied swathes of coastal western and central Africa, and their hinterlands, to western Europe and the Americas, to where millions of Africans were forcibly transported.[4] Trade networks, moreover, ran across Africa by 1800, connecting forest and woodland, savannah and desert. Many parts of the continent, therefore, had experienced several centuries of commercial relations with Europe, Asia, and the Americas; the nineteenth century, however, witnessed new developments in those relations and the incorporation of new regions into those trade networks.

Moreover, many of the key characteristics of Africa's modern relationship with Europe can be most powerfully demonstrated in the Atlantic zone, which is defined here as stretching from Senegal to Angola. In many respects, Atlantic Africa was something of a testing ground for European ideas about African culture, polity, and, perhaps most dramatically, economy; this was a zone which experienced enormous change in the course of the nineteenth century, faster in some areas than in others, but traumatic and permanent nonetheless. For our purposes, the most important "transition" – in fact the nineteenth century witnessed a series of "transitions" – was that from the slave trade to so-called "legitimate commerce" in Atlantic Africa.[5] There was no single or sudden transformation: an export trade in human beings, much to the despair of European humanitarians as well as, of course, millions of Africans, continued down to the 1860s. The difference between this phase of the slave trade and that which endured between the fifteenth and early nineteenth centuries was that it was held to be "illegal" in much of Europe and inimical to the advance of economic "modernity."

Finally, throughout this era of great creativity, Africans responded to external, and drove internal, change in a myriad of ways, despite experiencing what has been referred to as a global "reversal of fortune," as the result of which the continent fell behind Europe in economic terms.[6] The nineteenth century witnessed an escalation of the struggle to gain advantage from the burgeoning global economy, and to influence that system, despite the fact that the engines of industrial and financial control were now located outside Africa itself. In an era of destruction and construction, the processes which unfolded as Africans attempted to do so were frequently misunderstood by foreign observers.

States and Societies during the Atlantic Slave Trade

The slave trade had been devastating in many parts of Atlantic Africa, notably in terms of economic development – there can be little doubt that in some areas, the trade stunted economic growth and diversification – and demographic growth, with population levels at least remaining the same, if not declining, as a result of the systematic export of people. But it is important to observe that the slave trade had not been absolutely catastrophic: Africa survived. At the same time, the uncomfortable truth must be acknowledged that many Africans profited from the slave trade, mostly at the level of elites who built some of the most successful and dynamic state systems in sub-Saharan Africa on the basis of slavery and slave export. The institution of slavery, moreover, was of considerable antiquity in Africa, and in this sense, in some areas at least, it was no dramatic leap to sell slaves outside the community.

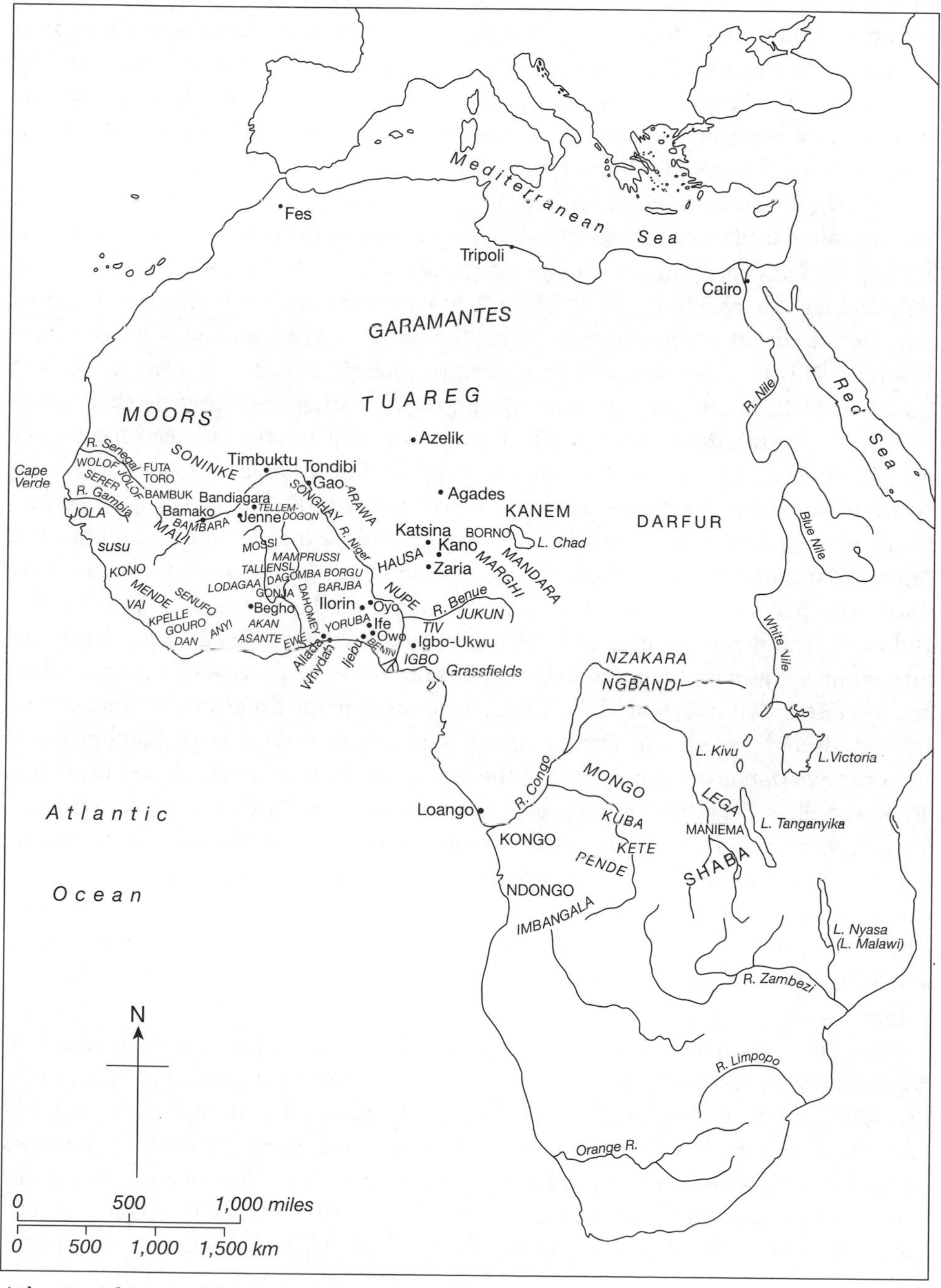

Atlantic Africa in the nineteenth century.

Atlantic and internal long-distance commercial systems had brought about major political, social, and economic changes among African states and societies by the end of the eighteenth century. It is also true, of course, that many of the societies involved in long-distance trade, exporting either slaves or other commodities, remained essentially *stateless* and decentralized; the Igbo of modern southeast Nigeria are one such example.[7] Nonetheless, in general, the major political consequence of such involvement was the creation of centralized, essentially mercantilist states, characterized by their fusing of political and economic power, and territorial expansion at the expense of smaller, weaker, or stateless communities. Political elites either controlled commerce or traders acquired political power. Across swathes of western and central Africa between the fifteenth and eighteenth centuries, militarized states arose, while imported firearms often facilitated the rise of small, well-armed minorities capable of dominating larger populations.[8] In broad terms, the slave trade resulted in an increased level of violence; wars were often fought deliberately for slaves, and such violence might be extremely destructive, sometimes involving the systematic devastation of weaker communities. This is demonstrable for the area of modern Angola, for example, where Ndongo and the Lunda empire became deeply involved in slave-raiding violence across swathes of central Africa, violence which continued well into the nineteenth century.[9] Angola, indeed, was one of the few areas where European traders – in this case Portuguese – were directly involved in the procurement of slaves, becoming permanently settled in the area of Luanda and its hinterland. By the middle of the eighteenth century, 10,000 slaves a year were being exported through the port of Luanda.[10] Yet slaves were just as often the product of wars fought for other reasons, as states formed and expanded. Benin, for example, sold slaves to the Portuguese in the fifteenth century while it was undergoing military expansion; once the process of expansion had run its course, Benin eschewed the selling of slaves, and the trade only resumed in the eighteenth century as Benin disintegrated.[11] Similarly, wars waged by expanding states such as Oyo, Dahomey, and Asante in the seventeenth and eighteenth centuries produced supplies of captives for the coast.[12] Ruling elites sold slaves when it suited them, often becoming wealthy in the process; as for the "logic" of participation in the trade, it is clear that the sale of people was deeply ironic given the concern of African rulers to maximize population growth. Powerful men sold slaves to acquire goods, goods with which to attract more personal followers: they sold people in order to acquire people, and from this perspective, there was clearly a separation of the collective from the individual interest.

One of the key areas of debate with regard to the impact of the slave trade relates to demography and endogenous economic growth. The former may be regarded as particularly important, given that one of the core themes in the continent's history has been the attempt to maximise population. The slave trade clearly involved a serious loss to Africa's productive potential. Labor was exported for a fraction of its value: slaves tended to be young, the most productive members of society. It is virtually impossible, however, to assess the demographic impact in any detail. The population of Atlantic

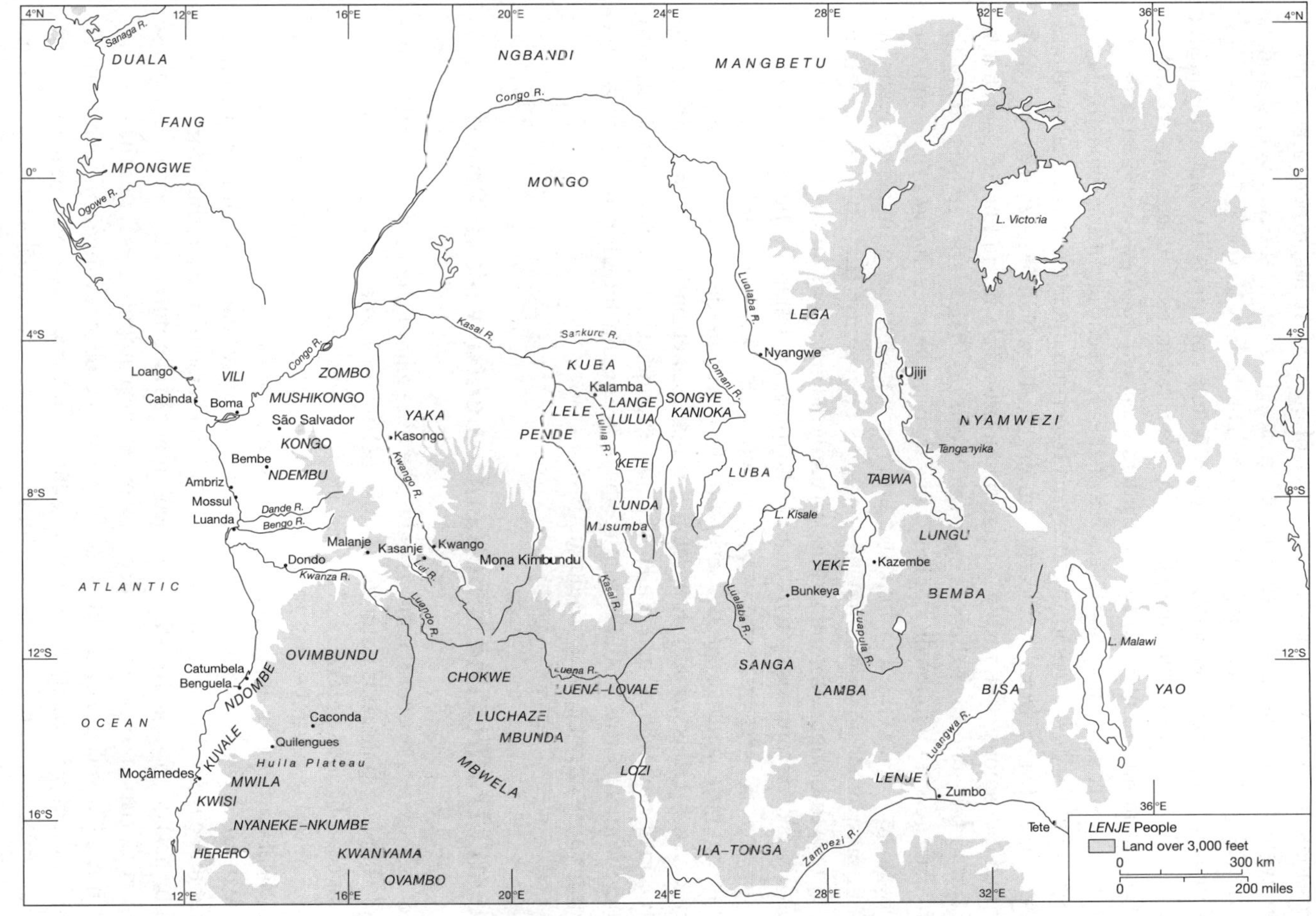

Central Africa in the nineteenth century. Source: From J. E. Flint (ed.), *Cambridge History of Africa*. Vol. 5 *c.1790–c.1870* (Cambridge, 1976), © 1976 by Cambridge University Press. Reprinted with permission from Cambridge University Press.

Africa at the beginning of the slave trade is unknown, and likewise, we have no way of knowing how fast (if at all) the population was growing, or how fast it might have grown if the slave trade had not happened. We can only speak in terms of general impressions. It is widely accepted that the area of modern Angola experienced depopulation, while other areas which were deeply involved – such as the Slave Coast and its hinterland – suffered retarded population growth at the very least.[13]

Overall, Atlantic Africa experienced no significant economic "development" during the era of the slave trade, although there are some instances of indigenous economies benefiting from involvement in the transatlantic system: Igbo and Asante textile and weaving industries expanded in the course of the eighteenth century, while the Benin brasswork industry benefited from the import of certain metals. Yoruba cloth was successfully exported to Brazil.[14] Clearly, the degree to which imported commodities destroyed indigenous craft, textile, and metal industries should not be exaggerated, at least not in the context of the late eighteenth century. The cloth industry along the Angolan coast was undoubtedly damaged, and there is evidence that local iron-smelting in Senegal was undermined by imported iron[15]; but the impact of imported manufactures in most other areas was nowhere near as destructive. Nonetheless, it remains broadly true that imported commodities certainly did little to stimulate change or innovation in African economic systems nor did the transport system of the Atlantic hinterland develop as a result of overseas contact. There was no significant export of agricultural produce from Africa, save what food was needed on slave ships for the Atlantic crossing; this would only develop during the nineteenth century. Moreover, the institution of slavery itself had in all probability expanded by the end of the eighteenth century; ironically, this would continue apace in the nineteenth century, to a large degree because of, not despite, abolition.

"Illegal" Traffic: The Nineteenth-Century Slave Trade

In the late eighteenth century, forces in Europe were gaining momentum for the abolition of the slave trade. It is a matter of some debate how potent particular factors are considered to be. Between the 1770s and 1800s, some, famously, argued for abolition on humanitarian grounds, with a curious alliance of Enlightenment humanism and evangelical outrage serving to publicize the unacceptable brutality of the trade itself. European intellectuals and church societies united in the belief in the universal right of all human beings to freedom and equality. The "movement" was, in that sense, a broad church: it brought together "Enlightened" men, profoundly anticlerical, and those driven by Christian conscience, spurred by evangelical impulse. As far as the Christian Church itself was concerned, this was the beginning of an evangelical revival which would see the rapid growth of missionary activity in Africa, as we will see in Chapter 8. The humanitarian argument was forcefully expounded by Jacque Pierre Brissot in revolutionary France, for example[16]; in Britain, the leading figures included Granville Sharp and William Wilberforce, the latter leading a massive public campaign in 1787–8, and industrial philanthropists such as Josiah Wedgwood, who produced the memorable

West Africa c.1865. Source: From J. E. Flint (ed.), *Cambridge History of Africa*. Vol. 5: *c.1790–c.1870* (Cambridge, 1976), Map 7; © 1976 by Cambridge University Press. Reprinted with permission from Cambridge University Press.

medallion depicting a slave in irons above the slogan, "Am I not a man and a brother?"[17] A handful of Africans also participated in the humanitarian movement: the writings and public speeches of Olaudah Equiano, for example, were influential in the 1790s. A former slave who had purchased his own freedom, he was educated in England, joined the ranks of the abolitionists, and became something of a celebrity, although more recently, questions have been asked as to the veracity of some of his claims. Nonetheless his public persona and his autobiography, the *Interesting Narrative* seemed at the time to bear out the great claims made for the value of exposure to civilizing Christian influences.[18]

One of the enduring outcomes of the slave-trade argument, apart from abolition itself, was the objectification of Africa, an imagined entity lying at the feet of the debaters with little (individuals such as Equiano excepted) to say for itself. Africa had become an "object," an issue or a question to exercise the great philanthropic and political minds of the day, and not a few lesser ones, too; and herein do we see a process by which "Africa" was being invented according to the concerns and the agenda of outsiders. It was a process which was to gather momentum through the nineteenth and indeed the twentieth centuries. As we shall see in a later chapter, the African Association was founded in London at the same time – the 1780s – as the slave-trade debate was gathering public momentum, and one of the stated aims of the Association was to wean the continent off the slave trade, diversify commerce and bring about a mutually beneficial, progressive, civilizing relationship which would "improve" Africa, heighten knowledge of it, and of course lead to commercial gains for Britain itself.[19]

The Association sought tangible gain in arguing for a change in the economic relationship between Europe and Africa. Moving and powerful though the broadly "humanitarian" arguments were, there can be little doubt that shifts in economic thinking, as well as in the profits to be had from the slave-based economy, also led to a more hard-headed reconsideration of the viability of the trade. Slave resistance, of course, had long made investors uneasy: mutinies on board ship were common enough, while the most notable slave revolt was that on the island of Haiti in 1791, under Toussaint l'Ouverture.[20] It is also the case that the revolutionary and Napoleonic wars which had engulfed Europe between the early 1790s, and 1815 had repercussions for international trade. Global shipping lanes were severely disrupted, including those linking Africa and the Americas, and the slave trade never fully recovered. More broadly, however, slave labor was no longer viewed as profitable by many western European economists: future economic growth, it was argued, lay in industrialized systems making use of free, waged labor, while profits from slave-based sugar production in the Caribbean, for example, had declined significantly in the second half of the eighteenth century.[21] Investment in manufacturing industry at home continued apace, particularly in Britain, and at the expense of plantation slavery overseas. This was not, of course, universally accepted, at least not immediately: slave labor would continue in the United States until the 1860s, and in Brazil, which was the single largest "illegal" importer of slaves in the nineteenth century.[22] Slavery itself would remain legal in the British empire until the 1830s.[23] This said, however, the abolition of the slave trade by the major European powers ushered in a new age of economic and political change, which is again why "c.1800" can be usefully employed as a notional watershed. There had been an important shift in economic thinking about Africa, which was increasingly regarded as a source of raw materials, and indeed a market for manufactured goods, rather than simply a source of slave labor. Industrialization in the northern hemisphere would be further fueled by the vegetable oil and rubber of "the tropics," while European manufacturers – many of whose companies had originally made their money in the slave trade – searched for markets abroad in which to sell cheaply made commodities.[24]

Denmark and Britain, two of the biggest slave carriers of the seventeenth and eighteenth centuries, were among the first to prohibit their citizens from participating in the trade, in 1803 and 1807 respectively; they were followed by the United States (1808), Holland (1814), and France (1817), although the last had toyed with abolition during the revolutionary years of the 1790s. At the Congress of Vienna in 1815, there was a general agreement among most European states that the slave trade should be abolished, although Portugal had argued for a ban only on the trade north of the equator. By the mid-1830s, most European states had outlawed the trade, but it was extremely difficult to enforce. The Atlantic slave trade died hard and continued through much of the nineteenth century, with several West African coastal states, for example Dahomey, refusing to abandon what was seen as an essential economic and indeed political activity. Widespread warfare among the Yoruba, too – examined below – produced large numbers of people for export. Swathes of central Africa, notably the region of modern Angola, also continued to be involved in the export of slaves, as it had been throughout the earlier period of the trade. The main destination for slaves in the nineteenth century was Latin America, although smaller numbers found their way further north. The Atlantic trade did, however, gradually decline in the course of the century and had largely disappeared by the 1870s and 1880s. This was in part due to the efforts of the British anti-slavery squadrons patrolling Africa's Atlantic coastline, but the real impact of such activity should not be exaggerated. Dwindling demand for slaves in the Americas, particularly from the middle of the century, and the expansion of "legitimate" commerce, were ultimately more important factors.[25]

One of the fundamental misjudgments made by European politicians, humanitarians, and philanthropists alike was the notion that slavery and "legitimate" commerce were mutually exclusive. In fact they could and did coexist. At any rate, African rulers pleaded that the slave trade was so deeply embedded in the political and social makeup of their states that it was impossible to stop, or at least to do so without bringing about major social and political upheaval. Gezo, the king of Dahomey, told a British official in 1848 that he could not possibly give up the slave trade: the army had to be kept active, and if Gezo himself tried to alter "the sentiments of a whole people" Dahomey would be thrown into anarchy and revolution, which "would deprive him of his throne."[26] These comments may have been rather disingenuous; in Dahomey, it was not in the interests of the ruling class to abolish the slave trade – over which it had complete control – and lose the privileges that went with it, and encourage production of palm oil, which would open up access to the lucrative overseas market to ordinary peasant producers.[27] The struggle to suppress the slave trade along certain stretches of the Atlantic coast and to spread the gospel of "legitimate" production, clearly led to increased European involvement in African politics across the region. Gezo was an example of the kind of recalcitrant ruler who in the 1840s and 1850s became the focus of much attention in the British Foreign Office; his refusal (or inability) to stop trading in slaves led to diplomatic missions and heightened political pressure.[28] In other areas, the British used military force, or the threat of it, to compel African rulers to accept their abolitionist demands. Gunboats might create favorable commercial conditions, the British discovered, but it also meant a usually unwelcome extension of formal political control, as in Lagos, a persistent slave-exporting city-state on the Yoruba coast, which was bombarded in 1851 and eventually annexed in 1861.[29] Thus, the increase in scale of European economic interest in Atlantic Africa led to growing levels of political and military intervention: this was limited at first, but it nonetheless laid the foundations for later outright partition.

Mineral and Vegetable: "Legitimate" Commerce

"Legitimate" commerce, as it has become known, increasingly supplanted the export of human beings and involved European demand for raw materials, natural resources, and agricultural produce from western and central Africa.[30] Yet it was far more than an economic system: it had moral and political implications, too, and indeed it has relevance for more recent debates concerning Africa's "modernization." This was trade which – like the slave trade before it – was of considerable economic benefit to Europe at a time of industrialization, and which, moreover, humanitarians hoped would bring economic and social progress to Africa. A great many African societies along the Atlantic coast, and to a rather lesser extent in the hinterland, participated in the export of such commodities as palm oil, groundnuts, and rubber; but in this era of transition, a number of societies experienced what have been called "crises of adaptation."[31] States whose socioeconomic and political structures were so geared toward the capture and export of slaves, or whose military ethos demanded the kind of cyclical military activity which resulted in the seizure of war captives, struggled to make the transition to agricultural exports. The era of the slave trade had produced, or at least strengthened, ruling warrior elites at the head of centralized political and economic systems; these elites now faced crises of adaptation in the era of "legitimate" commerce, in large part because they could not as easily control such trade or monopolize the supposed benefits coming from it. The very nature of the new economic system tended to undermine their internal power bases. While many states and societies did indeed make the transition successfully – with warrior elites finding new ways of controlling and adapting to the new economic reality, and indeed surviving until the onset of colonialism – others underwent profound social and political change or even collapse, with new groups becoming involved in overseas commerce and in some places challenging for political power. Everywhere, innovation and entrepreneurialism, often violent, were much in evidence.

Ultimately, it is clear that in contrast to other parts of the continent, parts of Atlantic Africa experienced much greater continuity between the nineteenth century and the colonial era in terms of export economies based on agricultural produce and other raw materials.

Demand for vegetable oils, notably palm oil, increased in line with the quickening pace of industrialization. The demand for palm oil in Britain, for example, had been on the increase since the 1770s, with production spanning much of the West African coastal forest from Sierra Leone to the Niger delta. Groundnuts were cultivated north of the palm-oil regions, and production was especially significant in the Senegal–Gambia region. Some societies attempted to grow and export cotton – in present-day southern Nigeria, in the Gold Coast, and in Senegal, notably – and these were certainly able to capitalize on the disruption of the world's cotton supply brought about by the American civil war in the 1860s. Rubber was also of growing importance: the demand for rubber was at first confined to European textile industries, but later tire manufacturers became involved. Wild rubber was being exported from parts of western and central Africa from the middle of the nineteenth century. Some people were ideally positioned to take advantage of the central African rubber trade, as well as the commerce in ivory; the Chokwe and Ovimbundu, for example, were successful as both producers and middlemen, and the Chokwe in particular were notable for making extensive use of slave labor in their commercial activity. Some cocoa was grown, at first on the offshore islands and then, toward century's end, on the mainland, while in Atlantic central Africa, the export of beeswax was also significant.[32]

The coastal zone in particular benefited from legitimate commerce, and this in itself denoted major socioeconomic, and thus political, changes. The transport of slaves from the interior to the coast had been relatively cheap, and straightforward – slaves, clearly, are self-transporting – but the transport of relatively bulky, low-value commodities such as groundnuts and palm oil was rather more expensive from the deeper hinterland, and so most of the production took place along the coast, where the best profits were also to be had. One long-term consequence of this economic-geographical imbalance was the migration of people from the interior to the littoral. Only in the colonial era was it possible for the West African interior to participate fully in the international economy, largely as a result of railway and later road construction.

Essentially, however, production techniques did not change, the expansion of legitimate commerce simply involving the cultivation of more land, using more labor. In fact, across West Africa, there was something of a labor shortage, as palm oil, for example, required larger amounts of labor in terms of both production and transportation to the market areas. The result – ironically, in view of humanitarian visions in Europe – was an increase across the region in the use of slave labor. The number of female slaves in particular expanded considerably across Atlantic Africa. Slaves were needed to meet demand for "legitimate" produce; they were also used in domestic food production. In the Congo–Angola region, the loss of large numbers of young men – the cumulative effect of several centuries' involvement in the slave trade – had resulted in a gender imbalance in many societies; local populations just about managed to reproduce themselves. With a decline in slave exports, population levels began to recover, and this in turn placed a strain on existing food resources, which meant using more domestic slaves to expand food production. Something similar occurred in the United States in the nineteenth century, where increased demand for cotton led to a dramatic expansion in the use of slave labor across the southern states. European humanitarians were uncomfortably aware that legitimate commerce had led to an increased use of slavery across Atlantic Africa; in time they would come to attribute this to the backward and brutal nature of African society itself, rather than explaining it in terms of Africa's economic relationship with Europe.

For those who owned slaves, however, the export trade opened up greater opportunities for participation than had been the case previously. In broad terms, the slave trade was organized by large-scale operators at the level of a monopoly; slave sellers or "producers" constituted a small number of elite entrepreneurs. In general, the people best placed to trade in slaves were political and military elites, especially as slaves themselves were usually generated through warfare, while slave-ownership was a crucial component in the exercise of political authority. Thus, what we can broadly term "warrior elites" had developed across Atlantic Africa, strengthening centralized political leadership. This was not necessarily true, however, of legitimate commerce, in which there were no special favors or advantages for centralized political or military authority. Unlike the slave trade, carried on largely at the level of the state, the very nature of legitimate commerce meant that it was rather easier to trade in small amounts; simply put, anyone with access to a small plot of land and family labor – again, often supplemented by domestic slavery, particularly women – could participate in the export trade. At the same time, free women were able to become involved in small-scale commerce in the course of the nineteenth century. Overall, there was arguably a greatly heightened level of social mobility where overseas commerce was most intense. West African warrior elites sometimes found their political and economic monopolies weakened and their revenues reduced; alternative pockets of power developed as access to the export trade widened, and the supposed benefits it bestowed, such as firearms and other "luxury" commodities, became more widely distributed. Sociopolitical disruption, even collapse, ensued in a number of states and societies as the nineteenth century progressed.[33]

In general, trade in "legitimate" produce tended to increase steadily – and in some cases dramatically – until the middle of the nineteenth century, when demand evened out somewhat; prices collapsed during the so-called "long" or "great" depression between the 1870s and the 1890s. Again very broadly, it can be argued that from the early nineteenth century until the 1870s, African producers enjoyed reasonably favorable terms of trade and a certain amount of economic power; with the collapse of prices in the 1870s and 1880s, however, there was a marked escalation in tension between Europeans and Africans, the latter feeling increasingly at the mercy of the former, and these commercial hostilities were to be a crucial factor in the European partition of West Africa, for example. Ultimately, Europe sought to protect its commercial interests from what were regarded as over-powerful African merchant-chiefs; and indeed, relations between Europeans and Africans had become increasingly problematic in the course of the nineteenth century, as a direct result of the changing economic structures brought about by the "new" commerce.

Although the terms of trade did indeed tend to be more favorable to African producers than previously, at least for the first half of the nineteenth century, the new commercial system in effect implied the economic empowerment of Europe at the expense of Africa over the longer term. Connected to the global economy, Atlantic Africa was now subjected to periodic shifts in demand and prices beyond its control. Indebtedness among African producers increased, with many coastal traders dependent on the credit advanced by European merchants; violence was often used to recover debts. To Europeans, moreover, over-powerful and ambitious African middlemen were becoming obstacles to the flow of trade and the realization of profit. Gradually, but with increasing frequency in the second half of the century, European traders – sometimes with the official backing of their governments – began to penetrate beyond the coast into the hinterland in an effort to bypass middlemen and buy direct from producers. Often the most efficient means of doing so was by river, and thus did the Niger, navigable in places, become increasingly important to British commercial concerns.[34] Combined with the anti-slave-trade activity mentioned previously, all of this denoted an ever greater European intervention in Atlantic African polity and economy, a process which formed the prelude to the actual partition of the region in the 1890s.

Ultimately, then, "legitimate" commerce did little to facilitate African economic growth, and many of the patterns of trade between Africa and Europe emerging in the first half of the nineteenth century in fact persist to the present day. This was the beginning of Africa's modern economic history, an era usually characterized as one of "underdevelopment."[35] Legitimate commerce was about the export of raw materials rather than finished products; the continent was never an equal partner in the global trading network. Three broad observations are worth making. First, levels of personal freedom declined as domestic slavery increased, while labor both free and unfree was now harnessed to the export trade rather than internal development and diversification. Second, European imports – these included a dizzying array of goods, but the most important were cloth, sundry manufactures, alcohol, and guns – did little to strengthen indigenous economies, and indeed in many respects weakened them over the longer term. And third, the independence of successful exporting societies was soon threatened by the interference of their European trading partners: commerce, ultimately, would lead to conquest.

Change and Continuity in Forest and Savannah

Change took many forms during the gradual transition from one commercial era to the next. While large empires such as Oyo and Kongo collapsed – though only partly, it must be said, as the result of explicitly commercial change – new states and communities came to prominence in the coastal forest and savannah zones. The small trading states of the Niger delta saw the emergence of powerful merchants as hereditary "kings," while among the Tio traders on the Congo River, kingship became largely ceremonial as real power passed to local merchant-chiefs.[36] Centralized states such as Dahomey and Asante, however, survived through the nineteenth century, and to some degree beyond; here, proto-national identities, potent military cultures, and monarchical systems of government strove to adapt in the face of threats both local and foreign.[37]

A great many Yoruba had entered the nineteenth century united within the Oyo empire, but Oyo was a state on the brink of collapse. It had been politically weakened by internal division and the dilution of the authority of the *alafin*, or king, while in economic terms, it was in a precarious position following the abolition of the slave trade: European buyers at the coast had dried up, as had the goods with which Oyo traders had purchased horses from northern merchants. Meanwhile, the Islamic jihad which had erupted in 1804 among the Hausa and Fulani further north – examined in Chapter 6 – posed a major threat to the empire. Whether Oyo was already in terminal decline, and the jihad merely hastened the process, or whether the empire might have recovered had it not been for the Muslim revolution, there can be little doubt that the latter was a significant factor in the destruction of a polity which had dominated the area of the Benin Gap and a swathe of the southern savannah for the previous two centuries. In 1817, a provincial revolt in Ilorin, in the north of the empire, erupted with the assistance of some Fulani jihadists, precipitating not simply the collapse of Oyo but a series of wars which would engulf the Yoruba for much of the nineteenth century. Muslim forces would continue to push south deep into Oyo territory.[38]

As conflict between the Oyo heartlands and Ilorin escalated, war broke out between Owu on the one hand, and Ife and Ijebu on the other, primarily over control of commerce. These wars combined to generate large numbers of displaced people, who themselves became a source of regional instability, living by plunder and carrying destruction over a wide area. The Oyo–Ilorin war reached its height in the early 1830s, when the old capital of Oyo was overrun, and largely destroyed; the empire's poor successor, "New Oyo," based in the forests to the south, ceased to play an active role in Yoruba politics. The empire's demise left a vacuum within which a series of Yoruba states competed violently with one another, while also attempting to defend Yoruba territory from Muslim encroachments from the north. There were principally four such states. Ijaye was frequently engaged in conflict with Dahomey to the west, which in making incursions into Yorubaland sought to take advantage of the collapse of its former overlord, the Oyo empire; Ibadan to the south of Ijaye was an important military power, engaged in conflict with the Fulani. The Egba, with their capital at Abeokuta, also fought Dahomey, and for this reason sought access to the coast in order to acquire the necessary firepower; and the Ijebu, located close to the coast north of Lagos, were transit handlers of firearms bound for the north, and this commercially dominant people were also heavily involved in the "illegal" slave trade, exporting the hapless victims of the violence. Indeed it was this which prompted the British to annex Lagos in 1861.

Thus the Yoruba fought with one another, as well as with foreign invaders, and the internecine conflict can be divided into approximately two phases. Between the end of the 1830s and 1878, Ibadan emerged as the single most powerful Yoruba state, following prolonged wars with the Egba and the Ijaye, the latter being largely destroyed in the early 1860s. Ibadan also benefited from British support, based on the notion that it offered the best chance for political and commercial stability. During the second phase, from 1878 to 1893, several Yoruba states coalesced in order to prevent a further expansion of Ibadan's power, but when no clear advantage accrued on either side, negotiations began – in 1886 – with a view to establishing a permanent settlement. Diplomacy was interspersed with outbreaks of violence, and it was only in 1892–3 when the British, still based at Lagos, imposed a *pax* on the warring parties.[39]

The violence of Yorubaland brought about dramatic changes, changes which to some extent can be used to highlight the impact of war in other parts of the continent.[40] There was demographic change, involving massive shifts in population as the Fulani advanced southward from Ilorin; people moved from the more open savannah southward into the forest, as indeed they had always done in the search for protection against men on horseback. Now, however, there occurred permanent migration, resulting in urban expansion, both the growth of extant towns and the creation of new, often fortified settlements. At the same time, the slave trade escalated dramatically along the coast of modern southwest Nigeria, marking a significant change from previous patterns of slave export in the area. In the eighteenth century, slaving among the Yoruba had been limited, owing largely to the fact that Oyo acquired most of its captives from further north, and slave exports had come from the areas adjacent to Yoruba country, notably the Niger delta to the east, and Dahomey and Asante to the west. But the jihad and the resulting Sokoto caliphate closed off supplies of slaves from the north, while the collapse of Oyo led to rather more systematic slave-gathering among the Yoruba themselves: war was a lucrative business. But war had other side effects. Islam spread into the region, following the expansion of Sokoto into Ilorin. Recurrent conflict engendered what can be acceptably described as a military revolution, evident, too, in other parts of the continent for many of the same reasons: the use of firearms became common, and a professional soldiery emerged, involving more systematic training and the development of complex tactics and strategy. As the nineteenth century drew to a close, the violence provided the British in particular with a justification for intervention, and indeed the Yoruba in some ways offered the best instance of a troubled, war-stricken people crying out for redemption and security, which only Albion could provide. Missionaries had already introduced a degree of British culture into coastal society and collected souls from among the displaced and defenseless; they helped shape official attitudes toward particular groups across the region and lobbied for intervention.[41] In the early 1890s, the British government answered the call, and local rivalries would now be played out in the context of the colonial experiment.

Ruler of a kingdom in transition: King Gezo of Dahomey, with Prince Badahun, in 1856. Source: BLM Collection/Alamy Stock Photo.

European propaganda, including that of the missionaries, targeted Dahomey as the source of much evil in the area.[42] The beginning of the nineteenth century found Dahomey a dynamic and expansionist state, able at last to throw off its long-standing subordination to Oyo – a relationship dating to the early eighteenth century – and, as noted previously, to launch incursions into Yoruba territory. These incursions were very largely economic in objective. Dahomey had been a successful slave-owning and slave-exporting state since at least the end of the seventeenth century: slaves were used extensively within the domestic economy, while others were exported, and others again were sacrificed according to ceremonies designed to honor the king and his ancestors. Slavery, thus, was central to Dahomey's economic, political, and social systems, and the result was a deep-rooted military culture, reflected in the fact that the army – using the firearms which were acquired through the actual export of slaves – was almost continually in action.[43] While the kingdom's traditional raiding grounds lay to the north and west, the collapse of Oyo facilitated manhunts among the Yoruba to the east – a strategy necessitated, indeed, by depopulation north and west of Dahomey. The kingdom was one of the most important "illegal" exporters of slaves along the nineteenth-century Atlantic coast: between the 1810s and the 1850s, under King Gezo, Dahomey financed wars of expansion through its dealings with slave-buyers at the coast, Brazilians among them, and defied British pressure to embrace the "legitimate" commerce being vigorously promoted on other parts of the coast. Gezo also took advantage of relative *lack* of pressure from the French, the efforts of whose own anti-slavery squadron were frequently undermined by official ambivalence – and indeed by the presence of French slave dealers on the coast itself. In the 1850s and 1860s, however, the slave trade finally went into steep decline, and Dahomey found itself compelled to consider alternatives; the result was palm-oil production, ironically using slave labor which thus expanded dramatically in the second half of the nineteenth century. Commercial rivalry fueled further conflict across the region, as states competed for access to the coast in the quest for the guns and ammunition vital to political and economic dominance. The wars between Dahomey and the Egba, beginning in the early 1840s and fought over control of key trade routes, demonstrate this; Dahomean forces were unsuccessful in their attempts to seize Abeokuta, the Egba capital, in 1851 and again in 1864, and indeed missionaries based at Abeokuta lobbied effectively for British moral, and some material, support for the Egba. Nonetheless, Dahomey remained powerful and active on the eve of the French invasion in the mid-1890s.[44]

In Asante, another powerful territorial state, a highly centralized administration took advantage of commercial opportunities during the eighteenth century; but although expansionist wars, as with Oyo, produced captives for export, Asante was never as dependent on the slave trade, and its underlying wealth lay in agriculture and gold production. There was competition in the course of the nineteenth century between two rival groups among the political elite. The "imperialist" party sought the generation of wealth through military aggression, while a "peace" party argued for the pursuit of the same goal through commerce. The decline of the slave trade along this stretch of coast, in evidence by the 1820s, propelled the "peace" party into a position of dominance, and by mid-century wealthy traders, engaged in "legitimate" commerce, had become honored and respected by the state. Asante had long been a successful commercial power, sitting astride a trade network which linked the savannah and the desert to the north with the Atlantic system, from whence, like Dahomey, Asante acquired firearms. The demise of the slave trade notwithstanding, guns were used for territorial expansion, and against the provincial rebellions which became endemic in an empire only loosely governed from the center by the nineteenth century.[45] To the south, along the coast, lay the Fante states, a source of trouble to Asante as they often instigated rebellion within the empire as well as blocking its access to European trading forts along the "Gold Coast." The Fante also had the British as allies, and the British themselves adopted an attitude to Asante similar to that toward Dahomey: Asante was a savage, tyrannical, slave-dealing empire, against whom the Fante must be protected, and while for much of the nineteenth century Britain was not interested in the acquisition of coastal colonies, it was prepared to become involved in local politics in order to protect commercial interests.[46]

The area of what would become the British Gold Coast colony thus provides a good example of "creeping imperialism," the term used to describe the piecemeal process by which European governments sometimes found themselves inextricably caught up in local

An aspect of Kumasi, capital of Asante, in the 1820s. Private Collection/The Bridgeman Art Library. Source: The New York Public Library/https://digitalcollections.nypl.org/items/510d47da-71ff-a3d9-e040-e00a18064a99/Public Domain.

politics. The British fought a series of wars with Asante through the nineteenth century, conflicts which were usually sparked by an Asante invasion of the coastal districts.[47] The British government was reluctant, however, to extend responsibility over the coastal forts, as in the 1820s, when following a brief period of colonial administration it withdrew, considering such responsibility expensive and troublesome. Later in the century, Britain adopted an increasingly hostile stance toward Asante: after the successful invasion of Asante in 1873–4,[48] Britain formally annexed the Fante states with a view to stabilizing trade, thus establishing the Gold Coast colony; they withdrew from Asante itself, however, and only in the 1890s would they return, this time on a rather more permanent basis.

Dahomey and Asante were examples of highly militarized, centralized, and territorial states with expansionist foreign policies driven to a very real extent by commercial interests. But in the Niger delta, or the "Oil Rivers," there were a number of much smaller states which relied on overseas trade perhaps even more heavily than the big polities further west. States such as Bonny, Calabar, and – later in the nineteenth century – Opobo were compact communities scattered among the innumerable mouths of the Niger, structured around trading "houses" which became the basic units of social and commercial organization. Each had its own informal area of commercial and political influence, which was used to gain access to European merchants; slaves had been important earlier in the century, but palm oil soon took their place, and indeed the delta became synonymous with oil for the

European (and especially British) trading companies which did business there. The social mobility made possible by commerce led to considerable instability: ex-slaves, for example, worked their way into the ranks of traders and demanded sociopolitical status commensurate with the wealth thus acquired. Wealth funded revolt, too, and this was common across the delta from the middle of the nineteenth century: most dramatically, perhaps, a swathe of Bonny's population migrated to found the new state of Opobo in 1869.[49] Nigerian palm oil lubricated European machinery and fueled European industrialization; yet, while the delta states had made the successful transition from slave trade to "legitimate" commerce, they were increasingly vulnerable to external developments over which they had no control. From the 1850s, antimalarial quinine and steam-powered gunboats facilitated the European advance up the Niger, and in so doing they were increasingly able to bypass the delta trading states, undermining the commercial power of the latter; moreover, in the early 1860s, the international price of palm oil began a gradual descent, while cheaper substitutes for palm oil were being found elsewhere during the last third of the nineteenth century.[50]

The experience of the Niger delta states highlights a key theme in the history of Atlantic Africa, and indeed of other parts of the continent, namely growing powerlessness in the face of global commerce. It is clear that Africans responded dynamically and creatively – if often violently – to the opportunities offered by overseas trade; it is also the case that African exports – whether in the form of human labor, or later in terms of agricultural produce and raw materials – made an ineffable contribution to economic growth in Europe and the Americas, and to cultural enrichment there, too. Yet they had less and less control over the system in which they increasingly invested in the course of the nineteenth century; the power to change it lay beyond the continent, and most of the real benefits flowed that way, too. It was a relationship between zones of the world characterized by a lack of both balance and equity, rooted above all in an economic mismatch between North and South which was becoming all the more marked by the late nineteenth century. From economic imbalance flowed political and cultural misunderstanding, and in many respects colonial invasion signified the crystallization of both disparity and misapprehension. Colonial rule may in some ways have represented a dramatic change in the relationship between Europe and Africa; but in fact, the core components of the relationship were present by the early nineteenth century, and remained in place deep into the twentieth, indeed beyond.

Notes

1 Ralph Austen, *African Economic History* (London, 1987), chap. 5.
2 See the papers by Ghislaine Lydon and Baz Lecocq in the "JAH Forum: Trans-Saharan Histories," *Journal of African History*, 56:1 (2015).
3 Milo Kearney, *The Indian Ocean in World History* (New York, 2004); *Journal of African History*, 55:2 (2014).
4 There is, of course, an enormous and expanding body of scholarship on this. For a useful introduction, see Paul Lovejoy, "The impact of the Atlantic slave trade on Africa: a review of

the literature," *Journal of African History*, 30 (1989). John Thornton, *Africa and Africans in the Making of the Atlantic World, 1400–1800* (Cambridge, 1998) is also a useful entry into a vast topic.

5 R.C.C. Law (ed.), *From Slave Trade to "Legitimate" Commerce: The Commercial Transition in Nineteenth-century West Africa* (Cambridge, 1995).

6 Daron Acemoglu, Simon Johnson, & James Robinson, "Reversal of fortune: geography and institutions in the making of the modern world income distribution," *Quarterly Journal of Economics*, 118 (2002).

7 David Northrup, *Trade Without Rulers: Precolonial Economic Development in South-eastern Nigeria* (Oxford, 1978).

8 Giacomo Macola, *The Gun in Central Africa: A History of Technology and Politics* (Athens OH, 2016).

9 David Birmingham, *Trade and Conflict in Angola: The Mbundu and their Neighbours under the Influence of the Portuguese, 1483–1790* (Oxford, 1966); John Thornton, *Warfare in Atlantic Africa, 1500–1800* (London, 1999).

10 Joseph C. Miller *Way of Death: Merchant Capitalism and the Angolan Slave Trade, 1730–1830* (Madison WI, 1988).

11 A.F.C. Ryder, *Benin and the Europeans 1485–1897* (Harlow, 1969).

12 By Robin Law, see for example *The Oyo Empire, c.1600–1836: A West African Imperialism in the Era of the Atlantic Slave Trade* (Oxford, 1977) and *The Slave Coast of West Africa 1550–1750: The Impact of the Atlantic Slave Trade on an African Society* (Oxford, 1991).

13 See for example the work of Patrick Manning, including: *Slavery and African Life: Occidental, Oriental, and African Slave Trades* (Cambridge, 1990); and "African Population, 1650–2000: comparisons and implications of new estimates," in Emmanuel Akeampong *et al.* (eds.), *Africa's Development in Historical Perspective* (Cambridge, 2014).

14 For detailed accounts, see Hopkins, *Economic History*, esp. chaps. 2 & 3; and Walter Rodney, "The Guinea Coast," in Richard Gray (ed.), *The Cambridge History of Africa. Vol 4, from c.1600–c.1790* (Cambridge, 1975).

15 P.D. Curtin, *Economic Change in Precolonial Africa: Senegambia in the Era of the Slave Trade*, 2 vols. (Madison WI, 1975); Iliffe, *Africans*, 150.

16 V. Quinney, "Decisions on slavery, the slave trade, and civil rights for Negroes in the Early French Revolution," *Journal of Negro History*, 55:2 (1970); and see also the collection of documents in *La Revolution Francaise et l'abolition d'esclavage*, 12 vols. (Paris, 1968).

17 'William Wilberforce, in the House of Commons, Pictures the Slave Trade in All Its Horror [12 May 1789]', in Harlow & Carter (eds.), *Archives of Empire*, II, 93–100; J.R. Oldfield, *Popular Politics and British Anti-Slavery: The Mobilisation of Public Opinion against the Slave Trade, 1783–1807* (Manchester, 1995).

18 Olaudah Equiano, ed. V. Carretta, *The Interesting Narrative and Other Writings* (London, 1995).

19 For example, Thomas Fowell Buxton, *The African Slave Trade and its Remedy* (London, 1840).

20 Among the many biographies and interpretations of this remarkable individual, see C.L.R. James, *The Black Jacobins: Toussaint L'Ouverture and the San Domingo Revolution* (New York, 1938); and Philippe R. Girard, *Toussaint Louverture: A Revolutionary Life* (New York, 2016).

21 J.R. Ward, "The British West Indies in the Age of Abolition, 1748–1815," in P.J. Marshall (ed.), *The Oxford History of the British Empire: Vol. II: The Eighteenth Century* (Oxford, 1998), 425.

22 For a useful introduction, see Boris Fausto, *A Concise History of Brazil* (Cambridge, 1999).

23 Andrew Porter, "Trusteeship, Anti-Slavery, and Humanitarianism," in Porter (ed.), *Oxford History of the British Empire*, III.

24 Martin Lynn, *Commerce and Economic Change in West Africa: The Palm Oil Trade in the Nineteenth Century* (Cambridge, 1997).

25 Herbert S. Klein *The Atlantic Slave Trade* (Cambridge, 2010), chap. 8.

26 Quoted in C. Newbury, *The Western Slave Coast and its Rulers* (Oxford, 1961), 51.

27 Robin Law, "Introduction," in Law (ed.), *From Slave Trade to "Legitimate" Commerce*, 5. But see, in the same volume, Elisée Soumonni, "The compatibility of the slave and palm oil trades in Dahomey, 1818–1858".

28 Brodie Cruickshank, "Report of his Mission to the King of Dahomey [1848]," in "Missions to the Kings of Ashanti & Dahomey: dispatches from the Lieutenant-Governor of the Gold Coast," Parliamentary Papers: Colonies (Africa), Vol 50 (Irish University Press series, 1971).

29 Kristin Mann, *Slavery and the Birth of an African City: Lagos, 1760–1900* (Bloomington & Indianapolis, 2007), 89ff.

30 Again, see the collection of essays in Law (ed.), *From Slave Trade to "Legitimate" Commerce*; also Hopkins, *Economic History*, chap. 4, and Austen, *African Economic History*, chap. 5. More recently, Robin Law, Suzanne Schwartz & Silke Stickrodt (eds.), *Commercial Agriculture, the Slave Trade, and Slavery in Atlantic Africa* (Rochester NY, 2013) is wide-ranging and comprehensive.

31 Paul Lovejoy & David Richardson, "The initial 'crisis of adaptation': the impact of British abolition on the Atlantic slave trade in West Africa, 1808–1820", and Martin Lynn, "The West African palm oil trade in the nineteenth century and the 'crisis of adaptation,'" in Law (ed.), *From Slave Trade to "Legitimate" Commerce*.

32 See for example Hopkins, *Economic History*; Northrup, *Trade Without Rulers*; K.O. Dike, *Trade and Politics in the Niger Delta, 1830–1885* (London, 1956); P. Martin, *The External Trade of the Loango Coast, 1576–1870* (Oxford, 1972).

33 See for example Susan Martin, "Slaves, Igbo women and palm oil in the nineteenth century," in Law (ed.), *From Slave Trade to Legitimate Commerce*. More broadly, see Suzanne Miers & Igor Kopytoff (eds.), *Slavery in Africa: Historical and Anthropological Perspectives* (Madison WI, 1977), and Suzanne Miers & Richard Roberts (eds.), *The End of Slavery in Africa* (Madison WI, 1988); Paul Lovejoy, *Transformations in Slavery: A History of Slavery in Africa* (Cambridge, 1983), esp. chap. 8.

34 For a useful overview, see R.A. Stafford, "Scientific exploration and empire," in Porter (ed.), *Oxford History, III*.

35 For the classic statement, see Walter Rodney, *How Europe Underdeveloped Africa* (London, 1973).

36 Jan Vansina, *The Tio Kingdom of the Middle Congo, 1880–1892* (Oxford, 1973); A.J.H. Latham, *Old Calabar, 1600–1891: The Impact of the International Economy upon a Traditional Society* (Oxford, 1973).

37 For example, Ivor Wilks, *Asante in the Nineteenth Century* (Cambridge, 1975).

38 See Law, *Oyo Empire*, esp. Part III.

39 For a still-useful study, see J.F. Ade Ajayi & Robert Smith, *Yoruba Warfare in the Nineteenth Century* (Ibadan & Cambridge 1964), which also contains an interesting primary account by a Captain Jones in 1861; and see also the major work by S.A. Akintoye, *Revolution and Power Politics in Yorubaland, 1840–1893* (London, 1971). These events are also narrated by one of the early, classic texts of African historical writing, Samuel Johnson's *History of the Yorubas, from the Earliest Times to the Beginning of the British Protectorate* (Lagos, 1921).

40 For this paragraph, in addition to Ajayi & Smith, *Yoruba Warfare*, see also Robert Smith, *Warfare and Diplomacy in Precolonial West Africa* (London, 1989).

41 This is explored in J.D.Y. Peel, *Religious Encounter and the Making of the Yoruba* (Bloomington & Indianapolis, 2000), chaps. 1 & 2.

42 Notably, by the explorer and British Consul in the Bight of Benin Richard F. Burton, see *Wanderings in West Africa: From Liverpool to Fernando Po*, 2 vols. (London, 1863); and *A Mission to Gelele, King of Dahome*, 2 vols. (London, 1864).

43 J.C. Yoder, "Fly and elephant parties: political polarisation in Dahomey, 1840–1870," *Journal of African History*, 15:3 (1974).

44 I. Akinjogbin, *Dahomey and its Neighbours, 1708–1818* (Cambridge, 1967); W.J. Argyle, *The Fon of Dahomey: A History and Ethnography of the Old Kingdom* (Oxford, 1966), esp. chap. 3; Smith, *Warfare and Diplomacy*, passim. For the commercial context, see Robin Law, *Ouidah: The Social History of a West African Slaving "Port", 1727–1892* (Athens OH, 2004).

45 Wilks, *Asante*; T.C. McCaskie, *State and Society in Pre-Colonial Asante* (Cambridge, 1995).

46 See also T.C. McCaskie, "Cultural encounters: Britain and Africa in the nineteenth century," in Porter (ed.), *Oxford History*, III.

47 These conflicts are of course dealt with in Wilks and McCaskie among others, but they also appear (in rather less sophisticated tones) in "popular" histories of nineteenth-century British military adventures: see for example Byron Farwell, *Queen Victoria's Little Wars* (London, 1973), and Ian Hernon, *Britain's Forgotten Wars: Colonial Campaigns of the 19th Century* (Stroud, 2003).

48 A useful contemporary account can be found in H.M. Stanley, *Coomassie and Magdala: the Story of Two British Campaigns in Africa* (New York, 1874).

49 Latham, *Old Calabar*; G.I Jones, *The Trading States of the Oil Rivers: A Study of Political Development in Eastern Nigeria* (Oxford, 1963); Dike, *Trade and Politics*. Lynn, *Commerce and Economic Change*, examines these developments from a wider perspective.

50 Lynn, *Commerce and Economic Change*.

3 Eastern Intrusions

Slaves and Ivory in Eastern Africa

While Atlantic Africa was undergoing the kinds of transformation described in the previous chapter, the experience on the other side of the continent was different in a number of respects. The period from the late eighteenth century onward witnessed the linking up of the eastern African interior with the international trade of the Indian Ocean, the Arabian peninsula, and the Persian Gulf via the Swahili city-states of the coast. In this period, at the same time as the Atlantic slave trade was in gradual decline, the eastern African slave and ivory trades were actually expanding rapidly. In large part, the escalation of these trades was closely linked to the economic system controlled by the sultanate of Zanzibar, which through the nineteenth century was the dominant commercial power on the Kenyan and Tanzanian coasts.[1] Serving as a transit handler for ivory and slave exports, as well as employing slaves on its own spice plantations, Zanzibar's influence stretched chiefly along the coast, but from the early nineteenth century, Zanzibari merchant caravans were also beginning to penetrate inland in search of sources of slaves and ivory. By the 1840s, they had reached Lakes Tanganyika and Victoria, and some penetrated even further, into the forests of eastern Congo where they carved out loose trading-and-raiding "empires."[2] A number of African states and societies became deeply involved in this rapid commercial expansion – which, indeed, could scarcely have happened without them – including the kingdom of Buganda north of Lake Victoria, which became a base for Arab traders and a major supplier of slaves and ivory; the Nyamwezi people of central northern Tanzania, who became renowned as caravan porters, guides, and traders in their own right; and the Kamba of southern central Kenya, who were important middlemen along a trade route of growing importance. Central-eastern African commerce was for much of the nineteenth century linked mostly to the Indian Ocean and western and central Asia, although after the opening of the Suez Canal in 1869, trade was also directed toward Europe.

A History of Modern Africa: 1800 to the Present, Third Edition. Richard J. Reid.

East African societies, similar to their counterparts in the western and central parts of the continent, were profoundly affected by trade. While Atlantic Africa in general saw the undermining of warrior elites, eastern Africa witnessed their emergence, with the appearance of military states and charismatic rulers who sought to control trade routes and benefit from commerce. Access to trade served to undermine extant ruling elites and social forms. At the same time, the nature of the commerce itself meant increased levels of violence, insecurity, and upheaval across swathes of the central east African interior.[3] Some peoples, notably the Yao of southern Tanzania, Malawi, and Mozambique, themselves became notorious slave raiders.[4] In very general terms, however, it needs to be borne in mind that the central-eastern African interior was less commercially developed than West Africa, notwithstanding the increasingly complex regional trading networks which emerged in the course of the eighteenth and nineteenth centuries. Low population densities inhibited the growth of sophisticated commercial systems like those of Atlantic Africa, although there were important exceptions, notably the interlacustrine zone. Nonetheless, across the entire region, the African response to long-distance trade was dynamic and interventionist, on the part of both relatively ancient states and the more recent products of this new age. As in the Atlantic zone, this was a violently creative era, involving new economic and political forms and a revolution in military affairs.

Trade was important further north, too, as commerce along the Red Sea expanded dramatically in the course of the nineteenth century and linked the Ethiopian region ever more closely with Europe, Arabia, and southern Asia. Firearms were increasingly important in deciding political strength, and they help explain – at least in part – the growing significance of the area of central and northern Ethiopia ("Abyssinia" according to an older designation) from the second half of the eighteenth century onwards.[5] The benefits to be had from access to commerce through Massawa, in particular, and Zeila were a factor in the heightened and violent competition between several states in the highlands. Between the 1770s and the 1850s, the unified highland Christian empire was an ideal only, as the centralized state disintegrated and several polities jostled for access to land, resources, and commerce; in the meantime, there was pressure from the south, as the Oromo migrated onto the plateau and became a political and military force to be reckoned with, even though many became assimilated into Amhara culture and society. Only in the 1850s, largely through brute force, did Tewodros bring about a kind of unity, and even then he spent most of his reign on campaign; but he laid the foundations for a larger, more stable empire-state which would continue to grow between the 1870s and 1890s under his two immediate successors, Yohannes and Menelik.[6]

Commercial Horizons: Slaves and Ivory

An East African slave trade had existed for several centuries, but it increased dramatically from the 1780s onward. There were several factors behind this. The expansion of the Russian empire had begun to cut off supplies of slaves from those regions to the Muslim world, which then looked to East Africa as a source whose potential had not been fully tapped. There was also heightened demand for slaves for the sugar and coffee

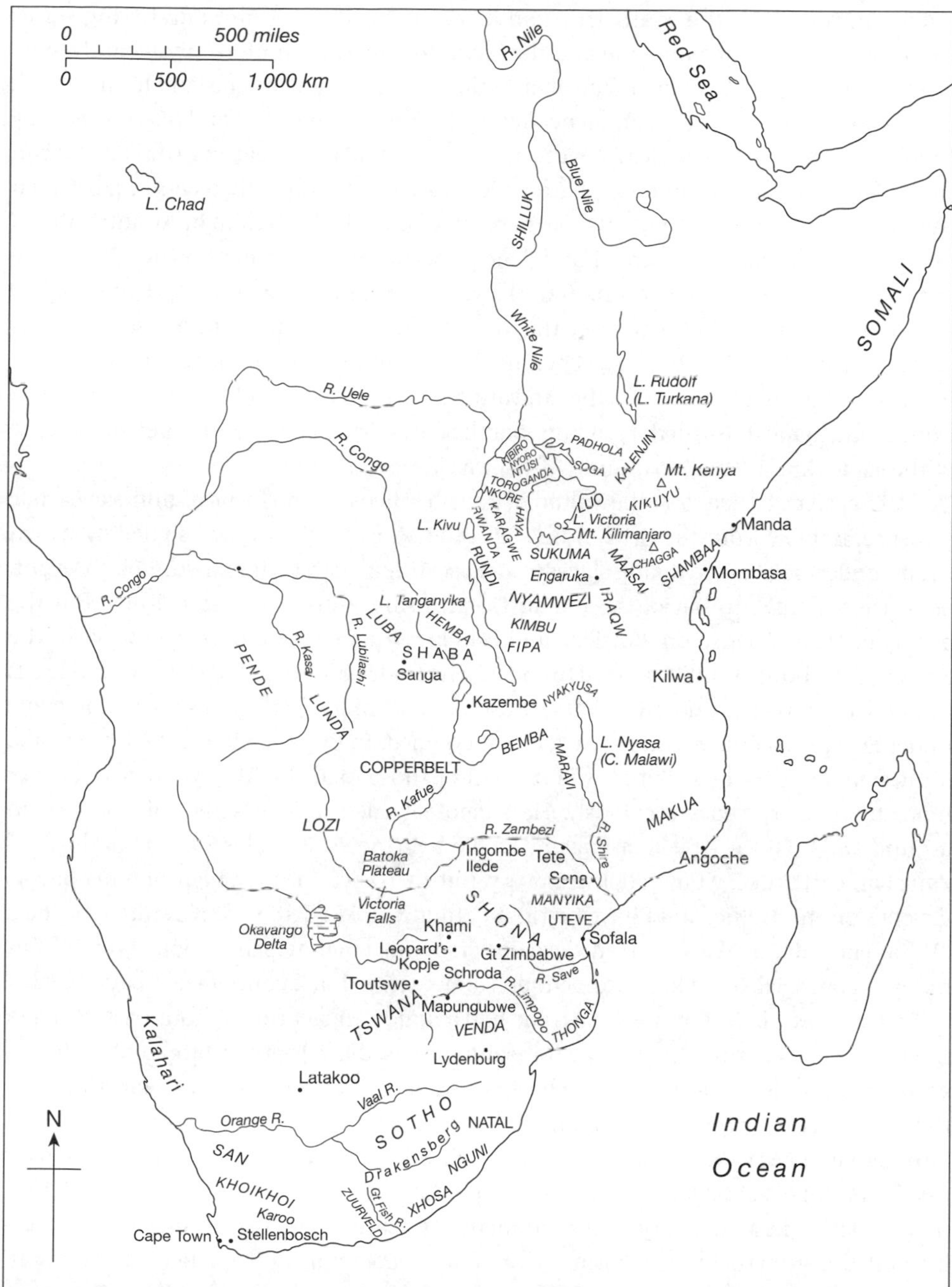

Eastern and southern Africa in the nineteenth century.

plantations on the French islands in the Indian Ocean, and these plantations were expanding from the 1770s. In the early nineteenth century, there was increasing demand from Brazil, as older sources declined along the Atlantic coastline and as plantations in Brazil itself expanded. Brazilian slave traders therefore began to make the longer journey from the southern Atlantic into the Indian Ocean, purchasing slaves from the region of Mozambique and the Zambezi valley. Even more significantly, new crops were being cultivated on Zanzibar itself, as well as on Pemba island to the north. Clove plantations in particular, owned by the islands' Arab rulers and often backed by Indian capital, absorbed slaves from the mainland. For all these reasons, the East African slave trade enter a new, intense phase which lasted approximately a century, between the 1780s and the 1880s. Figures are more difficult to establish than in Atlantic Africa, owing to the largely unrecorded and "illicit" nature of the trade; but by 1800 slave exports may have reached around 6,000 a year, rising to between 20,000 and 30,000 a year by the 1820s. At the peak of the trade in the 1860s, some 70,000 slaves a year were being exported. All these slaves came from the interior, with the raiding-and-trading frontier advancing ever further toward the Great Lakes and the area of eastern Congo; and again, it is worth recalling that the East African trade continued to increase at the same time as that in Atlantic Africa was in slow decline.[7]

Yet in eastern Africa, too, the Sultan of Zanzibar became the focus of anti-slave trade pressure, notably from the British. In 1822, the Moresby Treaty was signed by which Oman undertook to stop taking slaves from East Africa, with Britain assuming the right, as in the Atlantic, to patrol the Indian Ocean using anti-slavery squadrons. But the export of slaves for use on Zanzibar and Pemba remained legal until 1873, when the Zanzibari authorities finally agreed to end it.[8] The trade continued furtively in some areas until the early years of the twentieth century; but ultimately, clearly, as the region came under European control, the slave trade was doomed. In Buganda in the 1880s, Kabaka Mutesa made remarks strikingly reminiscent of those made by King Gezo of Dahomey more than thirty years previously. He supposedly declared to some missionaries in around 1881: "If the Queen of England would help me as she helps Sayyid Barghash of Zanzibar, certainly I would abolish slavery. But the power of my chiefs and my people depends on this traffic, and I have no right to hinder it." In 1883, he reiterated the idea: "What can I do? ... Those cursed slave dealers really rule my people. This I myself formerly encouraged, but it has assumed such dimensions that it cannot I fear be stopped."[9]

The rapid escalation of the slave trade had a major impact throughout East Africa in the nineteenth century. In general, it meant increased levels of warfare in the interior, with slaving violence destabilizing a host of societies. Such violence was exacerbated by the introduction of firearms, commonly traded by coastal merchants for slaves, although we need to be cautious about generalization; guns were often used as much for psychological effect as for the infliction of physical damage in the heat of battle.[10] Yet more broadly, the availability of guns influenced the breakdown of "traditional" authority and the growth of new forms of military leadership and political domination. Moreover, as in the Atlantic zone, the export of what was a potential labor force was profoundly damaging in societal and economic terms. This said, there were clearly opportunities for African traders to enrich themselves through involvement in the slave trade, both on a grand scale – for example leaders such as the Nyamwezi chief Mirambo, examined below – and on a much smaller scale, in the form of kidnapping. Nyamwezi, Yao, and Kamba peoples all seized their opportunities with gusto, acting as traders, middlemen, and porters. Some of the most dramatic sociopolitical changes took place among the Nyamwezi, who experienced a marked growth in economic inequality and the collapse of older political structures. In many areas, there was a breakdown in older subsistence systems, too, as ambitious young men neglected agriculture and pursued a life of commerce or war, or both.[11] This was an era of social flux and dramatic mobility, both upward and downward; new social systems, and new polities, were built on intergenerational conflict.

Ivory was also in increasing demand from the late eighteenth century: India remained an important market, but East African ivory was sought in Europe and North America, too, and throughout the nineteenth century, the European trade became ever more important, especially after the opening of the Suez Canal in 1869. It was, however, a finite resource and supplies dwindled as the century wore on; year on year, thousands of elephants were killed to meet demand, and the search for ivory was pushed ever deeper into the central African interior.[12]

While the kinds of goods being brought into Africa were fairly uniform across the continent, there was considerable dissimilarity in economic development between Atlantic Africa on the one hand and eastern Africa on the other. In the latter region, the export of slaves and ivory represented, as one historian has put it, "progress towards an inevitable dead end."[13] These were activities which were inimical to the region's long-term economic development: ivory was becoming increasingly scarce as the "elephant frontier" was pushed deeper and deeper into the interior, while slaves had no future as an export commodity as long as the region fell increasingly under European influence. This meant that as the nineteenth century drew to a close, central-eastern Africa faced a massive rupture with its economic past: slaves and ivory were abandoned, and export agriculture – representing the kind of "legitimate" commerce long practiced on the other side of the continent – was abruptly introduced under the auspices of newly established colonial regimes. Although ivory could be transported relatively easily through the organization of large caravans, only with railway construction could the eastern African interior be linked to the global economy in the way that the coast had been for several centuries.

The slave trade was arguably less widespread and less devastating in the Ethiopian region, although as the center of political gravity shifted north in the course of the seventeenth and eighteenth centuries, the Amhara and Tigrayans were dispatching up to 10,000 slaves per year through Massawa on the coast. Highlanders sometimes moved merchandise in their own caravans; but, loath as highlanders frequently were to travel to the hot coastal lowlands, increasingly the trade was in the hands of a distinct class of merchants, usually Muslim. In the nineteenth century, some slaves were themselves from the highlands, fetching high prices in Arabia; but increasingly, captives were brought from the western Ethiopian lowlands and eastern Sudan and were known derogatively as *shankalla*. Slaves were exported to the Arabian Peninsula, the Persian Gulf area, and to a lesser extent the wider Middle East. In addition to slaves, gold, ivory, skins, and spices were exported from the Ethiopian region, in exchange for firearms in particular; yet unlike in central-eastern Africa, firearms generally strengthened extant Amhara and Tigrayan political elites, largely through their ability to maintain commercial monopolies and control of trade routes between the coast and plateau; even so, as the nineteenth century progressed and commerce fanned out to some extent, a range of groups were better able to challenge states than previously. Criminality and rebellion flourished even as Tewodros and subsequently Yohannes unified the Ethiopian state.[14]

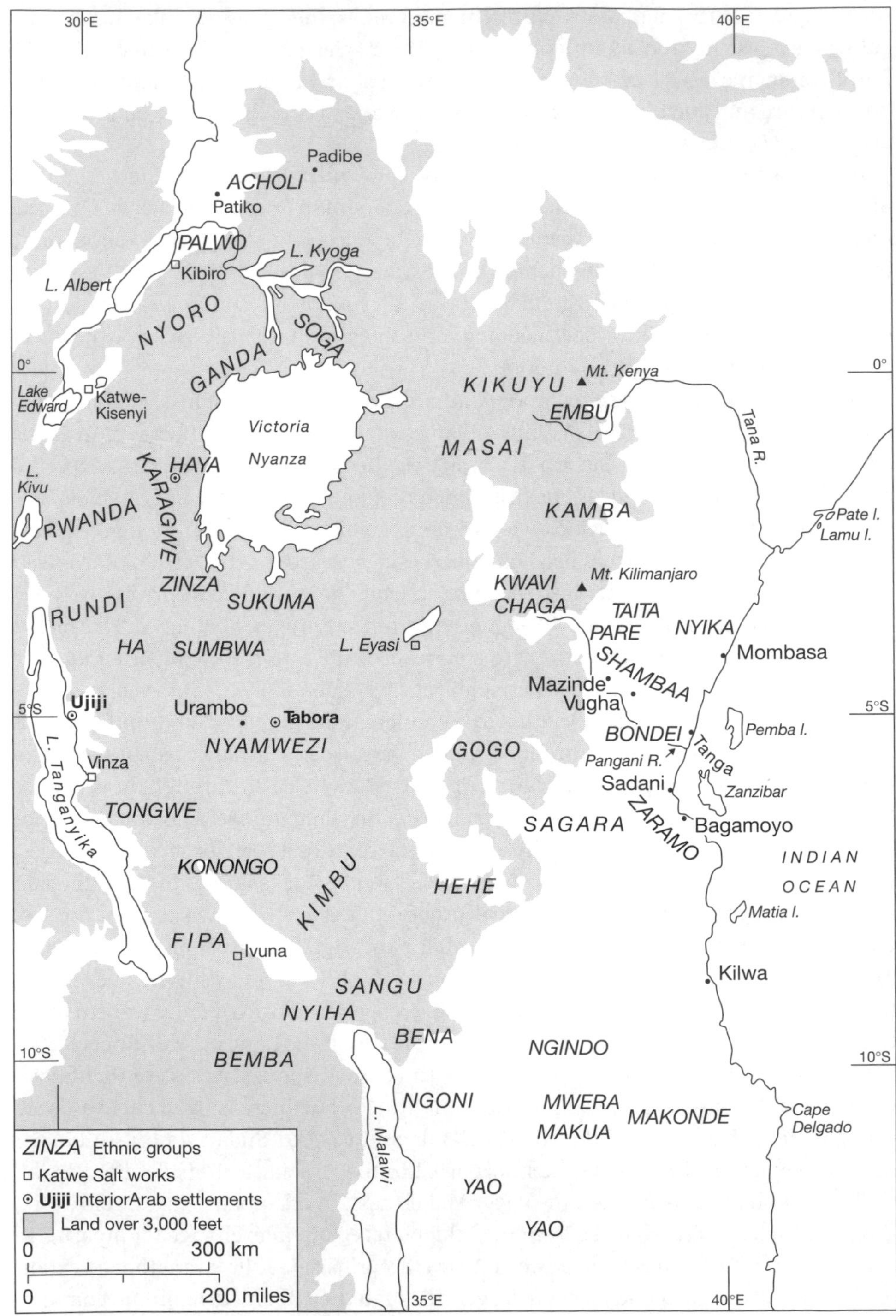

East Africa c.1870. Source: From J.E. Flint (ed.), *Cambridge History of Africa*. Vol. 5: *c.1790–c.1870* (Cambridge, 1976), p. 281, Map 10; © 1976 by Cambridge University Press. Reprinted with permission from Cambridge University Press.

The states and societies of lacustrine east Africa and the Ethiopian highlands alike were confronted with the problem that in order to gain access to global commerce, they had to do business with coastal communities which were frequently their adversaries. Nineteenth-century Ethiopian emperors may have laid claim to the Red Sea coast, based on some imaginative manipulations of the past, but the reality was that Massawa was administered by the Ottomans through the Egyptians. The latter had the power to bring trade to a halt, or otherwise to control it; increasingly obsessed with the idea of their isolation, Ethiopian ruling elites in the later nineteenth century would seek other means of accumulating firearms, as in the case of Menelik, who as king of Shoa traded with Europeans through Djibouti.[15] As emperor, Yohannes was forced to come to terms with his episodic religious tormentors at Massawa, Orthodox Christian supplier jostling with his Muslim buyers. Likewise, Mutesa, and, rather more dramatically, Mirambo were increasingly conscious of the fact that they were hostage to prevailing attitudes at Zanzibar, on which they depended for their guns, ammunition, and cloth. Participation in global commerce, Mirambo realized, required compromise and diplomacy, as well as force and bluster; the merchants of Zanzibar had rather more options in a stand-off than did their Nyamwezi suppliers.

Maritime Empire: Zanzibar

The East African coast has as long an international commercial history as anywhere on the Atlantic littoral – longer, indeed. Overseas contacts along the coast can be dated back centuries and perhaps millennia: the alternating patterns of the monsoon in the Indian Ocean facilitated seasonal journeys within an approximate triangle, linking India, Arabia, and East Africa. From central East Africa – by which is meant here modern Kenya, Tanzania, Mozambique, and the Zambezi valley – came ivory, gold, and slaves: trade in the latter, as we have noted, was of considerable antiquity but remained limited in scale until the late eighteenth century. This ancient commerce gave rise to Swahili culture along the coast, inspiring the foundation of a series of major coastal towns – for example Mogadishu and Mombasa – which were first and foremost trading settlements, combining African, Arabic, and Islamic culture, characterized by a high level of architectural achievement and enjoying considerable wealth.[16] The arrival of the Portuguese at the end of the fifteenth century spelled the end of what had been something of a "golden age": the Portuguese attacked and subdued much of the Swahili coast, and in so doing destroyed much of the rich commerce which was their lifeblood, although trade continued on a reduced scale with India and Arabia.

But the Portuguese conquest proved ephemeral. At the end of the seventeenth century, a fleet from Oman drove the Portuguese from most of the coastal settlements, with the exception of the southerly Mozambique littoral, and from this point, the Swahili coast was very loosely under the suzerainty of the Omani sultans. The latter began to assert their authority rather more vigorously toward the end of the eighteenth century, however, with a view to capitalizing on the Indian Ocean commerce, which was once more burgeoning; and the base of Omani expansion was the island of Zanzibar. The process is particularly associated with Sultan Seyyid Said, the energetic potentate who

An East African ivory porter in the mid-nineteenth century. Private Collection/The Stapleton Collection/ The Bridgeman Art Library. Source: The New York Public Library/ https://digitalcollections.nypl.org/items/510d47da-6e21-a3d9-e040-e00a18064a99/Public Domain.

in the 1830s went so far as to move his capital to Zanzibar permanently. Under him, the Omani–Zanzibari sphere of influence increased substantially and began to penetrate beyond the coast and into the interior: he organized both local and newly arrived merchant immigrants for the economic penetration and exploitation of the interior, and Zanzibari caravans had reached Lakes Victoria and Tanganyika by the end of the 1840s. When Seyyid died in 1856, his domains were basically split in two, and Oman and Zanzibar became to all intents and purposes independent of one another.[17] The government of Zanzibar strove to control the entire East Africa trade network along the coast of modern Kenya and Tanzania, and Zanzibar itself became the dominant force in East African commerce until the 1880s, when the European partition destroyed its sovereignty and its *raison d'être*.

Up until the early nineteenth century, then, Zanzibari and Omani merchants had operated mainly on the coast, dependent on African middlemen, among the most successful of whom were the Nyamwezi of modern west-central Tanzania. But it was only a matter of time before adventurous coastmen themselves began to follow the trade routes into the interior; wealthy coastal entrepreneurs financed caravans which traveled hundreds of miles west, often comprising several hundred people, and employing Africans as porters and guides.[18] Their security was based largely on the Arabs' possession of firearms. Between the 1830s and the 1850s, Arab merchants established permanent entrepots at Tabora, in the chiefdom of Unyanyembe, Ujiji on Lake Tanganyika, and at the capital of Buganda, at the north end of Lake Victoria. Among the most successful, and notorious, of these traders was "Tippu Tip," so named, apparently, after the retort of his firearms, who covered a vast area of modern Tanzania and Congo from the 1860s, raiding and trading, and establishing a considerable if short-lived sphere of influence. Tippu Tip was particularly successful in imposing himself politically on a number of societies; more generally, although this kind of penetration was essentially commercial in character, Arab traders in the second half of the nineteenth century attempted to assert political influence over African rulers, in order to secure commercial interests.[19] They had some success in comparatively decentralized and acephalous communities, but in others, powerful political establishments kept resident Arab traders under close supervision. In any case, Zanzibar itself exercised only the loosest control over these coastal adventurers, many of whom acted very much on their own accounts, Tippu Tip among them. But they all, to a greater or lesser degree, spread coastal culture, as well as Islam, into the interior: dress, architecture, and language were all influenced as representatives of heterogeneous Swahili civilization advanced across a broad zone bounded approximately by Lakes Malawi, Tanganyika, and Victoria.

Commercial pioneers: Seyyid Barghash, Sultan of Zanzibar (1870–88), with his advisors. Source: Photograph courtesy of the Peabody Essex Museum. Neg 13462.

Slaving violence in East Africa: the massacre of Manyema women at Nyangwe, c.1870. Source: The British Library Board, The British Library, B 224 DSC.

Statehood, Conflict, and Trade (1): The Lacustrine Zone

The area of the Great Lakes – in particular the northern interlacustrine zone around Lakes Tanganyika, Victoria, Edward, and Albert – was home to some of sub-Saharan Africa's most complex civilizations. The kingdoms of Buganda, Bunyoro, Toro, Ankole, Rwanda, and Burundi all had their origins before the nineteenth century and shared certain basic characteristics. They were the products of good rainfall and rich soil, facilitating a denser and more permanent level of population than is normally possible in Africa south of the Sahara. They shared much in the way of political culture, too, including the principle of strong, centralized kingship, which also had important symbolic and ritual dimensions. Kings of the lacustrine zone frequently ruled through provincial chiefs appointed directly by royal authority; and while chiefly lineages did indeed emerge, in addition to royal genealogies, appointments to such offices were often made according to merit, and certainly loyalty was rewarded. A key feature of kingship, moreover, was the absence (normally) of an obvious heir – royal kinsmen, for example, were often imprisoned or killed – which meant that succession was frequently a violent affair. Women generally enjoyed a higher economic and cultural status across eastern Africa than they did in the southern or western zones. In most of the kingdoms across the region, ruling dynastics claimed descent from migrating groups, with varying degrees of accuracy: the immigrant Nilotes, arriving in the area between the fifteenth and seventeenth centuries, did indeed spawn, or contribute to, a number of ruling lineages. Some would also come to claim divine status. Complex elite oral traditions developed around privileged status, underpinning the separateness of ruling classes and lineages, while privilege itself was maintained through elaborate systems of taxation and tribute. Immigrant pastoralists developed such systems in Rwanda and Burundi, where they became known as Tutsi, and in Ankole, where they were Hima; in these societies, they were patrons to agriculturalist clients, the Bantu-speaking farmers known as Hutu in Rwanda and Burundi, and Iru in Ankole.[20] In reality, there was a great deal of both cultural and economic interaction between these groups; but in many ways, cattle-keeping came to be regarded as something of an elite activity, associated with elevated status, and pastoralists as a superior caste. Only in the early twentieth century would these socioeconomic identities become solidified into "tribal" ones.

The dominant kingdoms of the northern lake region were Buganda and Bunyoro, two states with a history of intimate relations, both violent and otherwise. Bunyoro, which had evolved out of the earlier state of Kitara from the fifteenth century, had been the leading power in the region until, in the course of the seventeenth and eighteenth centuries, it had steadily lost ground to the expansionist and dynamic kingdom of Buganda, which enjoyed high levels of moisture, considerable agricultural fertility, and thus a dense and comparatively large population. A complex, competitive society, at the apex of which was the largely secular king or *kabaka*, who accumulated powers of appointment over the major chieftaincies in the kingdom, Buganda was characterized by a highly mercantilist foreign policy, which sought control of the region's economic resources and was driven by an advanced military culture. War was an instrument of policy in the reach for commercial, economic, and territorial hegemony. By the beginning of the nineteenth century, Buganda dominated the region north and west of Lake Victoria and would be – as we see in the following – in a strong position to meet the challenges of the age.[21] Bunyoro was weakened by internal political turmoil in this period and steadily lost territory in the course of the eighteenth century; it would, however, experience a period of resurgence from the 1860s and 1870s onward.[22] Further south, in the extremely fertile and well-watered hills north of Lake Tanganyika, lay the kingdoms of Rwanda and Burundi, also highly militarized, although Rwanda was the more successful, expanding aggressively in the course of the eighteenth and nineteenth centuries.[23] Of course, different political systems existed side by side: to the east of the centralized militarism of Buganda lay a loose confederacy of small principalities, the Soga; and likewise, to the north of Buganda and Bunyoro lay smaller, often "stateless," societies, peoples who lived along, and indeed in some ways represented, the fluid frontiers between expanding, hegemonic polities.[24]

In the nineteenth century, states engaged with one another in the context of both warfare and trade. Buganda's relations with its neighbors, for example, were pragmatic: trade and economic influence where possible, conflict when necessary, as the kingdom sought to build both a territorial and an "informal" empire.[25] Despite recurrent conflict, Buganda depended on healthy economic relations with Bunyoro, the Soga to the east, the pastoral states to the west, and a host of smaller states and societies to the south. However, interstate relations across the region became rather more volatile, more intense, and – in general – more violent with the expansion of long-distance, coastal-oriented commerce, the commercial network directed by Zanzibar. Control of trade and its benefits would increasingly drive interlacustrine relations, while trade itself – as in Atlantic Africa – would have major social and political consequences from the 1840s onward. Most of the states noted previously would strive to become involved in this commerce: only Rwanda and Burundi resisted the temptation for much of the nineteenth century, giving rise to their contemporary reputations for self-imposed isolation and hostility to all outsiders.

If some of the more remarkable developments in the lacustrine region involved political centralization and the predominance of the territorial state, the opposite was true in other parts of central-eastern Africa. Across modern Kenya and Tanzania, there were few centralized states of the interlacustrine model before the middle of the nineteenth century, while even ethnic identities were still fragile and continually evolving during the period under examination. Across much of this vast area, soils were thin and rainfall unreliable, and thus, agriculture was difficult and precarious: in the last decades of the nineteenth century, communities were still engaged in the struggle to colonize the land. In contrast to the interlacustrine zone, population densities were low, and settlement tended to be scattered – unlike in the area of Buganda and Bunyoro, where urban patterns had appeared long before 1800 – and therefore, the conditions for elaborate state formation were absent in many areas. With a tendency to live in small groups, people were able to move when land became infertile, or when political disputes arose; thus, while small chieftainships did emerge across Tanzania through the eighteenth and nineteenth centuries, these were flexible, and characterized by continual movement.

Nonetheless, the nineteenth century witnessed the arrival of new pressures, as the coastal commercial network spread inland; the result was the emergence within many societies of new forms of political organization in order to meet the new challenges and take advantage of the new opportunities, and leaders appeared – usually military, with much greater personal power than had been the case previously – to shape as well as to exploit new structures. This was most famously true among the Nyamwezi and the Kimbu. A similar situation developed in Kenya, where state formation had been likewise virtually absent before the nineteenth century: among the Nilotic pastoralists of the Kenyan interior (and of northern Tanzania), including the Maasai, age-regiment organization was more important than any centralized political control or personalized hierarchies. Alongside the Nilotes were smaller agricultural communities – notably the Kamba and Kikuyu – who both fought the Maasai over land and water, but who also intermarried and traded with them, and borrowed culturally from them.[26] Yet as the nineteenth century progressed, a number of societies underwent the same kinds of changes experienced in Tanzania: new forms of social and political structure emerged under stronger, more centralized systems of leadership. Similar to the Nyamwezi, the Kamba, too, would become energetic participants in global trade.

The themes of local entrepreneurship and the fluidity of identities are most dramatically manifest in the Nyamwezi, who did not exist as a "people" before the commercial and political dynamics of the mid-nineteenth century. These dry land grain farmers were, in cultural and linguistic terms, a loosely affiliated population group across western and northern Tanzania when they began to travel ever further afield, taking advantage of growing commercial opportunities; to people on or near the coast, they came from the west, and thus became "the people of the new moon."[27] As the nineteenth century dawned, the Nyamwezi had already developed trade routes which linked Buganda at the north end of Lake Victoria, Katanga to the south, and Zanzibar at the coast; they dominated this commercial network until the middle decades of the nineteenth century, when coastal traders began to penetrate the interior with their own caravans, discussed previously. Many Nyamwezi became porters for the wealthy Arab and Indian merchants; but conflict was inevitable with the newcomers, especially as the movement of large coastal caravans inland placed strains on local communities in terms of food supply, while antagonism also arose by the 1840s and 1850s over the establishment of customs duties by chiefs through whose territories the commercial highways ran.

As conflict escalated, coastal merchants sought increasingly to involve themselves in Nyamwezi politics – relatively straightforward, given the fragmented character of those politics – and backed one clan against another, or took up the cause of the politically disaffected, who were only too willing to accept such comparatively well-armed patronage. Through possession of firearms and the promise of commercial advantage, Arabs interfered in chieftaincy disputes and began to wield considerable power within chiefdoms. The process is exemplified by the case of Unyanyembe, on the main highway between the lakes and the coast, where civil war in the early 1860s saw heavy-handed Arab intervention, as merchant-adventurers backed first one *mtemi*, or chief, then another, in the pursuit of the best commercial arrangement. The Arab community was able to secure control of Tabora, which began to take on the character of a military garrison, especially as regional warfare, sparked by the sociopolitical breakdown and reconstruction brought about by commercial change, became more intense in the 1870s.[28]

Meanwhile, a violent new element was entering the region from the south, representing the far-flung effects of politico-military events in southern Africa examined in the next chapter. By the 1850s, groups of Ngoni, refugees from the Zulu revolution far to the south, were penetrating into the area of modern Tanzania, bringing destruction and a transformation in patterns of warfare and statehood. They attacked and pillaged across a wide area, living by plunder, although after a few years some had settled down to a more sedentary existence. Ujiji, for example, was attacked in the 1850s, while in the course of the 1860s and 1870s, Ngoni moved in various directions across central Tanzania. It is important to note, of course, that while the term "Ngoni" is commonly used to describe these groups, by the 1850s and 1860s, they were amalgamations of various absorbed and conquered peoples, imbued with the Ngoni military ethos. While some communities scattered on the approach of the Ngoni, others were absorbed, and others again copied the Ngoni model in order to survive, and thus became as militarized as the immigrants. Across the region, then, the Ngoni and their imitators brought about a revolution in terms of political structure and militarization and, just as new forces for commercial and social change were also entering the region from the coast, demonstrated the transformative power of violence. The changes which resulted, between c. 1850 and 1890, were often violent indeed.

Rising levels of conflict and endemic insecurity both gave rise to, and were exacerbated by, wandering gangs of desperate, cannabis-smoking young men, heavily armed, driven by the search for plunder and adventure. This was perhaps the single most important social phenomenon of the second half of the nineteenth century. These young men were the cause and the effect of social, political, and economic change, the symptom of both the destruction of old orders and the reconstruction of new ones. They came to be known generically as *ruga ruga*, a problematic term in so far as it denotes a young, unmarried, "professional" soldier, and one that is therefore rather more proscriptive than the phenomenon deserves. *Ruga ruga* might be petty criminals, living off plunder in the bush, or they might attach themselves to commercial caravans or the entourages of coastal merchants as mercenaries; crucially, they formed the backbone of the emerging military states which dominated swathes of the interior during the 1870s and 1880s.[29]

One of the most successful of these new states was that created by the Nyamwezi chief Mirambo. Born around 1840, Mirambo spent his youth as a caravan porter traveling to the coast before succeeding to a small chieftainship northwest of Tabora; he amalgamated this with another, overcoming his brother's claim in the process, building an army of *ruga ruga* with which to widen his political and military base, which was almost certainly at least partially inspired by the Ngoni. From the end of the 1860s onward, he incorporated surrounding chiefdoms by force and thus created a single unified state, with the urban and peri-urban district of "Urambo" at its center. Gathering ivory and livestock in tribute, he took control of the northern lacustrine trade routes and used his growing commercial power to accumulate firearms. Mirambo was a man of extraordinary talent: his state, which dominated a triangular section of territory between Unyanyembe, Ujiji, and Lake Victoria, was his personal creation; he usually led his army personally; and his ambition appears to have been the unity of the interior. In this sense, his violence, while it often appeared to the outsider to resemble the general lawlessness of the age, was constructive and creative; he believed in the supplanting of dozens of small chiefdoms with a handful of large, powerful states – of which his was to be one – in part to counter the growing power of the Arab merchants, the Zanzibar sultanate, and, later, the European presence at the coast. To this end, he sought alliances with other major regional players, notably Mutesa of Buganda, although his very presence was a threat to the Arabs of Unyanyembe, with whom he was at war for much of the 1870s and early 1880s. The strength of Mirambo's "empire" was, however, simultaneously its greatest weakness, namely its overdependence on Mirambo himself, and when he died in late 1884, the problem of lack of internal cohesion was one that his successor, Mpandoshalo, ultimately proved unable to address. By the end of the 1880s, on the eve of the German invasion, the state had largely disintegrated, disappearing as quickly as it had been created.[30]

Brilliant though Mirambo's career had been, it was not wholly unique, even if his peculiar vision for East Africa's political future may be considered as such. Another Nyamwezi leader, Msiri, built the commercial and military power of Garenganze, southwest of Lake Tanganyika, during the 1860s and 1870s, sitting astride a trade network which linked eastern to south-central Africa. Among the Kimbu, to the southeast of Mirambo, Nyungu-ya-Mawe carved out a loose hegemony in much the same manner as his rather more famous contemporary.[31] These states were innovative, dynamic, and violent responses to the opportunities of the age; yet they were as much rooted in criminality as political creativity, and therein lay the causes of their inherent instability. The forces that assisted their construction – in particular, a generation of youth able and willing to reject the values and patterns of behavior of its fathers and driven by a new set of social, political, and economic aspirations – were also those that rendered these new states unsustainable in the longer term. Individual leaders might command immense loyalty for a time, but the creation of stable state systems in which a wider community might invest proved rather more problematic. Despite Mirambo's attempts to historicize his warfare, and claim for Urambo a deeper political heritage,[32] he was ultimately unable to do what Shaka had done for the Zulu, for example. The *raison d'être* of the new states, in any case, was commercial freedom and military adventurism, neither of which would have been possible in the face of European hegemony. Nonetheless, the energy with which Africans engaged in global commerce and attempted to invent new political structures to channel these forces was an indication of what was to come under colonial rule.

The state-builder: Mirambo of the Nyamwezi, in the early 1880s. Source: Reproduced from London Missionary Society/Council for World Mission Archives.

While new African states were emerging, coastal traders were penetrating beyond Lake Tanganyika and into the eastern Congo, and through the 1860s and 1870s, they were carving out spheres of influence based on trading and raiding across swathes of the rainforest. The quest for ivory and slaves caused widespread disruption, as Arabs preyed on dislocated communities and built personal armies of armed slaves and retainers, in the process weakening extant sources of political authority. The region to the west of Lake Tanganyika was engulfed in violence, although some degree of order was imposed on the predatory chaos by the greatest predator of them all, Hamed bin Muhammad, otherwise known as "Tippu Tip." Tippu Tip epitomized the ruthless caravan merchant of the age: born in Zanzibar of Arab-African parentage around 1830, he was based at Tabora in the 1860s before moving into the ivory-rich region of Tetela in the eastern Congo in the 1870s. He carved out a considerable sphere of influence based on violence and sent caravans laden with ivory east to Zanzibar, passing through the territory of Mirambo with whom he generally had good relations. Tippu Tip became a wealthy man on the back of his commercial and military endeavors and was only undermined with the Belgian partition of the Congo, whereupon he retired to Zanzibar.[33]

Tippu Tip operated in areas where there was an absence of large, centralized states and was therefore able to impose himself and bend societies to his will; his respectful attitude toward Mirambo, however, indicates how even he needed to approach the stronger polity with considerable circumspection. Elsewhere in the region, indeed, Arab traders had markedly different experiences from those in Unyanyembe or eastern Congo. In the Kenyan interior of the 1860s, the Maasai, Kikuyu, and Nandi successfully resisted the penetration of Arab caravans, the latter attempting to bypass Kamba middlemen; indeed, the stereotype of the frightful Maasai in the interior was to some extent perpetuated by those African merchants wishing to discourage Swahili would-be entrepreneurs.[34] Around Lake Victoria, Arab traders were able to exercise a certain amount of political leverage in Karagwe, but at the north end of the lake, they encountered the Buganda kingdom, which they first reached in 1844. They traded successfully here, but generally on Ganda terms: they were closely supervised by Ganda authorities and were confined to the royal capital, where they had a residential quarter. They were generally not permitted to travel within or beyond Buganda, and when they were, they were accompanied by a Ganda escort. The two kabakas of the age, Suna (c.1830–57) and Mutesa (1857–84), profitably traded slaves and ivory in exchange for guns, cloth, and other commodities, which were highly prized in Buganda's competitive commercialized and militarized culture. Imported cotton cloth changed elite fashion as well as symbolizing changing socioeconomic aspirations, while guns found their way quickly into the military establishment, and Mutesa was particularly enthusiastic about the firearm's potential. Competition for control of trade across the Lake Victoria region prompted the Ganda to use military means to secure commercial interests; slave gathering was an increasingly important activity for the army itself, bringing the kingdom into conflict with its neighbors, such as Bunyoro, Busoga, and the other states to the west.[35]

The Ganda response to commercial opportunities, similar to that of the Nyamwezi, was dynamic and aggressive; by the 1870s, however, the army was beginning to overreach itself through territorial overambition. The Ganda military ethos was weakened by political tensions at the kingdom's center – generational conflict was in part reflected in allegiance to foreign faiths – while there is evidence that the increased use of guns by ill-trained soldiers was undermining the kingdom's military capacity. From the 1840s

Mutesa, kabaka of Buganda (c.1857–84), with his court, late 1870s. Source: Universal History Archive/UIG via Getty Images.

and 1850s onward, the Ganda sought to dominate lacustrine commerce by developing a fleet of canoes capable of traversing the lake from north to south. By the 1870s, Buganda had become one of the major exporters of slaves in the region, and its "navy" was a remarkable innovation, but the kingdom was unable to impose itself as firmly on the external political and economic landscape as Mutesa clearly hoped. By the end of the 1880s, Mutesa had been succeeded by Mwanga, a young man of little experience, and Buganda was experiencing heightened conflict with a resurgent Bunyoro, as well as internal religious and political tensions.[36] Ultimately, the Ganda would ally themselves with the British in the colonial subjugation of the surrounding region and indeed the name "Uganda" would be applied to the future colonial territory.

Statehood, Conflict, and Trade (2): Northeastern Africa

Through the seventeenth and eighteenth centuries, the Christian kingdom steadily shifted its center of political gravity northward, with a permanent capital established at Gondar, and the province of Tigray more fully incorporated into the state.[37] In large part, the expansion of trade on the Red Sea drew the nucleus of the modern Ethiopian state northward; but the migrations of the Oromo also constituted a mounting pressure from the south, and as the Oromo moved onto the highland plateau, they became a political, economic, and cultural force to be reckoned with, changing the very nature of *habesha*

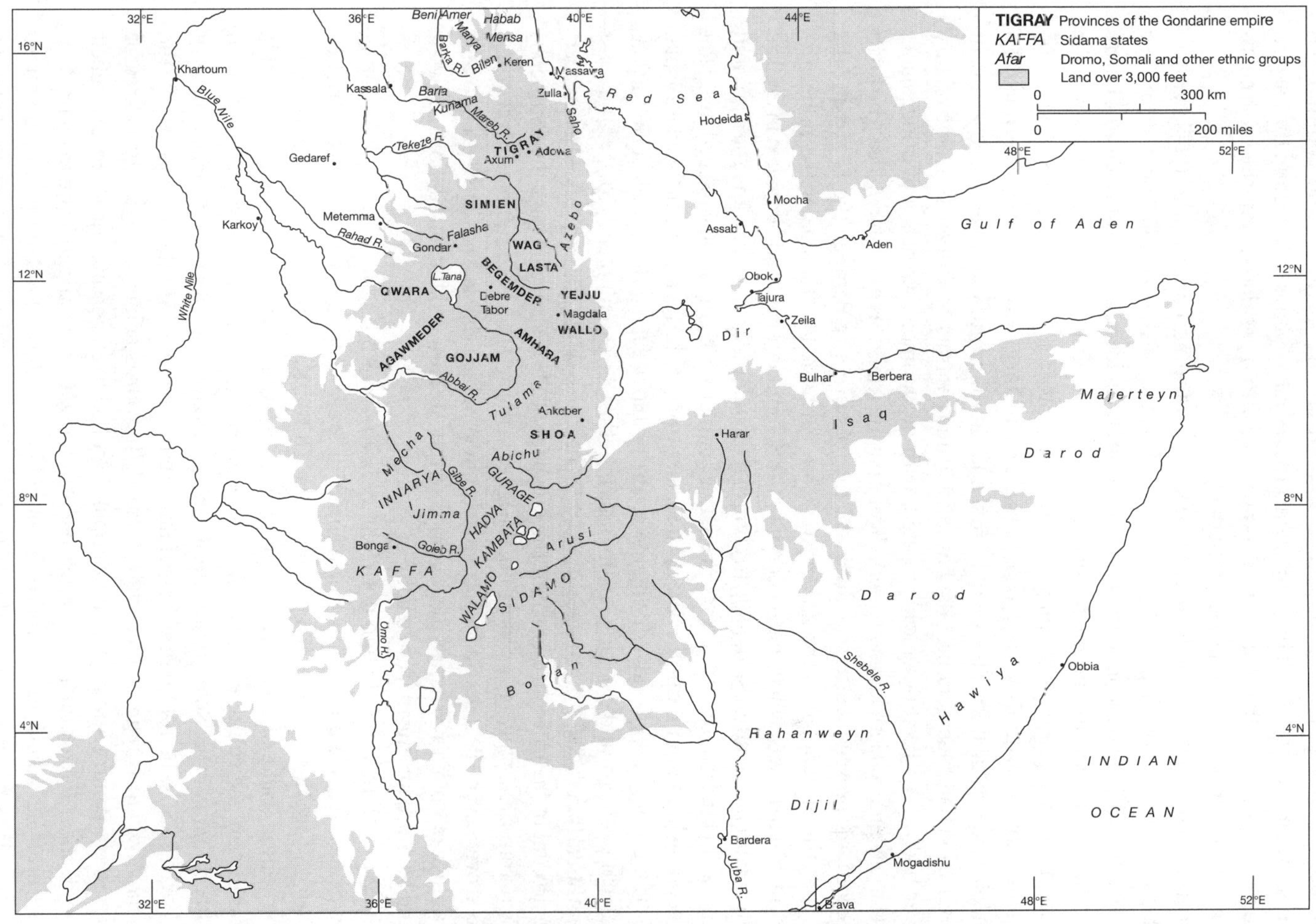

The Horn of Africa in the nineteenth century. Source: From J. E. Flint (ed.), *Cambridge History of Africa*. Vol. 5: *c.1790–c.1870* (Cambridge, 1976), © 1976 by Cambridge University Press. Reprinted with permission from Cambridge University Press.

society. Many were Muslim; but many others adopted the Orthodox Christianity that constituted the very foundation of Amhara and Tigrayan civilization, and were both absorbed into, and came to influence, Amhara culture. Some Oromo communities founded their own states, rubbing up against the *habesha* polities of Shoa and the eastern escarpment; in time, other individual Oromo would attain positions of considerable political and military power among the Amhara.[38]

In the second half of the eighteenth century, central authority in the fragile empire collapsed, and the Solomonic rulers – so-called because of the genealogical descent they claimed from King Solomon, a myth central to imperial ideology – were reduced to mere figureheads. To some extent, the political disintegration of the 1760s and 1770s was the culmination of a process stretching back several centuries. Ever since the decline of the ancient empire of Axum, the major commercial and military power in modern-day northern Ethiopia and central Eritrea between the first and eighth centuries CE, central government in the region had undergone periods of expansion and contraction; but political and military power had always been provincially rooted, with autonomous districts and principalities and largely independent kingdoms periodically paying tribute as much to an idea (the myth of Solomonic provenance) as to a physical center of authority. Between the 1770s and the 1850s – the era known as the *Zemene Mesafint*, Amharic for "the age of the princes" – provincial rulers were wholly independent of the Solomonic center, and engaged in cyclical conflict with one another, struggling to control regional trade, resources, and the signs and symbols of central authority. It was during this period that Tigray, ideally located to exploit burgeoning long-distance trade, became a major power in the region of northern Ethiopia, exercising control over Gondar during the governorship of *Ras* ("prince") Mikael in the late eighteenth century and reaching northwards into the Eritrean highlands toward the coast from the early decades of the nineteenth century onward. While Tigray amassed a considerable arsenal of firearms, further south the kingdom of Shoa struggled with the incursions of the Oromo, recapturing territory from the latter in the first half of the nineteenth century; indeed over several decades Shoa, particularly under Sahle Selassie, positioned itself to take advantage of commerce across the region, and the Amhara laid the foundations for what would later become the modern empire of Ethiopia.[39]

Violent regionalism – though not violence itself – was brought to an end by a young provincial renegade and member of a junior princely line, Kassa, from the district of Qwara on the edge of Amhara territory. In the 1840s, Kassa built up a reputation as an inspirational leader of men, his band of soldiers expanding to become an army capable of taking on the ruling elites of the region; renaming himself Tewodros, he claimed (rather dubiously) the Solomonic inheritance, and following a series of decisive battles in the early 1850s, he had himself proclaimed emperor in 1855, the year in which the *Zemene Mesafint* is regarded as having ended. Tewodros achieved a greater degree of unity across central and northern Ethiopia than had been possible for a century, albeit through sheer force, and indeed much of his reign was spent suppressing insurrection. For several years, however, Tewodros attempted to regularize land tenure and taxation, clip the wings of an over-powerful Orthodox Church, and instill a greater degree of professionalism and discipline in his army. Not unlike some of his North African contemporaries, he envisaged transforming Ethiopia into an industrial, commercial power, based on his understanding of what made Europe "great," and to this end, he welcomed Europeans whose expertise he sought to utilize in "modernizing" his army – largely through the ultimately unsuccessful import of artillery. In foreign policy, too, his vision was extensive – though somewhat less realistic than his domestic aspirations – and he sought religious, commercial, and political alliances with the European powers he considered his equals. Tewodros perceived Islam – embodied in the Egyptians and the Ottoman empire – as Christian Ethiopia's ancient enemy, and he demanded, among other things, the restoration of the Eritrean coast to Ethiopia and laid claim (based on the supposed Solomonic inheritance) to Jerusalem, which he bitterly lamented had fallen into the hands of the cursed Muslim.[40]

By the early 1860s, regional rebellion – often backed by a resentful clergy – was commonplace, notably in the north, where Tewodros lost control of much of Tigray and the Eritrean plateau. It was a vicious cycle of violence, for the harsher Tewodros became in attempting to suppress insurrection, the more stubborn and widespread such insurrection became, particularly among a peasantry increasingly hostile to the predations of the emperor's army. By 1866–7, an increasingly unstable Tewodros was confronted by an array of political enemies, including the young Menelik, king of Shoa, and his domain had shrunk to an area around the "fortress" of Magdala, on the eastern edge of the plateau. In the end, however, it was foreign intervention rather than internal uprising which destroyed him. In the mid-1860s, irritated and insulted by a perceived slight on the part of Queen Victoria – a reply to his letter had not arrived – he imprisoned a number of Europeans, including some Britons, and kept them in chains until amends could be made. In 1867–8, the British government dispatched an army – at a cost of some £9 million to the taxpayer, an enormous sum at the time – which landed at the Gulf of Zula on the Eritrean coast, marched into the highlands, and defeated Tewodros' dwindling army. The emperor shot himself rather than fall into British hands.[41] During a remarkable expedition, the British had been greatly assisted by the fact that Tewodros had so many enemies; their relatively uneventful march through potentially hostile Tigrayan territory, notably, had been facilitated by the cooperation of its governor, Ras Kassa, now a pretender to the Solomonic throne. The British released the European hostages and swiftly withdrew, taking Tewodros' young son, Alemayu, with them; after an unhappy education at Rugby school in England, the young man died after a short illness in 1879.

After a brief interregnum and a regional power-struggle, the Tigrayan Ras Kassa became emperor of Ethiopia as Yohannes IV in 1872 and continued the process begun by Tewodros in building a unified, expansionist state. Unlike Tewodros, however, Yohannes complemented military force with diplomacy and employed the age-old mechanism of intermarriage between regional ruling families to achieve political stability, in this case establishing a marriage alliance with Menelik, who aspired to the imperial throne but who now decided to bide his time. Yohannes did indeed bring about a degree of internal stability, but his horizons were clouded by the Egyptians on the coast. It was an uneasy, though symbiotic, relationship, made fraught by Yohannes' territorial claim over much of modern Eritrea and its littoral; the Egyptians evacuated under the auspices of the British in the mid-1880s, only to be swiftly replaced by the Italians, who already had a foothold further south on the coast, at Assab. Yet Yohannes' northern frontier, watched over by his faithful lieutenant Ras Alula, was only one of his causes for concern; another was the rise of the Mahdist state in the Sudan, in the northwest, and indeed Yohannes himself was killed in 1889 while fighting the Mahdists.[42]

With Yohannes' unexpected death came an end to Tigray's preeminence in the Ethiopian empire – Tigrayans would not claim leadership of Ethiopia again for another century – as power passed relatively smoothly to Menelik of Shoa. Between 1889 and 1906, when he suffered a crippling stroke (although he remained on the throne until his death in 1913), Menelik created modern Ethiopia. He immediately withdrew Ethiopian claims to the coast and ceded Eritrea to the Italians, and even after he overwhelmed an ill-planned Italian invasion at the battle of Adwa in 1896 – becoming the only African leader to permanently defeat an invading European army in the era of partition – he was unable or unwilling to continue into Eritrea and realize the ambitions of his predecessors. Nonetheless, victory at Adwa secured his northern frontier and ensured European recognition of Ethiopian sovereignty; not only did Menelik spare his state the colonial experience endured by the rest of the region but also he actively participated in the carving up of vast tracts of land to the south and east, demarcating his new empire with the agreement of the European colonial authorities in the territories adjacent to it. Amhara hegemony was extended into the rich agricultural Oromo lands to the south and into the Somali Ogaden; the new empire was controlled through the strategic garrisoning of troops and ruled through the careful distribution of territorial governorships. Like Tewodros before him, but rather more successfully, Menelik aspired to a "modern" Ethiopia and oversaw the building of a railway, a modern capital city in Addis Ababa, a banking system and a communications infrastructure. He employed European advisors and sent Ethiopians abroad for training.[43] Menelik's new state may have been an urban rather than a rural creation; but above all, it was the swift appearance of European embassies in Addis Ababa which signaled the recognition of an African sovereignty, a feat which no other polity in eastern Africa or beyond managed to achieve during this era of creeping foreign hegemony.

Notes

1 Abdul Sheriff, *Slaves, Spices and Ivory in Zanzibar* (London, 1987).
2 A.C. Unomah & J.B. Webster, "East Africa: the expansion of commerce," in John E. Flint (ed.), *The Cambridge History of Africa. Vol. 5, from c.1790 to c.1870* (Cambridge, 1976).
3 Richard J. Reid, *Warfare in Pre-Colonial Eastern Africa: The Patterns and Meanings of State-level Conflict in the Nineteenth Century* (Oxford, 2007).
4 E.A. Alpers, *Ivory and Slaves in East Central Africa* (London, 1975).
5 Richard Caulk, "Firearms and princely power in Ethiopia in the nineteenth century," *Journal of African History*, 13:4 (1972).
6 For a slightly outdated but still compelling account, Mordechai Abir, *Ethiopia, the Era of the Princes: The Challenge of Islam and the Reunification of the Christian Empire, 1769–1855* (London, 1968); also Sven Rubenson, *The Survival of Ethiopian Independence* (London, 1976), and for an accessible overview, Bahru Zewde, *A History of Modern Ethiopia, 1855–1991* (Oxford, 2001).

7 See the excellent range of studies in Henri Médard & Shane Doyle (eds.), *Slavery in the Great Lakes Region of East Africa* (Oxford, 2007).

8 Jan-Georg Deutsch, *Emancipation Without Abolition in German East Africa, c.1884–1914* (Oxford, 2006), 34–5.

9 Church Missionary Society (CMS) Archives: G3 A6/0 1883/71 O'Flaherty to Wigram, 28 February 1883.

10 Reid, *Warfare in Precolonial Eastern Africa*, 46–52.

11 Andrew Roberts, "The Nyamwezi," in Andrew Roberts (ed.), *Tanzania Before 1900* (Nairobi, 1968). See V.L. Cameron, *Across Africa*, 2 vols. (London, 1877), for a contemporary snapshot.

12 R.W. Beachey, "The East African ivory trade in the nineteenth century," *Journal of African History*, 8:2 (1967).

13 Andrew Roberts, "Nyamwezi Trade," in Richard Gray & David Birmingham (eds.), *Pre-Colonial African Trade: Essays on Trade in Central and Eastern Africa Before 1900* (London, 1970), 73.

14 M. Abir, "Southern Ethiopia," in Gray & Birmingham (eds.), *Pre-Colonial African Trade*; Caulk, "Firearms and princely power"; Alica Moore-Harell, "Economic and political aspects of the slave trade in Ethiopia and the Sudan in the second half of the nineteenth century," *International Journal of African Historical Studies*, 23:2/3 (1999). W.C. Plowden, *Travels in Abyssinia and the Galla Country* (London, 1868) is a rich contemporary source.

15 The best narrative account remains Harold G. Marcus, *The Life and Times of Menelik II: Ethiopia 1844–1913* (Oxford, 1975). For an interesting insight into the Djibouti connection, see Charles Nicholl, *Somebody Else: Arthur Rimbaud in Africa, 1880–1891* (London, 1998).

16 Derek Nurse & Thomas Spear, *The Swahili* (Philadelphia, 1985).

17 Norman Bennett, *A History of the Arab State of Zanzibar* (London, 1978); Richard F. Burton, *Zanzibar: City, Island, Coast*, 2 vols. (London, 1872).

18 Stephen Rockel, *Carriers of Culture: Labor on the Road in Nineteenth-century East Africa* (Portsmouth NH, 2006).

19 Norman Bennett, *Arab versus European: Diplomacy and War in Nineteenth-century East Central Africa* (New York, 1986).

20 A good introduction is J.-P. Chretien, *The Great Lakes of Africa: Two Thousand Years of History* (New York, 2003); see also David Schoenbrun, *A Green Place, A Good Place: Agrarian Change, Gender, and Social Identity in the Great Lakes Region to the 15th Century* (Portsmouth NH, 1998). For an older but still useful account, Roland Oliver, "Discernible developments in the interior, c.1500–1840," in Roland Oliver & Gervase Mathew (eds.), *History of East Africa* (Oxford, 1963), Vol. I.

21 M.S.M. Kiwanuka, *A History of Buganda: From the Foundation of the Kingdom to 1900* (London, 1971); Richard J. Reid, *Political Power in Precolonial Buganda* (Oxford, 2002); Henri Médard, *La Royaume du Buganda au XIXe siècle* (Paris, 2007).

22 Shane Doyle, *Crisis and Decline in Bunyoro: Population and Environment in Western Uganda, 1860–1955* (Oxford, 2006).

23 See for example Jan Vansina, *Antecedents to Modern Rwanda: The Nyiginya Kingdom* (Madison WI, 2004).

24 David William Cohen, *The Historical Tradition of Busoga: Mukama and Kintu* (Oxford, 1972); Ronald R. Atkinson, *The Roots of Ethnicity: the Origins of the Acholi of Uganda Before 1800* (Philadelphia, 1994).

25 Richard J. Reid, "The Ganda on Lake Victoria: a nineteenth-century East African imperialism," *Journal of African History*, 39:3 (1998).

26 C.H. Ambler, *Kenyan Communities in the Age of Imperialism* (New Haven CT, 1988).

27 Roberts, "The Nyamwezi"; also R.G. Abrahams, *The Peoples of Greater Unyamwezi, Tanzania* (London, 1967).

28 For a compelling first-hand account of the Unyanyembe crisis, see Speke, *Journal*, chap. V.

29 The rise of the *ruga ruga* phenomenon is described, if through a particular lens, in multiple contemporary European sources: see for example Henry Morton Stanley, *Through the Dark Continent*, 2 vols. (London, 1878, 1899); and Cameron, *Across Africa*.

30 The single best account of Mirambo remains Norman R. Bennett, *Mirambo of Tanzania, c.1840–1884* (London, 1971); for a local account based largely on oral sources, see J.B. Kabeya, *King Mirambo: One of the Heroes of Tanzania* (Nairobi, 1976).

31 A. Shorter, "Nyungu-ya-Mawe and the empire of the Ruga-Rugas," *Journal of African History*, 9:2 (1968).

32 This is attested to in the unpublished writings of a missionary, Ebenezer Southon: see London Missionary Society (LMS), SOAS Special Collections, Central Africa, Incoming, Box 3: Southon to Thomson, 28 March 1880, encl., "History, Country and People of Unyamwezi."

33 See his autobiography, tr. W.H. Whiteley, *Maisha ya Hamed bin Muhammed el Murjebi yaani Tippu Tip* (Nairobi, 1966).

34 One of the most exhaustive collective studies is Thomas Spear & Richard Waller (eds.), *Being Maasai: Ethnicity and Identity in East Africa* (Oxford, 1993).

35 Richard Reid, "Human Booty in Buganda: some observations on the seizure of people in war, c.1700–1890," in Médard & Doyle (eds.), Slavery.

36 For a dramatic contemporary account, see R.P. Ashe, *Chronicles of Uganda* (London, 1894).

37 Donald Crummey, *Land and Society in the Christian Kingdom of Ethiopia: From the Thirteenth to the Twentieth Century* (Oxford, 2000).

38 Mohammed Hassen, *The Oromo of Ethiopia: A History, 1570–1860* (Cambridge, 1990); P.T.W. Baxter, Jan Hultin, & Alessandro Triulzi (eds.), *Being and Becoming Oromo: Historical and Anthropological Enquiries* (Uppsala, 1996).

39 Abir, *Ethiopia, the Era of the Princes*; Marcus, *Life and Times*.

40 See Plowden, *Travels in Abyssinia*, for his earlier career; later analyses include H. Stern, *Wanderings among the Falashas in Abyssinia* (London, 1862) and H. Blanc, *A Narrative of Captivity in Abyssinia* (London, 1868). See also Donald Crummey, "The Violence of Tewodros," in B.A. Ogot (ed.), *War and Society in Africa* (London, 1972).

41 Stanley, *Coomassie and Magdala*; Clements Markham, *A History of the Abyssinian Expedition* (London, 1869). See also Darrell Bates, *The Abyssinian Difficulty* (Oxford, 1979) and, more recently, Philip Marsden, *The Barefoot Emperor: an Ethiopian Tragedy* (London, 2007). An excellent selection of contemporary Ethiopian material is brought together in Sven Rubenson et al (eds. & trs.), *Acta Aethiopica II: Tewodros and his Contemporariesm 1855–1868* (Addis Ababa, 1994).

42 Zewde Gabre-Selassie, *Yohannes IV of Ethiopia* (Oxford, 1975).

43 Marcus, *Life and Times*, and, for one of the best summaries of the epoch, Bahru Zewde, *Modern Ethiopia*. For a perceptive contemporary European account, see A.B. Wylde, *Modern Abyssinia* (London, 1901).

4 Southern Frontiers

Colony and Revolution in Southern Africa

Nineteenth-century southern Africa has much in common with the broadly defined "Atlantic" and "Indian Ocean" zones in the same period, not least in terms of expanding commercial networks, linking the region with a global economy, and increasing European influence. Yet southern Africa also had a markedly different experience in that the European presence there – which would eventually come to define the modern history of the region – was not merely commercial. Europeans came to the temperate coastal strip around the Cape of Good Hope as settlers, not just as traders; and at length, they would drift onto the inland plateau, an area of excellent pastureland free of the tsetse fly, where they encountered some of the most dynamic, expansionist African polities anywhere in sub-Saharan Africa in the nineteenth century.[1] Cooperation as well as conflict resulted; but in time, as foreign colony interacted with local politico-military revolution, it was conflict which would come to define the relationship between white and black south of the Limpopo River.

African State and Society to around 1800

Cattle were central to the growth of states, the creation of wealth, and the stratification of society south of the Zambezi before the nineteenth century. Cattle ownership meant political power and provided the material basis of early chieftainship; societies were based on polygamy, and economic systems depended on the extensive use of female labor, particularly in agriculture. The dry open grassland of modern Botswana witnessed the emergence of some of the earliest chiefdoms, characterized by hilltop settlements, which were based on a combination of cattle-keeping and cultivation. A similar

A History of Modern Africa: 1800 to the Present, Third Edition. Richard J. Reid.

socioeconomic system was responsible for the growth of Great Zimbabwe, a Shona state noted for its stone structures ("Zimbabwe" is Shona for "place of stone"), which reached its apex in the early fifteenth century. The prosperity of Great Zimbabwe was also based on gold-mining, which was a crucial activity on the plateau between the tenth and the eighteenth centuries. Great Zimbabwe would in time be supplanted by Mutapa, possibly founded by Zimbabwean emigrants, which would also take advantage of gold and regional trade networks, the latter linking the states and societies of central southern Africa with the Indian Ocean. Gold from the interior plateau financed the more southerly Swahili city-states, and aroused the avarice of the Portuguese, whose attempts during the sixteenth century to capture the central Zambezi valley from the direction of the coast were defeated by the resistance offered by Mutapa, and by disease.[2]

The southeastern lowveld would become the political powerhouse of the region, as far as African state and society was concerned, through much of the nineteenth century. Before about 1700, Ngoni-speakers – members of the Bantu language group – tended to organize themselves in small chiefdoms, a political pattern doubtless shaped by terrain: the numerous hills of the area are separated by valleys through which rivers, fed by relatively high rainfall on the plateau, flow into the Indian Ocean. A wide variety of grazing and farming resources characterizes the region, and this enabled small family homesteads to exist largely independent of one another, loosely related homesteads coalescing into small-scale chiefdoms; large numbers of neighboring Khoisan were also incorporated into these chiefdoms. However, the northern Ngoni in particular underwent significant changes in the course of the eighteenth century.[3]

After about 1700, a number of northern Ngoni chiefdoms expanded and absorbed smaller ones. The causes of this expansion in political scale remain a matter of speculation, but almost certainly, the process was connected to heightened competition over scarce resources. The introduction of maize into the area by the Portuguese at a time of unusually high rainfall probably led to a rise in population, and an ever greater area of land was brought under cultivation. Improved pasture, in turn, resulted in an increase in the size of herds of livestock, while the expansion of commerce – again with the Portuguese at the coast – doubtless acted, as it did in eastern Africa, as a force for state formation. Ever wealthier, more stable, and more populous chiefdoms sought to dominate increasingly lucrative trade routes to the Indian Ocean, and in particular, the struggle to control the export of ivory led to increased competition over the rich hunting grounds close to the coast.[4]

As the eighteenth century drew on, greater competition and enlarged political scale meant increased levels of militarism within the expanding chiefdoms. Age-sets, notably, long an integral part of Ngoni society, became more significant: the system by which childhood, adulthood (which usually meant warriorhood), and elder status were defined became one which in effect organized society into regiments, with standing armies created to aggressively pursue the objectives of the wider community. By the late eighteenth century, the northern Ngoni had amalgamated into three dominant and increasingly centralized, chiefdoms, namely the Ngwane under the chief Sobhuza, the Ndwandwe under Zwide, and Mthethwa under Dingiswayo. This last, a federation of smaller groupings, included the relatively obscure chiefdom of the Zulu. Whatever uneasy balance of power had been achieved between these three states, however, was shattered as the eighteenth century drew to a close: the period of prolonged high rainfall came to an end and appears to have been replaced rather abruptly by one of drought and famine. Control of scarce resources – chiefly in the form of well-watered pastureland and good farmland – now became critical to survival, and conflict increased sharply in the early years of the nineteenth century.[5] The struggle which ensued among the Ngoni led to dramatic new developments in the ongoing political and military revolution, which would have profound repercussions throughout the southern African interior, and indeed beyond.

War, Revolution, and the Zulu Impact

Much has been made – in contemporary literature, the popular imagination, and academic scholarship – of the rise of the Zulu and in particular of their most famous leader, and in some ways founding father, Shaka.[6] As we will see, there is much in nineteenth-century Zulu history to justify this feverish fascination, and in Shaka's personal history to support the various claims made for his political and military genius; but it is important to keep in mind the degree to which the Ngoni revolution began in the eighteenth century, when the Zulu were only a small part (and a relatively unimportant one at that) of a much wider process of political change. Shaka and the Zulu state which was in many ways, his personal creation took the changes in age-regimentation, battle-formation, weaponry, and political scale, and utilized these to stunning effect; but they were not Zulu innovations *per se*. It is also important to recognize that the events of the early nineteenth-century southern African interior have been the subject of some controversy. It has been suggested, for example, that the series of wars which engulfed the interior – known as the *mfecane*, derived from the Xhosa term meaning destitution and hunger, or *difaqane* ("scattering") in Sotho – and its effects were deliberately exaggerated by Europeans in order to justify colonialism, and later the *apartheid* state itself.[7] Nonetheless, the consensus of historical opinion accepts that the *mfecane* which eventually led to the emergence of the Zulu state originated among the Ngoni kingdoms of the Mthethwa, Ndwandwe, and Ngwane in the southeastern lowveld and involved a virtually permanent state of war over limited resources, the absorption of smaller chiefdoms across a wide area, and increasingly centralized and militarized kingship.[8]

The *mfecane* reached its height between approximately 1816 and 1819, during which period Sobhuza's Ngwane were expelled northwards, and in the ensuing conflict between the Ndwandwe and the Mthethwa, the former initially appeared to have the advantage following the death of the Mthethwa leader Dingiswayo. But a commander in Dingiswayo's army, Shaka, of the small chiefdom of the Zulu, rose to take control, defeating the Ndwandwe in a series of encounters which saw them, and several other Ngoni groups, fleeing north out of the area. These refugees scattered throughout southern-central and eastern Africa: Mzilikazi, leader of the Ndebele, crossed the Limpopo to settle in modern-day Zimbabwe, and others moved across the Zambezi into the area of modern Malawi. Here, they were a major influence on the Chewa in terms of culture

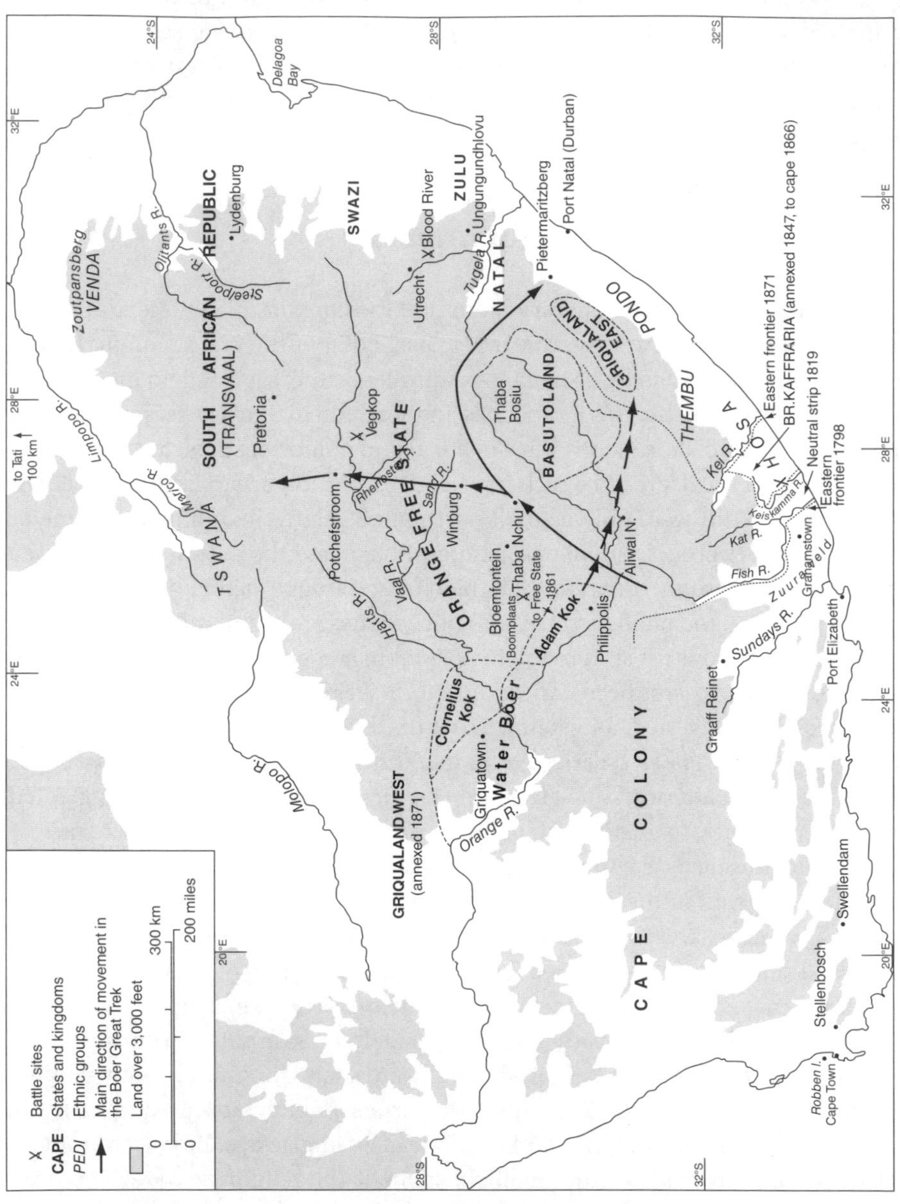

Southern Africa in the nineteenth century. Source: From J. E. Flint (ed.), *Cambridge History of Africa*. Vol. 5: *c.1790–c.1870* (Cambridge, 1976), p. 354;

and military organization. Other groups again wandered as far north as Tanzania by the 1840s and 1850s, reaching the shores of Lakes Tanganyika and Victoria having left considerable upheaval and destruction in their wake.[9] These groups would have a profound influence wherever they went, often becoming active in slave-raiding across the region, and coming into conflict with peoples already settled between the Limpopo and the Great Lakes. Emigrant Ngoni communities, fleeing the Zulu victory further south, would offer new models of state-building and the prosecution of warfare across the region in the decades following the *mfecane*. Other states and societies arose out of the need to defend themselves against the Zulu threat, notably the Sotho, led by Moshoeshoe, who established a mountain stronghold in the area of modern Lesotho and attracted a number of refugee groups. His diplomatic skills, moreover, were proverbial, and he retained the independence of his state through marital alliances with neighboring chiefs, and by playing the British and the Boers off one another.[10]

The significance of the Zulu was out of all proportion to their actual number, at least initially; yet the fact remained that by 1819, Shaka was established as the ruler of a highly centralized state which would be the dominant power in the region until its defeat and destruction at the hands of the British in 1879. Even following their conquest by the British, however, the Zulu would retain a powerful sense of "national" identity into the colonial period and beyond. The rise of the Zulu represented, again, a continuation, and indeed escalation of the political and military revolution begun several decades earlier, which involved a new model of political organization. The Zulu state was larger than anything in the region previously, transcending kinship and developing a new identity based on political and military power, and territorial unity; this was simultaneously a highly cohesive and aggressively expansionist society, as Shaka dispatched his regiments to prey on surrounding peoples by collecting tribute, or absorbing them completely into the kingdom. Newly conquered districts were assigned to chiefs appointed directly by Shaka, and eligible youth were conscripted; communities which continued to resist were either wiped out or forced to migrate out of reach of Zulu armies. Military innovations, based on those begun in the Ndwandwe and Mthethwa armies, included the creation of permanent regiments (the *amabutho*), highly disciplined and rigorously trained; the introduction of the short stabbing spear, which was put to more efficient use than the throwing spear; and the employment of speed and surprise in attack, together with the development of the "bull's horns" maneuver which involved the envelopment and destruction of enemies from the flanks. The system was highly centralized, with Shaka wielding direct control over active regiments. These regiments also had economic utility, with young men involved in herding cattle and hunting for ivory, while women cultivated for the state; regimental villages in the service of the state were established across the kingdom, and only when the members of the particular age-set had reached marriageable age was the village disbanded, the former warriors settling elsewhere to work their own farms.[11] In sum, the Zulu regimental system served to inculcate a larger "national" identity, eroding older regional and kin-based loyalties and facilitating a remarkable Zulu consciousness, based, at least initially, on a powerful royal cult centered on Shaka himself. Shaka was an authoritarian ruler, clearly, and much cruelty was attributed to him; he died as he had lived, murdered in 1828 at the instigation, if not by the hand, of his half-brother Dingane, who succeeded him. A standard view was that he had become deeply unstable, overseeing a veritable reign of terror characterized by periodic mass executions and that the power concentrated in his hands was such that he could only be removed by assassination.[12]

Vision of African genius: Shaka, king of the Zulu, c.1816–28. British Library/HIP/Topfoto. Source: Reproduced with permission of The Trustees of the British Museum.

The *mfecane* and the rise of the Zulu state have been interpreted in a variety of ways. The questions of why the *mfecane* happened when it did, and why it took the form it did, are vexed, as is the issue, noted previously, of the degree to which the whole notion of a region engulfed in violent conflict was a racist construct used to justify later white dominance. Some observers suggested that the patterns of warfare of the late eighteenth and early nineteenth centuries, and the emergence of the Zulu state itself, could be attributed to European influence and that Africans were imitating European models of command and battle. This racist assumption – which demonstrated a fundamental incredulity that Africans alone could be responsible for such an expansion of political scale, and such a revolution in military organization – was wholly groundless, and there is certainly no evidence that leaders such as Zwide, Dingiswayo, and Shaka were somehow exposed to and inspired by European models, even if the Portuguese at the coast had been able to provide them. Rather more seriously, interpretations which have aimed to explain the escalation of warfare in terms of competition for land and commerce are compelling. Population growth and consequent land shortage led to competition for pastureland and livestock, and this in itself was exacerbated by drought conditions. At the same time, although the role of trade should not be exaggerated – it was probably not as important a dynamic among the Ngoni as it was among the Nyamwezi or the Yoruba, for example – there can be little doubt that the *mfecane* cannot be fully understood without recognition of the role of commerce in ivory and slaves. This was growing in importance toward the end of the eighteenth century, and as other parts of Africa in the nineteenth century demonstrate, where there was growing global trade, there were attempts to monopolize it. Finally, the role of exceptionally talented individuals – most famously Shaka himself – must be acknowledged, and certainly contemporary Europeans tended to attribute much to Shaka personally.[13] While the events of the late eighteenth and early nineteenth centuries must be understood in the context of long-term socioeconomic processes, Shaka's own contribution was not inconsiderable: brilliant, opportunist, and ultimately unstable, he captured the imagination and built a state, and an identity, where none had existed previously. Yet the stories which proliferated about him – his supposed fear of old age, his extreme attachment to his mother, his sexuality (he never married) – were very often apocryphal, and no doubt designed to entertain Europeans around campfires in the decades following his death.[14]

Shaka's achievements look all the more dramatic considering the problems which came after; his successors, Dingane (1828–40) and Mpande (1840–72), had to contend with a greatly altered political environment. It is true that Dingane in particular lacked the military acumen and leadership talents of his half-brother, but this needs to be set alongside the advance of white settlement, which by the end of the 1830s had become a serious challenge to the Zulu. As the *voortrekkers* moved onto the interior plateau from the direction of Cape Colony, they grew in strength and confidence, and a clash became inevitable.

Cape Colonialism: White Settlement and the "Native Question"

The modern history of southern Africa has been characterized by a clash between Africans and Europeans, and the hegemony of the latter in the twentieth century served for many years to distort understanding of the region's past. Specifically, the "white" version of southern African history was that Bantu-speaking, iron-working farmers only crossed into what would become South Africa in the course of the seventeenth century, roughly, the same time that the first Dutch settlers were beginning to arrive. Thus, according to this thesis, Europeans encountered an "empty land," inhabited only by a few Khoisan, contemptuously dismissed as "Bushmen" and "Hottentots."[15] Historically inaccurate but politically convenient, the "empty land" thesis later provided the white minority with the justification they needed for claiming authority over a vast area. In fact, as we have seen, by the time the first European settlers had arrived, an array of African states and societies inhabited the region, from the Ovambo and Herero in Namibia and the Khoisan in southern Namibia and the southwest Cape, to the Sotho and Tswana of the central highveld, to the Ngoni-speakers of the southeast.

White settlement in southern Africa dates to the middle of the seventeenth century, when the Dutch East India Company established a small provisioning station in Table Bay. Over the ensuing century and a half, the "Boers" (Dutch for farmers) – or "Afrikaners," as they would become known – developed a distinctive identity, language, and culture. The frontier Boers in particular were tough, independent-minded, and Calvinist, and later developed a trenchant anti-Britishness; they came to regard the area around Cape Town, later Cape Colony, as theirs by right, claims underpinned by a distinctive racial and religious ideology. Initially trading with the Khoisan for food and water, they soon came into conflict with the African population, chiefly over access to grazing land which the Boers tended to occupy according to the principle of "right of conquest." Such conflict had become increasingly common by the late seventeenth and early eighteenth centuries, as ever greater numbers of Boers – *trekboers* – moved into the interior in search of good pastureland, particularly to the east. The Khoisan, confronted with Boer military superiority and introduced diseases (especially smallpox, carried by passing ships), responded either by becoming hunter-raiders attacking Boer farms or by withdrawing far to the north, away from the line of Boer advance, where they rebuilt their societies and retrieved a measure of independence. This policy was favored by those of mixed Khoi and European parentage especially. Many Khoisan, of course, accepted servile status within European society, working for Boers as herdsmen, hunters, and servants; very much a part of colonial society, they were nevertheless never accorded the rights of citizens.[16]

Although initially interracial relations in the Dutch Cape Colony were flexible and indeed common, racial attitudes hardened in time, and particularly during the eighteenth century. There may not yet have been a rigid system of racial classification, but there was a strong sense of hierarchy and relative privilege based on color; in large part, increasingly trenchant racialism was the result of clashes between European and

African on the expanding frontier over resources, while within the Colony itself status became increasingly linked to color and occupation. Most starkly, slave status was influenced by color: while slaves of "mixed" parentage were generally skilled labor, and indeed might even occupy positions of some responsibility, the worst, unskilled positions were filled by Africans themselves, or by those imported from Indonesia. Manual labor was undertaken by the lowliest of slaves, usually Africans, and this was rigidified from the late eighteenth century onwards; slavery underpinned Cape Colony society and economy, while slavery itself was increasingly defined by race – a portent for the future shape of South African state and society.[17]

Cape Colony remained under Dutch control until 1795, when it was seized by Britain during the French revolutionary wars, and was permanently under British control from 1806. From the 1820s, settlers of Dutch descent were joined by the first British emigrants, and tensions would quickly heighten between two white communities with markedly different sets of cultural values, languages, and visions for the future of the Colony. Boer hostility toward central colonial authority was already intensifying: in 1795, in the last weeks of Dutch control, there had been a brief trekboer rebellion, followed by another, suppressed by the British, in 1799. Both were motivated by the belief that the Cape government had failed to address trekboer concerns about land and security, a sense of betrayal and detachment which was an omen for the future of the region. In large part, clearly, the escalating tensions between two white communities stemmed from the fact of British administration, and Boer resentment of this would have dramatic consequences for the wider region. In the meantime, the question of the expansion and settlement of the eastern frontier of the Colony remained unresolved: white settlers had been gradually pushing the frontier eastwards, pressing in on the Xhosa people who, with their close-knit social structures and extensive herds, were becoming something of an obstacle, despite earlier economic cooperation and social interaction. Conflict became particularly intense from the 1770s as the Boers moved into the Zuurveld, an important Xhosa grazing area. However, the sporadic so-called "frontier wars" of the eighteenth and early nineteenth centuries failed to produce a lasting settlement.[18]

As the *mfecane* was unfolding in the deeper interior, important changes were taking place in the relationship between the Boer settlers and the newly arrived British administration. Boer government officials were replaced by British officials; and English was introduced into the education and legal systems. Further tensions mounted over the issue of African labor, toward which British policy was comparatively liberal. The granting of certain basic rights to African workers – such as the right to legally binding contracts and the right to take employers to court for breach of contract – horrified most Boers, who had long regarded Africans as little more than chattel labor, particularly important for poor white communities scarcely existing beyond the level of subsistence. At worst, Africans were vermin to be exterminated or at least driven out of view, as happened to many Khoisan; the British at the Cape were mere interlopers, urbanites whose "enlightened" and "liberal" views of "the native" were wholly disconnected from the realities of frontier life. Moreover, the British introduced a system of private land ownership, replacing the previous loan-farm system by which many Boers had occupied land on loan from the government; comparatively few could afford to hold land under the new rules instituted by an insensitive, English-speaking class of metropolitan administrators.

In addition to interference in long-standing practice at the official level, British missionaries increasingly found the Cape a field of great potential. They further alienated the Boer community by becoming the champions of the oppressed Khoisan, encouraging peasant farming at mission stations and involving themselves in court cases; missionaries also wielded increasing influence over government in their promotion of African causes, again notably in the sphere of labor. Perhaps the biggest blow to Boer sensibilities and economic requirements came in 1834, when slavery was abolished by the British administration in Cape Colony. This, again, was particularly disastrous to those poor white farmers struggling at the subsistence end of the colonial economy, who could not afford to pay competitive wages to free laborers.[19] The problem of "poor whites," indeed, would be a key dynamic in the shaping of South African society in the decades to come.

By this time, many Boers were beginning to consider the possibility of northward migration, of escaping beyond the frontier of the Colony, "into Africa" as it was known, away from British oppression. Indeed, those in the eastern Cape had been lobbying for government support in clearing the Xhosa from the area in order to make room for Boer settlement. But while the British demonstrated a willingness to interfere in Boer affairs within the Colony, they were not willing to assist those on its edges who complained of land shortage and of incursions by the Xhosa. The government refused to become involved in expensive wars or to countenance the equally troublesome extension of administration which successful campaigns would inevitably entail. Thus were land-hungry Boers compelled to consider crossing the frontier into the interior, in search of pasture and political freedom.

In the mid- and late 1830s, several thousand Boer families began moving north, in a process which later on became known as the "Great Trek." It was the stuff of mythology, the idea of a unified and cohesive migration – a kind of "exodus" – later becoming a cornerstone in emergent Afrikaner nationalism, celebrated in songs, poetry, and remembered heroism.[20] In reality, it involved a host of small, unconnected movements, hundreds of separate groups with little cohesion in terms of direction, and bound together only in their antipathy to the British and their desire for land. The voortrekkers ("those who trek ahead") of the 1830s and 1840s were mostly from the eastern Cape, and their migrations led to permanent white settlement in the interior of southern Africa. Yet the location of these "Boer republics" was influenced by concentrations of African population, or the absence of these: much early Boer settlement, for example, occurred in areas which had been temporarily vacated following the upheavals of the *mfecane*. In other areas, cooperation between Boer and African took place. In the region of the middle Vaal river, for example, the Rolong cautiously welcomed the voortrekkers as well-armed allies against the Ndebele; indeed it was a joint attack by the Boers and the Rolong against the Ndebele in 1837 which prompted the withdrawal of the latter north of the Limpopo. The Boers settled around the middle Vaal, and as they grew in confidence and strength, they were able to extract labor and tribute from the Rolong and the Tswana.[21]

To the north and east, small groups of voortrekkers lived nervously among rather stronger states and societies, notably the Swazi, and of course the Zulu themselves, whose presence was an obstacle to the acquisition of the attractive pastureland in the area. The relationship between Boer and Zulu was thus problematic from the outset, despite Dingane's initial attempts to convince the white newcomers that they could come to terms, and live in peace; whether he ever really believed this is difficult to know, but he acted precipitously in 1838 when he launched an attack on the Boers. A great many of the latter were killed; but Dingane now discovered, as many African rulers would after him, the significance of the new weaponry carried by the whites, who regrouped and inflicted a telling defeat on the Zulu at the so-called "Battle of Blood River" – the blood, that is, of the African.[22] Nonetheless, it is important not to overestimate the actual strength of the tiny Boer "republic" on the edge of the Zulu kingdom. Chary of unnecessary clashes with the Zulu, the Boers demonstrated a grudging respect for them and moved somewhat further south, establishing the "republic" of Natal. The Zulu themselves had been rocked by their initial conflict with the voortrekkers and suffered a civil war which saw the death of the hapless Dingane and his replacement by Mpande. Under Mpande, however, the kingdom recovered and continued to represent a significant obstacle to white domination in the area until much later in the nineteenth century.

Balances of Power to around 1870

The migration of the Boers out of Cape Colony had presented the British with a problem: should the recalcitrant voortrekkers be left to their own devices, or should some attempt be made to control them, or at least keep an eye on them? Initially, the British decided that control was necessary, annexing Natal in 1843 – an act which prompted the further movement of some Boers out of the area – and briefly taking control of the neighboring newly named Orange River zone in 1848. This was, however, considered too expensive, and indeed to all intents and purposes impracticable; and by the mid-1850s, Britain had recognized the political independence of the Boer "republics" of "Transvaal" and the "Orange Free State."[23] As Boers continued to expand into the highveld, they came up against the Sotho, who resisted but proved less troublesome than the Zulu, and in a series of conflicts through the 1850s and 1860s, the Sotho kingdom was greatly reduced in territorial extent; only a request for British protection, which was granted, apparently saved the kingdom from complete annihilation.[24]

The British had also been renewing older conflicts with the Xhosa further south. By the 1850s, the boundary had been extended to incorporate a considerable swathe of Xhosa territory, the Xhosa themselves being settled in the reserves which would later become a core feature of white-dominated southern Africa. Large numbers of Xhosa found themselves compelled to work on white farms across Cape Colony, an experience shared by the Africans of Natal. African peasant farmers were often tenants on white farms, either paying rent or handing over a percentage of their produce; in highland Boer territory, Africans might farm and keep livestock, in return for which they provided unpaid labor for their white landowners.[25]

Yet by the 1860s, overall, some degree of political and economic balance had been established across southern Africa between Africans and Europeans. White settlement had clearly advanced, and aggressively so in many areas, and Boers had taken advantage of areas depopulated or otherwise weakened by the *mfecane*. But in other areas, strong African states and societies successfully resisted European incursion, and indeed often intimidated the vulnerable frontier communities which scratched a living from farming and herding, or those white traders who did business with Africans. Africans also imported firearms as part of an increasingly lucrative interior trade, exporting such commodities as skins and ivory; they were thus greatly strengthened, and British merchants found they had little need or desire to interfere in the internal affairs of states as long as such trade continued to flow unimpeded. Indeed the British government was singularly disinterested in extending its territorial reach – whether into African or Boer territory – any more than was strictly necessary, which it was generally not. This, then, was the situation on the eve of the discovery of diamonds north of the Orange River at the beginning of the 1870s and of gold in the Transvaal in the mid-1880s. These finds would dramatically alter the balance of power, bringing about a veritable economic revolution which would ultimately destroy African self-sufficiency and lead to the creation of a capitalist economy by the end of the nineteenth century. It would lead, too, to the destruction of African political independence, at least temporarily.

Notes

1 South Africanist historiography has undergone more change than most over the last twenty years or so, but Shula Marks & Anthony Atmore (eds.), *Economy and Society in Pre-Industrial South Africa* (Harlow, 1980) and T.R.H. Davenport, *South Africa: A Modern History* (London, 1991) remain useful. More recently, see Carolyn Hamilton, Bernard K. Mbenga, & Robert Ross (eds.), *The Cambridge History of South Africa, Vol 1: From Early Times to 1885* (Cambridge, 2010).
2 For an excellent overview which has stood the test of time, see David Birmingham & Shula Marks, "Southern Africa," in R. Oliver (ed.), *The Cambridge History of Africa, Vol. 3: from c.1050 to c.1600* (Cambridge, 1977).
3 See J.B. Peires (ed.), *Before and After Shaka: Papers in Nguni History* (Grahamstown, 1983).
4 Jeff Guy, "Ecological factors in the rise of Shaka and the Zulu kingdom," in Marks & Atmore (eds.), *Economy and Society*.
5 John Wright, "Turbulent times: political transformations in the north and east, 1760s–1830s," in Hamilton, Mbenga & Ross (eds.), *Cambridge History*, Vol. I.
6 Carolyn Hamilton, *Terrific Majesty: The Powers of Shaka Zulu and the Limits of Historical Invention* (Cape Town, 1998); D. Wylie, *Myth of Iron: Shaka in History* (Scottsville, 2006).
7 Julian Cobbing, "The *mfecane* as alibi," *Journal of African History*, 29:3 (1988).
8 Again, see Wright, "Turbulent Times."
9 J.D. Omer-Cooper, *The Zulu Aftermath: A Nineteenth-century Revolution in Bantu Africa* (London, 1966); Carolyn Hamilton (ed.), *The Mfecane Aftermath: Reconstructive Debates in Southern African History* (Johannesburg, 1995).
10 Elizabeth Eldredge, *A South African Kingdom: The Pursuit of Security in Nineteenth-century Lesotho* (Cambridge, 1993).

11 There is a huge corpus of literature on the Zulu state. A sample would include the exhaustive but ageing Donald R. Morris, *The Washing of the Spears: The Rise and Fall of the Zulu Nation* (London, 1965; 2nd ed., 1989); Jeff Guy, *The Destruction of the Zulu Kingdom* (London, 1979); and, for military buffs, Ian Knight, *The Anatomy of the Zulu Army, from Shaka to Cetshwayo, 1818–1879* (London, 1999). See also B. Carton, J. Laband, & J. Sithole (eds.), *Zulu Identities: Being Zulu, Past and Present* (Pietermaritzburg, 2008).

12 E.A. Ritter, *Shaka Zulu: The Rise of the Zulu Empire* (London, 1955), and Peter Becker, *Rule of Fear: The Life and Times of Dingane, King of the Zulu* (London, 1964), are classics of the "bloodthirsty" genre.

13 For example, Nathaniel Isaacs, *Travels and Adventures in Eastern Africa*, 2 vols. (London, 1836).

14 For example, Ritter, *Shaka Zulu*, 13–14.

15 Jan Van Riebeeck (ed. H.B. Thom), *The Journal of Jan Van Riebeeck*, 3 vols. (Cape Town, 1952–58).

16 Robert Ross, "Khoesan and Immigrants: the emergence of colonial society in the Cape, 1500–1800," in Hamilton, Mbenga & Ross (eds.), *Cambridge History*, Vol. I.

17 Martin Legassick & Robert Ross, "From slave economy to settler capitalism: the Cape Colony and its extension, 1800–1854," Hamilton, Mbenga & Ross (eds.), *Cambridge History*, Vol. I; in A. du Toit & H. Giliomee (eds.), *Afrikaner Political Thought: Analysis and Documents*. Vol I: 1780–1850 (Cape Town, 1983).

18 Noel Mostert, *Frontiers:The Epic of South Africa's Creation and the Tragedy of the Xhosa People* (London, 1992); C.C. Crais, *The Making of the Colonial Order: White Supremacy and Black Resistance in the Eastern Cape, 1770–1865* (Johannesburg, 1992); Richard Price, *Making Empire: Colonial Encounters and the Creation of Imperial Rule in Nineteenth-century Africa* (Cambridge, 2008).

19 Legassick & Ross, "From slave economy," 285ff.

20 For example, Eric Walker, *The Great Trek* (London, 1934).

21 Johannes Meintjes, *The Voortrekkers: The Story of the Great Trek and the Making of South Africa* (London, 1973).

22 See Becker, *Rule of Fear*, esp. Part III.

23 See for example C.W. de Kiewiet, *British Colonial Policy and the South African Republics, 1848–1872* (London, 1929).

24 The story is effectively told in Peter Sanders, *Moshoeshoe: Chief of the Sotho* (London, 1975).

25 Legassick & Ross, "From slave economy"; Colin Bundy, *The Rise and Fall of the South African Peasantry* (London, 1979).

Part II Africa and Islam: Revival and Reform in the Nineteenth Century

Islam has been of immense importance in Africa's history: in terms of the role of external influences in shaping the continent's past, Islam was by far the most significant, at least until the nineteenth century and increasing European intervention. Although some of the most dramatic changes in African history in recent times have been brought about through interaction with Christian Europe – culminating, of course, in colonial occupation – Islam had already been transforming large parts of Africa for several centuries. Indeed, Islam in time came to form the basis of much African resistance to European expansion. The key point here is that across northern Africa, the Sahara, and the Red Sea region, Islam had long provided a framework for dramatic sociopolitical change and unified action which enveloped large areas. This is particularly clear from the late eighteenth century onward, an era which witnessed the re-emergence of reformist traditions across much of Islamic Africa.

Large areas of Africa have always been more Muslim than Christian: North Africa, clearly, has been Muslim for over a thousand years, a gradual process beginning with the Arab conquests in the seventh and eighth centuries and followed by the conversion of key groups and the migration of Arabic tribes across the Maghreb. West Africa is predominantly Muslim, a situation which came about largely as a result of the thriving trans-Saharan commercial network linking regions north and south of the great desert; this network expanded dramatically from the eighth and ninth centuries onward and facilitated the gradual filtering of Islam across the Sahara and into the savannah belt, where it was absorbed, initially at least, mainly by urban elites. Eastern and southern Africa, on the other hand, are predominantly Christian today, although Islam was also fundamental to the creation of a distinctive coastal civilization in East Africa, namely Swahili culture, combining African, Islamic, and Arabic influences, and it was of

A History of Modern Africa: 1800 to the Present, Third Edition. Richard J. Reid.

enormous significance in northeast Africa, where Muslims in Somalia, Ethiopia, and Eritrea had close ties to both North Africa and the Arabian peninsula. Islamic civilization is therefore as important as Christianity, and sometimes more so, in terms of the forces shaping Africa's own civilizations in the modern era. African Muslims, importantly, belonged to a global civilization which stretched beyond Africa itself, encompassing the Ottoman empire, Persia, and India, each of which had commercial and cultural links with Africa. African Muslims were part of a global community in which the exchange of information– for example, during the *hajj*, the pilgrimage to Mecca – generated political consciousness. Muslims were often well informed about developments in other parts of the world, and in the late nineteenth century, reactions to European imperialism were often based on knowledge of European actions elsewhere, for example, the subjugation of Muslims in India.

While there is, very broadly, a historical parallel in the growth of Islam and Christianity, there were important differences in their respective early periods, which would become hugely significant over time. In Europe since the Middle Ages, Christianity had gradually diminished in political importance, with a stark division emerging between secular and religious leadership; within Islam; however, faith and state were identified as one, with no distinction between religious and political affairs. Further, Christianity had begun in "failure": the systematic persecution of Christians by Rome meant that the early Christian church was an underground, disempowered movement, unconcerned with politics and government. But Islam was successful from the outset, seizing political power and within a matter of decades forging an empire through conquest; Muslim leaders were centrally concerned with how political authority should be ordered. As a result, Islamic law, government, and systems of taxation and property ownership were issues seen as indivisible from spiritual matters; in Christianity, such issues were largely secular. It is also important to note that in Islam, there is somewhat less of a religious hierarchy than in Christianity, and political leaders fulfill the role performed by the Christian clergy. There are, however, certain groups within Islam which claim special status, for example, the *ulama*, experts in the interpretation and application of Islamic law, and the *sufi*, mystics and ascetics who undergo meditation and physical exercise in order to achieve a closer relationship with God. In Africa, sufi brotherhoods have been vital in the spread of Islam and its adaptation to local circumstances.

It is a truism of Western scholarship that the Islamic world entered a period of stagnation and decline from the seventeenth century onward. According to this view, Islamic law became deeply inflexible and conservative, and precedent replaced independent judgment in its application. The period between the fifteenth and the seventeenth centuries had seen the three great Islamic civilizations of the early modern era – the Ottoman, Safavid, and Mughal empires – at their height, equaling and sometimes surpassing anything western Europe had to offer; but from the seventeenth century, it has been argued, no "progress" was achieved in political, social, or economic spheres. However, the idea of decline should not be exaggerated, and indeed a number of scholars have rejected the notion of an inherently stagnant Islamic system as a Eurocentric concept, a historical distortion born of burgeoning cultural hubris.

Nonetheless, what is clear is that Islamic history in the eighteenth and nineteenth centuries is characterized by three broad, closely interrelated themes. First, industrializing Christian Europe posed a serious challenge, in terms of its growing technological and military power. Ultimately, the age of imperialism, powered by industrialization, would culminate in the conquest of much of the Islamic world by European colonial powers, a historical process which continues to reverberate to the present day. European and Russian control and/or influence was extended into central Asia, India, the Middle East, and North Africa by the beginning of the twentieth century; and for the two preceding centuries, European expansion increasingly threatened the Muslim heartland. Napoleon's conquest of Egypt was a profound blow; Russian influence expanded in the Black Sea area following the Crimean War. The second two themes to some extent represent the response of Muslims to the expansion of Europe. The phenomenon of Islamic revivalism would sweep the Muslim world in the eighteenth and nineteenth centuries, seeking a restoration of "pure" or "fundamental" Islam, and a rigorous enforcement of the shari'a, Islamic law. In this context, it is worth noting that early Islamic history, and specifically the history of Muhammad himself, has provided generations of Muslims with a model and ideology of protest, resistance, and revolutionary change. Often, revivalist movements were also messianic, predicated upon the imminent arrival of the "Mahdi," or savior, who would come to restore pure Islam on earth; mahdism was most closely associated with Shi'ite Islam, the Shi'a historically having been critical of the early Caliphate on account of the fact that Ali (from whom they derived their name) had been the last direct descendant of Muhammad and that he had been usurped, indeed assassinated, by the Umayyads in 661. The rhetoric of these and other revivalist movements claimed that innovation within, and deviation from, pure Islamic law was fundamentally wrong; they were often violent, involving armed insurrection, namely *jihad*, or holy war. In many cases, their enemies were also Muslims whom they accused of being unbelievers, and not simply Christians or other "infidels." At the same time, a number of Muslim societies attempted to modernize and secularize – which usually meant an attempt to emulate European models – in order to meet the challenges posed by Western Europe. Often this involved the reduction of Islam in public life and the introduction of Western-style constitutions, legislatures, education, and taxation systems. African Islam must be understood in these contexts.

The origins of much nineteenth-century revivalism are to be found in the eighteenth century, and often lay beyond the African landmass itself. In Arabia, for example, Muhammad ibn 'Abd al-Wahhab (1703–1792) was a puritanical believer in the strict application of Islamic law; allied with a local chieftain, Muhammad ibn Saud, the Wahhabi movement preached the restoration of pure Islam. In India, the decline of Mughal power from the beginning of the eighteenth century coincided with the emergence of such figures as Shah Wali Allah (1703–1762), who founded a powerful revivalist school of thought which emphasized Islamic purity, the centrality of the Quran, and the study of Islamic tradition. Across the West African savannah, the Fulani were beginning to act as the inspiration behind a series of reformist Islamic movements, seizing power via jihad. Perhaps the most dramatic case of this was Uthman dan Fodio in what is now northern Nigeria, examined in greater detail in a later chapter. It is important to note, however, that these movements cannot simply be understood as reactions to European power: there existed a tradition of ongoing reform within Islam prior to the challenge of European imperialism, and certainly the cases of Arabia and West Africa represented such a tradition. Islamic revivalism which aimed at the moral rejuvenation of state and society was as old as Islam itself. Nonetheless, the failure of Muslim societies to prevent European encroachment was a powerful factor behind the demands for change – in the form of both revivalism and secular modernization – from the middle of the eighteenth century onward. Western imperialism and the modernization policies of certain indigenous regimes provided a new focus for popular revivalist leaders. Some of the latter used existing brotherhoods, others created new organizations by sheer force of personality. But all were concerned to unite anti-foreign or anti-government resistance with a message of imminent salvation, purification, restoration of holy law, or messianic deliverance.

5 Revival and Reaction

North African Islam

Old and New Identities: Brotherhoods of the Desert

In the centuries prior to 1800, northern Africa was characterized by the interaction between nomadic and sedentary groups. There is no doubt that this meant considerable conflict and dislocation, but these changes – setting the demographic pattern for much of the region – involved much peaceful cooperation as well as violent rivalry. There was also a major change in the nature of Islamic states themselves, a shift from the "early phase" in which political leaders attempted to copy the model provided by the first caliphs, to a new phase of restricted power and limited ambitions. Rulers were increasingly drawn from, and represented the interests of, particular ethnic groups, factions, or social classes; Muslim states no longer claimed both religious and secular leadership, but rather the sufi increasingly took over religious leadership in alliance with political leaders. Moreover, Islam could be a political weapon and could provide ideological cogency to larger material objectives. To some extent, for example, Islam had long provided Berber communities with a sense of brotherhood, facilitating contacts between pastoral communities and – perhaps even more relevantly, as in western Africa – among traders. It also provided Berbers with a common sense of purpose in their ongoing territorial struggle with the non-Muslim farmers of the Sahel belt south of the Sahara itself.[1] Above all, political life across North Africa was characterized by fragmentation and the primacy of local forces.

A large number of revivalist and fundamentalist movements appeared in the deserts and savannahs of Arabia and Africa during the modern era. The Wahhabi movement was challenging Ottoman rule from the 1750s onward, waging a war of purification against practices which, the Wahhabi asserted, had arisen since the time of the Prophet.

A History of Modern Africa: 1800 to the Present, Third Edition. Richard J. Reid.

In North Africa, Sidi Muhammad ibn Ali al-Sanusi in Libya sought more peaceful means through which to convince Muslims of the need to renew their faith, largely through expanding the membership of desert-based brotherhoods. Relations between the modernizing Ottoman authorities and the Sanusi communities in Libya were more peaceful than were relations between the Qadiriyya and the French in Algeria. The Qadiriyya, under 'Abd al-Qadir, rallied anticolonial resistance under the banner of pure Islamic values; 'Abd al-Qadir organized desert tribesmen into military units in creating his reformist army and utilized the sufi system of deference and authority. Sufism was also important in the Sudan, where subjection to the aggressive modernization of Egyptian rule provoked a violent reaction against the Turkish-speaking elite which dominated the Egyptian administration. Muhammad 'Ahmad ibn 'Abdallah, a sufi, declared himself the Mahdi, or promised savior, and mobilized his followers to expel the Egyptians in 1881. While the Mahdists' motives were markedly diverse, there can be no doubting the central importance of the charismatic figure of the Mahdi himself. We turn to this in Chapter 7.

Yet these movements, comprised of desert tribesmen, were only the most extreme forms of Islamic militancy operating in the nineteenth century. Other populist groups and associations flourished, including religious orders which represented older traditions, operating alongside neo-sufism in the urban centers of the Islamic world. But perhaps the key theme of nineteenth-century Islam was its regionalism. While there was a constant exchange of ideas across the Islamic world, and while the similarity of ritual might convey the idea that the Muslim world was a unified entity, Islam in this period expressed itself differently according to local circumstances and requirements. The call to jihad was frequent in the least-populated and peripheral zones of the Muslim world in the nineteenth century, and it had little impact beyond those groups immediately involved.

Trade and Conflict in the Mediterranean World: Ottoman and European Frontiers

The conquest of Mameluke Egypt by the Ottoman Turks in 1517 rendered that territory – not for the first time – a province within a western Asian empire. The significance of this would become clear over the next three hundred years. During the sixteenth century, Egypt was used as a platform from which to push south, both up the Nile valley into Nubia in modern Sudan, and into the Red Sea. Egypt thus became the base from which one of the great clashes of civilization in modern times began: the Ottoman advance into the Red Sea was partly a response to Portuguese incursions into the Indian Ocean, and the Ottomans took control of Massawa on the coast of modern Eritrea with a view to challenging the growing infidel presence further south.[2] But Egypt itself would come to achieve considerable autonomy within the Ottoman empire. The Mameluke aristocracy gradually regained its prominence in the seventeenth and eighteenth centuries, the heads of the powerful noble families taking the title of *bey*; at the same time, while the viceroys – with the title of *pasha* – had been in the first instance Turks appointed by Istanbul, these too began to establish dynasties of their own which through the eighteenth century came to rule essentially independently of Istanbul.

Egypt at the end of the eighteenth century was an Ottoman province largely in name only. The event which in many ways signaled the beginning of Egypt's modern history, however, was the invasion in 1798 by a Napoleonic army which was only repelled in 1801 by an alliance of Ottoman and British forces.[3] This marked the beginning of a growing Anglo-French rivalry over Egypt, which would dominate the territory's history in the later nineteenth century.

Romanticized Africa: Napoleon's invasion of Egypt portrayed in *The Battle of Heliopolis*, by Leon Cogniet (c.1850). Source: Photograph courtesy Mathaf Gallery, London.

Further west, one of the key themes of the sixteenth century was the competition for control of the western Mediterranean between Christian Spain and the Ottoman empire. By the end of the fifteenth century, a resurgent Spain had expelled the last Muslims from the Spanish mainland and had begun to seize key ports along the North African coast. Yet these ports would change hands repeatedly as Ottoman forces attacked Christian shipping in the western Mediterranean. While defeats of the Ottoman navy during the 1560s and 1570s – notably at Lepanto – limited Istanbul's ability to control the sea, the Ottomans did ultimately recapture Tripoli, Tunis, and Algiers, ensuring that the Maghreb remained within the Islamic world, until the age of European imperial expansion in the nineteenth century.[4]

Yet while the coasts and hinterlands of modern-day Algeria, Tunisia, and Libya were nominally provinces of the Ottoman empire, in reality, Istanbul had little effective control of them. Military government, benefiting from the lucrative trans-Saharan trade, developed largely autonomously in the coastal towns. The western Maghreb also witnessed the rise of the independent state of Morocco, a coalescence of Arab former nomads, in the first half of the sixteenth century. Morocco's emergence was significant in that it halted Ottoman expansion into northwest Africa and also involved the expulsion of the Portuguese from their Atlantic ports; at its height, under Ahmad al-Mansur, Morocco subdued the great West African savannah empire of Songhay, although it proved a temporary conquest. Despite a series of dynastic disputes and a range of internal power struggles, Moroccan unity was intact at the turn of the nineteenth century, even if the control of central government was confined largely to the urban centers and the Atlantic ports.[5]

At the beginning of the nineteenth century, the Ottoman empire remained the most powerful Islamic state in the world. Even so, it had encountered a series of problems since the late seventeenth century, notwithstanding an economic, intellectual, and cultural renaissance in the early 1700s. This period of Ottoman history witnessed a loss of power and territory. The nineteenth century saw a gradual dismantling of the empire, not least in North Africa, where several provinces were lost to European conquest, including Algeria (French settlement from 1830), Tunisia (France, 1881), Egypt (Britain, 1882), and Libya (Italy, 1911), as well as Morocco (France and Spain, 1912). The challenges of the nineteenth century prompted Ottoman rulers to introduce reforms aimed at the reduction of the role of Islam in public life. The traditional monopoly of the ulama in the fields of education and justice was undermined, as the Ottomans attempted to westernize their political, legal, and educational systems; they also introduced a western-style constitution, later suspended. The outcome was the gradual emergence of a new intelligentsia which espoused "Western values," in the broadest sense, and championed Western methods across many walks of life: in administrative and military affairs, in science and technology, in arts and literature.

However, religious courts and schools remained amid these waves of "modernization," with the result that the nineteenth century witnessed growing hostility between two competing sets of institutions and elites, namely Muslim "traditionalists" confronting those who believed that the empire's future lay with secular government and society. The process of secularization, indeed, was usually centrally imposed, Western in its

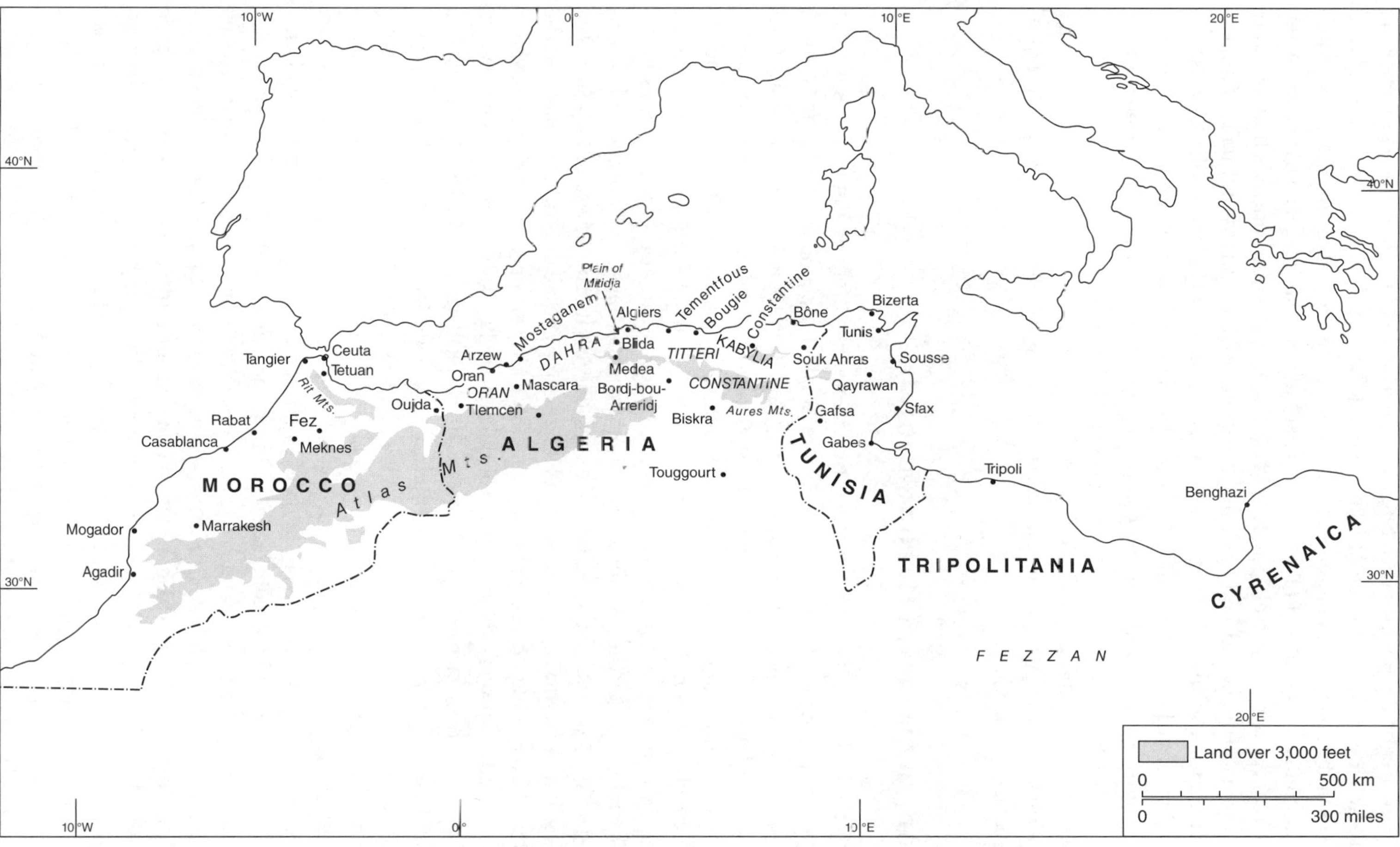

North Africa in the nineteenth century. Source: From J. E. Flint (ed.), *Cambridge History of Africa*. Vol. 5: *c.1790–c.1870* (Cambridge, 1976), p. 100, Map 6; © 1976 by Cambridge University Press. Reprinted with permission from Cambridge University Press.

form, and frequently popular with religious minorities – Christians among them – who clearly welcomed the reduction of Islam in public life. Muslims were thus often critical of government policy, and increasingly so when it was clear that the strategy of modernization did not actually halt European encroachment in the Mediterranean, or the Russian advance into central Asia. Herein lay the fundamental contradiction for many Muslims in the nineteenth century, namely that between Europe as the model of modernity and Europe as the colonizer, the *enemy*. This was a contradiction which by its very nature weakened the forces of political liberalism and secularism, simply because such forces were associated with European imperial aggression. Consequently, protest movements against Europe often targeted groups at home whose apparent support for European culture and political ideology seemed to be facilitating foreigners' imperial ambitions; in other words, "secular governments" were often seen as the agents of European colonialism.[6]

Changing Society (1): The Maghreb

Through the early nineteenth century, the nominally Ottoman states to the west of Egypt – Tripoli, Tunis, and Algiers – were increasingly independent of Istanbul; Morocco was already an independent monarchy. They had deep-rooted historic links with the eastern Mediterranean and also with the states and societies of the desert and savannah to the south, via trans-Saharan trade routes. But increasingly they looked north, from which direction they were confronted by the growing European imperial threat, particularly from the British and French, although Spain also had ambitions in the northwest corner of the continent. The threat was perhaps most dramatically manifested in Algiers, which, although it had undergone gradual decline since its peak in the sixteenth and seventeenth centuries, had long been a source of piratical trouble in the western Mediterranean, its corsairs regularly attacking European shipping. It was such piracy – and the perceived haughtiness of the *dey* of Algiers, Hussein – which provided the French with an excuse for its otherwise unprovoked invasion in 1830, but this was in fact undertaken with a view to bolstering the flagging monarchy at home. Algiers and Oran fell quickly; by 1832, French troops had also taken Bone to thc cast and were in control of a narrow coastal strip, which they hoped to keep. There was a certain amount of support on the part of the coastal townsfolk for French protection against the people of the mountainous interior, where the chief enemy of the French and their collaborators was 'Abd al-Qadir, leader of the local Qadiriyya. He displayed remarkable skill in holding together a range of groups in the interior under the banner of jihad against the infidel conqueror of the coast; ironically, perhaps, it was his formidable presence through the 1830s which drew the French south into the hills, with systematic conquest launched in 1841. The ensuing war was bitter and brutal, involving the massacre of civilians as well as clashes between the opposing forces; and Qadiriyya resistance continued after 'Abd al-Qadir's capture in 1847 (he was exiled to France, and thereafter to Damascus), down to the 1870s.[7] Even in the late nineteenth century, fighting was still taking place in the district of Kabylia.

With conquest of the territory which would become Algeria came large-scale white settlement. By the end of the 1840s, there were in excess of 100,000 settlers, mostly in the fertile coastal plain – where, from the viewpoint of the colonial administration, they were easier to protect than in the hilly interior – which was systematically cleared of its original inhabitants, the latter forcibly removed to designated areas. Colonial settlement continued to expand through the nineteenth century: by the 1880s, there were 350,000, including a number of Spaniards and Italians, who along with the majority of French Algerians remained poor farmers, and indeed many eventually abandoned their plots and drifted into the towns. As would be the pattern in other areas of white settlement south of the Sahara, only the large plantations backed by considerable capital were successful. In fact, the French governed largely through local elites, similar in pattern to the Ottoman system; but beyond this, Algeria loomed large in the French imagination at home. In time regarded as part of France itself, the territory played an increasingly large part in French politics, at home and abroad.[8]

Moreover, the French conquest had ramifications across the region, not least in the neighboring Regency of Tunis, which following events in Algeria felt sufficiently threatened to request a degree of British protection. Britain looked favorably on the Regency – its rulers had already shown modernizing tendencies, having clamped down on piracy in the central Mediterranean – and thus in the late 1830s, London offered protection against both the French to the west and the Ottomans to the east. Tunisia therefore became one of the more reformist-minded regimes of Islamic North Africa, abolishing slavery during the1840s and thereafter making moves toward constitutional modernization, in the late 1850s and early 1860s. European influence was considerable in Tunisia, indeed, through a powerful diplomatic presence – both British and French – and through the wealthy European trading community, which had much in common with an educated Tunisian middle class, on whose behalf constitutional reform was largely undertaken. The new constitutions, however, were largely window-dressing; and during the 1860s and 1870s, with the relative decline of British involvement in the area, France adopted a rather more aggressive position in Tunisia, at least partly in response to growing Italian interest in North Africa. By the time the French seized Tunis in 1881 – the restlessness of the "natives" in the interior provided the official excuse – the "scramble" for Africa was well under way, and the partition of the Islamic north was a dramatic demonstration of European hegemony.[9] So, too, was the British seizure of Egypt, as we see later.

In the early nineteenth century, the British had also supported the *pasha* of Tripoli, Yusuf Karamanli, against the Ottoman empire, a reward for the assistance he had rendered Britain against the French in Egypt in the 1790s; he was then able to extend his control over the Fezzan and developed an extensive network of contacts with states and societies further south, including the sultanates of Bornu and Sokoto. At the same time – and despite British patronage – Tripoli was one of the most significant slave-trading polities on the Mediterranean coast, as the terminus of long-distance trans-Saharan trade routes. After Yusuf Karamanli's death in 1830, civil war broke out, resolved by the reassertion of Ottoman authority by the early 1840s; but in fact, it was

Muhammad al-Sanusi, founder of the new order of the Sanusiyya, who established some degree of stability across the Fezzan, Cyrenaica, and the central Sahara, and as far south as Wadai and Bornu. The Sanusiyya spread across the region exhorting formerly feuding clans to return to a pure form of Islam and was remarkably successful in so doing – so much so, indeed, that the Ottoman governors in Tripoli were compelled to maintain good relations with the order, which had become the only guarantor of peace across the vast interior of present-day Libya. Sanusi merchants were also determined slave traders, and indeed in this region, the slave trade proved singularly difficult to suppress, surviving well into the twentieth century and only being brought to an end with the Italian conquest of Tripolitania and Cyrenaica, and once the French had moved into central equatorial Africa. Indeed, although the Italian conquest was officially complete by 1911–12, the Sanusiyya would continue to resist the Italians bitterly down to the 1930s.[10]

The kingdom of Morocco was the only state of the Maghreb not administered, nominally or otherwise, by the Ottomans. Morocco stubbornly resisted European influence, and restricted the activities of European merchants; its isolationism was especially pronounced in the early nineteenth century under Sultan Mawlai Sulaiman, who resisted all efforts on the part of European diplomats to discuss the slave trade. But regional events soon had a profound impact on the kingdom: the Moroccans under Sultan 'Abd ar-Rahman assisted 'Abd al-Qadir in his struggle against the French in Algeria, which provoked a French incursion in 1845. Immersed in Algeria, France could ill afford the complication of involvement in Morocco; but in the meantime, a renewed threat came from the Spanish, in possession of the ports of Melilla and Ceuta, and now claiming that these were being continually harassed by hostile locals, with some accuracy. Spain dispatched an army which inflicted heavy defeats on the Moroccans, who in 1860 brought the brief conflict to a close by agreeing to pay the Spanish a hefty indemnity. It was the beginning of the end of Moroccan independence, for in order to pay the indemnity the Moroccans had to raise a loan in Britain, which awarded the British a degree of control over Moroccan commerce. In part, the kingdom's problems had stemmed from an inability to exercise authority over all of its subjects; this had provoked the conflict with Spain, and through much of the nineteenth century threatened to destabilize the state. Under Sultan Mawlai al-Hasan, between 1873 and 1894, the state was greatly extended, Mawlai al-Hasan successfully bringing to heel swathes of northern Mauritania and the area of the Atlas mountains by subduing disloyal and rebellious groups; continual campaigning strengthened the state, and although European influence and colonial occupation were encompassing the kingdom on all sides, Morocco achieved a remarkable degree of autonomy and stability until the early twentieth century. Only in 1912 did Morocco finally fall under European control, partitioned between the Spanish and the French.[11]

In the course of the nineteenth century, the Maghreb had been subjected to European military aggression, colonial occupation, and diplomatic pressure, and the Ottoman empire had been gradually undermined and ultimately dismantled. The response to an increasingly Europeanized Mediterranean Sea in some places had been reform and "modernization" – of military structures, economies, political systems. Yet in other areas, in the Sahara and on its fringes, the response had been an increasingly militant and fundamentalist Islam, and again it is clear that across swathes of Islamic North Africa European control was scarcely possible, as the Qadiriyya and – in particular – the Sanusiyya demonstrated. Even in those places where the European military and political presence was apparently strongest, the seeds were sown in the late nineteenth century for the Islamic and nationalist movements of the twentieth; and nowhere was the clash of civilizations more dramatic than in Egypt.

Changing Society (2): Egypt

In the wake of the French invasion in 1798, Egypt embarked on a process of dramatic change which would see the destruction of the Mameluke aristocracy and the emergence of a new political and military system, which was largely the creation of the Macedonian Muhammad Ali. The latter, a ruthless, far-sighted, and talented leader and administrator, was an officer in the Ottoman army which had expelled the French in 1801; surrounded by a loyal corps of Albanian soldiers, he had positioned himself as the most powerful military leader in Cairo by 1805, and the following year was appointed governor of Egypt by the Ottoman sultan. If the sultan thought he had reconquered Egypt for the empire, he was to be disappointed: after an unsteady beginning, in which he had to deal with a range of opposition, Muhammad Ali established a military dynasty of his own and achieved de facto independence from Istanbul. Employing European advisors, he created a huge army, which was initially used against the Wahhabis in the Red Sea area – puritanical Islam had no place in the modern state which he and his successors envisaged for Egypt – and within a few years Muhammad Ali's forces had cleared the Wahhabis from the Hijaz and restored the holy places of Islam to their Ottoman rulers. Egyptian hegemony was extended down the Red Sea, and in 1846, the ports of Suakin and Massawa were leased by Istanbul to Cairo. The army was an enormous burden to the treasury, and Muhammad Ali also sought to reform Egypt's economic and indeed industrial base, expanding the taxation system and enforcing the production of cotton; huge growth in cotton production through the nineteenth century was made possible by extensive irrigation programs. Ever innovative and attracted to European models of administration and education, Muhammad Ali set up technical schools, while an elite was sent to Europe for training; he imported European technology in attempting to lay the foundations for an industrial revolution of sorts, involving the manufacture of arms and textiles, for example. Government was founded upon a reformed military bureaucracy.[12] Egypt thus witnessed the creation of a new landowning and bureaucratic middle class, which over several generations would become involved in politics, administration, the law, and journalism – a "modernizing" class whose activities were underpinned by a lower order that remained comparatively unchanged, namely the peasantry marshaled to grow cotton, Egypt's major source of external wealth. In later decades, notably, the scions of Egypt's new middle class would find their social status undermined by the British and would embrace new forms of anticolonial nationalism.

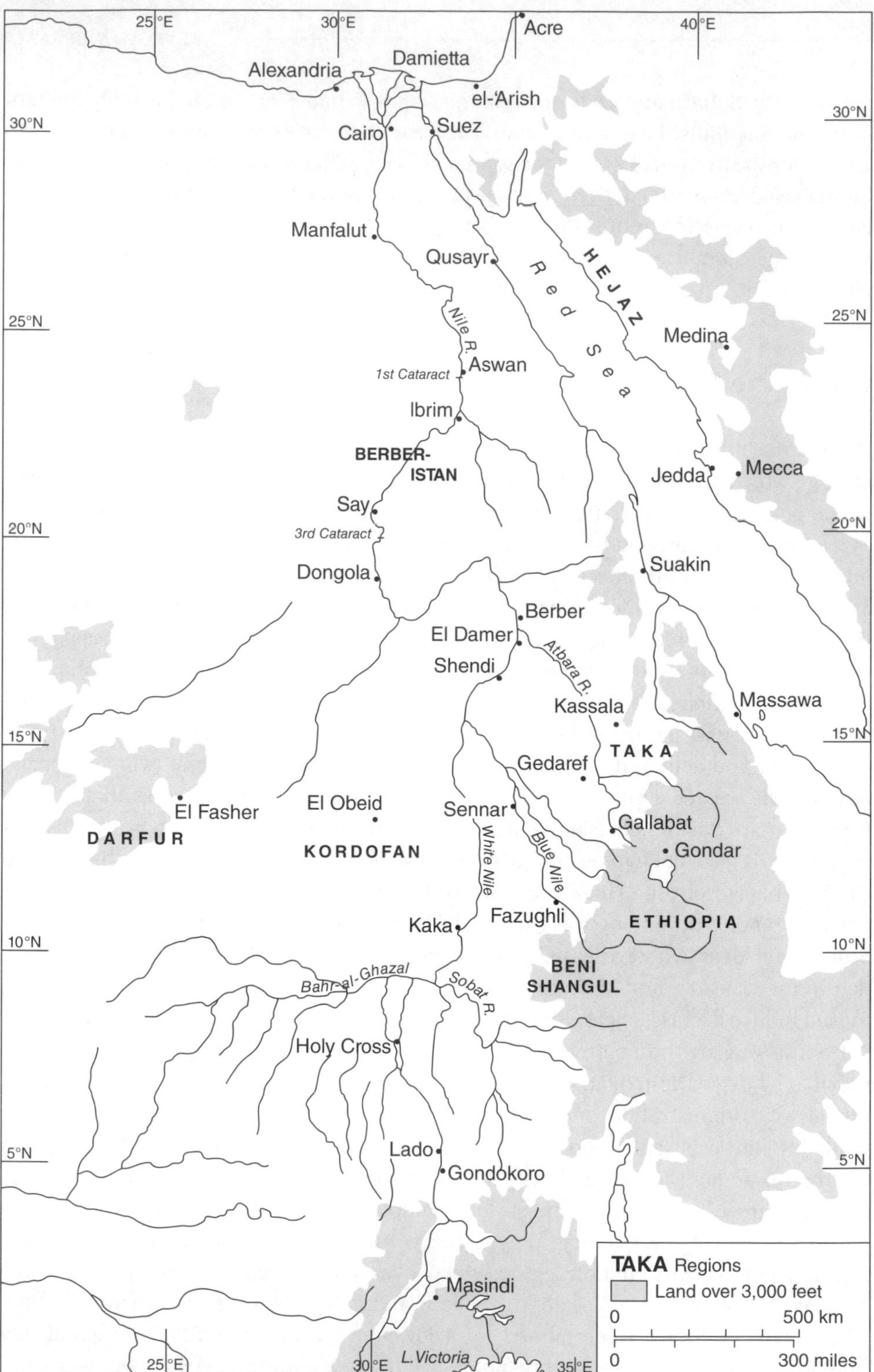

Egypt and the Nile Valley c.1800. Source: From J. E. Flint (ed.), *Cambridge History of Africa*. Vol. 5: *c.1790–c.1870* (Cambridge, 1976), p. 12, Map 1; © 1976 by Cambridge University Press. Reprinted with permission from Cambridge University Press.

In the meantime, Muhammad Ali also looked southward, into Sudan: in the early 1820s, a series of campaigns saw Egyptian forces overcoming the Funj sultanate, as well as the last remnants of Mameluke opposition. In 1824, the Egyptian capital was established at Khartoum, where the Blue and White Niles meet. Further southward incursions would continue in the decades to come, toward Kordofan and into the Nuba mountains, while Khartoum-based traders and soldiers would reach as far as the lacustrine kingdoms of East Africa by the 1860s and 1870s; Egyptian rule of Sudan was only shattered by the Mahdist revolt in the 1880s.[13] Importantly, the Egyptian presence in both Sudan and the Red Sea facilitated an expansion of trade, with many becoming rich on the proceeds of the regional slave and ivory trades along the Nile, fed by incursions into south Sudan, and the eastward-bound commerce on the Red Sea, increasingly used by Europeans as a route to India and East Asia. Egyptian expansion in Sudan would also lead to conflict with the other great expanding state in the region, namely Ethiopia under emperors Tewodros and Yohannes.

In time, it was the commercial and strategic importance of the Red Sea to the British in particular which would be the undoing of the independent Egypt created by Muhammad Ali – and for this reason, he consistently opposed the building of a canal linking the Red Sea to the Mediterranean. But even before this, he was a cause for concern in European capitals, where he was perceived as becoming over-mighty and a threat to stability in the region. The British, moreover, had committed themselves to the defense and maintenance of the ever-weakening Ottoman empire, and Muhammad Ali needed to be brought to heel. It was Muhammad Ali's expansion into the Levant in the early 1830s that caused great anxiety in Istanbul: an Ottoman expedition dispatched in 1839 to wrest the provinces of Syria and Palestine from Egyptian control ended in defeat and humiliation for the sultan, at which point Britain and several European allies stepped in to force Muhammad Ali to withdraw. In the late 1830s and early 1840s, he had his wings clipped even further when he was forced to reduce the size of his army – from close to 200,000 men to some 18,000 – and to end the monopolies he had set up which excluded Europeans from Egyptian markets.[14] This effectively ended Muhammad Ali's industrial ambitions, and from the 1840s onward, the Egyptian economy became both largely agricultural and exposed to ever greater European influence and indeed management. The Egypt he had created was only partially "modernized," limited by European wariness of this "oriental despot" and prone to European intervention; it was a pattern which was repeated across Islamic North Africa, and ultimately caused a profound cleavage within Islam itself.

Muhammad Ali died in 1849, and uncertainty as to how to deal with Europe and what Europe represented was manifested in the reigns of his immediate successors, Abbas I (1849–54) and Muhammad Said (1854–63). Abbas was wary of Europe and its ideas, while Muhammad Said conversely fell under the influence of an inner circle of European advisors. In any case, the expansion of European influence was seemingly inexorable – as was European settlement, with tens of thousands coming to reside in Egypt in the middle decades of the nineteenth century – especially during the "modernizing" reign of Ismail (1863–79), who took the old Persian title *khedive*. Ismail, educated in Europe, pursued his grandfather's dreams of a modern, industrial Egypt; the construction of the Suez Canal had begun in 1859, but it was completed under Ismail, in 1869. Under the *khedive*, railways were built, modern communications installed (in the form of the telegraph), and cities redesigned; Ismail dreamt of a Cairo that would look like Paris. But all this required capital, and it was the enormous loans raised in Europe – and the enormous rates of interest which accompanied them – which made

Cairo in the mid-nineteenth century. Syndics of Cambridge University Library, Tab. b.13. Source: Reproduced with permission of University of Cambridge.

Ismail's Egypt increasingly vulnerable to the predations of European politicians and creditors alike. Such rapid externally funded "modernization" would have some of the same consequences for a number of African states in the 1960s and 1970s, for European ideas of "modernity" came at a price. In 1875, Ismail was compelled to sell his shares in the Suez Canal to pay some of his mounting debts, but it offered only temporary relief, for by the end of the decade, the Egyptian government was bankrupt. Meanwhile, a Briton, General Charles Gordon, had been foisted upon the Egyptians as governor of Sudan, his mission being to suppress the slave trade there. The year 1879 witnessed the overthrow of Ismail and the arrival of European experts whose job it was to oversee Egypt's finances; Ismail's successor, his son Tawfiq would find his freedom of action increasingly impaired and his country's sovereignty compromised.[15]

Egypt offers one of the most dramatic examples of a secular government being targeted because of its perceived role as an agency of European colonialism. The revolt in 1881 of Ahmad Urabi Pasha, an army officer and government minister, channeled the popular protests which had themselves been provoked by growing foreign economic and cultural influence over the government in Cairo. As riots erupted in Alexandria, the British dispatched an army in 1882 and brought the protestors to heel; Urabi Pasha's forces were defeated, and he himself was exiled.[16] In fact, it had not been the intention of the government in London to stay in Egypt: the idea had been to remove the troublemakers, stabilize a friendly and trustworthy regime, and pull out. But as the country descended into chaos, the British found this plan unworkable. In seizing Egypt, Britain acted to the exclusion of the French, who also had financial interests there, but who were paralyzed by political crisis at home; British action, moreover, sent shock waves across the Islamic world and was one of the key moments in the escalating European partition of the continent. Yet even as the British took control in Cairo, events were unfolding more than a thousand miles to the south, in Sudan, which would soon consume the region. The Mahdist revolt would lead to the expulsion, albeit temporarily, of the Anglo-Egyptian administration in Sudan, and for a time, the resultant state would defy the British empire. We return to this in Chapter 7.

Notes

1 One of the best surveys is Ira M. Lapidus, *A History of Islamic Societies*, 2nd ed. (Cambridge, 2002), 299–336.

2 Jonathan Miran, *Red Sea Citizens: Cosmopolitan Society and Cultural Change in Massawa* (Bloomington & Indianapolis IN, 2009), 38ff.

3 For wide-ranging analysis, M.W. Daly (ed.), *The Cambridge History of Egypt. Vol II: Modern Egypt, from 1517 to the End of the Twentieth Century* (Cambridge, 1998).

4 Douglas A. Howard, *A History of the Ottoman Empire* (Cambridge, 2017), chaps. 3 & 4.

5 Lapidus, *History of Islamic Societies*, 319ff.

6 See John L. Esposito, *Islam: The Straight Path* (Oxford, 2005), chap. 4, for an overview of the debates within Islam in the nineteenth century; also Lapidus, *History of Islamic Societies*, 453–68.

7 R. Danziger, *Abd al-Qadir and the Algerians* (New York, 1977).

8 C.-R. Ageron, *Modern Algeria: A History from 1830 to the Present* (London, 1991); J. Ruedy, *Modern Algeria: The Origins and Development of a Nation* (Bloomington IN, 1992); James McDougall, *History and the Culture of Nationalism in Algeria* (Cambridge, 2006).

9 Kenneth Perkins, *A History of Modern Tunisia* (Cambridge, 2014), esp. chap. 1; L.C. Brown, *The Tunisia of Ahmad Bey* (Princeton, 1974).

10 John Wright's republished *A History of Libya* (London, 2012) remains a pacey read; see also Dirk Vandewalle, *A History of Modern Libya* (Cambridge, 2014), chaps. 1 & 2, and the older A.A. Ahmida, *The Making of Modern Libya* (New York, 1994). The famed anthropologist E.E. Evans-Pritchard's colonial-era study, *The Sanusi of Cyrenaica* (Oxford, 1949), is also a revealing account.

11 Among the best accounts of the modern kingdom are C.R. Pennell, *Morocco Since 1830: A History* (London, 1999); and, more recently, Susan Gilson Miller, *A History of Modern Morocco* (Cambridge, 2013).

12 A.L. al-Sayyid, *Egypt in the Reign of Muhammad Ali* (Cambridge, 1984); P.J. Vatikiotis, *The Modern History of Egypt* (London, 1980).

13 P.M. Holt & M.W. Daly, *A History of the Sudan: From the Coming of Islam to the Present Day* (Harlow, 2000), chaps. 3–5, provides a useful overview.

14 For the narrative detail, P.M. Holt, "Egypt and the Nile Valley," in Flint (ed.), *Cambridge History*, Vol. 5, 22–33.

15 Ibid., 33–50.

16 Alexander Schölch, "The "Men on the Spot" and the English occupation of Egypt in 1882," The Historical Journal, 19:3 (1976).

6 Jihad

Revolutions in Western Africa

Islam in Western Africa to the Eighteenth Century

Islam had been introduced to West Africa from the north a millennium before the nineteenth century, via the trans-Saharan trade. Berber merchants carried Islam across the Sahara to the states and settlements of the western savannah, where ruling elites, urban populations, and local traders generally embraced the faith before rural populations did. The earliest conversions are believed to have taken place before the beginning of the ninth century. The main advantages of Islam to sub-Saharan traders were literacy and the fact that Islam brought about a sense of brotherhood and cooperation between merchants north and south of the desert. This was a period, therefore, of both cultural and economic interaction between the Maghreb and the savannah, and within West Africa itself. Traders on the southern fringes of the desert who converted to Islam pushed commercial and religious frontiers southward, and trade migrations led to the creation of Muslim settlements at strategic points across the region.[1]

Rulers and traders who converted had an eclectic approach to Islam and adapted it to fit existing features of West African religion, which continued to be influential. Thus, although local religion allowed for the existence of a creator god – approximately compatible with the monotheism of Islam – such creators were no longer regarded as taking a direct interest in the physical world, with greater emphasis placed on a pantheon of deities with occupational functions. Other features of local religion which were retained included the spirits of ancestors, the guardians of specific lineages and ethnic groups; and diviners, who possessed extraordinary authority and who were responsible for identifying those guilty of witchcraft and sorcery. However, the "intellectual theory" of conversion suggests that for many Africans, the creator god was associated with the outside world and was thus unimportant as long as the outside world was relatively insignificant. But as the latter encroached on states and societies – in this case, the expansion of trade with peoples north of the Sahara – there was a revival in interest in monotheism and the creator god himself.[2] Thus, the expansion of the West African worldview was attended by conversion to Islam – just as, rather later, in other parts of the continent, there would be conversion to Christianity.

As demand for West African gold expanded between the ninth and eleventh centuries, so did the kingdom of Ghana, and so did Islam; Ghana's capital contained a "Muslim quarter" in the eleventh century, and its rulers employed literate Muslims as secretaries. The kingdom itself became Muslim in the 1070s, whether voluntarily, or as a result of Almoravid conquest (as claimed in the Arabic sources), is unclear. Later, the empire of Mali – Ghana's successor as the predominant power in the West African savannah – was recognized as a Muslim state by the early fourteenth century, although the broad mass of the population continued to adhere to local beliefs. The extent to which West African rulers promoted Islam and were generally regarded as "good Muslims" in the Arabic sources varied from reign to reign. Mali's Mansa Musa (1312–37) made the pilgrimage to Mecca, patronized Islamic learning, and built a mosque at Gao; he sent scholars to North Africa, and some returned to set up centers of learning, notably at Timbuktu. Songhay's Muhammad Ture (1493–1528) was an enthusiastic exponent of Islam, waging jihad against the Mossi, going on the *hajj*, and getting himself appointed as caliph of the "Sudanic belt" of West Africa. In between, there were rulers who were seen as less sympathetic to Islam, such as Songhay's conquering hero Sonni Ali "the Great" (1464–92).[3]

Religious and economic networks spread across the West African savannah, particularly in the decades following the collapse of Songhay. Scholarly lineages, which grew around individuals noted for their legal expertise and personal insight, were crucial in spreading belief in Islam (including belief in miracles) and providing political mediation. The Kunta family was one such lineage: initially influential in Mauritania and the Senegambia area, between the sixteenth and the eighteenth centuries the Kunta spread to Bornu, Hausaland, and the middle Niger where they established important colonies.[4] Through the Kunta, moreover, the Qadiriyya brotherhood spread throughout the region. Further south, in the forest, other Muslim communities were formed among traders and farmers: through commercial links and kinship ties, the Dyula or *wangara* – the terms have often been used interchangeably, denoting networks of merchants, at least in origin – established communities along trading routes and, through marriage with unbelievers, spread Islam itself.[5] These were essentially Muslim missionaries; but not all West African Muslims were possessed of a proselytizing spirit. While in some areas Islam had a powerful influence over political elites and Muslims became incorporated into broader society – notably in the kingdoms of Gonja and Dagomba, west of the Volta River – in others they constituted relatively isolated enclaves, even if they might have some political importance. This was the case in Asante, for example, where a small Muslim community in the capital Kumasi served as translators, advisors, and diplomats, but made no great effort to convert the wider populace nor to integrate with it.[6]

Alongside the conversion of political elites, there had developed a local tradition of Islamic learning, with indigenous scholarship in Arabic emerging from the fifteenth century, particularly in Timbuktu, the most important center of both commerce and scholarship in the West African savannah.[7] Yet Muslims remained a minority, confined largely to the class of traders and the courts of rulers. Islam was thus primarily an urban religion, little developed beyond the towns; the shari'a, the code of Islamic laws, was not enforced with any particular rigor. But in the eighteenth and nineteenth centuries, there was a series of movements in West Africa which had as their stated objective the purification of Islam across the region and the enforcement of shari'a law; they sought to achieve this through jihad, often winning popular support among peasants who had begun to embrace Islam much more fervently than previously and who were prepared to challenge, as they saw it, corrupt and indolent ruling elites who were Muslim in name only. In many ways, these drew on deep traditions of Islamic militancy across both savannah and the Sahara to the north. Islam had long been mobilized, for example, by communities competing for space along the desert edge, while the wider region had a history of producing visionary religious leaders aspiring to perfect theocracy. The movements of the eighteenth and nineteenth centuries, however, were marked by especial vigor and interconnectedness, while in many respects the states they made – and the means by which they made them – represented part of the unfolding revolution in military and political affairs across much of Africa in the same era. There were close parallels with movements north of the Sahara: common themes included calls for the enforcement of shari'a law, the elimination of "pagan" Muslims failing to fulfill their duties, and the powerful influence wielded by revivalist brotherhoods. There may be an argument for the North African movements inspiring those further south; but there were particular circumstances in the southern desert and savannah, specific forces for change within West Africa which contributed to distinctive, independent revivalist movements. The most dramatic of these was the 1804 jihad in Hausaland, and the 1852 uprising of the Tukolor; but these had themselves been influenced by two earlier jihads in the regions of Futa Jalon (1725 to c. 1750) and Futa Toro (1769–76). All of these involved, to a greater or lesser degree, sedentary Muslim communities allied with the pastoralist Fulani people, who were instrumental in the spread of West African Islamic revivalism.

The Wandering Fulani

By the beginning of the seventeenth century, much of the West African savannah, a huge area north of the forest belt, was at least nominally Muslim. Yet it was not only trade which facilitated the spread of Islam but also the migration of people over several centuries which resulted in much cultural interaction, the exchange of ideas as well as commodities. People migrated for many reasons, including drought and crop failure, and political upheaval and oppression; the regional slave trade was also a force for demographic change, involving the carriage of culture as well as people from place to place. One of the most important long-term migrations was that of the Fulani, or

"Fulbe." Originating in the area of the middle Senegal, the pastoral Fulani drifted eastwards over several centuries; vulnerable to climatic change, they migrated slowly across the savannah in search of better pasture and had spread across much of the region between the Senegal and the Niger by the seventeenth century. By the beginning of the nineteenth century they were most numerous in the area of modern northern Nigeria.

The Fulani mostly retained their distinctive language, culture, and economy in the areas where they settled, but in some places, they came under increasing pressure from agricultural populations who often resented the intruders and restricted their grazing and trading rights. This sense of isolation may explain their readiness to embrace Islam, which offered a common sense of purpose and protection in the midst of potential enemies; Islam provided the Fulani with an alternative model of government and a belief system with which to confront oppressive agricultural rulers who might *claim* to be Muslim but who clearly neglected the shari'a. As they moved, the Fulani also regularly came into contact with Muslim traders and other Muslim peoples, such as the Tuareg; certainly they were largely Islamized by the early eighteenth century, and from their number were drawn many of the leading Muslim scholars in the region. Some of these began to preach the need for jihad against the unbelievers and would be instrumental in the outbreak of several Islamic revolutions in the eighteenth and nineteenth centuries. They were, again, influential in fostering the jihads of Futa Jalon and Futa Toro in the early and mid-eighteenth century.[8]

Among those who would be their enemies were the Hausa, a group which had emerged from a mixture of southern Saharan nomads and farmers of the northern Nigerian savannah. The economic basis of the Hausa was agriculture, bolstered by some manufacturing and commerce, and they, too, had developed close contacts with trans-Saharan Muslim traders. As with many others, trade exposed the Hausa to Islam; by the fourteenth century, the Hausa urban elite had become Muslim, and in the centuries that ensued, swathes of the peasantry would follow suit. Hausaland was torn by warfare between individual city-states, resulting in the heavy taxation of the peasantry by ruling elites eager to fund conflict; at the same time, rulers increasingly resorted to the illegal capture of fellow Muslims as slaves for export. In the eyes of the Muslim Hausa peasantry, their rulers were corrupt, oppressive, and ever less mindful of Islamic law, and thus was the scene set for the "holy war," which would sweep the region in the early nineteenth century in conjunction with the Fulani.[9]

Prophets and Warriors

By the beginning of the nineteenth century, then, there had emerged across the West African savannah networks of Muslim clerics who aspired to a return to a purified Islam, based on the life of the Prophet; this, they argued, was incompatible with local religions. Many had been to Mecca and were imbued with messianic zeal. Uthman dan Fodio (born 1754, died 1817) came from a Fulani family already steeped in Islamic learning, and the young Uthman began preaching in the state of Gobir in the 1770s. Central to his message was the need to enforce the shari'a, and his criticisms of the governing elites who were Muslim only in name became ever more trenchant; a dedicated community formed around him, much to the alarm of the authorities in Gobir, who attempted to restrict his movements. His reputation spread across Hausaland, based largely on his critiques of government corruption, injustice, and ungodliness, a platform which served to attract an eclectic array of followers, many of whom – as we see below – were not simply, if at all, interested in the restoration of pure Islam, but were more concerned with the creation of a new political and indeed ethnic order. Nonetheless, a great many did indeed believe him to be the Mahdi, the savior and restorer of fundamental Islam, a notion which Uthman himself tended to play down, at least in later years; he did, however, believe he had the ability to perform miracles. Uthman condemned the authorities for illegal taxation, their condoning of polytheism, the practice of enslaving other Muslims, and infidel ceremonial and other social practices.[10]

Official persecution intensified, and Uthman ultimately left Gobir, in so doing performing the *hijra*, the act of withdrawal out of reach of infidel government; and, following the precedent clearly established by the Prophet Muhammad himself, jihad soon followed, erupting in 1804. By 1810, most Hausa states, including Katsina, Kano, and Gobir, had been seized by a motley array of Muslim forces, including a number of disaffected Hausa, and Uthman and his disciples controlled virtually the entire region; the jihad reached as far east as Nupe and the area south of Lake Chad, and as far south as Yoruba territory in the coastal forest belt. Within a few short years, a new empire across much of present-day northern Nigeria and northern Cameroon had been created out of, among other things, a revolution against infidelity to God, and the Sokoto Caliphate was the single largest polity in nineteenth-century West Africa, surviving into the colonial period.[11] Uthman himself retired from political life, dedicating the remainder of his days to monasticism, while his brother Abdullahi and son Muhammad Bello took over government; indeed, they carried the revolution further, inciting more uprisings in neighboring states, and invading Ilorin, the northern province of the tottering Oyo empire, in so doing pushing Islam deep into Yoruba territory.[12] Islam was also rejuvenated within Hausaland itself, although the extent to which some of the participants in the Hausaland revolution were genuinely motivated by faith is a matter of some debate.

The territory of the new caliphate was organized into emirates, many of which corresponded to pre-jihad Hausa states, and which were answerable to the Caliphs. The Emirs themselves relied on military force and also on the legitimacy which derived from their association with prominent Fulani lineages. In some respects, Sokoto was a slightly reformed version of the old Hausa monarchical system, and the indirect rule which operated in many provinces meant that Islam was only selectively applied. Nonetheless this was an Islamic state, arguably the most potent in nineteenth-century Africa, and through Sokoto, Hausaland was fully part of the Islamic world. The Caliphate was ultimately governed through Islamic administration, its legal system maintained and interpreted by Muslim judges, and its taxation and land tenure systems based on Islamic practice. An enormous population of enslaved infidels underpinned the economy.[13] Mosques and schools were built to convert the non-Muslim population, and scholarship was encouraged by the state; the scholars of Sokoto were mostly associated with the Qadiriyya, but in time the Tijaniyya would also be represented. Sufism was widespread.[14]

The creation of Sokoto was a source of inspiration elsewhere across the savannah belt, leading to the formation of states based on revitalized Islam, as in Bornu and Masina.[15] In particular, Sokoto was the inspiration behind the foundation of the Tukolor state. Here, too, people related to the Fulani were instrumental in the fomentation of discontent, and the leader of the broad movement which emerged, al-Hajj Umar Tal (1794–1864), was a distinguished scholar who had undertaken the pilgrimage to Mecca and spent time at Sokoto. He railed against both pagans and lapsed Muslims, and as the West African head of a new brotherhood, the Tijaniyya – which he had introduced to Sokoto during the 1830s – Umar came into conflict with local authorities, as Uthman had done in Gobir. In articulating popular grievances against governing elites, he attracted a large following among the displaced and marginalized, who came together under the banner of Islam. In 1852, he declared a jihad on the upper Senegal River. As the French looked on from their coastal base to the west, Umar conquered a swathe of territory across the Senegal interior and indeed further east. He made war on Masina, an act which was condemned by his enemies as illegitimate – it involved conflict with fellow Muslims – and the Tukolor state ultimately proved somewhat less durable than Sokoto as a result. Following Umar's death in 1864 at the hands of a coalition of enemies, the "empire" – unconsolidated and fraught with internal tensions – deteriorated into civil war. Nonetheless, the religious impact of Umar's revolution was rather more significant: as Sokoto had done, the short-lived Tukolor state revitalized Islam across the western savannah, on the eve, importantly, of French encroachment into the area. Umar's followers, indeed, created a state in Hamdallahi, extending across the western part of present-day Mali, which was only overwhelmed by the French in 1893.[16]

Yet interpretations of these jihads vary: while on a certain level, they can be seen as being genuinely concerned with religious reform, on another they may be interpreted as representing the crystallization of deep-rooted interethnic tensions, or as insurrections against political and economic repression. The spiritual interpretation, of course, was the "official" view of the leaders themselves and of their chroniclers, who claimed that Islam was being purified through the legitimate employment of violence, jihad, against unbelievers. Again, a framework, as well as precedent, for spiritually motivated action of this kind had existed in the region for several centuries, and in many respects, jihadist leaders were merely galvanizing and extending extant networks of faith. But in fact, the use of the term "jihad" in this context is problematic. War against oppressive "infidel" or non-Muslim rule is in theory obligatory for all Muslims; but the uprisings of the West African savannah were often against Muslims who were believed not to be adhering to the shari'a, and therefore, it might be suggested that there was a difficulty about the actual legitimacy of these particular jihads, as they frequently targeted Muslims from other brotherhoods – as was the case for the Tijaniyya, for example – rather than "infidels" *per se*. Thus, it seems safe to propose that Islamic "revivalism" cannot be seen as the sole factor behind the insurrections and indeed for many people involved was probably completely absent.

To a very real degree, then, they can also be interpreted as ethnic conflicts. This was particularly true across Hausaland, where much of the leadership and support for Uthman's revolt came from the pastoral Fulani, who believed themselves to be oppressed at the hands of the agricultural and indeed increasingly urban Hausa. And while, as we have seen, many Fulani were indeed dedicated Muslims, many in fact were not, and almost certainly the latter were motivated more by a sense of ethnic solidarity than religious zeal. Ethnic "consciousness" was clearly important; and linked to this, the socioeconomic interpretation is also an attractive one. The Hausaland and Tukolor revolts had in common the articulation of discontent around political and economic issues as well as moral and religious ideas. Most prominent was the question of taxation, and in particular the *jangali* or cattle tax – again hitting the Fulani especially hard – which was seen as brutal, illegal, and un-Islamic. In that sense, the prophets and warriors of revivalist Islam represented a pastoralist militancy born of the long-standing struggle for land rights. Slavery was also a thorny issue: enslavement was commonly practiced by ruling elites, notably among the Hausa, even though the enslavement of Muslims was prohibited (although it was permissible for everyone else). Overall, then, jihad was at least partially motivated by socioeconomic repression, and the resulting conflict was broadly between pastoralists and agriculturalists, reflecting, perhaps, competition for access to and control of regional resources. Clearly, a combination of all these factors lay behind the uprisings of the eighteenth and nineteenth centuries, in what can be termed "coalitions of interests."

Whatever the motives of particular individuals or groups, Islam became much more deeply rooted in the states and societies of the West African savannah; there were many more West African Muslims at the end of the nineteenth century than there had been in the middle of the eighteenth. As European colonial invasion gathered pace between the 1870s and the 1890s – the French pushing across the savannah from Senegal, the British penetrating north of the forest from the Nigerian coast – Islam provided a greater unity of purpose and action in terms of resistance than was the case in many other parts of the continent. Muslims offered more concerted and unified resistance to the European infidel, and indeed were obliged – again in theory – to fight rather than submit to non-Muslim authority; Islam thus provided a unity which transcended ethnicity and language in certain areas. Yet the opposition to European imperialism was never fully effective, in large part because it was undermined by sectarian rivalry, in particular between competing brotherhoods. Moreover, Europeans often tackled the potential threat of Islam by adopting a conciliatory stance toward Muslim authorities, who were co-opted into the colonial system and offered considerable autonomy. The classic instance of this was the British in Northern Nigeria, where, having militarily subjugated the Sokoto Caliphate, they governed through the Fulani and Hausa aristocracy and avoided interference in day-to-day administration.

As for Umar's state and its successor in Hamdallahi, it also involved the enforcement of Islamic practice and outlawing of infidel ceremonies; but it was rather weaker economically than Sokoto, dependent as it was on predatory warfare. The state was a major exporter of slaves; and more widely, violence, though initially inspired by the concept of jihad, became endemic across the region. In the wake of Umar's death, jihad erupted among the Wolof people of the Senegambia region; it was remarkably violent, involving widespread destruction and the enslavement of non-Muslims, but it did lead to the conversion of substantial numbers of Wolof.[17] To the southeast, earlier in the nineteenth century, religious violence had also erupted in the region of Toron and Konyan, led by Mori-Ule Sise. When he was killed in 1845, his cause was at length taken up by Samori Ture, who belonged to a *wangara* family, and in the course of the 1860s and 1870s, he built up a substantial personal army and brought a large area under his sway. His state was essentially a military one, administered through military governors and through an army which depended on imported firearms and horses, which he paid for through widespread slave-raiding; but in the 1880s, he attempted more systematic Islamization, trying to enforce Islamic law and patronizing Muslim scholarship. Much of his support came from fellow *wangara* who had benefited from Samori's encouragement of regional commerce. However, following considerable resistance, he quickly retreated from his Muslim policy and concentrated on military and political consolidation, particularly in the face of French aggression, which forced him to shift eastward in the course of the 1890s.[18] As we see in a later chapter, he was eventually defeated and exiled by the French.

Samori was the last of the great Muslim military leaders and state-builders of the nineteenth century. It was the end of an era which had witnessed the rallying of a range of different groups in society under the banner of jihad, from religious scholars and teachers, to oppressed ethnicities, to aggrieved and exploited peasants. These different groups were inspired, clearly, by a range of motives. But Islam had been the vehicle for struggle at the local level and also for the creation of larger, militarized, expansionist states, many of which participated in the trans-Saharan and Atlantic slave trades, as well as for moral and spiritual reform and renewal. It was an era which undoubtedly witnessed the rejuvenation of Islam in those parts of West Africa where it already had roots of considerable antiquity, the spread of Muslims into new areas, and the conversion of the peoples of those areas to Islam. West African Muslims' contribution to Africa's nineteenth-century revolutionary age – an age of conflict as well as creativity – was therefore a significant one indeed, and their actions would have profound repercussions throughout the twentieth century. Across the region, messianic movements had preached that the nineteenth century – the thirteenth century in the Muslim calendar – would witness a return to a pure Islam and the subjection and conversion of the unbelieving world. In fact, such revivalism was in part driven by, and in part coincided with, the expansion of that unbelieving world, manifest in European imperialism. There would be no conquest of the European infidel; the interaction with Europe would be rather more complex than that.

Notes

1 For a classic study, see J.S. Trimingham, *A History of Islam in West Africa* (London, 1970); also P. Clarke, *West Africa and Islam* (London, 1982) and M. Hiskett, *The Development of Islam in West Africa* (London, 1984). A recent forum in the *Journal of African History* involving contributions from Jean-Louis Triaud, Scott Reese and Benjamin Soares explores the construction of Muslim identities south of the Sahara: see "JAH Forum: Islam in Sub-Saharan Africa," *Journal of African History*, 55:1 (2014).

2 J.D.Y. Peel, "Conversion and tradition in two African societies: Ijebu and Buganda," *Past and Present*, 77 (1977).
3 N. Levtzion, "The western Maghrib and Sudan," in Oliver (ed.), *Cambridge History*, Vol. 3; E.W.Bovill, *The Golden Trade of the Moors*, 67–97, 108–95.
4 Lapidus, *History of Islamic Societies*, 409–10.
5 Paul Lovejoy, "The role of the Wangara in the economic transformation of the Central Sudan in the fifteenth and sixteenth centuries," *Journal of African History*, 19: 2 (1978).
6 See Wilks, *Asante*.
7 See N. Levtzion & J.F.P. Hopkins (eds.), *Corpus of Early Arabic Sources for West African History* (Princeton, 2001), for a useful anthology of source material.
8 Humphrey Fisher, "The central Sahara and Sudan," in Gray (ed.), *Cambridge History*, Vol. 4.
9 For a useful summary, see N. Levtzion, "Islam in the Bilad al-Sudan to 1800," in Levtzion & Pouwels (eds.), *History of Islam in Africa*.
10 Mervyn Hiskett, *The Sword of Truth: the life and times of the Shehu Usuman dan Fodio* (New York, 1973).
11 The standard accounts remain Murray Last, *The Sokoto Caliphate* (London, 1967); H.A.S. Johnston, *The Fulani Empire of Sokoto* (London, 1967); and J.P. Smaldone, *Warfare in the Sokoto Caliphate* (London, 1977). For a more recent attempt to place these events in a wider, indeed global, context, see Paul E. Lovejoy *Jihad in West Africa During the Age of Revolutions* (Athens OH, 2016).
12 Robin Law, "Making sense of a traditional narrative: political disintegration in the kingdom of Oyo," *Cahiers d'Etudes Africaines*, 22 (1982).
13 Paul E. Lovejoy, "Plantations in the Economy of the Sokoto Caliphate," *Journal of African History*, 19: 3 (1978).
14 Again, see Last, *Sokoto Caliphate*; B.G. Martin, *Muslim Brotherhoods in 19th-Century Africa* (Cambridge, 1976); and also R.A. Adeleye, *Power and Diplomacy in Northern Nigeria, 1804–1906* (London, 1971).
15 For example, Vincent Hiribarren, *A History of Borno: Trans-Saharan African Empire to Failing Nigerian State* (London, 2017); Louis Brenner, *The Shehus of Kukawa: A History of the al-Kenemi Dynasty of Bornu* (London, 1973).
16 David Robinson, *The Holy War of Umar Tal* (Oxford, 1985).
17 See for example Martin A. Klein, "Social and economic factors in the Muslim Revolution in Senegambia," *Journal of African History*, 13: 3 (1972).
18 The classic work is Yves Person, *Samori, une révolution Dyula*, 3 vols. (Dakar, 1968–75).

7 The Eastern Crescent

The Islamic Frontier in Eastern Africa

Swahili Islam: Coastal Frontiers in the Nineteenth Century

Swahili – the term denotes a culture and a civilization, as well as a language – was born of the remarkable fusion of African and Arabic elements along the Indian Ocean coast between modern Somalia and Mozambique. The rise and rapid diffusion of Islam provided a major boost to Indian Ocean commerce, and the first Muslim migrants from southern Arabia and the Persian Gulf began settling along the northern section of the east African coast in the eighth century. They intermarried with the local populace, including ruling elites, and their presence facilitated trading relations between the African littoral and the expanding Muslim world. The rise of settlements at Mogadishu, Barawa, and the Lamu Islands was linked to the expansion in demand for African ivory and, later, gold, and Muslim migration increased over the ensuing centuries; from this dynamic interaction, Swahili civilization emerged. The term itself, derived from the Arabic for coast, literally meant "the people of the coast," and in a linguistic sense, it was a Bantu African language infused with Arabic words, probably emerging in the Lamu Islands–Tanu valley area of modern Kenya. In time, it developed as a written language using Arabic script. Yet "Swahili" came to mean much more than this: between the tenth and the fourteenth centuries, it became a distinctive coastal culture, Islamic in religion, centered around a series of commercial city-states. Muslim immigrants moved ever further south, and were instrumental in the creation of settlements at Zanzibar, Mafia, Pemba, and Kilwa, many of these located on islands a short distance from the African mainland. The distinctive architectural styles which emerged in these settlements – stone-built mosques, residential quarters, and palaces – represented a fusion of African and Arab styles; Swahili material culture was the manifestation of an

A History of Modern Africa: 1800 to the Present, Third Edition. Richard J. Reid.

artistic achievement unique to coastal eastern Africa. New towns and ruling dynasties proliferated, the latter known as "Shirazi" because they traced – or claimed – ancestry from Shiraz in the Persian Gulf. By the thirteenth century, there were some forty Swahili towns between Mogadishu in the north and Sofala in the south; the larger towns, including Mogadishu itself, Mombasa, Malindi, Zanzibar, and Kilwa, generated considerable wealth through trade, and were compact, self-governing sultanates. As for Islam itself, this was largely confined to ruling elites, for while some ordinary townspeople might also be Muslim, the African majority was not, as yet.[1]

Indigenous coastal religion was based upon the notion of a universe in which the physical and moral worlds, natural and supernatural, were one; moral actions had physical consequences. Emphasis was placed on the spirits of ancestors, who were the arbiters of appropriate social discourse and moral behavior, while the spirits of nature, as well as malevolent spirits, played a critical role in everyday life. Each coastal settlement was essentially a spiritual microcosm, a moral and religious universe in miniature, with its own specific spirits and guardians, and to move to another settlement was to cross into another such universe. However, urban dwellers operated in the context of a much wider world and were involved in a commercial network which linked continents either side of the Indian Ocean. They inhabited a macrocosmic universe, shared by peoples with different languages, ancestors, occupations, and in this environment local belief systems were too narrow. A more universal set of beliefs was required; and thus, in many ways not dissimilar to the experience of West Africa, many townspeople adopted Islam. In so doing, they were adopting a set of beliefs and a framework for action and discourse which were held in common by people across the Indian Ocean world. While it is difficult to assess the impact Islam had on Swahili society in earlier centuries, it is clear that stone mosques had appeared in the major settlements by the twelfth and thirteenth centuries; however, as in the West African savannah, conversion was confined to the commercial class, who employed Islamic law and custom to facilitate trade.[2] Islam, in sum, offered access to overseas commerce, as well as providing an identity which transcended local loyalties. At the same time, however, it is important to note that microcosmic and macrocosmic universes were rarely mutually exclusive. People frequented both, and local spirits were appeased and protection from witchcraft offered, within the context of Quranic law. Two sets of belief systems coexisted interdependently, and it was this which made for the dynamic synthesis that was Swahili civilization.

As in other parts of the world at the same time, Islam along the East African coast was soon challenged by Europe, in the form of the Portuguese flotilla which rounded the Cape of Good Hope and arrived at the southern end of the Swahili coast in 1498. It was a coincidental discovery for the Portuguese, who now saw the seizure of Swahili trade as part of the increasingly global mission to destroy Muslim control of the rich commerce with India. They attacked and demanded the surrender of the coastal settlements in the name of holy Christian war, and in the course of the sixteenth century, Swahili resistance was gradually overcome. It was a process of conquest which culminated in the construction of Fort Jesus at Mombasa in 1599, the symbol as well as the center of Portuguese control in East Africa. As described in Chapter 3, however, the expulsion of the Portuguese from most of their coastal possessions at the end of the seventeenth century led ultimately to the creation of a new commercial empire centered on Zanzibar, and the eighteenth and nineteenth centuries witnessed the gradual expansion of Islam into the East African interior.

Islam in the Central East African Interior

The commercial expansion of the Zanzibar sultanate from the early nineteenth century led to the gradual penetration of Islam into the eastern African interior, although much less systematically than in the western part of the continent. It was also used for different purposes and employed in a range of contexts. Islam was perhaps most enthusiastically embraced in Buganda, where, upon the arrival of the first coastal merchants in the 1840s, the royal court welcomed not only cloth and firearms but also, in time, the faith itself; yet Islam had both commercial and political utility. In particular, Kabaka Mutesa envisaged Islam as a possible state religion which might be used to control the powerful spirit-mediums of indigenous belief; he proclaimed himself Muslim, possibly in the late 1860s, and encouraged others to follow suit. His was an insincere attachment, however, and in the middle of the 1870s, he found himself compelled to execute a number of young chiefs who had defied his authority on the grounds of Islamic principle. A number of Ganda, indeed, used imported religion for that very reason. Mutesa, ultimately, sought to balance Christianity and Islam against one another, claiming to be interested in all religions; but Muslim as well as Christian influences introduced profound instability into Ganda political society, instability which would manifest itself in civil war – ostensibly fought around allegiance to foreign faiths – at the end of the 1880s.[3]

Further south, Yao traders, long receptive to coastal culture, adopted Islam in the second half of the nineteenth century, and more broadly, Islam filtered into the coastal hinterland of Tanzania, where mobile young men – excited by the lure of commerce and adventure – used it to free themselves from more traditional social and political constraints.[4] In the deeper interior, however, Islam was most visible in the commercial entrepots established by Swahili-speaking merchants, notably at Tabora and Ujiji. Passing European travelers might despise coastal entrepreneurs as grasping troublemakers who made a mockery of true Islam, and African chiefs themselves were often less than enthusiastic about these new settlers, upon whom they nonetheless increasingly depended for commerce.[5] But they had a significant impact across central Tanzania, on the shores of Lake Tanganyika, and in the forests of eastern Congo. It is perhaps true that Islam was not best represented by the commercial representatives of the Zanzibar sultanate, but through intermarriage with local elites, the accumulation of entourages, and the trading-and-raiding network which they pioneered across lacustrine Africa, they did claim isolated converts, carried a form of the faith into new areas, and left an indelible mark on those communities within which they settled. There was an increasing demand, for example, for Islamic medicines and the "magical" knowledge available from coastal traders moving inland; and perhaps most important of all, the second half of the nineteenth century witnessed the adoption of Swahili as a language across a broad arc encompassing present-day southern Uganda, Tanzania, eastern Congo, Malawi, and northern Mozambique.

Overall, however, the impact of Islam in the central eastern African interior was much less than in West Africa in the nineteenth century, although the comparison is in a sense inappropriate, given the greater antiquity of Islam in the western savannah. Buganda and the area around Lake Nyasa were probably the areas in which most East African Muslims were concentrated; chiefs involved in long-distance trade sometimes became Muslim, or at least went through the motions of doing so, while Islam also took root among those displaced and uprooted by war and slavery in the second half of the nineteenth century. But more broadly Islam would grow rapidly from the early twentieth century and would vie with Christianity as the chief imported faith in certain areas.

Cross and Crescent in Northeast Africa

The first Muslims in Africa arrived on the Eritrean coast. Exactly *when* is a matter of debate; but the first mosque on the continent was in Massawa and may have been built by members of the Prophet's own family, in the 620s or 630s, sent there for their own safety amid the turbulence of Muhammad's revolution. The Red Sea was a natural channel of communication and exchange between northeast Africa and the Arabian peninsula and the Middle East; but by the tenth century, with the founding of ports such as Zeila, Islam was advancing into the region of modern-day Somalia, Djibouti, Ethiopia, and Eritrea from the direction of the Somali coast.[6] In some ways, we might see the defining characteristic of this process as a fundamental struggle between Christianity and Islam in the region, a struggle for hegemony which continues to the present day. There was clearly much religious conflict in the region's history, as Islamic authority expanded and periodically challenged the Christianity of the Ethiopian and Eritrean highlands. But we need to be careful not to exaggerate this. There was a great deal of cooperation and peaceful coexistence, notably, again, in the commercial arena. Much of the history of the region has been distorted by the anti-Islamic biases of precolonial European travelers and missionaries, while in medieval Europe, the Portuguese became obsessed with the idea of the "kingdom of Prester John," a Christian kingdom somewhere in "the East," surrounded by hostile Muslims.[7] The Ethiopian state itself deliberately cultivated such an image, defining itself ideologically through its religion: a kingdom (or a series of kingdoms, in fact) deep in the highlands, isolated from the Eurasian core, Muslims pressing in on the gates. On many levels, the Bible loomed large in the highland imagination, and the Christian polity saw itself as a second Israel, defending the faith against a host of external enemies, both Muslim and pagan.[8] It was an idea which had a powerful influence on Ethiopian art, which represents one of the most vibrant aesthetic traditions on the continent. Ethiopian painting frequently depicted the Christian struggle against evil opponents, and indeed the saintliness of the Ethiopian people themselves as well as their spiritual and political leaders. The concept was very much present in the late nineteenth century, when Ethiopia was perceived as a "Christian island set in a stormy Muslim sea" and therefore deserving of special attention.[9] In the twentieth century, Emperor Haile Selassie would likewise portray Ethiopia as the friend of the Christian West on the doorstep of a hostile Islamic world.

The Shoan-based Christian kingdom had survived sustained and well-organized Islamic attack in the mid-sixteenth century, partly through the timely intervention of a party of Portuguese musketeers; the Christian Church was thus preserved, but this prolonged period of violent conflict had weakened Ethiopia, facilitating the advance into the southern highlands of the pastoral Oromo. The Cushitic-speaking Oromo came from the grasslands northeast of Lake Turkana, and advanced to occupy the southern third of present-day Ethiopia by the end of the sixteenth century in their quest for better pastureland. They also moved onto the Harar plateau. Many converted to both Christianity and Islam in the process; the Muslim Oromo were often portrayed in the contemporary literature as barbarous hordes, closing in on Christian "fortress Ethiopia." They moved into the Shoa and Afar regions and transformed Harar into a Muslim settlement of no little significance; in the mid-seventeenth century, the Harar sultanate became an important regional power through its commercial and political contact with the Funj sultanate in Sudan, and through trade links across the Horn and with the Red Sea. Harar remained important down to the second half of the nineteenth century and was eventually absorbed into Menelik's expanding Christian empire.[10] The progress of the Oromo coincided with, and probably partly caused, the movement of the Amhara north and west, as the center of political gravity of the *habesha* state edged toward the Red Sea coast. In their search for trading contacts with the Ottoman Turks at Massawa, the Amhara established a permanent capital at Gondar, and in the course of the seventeenth century, they became heavily involved in the slave trade, exporting perhaps 10,000 slaves a year through Massawa.[11] In the eighteenth century, however, the collapse of centralized authority in the Ethiopian highlands rendered the kingdom a unified polity in name only and facilitated the further expansion of the Oromo into the Ethiopian heartland. Meanwhile, the expanding trade networks with the Red Sea greatly benefited Muslim merchants, who came to constitute a distinct class – known as *jiberti* – across the central and northern Ethiopian highlands. In this way was there both conflict and cooperation between Muslim and Christian in the area of modern Ethiopia, although in the second half of the nineteenth century a succession of Christian *habesha* rulers would use the rhetoric of holy war in appealing to European governments for assistance. The major confrontation between Christianity and Islam, however, now came in the north, in the form of Egyptian expansion into the Sudan, as well as along the Eritrean coast and parts of the Eritrean hinterland.

Sufism as well as commerce facilitated the spread of Islam across the region: the Qadiriyya, for example, expanded from the direction of Harar, where it had been long established, into Somalia and Eritrea in the course of the nineteenth century. In Eritrea, too, reformist movements such as the Mirghaniyya were in evidence in the second half of the nineteenth century; here, through settlement and intermarriage, widespread conversion was achieved as well as the absorption of political lineages. The Salihiyya and the Ahmadiyya were active among the Somali.[12] Indeed the Somali themselves were as important in their region as the Oromo were elsewhere in pushing forward Islamic frontiers, a process of migration which dated back several centuries. By the seventeenth and eighteenth centuries, Muslim Somali communities had occupied the Ogaden, and much of the coast of the geographical Horn between Zeila and Berbera in the north and Mogadishu in the south.[13] They went on to push into northern Kenya, and through a patchwork of tribal and spiritual affiliations, the Somali by the nineteenth century constituted an Islamic population sitting adjacent to that of the Oromo, thus dominating an enormous swathe of northeast Africa. In the late nineteenth and early twentieth centuries, with the encroachment of Italian and British colonialism, the Somali were as resilient as their Muslim brothers in Libya in resisting the infidel.

Between the 1840s and the 1860s, an increasingly aggressive Egyptian presence was established in southern Sudan and the present-day western lowlands of Eritrea and was creeping into the Christian highlands. The creation of the administrative province of Takrur and a fortified outpost at Keren posed a direct threat to the Ethiopians, as did the consolidation of Egyptian control of Massawa, leased from the Ottoman authorities, on the Eritrean coast. Those who were necessary as trading partners to the Christian highlanders were also religious and political antagonists, and this contributed to the Ethiopian sense of encirclement, as well as to the growing frustration at the apparent indifference of European powers who were supposed to be the Ethiopians' spiritual allies. The Christian militancy of nineteenth-century Ethiopia was driven in large part by the supposed Muslim threat – a threat lodged deep in the highland Ethiopian historical imagination. In the mid-1880s, Britain arranged for the Egyptians to withdraw from Keren and Massawa, but, much to Emperor Yohannes' irritation, only to oversee the arrival of the Italians in their place.[14] By the end of the 1880s, Italy had laid the foundations of the colony of Eritrea, and the Muslims of the area – as well as the Christians of the northern highlands, of course – would come under Italian rule in the course of the 1890s.

Islam on the Nile

Islam had been pushing southward from Egypt, up the Nile valley and into the area of modern Sudan, for several centuries prior to 1800. While governance of the most powerful state to emerge in the region, the Funj kingdom, rested upon local ideas of quasi-divine kingship, Islam was increasingly important: Muslim holy men, for example, known locally as *faqis*, established a patchwork of lineages which were critical in political mediation and in the spread of Islamic belief among the broader populace of the central Nile valley. Venerated as workers of miracles, *faqis* were also scholars of Islamic law, interpreters of the Quran, and builders of schools; they also belonged to sufi brotherhoods, which were thus dispersed through the Sudan, including, between the fifteenth and the eighteenth centuries, the Shadhiliyya, the Qadiriyya, and the Majdhubiyya. Muslim influence was particularly potent in the eighteenth century as the Funj kingdom disintegrated into civil war; disconnected from their own rulers, and exposed to cyclical violence as well as aggressive, unregulated commerce, the broader population increasingly turned to the *faqis* for succor and guidance. Funj itself was conquered by the Egyptians in the early 1820s.[15] Islam grew in other areas, too: to the west, the modern Darfur sultanate had its roots in the creation of a new dynasty in the late seventeenth century which applied (albeit selectively) shari'a law, elevated Islam to a royal cult, and patronized the construction of mosques. By the late eighteenth century – and in particular under 'Abd al-Rahman al-Rashid, who reigned between 1786 and 1801 – Darfur had consolidated itself into a major regional power, governing in part through Muslim holy men who had increasingly supplanted an older territorial administrative elite. In many respects, indeed, Darfur sat on an enormous crossroads which linked the western savannah and desert with the Nile valley and Egypt; the crossroads was commercial as well as spiritual, and traders and sufis alike enjoyed the protection of the sultans in the eighteenth and nineteenth centuries.[16]

Sudanese Islam had taken a particular form, but with Egyptian encroachment into the area in the course of the nineteenth century came new threats. The founding of a new capital at Khartoum in the 1820s was followed by increasingly aggressive commercial, military, and religious incursions into southern Sudan, including the upper Nile and equatorial regions, and the area of Bahr al-Ghazal and Darfur by the mid-1870s. The Egyptians brought their own brotherhoods and holy men and teachers; they also, in the 1870s, brought a Christian, in the form of General Gordon, appointed governor of the Sudan with a view to suppressing the slave trade so important to Muslim merchants. Foreign incursions, in particular the undermining of local holy men, led to the expansion of reformist sufi brotherhoods. The growing popularity of some of these in fact dated to the late eighteenth century, but in the course of the nineteenth century, sufism became the main vehicle of anti-Egyptian resistance. One of the most prominent was the Sammaniyya order, brought into Sudan by Ahmad al-Tayyib ibn al-Bashir around the beginning of the nineteenth century and increasingly influential among local communities and indeed frequently distant from political elites. From their number would come the leader of the Mahdist revolt in the 1880s, Muhammad Ahmad. Another branch of reformist teaching was introduced by Muhammad al-Majdhub in the early nineteenth century, and in time, the Majdhubiyya would encourage militant resistance to Egyptian rule. But others became politically important in different ways, such as the Khatmiyya, which in fact worked with the Egyptian administration.[17]

Revolt against Egyptian rule broke out among the nomads west of the Nile, particularly the Baqqara, Arabic-speaking pastoralists of Kordofan and the Nuba mountains, who had long been resentful of Egyptian interference, and in particular, their systems of taxation. It did not catch on immediately among the Arab populations on the banks of the Nile itself, who were less persuaded as to the possibility of success and of the legitimacy of the message. The conveyer of that message was Muhammad Ahmad, Sammaniyya teacher, *sheikh* and, in 1881, self-proclaimed Mahdi, or savior, promising to restore Islam to a pure state. He preached the enforcement of the shari'a, and the emulation of the Prophet's life. His Baqqara forces swept across much of the region to the west of Khartoum in 1882–3, by which time the significance of the movement had become clear to the riverain Arabs – who began to join it – and to the British, who acted too late to prevent the capture of Khartoum and Gordon's death in 1885. Between 1881 and 1885, the Mahdi had conquered in order to bring about Islamic revolution; but after his death, his successor – his chief military commander Abdallahi, who took the title *khalifa* – created a rather more secular state which kept the British and the Egyptians at bay even as the "scramble" for the region was under way. Centralized military government characterized the khalifa's administration of the sprawling new state, while his Muslim policy was fundamentally aimed at standardizing Islamic practice and eradicating localism. While the Mahdists' existence was a constant affront to the British to the north, the Islamic state also pressed in on the Ethiopians' northern frontier through the late 1880s and 1890s; but only in 1898, finally, and at considerable expense, did the British successfully reconquer the Sudan, defeating the Mahdist forces at Omdurman near Khartoum.[18] As for Darfur, it was initially largely left to its own devices, and not until 1916 would the British consider it expedient to bring the sultanate into the Condominium Sudan.

Yet even after their military defeat, the Mahdists retained considerable popular support, and in its appeal beyond narrow regional or "tribal" interests, Mahdism laid the foundations, to a very real degree, for the later emergence of Sudanese nationalism, at least in the north of the territory. This was true, indeed, across much of Islamic Africa in the late nineteenth and early twentieth centuries, among the Sanusiyya in Libya and the Somalis in Egypt, and further west across the Maghreb. Anti-imperial resistance – in some cases, as we have seen, markedly prolonged – combined with the powerful influence of sufism and a range of militant brotherhoods to create frameworks within which modern nationalism would flourish in fighting European colonialism. The subjugation of much of the Islamic world at the end of the nineteenth century represented a new phase in the story of conflict and coexistence between Christian and Muslim.

Notes

1 Nurse & Spear, *The Swahili*; A.M. Mazrui & I.N. Shariff, *The Swahili: Idiom and Identity of an African People* (Trenton NJ, 1993); Pat Caplan, ""But the coast, of course, is quite different": academic and local ideas about the East African littoral," *Journal of Eastern African Studies*, 1:2 (2007). See also G.S.P. Freeman-Grenville, *The East African Coast: Select Documents* (Oxford, 1962).

2 Randall L. Pouwels, "The East African Coast, c.780–1900 C.E," in Levtzion & Pouwels (eds.), *History of Islam*; and by the same author, *Horn and Crescent: Cultural Change and Traditional Islam on the East African Coast, 800–1900* (Cambridge, 1987).

3 Michael Twaddle, "The Muslim Revolution in Buganda," *African Affairs*, 71 (1972); Michael Twaddle, "The emergence of politico-religious groupings in late nineteenth-century Buganda," *Journal of African History*, 29:1 (1988); Apolo Kagwa (tr. & ed. M.S.M. Kiwanuka), *The Kings of Buganda* (Nairobi, 1971), 166–7. Also A.B.K. Kasozi, *The Spread of Islam in Uganda* (Nairobi, 1986) and Michael Wright, *Buganda in the Heroic Age* (London, 1971).

4 David C. Sperling, with additional material by Jose H. Kagabo, "The Coastal Hinterland and interior of East Africa," in Levtzion & Pouwels (eds.), *History of Islam*.

5 See for example E.C. Hore, "On the twelve tribes of Tanganyika," *Journal of the Anthropological Institute*, 12 (1883).

6 J.S. Trimingham, *Islam in Ethiopia* (London, 1965).

7 John Sorenson, *Imagining Ethiopia: Struggles for History and Identity in the Horn of Africa* (New Brunswick NJ, 1993), 24–5.

8 It is the underpinning idea in the great chronicle, and (to some extent) national literary epic, the *Kebre Negast*: see for example M. Brooks (ed & tr.), *A Modern Translation of the* Kebra Nagast (*The Glory of the Kings*) (Lawrenceville NJ, 1995).

9 For example, G.H. Portal, *My Mission to Abyssinia* (London, 1892), 81.

10 Mohammed Hassen, *The Oromo of Ethiopia: A History, 1570–1860* (Cambridge, 1990). See also Richard F. Burton, *First Footsteps in East Africa*, 2 vols. (London, 1856) for a compelling, if challenging, mid-nineteenth century account of Harar.

11 See Abir, *Ethiopia, the Era of the Princes*; and Donald Crummey, *Land and Society in the Christian Kingdom of Ethiopia, from the Thirteenth to the Twentieth Century* (Oxford, 2000).

12 Lapidus, *History of Islamic Societies*, 437.

13 I.M. Lewis, *A Modern History of the Somali* (Oxford, 2002), chap. 2.

14 These events are given accessible treatment in Sven Rubenson, *The Survival of Ethiopian Independence* (London, 1976); Bahru Zewde, *A History of Modern Ethiopia, 1855–1991* (Oxford, 2001); and Harold Marcus, *A History of Ethiopia* (Berkeley CA, 2001). See also two pieces by Richard Caulk: "Religion and state in nineteenth-century Ethiopia," *Journal of Ethiopian Studies*, 10:1 (1972); and "Yohannes IV, the Mahdists and the Partition of North East Africa," *Transafrican Journal of History*, 1:2 (1972).

15 R.S. O'Fahey & J. Spaulding, *Kingdoms of the Sudan* (London, 1974), Part I; Holt & Daly, *History of the Sudan*, chaps. 2 & 3.

16 R.S. O'Fahey, *The Darfur Sultanate: A History* (New York, 2008).

17 Holt & Daly, *History of the Sudan*, Part II; R. Gray, *A History of the Southern Sudan, 1839–1889* (London, 1961).

18 P.M. Holt, *The Mahdist State in the Sudan, 1881–1898: A Study of its Origins, Development, and Overthrow* (Oxford, 1970) remains one of the single best studies.

Part III Africa and Europe: Commerce, Conflict and Co-option, to c.1920

Africa and Europe have had a long and complex relationship, and the two continents' economies have been interlinked just as their interaction on a cultural level has been characterized by a series of misunderstandings as well as reciprocal borrowing. In the nineteenth century, this led ultimately to the partition of Africa by several European governments, but in many ways, the "colonial moment" has distorted our understanding of Afro-European relations over the longer term. As reflected in the Eurocentric terms "old world" and "new world," the African landmass, unlike the Americas, had dealings with Europe since antiquity: northern Africa, notably, has long had commercial and cultural links with southern Europe, while sub-Saharan Africa's relationship with Europe, though somewhat less direct before the fifteenth century, was of increasing importance.

Europe's modern perceptions of Africa essentially date from the era of the Atlantic slave trade, and particularly from the latter half of the eighteenth century, when among apologists for the slave trade and humanitarian abolitionists alike there developed the idea that Africa was a land of savagery and bloodthirstiness, a primitive continent forgotten by progress and civilization, crying out for redemption. For defenders of the trade, the traffic in human beings was not only acceptable because Africa was doomed in any case but also necessary because the transportation of slaves to the Americas offered them an "escape" from the terrible fate of living in Africa itself; in any case, slave traders were simply buying up the surplus produced by endless wars, purchasing individuals who would normally have been put to death according to savage custom. For abolitionists, Africa needed Europe to rescue it from itself, to "modernize" it, to bring it into the fold of Christian civilization. Both views, clearly, were based on racial concepts of Africans and their societies, rooted in the notion of the African as childlike and in

A History of Modern Africa: 1800 to the Present, Third Edition. Richard J. Reid.

pseudoscientific theories relating to physical types popular from the eighteenth century onward. The racism which emerged during, and as a direct result of, the slave trade would harden through the nineteenth century and beyond; the rhetoric surrounding the abolition of the slave trade in the early nineteenth century would be echoed at the end of the century during the "scramble" for Africa.

We have seen in an earlier chapter how the "legitimate" commerce which increasingly supplanted the slave trade brought with it heightened European interest in the continent, a fascination ultimately rooted in abolition and commercial "legitimacy." First, Europe was increasingly seized by the need to "explore" Africa. The slave trade, Europe's primary economic connection with sub-Saharan Africa, had not required extensive knowledge of Africa itself: Europeans had rarely needed to venture beyond the coast, even had they been able to, and they certainly did not need to know where slaves were coming from. The "new" commercial requirements of the nineteenth century, however, aroused scientific interest in Africa, in terms of its potential resources and productivity, its geography and climate, and its major centers of population. There was an increasing interest in what lay in the interior, driven in large part by a desire to exploit the continent's economic potential. In this way, there was a powerful commercial motive behind exploration from the early nineteenth century onward, and this was combined with – and often disguised by – a spirit of scientific enquiry, manifest in the organization of expeditions financed by learned institutions which aimed at the penetration of the interior in search of "knowledge." Sometimes, indeed, such expeditions were genuinely scientific endeavors; but rarely were they of no commercial value. And the major focus, for much of the nineteenth century, was Africa's rivers: explorers sought to chart the Niger, Congo, Nile, Zambezi, searching above all for the navigability which held out the promise of commercial gain. In the process, of course, European travelers collected enormous amounts of data – albeit often of questionable reliability – on the peoples, power centers, products, and trade networks of the regions they passed through.

Second, Europe and North America in the eighteenth century had witnessed an evangelical revival, an attempt by the Church to reassert itself in the face of the twin assaults of "science" and "reason," and of growing secularism in the West. An important part of this revival was the emergence of a powerful missionary impulse, evident in the call to go forth into the world and preach God's word, particularly among "heathen," savage, and uncivilized peoples. The Church movement, moreover, was closely linked to the humanitarian abolitionist movement aimed at the destruction of the evil that was the slave trade; many abolitionist campaigners were themselves evangelical Christians, committed to what they saw as the intertwined goals of ending slavery and preaching the Gospel. Africa, thus, became a target for missionary activity: in the course of the nineteenth century, a number of evangelical Protestant orders were later joined by several Catholic societies.

Importantly, missionary activity and exploration were often indelibly intertwined. Many explorers were themselves missionaries, advancing scientific and commercial knowledge while finding willing souls for Christ at the same time: indeed the two were increasingly seen as inseparable, as Christian converts in the interior would surely assist commercial development. David Livingstone, in southern and eastern Africa, became the most celebrated "exploring missionary" of the age, though his ability to win converts was less impressive than his geographical "discoveries," and the physical endurance required to achieve these. Moreover, exploration itself, of course, opened up new areas for missionary activity, with bibles often following in the wake of scientific-commercial expeditions.

It is perhaps debatable the degree to which missionaries and explorers later became the agents of European colonialism, though some undoubtedly were, and many others at least created the political and moral framework within which conquest would take place. As the nineteenth century advanced, a number did receive either implicit or explicit support from their own governments; and missionaries in particular lobbied hard for political intervention, pressurizing governments to give them official support and to shoulder their civilizing responsibilities. Public pressure of this kind took place at a time – the last decades of the nineteenth century – when there was a growing belief in Europe's civilizing mission in Africa, the "white man's burden," in the words of Rudyard Kipling. European governments, as we will see in Chapter 9, rarely intervened in Africa on the back of the missionary lobby alone, and usually acted in response to supposed commercial opportunities, or in order to offset strategic threats from rival European powers. But the kind of imagery projected by missionaries and travelers was extremely powerful for politicians and public alike and had a great influence on popular perceptions of Africa as the nineteenth century progressed. As for explorers, these were increasingly employed – quietly or otherwise – as commercial agents, working for government-chartered companies and pushing into the interior to discover the continent's economic potential. Henry Morton Stanley, traversing the Congo basin in the pay of King Leopold of the Belgians, is perhaps the most noted example of this. Moreover, Europeans in this context – especially missionaries – were the forerunners of cultural imperialism, and much of what they did in Africa involved at least the implicit assumption of the essential superiority of European civilization. In condemning much of what they saw of African culture, religion, and society as the work of the devil, or at least as the product of savage heathenism, their very presence was meant to demonstrate to Africans their fundamental inferiority, clearly one of the keystones in the foundations of European colonial rule. More enduringly, missionary work and exploration signaled an exercise in objectification of Africa by Europe, part of an ongoing (if increasingly unconscious) process of self-validation. Through didacticism and data collection, Europeans elevated themselves above Africans, who thus lay prone and primordial beneath them.

All this said, however, it is important not to exaggerate the actual impact Europeans had in Africa before the last 20 years of the nineteenth century. Missionaries operated, as they had always done, in small, isolated groups, tolerated by African rulers who believed they might be used to local advantage. Explorers, sometimes treated with hostility or mild contempt, and doubtless greeted with amusement, were rarely regarded as a significant threat but were there to be exploited for commercial or other gain. Before 1880, Europeans in the African interior were vulnerable, often insignificant individuals, passing through African societies with minimal impact. Overall, indeed, the

European presence in Africa remained largely coastal, as with the French in Algeria and Senegal, the British in Sierra Leone and the Gold Coast, and the Portuguese in Angola and Mozambique. Only in southern Africa was there a sizeable white colonial presence. We should not, therefore, make the mistake of assuming the inevitability of European conquest at the end of the nineteenth century. For much of the nineteenth century, no European power would have envisaged such a scenario; official policy toward Africa, rather, was characterized by vacillation and a reluctance to commit to any greater expense than was necessary in terms of what can loosely be termed "imperial ambition." The British were unwilling to expand in the Gold Coast and in Cape Colony and were indecisive in both areas; likewise, the French in Senegal. Neither Britain nor France, the two leading powers on the African continent, were convinced of the value of or the need for colonial possessions there, and thus, while we might identify missionary and exploratory activity as denoting growing European interest, this in itself did not in any way represent some form of transcontinental imperial ambition.

And yet, in the last quarter of the nineteenth century, "conquest" – in the broadest sense of that term – was indeed what happened. An important reason behind this – perhaps the main reason – has been discussed in Part I and relates to "legitimate" commerce and the growing belief in the need to intervene directly in African society and economy if profit was to be realized. It was assumed at the outset of the nineteenth century that "legitimate" commerce would bring stability and peace to Africa and that the doctrine of "free trade" (rather loosely interpreted, admittedly) would allow the economic exploitation of Africa with a minimum of political commitment. But it was increasingly clear that this was not the case. If trade was to flow freely, if resources were to be profitably exploited, if Africa was to constitute a stable market for European products, and if capital investment was to be protected, then political control was required. Again, this linked with burgeoning racial thought, which now assumed that Africans were childlike and irrational, incapable of modernizing themselves, or of stabilizing their war-torn, bloodied, and splintered kingdoms and societies. It was, again, the most extraordinary exercise in objectification, in which Europeans imagined Africa according to their own fears, anxieties, and prejudices – many of which have in fact endured beyond the late nineteenth century and proven remarkably resilient. The Africa that was then imagined by Europe hovers phantom-like in the Western imagination still.

The so-called Scramble for Africa is more complex than perhaps it may initially seem, however. In the first instance, of course, the multitude of European invasions of the continent between the 1870s and the 1900s were made possible by industrial and technological superiority, a superiority which by the late nineteenth century was most dramatically manifest – at least from the African perspective – in military supremacy. Thus was the desirability of subjugating the continent doubtless greatly enhanced by the ability to do so. Much of the story of the Scramble involves the description of Africans as victims, in the context of the internal power politics of Europe itself which gave rise to an international rivalry with both Africa and many parts of Asia as prey. The economic competition between industrial nations led to the search for both raw materials and captive markets; the political rivalry and the quest for international prestige manifested itself in the acquisition of African territory. But while many forms of "conquest" did indeed take place, the term itself is often misleading, and the political and economic "remaking" of Africa in the late nineteenth century was as much a matter of negotiation as of physical imposition. This was no one-way traffic: Africans manipulated European ideas and exploited their fears; African manpower, mobilized by the momentous violence of the nineteenth century, was involved in the Scramble itself – which was thus expedited by local knowledge and military skills. Africans, as we shall see, were active participants in the various processes of reinvention and reconstruction which unfolded in the late nineteenth century, and the colonialism which resulted was as much the product of African creativity as of European firepower.

The "Scramble" was just that: a largely uncoordinated, often headlong rush from the coast into the hinterland and beyond, a multitude of military advances and engagements interspersed by diplomatic interactions, which resulted – ultimately – in the demarcation of some of the most bizarre territorial entities in modern global history. Maps may have been drawn in European capitals; but the process of partition itself involved both Africans and Europeans, and indeed the latter could not have come to govern the vast continent without the former. Certainly, the arrangements through which many colonial territories came into being necessarily involved African intellectual input, African political ingenuity, and African manpower. African responses were diverse in the extreme, and peoples frequently attempted more than one tactic simultaneously with the same goal in mind. While some bent European "invasion" to their own ends, and indeed engaged in some more localized invasions of their own through the vehicle of European hegemony, others took up arms and fought, and died, sometimes in great numbers. States and societies responded according to local or at best regional exigencies, and as many saw opportunities in European encroachment as saw threats. In some areas, a greater unity of purpose in resistance was achieved, notably under the banner of Islam: across North Africa, notably, Islam offered larger territorial and ideological cohesion than was possible in the savannahs and forests further south. And in Libya and Morocco, for example, such resistance continued beyond the First World War, during which period in most other areas armed opposition was finally subdued. But across the continent, whatever the nature of their response or contribution to new political realities, Africans everywhere were instrumental in the shaping of colonial structures and policies; meanwhile, the African response to colonial political, economic, and cultural authoritarianism would continue to evolve.

In the early 1900s, the groundwork was laid for the creation of the modern African nation-state, an essentially indigenous entity, for all Europe's military superiority, but infused with European imports and impositions. Colonial regimes varied in the detail across the continent, but with the partial exception of those of longer standing – South Africa, or Algeria – all found themselves in the 1890s and 1900s confronted with a similar range of novel problems. Colonial states aimed to establish territorial hegemony, which meant the ability to exercise practical political sovereignty – in effect the possession of a legal monopoly on the use of force – within a defined area. The militarism of the colonial state was inherent, in most cases flowing directly from the violence involved in the creation of the state itself. Colonial armies making use of African recruits formed the basis of security in the vast majority of new territories. Violence, or the threat of it, was thus the means by which control was maintained, although – as we shall see later in the book – the overt militarism of the early colonial state would recede in most territories by the 1920s. Certainly, in some respects, the First World War can be seen as the culmination of the period of partition, in terms of the stabilization of systems and the establishment (with some notable exceptions) of military security. Following directly from this was the need to establish stable government, no easy task in those territories acquired through force of arms. New strategies of governance were required, preferably (and in some areas necessarily) involving minimal expense. In this context, there was considerable diversity across the continent; while indirect rule was favored in some territories, others were characterized by more direct forms of administration, and others again were selected for white settlement, systematic or otherwise.

At one time, it was common to understand the African response in terms of either "resistance" or "collaboration": Africans either fought and were ultimately subjugated by force of arms or else they accepted the arrival of Europeans and cooperated with their new masters, recognizing that resistance was, indeed, futile. This dichotomy is unhelpful, as is that between "primary" and "secondary" resistance, another concept developed in the 1960s distinguishing initial resistance to European invasion from anti-colonial revolts a few years later. It is necessary, rather, to view African responses in a more holistic manner and to understand that while some societies did indeed take up arms against colonial armies, others adapted political and indeed cultural norms and not only "resisted" in more subtle ways but also shaped the colonial system to their own ends. Anti-colonial violence, meanwhile, was itself interspersed with diplomatic overtures and attempts to reach mutually beneficial arrangements and was constrained by political and economic exigencies. Ultimately, European intrusions were absorbed into long-term African processes of internal change.

8 The Compass and the Cross

By the eighteenth century, "Africa" – in so far as such an entity can be said to have existed – had long been a source of fascination in the Eurasian world. It had loomed large in the imagination since Greek and Roman traders had nibbled at the Mediterranean and Red Sea edges of the continent in the late pre-Christian and early Christian eras. But beyond the coasts of northern and northeastern Africa, this vast continent was shrouded in mystery, and it remained so for many centuries, down to the European late Middle Ages when West Africa was the "land of gold" of contemporary Spanish maps, the gaps filled by myths and fantastic tales. The Portuguese were the trailblazers, creeping around the Atlantic coast of northern, western, and central Africa in the course of the fifteenth century. Their mission – characteristic of the late crusading spirit in which such voyages were made – was a combination of economic aspiration and religious zeal. With the expansion of the slave trade in the course of the sixteenth and seventeenth centuries, the Portuguese were joined by the French, Danish, Dutch, and English, among others, and the religious aspect subsided somewhat in favor of the economic motive. Nonetheless, the element of cultural exchange in this burgeoning relationship remained crucial, as perceptions of the continent became increasingly shaped by the slave trade itself, which in turn generated some of the more enduring images of the nature of African state and society. These images persisted, indeed hardened, even as the slave trade receded and as Europeans began to probe beyond their coastal forts.

A History of Modern Africa: 1800 to the Present, Third Edition. Richard J. Reid.

Interested Gentlemen and Learned Bodies: Explorers and Exploration

From the Enlightenment onward, there was heightened scientific, intellectual, and commercial interest in Africa; it was also, importantly, a period in which such curiosity could be fed by technological progress. In part, this interest was linked to the slave-trade debate, which was increasing in intensity in the second half of the eighteenth century, and manifested itself in the foundation, in London in 1788, of the "Association for the Promoting the Interior Parts of Africa," commonly known as the "African Association." It was one of several such scientific and intellectual organizations founded in the late eighteenth and early nineteenth centuries, associations of learned men concerned with ethnology, geography, botany, folklore, and the like. These included, in Britain, the Bengal Asiatic Society, established in 1784; the first of many geographical societies, the Paris-based Société de Geographie, in 1821; and in Germany, the Berlin Geographical Society (Gesellschaft für Erdkunde zu Berlin), founded in 1828. In London, the Royal Geographical Society was established in 1830 on the principles of the African Association, the chief founder of which was Sir Joseph Banks, man of letters and distinguished botanist, who had traveled with James Cook in his voyage around the world twenty years earlier. The African Association, like Banks himself, in many ways embodied the "Enlightenment" age. It had a number of aims – the location of fabled gold-rich Timbuktu was an early obsession – but central among them was to "diversify" African trade, promote the trade in commodities other than human beings, and in so doing exploit the continent's natural resources.[1]

It was all supremely rational: scientific enquiry and humanitarian endeavor were linked unashamedly to commercial gain. It was an alliance of interests, representative of an ethos which would come to define Europe's approach to much of the non-European world in the course of the nineteenth century.[2] The at least implicit assumption behind the African Association was that Africa must be "improved" through energetic outside intervention; it could not happen otherwise. Growing opposition to the slave trade would not lead to a diminution of European involvement in Africa but quite the reverse: it represented a growing sense of obligation to Africa. In particular, it would be Britain's self-appointed role to actively promote the export of Africa's natural produce, which would turn lead inevitably to the death of the slave trade. Crucially, the growing demand for knowledge about Africa was intimately linked to "legitimate" commerce itself: unlike the slave trade, the new commercial system, as we have seen, required some knowledge of the transport potential of river systems, available raw materials, and centers of population as markets for European goods. These quests would often be at the heart of the exploratory expeditions of the nineteenth century.[3]

The "improvability" of Africa is thus a theme which is present from the late eighteenth century onward. It would lead to controversy over time, for not everyone agreed that Africa *could* be improved, whether by outside intervention or not. We have observed this in the context of the slave–trade debate, with defenders of the trade arguing that Africa was *inherently* backward, and that little could be done to alter this. Yet the other key concept here, just as abstract, was that of Africa's *interior*: the continent was seen as a curiously closed entity, something which could be opened up and have light shed upon it; Africa had "interior parts" that promised much but which needed, in the spirit of the age, to be examined scientifically. The image of Africa as medical experiment would develop in the course of the nineteenth century: explorers sought to journey to its "heart," sometimes via the rivers which were its "veins." This was a continent riddled with disease, both real and imagined, including that which supposedly crippled its cultures, societies, and political practices. Livingstone and other missionaries would later talk of Africa in terms which suggested that it required examination, diagnosis, and cure. The African Association, then, represented the desire for new knowledge about this huge, unknown section of the "Old World"; ignorance, indeed, was a matter of shame in that enlightened age, according to the preamble to the Association's manifesto. Moreover, the wealth that could be derived thence would in turn bring benefit and progress to peoples "hitherto consigned to hopeless barbarism and uniform contempt," in the words of the Association's secretary Henry Beaufoy.[4]

In the decades that followed, many would venture forth among those peoples, and in nineteenth-century Britain, the Royal Geographical Society (RGS), in many respects the direct descendant of the African Association, instigated and directed many of the most important expeditions. Between the 1830s and the 1880s, African exploration became a source of public fascination; more importantly, it represented a frontier, of commercial and scientific knowledge, of burgeoning racialism, and, increasingly, of protoimperial expansionism. British naval involvement was prominent in exploration as long as the focus was primarily upon the navigation of rivers; once that focus had shifted, however, to the crossing of the landmass, particularly from the 1850s, the navy's involvement faded, and the RGS became the driving force behind much Victorian exploration. Sir Roderick Murchison, a geologist, provided dynamic and patriotic leadership: he was committed to the notion of exploration as serving British national interests, and therefore deserving of support from public funds, and believed that science and empire were indelibly intertwined. Murchison dominated exploration for a generation, until his death in 1871, and won considerable government support through his ability to balance three crucial dimensions of Victorian exploration: satisfying the Victorian public's thirst for overseas adventure and drama, which many explorers undoubtedly supplied; the spirit of scientific enquiry and quest for knowledge; and commercial interest, in terms of the location of sources of raw materials and of potential markets. The RGS combined the rhetoric of imperialism and humanitarianism with the interests of science.[5]

European explorers were preceded by some centuries by Arab explorers: during Europe's Middle Ages, Arab merchants and adventurers were traveling across northern, western, and parts of eastern Africa, leaving behind some invaluable first-hand accounts.[6] Europe only began to probe around the edges of the continent in the fifteenth century; and many of the early "explorers" were missionaries, such as those arriving in Kongo and Ethiopia in the course of the sixteenth century. What might be termed the "vocational" or professional explorer was slower to emerge, only becoming prominent in the latter half of the eighteenth century. James Bruce's quest for the source of the

Nile in Ethiopia and Sudan in the 1770s was followed by a sequence of explorers in West Africa concerned with the length and pattern of the Niger. Mungo Park, under the aegis of the African Association, attempted to trace the course of the Niger in the 1790s and early 1800s; he died on a return trip in 1806. Mungo Park had reached Timbuktu, and a few years later, Rene Caillie also entered the fabled city in 1827, although his description of the town was disbelieved. Denham, Clapperton, and Oudney journeyed south from Tripoli in the early 1820s, and the expedition reached Sokoto, the capital of the great West African caliphate, in 1824. Yet the trans-Saharan route was considered too hazardous, not to mention too long, and the West African coast was increasingly the preferred starting point. Hugh Clapperton and Richard Lander traveled from the trading port of Badagry to Kano between 1825 and 1827, though Clapperton died en route. Lander and his brother John, reaching Bussa overland, then followed the Niger to its mouth in 1830. European merchants were excited to learn that the Niger was navigable in places, and the region as a whole aroused the avarice of manufacturers and financiers. In the early 1850s, Dr. Heinrich Barth, German but funded by British interests, carried out extensive journeys across the West African savannah and examined the area of the Niger bend, with a view to assessing the commercial potential of the region; similar to Clapperton before him, Barth used Tripoli as the "gateway to Africa," traveling south across the Sahara.[7]

Malaria, however, was the great obstacle to progress. In 1841, the expedition mounted by the British government to travel up the Niger with a view to exploring commercial opportunities ended in disaster, with some fifty Britons dying, mostly of malaria, before the entire enterprise was abandoned. The mosquito prevented further European penetration until the 1850s, when the discovery that quinine offered some protection against malaria greatly quickened the pace of exploration. This was demonstrated during the government-funded expedition of Dr. William Balfour Baikie up the Niger in 1854.[8] Within a few years, British steamers were operating on the river. Between the 1850s and the 1870s, the Niger was joined in the pantheon of European geographical "discoveries" by the great river-systems of the Nile, Zambezi, and Congo, as genuine scientific interest was compounded by the promise of such rivers as commercial arteries. In southern Africa, it was often missionaries who were the pioneers of exploration. Robert Moffat had reached the area of modern Botswana by the 1840s, and his son-in-law, David Livingstone, achieved some of greatest feats of the age in this context: he crossed the continent from Luanda to the mouth of the Zambezi in the mid-1850s. In the same period, Richard Burton and John Speke reached Lake Tanganyika, while Speke and James Grant later located the source of the White Nile at the north end of Lake Victoria and demonstrated navigable possibilities upstream of Khartoum. Livingstone traced the course of the Zambezi and Shire rivers between 1858 and 1864 and spent the last years of his life charting the tributaries of the Congo. Verney Lovatt Cameron traversed Africa from the Indian Ocean to the Atlantic in the mid-1870s, while a little further north Joseph Thomson explored the area of modern Kenya. Henry Morton Stanley, one of the iconic figures of the Victorian age, continued Livingstone's work – somewhat self-consciously, indeed – in crossing the continent from east to west and charting the course of Lualaba and Congo rivers. Stanley's expedition, funded by the Belgian King Leopold, demonstrated the commercial possibilities of the Congo river basin on the eve of the Scramble for Africa. Stanley returned to Africa in the late 1880s, journeying through the forests of northern Congo and into Uganda, ostensibly to "rescue" the beleaguered governor of Egyptian Equatoria, Emin Pasha.[9] Expeditions were frequently organized with the specific aim of compiling hard data, acquiring information related to commercial opportunities, population groups, resources, states, and societies. "Legitimate" commerce, again, lay at the core of these quests, requiring much greater knowledge than the eighteenth-century slave trade had done, and thus exploration was given a significant impetus by the new economic orthodoxy of the age: this was not simply a quest for knowledge for the sake of it – although there was an element of this in many expeditions – but knowledge for a purpose.

Creeping Hegemony and the Invention of Africa

A multitude of travelers left behind an enormous body of literature. The material itself is problematic for the historian, who often relies heavily upon it to reconstruct particular societies in the precolonial era, yet who must also be mindful of the context in which it was produced. In a sense, this is a tension which is impossible to resolve: the sources which Europeans left behind are often the only ones we have for a given place at a given time, and yet by their very nature, they are characterized by misunderstanding, willful or otherwise, and contributed to the "invention" of Africa by means of a creeping literary hegemony.[10] In the nineteenth century, exploration was itself an expression of cultural hubris, most clearly manifest in the notion of "discovery." One of the key premises of nineteenth-century thinking about Africa was that the continent was there to be "discovered"; the literature itself is replete with references to how Europeans "discovered" lakes, river sources, waterfalls, mountains, and in the European imagination, these were all part of a wild and undeveloped landscape in which Africans are usually static, background figures, the ignorant and unresponsive recipients of the staggering geography which surrounds them. The African does not "discover" his landscape: he is simply *there*, as part of it. He is at the edge of humanity, often bemused at the strange obsession of the white man with geography in a way that reinforces the African's genetic ignorance. The African is the white man's guide through the wilderness; he is the armed guard of the explorer's caravan, the translator, the carrier of stores, and the gatherer of food and water, and sometimes even a companion. But any affection from the European is always in response to and conditional upon the African's loyalty and faithful service; and he is always on the edge of the story, one-dimensional, trapped by birth in an environment which is as primitive as the physicality of the terrain is beautiful.

Nonetheless, many explorers also attempted to produce histories of the societies through which they passed, and these are often even more problematic for the historian than the supposed eye-witness account. The second volume of Bruce's mammoth account was dedicated to the history of Ethiopia, apparently based on royal chronicles and ecclesiastical manuscripts, and numerous conversations with well-placed individuals. Many others would follow in his footsteps, attempting to reconstruct the history of societies which they deemed worthy of attention – later a crucial element in the establishment of the early colonial state. Europeans' accumulation of knowledge was a form of assumed power over indigenous peoples: as the historian Robert Stafford put it, indigenous peoples' "control over their destinies could be eroded as surely by map coordinates and museum specimens as by steamships, bullets, and treaties of concession."[11] Nor were African rulers wholly unaware of this: there is much evidence of African suspicion about European motives behind the collection of natural specimens, the charting of river courses, and the search for mountain ranges. As the nineteenth century wore on, and Africans' own knowledge of the expanding European presence along certain stretches of coastline grew, so this suspicion grew in proportion; some would begin to mutter that the white man was here to "eat up" the land, that soon the lone explorer, and indeed the Bible-wielding missionary, would be followed by armed invading hordes. Such mutterings were scarily prophetic.

Explorers frequently saw themselves as pioneers of European civilization and the civilizing mission. Sometimes this was self-appointed: Stanley, for example, carried the British and American flags in the 1870s while marching across central Africa, but reports of his brutality resulted in a flurry of messages from the British Foreign Office demanding that he remove the Union Jack from the head of his caravan. Yet Stanley still felt able to represent the Christian mission, calling for missionaries to come to Buganda.[12] Speke likewise saw himself as something of a British ambassador, talking at length to Kabaka Mutesa about the Bible and British military might; Burton, an admirer of Islam, was wholly disparaging about African culture and society but still made a case for intervention to improve the "African condition."[13] As to the writings that resulted, these were clearly crucial in informing Europe's view of Africa. As a Victorian geographical order was imposed on the African landscape, and the continent mapped out in a wider physical and moral universe, states and societies themselves were described with varying degrees of contempt and despair, although a degree of admiration was reserved for those kingdoms regarded as lying a little higher up the scale of civilization. Explorers' detailed descriptions of African life were crucial in informing public and political opinion; and Victorian Britain, for example, offered a swelling market for travel literature, and a public hungry for titillating tales of savagery, dark and bloody deeds, cannibalism, human sacrifice, and sexual abandon. What is clear, however, is that exploring Europeans were frequently the unwitting witnesses to a dramatic transformation in political, military, and economic affairs across Africa; their accounts offer rich pickings for the historian, even if great care is needed to navigate their deeply problematic prejudices, and even if they themselves misunderstood a great deal of what they observed.

By the end of the 1880s, the golden age of African exploration was largely over. In some ways, so assiduous had they been in the middle decades of the nineteenth century that explorers had virtually made themselves redundant; but more significantly, the age of colonial expansion saw them largely sidelined. Explorers were no longer necessary in an age of invasion, in which colonial officials, army officers, and, frequently, missionaries pushed the imperial frontier forward; sometimes they played the part of explorers, as did the officials sent on diplomatic missions to the courts of kings during the 1880s and

1890s. It is clear, however, that the explorers' contribution to the age – to the imperial adventure, the shaping of popular imagery about Africa, and to the formation of some of the more enduring notions about the African past – had been absolutely fundamental. Yet the impact of missionaries was to prove even more enduring over the long term.

European Missionary Activity in Africa to around 1800

European missionary enterprise in sub-Saharan Africa dates to the Portuguese, who dispatched missions to Ethiopia and the kingdom of Kongo in the fifteenth and sixteenth centuries, while the area around the port of Mozambique was also a base for this early Christian activity.[14] Such missionary work was closely associated with the expansion of Portuguese power overseas and more broadly can be seen as representative of the crusading, anti-Islamic ethos characteristic of Europe's worldview in the late Middle Ages. But the Portuguese were also searching distant lands for allies: in late medieval Europe, legend had spoken of a great Christian kingdom somewhere in "the East," where it lay surrounded by Muslim and heathen enemies. This kingdom was powerful in the imagination: rich, strong, and mysterious, it was above all a potential ally for the Portuguese in the struggle against Islam, and the Europeans determined to locate and befriend the great king, the "Prester John," the "priest king," of contemporary literature. There was indeed a Christian kingdom in the so-called "Orient," but it turned out not to be where the Portuguese – who thought of India – had imagined it. That kingdom was "Ethiopia," which Portuguese missionaries reached in the early sixteenth century. Many of them were less than impressed: it appeared backward and poverty-stricken, its armies poorly equipped, and its inhabitants lazy and degenerate. Even its Christianity, which was Orthodox, drew sighs of despair from the ardent Franciscans who first beheld it; this was a corrupted, superstitious form of Christianity, whose priests were isolated in their mountain habitat, separated by their harsh and savage environment from God, and from Rome.[15] And yet, it was *Christian*, after a fashion, and this, combined with the belief that it might yet be brought back to the righteous path, motivated the Portuguese to intervene militarily in the 1540s when the kingdom was invaded by a Muslim army from the south.

Around the same time, their brethren had arrived at the court of the king of Kongo, a short distance from the central Atlantic coast. Portugal established diplomatic relations with Kongo at the beginning of the sixteenth century, impressed by this wealthy empire situated in a fertile agricultural region and collecting tribute across a wide area. The Kongolese elite sought teachers and craftsmen from the Portuguese, as well as soldiers; but the issue of foreign contact quickly divided the governing class, and political factions arose, with one group favoring interaction with the Portuguese and another advocating their expulsion. It was the former faction which carried the day – as in Ethiopia a few years later, the Portuguese lent musketeers to the cause – and a new king, a Christian convert, Afonso (1506–43), opened communications with the King of Portugal and the Pope himself. As others would do in the centuries to come, Afonso recognized the political potential of Christianity and used the new faith to increase his own authority through the development of a royal cult and to undermine local religious leaders. It was, however, a poisoned chalice: through the sixteenth and seventeenth centuries, as the kingship became increasingly dependent on Portuguese support, royal authority lost legitimacy across the kingdom, leading to its fragmentation, while Christianity itself hardly took root among a populace which regarded it as the manifestation of hostile foreign intrusion.[16]

In the early seventeenth century, Portuguese Jesuits attempted to convert the Abyssinian emperor to Catholicism, causing – not for the last time in the field of Western missionary endeavor – massive internal upheaval and bloodshed, as the country descended into a civil war in which the loyalties of the participants were divided between the old and the new, the Ethiopian church and this new form of Christianity.[17] If most Ethiopians were largely unimpressed by – indeed often contemptuous of – the faith of the *ferenjis* (or Europeans, from "Franks"), a muddle of myths and curious misconceptions in Europe had given rise to a certain respect for the kingdom by the nineteenth century. The original myth of Prester John, apparent biblical and classical knowledge of "Ethiopia," and the fact that the kingdom was indeed Christian after a fashion, all combined to fascinate and intrigue Europeans. Here were people damaged by their cultural and physical environment, but which nonetheless represented a curious Christian throwback, and which had – most admirably of all – repeatedly resisted in the face of Muslim enemies. Perhaps, after all, this *had* been the realm of the priest king, now fallen some way from grace, and as such "Ethiopia" was awarded a special place in the imagination of Christian Europe. It was flawed but improvable; its Christianity might frustrate missionaries, but it was, in a sense, worthy of some veneration as a historical and cultural oddity unique in a continent that otherwise showed few signs of such "advancement."

It was only in the mid- to late eighteenth century that British missionaries entered the fray, by which time Catholic influence, outside the core Portuguese settlements of Angola and Mozambique, had begun to wane. The Protestant churches now provided new impetus to missionary activity, although the Roman Catholic Church would later rejoin the struggle, notably the French White Fathers from the late 1860s, operating from their base in Algiers. Roman Catholic missionaries were also active in Gabon and Senegal, and later in southern Nigeria. Foremost behind the Protestant surge was the Anglican Church Missionary Society (CMS), founded in 1799, which – alongside such organizations as the London Missionary Society and the Wesleyan Methodist Missionary Society – would be to missionary work in Africa what the Royal Geographical Society was to exploration in the same period.[18] But while exploration was by and large, and increasingly, successful, missionary endeavors – with one or two notable exceptions – were noted only for their failure in the early decades of the nineteenth century. In truth, despite the evident energy of the would-be proselytizers, missionaries made very little progress in sub-Saharan Africa before the mid-nineteenth century. They were, and often considered themselves to be, wandering in the wilderness, a dark, godless environment in which the devil reigned supreme and into which the rays of light could scarcely penetrate.

Evangelical Humanitarians: Missionary Revival

The evangelical revival which swept Western Europe and North America in the late eighteenth century was closely linked to the humanitarian abolitionist movement. Evangelical eyes turned on Africa – as they also did on China and India – as a field ripe for Christian missionary endeavor, in both converting the heathen world and preaching against such evils as slavery, and other assorted social and cultural abominations. This Christianity was intimately tied to European cultural values, and the link would harden in the course of the nineteenth century: emphasis was placed on the adoption of European dress and a strict puritanical morality, and there was opposition to dancing, drinking, nonreligious singing, and sexual freedom outside the sanctity of marriage. In effect, this meant condemning huge swathes of African culture and society, and particular scorn was reserved for polygamy. Missionaries were the pioneers of the civilizing Christian enterprise, while in Britain, evangelical philanthropists such as Wilberforce and Wedgwood were, in a sense, "domestic" missionaries, fighting the good fight (against the slave trade) on the home front.[19] Missionaries often saw themselves as pioneers of "legitimate" trade, forging the link between Christianity and healthy commerce in the popular imagination: they would carry the "three Cs" into Africa, namely Commerce, Christianity, and Civilization.[20] Missionary societies themselves were the forceful and revitalized response to the secularism of the Enlightenment, seeking to put God back at the center of the political and social debates of the day – and, in Britain, at the center of imperial responsibility. Similar dynamics were at work across Europe: the Society of Mary, founded in France in 1817; the Italian Pallottines, active from 1835; the Society of African Missions, based in Lyons, established in 1868, and the Society for Missionaries in Africa, in Algeria in the same year; the Anglo-Dutch Mill Hill Fathers, founded in London in 1866; the Belgian Sheut Fathers in 1860; and in 1875, the Society of the Divine Word in Germany. US missionaries were increasingly active, too, notably under the auspices of the American Board of Commissioners for Foreign Missions, created between 1810 and 1812. It is in the British context, however, that the role of the Christian mission in the global civilization project is best illustrated.

Many things would be done to and about Africa in the name of God through the nineteenth century. "Christian conscience" was almost always at the heart of stated British policy toward Africa, at least in terms of public rhetoric, if not always of hardheaded political decision-making. British statesmen were as sure of the responsibilities that Britain carried as a Christian nation as they were of its military and economic might. Missionaries would indeed often be seen as the agents of the imperial project, and as such they were often at the forefront of British expansion and informal influence, at the heart of the "modernizing" project to combat godlessness and superstition and backwardness. The centrality of missionaries to actual government policy is perhaps best demonstrated in the case of Sierra Leone, the "Province of Freedom," from the 1780s onward, which also offers the best example of the alliance of government and missionary interests in practice.

Sierra Leone was the great Georgian experiment, embodying the notion of humanitarian brotherhood. A new country was created where former slaves could begin life afresh, in freedom and in hope, where they would be exposed to the learning of new skills and shown the profit to be had through the fruits of their own free labor. In this sense, Sierra Leone must also be seen as part of the campaign for the spread of "legitimate" commerce. Moreover, it represented the perfect evangelical field: missionary work is never more successful than when carried out among the displaced, the rootless, and the traumatized, and so it was in Sierra Leone. The first community there came from England; and from the early nineteenth century, newly liberated slaves would be landed at Freetown by British naval squadrons to join the ranks of Christian farmers. Many of the hopes for the colony would prove groundless, however, and indeed were utterly naïve; but a lasting British colony was indeed established there, and a dynamic community of ex-slaves did develop over the ensuing decades.[21] In the first half of the nineteenth century, similar resettlement projects for freed slaves were established under American auspices in Liberia from the 1820s – Liberia was actually granted independence in 1847 – and by France in Libreville, in present-day Gabon, from 1849. Importantly, Sierra Leone also embodied the notion of "assimilation," with its Francophone equivalent in Senegal, on the coast of which a Franco-African community dated to the 1650s. Assimilation represented the belief that the "natives," through exposure to British culture, commercial practices, and above all Christian faith, could be expected to *be British*, to become literally assimilated into British culture. Education, baptism, and cultural assimilation – in dress, manners, and speech – would create enlightened Africans in that dark continent. Olaudah Equiano, himself an enthusiastic champion of the Sierra Leone project back in England, was the embodiment of the notion.[22] Freetown itself was even designed to look like a small English provincial town, with its two-storied houses, schools and churches, and tree-lined avenues. Fourah Bay College, founded in 1827 by the CMS, would provide a gateway into the higher echelons of British culture; half a century later, in 1876, the College was affiliated to Durham University, enabling it to confer British degrees.

Assimilation, then, the creation of "black Englishmen," was indeed the ultimate goal of the British civilizing mission – for a while, at least. Something similar, though in a very different political and cultural setting, was pursued in India during the same period. Belief in the inherent superiority of white civilization was the foundation of the experiment; only the natives' obedient emulation was required, and it was difficult to imagine how they could refuse. It represented a new concern for "primitive peoples": the treatment of "native races" and "subject peoples" was no longer a matter of indifference. It was, in fact, the hallmark of the progressive mission in Africa. Thomas Buxton, evangelical humanitarian, wrote at the end of the 1830s:

> Legitimate commerce would put down the slave trade, by demonstrating the superior value of man as a labourer on the soil, to man as an object of merchandise; and if conducted on wise and equitable principles, might be the precursor, or rather the attendant, of civilisation, peace and Christianity, to the unenlightened, warlike and heathen tribes who now so fearfully prey on each other, to supply the slave markets of the New World. In this view of the subject, the merchant, the philanthropist, the patriot, and the Christian, may unite.[23]

In light of these noble aspirations, Buxton formed the African Civilisation Society in 1839, and – despite some misgivings – had the support of government for a time. Political and humanitarian interests united as the British government agreed to finance an expedition up the Niger River in order to make contact with friendly chiefs, make treaties, and gather information on areas of possible agricultural and commercial settlements in the interior. The expedition, departing for West Africa in May 1841, was something of a disaster: almost a third of the contingent died of fever, and the whole affair had to be abandoned. The African Civilisation Society collapsed soon afterwards. Humanitarian endeavor was damaged by the affair, but not irreparably, as humanitarianism retained considerable influence in subsequent governments. However, it served to remind statesmen of a compassionate bent – such as Lord Palmerston, British foreign secretary during much of the 1830s and 1840s, and prime minister 1855–8, and again 1859–65 – that they could not afford to be overly sentimental. An important principle was established, present down to the partition of Africa, whereby official support for humanitarian endeavor could only be guaranteed once it was clear that British national interests more broadly – whether commercial or strategic – were also being served.[24]

Palmerston embodied much of the ethos of the age. Deeply committed to the suppression of the illegal slave trade, he saw it as one of his missions to build up what he called "the moral weight and political influence of England." It was certainly no coincidence that Lagos was annexed while he was in office. For Palmerston, trade was civilizing: the development of trade was a means to the end of achieving that political and moral weight. There was no question of commerce for commerce's sake, but rather trade, as he put it, "begets kindly feelings,"[25] while through trade a commercial and political framework could be developed whereby alliances could be formed, moral advancement effected, and Britain's undoubtedly immense power could be utilized to some greater and higher good. Missionaries were so often at the moral frontier of empire in the nineteenth century, but it was a difficult and lonely frontier indeed.

The Christian Impact on Culture, State, and Society

There are many stereotypes of the missionary in nineteenth-century African society; but perhaps the two which follow are among the most compelling. One depicts the unbending, evangelical thunderer, marching around red-faced in the tropical sun in cassock and robes, railing with futile courage against the savagery of the environment that surrounds and ultimately kills him; the other describes the radical maverick, absorbed into indigenous society, the defender of indigenous rights, and the protector of cultures, who, while still conscious of the failings of those cultures, speaks local languages and acts as a thorn in the side to colonial administrations which could hardly share his devotion. In truth, while these images were at times accurate, there were many "types" of missionary in the nineteenth century, and the Christian impact was variable as a result.

African religions and political institutions proved stubbornly resistant to Christian theology. There were many reasons for this, of course, some doubtless "personal" – and for our purposes, in a sense, impossible to measure, just as in the case of actual conversion – and others related more to the public and cultural life of African societies. People do not convert *en masse* to new religions unless they have very good reasons for doing so; and for much of the nineteenth century, few such reasons existed, and missionaries certainly did not provide many. In terms of political elites, whose power was so often rooted in the control of indigenous religion and in their links with the supernatural, Christianity was a clear threat to their authority, as Islam indeed could be in other areas. This was true of priests and spirit mediums as well as of kings and chiefs. In purely theological terms, the fundamental principle of Christianity – that of monotheism – was in many senses alien to polytheistic societies. In many African religions, there was indeed a "creator god," but this figure was often distant, unconnected with everyday life, and retired from the real concerns of people who turned much more to functional deities, such as those associated with rain, fertility, war, and so on.[26] This polytheistic dimension made it very difficult for Africans to relate to the concept of one, omnipotent god who could tolerate no others: this was both subversive and downright dangerous. However, it has been argued by one historical anthropologist that this began to change as the presence of Europeans and other foreigners increased in certain areas, resulting in a shift in Africans' worldview in the course of the nineteenth century.[27] According to the "intellectual theory," discussed in Chapter 6 in relation to Islam, in much African religion the creator god was often associated with the "outside world," with a macrocosmic universe that was, in relatively isolated and self-contained communities, quite irrelevant to most people's lives. As the "outside world" encroached, however, in the form of expanding overseas trade networks, or of European missionaries, explorers, and eventually soldiers and colonial officials, the creator god became much more relevant. In periods of such change, Africans, it is argued, became more receptive to global, monotheistic faiths, Islam as well as Christianity.

Missionaries would frequently bemoan the fact that Islam had such a strong grip: this was true notably in West Africa, and also in East Africa, which missionaries reached rather later in the nineteenth century.[28] Missionaries thought they could attribute this to Africans' innate backwardness, while the primitiveness of the latter rendered them rather more likely to be drawn to the Muslim faith (or a corrupted version of it) than any other. But the uncomfortable question remained of how Christians could make inroads into Islam and of why so few Africans seemed drawn to Christianity. One of the problems – recognized, indeed, by successive generations of missionaries – was that Christian teaching was rather more proscriptive *vis-à-vis* African culture than was Islam. Most obviously, again, nineteenth-century missionaries abhorred polygamy, while Islam did not. Missionaries poured disapproval on African singing, dancing, drumming, as the work of Satan himself, and were appalled at Africans' apparent tendency toward sexual abandon and promiscuity. Islam, it seems, had always been rather more adaptive or at least had been interpreted as such by Africans who had embraced the faith.

Where Christianity was adopted, in whatever form, it was likewise a matter of adaptation to indigenous religion. Religious syncretism involved the selection and interpretation of certain elements of Christian ceremony – as happened with Islam, too – and the absorption of these into existing practice.[29] And it is true that some *did* show interest in Christianity, though it is not always easy to assess to what degree this was genuinely "spiritual," and to what degree politically or economically expedient. Either way, it is revealing of Africans' receptivity toward representatives from the wider world. One of the most dramatic illustrations of this was among the Xhosa, some of whom had absorbed radical Christian ideas – notably those related to the end of the world – by the mid-nineteenth century. In 1857, many Xhosa were persuaded by their own prophets to kill their livestock in anticipation of the rebirth of the community and the destruction of European power in the region. The cull took place against a backdrop of livestock disease and European encroachment, and indeed with the Xhosa thus weakened, the Cape Colony administration was able to take control of a swathe of new territory with relatively little fuss.[30] More broadly, Christianity offered the advantage of literacy, which a number of ruling elites were eager to acquire; Islam, of course, offered the same benefit. Missionaries were also seen as agents of a lucrative commercial network of which rulers were keen to take advantage; indeed some missionaries did indeed engage in trade in a range of goods, sometimes even guns. Outward-bound missionaries made sure to take plenty of trade goods with them, as this was believed to be a good way of winning confidence and ingratiating oneself into royal courts; and in the process, missionaries made a point of portraying Muslim traders as cheats and scoundrels, and Christians as fair and honest, all in the name of "legitimate" commerce.[31] But commercial activity was also important for the mission stations themselves, which needed to be reasonably self-supporting. While benign or generous chiefs might keep their Bible-wielding guests supplied with food and other necessities, in other situations they were left to fend for themselves, to build their own shelter and trade in the marketplace like anyone else.

For the disadvantaged in society, Christianity offered some degree of protection. Mission compounds were sanctuaries during war, while some were hiding places for slaves who were offered freedom and salvation at the same time. Controversially, in the eyes of their Anglican colleagues at least, the French White Fathers in Buganda engaged in the internal slave trade and purchased captives as converts, particularly children. Yet the same thing happened among the Yoruba, which by the 1840s and 1850s had become one of the major areas of missionary activity.[32] One of the most important strategies for proselytization was the use of "native" converts to actually undertake much of the grassroots mission work. The precedent was established by Philip Quaque, born in the Gold Coast in 1741 and sent to Britain where he became the first African to be ordained by the Church of England; he returned home in 1766 to preach the gospel.[33] He would be followed by others, notably ex-slaves, from Sierra Leone, who would find themselves dispatched across various parts of West Africa to spread the Word. The most famous of these, later in the nineteenth century, was Samuel Crowther. Quaque and many who followed in his footsteps had just as much trouble as the white missionaries in that their preaching usually fell on deaf ears; they were no less "foreign" than their white counterparts, and their message no less alien. They were culturally displaced, curious individuals in the eyes of the Africans who were the targets of their sermons.

Nonetheless, as previously discussed, Sierra Leone itself was one of the missionary "success stories" of the late eighteenth and early nineteenth centuries, hardly surprising given that it represented, in more than one sense, a captive audience. Sierra Leonean Christianity, moreover, can in some respects be seen as the forerunner of the much later "Africanization" of Christianity. Another area of relative success was southern Africa, where the displaced and downtrodden Khoisan and others of Cape Colony were drawn to the Christian message, and where the mission compound again offered sanctuary and compassion, albeit of a rather strict moral kind.[34] In this region, Robert Moffat achieved public fame in the 1840s, though it was his protégé David Livingstone who would go on to become Victorian icon *extraordinaire*, combining evangelical endeavor with exploration and the need to "open up" the continent to "legitimate" trade during his travels in southern and central Africa between the 1840s and the early 1870s. Livingstone's call for greater missionary efforts inspired a new surge in activity, including the creation of the Universities' Mission to Central Africa (UMCA), by the 1860s. This renewed commitment would, in time, coincide with the era of partition, in which missionaries would play a prominent role – not necessarily as the overt agents of imperialism, although this would sometimes be the case, but certainly as the pioneers of increasing European influence and cultural penetration, tacitly or otherwise backed by government.

Livingstone combined evangelical conviction with scientific curiosity, and spent years in southern and central Africa mapping the landscape, searching for the sources and the feeders of the Congo River system and observing indigenous peoples. In so doing, he was the embodiment of Victorian humanitarian conscience, railing against the slave trade and calling for Britain's youth to commit themselves to missionary work: his famous description of the African slave trade as the "open sore of the world" encapsulated Britain's conceptualization of the continent as a place of suffering, awful backwardness, sin, and savagery.[35] Although Livingstone himself would not live to see the "scramble," he contributed to the creation of the rhetorical and moral context for Britain's eventual "humanitarian conquest" of the continent. Livingstone was a Victorian icon, and in some respects, his legacy has been considerable in the West. He died somewhere west of Lake Tanganyika in 1873 and swiftly became one of the most celebrated "martyrs" to Africa, a man who literally gave his life to the improvement and salvation of the continent. In one of the great tales of the Victorian age, his servants – Susi and Chuma – removed his heart and buried it under a tree close to where he had died; they disemboweled and preserved the corpse, and traveled with it and his last remaining possessions, via Zanzibar, back to England, where the great man was interred in Westminster Cathedral. Susi and Chuma were briefly feted, and Livingstone's last diaries were speedily edited by his friend Horace Waller, and published in 1874.[36]

The story of "Uganda" is informative in this context and demonstrates some of the dynamics of the age admirably; the kingdom of Buganda ("Uganda" was the Swahili rendering of the name) caught the popular imagination and would become something of a *cause celèbre* in the last years of the nineteenth century. In early 1876, Henry Morton Stanley, the pre-eminent explorer of the age and the self-anointed heir of Livingstone, published his letter in the *Daily Telegraph* in which he made a plea for missionaries to come to Buganda, the kingdom in which Stanley himself had just spent some time.[37] Here, he declared, they would find an intelligent and interested ruler, at the head of a people crying out for redemption and a way out of the darkness that surrounded them; this was a field ripe for Christian endeavor. Kabaka Mutesa had indeed shown an interest in Stanley's Bible, as he had in Speke's some years earlier; this was true despite the fact that by the time Stanley arrived in 1875 Mutesa was nominally Muslim. The response to Stanley's letter was swift and purposeful: in 1877, the first CMS missionaries arrived among the Ganda to take on the task of wresting the kingdom from the forces of Islam and paganism. Among the earliest members of the station, and one who would dedicate the rest of his life to the work, was the Scot Alexander Mackay, eminently practical (he was a skilled craftsman) and uncompromising in his vehement hatred of Catholicism. He was also impervious to local sensitivities and was prone to angry outbursts at the royal court against both Islam and the dominant role played by spirit mediums and local deities. His dismay – and indeed that of his colleagues – when in 1879 the French Catholic order, the White Fathers, arrived in Buganda is not difficult to imagine.[38] There then followed the somewhat degrading sight – though no doubt amusing to at least some of the Ganda who beheld it – of Protestant and Catholic missionaries haranguing one another at the royal court in front of the kabaka, whom they were trying to persuade of the righteousness of their own particular faith and the fundamental wrongheadedness of their rivals.

Both enjoyed some success in converting the elite of Ganda society. Many chiefs became either Protestant or Catholic – in addition to those who were already Muslim, or claimed to be – while also holding onto their old gods tightly enough to cause despair among the missionaries and sow the seeds of doubt that they had genuinely converted. The upper echelons of Ganda political society sent their children to the mission compounds to learn to read and write and have them baptized; Mutesa sent his court pages and junior chiefs there for the same reasons. As for Mutesa himself, a clever individual who kept his thoughts very much to himself, there is little doubt that he played a number of groups off one another in the late 1870s and early 1880s: the CMS, the White Fathers, Muslim traders, his own spirit mediums who maintained a powerful hold over the royal court. He gave enough encouragement to the missionaries to keep them hopeful, without convincingly committing himself to anything; but there seems little doubt that he was genuinely interested in the Christian God, and his patronage facilitated the spread of the Christian faith among his own chiefs. How successful Mutesa actually was in controlling the new forces entering his kingdom, however, is a matter of debate.[39]

The Ganda universe was changing. Christianity attracted followers, as did Islam, because it seemed to offer social and political opportunities, literacy, and access to trade; at the same time, there were new threats to the political and moral order. When Mutesa died in 1884 – Mackay supervised the manufacture of a European-style coffin – he was succeeded by his son Mwanga, who as a boy had frequented the CMS compound, but who as kabaka launched a persecution of both missionaries and Ganda converts. A number of the latter were put to death, their martyrdom belonging to the Ganda tradition of honor as much as it was inspired by new faith. Life for the missionaries themselves became difficult, although stalwarts such as Mackay refused to leave. Mwanga behaved like a man caught, confused, in the headlights of change; his persecution of Christians can be seen as something of a struggle for the soul and the future of the kingdom itself. When in 1885 Bishop James Hannington, appointed to take charge of the Nyanza mission, decided to travel to Buganda via the "eastern" route – across present-day Kenya, rather than from the south – he was warned that the Ganda "traditionally" regarded any approach from this direction as a hostile act. He ignored the advice and was killed by a group of Ganda on the eastern frontier of the kingdom.[40] Thus was the CMS, and African missionary work more broadly, given another martyr, albeit one that might have been avoided; but more importantly, perhaps, Hannington's murder merely highlighted the deep tensions opening up within Ganda society, namely a willingness to embrace the new and the foreign versus a deep-seated fear of forces advancing inexorably from distant horizons.

Mission and Empire

From the 1860s and 1870s onward, the missionary endeavor developed new impetus and was increasingly at the forefront of imperial expansion and the spread of European influence. French Catholic missionaries, for example, were in the vanguard of the Third Republic's creeping imperial project, especially in coastal West Africa, and in the Congo basin.[41] The German explorer and empire-enthusiast Karl Peters sought spiritual sanction for his efforts when he initiated the Evangelical Missionary Society for German East Africa in the mid-1880s.[42] Almost universally, ideas about imperial ambition and responsibility – at least as expressed in the public sphere – were dignified with the language of the Christian mission. In the middle of the nineteenth century, as we have seen, British Prime Minister Lord Palmerston had laid down the policy framework whereby, although Britain had moral responsibilities in the world, and perceived itself as the Christian conscience of the civilized world, morally motivated intervention should coincide with genuine strategic or commercial interests. Thus, while missionaries were not necessarily part of the imperial project, and while "Christian conscience" alone did not shape British policy decisions, missionaries were nonetheless a constant reminder of Britain's expanding role in the world in the age of the "new imperialism" of the late nineteenth century. They both reflected Britain's self-image, representing metropolitan Christian impulses, and in turn informed and influenced public opinion and political decision-making. Livingstone's martyrdom had fixed the "dark continent" firmly in the late Victorian imagination; and it was subsequently argued that the Bible and the Flag must go together if Britain's moral destiny was to be wholly fulfilled.[43] This was certainly the argument of the Christian humanitarian as the century drew to a close: even if no clear strategic or commercial motive for intervention could be discerned, should not Britain still shoulder her moral responsibilities? Could Britain turn her back on savage and benighted peoples in desperate need of salvation?

This said, the situation in the middle decades of the nineteenth century presented a grim picture for the Christian mission in Africa. Missionaries had made little impact, beyond the areas noted previously; many had died for the cause. War and disaster apparently stalked the societies in which missionaries strove to overcome the forces of darkness. In Britain in the 1860s, the Church of England found itself once again on the defensive following the publication of Darwin's *Origin of Species*, and the wave of critical questioning which swiftly ensued. Yet as the political and racial attitudes of the age shifted, and Africa came under closer scrutiny, missionaries were able to reposition themselves at the frontline in the age of expansion.

Frustrated by lack of progress, missionaries increasingly looked to governments at home for support in changing African society, to make it more amenable to the spread of Christianity; they lobbied for political or military protection from their governments, which might respond positively when it suited their broader strategic or commercial interests. The area of Lake Nyasa – present-day Malawi – witnessed some of the most intense activity on the part of British missionaries, in large part representing Livingstone's legacy; here, the "Christianity and Commerce" lobby argued during the 1880s for intervention in order to crush the slave-traders who were particularly powerful in the region. When the British government finally did declare a protectorate, in 1889, it was primarily motivated by the desire to prevent Portuguese encroachment from the east, but the missionaries' work provided a powerful humanitarian argument, too.[44] British missionaries were active promoters of imperial authority across southern Africa, for example encouraging Tswana chiefs to seek the British government's protection against the Boers; and among the Ndebele, in 1888, it was a missionary who deceived the king, Lobengula, by mistranslating the treaty by which the latter signed away a swathe of his territory to Cecil Rhodes' business concerns. This somewhat base treatment of Lobengula was justified by the depiction of the king as a savage potentate who was an obstacle to the progress of Christianity in the region. French and German missionaries were likewise successful lobbyists of – and often severe irritants to – their own governments when it came to shouldering their "moral" responsibilities in Africa.[45]

The death of Bishop Hannington, noted previously, caused outrage in Britain; and now "Uganda," as it was popularly known, was becoming something of a *cause celèbre* in Britain. The inroads made by missionaries into Ganda society enabled the CMS, allied with various humanitarian groups, to lobby for government intervention in the region. The lobbying became all the more urgent once the kingdom descended into civil war in 1888, with the factions ostensibly divided according to allegiance to a foreign faith, Protestantism, Catholicism, or Islam.[46] Christian conscience and supposed commercial potential prompted the establishment of a semi-official presence in Buganda, in the shape of the Imperial British East Africa Company (IBEAC); the kingdom's location at the headwaters of the Nile was also a significant factor, as Britain increasingly viewed particular localities in broader geopolitical terms. The IBEAC was in financial trouble by the early 1890s, and in 1894, the Liberal government of Rosebery agreed, somewhat reluctantly, to declare a protectorate over "Uganda." Missionaries had acted as the pioneers of imperial expansion, and the fact that the territory had been to some extent "Christianized" in advance of the imperial takeover was critical in the process. The "Uganda question" exercised the British popular imagination in the early and mid-1890s, representing a test case for the civilizing mission supposedly pursued since Palmerston. So Britain stepped in, and the famous *Punch* cartoon of the time captured that sense of moral duty, with John Bull as the patriarch, wearily taking the abandoned African baby into the orphanage.[47] Buganda itself captured the imagination as the relatively advanced African civilization, morally receptive and usable as a local agency of moral regeneration in the wider region – and, shortly, an agency of imperial control.

The role of missionaries in this process was fundamental, and it was significant among the Yoruba on the other side of the continent, too, where missionaries highlighted the need for intervention against the ravages of the slave trade and the terrible consequences of interminable war across the region. As we saw in an earlier chapter, missionaries were instrumental in the depiction of Dahomey as a source of instability and violence, preying on the Egba, attacking Abeokuta (where a number of missionaries themselves were located), and engaging in the "illegal" traffic in human beings. As in Buganda, missionaries acted as Britain's conscience; and while they may have played a minimal role in Britain's eventual decision to extend formal control, they had created a moral framework within which this could be done.

Missionaries were critical in the projection of some of the more enduring images surrounding Africa in the late nineteenth and early twentieth centuries; as with those of explorers, their published accounts were popular, the interest in the crusading Christian spirit overseas being very largely inspired by the martyrdom of Livingstone. It was the publicity surrounding missionary endeavor which kept religious societies afloat in lean years, and through which missionaries were able to lobby national parliaments and arouse public opinion when it mattered. Moreover, similar to the exploration literature of the age, their work constitutes some crucial primary source material for historians in the reconstruction of the societies in which they worked; again, as with explorers, they were reporting on an era of dramatic and frequently violent change in Africa, even if they usually failed to comprehend the meaning and direction of such change. At the same time, missionary writings informed views about race at home, as well as reflecting the hardening racial views of the age: Samuel Crowther, the first West African bishop of the Niger diocese, was replaced toward the end of the nineteenth century by a Briton, and an African would not hold the position again until the 1950s. Missionary discourse reflected the debate about whether certain "negro peoples" were capable of improvement; many would despair that so many baptized Africans simply appeared to be going through the motions, providing no real evidence of spiritual transformation. This, it was argued in the late nineteenth century, would only be achieved with political and military backing; the full weight of imperial power would be necessary to drive home the gospel. And yet it is important to note that equally there were missionaries who disapproved of the imperial project and who condemned the violence which attended it.

Missionary writing heightened "knowledge" of Africa, as it did of Asia and the Pacific, too, notable considering that many missionaries had had scant education themselves. They were, in many ways, pioneer anthropologists and historians working and living among societies in ways that few other Europeans did and accumulating data of variable quality on custom, culture, and history. They were often proficient in local languages, many of which they committed for the first time to writing, usually in the process of translating the Bible into local vernaculars. They recorded local histories and traditions, codifying local knowledge.[48] If missionaries heightened European knowledge of Africa – or, more appropriately, clarified European perceptions of the continent – they also contributed to the emergence of new identities in Africa itself, in the process of assisting in the creation of pools of received knowledge within many communities. Through their work on local languages, they contributed to the invention of "tribal" identities where none, or only loose associations, had existed previously. Yet this was, again, no one-way relationship. Africans manipulated missionaries, and their need for information, in a myriad of ways; by committing to writing local tradition, missionaries enabled elites to justify and consolidate particular versions of the past through the new-found power of literacy, thus enhancing their position in the new Afro-European colonial order. Above all, in the longer term, millions of Africans embraced Christianity and made it their own, using the principles at the core of the missionaries' teaching to found their own communities of faith and to challenge colonial rule itself.

Notes

1 Anthony Sattin, *The Gates of Africa: Death, Discovery and the Search for Timbuktu* (London, 2003).

2 See for example Roy Porter, *Enlightenment: Britain and the Creation of the Modern World* (London, 2000).

3 For context and an excellent overview of the period, see McCaskie, "Cultural Encounters."

4 Quoted in R. Hallett, "The European approach to the interior of Africa in the eighteenth century," *Journal of African History*, 4:2 (1963), 203.

5 R.A. Stafford, *Scientist of Empire: Sir Roderick Murchison, Scientific Exploration, and Victorian Imperialism* (Cambridge, 1989).

6 Among the most notable is that of Ibn Battutah from the fourteenth century: see Tim Mackintosh-Smith (ed.), *The Travels of Ibn Battutah* (Basingstoke, 2002).

7 Sattin, *Gates*; Christopher Hibbert, *Africa Explored: Europeans in the Dark Continent, 1769–1889* (Harmondsworth, 1984); R. Hallett, *The Penetration of Africa: European Enterprise and Exploration, Principally in Northern and Western Africa up to 1830* (London, 1965). For a more general account, see the still-readable V.G. Kiernan, *The Lords of Human Kind: European Attitudes to the Outside World in the Imperial Age* (London, 1969).

8 E.W. Bovill, *The Niger Explored* (London, 1968).

9 These travellers left behind a substantial body of literary work, of variable quality: for example, David & Charles Livingstone, *Narrative of an Expedition to the Zambesi and its Tributaries* (Stroud, 2005; first pub., 1865); H. Waller (ed.), *The Last Journals of David Livingstone in Central Africa, from 1865 to his Death*, 2 vols. (London, 1874); R.F. Burton, *The Lake Regions of Central Africa*, 2 vols. (London, 1860); J.H. Speke, *Journal of the Discovery of the Source of the Nile* (Edinburgh, 1863); V.L. Cameron, *Across Africa*, 2 vols. (London, 1877); H.M. Stanley, *Through the Dark Continent*, 2 vols. (London, 1878); H.M. Stanley, in *Darkest Africa*, 2 vols. (London, 1890).

10 T. Youngs, *Travellers in Africa: British Travelogues, 1850–1900* (Manchester, 1994); Laura Franey, *Victorian Travel Writing and Imperial Violence: British Writing on Africa, 1855–1902* (Basingstoke, 2003).

11 R.A. Stafford, "Scientific exploration and empire," in Porter (ed.), *Oxford History*, Vol. III, 302.

12 He did so in a letter to the London *Daily Telegraph*: see Harold Ingrams, *Uganda: A Crisis of Nationhood* (London, 1960), 7–10.

13 Burton, *Lake Regions*; Speke, *Journal*.
14 For a useful overview, see David Maxwell, "Christianity," in John Parker & Richard Reid (eds.), *The Oxford Handbook of Modern African History* (Oxford, 2013).
15 For example, Fr. Jerome Lobo (tr. Samuel Johnson), *A Voyage to Abyssinia* (London, 1789); J.H. Arrowsmith-Brown (ed. & tr.), *Prutky's Travels in Ethiopia and Other Countries* (London, 1991).
16 John Thornton, "The development of an African Catholic Church in the Kingdom of the Kongo, 1491–1750," *Journal of African History*, 25:2 (1984).
17 Crummey, *Land and Society*, 67–72.
18 Brian Stanley, *The Bible and the Flag: Protestant Missions and British Imperialism in the Nineteenth and Twentieth Centuries* (Leicester, 1990); Andrew Porter, *Religions Versus Empire: British Protestant Missionaries and Overseas Expansion, 1700–1914* (Manchester, 2004).
19 For example, William Wilberforce, *A Letter on the Abolition of the Slave Trade, Addressed to the Freeholders of Yorkshire* (London, 1807).
20 Fidelis Nkomazana, "Livingstone's ideas of Christianity, commerce, and civilisation," *Pula: Botswana Journal of African Studies*, 12:1–2 (1998).
21 The classic study is Christopher Fyfe, *A History of Sierra Leone* (London, 1962).
22 Olaudah Equiano (ed. Vincent Carretta), *The Interesting Narrative and Other Writings* (London, 2003; 1st ed., 1789).
23 Thomas F. Buxton, *The African Slave Trade and its Remedy* (London, 1967; 1st ed., 1839–40), 306.
24 Martin Lynn, "British policy, trade, and informal empire in the mid-nineteenth century," in Porter (ed.), *Oxford History*, Vol. III, esp. 107–13.
25 Quoted in F.R. Flournoy, *British Policy Towards Morocco in the Age of Palmerston (1830–1856)* (London, 1935), 69–70.
26 For a useful survey, see Robert M. Baum, "Indigenous African Religions," in Parker & Reid (eds), *Oxford Handbook*.
27 For example, see R. Horton, "African conversion," *Africa*, 41 (1971); J.D.Y. Peel, "Conversion and tradition in two African societies: Ijebu and Buganda," *Past and Present*, 77 (1977).
28 Roland Oliver, *The Missionary Factor in East Africa* (London, 1965).
29 See for example John K. Thornton, "Afro-Christian Syncretism in the Kingdom of Kongo," *Journal of African History*, 54:1 (2013).
30 J.B. Peires, *The Dead Will Arise: Nongqawuse and the Great Xhosa Cattle-Killing Movement of 1856–7* (Johannesburg & London, 1989).
31 It is a recurrent theme in A.M. Mackay (ed. by his sister), *A.M. Mackay, Pioneer Missionary of the Church Missionary Society to Uganda* (London, 1890).
32 J.F.A. Ajayi, *Christian Missions in Nigeria, 1841–1891* (London, 1965); E.A. Ayandele, *The Missionary Impact on Modern Nigeria, 1842–1914* (London, 1966).
33 Vincent Carretta & Ty M. Reese (eds.), *The Life and Letters of Philip Quaque: The First African Anglican Missionary* (Athens GA & London, 2010).
34 Elizabeth Elbourne, *Blood Ground: Colonialism, Missions, and the Contest for Christianity in the Cape Colony and Britain, 1799–1853* (Montreal, 2002).
35 Oliver, *Missionary Factor*, 34.
36 Waller (ed.), *Last Journals*.
37 See footnote 11.
38 Mackay, *Pioneer Missionary*.
39 Michael Twaddle, "The emergence of politico-religious groupings in late nineteenth-century Buganda," *Journal of African History*, 29:1 (1988).

40 Mackay, *Pioneer Missionary*, 262, 265, 267–8.

41 James Patrick Tudesco, "Missionaries and French Imperialism: the role of Catholic missionaries in French colonial expansion, 1880–1905," PhD Dissertation, University of Connecticut, 1980.

42 See Sebastian Conrad, *German Colonialism: A Short History* (Cambridge, 2012).

43 J.M. Mackenzie, *David Livingstone and the Victorian Encounter with Africa* (London, 1996); B. Pachai (ed.), *Livingstone, Man of Africa: Memorial Essays, 1873–1973* (Harlow, 1973).

44 By the eminent historian of Malawi, the late John McCracken, see: *Politics and Christianity in Malawi, 1875–1940* (Cambridge, 1977); and *A History of Malawi, 1859–1966* (Woodbridge, 2012).

45 J.D. Omer-Cooper, *History of Southern Africa* (London, 1987), 131–2; for wider context, Andrew Porter, "Religion, Missionary Enthusiasm, and Empire," in Porter (ed.), *Oxford History*, Vol. III.

46 Ashe, *Chronicles*.

47 In H.B. Thomas & Robert Scott, *Uganda* (London, 1935), frontispiece.

48 Toyin Falola, "Mission and colonial documents," in John Edward Philips (ed.), *Writing African History* (Rochester NY, 2005).

9 "Whatever Happens ..."

Towards the Scramble

There has always been a temptation to see the Scramble for Africa in terms of discontinuity, a view apparently borne out by the bare facts: between the end of the 1870s and the end of the 1890s, Europe engaged in a sudden, largely uncoordinated partition of this vast region of the world with seemingly little warning. At the end of the 1870s, most of the continent was still in African hands, notwithstanding spreading European influence in some areas, largely economic; yet within the space of twenty years, the entire continent – with the exceptions of Ethiopia and Liberia – was under European colonial rule.[1] The drama of the Scramble is evident in the fact that c.1880 the "foreign presence" scarcely extended much beyond coastal enclaves or loose spheres of influence along the littoral, with notable exceptions at either end of the landmass – the British and the Boers in South Africa, and the French in Algeria. The Portuguese were confined to a coastal "empire" in Angola and Mozambique, likewise the French in Senegal, Cote d'Ivoire, and Gabon, and the British in Gambia, Gold Coast, Lagos, and Sierra Leone, with a loose commercial influence in the Niger Delta. In eastern Africa, the influence of the Zanzibar sultanate was similarly restricted to the islands and coastal settlements, notwithstanding the penetration of caravans into the interior.

There is, however, much to be said for thematic continuity, for many of the ideas, rhetoric, and policy considerations which attended and drove partition had been present since the late eighteenth century, and certainly since the abolition of the slave trade and the struggle to "modernize" African society in economic and political terms. The nineteenth century witnessed a gradual hardening of attitudes which created the moral, intellectual, and cultural climate within which the European invasion took place. Of course, in terms of immediacy, there was a range of strategic and commercial decisions taken by European governments, and by the proverbial "men on the spot," the

A History of Modern Africa: 1800 to the Present, Third Edition. Richard J. Reid.

army officers and consuls and administrators at the "edge of empire." But these decisions must be understood in terms of the long-term themes examined in previous chapters: the burgeoning scientific interest in the continent; the struggle against the slave trade and consequent discourses regarding the economic and thus political "modernization" of Africa; the evangelical drive and the interventionism made possible by "Christian conscience"; and increasingly racially charged interpretations of the nature of African polity, society, and culture.

Africa and Theories of Imperialism

Debate has abounded for several decades over the factors behind the European partition of the continent, and there are certainly several interpretations to choose from, as indeed there are when it comes to understanding the phenomenon of nineteenth-century imperialism more broadly.[2] Again, however, it is clear that we can interpret the events of the late nineteenth century in terms of continuity, rather than discontinuity. It is also possible to suggest that the period c.1880–1914 witnessed a conjunction of processes, some of which had their roots in the era of the European Enlightenment and the Atlantic slave trade. It is important to consider the timing of the European invasion, in terms of certain political, economic, and cultural processes unfolding both inside and outside Africa itself.

One standard – although in some respects rather dated, and certainly Eurocentric – explanation focuses on events outside Africa in the second half of the nineteenth century: European rivalries are often cited as an important dynamic, and although competition among European states was obviously nothing new, this was complicated by the emergence of a united Germany from the 1870s, leading to new and heightened tensions within Europe. The relative balance in place since Napoleon's defeat and the Congress of Europe was shattered; and shifts in the balance of power led to a number of European states to seek to bolster their international positions through acquisition of territory overseas. "Compensation" was thus sought in Africa. The British pursued "defensive imperialism" in response to rising German power, while the French searched restlessly for national prestige in the years following its defeat at the hands of Bismarck in 1870–1. France, it has been argued, was in no position to confront Germany directly, but it *could* use imperialism as an aid to recovery. Once this process was under way, Germany itself – despite Bismarck's deep misgivings – also sought territory in Africa in order to maintain the *new* European balance of power. Bismarck was depicted by the historian A. J. P. Taylor, for example, as the master of European diplomatic wrangling, using Anglo-French rivalry over Egypt to sow mistrust between them and thus strengthen Germany's own position inside Europe.[3] In other areas, colonial disputes were conjured up overseas in order to create arguments within Europe and thus facilitate intricate alliance systems. Empire in Africa, according to this reading, was mere sideline to the real business of European politics, useful only in so far as it might strengthen particular powers inside Europe.[4]

And so there followed a domino effect: many smaller or less secure European nations sought colonies as a prerequisite to national prestige, or to affirm their arrival as "great powers." The British and French remained the major players, ending up with the lion's share of territory between them. Others were Portugal, also with a coastal presence on both sides of the continent of some antiquity; King Leopold of the Belgians (*not* the Belgian government itself until much later) in the Congo basin; Spain, mostly north of the Sahara; Germany, eventually acquiring territory in the west, east, and south of the continent; and Italy, coming late to the Scramble and never entirely convincing as an imperial power. The Danes and the Dutch, erstwhile participants in the slave trade, had long since dropped out of the race, selling their tiny coastal possessions to the British in the course of the nineteenth century; but in general across western and central Europe, there was a fear of exclusion which drove governments to acts of otherwise irrational colonial expansion.

This political interpretation has some limited value but needs to be seen for what it is, namely an exercise in blatant Eurocentrism. The partition has also been interpreted in the context of *economic* developments in Europe. The argument is that by the 1870s and 1880s, the industrial supremacy enjoyed by Britain for much of the nineteenth century was being challenged by France, Germany, and the United States. Previously, "free trade" – or a particular interpretation of it – had suited the British as the largest producers of the cheapest manufactured goods, while they also possessed the largest naval capacity to transport these goods to distant markets. Free trade, in other words, worked fine as long as serious competition was largely absent. But as much of Western Europe and North America industrialized, competition for markets increased markedly; European merchants, finding demand in their home markets declining – especially during the economic downturn between the early 1870s and the mid-1890s – turned increasingly to overseas markets (Africa included) in which to sell textiles, hardware, firearms, and so on. Global competition increased sharply, and free trade gave way to protectionism, namely the establishment of colonial territories from which rival European powers could be excluded or at least heavily taxed. In the British context, one influential thesis – by P. J. Cain and A. G. Hopkins – proposes that a key role was played by financiers, or "gentlemanly capitalists," in driving forward a remarkable commercial expansion across the globe.[5]

For our immediate purposes, however, the problem with many economic interpretations is that Africa itself accounted for only a small percentage of the exports which this overseas rush involved in the last third of the nineteenth century. British manufacturers, for example, sought markets in Europe itself, the "white dominion" territories, India, the United States, and Latin America before Africa. Nonetheless, we should not overstate this, for the point is not to consider Africa in this context in comparison with other parts of the world, but rather to consider the peculiar circumstances which characterized Europe's involvement in the continent. It is also the case that many European merchants were convinced of the existence of vast untapped wealth and copious raw materials in the African interior; this had already been suggested by the oil and rubber of the coastal tropical forests and later by the diamonds and gold of southern Africa. European states believed in their capacity and indeed their right to control these resources directly. Much of this was based on the notion of Africa's *potential*, namely that at some point in the future swathes of "tropical Africa" would become hugely profitable. Often these hopes were wildly unrealistic, as the French discovered after acquiring a sizeable chunk of the western Sahara; but the role they played in policymaking can never be discounted.

Again, partition needs to be understood in terms of relations between Africans and Europeans in this period, particularly against the backdrop of "legitimate" commerce. It was deemed necessary to control African society directly, but neither China nor Latin America, for example, came in for the same treatment. For several centuries, Europe had taken from Africa what it needed without political intervention; but the process of commercial change, as we have seen – from the gradual suppression of the slave trade to the development of "legitimate" commerce – had led to ever greater involvement and indeed, sometimes, military pressure to induce to Africans to cooperate in their own "modernization." The historians Robinson and Gallagher argued for a "peripheral" theory of imperialism, which rejected older "centrist" or metropolitan interpretations and which described an expanding frontier along which the British relied heavily on local "collaborators" or partners to sustain an "informal" empire.[6] The British, on whom Robinson and Gallagher concentrated, preferred this because it was comparatively cheap; but once such "collaborative" regimes on the periphery collapsed, Britain was compelled to involve itself directly in those societies in order to protect its interests. According to this view, Europe was sucked into Africa; and it is certainly the case that Africa's violent transformation provided openings – and, crucially, leverage – for European powers. Creeping imperialism involved gradual, and indeed often deeply reluctant, political involvement in order to establish military security and financial viability. Yet it is important to note that there was no systematic imperialism in Africa before the 1870s, nor tactical consistency from one government to the next, whether in London or Paris or Lisbon; there was, rather, reluctance and vacillation and a fair amount of thrift. There was even inconsistency within governments at home: in Britain, for example, Gladstone's Liberal administration was publicly anti-empire in principle, and yet it presided over some of Britain's most aggressive expansion during the first half of the 1880s.[7] But crucially there was also a general sense of what Africa was and what it needed to become, in economic as well as cultural terms, and – as we have seen – a vaguely defined "strategy" concerned with how to bring this about. By the 1870s and 1880s, it had become clear that economic penetration would not proceed peacefully or smoothly without intervention; the "free market" was no longer sufficient to deliver what Europe needed, and obstacles had appeared which only imperialism could remove.

This was compounded by the rise of racialism in Europe, involving as it did the idea that Africans could not be left alone to create conditions conducive to healthy economic development. Problems of local disorder threatened trade and investment and required direct and forceful solutions; there was also the problem of the apparent fragmentary nature of African political systems, manifested in the existence of numerous small states, all seeking to levy taxes on and to control their part of the trade. In some cases, African rulers attempted to use their political power to maintain their positions as middlemen, and Europeans increasingly believed it necessary to crush such leaders in order to make trade run more smoothly. Culturally and politically, Africans stood in the way of economic modernity.

Race and Culture

One of the most important elements in the story of European invasion is racialism, or more precisely shifting European attitudes toward the "races" of Africa.[8] It is not always given its due place in the standard narratives, owing partly, no doubt, to the odiousness of the subject itself, and also perhaps to the idea that it can be "taken for granted," that *of course* imperialism is rooted in the assumption of superiority over another people or culture, often, though not exclusively, based on skin color. It is, however, dangerous to overlook the subject because in many ways, it goes to the very heart of the historical relationship between Africa and Europe in the timeframe encompassed by this book.

European attitudes toward race hardened in the course of the nineteenth century. Ideas about assimilation and the improvability of "the native" – embodied, for example, in the case of Sierra Leone – gave way to a growing sense of disillusionment about the native "character," his natural intelligence, his capacity for change. There developed a profound contempt among missionaries and others for what they saw as the mere "mimicry" of Africans, who crudely and comically aped European culture, manners, and dress.[9] This view was shared by many and was developed by Sir Garnet Wolseley, commander of the British forces against the Asante in the 1870s, and his lieutenants, who constituted the so-called "Wolseley Ring." The "Ring" tended to highlight the intrinsic bloodthirstiness and savagery of Asante culture and custom, but it also argued that this "natural state" was always preferable to the semi-westernized Africans of the British Gold Coast colony. The latter were contemptible; the Asante were at least "true." Any attempt, argued the Wolseley Ring – which dominated British military thinking about Africa until the early 1900s – to assimilate the African into "English" culture was bound to produce a rootless, pathetic caricature.[10] At any rate, "natives," in short, were not as committed to genuinely improving themselves as it was hoped they might be nor indeed were they as grateful as they should have been when it came to grasping the opportunities provided through exposure to European civilization. The slave trade proved singularly difficult to suppress, for example; and this led some to consider that perhaps the African was not actually "salvable" after all, at least not when left to his own devices. The notion of the irresistible power of "legitimate" commerce died hard; however, many continued to believe through the middle decades of the nineteenth century that it would take root in time and that Africans would come to see the value of producing palm oil, growing certain crops, selling rubber, and so on. Many did, as we have seen; but things were not improving as quickly as had been envisaged, and there was a growing disenchantment with the notion that Africans could improve themselves. Perhaps the civilizing mission would need to go further. In East Africa, too, the slave trade was actually *increasing*, and here the finger of blame could be pointed at those dark, isolated zones of the interior where the light of Christianity had scarcely penetrated, and where instead God-forsaken societies were at the mercy of voracious, grasping Muslim merchants. The battle might have to be taken to the region itself, against Islam, or what passed for Islam in those neglected parts.

Much of this was directly linked to changing racial thought in the course of the century. Changes in such thinking were spurred by a series of global events clustered together in mid-century. The Indian uprising of 1857–8, followed by rebellion in Jamaica in 1865 – not to mention the American civil war of the early 1860s – carried the question of native ingratitude to the fore, as well as throwing open the whole question of dealings with other "races." The achievements of Lincoln's Union notwithstanding, in the imperial context the "black races" were increasingly seen as irredeemably savage, brutal, and ignorant; in the wake of the violence in the Caribbean and across the Indian subcontinent, perhaps, many believed, the time had come to treat them differently. Thus did the whole issue of "race" become a prominent one in mid-nineteenth-century Europe, as well as in the Americas.

Darwin's *Origin of Species*, published in 1859, highlighted some key strands of thought in terms of racial science, but in fact, Darwin contributed very little to a debate which had its roots in the late eighteenth century. The Western European Enlightenment had produced the notion of the "noble savage" – associated particularly with Rousseau – as the model of man untouched by the vices of civilization and at peace with himself and his environment.[11] Linked to this was the belief in the potential for the salvation of man: the "savage" was an innocent, ripe for education and improvement. At the same time, however, others argued that the "savage" could be sinister and was capable of evil and depravity if left without guidance. The discourse between proponents of these two models grew ever more intense – and indeed relevant – during the debate surrounding the abolition of the slave trade, and it fed into new forms of scientific enquiry toward the end of the eighteenth century. Discussion of racial difference was part of a broader movement toward the classification of species and the attempt to measure differences in physical as well as behavioral ways.

From these debates, very broadly, emerged the monogenist and the polygenist camps during the nineteenth century. Monogenists drew their inspiration from the orthodoxy of the Scriptures: all men were descended from Adam and Eve, therefore all types of human – regardless of skin color or physical type – possessed a common origin. Subsequent differences were explained by environmental factors: Europeans, for example, had been favored and thus represented the most advanced form of human development, while other peoples had been less fortunate. Yet according to this line of thought, the lot of degenerate peoples *could* be improved if the sociopolitical and cultural environment itself could be altered. The polygenists, however, held that all races had evolved separately, and this certainly appeared to make sense in the context of nineteenth-century political realities, in terms of the global domination of the "white race" over all others. There was no common point of origin, they argued, and indeed cross-breeding would only lead to degeneration and genetic weakness: strength was rooted in purity. In this way, the polygenists argued that the "black races" had a naturally inferior status because of distinct origins, while the monogenists contended that this inferior status was conditional upon distinctive historical and environmental factors at work since the point of common origin. Yet did these "scientific" (in the loosest sense of that word) debates actually inform racial attitudes or were they in fact the product of the latter? Again, there were social and political events in the course of the nineteenth century which prompted Europeans to develop new ideas about race: the importance of war and rebellion in the Americas in the 1860s has been noted. But there were also deeper processes unfolding as the century wore on. Notably, as indigenous peoples took up Christianity, or gained access to European education, or adopted European modes of dress and manners – all these, ironically, having been promoted as part of the civilizing mission, especially in France and Britain, and then later despised – they became a threat to the social and political order. Regardless of whether or not Africans were contemptible "mimics," it became ever more difficult to maintain the all-important social distance between rulers and ruled, and new interpretations of "race" thus became necessary, notably in India but later, too, as we shall see, in Africa. Seen from this perspective, "race" was in fact a deliberate construct necessitated by sociopolitical change.[12]

Nor were racial attitudes a European preserve. Discrimination based on skin tone, language, environment, and economic practice is evident across nineteenth-century Africa, although this was rarely so impermeable that it precluded various degrees of integration and certainly interaction: "identity" was so often a matter of pragmatism. Such flexibility notwithstanding, however, Africans used "race" and culture as much as Europeans did to justify expansion, expropriation, and servitude, and this was most visible among state-building elites. These same elites would often become the partners of colonial administrations, and there can be little doubt that in the western savannah, in the Ethiopian highlands, among the eastern African lakes, European notions of "racial hierarchy" were frequently influenced by those of Africans themselves, although as we will see Europeans codified these in ways which would have been, on the whole, unthinkable before the onset of colonial rule.

In this context, at least, then, imperialism was ultimately rooted in notions of *race*, and in its late nineteenth-century manifestation, imperialism was the practical ability to act upon these notions, to give them practical applicability through the deployment of superior material culture. Above all, racialism made the use of force, the employment of the means of destruction, justified. Racist thought was instrumental in depicting Africans as childlike and irrational, bloodthirsty and brutal, and their politics and cultures as deeply flawed and intrinsically unstable. The "modernization" of Africa would now involve the death of, as well as the imposition of notions of "progress" upon, the "native"; the latter would, however, have a great deal to say about both.

Disorder and Civilizing Violence: Political and Economic Justifications

There was, in the course of the nineteenth century, a growing belief in the need for more forceful intervention in African society. Some states and societies stubbornly refused to halt the slave trade. Humanitarian, or more specifically missionary, representations of the resultant violence could compel governments into action, as among the Yoruba from the 1850s and 1860s onward. The British annexation of Lagos in 1861 was a relatively rare act of direct military intervention in Africa – rare, that is, in the pre-1880 context – but it indicated a readiness to intervene in the enforcement of "legitimate" commerce if necessary. Asante and Dahomey were increasingly seen as despotic and barbaric slaving states, as we have seen, and Asante was the focus of British military intervention on several occasions through the nineteenth century. Persistent Wolof involvement in the slave trade, meanwhile, provided the French with all the justification they needed for punitive campaigns up the Senegal River in the 1860s and 1870s.[13] Moreover, societies struggling with the internal pressures of transition from slave trade to legitimate commerce might undergo periods of collapse, civil upheaval, and protracted conflict, and also required some degree of intervention or a more or less permanent consular presence. It appeared as though Africa's economic "modernization" could not proceed without outside help. Combined with the hardening racial attitudes of the era, the opinion was being formed that African society was indeed fundamentally flawed – violent, unstable, and fragmented. If the promised commercial benefits were to be realized, and if Africans were to be lifted from their natural state of economic poverty and endless petty feuds, then perhaps more direct intervention was needed.

When in 1898 the French (but British-based) poet Hilaire Belloc penned his oft-quoted couplet, it seemed to pithily summarize the age of "high imperialism":

> Whatever happens we have got
> The Maxim gun, and they have not.[14]

Ultimately, "our" technology – represented here by the rapid-firing machine-gun invented by Hiram Maxim – would be more than sufficient to quash resistance and deal with any unforeseen circumstances that might arise. "They" were the peoples of the non-European world – Africans, Indians, Southeast Asians, Pacific Islanders – destined to be subject to white empires. At the heart of the "relationship" was *violence*: the machine-gun would resolve the matter and remove any ambiguity about the nature of the relationship. The following year, Kipling produced his poem "The White Man's Burden," concerned in the first instance with the United States' conquest of the Philippines, but with a much wider applicability to the European imperial mission. Kipling – the "poet of empire" – called upon youth to go forth and fight "the savage wars of peace," a duty which was indeed the "white man's burden." There is a darkness to Kipling's lines which is wholly lacking from Belloc's rhythmic jollity: here, violence was necessary in order to bring about "peace," necessary to bring to order

> Your new-caught, sullen peoples
> Half devil and half child.[15]

The concept of an imposed peace, a civilized order brought about through violence, was at the heart of much late-nineteenth-century thinking about Africa. For the British, the *Pax Britannica* was the desired end result, and for many – notably Joseph Chamberlain, colonial secretary in the late 1890s and early 1900s – the means were by and large irrelevant, although the approach had its critics, chiefly from the Left in British politics. Chamberlain, one of the most forceful advocates of the "new imperialism" of the age, reserved his worst contempt for the "little Englanders" who were pessimistic, squeamish, and small-minded about Britain's imperial destiny. As he declared in a speech made in 1897:

> In carrying out this work of civilisation we are fulfilling what I believe to be our national mission ... I do not say that our success has been perfect in every case, I do not say that all our methods have been beyond reproach; but I do say that in almost every instance in which the rule of the Queen has been established and the great Pax Britannica has been enforced, there has come with it greater security to life and property, and a material improvement in the condition of the bulk of the population.

Violence was necessary, however regrettable the resultant deaths might be:

> No doubt ... there has been bloodshed, there has been loss of life among the native populations, loss of still more precious lives among those who have been sent out to bring these countries into some kind of disciplined order, but it must be remembered that that is the condition of the mission we have to fulfil.

"Black tyrants" stood in the way of the mission, and they had to be removed. Chamberlain reminded his audience that "here are, of course, among us ... a very small minority of men who are ready to be the advocates of the most detestable tyrants, provided their skin is black." But he reserved the greatest of his anger for the "imaginary philanthropist" who sat "cosily by his fireside ... denouncing the methods by which British civilization was promoted." Ultimately,

> you cannot have omelettes without breaking eggs; you cannot destroy the practices of barbarism, of slavery, of superstition, which for centuries have desolated the interior of Africa, without the use of force ... [I]f you will fairly contrast the gain to humanity with the price which we are bound to pay for it, I think you may well rejoice in the result of such expeditions ...[16]

It was the classic defense of the arch-imperialist, and it continued to be made by many through the twentieth century; indeed, in our own era, it has its echoes in the arguments made for armed (and of course "humanitarian") interventions across the globe to remove obstacles to economic and political "development."

This imperialism did, however, have its critics. In France, a new imperial strategy aimed at the restoration of national greatness had been championed, for example, by Jules Ferry, prime minister in the early 1880s; but it was the cause of much discomfort in certain quarters. In 1900, the literary magazine *Revue des Deux Mondes* referred to imperialism "creeping unnoticed like bacteria, in the blood of the crowd, poisoning it and weakening its conscience."[17] Much of the blame, however, was laid at the feet of the British. Emile Zola warned of "English" ambitions "to make herself mistress of the most important posts in the world," an ambition which "may lead her to extremes."[18] And in Britain itself, there were deep misgivings.[19] An editorial in *Review of Reviews*, from 1899, opined that "future generations will smile at the glee with which serious statesmen risked war and the wreck of civilization in order to increase the area of the African map over which their country's influence is recognized as supreme." Notably, the piece incorporated a German cartoon which represented the map of Africa as a human skull.[20] Many were especially outraged by British actions during the second Boer War

(1899–1902): the Boers' right to self-determination was vigorously defended by the British left, which worried that the "civilizing mission" was being tarnished. Nonetheless, while the Boers may have excited particular sympathy, the treatment of supposedly ignorant and illiterate African chiefs caused dismay, too. These critics considered the duplicitous and violent treatment of Asante, or the Ndebele, unbecoming of British civilization. Beatrice Webb of the Fabian Society in London deplored the "pecuniary self-interest" of British empire building and wrote damningly of the empire builders themselves, who "have neither the knowledge nor the industry to be professional administrators or skilled soldiers."[21] The idea that British power lacked moral direction was taken up by J. A. Hobson, one of the most articulate critics of imperialism, who in 1902 wrote despairingly of the jingoism of the age and the militaristic tendencies of the largely redundant "leisured classes." Hobson had little doubt as to the inferiority of the "lower races"; his concern was the kind of nation that Britain had become in taking out its excess animal aggression on poorer, weaker, and less developed peoples.[22] The means of destruction employed in the extension of empire undermined the civilizing mission from the outset.[23]

Nonetheless, what most agreed upon was the desirability of bringing progress and order and civilization into the world. Chamberlain believed it could only be done by force; Hobson believed force destroyed the chances of progress from the beginning. They disagreed over the means, but not the end; and neither doubted that there were indeed "backward" and "lower" races in the world which needed saving. Technology brought death, but it must also bring progress; and as we shall see in a later chapter, this would become one of the core concerns of colonial administrations across the continent, namely how technology might be deployed to engender "development" and "modernization" among the benighted peoples of Africa. In reality, however, such "progress" was rather more ambiguous than the killing which had preceded it.

Notes

1 One of the single best accounts remains John Lonsdale, "The European scramble and conquest in African history," in Oliver & Sanderson (eds.), *Cambridge History*, Vol. 6.

2 See for example Wolfgang J. Mommsen, *Theories of Imperialism* (London, 1981); Anthony Brewer, *Marxist Theories of Imperialism: A Critical Survey* (London, 1980).

3 A.J.P. Taylor, *Germany's First Bid for Colonies, 1848–1884* (London, 1938). See also A.J.P. Taylor, *The Struggle for Mastery in Europe, 1848–1918* (Oxford, 1954).

4 For example, F.R. Bridge & Roger Bullen, *The Great Powers and the European States System, 1814–1914* (Harlow, 2005).

5 P.J. Cain & A.G. Hopkins, *British Imperialism 1688–2000* (London, 1993, 2002).

6 R. Robinson & J. Gallagher, *Africa and the Victorians: The Official Mind of Imperialism* (London, 1961).

7 Bernard Porter, *The Absent-Minded Imperialists: What the British Really Thought about Empire* (Oxford, 2004), 165–7.

8 Curtin, *The Image of Africa*; D.A. Lorimer, *Colour, Class and the Victorians: English Attitudes to the Negro in the Mid-Nineteenth Century* (Leicester, 1978); G.W. Stocking, *Victorian Anthropology* (New York, 1987).

9 Burton, *Wanderings in West Africa*; see also M. Daunton & R. Halpern (eds.), *Empire and Others: British Encounters with Indigenous Peoples, 1600–1850* (London, 1999).
10 McCaskie, "Cultural Encounters."
11 Jean-Jacques Rousseau (ed. G. Boroson), *Discourse on the Origin of Inequality* (New York, 2004). See also Adam Kuper, *The Reinvention of Primitive Society: Transformations of a Myth* (Oxford, 2005).
12 In addition to the references in footnote 8, see for example Kiernan, *The Lords of Human Kind*; Edward Said, *Orientalism* (New York, 1978); Paul Rich, *Race and Empire in British Politics* (Cambridge, 1986); Kenan Malik, *The Meaning of Race: Race, History and Culture in Western Society* (New York, 1996).
13 John D. Hargreaves, *Prelude to the Partition of West Africa* (London, 1963), chap. 3.
14 Hilaire Belloc, *The Modern Traveller* (London, 1898).
15 Rudyard Kipling, "The White Man's Burden" (1899), in Elleke Boehmer (ed.), *Empire Writing: An Anthology of Colonial Literature 1870–1918* (Oxford, 1998), 273.
16 Joseph Chamberlain, "The True Conception of Empire" (1897), in Boehmer (ed.), *Empire Writing*, 213–14.
17 Quoted in R. Koebner & H.D. Schmidt, *Imperialism: The Story and Significance of a Political Word, 1840–1960* (London, 1964), 244. Author's translation.
18 In ibid., 244. Author's translation.
19 This was the case at least within those sections of society which were aware of imperial policy: Bernard Porter has argued that many Britons were in fact either unaware of their country's role in the world, or did not care much either way. See *The Absent-Minded Imperialists*. Yet empire clearly had a profound influence on Britain itself: Andrew Thompson, *The Empire Strikes Back? The Impact of Imperialism on Britain from the Mid-nineteenth Century* (London, 2005).
20 B. Harlow & M. Carter (eds.), *Archives of Empire, Vol. II: The Scramble for Africa* (Durham NC, 2003), 81.
21 Beatrice Webb (ed. B. Drake & M. Cole), *Our Partnership* (London, 1948), 194–5.
22 J.A. Hobson, *Imperialism: A Study* (London, 1902, 1938), Part II.
23 See also Bernard Porter, *Critics of Empire: British Radicals and the Imperial Challenge* (London, 2008).

10 Africans Adapting

Conquest and Partition

Explaining the "Conquest"

There was no single European "invasion" of Africa, but rather a multitude of invasions, uncoordinated (on the whole), frequently unconnected (in a continental sense), and often piecemeal.[1] This said, however, from a strictly military point of view, the Scramble for Africa took place with relative ease as far as nineteenth-century colonial campaigns are concerned. Clearly, the desirability of intervention was greatly increased by the ability to do so; greater military difficulty may have led to a reluctance to become involved beyond a certain point, and Africa might have experienced something similar to China in the same period, in other words, hinterland spheres of commercial influence and a system of coastal enclaves. As it happened, conquest was effected by relatively small military forces, generally involving an insignificant commitment of resources and costing very little. There were important exceptions, of course: in Britain's case, the reconquest of the Sudan in the late 1890s was comparatively expensive, as was the second Boer War in Transvaal between 1899 and 1902, which in the end involved more than half a million British troops. But more often, the subjugation of particular areas involved small armies: the French, for example, conquered a swathe of the western savannah using little more than 4,000 soldiers.[2]

Nonetheless, it needs to be borne in mind that these small armies were composed mostly of African soldiers, under the command of European officers. The European partition, in other words, was undertaken using African manpower which had become available owing to massive social and political dislocation across the continent in recent decades. Viewed in the long term, indeed, the Scramble in many ways involved the co-option of Europe into *African* patterns of violent change, the "military revolution"

A History of Modern Africa: 1800 to the Present, Third Edition. Richard J. Reid.

which had been unfolding since the early nineteenth century. African combat skills, in many areas honed in the course of long-term military upheaval, were deployed during the era of imperial expansion, in addition to pools of local knowledge. The turbulence of the nineteenth century had involved heightened levels of violent competition between states and societies, in turn providing Europeans with opportunities to exploit long-running local rivalries; with skill, and some luck, Europeans could exercise considerable local leverage with a minimum of effort. Overall, then, the Scramble must be seen as an extension of Africa's violent – and dynamic – nineteenth century.

The technological disparity between Europe and Africa was clearly significant. In the broadest terms, Europe had enjoyed a growing technological supremacy globally since the fifteenth century; by the nineteenth century, this had become insurmountable for most African and Asian peoples on the receiving end of European imperialism.[3] In particular, the development of military technology, especially in the field of firearms, gave Europe an enormous advantage in the closing decades of the nineteenth century. Increasing range and accuracy of firepower culminated in the development in the 1860s of breech-loading rifles and of machine-guns with rapid-fire mechanisms, the best of which was the Maxim gun, at the end of the 1880s. Breech-loaders and Maxims proved decisive in a number of colonial campaigns, as African armies, whether on foot or horseback, could be cut down before they had a chance to fight at close quarters, a critical European advantage.[4] Caution needs to be exercised here, however: these weapons were not readily available for much of the 1880s and 1890s, and European-led armies frequently made use of older firearms which were only replaced in the course of the 1890s and 1900s. More important, in many respects, was the technological advantage in logistics and communications provided by the steamship and the telegraph.[5]

Many African societies did, of course, possess firearms, and often large numbers of them, as was the case among the coastal West African states, where a range of musketry was in use by the end of the eighteenth century, and in the Ethiopian highlands. Across the Tanzanian and Ugandan interiors, too, states accumulated large numbers of firearms in the second half of the nineteenth century.[6] Often, however, these weapons were obsolete, inaccurate if used without training, and even dangerous. Only in Ethiopia were modern guns successfully acquired: Menelik, first as king of Shoa, then as emperor, accumulated modern weaponry from an array of commercial sources at the southern end of the Red Sea and was able, famously, to defeat the Italians at the battle of Adwa in 1896. Nonetheless, Europe was increasingly unwilling to sell such weaponry to Africans, and in the course of the 1880s and 1890s, several bans were put in place to this effect. The further disadvantage for African societies, of course, was that most societies were unable to manufacture their own guns and ammunition, although there were some interesting exceptions.[7]

The dangers of technological determinism are clear enough, however, and differences in military organization and training were arguably more important than the weaponry itself. Firearms, of course, were generally only effectively used with drill and discipline. While Europeans had professional armies at their disposal, with superior methods of training and structure, African armies tended to be militias rather than regular professional corps, called up when necessary or desirable; with some important

Ethiopian depiction of the battle of Adwa, 1896. © The Trustees of the British Museum. Source: PvE/Alamy Stock Photo.

exceptions, they were not as tightly structured in the field, and placed greater emphasis on individual valor than on collective discipline. In this way, combined with superior firepower, relatively small European forces could overcome often very large African armies. While the Zulu, for example, could successfully ambush an unprepared British force in January 1879, they were no match for the full might of the British army some months later.[8] Again, the Italo-Ethiopian clash at Adwa was the exception, and here the Italians were defeated as much by their own incompetence and the sheer numbers of gun-wielding Ethiopians as by Ethiopian methods, organization, and planning.[9]

In a few areas, guerrilla warfare against European invaders was preferred to the pitched battle in open country, and this certainly made tactical sense given the European advantages outlined previously. In some cases, African guerrillas kept European troops occupied for years. Had these tactics been more broadly applied, it is possible that, while Europeans may not have been driven out, they might eventually have had occasion to consider the implications of long-term commitment, involving ever more money and resources in the prosecution of expensive and draining low-level wars. But in fact, most African societies did not adopt the guerrilla method, in many cases because local economies were unable to withstand the strain of this kind of warfare, especially considering the environmental catastrophes discussed in the next chapter. Only in the 1950s and 1960s would guerrilla wars – often, ironically perhaps, drawing on the inspiration of resistance in the 1880s and 1890s – become more common against some of the continent's more intransigent colonial regimes.

From the European perspective, Africans fought piecemeal, disunited, and uncoordinated, and this weakened resistance from the outset. The premise on which this argument is based, however, is deeply flawed. "Africa" did not exist, except in the European imagination, and thus nor did "Africans"; and accordingly, "they" could hardly have acted in some kind of continental or even regional unison. We continue to use the term for the sake of convenience in the nineteenth-century context, but otherwise, the appellation has no meaning. Clearly Europeans, possessing a larger political and geographical "vision" than was available to Africans, were able to exploit rivalries and divisions between states and societies. Again, the intensification of conflict across nineteenth-century Africa provided leverage for Europeans, and heightened competition meant local allies, manpower, and skills. In sum, Africans had different conceptions of what the European presence meant; Europeans were seen by some as trading partners, or political allies against older local adversaries, and by others as enemies. Sometimes Europeans were seen as protectors and liberators, particularly (and often prematurely) in the context of the abolition of slavery. Much depended on local circumstances. More concerted and unified resistance was possible in Muslim areas, Islam providing a unity unavailable to non-Muslims. The Sanusiyya in the area of modern Libya, notably, resisted the Italians until the 1930s, while swathes of the Algerian interior remained outside French control throughout the nineteenth and much of the twentieth centuries. Even here, however, such unity could be undermined by sectarian rivalry, since the brotherhoods of the desert could clash with one another as much as with the metropolitan infidel.

As for the Scramble itself, it is no straightforward matter to identify the moment at which it can be said to have begun; suffice to say that a series of events between the mid-1870s and the early 1880s accelerated the process by which the continent came under increasing European control and/or influence.[10] These events were fundamentally unconnected; although with the benefit of hindsight, they can be seen to represent different parts of a broader phenomenon. British influence was solidifying in the Gold Coast and Niger Delta, King Leopold of the Belgians was taking an active interest in the Congo basin, and the French were beginning to expand their colony at Senegal, instigating the building of a railway which would eventually link the Senegal settlement to the upper Niger valley. Leopold's involvement in the Congo basin was a cause for concern in both London and Paris; but fundamentally, much of this can be seen in terms of growing rivalry between the British and the French, each perceiving that the other was threatening their commercial position. As the 1880s dawned, meanwhile, events in the nominally Ottoman province of Egypt raised the stakes in this unfolding rivalry. British and French investors were largely in control of Egyptian finances, while it was a French company which controlled the vital Suez Canal; but it was the British government which acted swiftly in 1882 to suppress the nationalist uprising and extend formal political control over the turbulent territory, sparking intense competition with the

French over the Nile Valley. British and French armed parties met at the small town of Fashoda in Sudan in 1896, but a seemingly imminent war was swiftly averted.[11] In another part of North Africa, indeed, European rivalries led to informal influence being transformed into imperial presence. Unwelcome Italian interest in Tunisia, as well as supposed local disturbances, forced the French into seizing Tunis in 1881.[12]

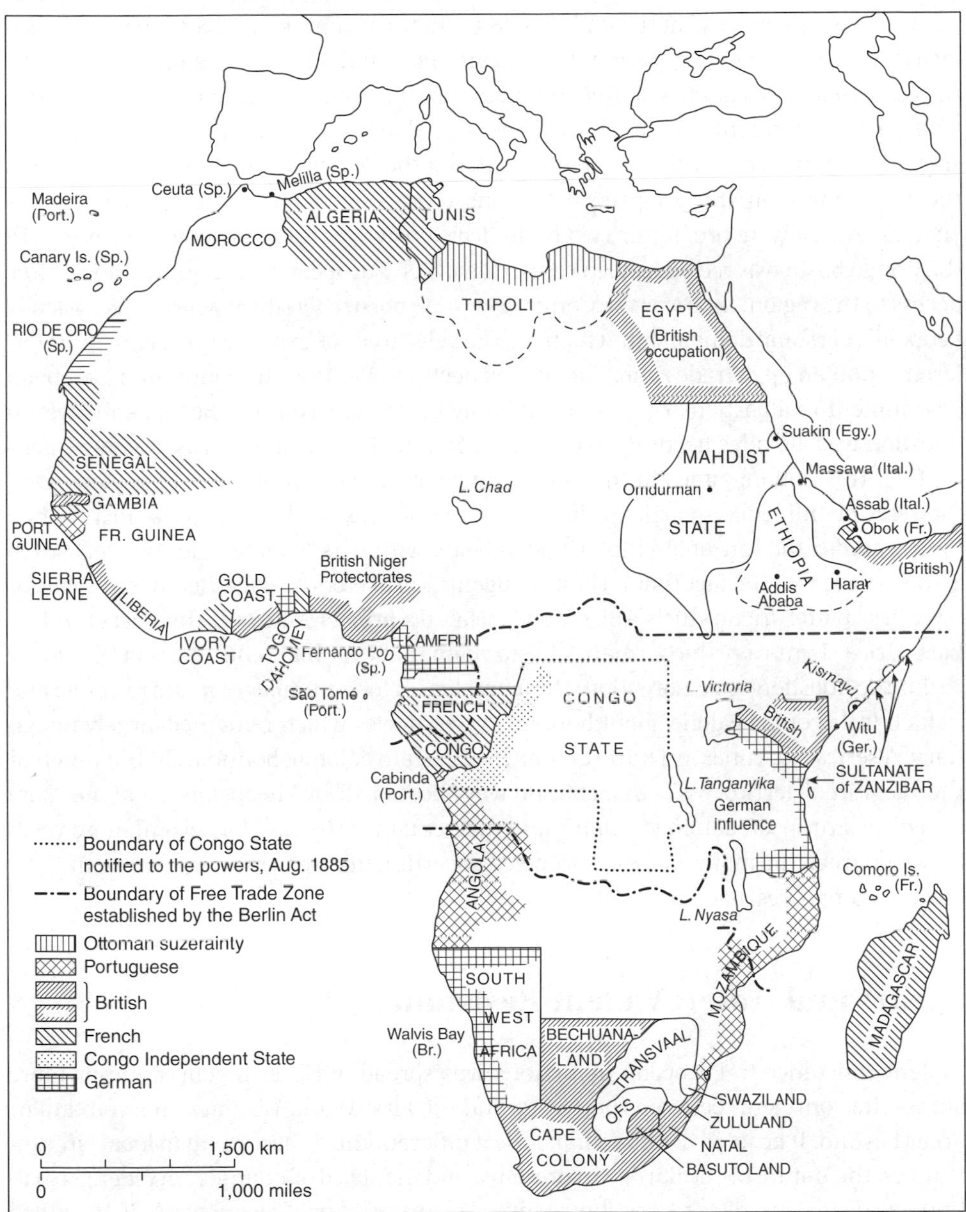

The early phase in the partition of Africa, to c.1887. Source: From R. Oliver and G.N. Sanderson (eds.), *Cambridge History of Africa*. Vol. 6: *1870–1905* (Cambridge, 1985), p. 140, © 1985 by Cambridge University Press. Reprinted with permission from Cambridge University Press.

As for Germany, Bismarck was unconvinced of the usefulness of African colonies but was even more unwilling to see Britain and France acquire more than their fair share. In the early 1880s, the German factor became crucial. In 1884, Bismarck finally declared protectorates over Togo and Cameroon, and over South West Africa; and at the same time, the wily old chancellor called for an international conference to discuss what many feared was becoming a dangerous situation in Africa. The Berlin "West Africa Conference," held at the end of 1884 and the beginning of 1885, was attended by a host of heads of state, national representatives, and other interested parties, and a range of issues was discussed. But the main topics of concern were the threat to "free trade" posed by recent activity on the Niger and Congo rivers and the need to arrive at some form of international agreement regarding the demarcation of boundaries across the continent. From this perspective, the long-term political implications of this conference for Africa were profound. Two main decisions were taken. Leopold's authority in the Congo basin was recognized, in return for which European traders were allowed free access to the region; thus was the Congo Free State born, a territory which was basically Leopold's personal domain, but which was largely "free" of excessive government interference and an open trade zone. The second decision was that the claims of a European government to a particular region would only be recognized if the European power in question was already effectively in control of that region. Bismarck was largely responsible for this notion, aimed in the first instance at undermining the British concept of "spheres of influence," particularly in the area of present-day Tanzania. Britain had long regarded the Tanzanian hinterland as being within its "sphere of influence," but in 1885 – based on the fact that a German agent, Karl Peters, had gathered a number of "treaties" with African chiefs – Bismarck declared a protectorate over this vast chunk of East Africa. Thus were the Germans able to claim that they had "effective occupation."[13] As for the question of demarcation, this rumbled on for a number of years to come, and in fact, little could be done about borders for territories which remained largely imaginary. A series of treaties in 1890–1 confirmed certain colonial boundaries, but much of the "acquired" territory was in fact in no way "occupied" by Europeans, let alone "governed" by European administrations, and this remained the case for several more years in some areas. In many places, European governments were initially represented by trading companies, backed by military force.

Spears and Water: Violent Resistance

Violent resistance to European incursions was spread out over a generation or more across the continent, between the 1880s and the First World War, and in a handful of areas beyond. It erupted in different places at different times, according to local circumstances, the nature of the European presence and the speed of change. An older generation of historians divided resistance into "primary" and "secondary": if so-called "primary" resistance took place in the 1870s and 1880s, then a series of rebellions in the 1890s and 1900s – the Shona and Ndebele in Rhodesia, the "Red Shawls" in Madagascar, the Herero in South West Africa, the Zulu in South Africa, "Maji Maji" in

Tanganyika – constituted "secondary" resistance.[14] Primary resistance, according to this view, tended to be *defensive* in nature, undertaken to maintain sovereignty in the face of foreign encroachment, while secondary resistance was *offensive* because it took place where colonial rule was already established. Primary resistance was led by an "old elite" rooted in the precolonial era, while later rebellions were led by "new" men; primary resistance tended to be secular, while subsequent revolts contained a powerful spiritual dimension. Some of these distinctions are certainly discernible; but in general, the strict demarcation between "primary" and "secondary" is dangerous because in some cases, rebellion erupted where there had been no prior "resistance," and in others, there was a clear line of continuity between various clashes with the colonial power, certainly in the minds of local participants themselves. More broadly, the era of imperial violence between c.1880 and c.1920 must be understood as the culmination of a century of dramatic military and political change across Africa – into which Europe was ultimately co-opted, introducing a number of novel dynamics in the process.

Again, Europeans were often able to exploit local rivalries, as the French discovered when they advanced into the western savannah from the direction of Senegal at the end of the 1870s. The main obstacles to French imperialism in the region were the Tukolor and Mandinke empires, under Ahmadu Seku and Samori respectively, neither of which could set aside their competition for hegemony, and indeed the Tukolor made a series of agreements with the French which they believed secured them against attack. In violation of the agreement, the French built a string of forts across southern Tukolor; yet Ahmadu still harbored hopes of peaceful coexistence, going so far as supporting the French in their campaign against Futa Bondu in the mid-1880s. A Senegalese force, however, attacked the Tukolor in 1889 and had subdued the great Islamic state by 1893. A similar approach – the making of temporary agreements for the sake of convenience – was adopted by the French against the Mandinke, though Samori was in some ways a more formidable opponent than Ahmadu, commanding 30,000 well-armed and trained soldiers. When the French invaded in 1891, Samori was weakened by internal revolt, but he still managed to keep up a mobile resistance for several years. Yet his scorched-earth tactics, while slowing up the French advance, also brought agricultural ruin to the region, and Samori was forced to sue for peace in 1898.[15] Islam, again, facilitated a unity of purpose in resistance to European incursion in the West African savannah, witness the struggle offered to the French by Rabih ibn Fadl Allah in the area of modern Chad. Compact, centralized states were often the easiest to crush, as the French, again, demonstrated in their rapid defeat of Dahomey in 1893; conversely, although the French proclaimed the colony of Cote d'Ivoire in the same year, it was another twenty years before an array of decentralized communities in the forest could be considered subjugated. The British encountered similarly tough resistance among the forest chiefdoms of the Igbo, in southeast Nigeria, many of which refused to acknowledge British suzerainty until 1910. Above all, these expeditions were in many ways self-fueling and took on a momentum of their own.[16]

A British force had conquered Asante in 1874 but had withdrawn for reasons of economy; only in the mid-1890s, with Asante power resurgent and the French advancing into the northern interior, did Britain move inland again, this time establishing a protectorate over the region. The Asante army remained sufficiently intact to confront the British once more in 1900, and only after a brutal struggle was the rising crushed, Britain thereafter proclaiming the colony of the Gold Coast.[17] Meanwhile British influence over the coast of present-day Nigeria was expanding: Lagos had been under direct control since 1861, but by the mid-1880s, this had been extended into a virtual trading monopoly over the Niger Delta under the National African Company. Decisions taken at the Berlin Conference moved Britain to declare a protectorate over the Delta, with the newly formed Royal Niger Company appointed to rule the lower Niger on behalf of the British government. Military campaigns in the area were largely motivated by the desire to remove troublesome middlemen who were seen to be impeding commerce; and through the 1890s, these campaigns were extended deeper into the hinterland, past the northern edge of the forest and into the savannah. As the French discovered further north, the British were able to exploit local rivalries, enabling them to face one opponent at a time. Yoruba territory was conquered during 1892–3; the centralized state of Benin fell, similar to Dahomey, relatively swiftly in 1897, whereupon the British plundered the kingdom's most valued treasures. The Sokoto Caliphate offered more prolonged resistance, the war there lasting between 1900 and 1903.[18]

In some areas, of course, there was no physical "conquest," as such, at least not initially. Rather, there was the making of "treaties" which African chiefs regarded, no doubt, as pacts of friendship but which European agents carried back as evidence of effective occupation. Thus did the French explorer de Brazza lay the foundations for his country's claims over a swathe of the Congo basin by concluding a treaty in 1880 with the Tio chief Makoko, who, it was claimed implausibly, had ceded sovereignty to France. Further south, Henry Morton Stanley was forcing his way down the Congo River, and in so doing represented the Belgian monarch Leopold II's interests. In all probability, Makoko believed the treaty he signed with de Brazza gave him an ally against proxy Belgian encroachment. Either way, at the Berlin Conference, the French claimed territory north of the lower Congo, and de Brazza was dispatched to collect more treaties from chiefs who were offered gifts of cloth, manufactured goods, and alcohol. Certainly, as with Makoko, these chiefs had little understanding of the treaties' implications. By the end of the 1880s, de Brazza had used a Senegalese force to establish an administrative and commercial presence; but there was little resistance from Africans, largely because there was little to resist. So it was further northeast, where by the early 1890s the French had (on paper at least) established the equatorial colonies of Gabon, Middle Congo, and Ubangui-Chari, meaningless boundaries scything through tropical forest and savannah; again, Africans scarcely noticed, and only later took up arms with the arrival of commercial companies.[19]

While the French were carving out territory in the equatorial zone, further south Stanley's adventures in the Congo basin had established the Congo Free State for his employer Leopold, officially recognized at the Berlin Conference. It was a vast personal empire, bizarre in shape and violent in nature, stretching from the Atlantic to the Great Lakes. Arab traders in the east quickly found themselves isolated from Zanzibar, and the opportunistic Tippu Tip accepted the governorship of the eastern provinces; the lucrative ivory trade now flowed west instead of east, its direction through much of the nineteenth century. Yet many Arabs and other coastal traders were not yet reconciled to Belgian overlordship, represented by the largely mercenary Force Publique, and resented the restrictions placed on their commercial activities. Their resistance was largely overcome in the early 1890s and marked the transition from one era of hegemony to another.[20] In any case, Zanzibar itself was no longer the force it had been and had problems of its own: British support for the sultanate was diminishing by the end of the 1870s, and by the mid-1880s, the Germans had muscled in on the region. Karl Peters did the job for Bismarck in central East Africa which de Brazza had done for the French government further west, and in 1885, Germany declared a protectorate over present-day Tanzania. An agreement with Britain and the (almost) straight line which resulted demarcated German from British East Africa (Kenya), and as in other areas a private company was given responsibility to administer the territory on behalf of the German government. It was a violent administration. The Germans were compelled to overcome Unyanyembe by force, while demands for tax and labor provoked resistance across the territory. A major uprising by the Swahili along the coast in 1888–9 was only crushed following the arrival of reinforcements, at which point the German government took over direct control of the colony. The Hehe in the south fought until the end of the 1890s. In the north, the resistance put up by the Maasai, however, was greatly weakened by the rinderpest epidemic sweeping down from northeast Africa.[21]

It was in the southeast of the territory, however, that the Germans were later confronted with their greatest challenge. The Maji Maji revolt erupted in July 1905 as pressure mounted from the colonial authorities to grow cotton for export. Farmers were forced to abandon their own cultivation, often at a critical point in the agricultural calendar, and saw little profit in return for the cotton they produced. The rebellion spread rapidly over a wide area; yet there is little evidence of prior planning, and it appears to have been genuinely spontaneous, nor was there any central leadership or command structure directing the insurgency. Religious ideology, however, represented by priests across the territory provided coherence, facilitating unity, and encouraging a belief in the supernatural to overcome European weaponry. The word *maji* referred to a supposedly magical water which was sprinkled on the body and which would provide immunity against German bullets. Belief in the spirit world brought unprecedented unity and made rebels confident of success; however, after some initial, and rapid, gains – the Germans were caught wholly unaware – colonial military superiority made itself felt, and belief in the potency of the *maji* was quickly undermined. Through 1906, disunity and German scorched-earth tactics weakened the revolt, which was finally crushed early the following year. The cost had been horrendous: 26,000 Africans had died, and upwards of a further 50,000 may have perished in the famine which resulted from scorched-earth tactics. In the aftermath, however, the Germans took care not to provoke another uprising, committing more resources to development, and mission schools and clinics, in particular; many farmers in the former rebel areas took to growing cotton voluntarily, suggesting that the violence had not been in protest at the cultivation of cotton in itself, but the coercion involved. Importantly, however, the revolt demonstrated, however briefly, the potential for multiethnic anti-colonial protest over a wide area, and as such, Maji Maji served as an inspiration for a later generation of Tanganyikan nationalists.[22]

For some societies, the European presence was strategically advantageous. At the north end of Lake Victoria, the Imperial British East Africa Company (IBEAC) sought to establish influence over the Protestant elite in Buganda, a kingdom which at the dawn

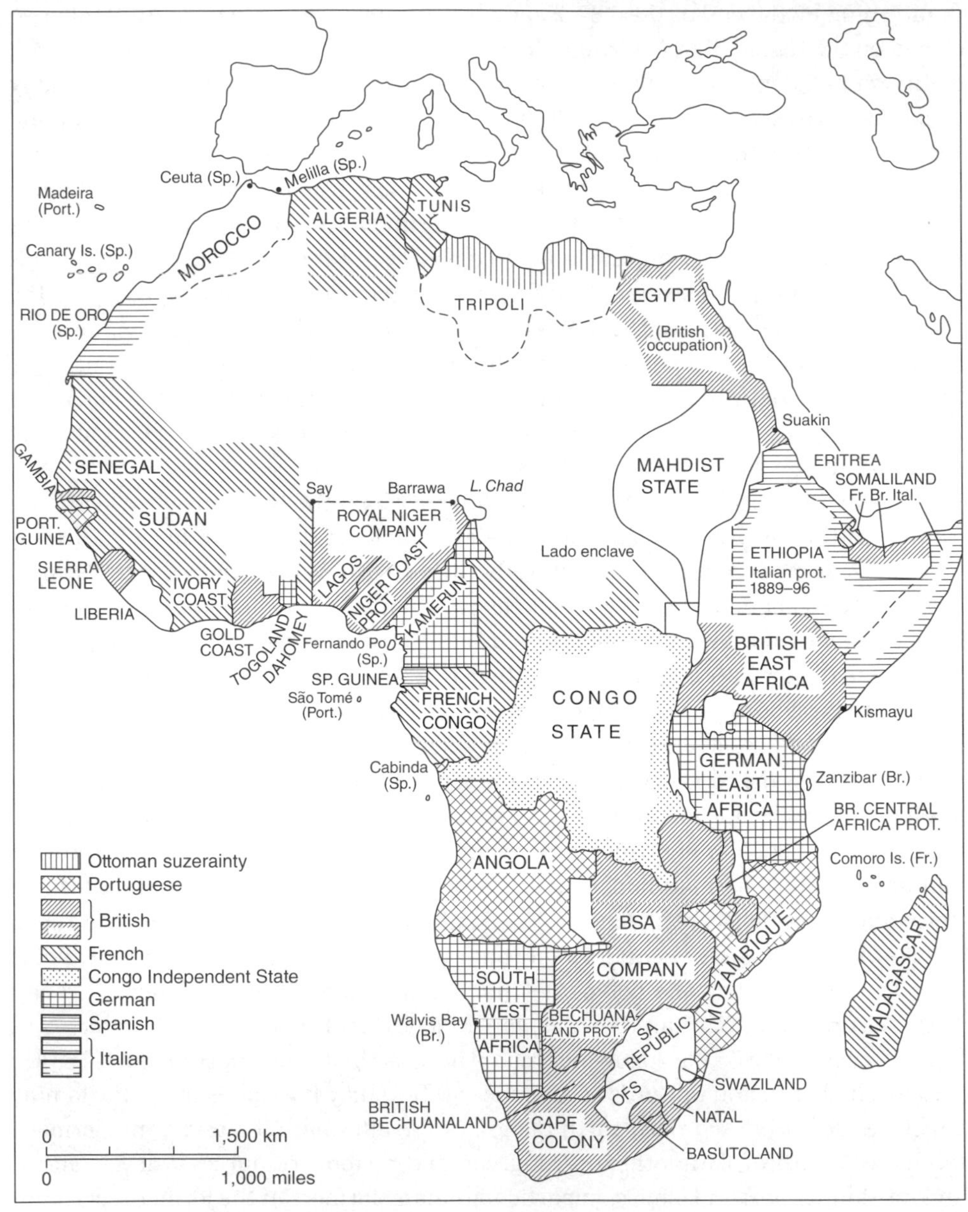

The partition continued: Africa c.1895. Source: From R. Oliver and G.N. Sanderson (eds.), *Cambridge History of Africa*. Vol. 6: *1870–1905* (Cambridge, 1985), p. 146, © 1985 by Cambridge University Press. Reprinted with permission from Cambridge University Press.

of the 1890s was still fragile following the "religious wars" which had seen the deposal, then restoration, of the unstable Mwanga. The young Lugard allied himself to this elite, which came to value British assistance in bolstering its own position; when the IBEAC experienced financial difficulties in 1893–4, the British government – somewhat reluctantly, and following some vigorous lobbying at home – declared a protectorate over "Uganda." In the course of the 1890s, the Ganda assisted politically and militarily in the subjugation of surrounding kingdoms, including Bunyoro, Toro, and Ankole. Nyoro resistance in particular was determined and continued until the late 1890s, by which time Mwanga had also attempted to stage his own revolt against the British, and was exiled – along with his old adversary, Kabarega of Bunyoro – to the Seychelles for his trouble. Mwanga's insurrection notwithstanding, Buganda was regarded as the ideal subimperial agency in the region and was rewarded with a favored status within the protectorate.[23] The IBEAC was also active in British East Africa – the future Kenya – but here too the government soon took over direct control, in 1895. As they had in Tanganyika, the coastal Swahili rose up – the "Mazrui rebellion" – for several months against the British; as in French central Africa; however, there was initially little violence of note in the Kenyan interior, largely because the implications of European rule did not become clear until the early 1900s, with the building of the railway from the coast to Uganda and the arrival of the first white settlers.[24]

Across tropical Africa, a combination of political paranoia, commercial optimism, and geopolitical jostling drove the carve-up forward; but in southern Africa, economics were at the heart of a regional scramble for territory, which in many respects represents a unique set of circumstances. The "mineral revolution" defined the modern history of southern Africa, beginning with the discovery of huge diamond fields between 1869 and 1871 to the north of Cape Colony, in territory governed by independent African chiefdoms but claimed by neighboring Boer "republics." As thousands of speculators flooded the region, the Cape government resolved to take the territory for itself: following the decision of a land court that a local Griqua chief was the rightful owner of the land, the same chief requested Boer protection, but the British swiftly annexed the area anyway, naming it "Griqualand West." The role of capital, backed by British political power, now became critical: although initially worked by individual diggers employing African labor, the mines by the late 1870s had become enormous open pits requiring machinery to exploit them effectively. Only companies with the necessary capital could provide this machinery, and within a decade, the entire diamond area had come under the control of a single such company, De Beers, with close links to the government at the Cape. The process witnessed the rapid growth of a cash economy: the city of Kimberley emerged swiftly, offering a market for agricultural produce, an opportunity to which both African and European farmers responded readily. This in itself led to renewed competition over the best arable land. Particularly significant for the future development of the region, however, was the expansion of migrant labor, as Africans flooded the Kimberley area in search of work: 50,000 a year were employed in the Kimberley mines in the 1870s.[25]

The balance of power between African and Europe that had been achieved in the middle decades of the nineteenth century was now shattered, as the British looked to create a southern African federation whose prosperity would be guaranteed by diamonds; an important part of this plan was the destruction of remaining African kingdoms, and also the exclusion of circling European rivals. In 1877–8, for example, the Xhosa did much as they had done in the eighteenth and early nineteenth centuries and put up such determined resistance that the British were forced to abandon the attempt to seize any more Xhosa territory, at least in the interim; the Xhosa were left with a substantial amount of "reserve" land.[26] The greatest threat to white hegemony, however, came from the Zulu, under the rule of Cetshwayo since 1872. In January 1879, a small British force advanced into the kingdom but was largely wiped

"The aftermath at Omdurman," from the *Illustrated London News*, 1898. Source: Reproduced with permission of Mary Evans/ILN Pictures.

out at the battle of Isandlwana; this was a blow both to plans for federation and to British pride, although after several months' campaigning, a reinforced British army eventually defeated the Zulu army and captured Cetshwayo. Britain effectively destroyed the Zulu kingdom in its nineteenth-century guise, dividing the polity into several parts; violent factionalism led to civil war, the tragedy of which was compounded by famine, and in 1887, Zululand became a crown colony. The Zulu would violently confront the state one more time, through the Bambatha uprising in 1906, which was quickly crushed.[27]

In the meantime, the Boers remained a problem. In 1877, by mutual agreement, Britain had annexed Transvaal, weakened by its sporadic conflicts with the Zulu; but within three years, the Boers decided British "protection" was no longer necessary and, resentful of both lost sovereignty and heavy taxation, launched a rebellion in 1880 which again – as with setbacks against the Zulu the previous year – exposed certain British military weaknesses. In 1881, Britain withdrew from Transvaal, no longer prepared to accept the cost and effort which the creation of a federation would evidently entail. Yet the situation was further complicated when in 1886 gold was found in central Transvaal. Subsequent industrial development was on an even more dramatic scale than that witnessed at Kimberley. Johannesburg swiftly became the largest city in sub-Saharan Africa, and by the early 1890s, gold mining was concentrated in the hands of a small group of large companies. Political tensions heightened dramatically. The Germans had already established a presence in adjacent South West Africa, following which Britain moved to annex the Tswana chiefdoms, who had requested protection against the Boers, amalgamating these into the protectorate of "Bechuanaland" (modern Botswana) in 1885. Following the discovery of gold, Britain became concerned to prevent a regional linkup between the Germans and the Transvaal Boers, seen by many (including the Germans and the Boers) as a "natural alliance." At the same time, President Kruger of Transvaal imposed heavy taxes on the *uitlanders* (foreigners) in whose hands gold-mining largely rested and who were denied full political rights. Rhodes sought to topple the Kruger government, but the chief consequence of the abortive and embarrassing "Jameson raid" of 1895 was heightened anti-British feeling inside Transvaal. Britain pressured Kruger to introduce reforms favorable to British interests, and to grant political rights to *uitlanders*, while at the same British forces massed on the Transvaal border; Kruger's declaration of war in October 1899 sparked the second major conflict between the British and the Boers within twenty years. There were early victories for the Boers, and blunders on the part of the British which prompted some national soul-searching; reinforced by some 500,000 men, however, the British force had captured the key Boer towns by the middle of 1900 and employed scorched-earth tactics and concentration camps to subdue the population. The Boers sued for peace in 1902, but the flames of "Afrikaner" nationalism had been fanned by British brutality. This was true despite the fact that Britain now sought to accommodate the Boers, and in 1910, Boer republics and British colonies were joined under the Union of South Africa. Continued white domination of the region was assured, but political conflict between the two white communities would also continue to fester, to the detriment of the African.[28]

Mineral discoveries, moreover, inspired imperial avarice, fueled by dreams of wealth in the deeper interior. British industrialist Cecil Rhodes became seized by the notion that more gold lay north of the Limpopo, in the region of the ancient Zimbabwe kingdom, and by this time inhabited by the Shona and Ndebele. King Lobengula of the Ndebele kingdom was tricked into signing away rights over his own territory to Rhodes' British South Africa Company (BSAC), which moved into the area in force in the early 1890s, laying the foundations for the colony which Rhodes modestly named Rhodesia (later Southern Rhodesia) with the backing of the British government. In 1890, the first armed column occupied a swathe of Shona territory and established farms. But expectations of gold deposits were soon disappointed, although in their frantic search, they caused irreparable archeological damage. The Ndebele were worsted in a serious clash with the pioneer farmers in 1893; in 1896–7, both Shona and Ndebele rose against the occupiers in a rebellion – known as the "Chimurenga" – which came close to expelling the white colonists from the territory, but Rhodes received reinforcements from the Cape, and the insurgents were eventually subdued. The spirit of the uprising lingered, however, and – as with Maji Maji in Tanganyika a few years later – a later generation of Zimbabwean nationalists would draw on the memory of it to historicize their own struggle.[29]

The BSAC was also instrumental in the subjugation of modern Malawi, where the Central African Protectorate (Nyasaland according to a later appellation) was proclaimed in 1889, in part to offset Portuguese advances from Mozambique. Harry Johnston's small force clashed with the Yao, Swahili, Chewa, and Ngoni in the course of the 1890s, confrontations which were justified in the name of suppressing the slave trade but which resulted in the crushing of the chief African polities in the region. Johnston continued the "pacification" work of the BSAC in the area of Northern Rhodesia (modern Zambia), too, where the Bemba – weakened by their sudden commercial isolation – were overcome relatively easily and where the Ngoni experienced the Maxim gun at first hand.[30] The violence employed by the British was mirrored elsewhere in the region. The Portuguese themselves used African armies to extend authority in Mozambique, to the extent that this was as much a series of inter-African wars exploited by Portuguese officers as it was a Portuguese "conquest," and the situation in Angola was not much different: here, however, armed resistance was robust, and it was really only by the beginning of the First World War that Portugal could claim to be in control of the territory.[31] The Germans were also involved in brutal wars of conquest against the Herero and Nama in South West Africa, and eventual victory was in large part facilitated by the cattle disease which devastated pastoral economies. The Herero revolted in 1904 and were once again crushed with appalling violence – nothing less than genocide – although it took until 1907 to do so.[32]

According to most standard accounts, the era of the Scramble was largely over by the early 1900s. But in Angola and among the Somalis, resistance continued until the First World War and the 1920s respectively, and only then could these territories be considered in any way "pacified." In British Somaliland, Sayyid Muhammad Abdille Hassan fought the foreign invaders until his death of natural causes in 1920, while the Italians did not subdue the northern part of their own Somali territory until the end of the decade.[33] Libya was not formalized as an Italian colonial territory until the period between 1911 and the First World War with the military conquest of Tripolitania and Cyrenaica, and even then, as we have noted, the Sanusiyya in Libya kept Italian colonial armies (Eritreans among their number) occupied well into the 1930s. The Qadiriyya lurked in the Algerian Sahara and defied the French for many years. Morocco was only

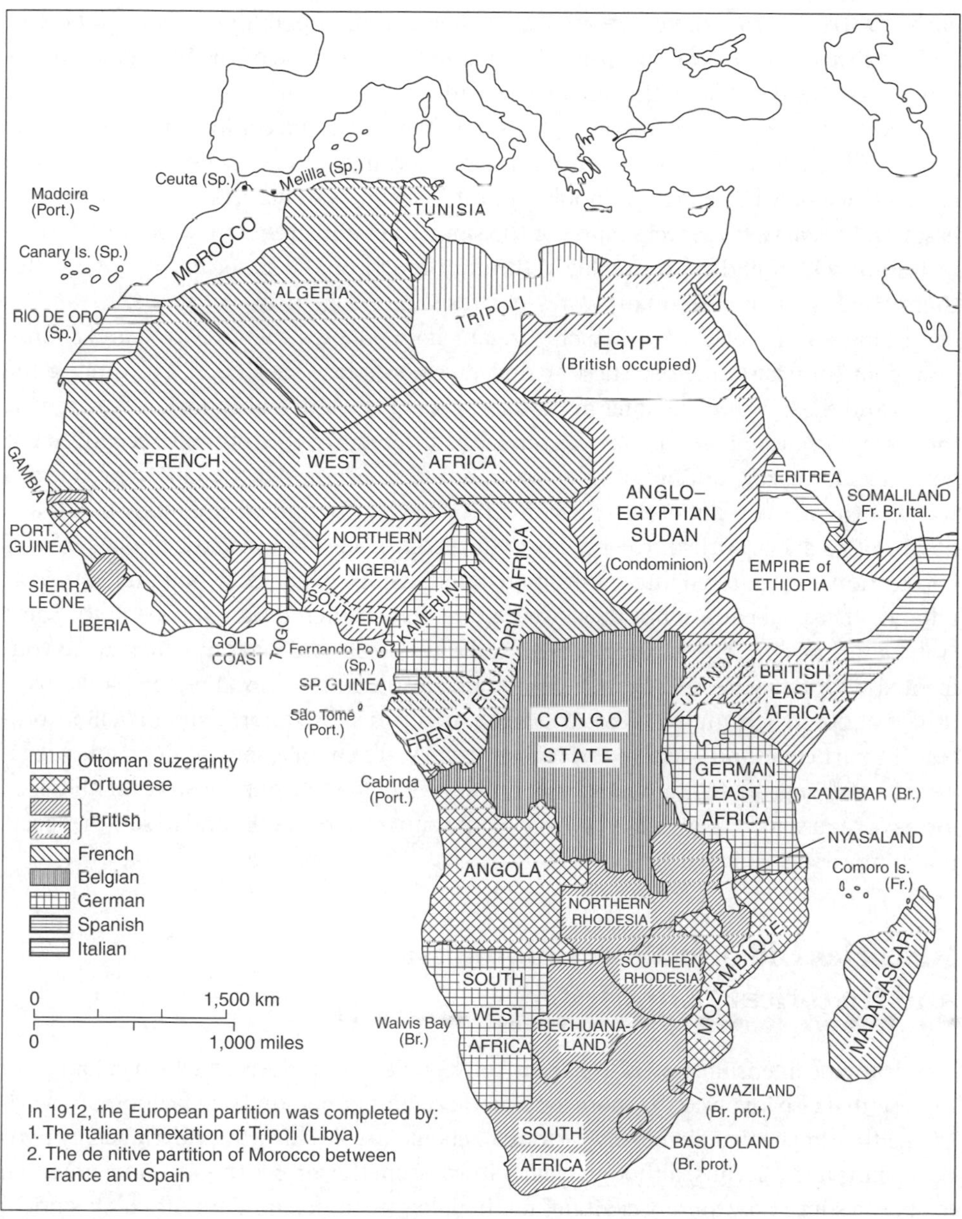

Partition complete: Africa c.1902. Source: From R. Oliver and G.N. Sanderson (eds.), *Cambridge History of Africa*. Vol. 6: *1870–1905* (Cambridge, 1985), p. 152, © 1985 by Cambridge University Press. Reprinted with permission from Cambridge University Press.

brought under European control in 1912, Spain taking the northern coastal portion and France the rest, following a period of intense rivalry which the Germans had attempted to exploit. But resistance against both European powers was sustained into the 1920s, and indeed beyond in the case of the French; the Spanish were confronted with the guerrilla tactics of 'Abd al-Karim in the Rif until his defeat and surrender in 1926, and France could not claim full control of Saharan Morocco much before the early 1930s.[34] Across the entire region, outside the metropolitan centers and beyond coastal strips and areas of European settlement, the deserts belonged very much to the same people as they had in the nineteenth century.

Overall, "resistance" is in many respects a problematic term, conjuring up a simplistic image of the African warrior pointing his spear proudly but senselessly at modernity. His violence may be somehow "noble," but it is savage and atavistic, and his defeat is assured. In reality, these were many of the same wars and attendant processes of militarization which had been unfolding through much of the nineteenth century. But there were, in any case, many ways of "resisting," which we must understand as describing a range of ways in which Africans both adapted themselves to and shaped new political environments. These included requests for "protection," as among the Sotho and the Tswana, and later in the case of King Lewanika of Bulozi. A Eurocentric interpretation would see this as a surrender of sovereignty, the ultimate recognition of colonial supremacy; but neither the Sotho nor the Tswana nor the Lozi viewed it this way. For them, it was about the *preservation* of sovereignty, and an eminently pragmatic means of so doing. African rulers may at times have failed to grasp the implications of "protection" and entered into subordinate relationships which they had understood as alliances between equals; but these were nonetheless entered into in good faith. Some states and societies chose to fight from the outset, especially those which were confronted with an aggressive European presence in the initial period of the "scramble"; others chose to fight much later. As developments in subsequent years indicate, "protest" in particular and "adaptation" more broadly are complex phenomena and take a variety of forms. In subsequent chapters, we will come to examine some of these, as forms of "resistance" became ever less violent, rather more subtle, and in some respects much more sophisticated.

Histories Old and New: Colonialism and Historical "Knowledge"

The dramatic intensification of relations between Europe and Africa which colonialism represented also involved the more systematic accumulation and codification of *knowledge*, either implicitly or explicitly historical, about Africa. This was undertaken by both Europeans and Africans, although clearly it was from the former that the impetus came to apply a supposedly more "scientific" methodology to understanding Africa's historical and "ethnographic" development. The phenomenon was absolutely crucial to the colonial system and indeed has had repercussions far beyond the achievement of African independence. The attempt to historicize African society was not novel in the late nineteenth and early twentieth centuries; there was a long tradition of this in European writing about Africa, as many travelers, missionaries, and armchair geographers alike sought to produce "ethnographic" studies, descriptions of "tribes" and customs, histories of wars and great leaders. At the end of the eighteenth century, for example, James Bruce's mammoth account of a journey to Ethiopia included an entire volume dedicated to the history of the region[35]; at the same time, on the other side of the continent, the slave trader Archibald Dalzel wrote his *History of Dahomy*, which was largely a pro-slave trade polemic and in which the historical reconstruction was aimed at demonstrating the kingdom's innate savagery.[36] While these histories were driven by particular interests – support for a cause and self-aggrandizement – they represent an early attempt to represent "historical fact" and to produce "incontestable knowledge."

In the mid-nineteenth century, as exploration gathered pace, so the historical narrative became increasingly common. Nowhere is this more dramatically demonstrated than in the East African Great Lakes region, where in the early 1860s, Speke drew up the first king-list for Buganda and the surrounding area as part of what he called the "legendary history" of the region. Speke described how the kingdom of Buganda was formed by an invasion of lighter-skinned peoples from the north, which came to be known as the "Hamitic myth": statehood and anything approaching "civilization" in the area (i.e. the Ganda kingdom) had its origins, in effect, *outside* Africa. Speke, albeit in a rudimentary way, had set the parameters for the region's history.[37] Several years later, Stanley devoted a little more time to the reconstruction of Buganda's history, and expanded Speke's king-list to a remarkable thirty-five monarchs, describing their stories with customary panache.[38] More lists followed: through the 1870s and 1880s, missionaries and travelers produced their versions, sometimes with minor differences, but each clearly contributing to what was becoming a body of "received knowledge." The "history of Buganda" was taking shape, and in the early 1890s, the CMS missionary Robert Ashe produced the first explicitly historical account of the kingdom, his *Chronicles of Uganda*.[39]

Crucially, this was a process over which African elites had an enormous amount of control. Various lineages, political groupings, and significant political figures had their own versions of Buganda's past, and put these forward when given the opportunity to do so. In the 1890s, orality gave way to literacy, as chiefs in a position to do so were able to commit to writing versions of the past and key historical "truths," and hence make important claims about the kingdom's present. Access to the written word meant power, as literacy gave rise to dominant narratives and received wisdoms which, once written, appeared to have permanence and rectitude, especially in a technophile society such as Buganda. This is most clearly exemplified in the case of Apolo Kagwa, chief minister of Buganda in the early period of colonial rule, Christian convert and close friend of missionaries and governor alike. When he wrote his *Kings of Buganda* in the early 1900s, he was able to put into writing his preferred (and the dominant) version of the Ganda past. At times, his book bore a close resemblance to the Bible, the other major text of the age in the Luganda language, the significance of which was enormous. The Bible was understood by Christian Ganda to be "absolute truth," and thus, the literary form was in turn held to facilitate the expression of absolute truth in a way that mere orality did not; and Kagwa's book is indeed Biblical in form. It has a Genesis-style opening – complete with a

Ganda take on the Fall of Man through the misdemeanors of woman – and its genealogical format reads like Old Testament scripture, with descriptions of the Ganda kingdom's highs and lows unfolding like the triumphs and travails of the Israelites; its judgments of particular kings and princes are moral and righteous. Kagwa knew his Bible; and he also knew he had rivals in the Ganda political establishment under the British with their different versions of the kingdom's past. His *Kings of Buganda* can thus be seen as an attempt to write those rivals out of the political scene and place the absolute truth before all.[40] A West African example of the production of historical truth in written form is the Reverend Samuel Johnson's weighty tome, *The History of the Yorubas*. Johnson, a Yoruba himself, attempted to place in both moral and historical focus the evolution of the Yoruba people, their trials and tribulations, and destiny expressed in the form of a narrative that again was clearly inspired by acquaintance with the scriptures.[41]

While Kagwa was attempting, through historical "knowledge," to clearly define an extant Ganda "state," to strengthen the balance of power within the new colonial framework, Johnson, in clarifying the meaning of the Yoruba as a distinct historic and "national" identity, was building on earlier missionary innovations in thus defining the Yoruba. Through the spread of literacy, and the endeavors of missionaries to translate the Bible into vernaculars, "ethnic" or "national" identities were being formed around language; the Yoruba, such as Johnson was defining them, had scarcely existed before the middle of the nineteenth century, and yet his account of their history was meant as the definitive statement on Yoruba identity and place in the modern world. Language and literacy, in other words, had led to the production of new forms of "knowledge" about identity, loyalty, and belonging. In a somewhat different context, the Ganda Christian elite (especially Protestant) was articulating to the British a particular interpretation of their own "national" history. The Ganda did not "resist" colonialism in the traditional sense of that word, excepting Kabaka Mwanga's brief and doomed rebellion in 1897; they did not need to. They used the creation and manipulation of historical "knowledge" to consolidate and indeed advance their position within the Uganda Protectorate. Their ability to articulate a "great state" history, to provide the British with a historical narrative which described and justified their dominant position in the region, was an important factor in persuading the British to award Buganda a similarly dominant – indeed greatly enhanced – position in the colonial state, at the expense of other, less well-regarded precolonial entities such as Bunyoro. Historical "knowledge," again, meant current power. In a variation on the theme, Asante in West Africa in the second half of the nineteenth century had been a state in crisis: dynastic conflict, for example, had led many Asante to flee to the British territory on the coast, where they exposed themselves to commerce and British cultural influences. In exile, they agitated for, and finally supported, the British invasion of the state in the 1890s – and as they did so they won access to the prestigious positions of chiefly power in Asante. After 1900, the British used these people to govern the newly conquered territory, and these supposedly progressive, intelligent, and commercially motivated individuals were now regarded as being "ideologically reconciled" to the new imperial order. It is clear that British overlords relied heavily on these chiefs to carry out the day-to-day governing of the territory for them – and in this sense the relationship between African chief and white overlord was based on the ignorance of the latter.[42]

The African initiative in the generation of such "knowledge" is clear enough. This was not merely a question of "invention," moreover; these were histories ready for the telling, and the re-telling. But their production was also spurred by the desire – indeed, the *need* – on the part of Europeans in the late nineteenth and early twentieth centuries to peer into the seeming abyss that was Africa's past and to make sense of it, to study and understand the African "condition" in historical context. In one sense this was an extension of the earlier endeavors of explorers to reduce the "wild" and "exotic" African landscape to a comprehensible set of data, to have mountain ranges marked and crossed, rivers traced, lakes named, and navigated. This was as critical an element of control as the possession of superior weaponry. The period either side of 1900, thus, saw the first serious application of the disciplines of history, anthropology, ethnography to Africa, notwithstanding the fact – discussed in the introductory chapter – that of course Africans were not really believed to have a history as such, at least not in the European sense of the term. To lack writing was to lack history, and for this reason, Ethiopia drew a certain measure of admiration, as did the Arabic-speaking northern zones of the continent; indeed such cultural anomalies as Ethiopia and Egypt were more easily understood if they were simply detached from the rest of Africa, which is precisely what happened. More broadly, Africans had "myths" and "legends," among which Europeans had to discern some indication of relative sophistication.

For Europeans, the acquisition of such "understanding" was a core component of the imperial mission, and, as with the domination of the landscape, reinforced notions about European supremacy – ironically, given that Africans saw the process rather differently. It also had an eminently practical function: in studying Buganda, for example, or the Tutsi in Rwanda and Burundi, or the Yoruba in Nigeria, Europeans were identifying appropriately "advanced" groups through which to govern and who could be the agencies of imperialism. The colonial project could hardly have functioned without them. In turn, Africans responded to this demand by cultivating histories and manipulating their own knowledge-bases: knowledge, like cash crops, was supplied according to the needs of the new political market. Thus, the era between the 1880s and 1920s – a period of considerable political and social upheaval – was an era of "histories in the making"; and the cultivation of knowledge at this time would in some areas fundamentally shape the colonial state and define the colonial experience.

Realities Old and New: Colonialism and Political "Knowledge"

The early colonial state depended on "knowledge of the native" and was to a very real degree shaped around what was perceived to be the nature of African political structures, styles of leadership, sense of "tradition." In developing historical knowledge, African ruling groups sought to articulate notions of regional dominance and hierarchy, and in so doing adapted themselves to new political and social realities. In many ways, this was a process of *reinvention*; this is not to suggest that all such histories and articulations were based on falsehoods, however, but rather that they often represented reconstructions – or, perhaps, the repackaging – of older identities and remembrances. From the European perspective, meanwhile, elites, "states," and indigenous structures were often identified as suitable means through which to govern, and such elites sometimes even became "partners" in the colonial project. Thus, "knowing the native" was crucial to the creation of a stable political system, and for Africans, "knowing the European" was vital to repositioning and advancement within the new order.

Frederick Lugard was one of Britain's great imperial practitioners, having been instrumental in the creation of two key sub-Saharan territories, Uganda and Nigeria. In his classic explanation of the British imperial mission, *The Dual Mandate in British Tropical Africa*, first published in 1923, he declared:

> It was the task of civilisation to put an end to slavery, to establish Courts of Law, to inculcate in the natives a sense of individual responsibility, of liberty, and of justice ... above all, to see to it that the system of education should be such as to produce happiness and progress. I am confident that the verdict of history will award high praise to the efforts and the achievements of Great Britain in the discharge of these great responsibilities. For, in my belief, under no other rule ... does the African enjoy such a measure of freedom and of impartial justice, or a more sympathetic treatment, and for that reason I am a profound believer in the British Empire and its mission in Africa.[43]

At the heart of this "success" was the system of indirect rule. In essence, the system involved governance through indigenous chiefs and extant hierarchies, following imperial "conquest" whether violent or peaceful. In this sense, there was nothing especially novel about indirect rule: it is an ancient mechanism of governance, utilized by empires across time and space. Under the British, however – and to a lesser degree the French – it was elevated to a political philosophy, and one of the central tenets of the civilizing mission; the British were proud, moreover, of its intrinsic flexibility and pragmatic nature, which were held to be virtues and not simply reflections of expedience. Each subject kingdom and society, each province or district, was to be governed according to its needs and its own practices; and where these were somehow inappropriate or indeed lacking entirely, colonialism would amend or introduce them accordingly. There seemed no better way to inculcate in the "native" a sense of deference and tradition, to open him up to the influences of European civilization, than to make him a part of it, and on his own terms. Of course, the system could only work through the development of some "knowledge" of the "native" himself, and the system certainly *implied* such knowledge, derived in large part from the historical constructions which were emerging in this period. Yet it is crucial to keep in mind that this was above all a partnership between "governed" and "governing"; it was in many respects a two-way relationship, each side informing (or misinforming) the other, if at times unwittingly.

In some respects, indirect rule was also the culmination of ongoing racial debates, with their roots in the nineteenth century. Here, it is important to note the concepts of "assimilation" and "association." According to assimilationist thinking in the earlier nineteenth century, African cultures were flawed, inefficient, and backward, but they were also ultimately improvable. Through commerce and Christianity, Africans could be "saved," and Sierra Leone was the laboratory in which this grand theory could be tested. There was limited success, as the colony did indeed produce "black Englishmen" of a certain kind, among them clergymen who carried the gospel across the region. In Senegal, the French attempted something similar: here, following the 1848 revolution, Africans were declared to be citizens of France and accordingly awarded representation in the National Assembly. The belief was that Africans could be fully assimilated into European culture, given the correct tutelage.[44]

However, in the second half of the century, there was a shift away from assimilation and toward "association," in both Britain and France. Racial attitudes hardened from the 1860s and 1870s, as we have seen, and Richard Burton was one of those who despaired at the inability of "Europeanized" Africans to do anything other than to mimic, to simply go through the motions, looking ridiculous and making a mockery of European culture. While in Senegal, the majority of Africans became "subjects" rather than citizens – the privilege of citizenship was restricted to a minority of permanent residents in the coastal towns – Sierra Leone was regarded as a failure; and although a Senegalese elite might continue to progress through the French higher education system and into the upper echelons of French culture, they were merely a reminder that the vast majority could only be associated with, not assimilated into, European civilization. Distance was placed between the European and the African and that distance would remain no matter how much the latter attempted to emulate the former.

To a considerable extent, the philosophy was evident in indirect rule, which systematized distance between ruler and ruled, although the methods of applying these general (and often unspoken) principles were complex and varied across the continent. For the British, it originated among the Hausa and Fulani of northern Nigeria. Having subdued the Sokoto Caliphate by military means between 1900 and 1903, Lugard transferred substantial authority back to the emirs. The latter were obliged to recognize that they were part of a unified, hierarchical system at the apex of which was the British crown; indeed, as in India, this led to a royal "cult" of a sort in some areas. The Fulani were prepared to come to such an understanding with the British: they themselves were relative newcomers to political power, which dated, as we have seen, to the jihad of the early nineteenth century and to work within the framework of British imperial power cemented their position – especially as the British were prepared to treat Islam in the region with considerable respect. Indeed, the Sokoto Caliphate was influenced in its approaches to the British by two further considerations. Firstly, the ruling elite decided to follow Islamic precedent and submit in body but not in mind; the physical independence of the state was regarded as something temporal, but the rulers of Sokoto could preserve the integrity of Islam for the next world. Secondly, and rather more pragmatically, there was concern among Sokoto's Fulani rulers about the growing belief among certain elements of the population in the imminent arrival of the Mahdi, the savior who would come to restore pure Islam. Following jihad in the early nineteenth century, the Sokoto state had gone to great lengths to discourage the notion; but Mahdist expectation was rife in the early 1900s – as it was in other parts of the Islamic world in this period – and the British themselves were caught up in Mahdist violence in 1906. The leaders of Sokoto allied themselves with their infidel conquerors in suppressing the revolt: while Britain had guaranteed the survival of orthodox Islam, the Sokoto elite were grimly determined not to let extremist elements disturb the mutually beneficial arrangement thus arrived at.[45]

In North Africa, too, European administrations adopted strategies of noninterference in Islam itself and governed largely through extant indigenous elites, though from the late nineteenth century onward these were increasingly challenged by Muslim reformists and new nationalist movements. The French had long governed coastal Algeria through existing political systems and utilized a small Tunisian middle class further east. In Egypt, the British initially used the court of Khedive Tawfiq (1879–92) and attempted to use that of his son Abbas Hilmi (1892–1914); the consul-general in Cairo, Sir Evelyn Baring (Lord Cromer), was able to intimidate the nationalist-leaning Abbas through the threat of military force, but nationalist opposition would continue to grow. In Libya, the difficulties the Italians faced in actually "stabilizing" the territory forced them to attempt compromise with the Sanusi authorities, permitting provincial councils and maintaining a respectful distance in the early 1920s; but the arrangements were fragile, and relations remained hostile through the 1920s.[46]

As a rule, south of the Sahara, resident British officers were scattered through colonial territories to adjudicate in disputes, to represent the highest imperial authority, and generally to ensure that the system functioned smoothly. "Native Treasuries" were established, with responsibility for tax collection devolved to African rulers, who were able to generate some income for themselves through it; and as far as possible, the "native" should learn to administer justice through local courts. The whole system was based on the principle of "traditional legitimacy," utilizing African rulers who were, in the eyes of the broad populations of particular districts, their legitimate overlords. It was developed in Northern Nigeria between 1902 and 1906; from 1906 until 1914, it was applied to the rest of Nigeria, and thence to a number of other territories across British tropical Africa. Problems arose when it was necessary to create overlord chiefs where none had existed previously, in turn undermining the entire notion of "legitimacy" through the invention of so-called "traditional" authority. A Nigerian example was the Igbo, highly decentralized at the point of conquest; but the British created chieftaincies in a form which bore little resemblance to anything which had gone before and imposed these on communities which could thus hardly regard them as "legitimate."[47] Africans at the very least questioned, were skeptical about, and even rebelled against, those chiefs placed in positions of authority over them where none had existed previously. In northern Sudan, they were soon bypassed, indeed, and were perceived to have little real power; somewhat later, in Tanganyika, where the British searched for evidence of precolonial statehood and hierarchy, and then, where they did not find it, invented it anyway, such chiefs were regarded with contempt by Africans themselves. In these contexts, British lack of knowledge, and the failed attempts to create such "knowledge," let them down in pursuit of governance. Even so, more generally, the actual level of "invention" involved in this process can be too easily exaggerated.[48] European administrations also frequently made use of existing political structures, and harnessed (whether wittingly or not) long-term processes of political evolution and adaption which were particularly characteristic of Africa's dramatic nineteenth century. The external interventions of the late nineteenth century often represented only the latest element – albeit, in many cases, a markedly influential one – in the continent's political development, a process encompassing the distinctively African traits of creativity, mobility, and adaptability.

In other areas, there were different problems with the imposition of indirect rule. In the Uganda Protectorate, the British took the highly developed administrative structures of the nineteenth-century Buganda kingdom and spread these beyond Buganda itself, transposing them on peoples around the Protectorate whose resentment of the hegemonic Ganda thus quickly heightened. In Rwanda and Burundi, the Germans and later the Belgians misread the precolonial relationship between Hutu and Tutsi, simplified it, and placed the Tutsi monarchy and political elite in a position of much greater authority than had been the case previously. In so doing, the Belgians in particular created a cheap and effective system of indirect rule, but one which contained the seeds of catastrophe for the future.[49] In expanding settler societies, however – Kenya, Southern Rhodesia, Algeria, and of course South Africa – the principles of indirect rule were unthinkable, both to European governments and to white settlers themselves. The latter in particular demanded ever greater control over African labor, taxation, and resources; here, systems of administration would be very different, with profound implications for the political development of those territories. "Direct" rule was therefore common in territories of white settlement, where colonists quickly perceived that indirect rule would award unpalatable levels of local authority to chiefs[50]; and more direct systems of administration were also put in place in parts of Francophone West Africa, for example. Here, local lineages found their powers greatly curtailed through the imposition of *chefs de canton*; thus French administrators created a new political class which was often drawn from the local population, but which was expected to be loyal and answerable directly to the colonial authorities themselves.[51]

Lugard, foremost advocate of the principles of indirect rule, elevated the system to something of a political philosophy. Yet in many respects, indirect rule was a response to the perennial problem of limited resources, and in areas with ready-made political resources – strong and established systems of government, such as in Northern Nigeria, or Uganda, or Rwanda – the temptation to make use of these proved too great. The relative ease with which they were set up can also be explained by the evident willingness, again, of elites to participate. Partnerships were thus forged after the dust of battle had settled. The Fulani of Northern Nigeria, as we have seen, were still in some ways recently arrived aliens, certainly as a ruling elite; their willingness to work with the British betrayed their self-consciousness as a *parvenu* ruling class. Elsewhere, the Ganda of Uganda, and the Tutsi of Rwanda and Burundi, seized with alacrity the opportunities to cement their sociopolitical status in the new order. The British later, in the 1930s, extended indirect rule systems to their central and southern African territories, including Northern Rhodesia, Nyasaland, Swaziland, Basutoland, and Bechuanaland.[52]

Moreover, the system had some wider political and cultural implications, which have already been alluded to. In time, indirect rule provided an ideological justification for not sharing power with an increasingly politically conscious, mission-educated African elite, emerging by the 1920s to vie with and eventually directly challenge the "traditional" elite who were seen by them as the upholders and agents of colonial rule. From

New order in Uganda: the young Kabaka Daudi Chwa at Namirembe Cathedral, Kampala, 1902. Source: ©The British Library Board, British Library, W24/2136 DSC.

the British perspective, indirect rule maintained the distance between themselves and the African, ensuring that such chiefs were only *associated* with European civilization, kept firmly in their place in the firmament of ancient tribal tradition. For the same reasons, it would be many years before colonial authorities would trust the new elite who

Lord Lugard and Northern Nigerian chiefs, London Zoo, c.1925. Hulton Archive/Getty Images. Source: Reproduced from Fox Photos/Stringer.

were themselves the products of the colonial system. Indirect rule enforced the idea of "tribal identity," a concept with which we will deal in more detail later. Ultimately, "modernization" was to be applied only selectively; indirect rule maintained, indeed created, "tribal" divisions, and militated against the emergence of nationalism. Lugard himself had cautioned against modernizing the African too quickly, as the "native" mind would not be able to cope with rapid change and sudden influx of new ideas; he functioned best in his "traditional" environment, into which modernity would only be introduced gradually. "Tribalism," in many respects, would become ever more entrenched in the later colonial period and would indeed militate against the growth of territorial nationalism; but for Europeans in the late nineteenth and early twentieth centuries, tribalism ensured the perpetuation and indeed hardening of a system of hierarchy, patriarchy, social order, and control, in which everyone understood the system and their place in it. Local aristocracies were conceived as subordinate partners in the imperial project; African chiefs and kings were part of a hierarchical system of rule and therefore should be accorded such ceremony and pomp as befitted their status.[53] They were awarded displays of official respect on such ceremonial occasions as coronations, investitures, birthdays, and jubilees. In Uganda, for example, the British built a public school at Budo, the site on which Ganda kabakas had been crowned, on the outskirts of

Kampala for the education of the children of the Ugandan elite; thereafter, the coronation of Ganda monarchs took place in the college chapel, combining British and African ceremonies, and in this way, it has been argued, did the institution of kingship in Buganda become an Anglo-African invention. Nonetheless, again, the degree of "invention" can be exaggerated, and too often, these acts of creativity are attributed to the peculiar dynamism of the colonial encounter.[54] Ultimately, such developments need to be understood in the context of long-term processes of political evolution into which Europeans were tapping – often with some dexterity, it must be said – and into which Africans frequently co-opted Europeans. In some areas, "traditional" systems of hierarchy and deference were created where none had existed previously, as in southern Nigeria, or in Tanganyika; but just as often, Europeans were utilizing African systems of authority, whether comparatively well established or emergent and novel. Indirect rule was supposed, above all, to be about *legitimization*, the management of systems of governance through which the civilizing mission and the stability of the colonial order could best be achieved. Yet the processes by which this was accomplished – and the reasons why it sometimes failed – must be considered in the context of nineteenth-century political development and energetic experimentation on the part of Africans.

Bush Wars and Distant Shadows: Africa in Global War

The First World War may have been, in provenance at least, a European conflict, but each colonial power sought to wring the most from its African possessions in terms of both manpower and material. In some areas, of course, the passage into global conflict was invisible, and the impact scarcely noticeable; for some communities, the experience of colonial administration in 1918 was much as it had been in 1914. And yet the larger picture suggests that the 1914–18 conflict brought about significant change, not only in terms of metropolitan thinking about African empires but also among a range of sociopolitical groups within African society itself. Moreover, the First World War erupted at a time when most colonial states were attempting to consolidate after the violence and upheaval of the previous two decades or more; indeed in some areas, it can be considered the end of Africa's "long" nineteenth century, and certainly the concluding phase of the Scramble.[55]

The German territories of Togo and Cameroon were invaded by British and French forces from west and east in late 1914. Fighting erupted swiftly despite the fact that there was an exchange of telegrams between German and Allied colonial officials about the possibility of putting in place a local armistice, so as not to present the "native" with the undignified sight of white men killing one another. The long, thin territory of Togo was overrun relatively easily, but the battle for Cameroon – extending into the mountains and forests of the colony's interior – dragged on until 1916. German South West Africa was poorly defended – indeed it was virtually impossible to defend in any case, for few colonial boundaries had been drawn up with the idea of defense from external attack in mind – and was swiftly occupied by South African forces, an occupation which would have long-term political implications for the territory: in effect, the South

Africans would remain for over seventy years. But it was in eastern and central Africa that the fighting was most bitter, where the consequences were most devastating for the region, and where the campaign matched the duration of the conflict in Europe. British, African, and South African forces were engaged in combat with German forces across a huge swathe of the region between Kenya and Mozambique. Even after Tanganyika was effectively occupied by the Allies, the German commander von Lettow-Vorbeck led his loyal troops on a remarkable campaign of attrition through Portuguese Mozambique, Nyasaland, and northeastern Rhodesia, keeping the Allies engaged month after month, year after year, through a skilled combination of set-piece confrontations and guerrilla war. Von Lettow-Vorbeck's motley collection of regular African troops, renegades, and a handful of German officers proved more than a match for the combined forces of the Allies and remained essentially undefeated: he only surrendered upon hearing of the armistice in Europe in November 1918.[56]

In the course of the East African campaign, between 750,000 and 1 million Africans were forced into service as porters, hauling the equipment of the opposing armies through forest and swamp, across scrub and over mountain. Around one in five died, mostly from disease. Local economies were ravaged by the requisitioning of cattle, crops, and young men as the fighting ebbed and flowed. Scorched-earth tactics were common and were practiced by both sides, well versed as they were in them: the Germans drew on their experience of suppressing revolts in Tanganyika and South West Africa just a few years later, and the British recalled the effectiveness of their targeting of civilians during the second Boer War. Villages were burnt, and harvests put to the torch when they could not be seized; chronic food shortage, if not outright famine, was the result in areas affected directly or indirectly by the combat, notably Rwanda between 1916 and 1918. Disease killed porters and devastated communities, too; but the scale of the influenza epidemic which swept across swathes of western, central, and eastern Africa in 1918 and 1919 was unprecedented. It came from Europe, and spread rapidly from coastal areas inland, bacteria following the same lines of transport and communication that had carried troops, supplies, and news from the metropole. Numbers of deaths are impossible to estimate, but they count in the thousands.[57]

Ironically – as during the wars of conquest a generation earlier – most of the soldiers on the opposing sides were African, under comparatively tiny numbers of European officers. The exception was South Africa, where in the newly created union, black Africans were recruited but prohibited from carrying firearms for use against whites: after all, it had only been a few years since the Germans in neighboring South West Africa had been the champions of the Boers themselves. Elsewhere, conscription was systematic and often brutal. The British recruited troops from their West African colonies to fight on the other side of the continent; French recruiting sergeants traveled from village to village, from the coastal forests into the savannah, rounding up young men for service, of whom 150,000 were dispatched to the Western Front in France and Belgium to compensate for spiraling casualties among the French themselves. They also recruited men from Algeria. Of these, 30,000 were killed in action; and for the survivors, the experience of combat in Europe was politicizing. Indeed, increasingly aggressive attempts by the French authorities to conscript troops from West Africa were greeted with resistance and in some areas outright insurrection. Conscription itself became known bitterly as the "blood tax" among Africans, while the military campaigns prosecuted by the French to suppress local armed resistance actually brought the Scramble to a conclusion. These campaigns witnessed the final subjugation of significant chunks of French West Africa which had not been brought fully under control since being carved up in the 1880s and 1890s. Now, in the course of 1915 and 1916, French administrators created new lines of communication with formerly unimportant chiefly lineages which were useful in aiding recruitment and thus did the exigencies of the war lead to a further modification of systems of governance.[58]

The African refusal to participate in the Europeans' war was manifest in various ways. In the French territories, for example, young men frequently fled across borders into neighboring territories, hiding out until recruiting sergeants had moved on. Such "protest migrations," as they have been called – common, too, in the avoidance of tax and demands for labor – were comparatively more common than the acts of self-mutilation which nonetheless occurred as a means of avoiding service. Indeed, recruitment drives were, from the African perspective, simply the latest in a series of intolerable impositions which had begun with demands for tax and labor. In the French army, there were instances of desertion and insubordination among African troops, notably those from French North Africa.[59]

Uprisings which were ostensibly against conscription were in fact in many cases the crystallization of long-term and deep-seated grievances, festering since the late nineteenth century. Thus, there was armed resistance against the British in Nigeria and the French in Dahomey; the Barwe people rose up against the Portuguese in Mozambique in 1917. Islam, again, provided the framework for a series of rebellions across the French-controlled West African savannah and in North Africa. The Muslim Tuareg launched a series of attacks against the French in Niger in 1916–17. In this context, it is important to note the role of the Ottoman empire, which had entered the war on the side of Germany in late 1914; for the Ottomans, who had envisaged universal jihad across the colonial world – to the relief of the Germans themselves, no doubt, it never materialized – the outbreak of the European war represented an opportunity to reclaim lost territory across North Africa. In French Morocco, 'Abdal-Malik organized anti-colonial revolts, and local anti-conscription disturbances also occurred in Algeria. The most concerted resistance, however, came from the Sanusiyya, who were funded and armed by the Germans and the Ottoman empire. In Libya, the Italians were not yet secure, and thus represented something of a soft target: in early 1915, they were defeated by the Sanusiyya in the Misurata province. Later that year, the Sanusiyya extended their operations across the border and launched offensives against the British in Egypt. In 1916, however, with the emergence of the pro-British Sayyid Idris al-Sanusi in Cyrenaica, a truce was negotiated with the Italians in Libya, and more peaceful relations were secured with the British themselves in Egypt. But the Sanusiyya were also busy further south, attacking bases in the French Sahara in 1916 and launching an assault in Niger; only with the support of British forces in Nigeria were the incursions reversed.[60]

With the outbreak of war, the British clamped down hard on Egypt, declaring a protectorate, cutting all links with Istanbul, deposing Khedive Abbas, and suppressing all political activity deemed "nationalist."[61] In the Sudan, the British used the complex weave of events north of the Sahara to extend their control westwards, toward the Darfur sultanate, which had been largely autonomous of Khartoum since the 1870s. Following Sultan Ali Dinar's flirtation with the Sanusiyya in 1915, in early 1916, the British governor of Sudan, Wingate, launched an assault on Darfur, and quickly subdued it, but he also sought good relations with the sufi orders in order to stabilize a potentially volatile region.[62] The French, indeed, attempted to do much the same in Morocco and Algeria, and in this way, the potential threat of Islam was offset to some degree.

Militant Christianity played its part, too, most dramatically in Nyasaland where in 1915 the preacher John Chilembwe led a fierce but short-lived insurrection. One of its central grievances was the large-scale conscription of Africans and the heavy death toll wrought by the early campaigns against the Germans.[63] There were other more peaceful but locally potent apocalyptic and millenarian Christian movements in Nigeria, Cote d'Ivoire, and Northern Rhodesia, in which leaders preached, variously, the imminent end of the world and the second coming of Christ, the destruction of European rule, and the moral necessity for disobedience to the colonial state. In rather different political and cultural circumstances, in South Africa a group of Afrikaners rose in October 1914, an uprising inspired by both hatred – the term is not too strong – of the British, and sympathy for the Germans. It was swiftly crushed, as their African counterparts were elsewhere.[64]

Meanwhile, nascent colonial economies suffered a setback during the war years, and economic hardship was felt across the continent, another cause for social unrest. Trade declined, for example the formerly thriving commerce that had existed between British and German territories in West Africa; prices for export produce fell markedly, reflecting a global downturn more generally. Governments maintained tight control over prices and wages, which meant that producers and labor forces suffered, despite the fact that demand for certain raw materials increased between 1914 and 1918 as European economies gradually transferred to a war footing. At the same time, however, the prices which African consumers had to pay for imports climbed steadily during the war years. Combined with requisitioning, forced labor, the compulsory cultivation of certain crops, and of course military conscription, the war witnessed straitened social and economic circumstances for millions of Africans.

In many ways, the First World War saw the final establishment of colonial systems across the continent, systems which from the early 1920s onward were able to more efficiently control, shape, and exploit the environments in their charge; and in that sense, the war can be described as heralding the age of colonial rule at its height, its most effective, and its most clearly articulated. Moreover, as the historian Bill Freund put it, the First World War "probably marked the last high point of the reign of crude force": the era of conquest drew to a close, as well as that of "consolidation," broadly defined.[65] From the beginning of the 1920s onward, soldiers repaired to their barracks, and market forces became more important than – or at least as important as – rapid-firing machine-guns. The commercial economy was now to define colonial society, as overt militarism receded.

At the same time, however, the experience of the war left an indelible impression on societies and communities across the continent. Those Africans who had been privy to the sight of Europeans killing one another would not easily forget it nor would those who had experienced the hardship wrought by the conflict: they had been witness not only to the brutal ambiguity of colonial rule but also to the weaknesses and deeply flawed "humanity" of European civilization. The experience of the war also gave rise to some of the earliest quasi-political associations and organizations among Africans which were symptomatic of what we can call "protest identities." The process of politicization *vis-à-vis* the realities of the colonial state had begun, for many, in the aftermath of invasion and conquest; but the war pushed it forward for many more. It was as true among peasants and workers as it was among those educated Africans who had been required to fill the junior administrative and clerical positions temporarily vacated by Europeans on military service. These Africans in particular had had their social and political horizons broadened; subtly empowered by the experience, they would become an important class in the post-war period, increasingly disillusioned with the indirect rule system and the chiefly class which upheld it. This was a system which, they now understood, denied them access to political responsibility and locked them into an apparently immutable status.

For some, then, there were heightened political sensitivities, and in many ways for the first time, events on a global stage made some Africans aware of their place in the world. The deliberations at the Versailles Conference – and in particular reportage of US president Woodrow Wilson's Fourteen Points and the later covenant of the League of Nations – attracted the attention of increasingly politically active Africans, notably across British West Africa where there was a growing, if low-level, clamor for greater representation in local government. In South Africa, the South African Native National Congress, founded in 1912 and later (1923) to become the African National Congress (ANC), petitioned King George V for representation at the Versailles Conference. The movement outlined Africans' wartime contribution and reminded the king that one of the principles of the peace was the right to self-determination and freedom from oppression. The British government, however, rejected outright the notion of permitting an African delegation to attend the conference, stating that in any case the whole affair would constitute interference in the Union of South Africa's internal affairs. Nonetheless, it signified an awareness of their plight on a global stage which few Africans would have possessed even a decade earlier and thus had African protest identity entered a new phase.

This was even more clearly demonstrated, perhaps, in Egypt, where nationalists were growing increasingly impatient with the heavy-handed British presence. Several leading nationalist figures, mostly members of the Umma party which advocated gradual, peaceful transition rather than violent confrontation, petitioned Wingate for an opportunity to negotiate an end to the British protectorate. Initially, the British questioned the right of the petitioners to speak for Egypt, at which point the latter gathered broad support for their *Wafd*, or delegation; their activities having been severely curtailed by Britain, the Wafd dispatched petitions to the Versailles Conference. The British misunderstood the increasing popularity of the Wafd and were taken aback by the eruption of territory-wide violent protest in 1919, prompted by the detention of the leading nationalist Sa'ad Zaghlul. General Allenby was dispatched by London to suppress the violence, which he did, but he also released Zaghlul who proceeded to transform the Wafd into a formal political party, of which he was president. The Wafd under Zaghlul now became the major movement of anti-British resistance, although further challenges would confront it in the early 1920s. Post-war talk of self-determination also stirred nationalist movements in Algeria and Tunisia; in the period following the armistice in Europe, there was an uprising in the Moroccan Rif under the leadership of 'Abd al-Karim, while the Sanusiyya renewed their war with the Italians in Libya.[66]

At Versailles in 1919, among the other issues of great import on the agenda was the question of defeated Germany's occupied colonial territories. In one sense, the fate of these territories was something of a foregone conclusion: the victorious Allies would parcel them out amongst themselves, as the ideas of their becoming in some way self-governing or of returning them to a humiliated Germany were out of the question. Thus the British and French, for example, shared Togo – the British eventually incorporated their western portion into neighboring Gold Coast, while the French administered their share separately – and Cameroon, where France acquired around four-fifths of the colony and Britain the remainder, bordering Nigeria. The British also acquired responsibility for Tanganyika. Belgium was awarded the comparatively small beer of Rwanda and Burundi, which lay on the northeast border of the Belgian Congo, while the Union of South Africa was to administer the former territory of German South West Africa.

Yet times had changed. The era of rampant high imperialism had passed, at least in terms of rhetoric; the mere land-grabbing of the 1880s and 1890s was no longer acceptable. The Versailles treaty stipulated that the former German colonies were to be administered by the various European governments on behalf of the newly founded League of Nations; according to the rhetoric of the League, these African territories were to be held in trust, with their administrations preparing them for eventual self-government, and protecting "native" interests in the meantime. Thus was the Mandate system created, and although to all intents and purposes impotent to enforce any "recommendations" – in any case the two most powerful members of the League were the two largest colonial powers, Britain and France – the Secretariat of the League did regularly dispatch inspection teams to the various territories in order to report on their "progress."[67] The reality may have been that these newly acquired territories were governed much like any other; and yet a new ethos was evident, and a new set of principles put in place – to some extent enshrined in the League's own covenant – by which the "less developed" peoples of the world should be managed and prepared for their own political and cultural maturity. This was guardianship, no mere tawdry imperialism, according to the rubric of the age; the concept would take root in the course of the 1920s and 1930s, an era which arguably witnessed the establishment of precedents for present-day Western attitudes toward "development" and "management."

Notes

1 Lonsdale, "The European Scramble"; Thomas Pakenham, *The Scramble for Africa 1876–1912* (London, 1991); M.E. Chamberlain, *The Scramble for Africa* (London, 1999); Colin Newbury, "Great Britain and the partition of Africa, 1870–1914," in Porter (ed.), *Oxford History*, Vol. III.
2 See the accessible and nicely illustrated Douglas Porch, *Wars of Empire* (London, 2001).

3 William H. McNeill, *The Pursuit of Power: Technology, Armed Force, and Society, Since A.D. 1000* (Chicago, 1982).

4 Bruce Vandervort, *Wars of Imperial Conquest in Africa, 1830–1914* (London, 1998).

5 Daniel R. Headrick, *The Tools of Empire: Technology and European Imperialism in the Nineteenth Century* (Oxford, 1981); Robert Kubicek, "British expansion, empire, and technological change," in Porter (ed.), *Oxford History*, Vol. III.

6 See two special issues of the *Journal of African History* on "Firearms in Sub-Saharan Africa," 12: 2 (1971) and 12: 4 (1971).

7 For example, Martin Legassick, "Firearms, horses and Samorian army organisation, 1870–1898," *Journal of African History*, 7:1 (1966).

8 Jeff Guy, *The Destruction of the Zulu Kingdom: The Civil War in Zululand, 1879–1884* (London, 1979).

9 For contemporary assessments, see for example G.F.-H. Berkeley, *The Campaign of Adowa and the Rise of Menelik* (London, 1902); A. Wylde, *Modern Abyssinia* (London, 1901); Richard Pankhurst (ed.), *The Ethiopian Royal Chronicles* (Addis Ababa, 1967), 166–194. Also Paulos Milkias & Getachew Metaferia (eds.), *The Battle of Adwa: Reflections on Ethiopia's Historic Victory Against European Colonialism* (New York, 2005).

10 Robinson & Gallagher, *Africa and the Victorians*; Pakenham, *Scramble*.

11 Patricia Wright, *Conflict on the Nile: The Fashoda Incident of 1898* (London, 1972); G.N. Sanderson, *England, Europe, and the Upper Nile, 1882–1899: A Study of the Partition of Africa* (Edinburgh, 1965).

12 Mary Dewhurst Lewis, *Divided Rule: Sovereignty And Empire in French Tunisia 1881–1938* (Berkeley CA, 2014), esp. chap. 1.

13 See the English translation of Karl Peters' account of his various adventures, *New Light on Dark Africa* (London, 1891); also Sebastian Conrad, *German Colonialism: A Short History* (Cambridge, 2012).

14 T.O. Ranger, "Connexions between Primary Resistance Movements and Modern Mass Nationalism, I & II," *Journal of African History*, 9:3 & 9:4 (1968). See also A. Isaacman & B. Isaacman, "Resistance and collaboration in southern and central Africa," *International Journal of African Historical Studies*, 10:1 (1977).

15 See Person, *Samori*.

16 J.D. Hargreaves, *West Africa Partitioned* (London, 1974).

17 David Kimble, *A Political History of Ghana* (Oxford, 1963); Wilks, *Asante*.

18 For useful overviews, see Yves Person, "Western Africa, 1870–1886," and J.D. Hargreaves, "Western Africa, 1886–1905," in Oliver & Sanderson (eds.), *Cambridge History of Africa*, Vol. 6.

19 A.S. Kanya-Forstner, *The Conquest of the Western Sudan: A Study of French Military Imperialism* (Cambridge, 1969).

20 Norman R. Bennett, *Arab versus European: Diplomacy and War in Nineteenth-century East Central Africa* (New York, 1986).

21 John Iliffe, *A Modern History of Tanganyika* (Cambridge, 1979), chap. 4.

22 For a useful collection of primary sources, see G.C.K. Gwassa & J. Iliffe (eds.), *Records of the Maji Maji Rising* (Nairobi, 1967). There is now a substantial body of scholarship relating to Maji Maji. A sample would include: John Iliffe, "The organization of the Maji-Maji rebellion," *Journal of African History*, 8:3 (1967); G.C.K. Gwassa, "African methods of warfare during the Maji Maji war of 1905–7," in B.A. Ogot (ed.), *War and Society in Africa* (London, 1972); P. Redmond, "Maji Maji in Ungoni: a reappraisal of existing historiography,"

International Journal of African Historical Studies, 8:3 (1975); Felicitas Becker, "Traders, "big men" and prophets: political continuity and crisis in the Maji Maji rebellion in southeast Tanzania," *Journal of African History*, 45:1 (2004). See also John Iliffe, *Tanganyika under German Rule 1905–1912* (Cambridge, 1969).

23 D.A. Low & R.C. Pratt, *Buganda and British Overrule, 1900–1955* (London, 1960); D.A. Low, *Fabrication of Empire: the British and the Uganda Kingdoms, 1890–1902* (Cambridge, 2009).

24 John Lonsdale & Bruce Berman, "Coping with the contradictions: the development of the colonial state in Kenya, 1895–1914," *Journal of African History*, 20:4 (1979).

25 Robert Vicat Turrell, *Capital and Labour on the Kimberley Diamond Fields, 1871–1890* (Cambridge, 1987).

26 The Xhosa experience is eloquently explored in Richard Price, *Making Empire: Colonial Encounters and the Creation of Imperial Rule in Nineteenth-century Africa* (Cambridge, 2008).

27 Shula Marks, *Reluctant Rebellion: The 1906–8 Disturbances in Natal* (Oxford, 1970); and for a broader survey, D.M. Schreuder, *The Scramble for Southern Africa 1877–1895: The Politics of Partition Reappraised* (Cambridge, 1980).

28 One of the best recent contributions to a substantial body of literature on the war is Bill Nasson, *The South African War, 1899–1902* (London, 1999). See also his study of these events from the African perspective in *Abraham Esau's War: a Black South African War in the Cape, 1899–1902* (Cambridge, 1991).

29 D.N. Beach, "Chimurenga: the Shona risings of 1896–97," *Journal of African History*, 20:3 (1979); T.O. Ranger, *Revolt in Southern Rhodesia, 1896–97* (London, 1967).

30 Andrew Roberts, *A History of Zambia* (New York, 1976), 162–70.

31 E.V. Axelson, *Portugal and the Scramble for Africa* (Johannesburg, 1967).

32 David Olusoga & Casper W. Erichsen, *The Kaiser's Holocaust: Germany's Forgotten Genocide and the Colonial Roots of Nazism* (London, 2010). See also Jan-Bart Gewald, *Herero Heroes: A Socio-political History of the Herero of Namibia, 1890–1923* (Oxford, 1998).

33 I.M. Lewis, *A Modern History of the Somali* (Oxford, 2002), chap. 4.

34 See for example Michael Brett, "The Maghrib," in A.D. Roberts (ed.), *The Cambridge History of Africa. Volume 7: 1905–1940* (Cambridge, 1986).

35 James Bruce, *Travels to Discover the Sources of the Nile, in the Years 1768, 1769, 1770, 1771, 1772, and 1773*, 5 vols. (London, 1790).

36 Archibald Dalzel, *The History of Dahomy* (London, 1793).

37 Speke, *Journal* esp. chap. 9.

38 Stanley, *Through the Dark Continent*, Vol. I, chap. 14.

39 Ashe, *Chronicles*.

40 *The Kings of Buganda* was published in English translation in 1971; the original Luganda text, *Basekabaka be Buganda* first appeared in 1901.

41 Rev. Samuel Johnson, *The History of the Yorubas* (London, 1921).

42 McCaskie, "Cultural Encounters," 680.

43 Lugard, *Dual Mandate*, 5.

44 Patrick Manning, *Francophone Sub-Saharan Africa, 1880–1995* (Cambridge, 1998), 59–60.

45 P.K. Tibenderana, "The role of the British administration in the appointment of the emirs of Northern Nigeria, 1903–1931," *Journal of African History*, 28:2 (1987).

46 Vandewalle, *History of Modern Libya*, chap. 2; Afaf Lutfi Al-Sayyid-Marsot, "The British Occupation of Egypt from 1882," in Porter (ed.), *Oxford History*.

47 A.E. Afigbo, *The Warrant Chiefs: Indirect Rule in Southeastern Nigeria, 1891–1929* (Harlow, 1972).

48 Thomas Spear, "Neo-traditionalism and the limits of invention in British colonial Africa," *Journal of African History*, 44:1 (2003).

49 Gérard Prunier, *The Rwanda Crsis: History of a Genocide* (London, 1995), 23ff; also René Lemarchand, *The Dynamics of Violence in Central Africa* (Philadelphia, 2009), chap. 3.

50 For a wide-ranging exploration of the phenomenon, see Susan Pedersen & Caroline Elkins (eds.), *Settler Colonialism in the Twentieth Century: Projects, Practices, Legacies* (New York, 2005).

51 Michael Crowder, "Indirect Rule: French and British style," *Africa*, 34:3 (1964).

52 Lord Hailey, *An African Survey* (London, 1938), is a rich resource. This mammoth tome was republished in revised form in 1956. For an African perspective, see Tshekedi Khama, 'The principles of African tribal administration', *International Affairs*, 27:4 (1951).

53 See also David Cannadine, *Ornamentalism: How the British saw their Empire* (London, 2001).

54 T.O. Ranger, "The invention of tradition in colonial Africa," in E. Hobsbawm & T.O. Ranger (eds.), *The Invention of Tradition* (Cambridge, 1983); and see his later revision of the argument in "The invention of tradition revisited: the case of Africa," in T.O. Ranger & O. Vaughan (eds.), *Legitimacy and the State in Twentieth-Century Africa* (London, 1993). Also Spear, "Neo-traditionalism."

55 Much of the following is based on a substantial and growing body of work on Africa and the First World War. A sample would include: "World War I and Africa," special issue of the *Journal of African History*, 19:1 (1978); M. Page (ed.), *Africa and the First World War* (London, 1987); J.H. Morrow, *The Great War: An Imperial History* (London, 2004); Hew Strachan, *The First World War in Africa* (Oxford, 2004); Edward Paice, *Tip and Run: the Untold Tragedy of the Great War in Africa* (London, 2007).

56 See Paul von Lettow-Vorbeck's own memoir, published in English as *My Reminiscences of East Africa* (London, 1920), reprinted in facsimile in 2009.

57 Ross Anderson, *The Forgotten Front: the East African Campaign, 1914–1918* (Stroud, 2004).

58 For a local interpretation of events, see Joe Lunn, *Memoirs of a Maelstrom: a Senegalese Oral History of the First World War* (Oxford, 1999).

59 Morrow, *The Great War*, 144–7; Francesca Bruschi, "Military collaboration, conscription, and citizenship rights in the Four Communes of Senegal and in French West Africa (1912–1946)," in Heike Liebau *et al* (eds.), *The World in World Wars: Experiences, Perceptions, and Perspectives from Africa and Asia* (Leiden, 2010). Also C.M. Andrew & A.S Kanya-Forstner, "France, Africa, and the First World War," *Journal of African History*, 19:1 (1978).

60 E.E. Evans-Pritchard, *The Sanusi of Cyrenaica* (Oxford, 1949).

61 Tom Little, *Modern Egypt* (London, 1967), 69–70.

62 M.W. Daly, *The Sirdar: Sir Reginald Wingate and the British Empire in the Middle East* (Philadelphia, 1997), Part II.

63 The classic study is G. Shepperson & T. Price, *Independent African: John Chilembwe and the Nyasaland Native Rising* (Edinburgh, 1958); and see the primary source material in John McCracken (ed.), *Voices from the Chilembwe Rising: Witness Testimonies made to the Nyasaland Rising Commission of Inquiry, 1915* (Oxford, 2015).

64 Paice, *Tip and Run*, 125–9.

65 Bill Freund, *The Making of Contemporary Africa* (Basingstoke, 1998), 112.

66 Brett, "The Maghrib," 288ff; M.W. Daly & G.N. Sanderson, "Egypt and the Anglo-Egyptian Sudan," in Roberts (ed.), *Cambridge History Vol 7*, 742–5.

67 Susan Pedersen, *The Guardians: the League of Nations and the crisis of empire* (Oxford, 2015), esp. Part I.

Part IV Colonialisms

The British, French, Portuguese, Belgians, and Italians shared certain core objectives. In particular, colonial administrations sought to create a base of revenue, a system of taxation which ensured that the territory would pay for itself. Self-sufficiency was the objective; Africans would be made to pay for their own control. For many, the first real sign of loss of sovereignty was the imposition of a poll or head tax; the collection of tax was not only absolutely fundamental to the functioning of the colonial state but it was also in many ways its key *purpose*. Often, police forces were almost entirely associated with tax collection, empowered as they were to seize the property of defaulters and make arrests; they could be the most visible, and the most dreaded, manifestation of conquest. In addition to poll or head taxes, customs duties were put in place, as administrations sought to generate income via the burgeoning commerce which was itself a core part of a further key objective, namely the compelling of Africans into a labor pool to ensure the expansion of the market economy. The aim was to create a system of wage labor, while at the same time expanding the production of cash crops and minerals. Along sections of the western African coast, commercial agriculture was already relatively well established, as we have seen, in some places dating to the late eighteenth and early nineteenth centuries. In these circumstances, the colonial state needed only to provide seeds and encouragement. But in areas where such agriculture was less developed, notably on the eastern side of the continent, force might be employed, as farmers sometimes needed to be coerced into producing certain crops. The Germans found this necessary in Tanganyika, where the cotton gospel was received somewhat less enthusiastically than in British Uganda, for reasons we will explore in due course. In settler societies such as Kenya, Africans were compelled into a labor market designed to service an economy run by and for European planters. In southern Africa, similarly, the rapid

A History of Modern Africa: 1800 to the Present, Third Edition. Richard J. Reid.

growth of the mining economy was attended by the emergence of a network of migrant labor which traversed the region. Yet while in some areas direct coercion was used to integrate Africans into the market economy, from the 1920s onward, such compulsion was largely unnecessary, as willing participation became the norm. In many territories, Africans became enthusiastic and successful cash-crop farmers, and more broadly, entry into the labor market was necessary in order to pay taxes and feed families.

These, then, were the central objectives of colonial administrations – and in many cases, it was not until the First World War or shortly afterward that they were achieved. But in time, there were other huge swathes of public life which demanded attention, for example in terms of the provision of health care and education and the delivery of "development." In principle, the rhetoric of the "civilizing mission" required that the state take an active role in this, particularly for the British and French. Yet in fact, the state remained small in many spheres of African life for many years. Until the 1920s, the education of Africans remained largely in the hands of mission schools – for example, the Anglican Church Missionary Society in British Africa or the White Fathers in the Francophone zone – which often had an uneasy relationship with the colonial authorities. Only between the wars did state school systems begin to develop. So too with health care, in which the involvement of the early colonial state was minimal and in which missionaries, again, were instrumental, seeking to provide both spiritual and physical well-being. Again, only in the 1920s and 1930s did the state begin to provide a more comprehensive health-care system. In these spheres was the colonial state, at least in the short term, largely ineffective in "transforming" African society. Similarly, in the context of environment, colonial invasion brought catastrophe in some areas; but it was many years before the state became concerned to intervene in rural life with a view to "improving" farming techniques and preventing environmental degradation. Before the 1930s, the effectiveness of agricultural departments established for the purpose was extremely variable.

Overall, then, one of the most important issues to consider with regard to colonial regimes generally is the extent to which the state transformed African society. It is a matter of debate as to whether or not colonialism really did leave an indelible mark on African society, politics, or indeed culture; what is clear, however, is that colonialism tied the continent firmly to the international economy. The key was the transport revolution which colonial rule engendered. In the nineteenth century, the prevalence of head-porterage across huge distances meant that heavy, bulky items of low value were not worth carrying. Colonial rule transformed "internal" economic systems through the exposure of societies to global demand for certain commodities and through the construction of railways and, from the 1920s, road networks, which made transport cheaper and therefore made production for the international market more viable. This process was truly seminal for many communities. In this sense, the colonial experience was indeed a formative one, and colonialism facilitated new means by which Africans continued to develop and interact with the rest of the world. Yet the state itself was still often largely insignificant in many walks of life, while the actual transformation which came about in the early decades of the twentieth century was as much the product of African initiative as it was the outcome of colonial investment.

In the years after the First World War, colonial systems became more stable, the theories justifying them more articulate, and the economic systems underpinning them more efficient. Among Africans, in the wake of the violence of the late nineteenth and early twentieth centuries, there was a recognition, in most territories, of the futility of armed resistance – this would rarely be attempted again until the 1950s and 1960s – and indeed the overtly militaristic dimension of colonialism receded somewhat. Yet "adaptation," in the broadest sense of that term, continued apace, and there were indeed many ways of adapting to the system. New modes of resistance, initiative, and self-expression reflected new identities and the emergence of new forms of group consciousness, which was sometimes "tribally" rooted, ethnic or linguistic, and sometimes transcended such ethnic and even territorial boundaries, reflecting wider socioeconomic changes. New lines of Islamic thought – some of which had their roots in late nineteenth-century Egypt – were emerging in the period between the 1920s and 1940s, seeking to reconcile modern political realities with spiritual rejuvenation. Thus were Africans able, increasingly, to impose themselves on the system and change it in subtle but important ways. From this perspective, it is important to acknowledge *African* agencies of change, and not simply assume – as has often been the case – that the colonial state possessed a monopoly on transformative capacity.

By the 1920s and 1930s, indirect-rule chiefs were established across swathes of colonial Africa and were essentially salaried officials upholding some of the key administrative and ideological principles of the colonial system. Often, as in Nigeria, or Uganda, or the Gold Coast, they operated as agents of colonial rule, collecting taxes and administering justice, and being decorated with titles, honors, and medals which were distributed in recognition of the supposedly vital and progressive role of this chiefly class in liaising between the state and its subjects. Chiefs had access to mission education and were thus essential in the articulation of the notions of "progress" and "development" so important in colonial rhetoric. Yet mission education expanded and also facilitated the emergence of a new educated elite which would increasingly challenge the old system, feeling itself excluded from social status and political authority.

In the 1920s, some Africans, at least, believed that colonial rule did indeed offer a chance for progress and possessed the capacity to improve Africans' lives. According to this interpretation, the colonial "mission" had been understood and might be invested in. Colonialism seemed to provide security and stability. The 1920s saw a decline in violence, in the most general sense: the process of "pacification" begun in the 1880s and 1890s had been largely completed by the First World War, armed resistance and insurrection had been crushed, and banditry and crime had been reduced to insignificant levels. "Peace" had been imposed on African society, and this had opened up economic and social opportunities – for entrepreneurial endeavor in terms of cash crops, for migration, for new forms of social status. For some, commercial agriculture facilitated relative economic prosperity, notably among those communities which responded energetically to the opportunities presented by cash-crop farming. The *pax colonia* also had demographic repercussions, as many regions experienced population growth following the predations and catastrophes of the 1890–1920 period. Indeed, the "ambiguity" of colonialism lay in the fact that while it brought with it massive dislocation,

Imperial relations: the king of Asante and the governor of the Gold Coast, 1935. Source: Reproduced with permission of The National Archives UK, ref. CO1069/44.

new diseases or more virulent versions of old ones, and environmental disaster, it also possessed the technological and organizational power to address these crises – and in so doing, it had the capacity, through medicine, for example, to control African bodies (and souls) much more effectively. In terms of education, mission schools and institutions of further or higher education seemed to underpin the notion of colonialism as progressive and enlightening. In the British sphere, Livingstonia School in Nyasaland, Fourah Bay College in Sierra Leone, or Makerere College (later Makerere University) in Uganda were undoubtedly elitist; but they produced people who appeared, at least, to have a stake in the system, from which they had clearly benefited. The same was true in Egypt and across the Maghreb, although here change was already afoot. In this context, the colonial system would later backfire on its overseers, of course, as such education involved exposure to ideas about democracy and nationalism; but in the short term, at least, the appearance of a skilled and literate African middle class, however small, seemed to bear out the claims made by colonial theorists for the civilizing and enlightening propensities of colonialism itself.

Things changed, however – as they did globally – in the 1930s. Older elites increasingly found themselves out of step with socioeconomic change; in some places, for example in Uganda and the Gold Coast, they were found to be unable or unwilling to protect the interests of their "constituents," and increasingly distant from the concerns and grievances of an ever more commercialized peasantry and the expanding urban population alike. In the 1930s, the system would be increasingly challenged and not only by the new elites who were the beneficiaries of relatively advanced education. The socioeconomic hardships of the Great Depression engendered heightened levels of political consciousness and new forms of protest, as disillusionment with the system set in. Within colonial administrations, too, attitudes toward governance in general and indirect rule in particular began to change in the 1930s. In many respects, the interwar years witnessed the completion of colonial society, under construction since the late nineteenth century, and thus saw colonial rule at its height: administrations were more complex, more experienced, and more efficient. Yet throughout this period, and especially during the Depression, there were signs of weakness; cracks were appearing in the edifice. There was growing disillusionment with the philosophies underpinning the colonial order; officials frequently bemoaned the directionless nature of the system, its inherent brutality, and the fact that it did not seem to be "improving" Africans' lives in any meaningful way. The "mission" came under critical scrutiny, or was rejected outright, as in the case of North African spiritual and nationalist movements able to draw on deeper historical experiences of dealing with Europe.

An important outcome of this was a move toward greater colonial intervention in African societies and an enlargement of the state itself, at least in sub-Saharan Africa. To a considerable extent, this was aimed at economic gain; but it was also accompanied by a recognition of the need for greater political inclusiveness and of the fact that Africans might, at some point in the future, be brought into government and become, in one way or another, "self-governing." Ultimately, this happened much more quickly than was originally envisaged; but certainly the roots of the process can be found in the second half of the 1930s and the war years. Indirect rule was seen increasingly as unrepresentative, archaic, and conservative, while at the same time, on a practical level, the Depression itself had a detrimental effect on the revenues available for the system and the salaries of the chiefs themselves. Awareness of the hardships brought about by the Depression led to a shift in colonial thinking – at least in the case of Britain and France, if not Belgium, Portugal, and Italy, and certainly not in the case of settler territories. The new line of thought suggested that the state should take greater care of its subjects and that Africans must be protected as much as possible from the vagaries of the global economy. This was accompanied by the inevitable dosage of paternalistic humanitarianism, but ultimately, it was aimed at the achievement of social stability and offsetting the threat of unrest. Subjects needed to be bound more securely to the system; ultimately, both heightened levels of loyalty and improved and more efficient productivity would go hand-in-hand. As indirect-rule chiefs were increasingly marginalized, and as colonial regimes sought to maximize efficiency and stabilize society, colonial rulers were unwittingly paving the way for the incorporation of the new elites they had long excluded; and these changes would facilitate the new forms of protest and identity which came to the fore during and immediately after the Second World War.

The war itself would prove something of a turning point for colonial regimes both north and south of the Sahara, in terms of North African nationalists' ability to build upon prewar political protest, and the emergence of the more cogent articulation of political and economic grievances across sub-Saharan Africa. All in all, the impact of the war was such that by 1945, half way through a turbulent and critical decade, it was clear that both Europe and Africa had entered new chapters in their respective narratives and that new conversations would be required between colonizer and colonized – perhaps for the first time since the consolidation of imperialisms in the early 1900s.

11 "Pax Colonia"?

Empires of Soil and Service

Core colonial objectives included the need to render territories both militarily stable and economically viable. In terms of the development of colonial economic systems, we are concerned with three broad models. First, the indigenous cash-crop economy was largely in the hands of African peasant producers and developed across a broad belt encompassing tropical western, central, and Eastern Africa, and was also found in the Mediterranean zone; second, the settler cash-crop economy involved territories such as Kenya in which production was in the hands of white settlers or organized through plantation systems backed by European capital; and third, the "industrial-urban" economy emerged as a result of mining, for example across southern and central Africa.

The belief that African society would be "naturally" improved through exposure to European commerce was gradually superseded, by the end of the nineteenth century, by the notion that any modernization would have to be engendered through outside intervention, in the form of the imposition of a political infrastructure which would facilitate material advancement. Such supposed altruism, of course, was not to be mistaken for economic irrationality: there was plenty of mutual benefit to be had, the entire project being presented as "good" for metropolitan trade and industry, and providing a wealth of opportunities for enterprising businessmen. As Lugard put it from the British perspective:

> It is ... also of great moment that the British democracy, faced with problems which portend great changes in our social organisation, should understand the relation which our overseas dependencies bear to the economic well-being of this country – how vital to our industrial life are the products of the tropics, and its markets for our manufactures. It is indeed essential that democracy should take an intelligent and well-informed interest in questions which affect the Empire of which it is the inheritor and trustee.[1]

A History of Modern Africa: 1800 to the Present, Third Edition. Richard J. Reid.

The key point was that none of this could be entrusted to African state and society; rather, responsibility for the material advancement of Africa, and for the commercial opportunities thus presented, lay with Britain itself, and the colonial administration which must come after the violence of "pacification."

The project to "transform" the African environment, moreover, had its roots in earlier nineteenth-century notions about the need to "map" the continent, to chart and comprehend the African landscape. One of the most visible manifestations of the application of technology lay in transport infrastructure. Roads and railways were held to have "opened up" the African interior, and indeed mechanized transport did have transformative power in some areas. The Uganda Railway exemplifies this and was an engineering feat of considerable note. Built using both local and Indian labor imported for the purpose, the railway was constructed between 1896, when work started at Mombasa, and 1901, when the first locomotive ran into Kisumu on Lake Victoria. In so doing, it sliced across the coastal belt, rose into the Kenyan highlands, and ultimately linked the lacustrine interior to the Indian Ocean.[2] It represented a conquest of the environment which was doubtless unimaginable a generation or two earlier, and similar projects would be launched across Africa between the 1900s and the 1940s, bold manifestations of the supposedly transformative power of the colonial state.

Monopolies on Violence

First, however, there was the question of security. Africa was largely subdued, and consequently policed, by Africans themselves. Considerable swathes of the continent were "conquered" during the 1880s and 1890s by colonial armies which frequently comprised a large African rank-and-file under a comparatively tiny number of European officers. From the early 1900s, the practice of recruitment of Africans into colonial forces became more systematic, and by this process did Africans themselves make the transition from being aggressive, warlike savages to being disciplined, loyal servants of the new order, a metamorphosis which tells us much about the evolving relationship between Europe and Africa. In sum, Africans who had been alternatively apostrophized as warlike, savage, lazy, and so on, became, under the colors of European regiments, fine upstanding troops and progress incarnate. Frederick Lugard was hardly untypical in believing that Africans understood force and force alone, arguing for Europe's moral right to intervene in what he described as the continent's interminable internecine warfare.[3] However, while Africa's soldiers were in general seen as benighted savages in the precolonial era, colonialism brought new order and rectitude. It was fundamental that Europe's militarism was of a higher kind, and its wars grander and nobler; by a curious twist of logic, then, Africans who served in European armies were exposed to the civilizing mission, as much as were those who sat at the feet of missionaries.

The practice of indigenous recruitment had a long history in Africa, as it had in Asia and North America. The French had recruited local men into their colonial force in the coastal settlement of Senegal, the Tirailleurs Sénégalais, since 1857; Britain had raised local levies at their Gambia and Sierra Leone outposts since the early nineteenth century. Along the Gold Coast, and in the Niger Delta, too, African militia had been used to protect trading stations and deployed in the intermittent, low-level conflicts with peoples in the hinterland since at least the early 1800s, and even earlier in some places: in the seventeenth century, English merchants had used locals to defend trading posts, and on the lower Niger these evolved into corps known as the "Oil Rivers Irregulars," or "the Forty Thieves." In the course of the nineteenth century, Europeans were able, again, to take advantage of the sociopolitical turmoil produced by the rise and fall of states, and the predations of the slave trade. Between the 1880s and the early 1900s, a number of African forces were established which participated in the partition and subsequent control of European African empires; Europe thus harnessed the process of militarization unfolding across Africa, and utilized African combat skills and local knowledge without which, indeed, the partition would have been impossible. These forces would become the representatives of European armed might, the upholders of order, and one of the most visible and durable reminders of the conquest itself. Motley bands of armed and loosely trained militia acquired a more regimented and official role. In the British sphere, the Royal West African Frontier Force was founded in 1897 to defend and control the vast new territory of Nigeria, while the West African Regiment was raised in 1896 to do the same job in Sierra Leone. In East Africa, many of the troops involved in conquest, counterinsurgency, and anti-slave-trade activity were brought from India – Sikhs and Punjabi Muslims – commanded by British officers seconded from the Indian Army. But Africans were also recruited, many from Sudan initially, and later from the territories about to become known as Uganda and Kenya. In 1902, a number of territorial units were amalgamated into the King's African Rifles, although each new colony was responsible for recruiting and maintaining its own forces; in the same period the Germans set up the *Schutztruppe* in their East African territory. In northeast Africa, the British were involved in reforming the Egyptian army after the Sudanese revolt of the early 1880s, and at the end of the 1890s, it was an Anglo-Egyptian army making use of Sudanese recruits which finally defeated the Mahdist state. In the 1920s, the Sudan Defence Force was founded, and the pattern was replicated elsewhere: in 1914, the Somaliland Camel Corps was established to suppress local revolts, for example.[4]

Troops were often recruited over long distances, with essentially "alien" groups being used to pacify and police newly acquired territories. These armies, moreover, were often small, commanded by even smaller numbers of European officers, reflecting both financial constraints and local exigencies, it often being unnecessary to maintain larger forces. Lugard's West African Frontier Force, charged with policing northern Nigeria, numbered some 2,000–3,000 African troops under little more than 100 European officers, but this force was huge in comparison to the little army set up by Harry Johnston in Nyasaland, administered by less than 100 Indian troops and a couple of European officers. Military control was thus tenuous in many territories. Across the whole of their West and Equatorial African territory on the eve of the First World War, for example, the French colonial army did not exceed some 13,000 men. In the early 1900s, the British had a little more than 11,000 soldiers across sub-Saharan Africa, under the command of 300 officers and NCOs.[5] During the First World War, however, conscription expanded dramatically, particularly in the French territories, and the Tirailleurs

Sénégalais would play a significant part in the action on the Western Front.[6] Yet in the early years of colonial rule, armies and police forces were as important for the collection of taxes as they were for the maintenance of internal order, and certainly were rarely used for external defense or offense, the two world wars being the notable exceptions. Indeed, it was the need to make tax collection more efficient – critical in rendering colonial territories capable of paying for themselves – that prompted governments to increase expenditure on police and army, in the form of metropolitan grants-in-aid in the years between partition and the First World War. By 1914, however, these grants had mostly been abolished, with responsibility for military administration devolved to colonial officials. Thereafter, with processes of "pacification" largely complete – with some important exceptions – armies were confined to barracks, or deployed on periodic patrols of troublesome areas not yet fully under civil administration.

In large part, again, the nature of colonial armies and police forces was a matter of expedience, as it was much cheaper to recruit locally; early colonial administrations often operated within severe budgetary constraints. Logistically it was preferable, too, as the raising of indigenous forces removed the need to deploy professional metropolitan armies. Through the nineteenth century, on those relatively rare occasions when it was necessary, the British had fought wars in Africa with one eye on the cost, only very occasionally doing something extravagant with taxpayers' money – such as the expedition mounted to rescue Emperor Tewodros' hostages in Ethiopia in 1867–8. Europeans also found it relatively easy to recruit among displaced and rootless peoples, for the same reasons that missionaries often found souls among them: military service provided stability, identity, a salary, and socioeconomic advantages more broadly. During the Scramble, for example, communities devastated by slave raiding, drought, and earlier colonial campaigns were fertile hunting grounds for recruitment officers. The Belgian Force Publique in Congo Free State exemplifies the pattern and also demonstrates the grim consequences of governance on the cheap: the Force Publique was a motley collection of the displaced and brutalized, who engaged in violent extortion to such a degree that the resultant scandal brought Leopold's commercial project to an ignominious close.[7] Indigenous recruitment was also important in terms of European interpretations of the "character" of particular peoples. Ideas developed of how certain peoples were particularly well-suited to military service, because they understood "loyalty," or because they were "docile," uncomplicated by the vices of civilization; above all, Europeans were interested in "martial" peoples, those who were militaristic and warlike, but who could also be disciplined in the service of the state.

Notions about "martial races" were essentially imported from India into Africa, and thus involved the idealization of recruits from savannah and mountainous areas – where peoples were "masculine" and warlike – and suspicion of those from coastal and lowland regions, where peoples were tainted with the "vices" of civilization and had developed "feminine" traits.[8] In West Africa, for example, the British and French tended to recruit among the peoples to the north, in the savannah belt. Early allies and partners in initial colonial conquest, however, did not necessarily constitute pools of recruits later on: in Buganda, for example the Ganda may have assisted the British in the establishment of the protectorate, but thereafter they contributed little in the way of manpower to the colonial army. In Uganda, rather, it was again the peoples of the north who were recruited, notably the Acholi and other smaller groups close to the Congolese and Sudanese borders. In Kenya, soldiers were drawn predominantly from the Kamba and the Kalenjin, rather than from the supposedly "militaristic" Maasai. Such ethnic imbalances in colonial armies, moreover, would have important consequences for the national armies which succeeded them. Only in particular territories – in Algeria, where the French metropolitan army was deployed, or in South Africa, where African "soldiers" were not trusted enough to be armed – did colonial armies remain predominantly white.

Slaves and Labor

One of the stated aims of the "civilizing mission" had been to crush the last vestiges of the slave trade and bring an end to the practice of slavery across the continent. Just as the abolition of the slave trade in the first half of the nineteenth century had not brought the commerce to an end, however, so the onset of colonial rule did not end slavery itself – in part because it was so widespread in African polity and society, and in part because it was not in the interests of sociopolitical stability to abolish it. Colonial authorities approached the abolition of domestic slavery with caution, conscious of the economic cost and potential social and political upheaval involved in abruptly emancipating the slave population. Slaves constituted an essential part of the economic systems upon which colonial states depended in their early years, and so in many territories, the legal basis of slavery was simply not recognized, but slaves were discouraged from actually leaving their masters – for example by preventing them from owning land and not assisting them to "resettle." Even where the authorities declared that slavery had no legal basis, for example in Zanzibar in 1897, former slaves continued to work on the plantations, which were so critical to the island's economy, much as they always had. Indirect rule in northern Nigeria meant that the British were reluctant to interfere too much in domestic arrangements, and slavery was abolished only with the caveat that slaves had to purchase their own freedom: thus slavery continued until it was finally made illegal in 1936. Elsewhere, notably along the East African coast, slave-owners were compensated if their slaves departed, but this was not universally practiced by the British. Slavery continued in the Portuguese territories well into the twentieth century, despite having been outlawed in 1878, and it persisted in Ethiopia until at least the interwar years, in a somewhat different sociopolitical setting, given Ethiopia's sovereign status. Certainly African employers and ruling elites often treated formally "free" labor as mere slaves; in their minds the legal distinction was irrelevant. On some parts of the West African coast, for example in the cocoa-producing areas of Nigeria and the Gold Coast, slave labor was central to the cash-crop economy. Its gradual disappearance certainly undermined the power of elites in many areas to control labor, which was placed on a wage basis, although such elites sought ways (political and otherwise) of compensating for this.[9]

At the same time, of course, "freedom" is relative. Early colonial states had relied on runaway and "freed" slaves for their armies and police forces. Hundreds of thousands of former slaves, notably in the French western and equatorial zones, became part of the forced labor so essential to the early functioning of colonial economies. Former slaves, too, entered the migrant labor system in Southern and Central Africa, and more broadly, the expanding cash economy meant that there were employment opportunities for formerly unfree male labor. They migrated to cash-crop areas across West Africa. Men did rather better than women, however, and frequently, the dependent status of women hardly changed with emancipation.

With the slave trade suppressed, however, and the illegality of slave status gradually enforced across the continent, slavery had largely disappeared by the middle of the twentieth century, even if some of the forms of labor which replaced it were hardly less odious or exploitative. But the new socioeconomic opportunities and patterns of change wrought by colonial rule meant that the institution of slavery slowly withered. In part this was also down to humanitarian action, such as the activities of the British Anti-Slavery and Aborigines Protection Society in the 1920s, which resulted in the League of Nations taking a greater interest in the suppression of slavery and forcing colonial administrations to report regularly on the issue.[10] Slave-raiding and trading was reduced to an underground activity, though it continued in remote areas, as it does to the present day, especially in the Sahel belt and across the Sahara: indeed in the early twenty-first century, there has been a resurgence in the traffic in people.

Cash Crops

Markets and raw materials were the primary economic needs of European colonialism, and initially, in many areas, responsibility for developing these and "opening up" the interior was given to private companies – in the British sphere, for example, the Royal Niger Company, the British South Africa Company, the Imperial British East Africa Company – which also represented attempts at administration on the cheap. In France, the Marseilles-based Compagnie française de l'Afrique occidentale was one of the earliest monopolist trading companies on the West African coast, which in the 1890s and 1900s was operating alongside such firms as the Société coloniale de la côte de Guinée and the Compagnie française du Commerce Africain. As with the British firms – and the German companies operating out of Bremen and Hamburg – these businesses were at the commercial, and indeed political, frontier of the expanding colonial state.[11] This was quickly discovered to be inefficient, however, as such trading concerns struggled to make themselves viable – many went bankrupt as a result of mismanagement and African resistance, for example – while administration was often amateurish and could be somewhat heavy-handed. Most companies had been superseded by governmental authority by the beginning of the 1920s. Moreover, the system was open to abuse, as companies above all pursued private profit, often violently, and were scarcely interested in long-term investment. The Congo Free State witnessed some of the worst abuses on the continent: here, so-called "vacant" (in other words, expropriated) land was leased to private companies from the state government, which received a percentage of profits. The main focus around the early 1900s was wild rubber, stimulated by the motor industry in Europe and North America. Companies employed what were effectively armies of the displaced – often ex-slaves – to collect rubber, terrorizing communities in the process; it was a brutal commercial free-for-all, involving the destruction of villages which refused to cooperate and arbitrary executions, atmospherically captured at the time in Joseph Conrad's novella, *Heart of Darkness*.[12] As a "system" it was, however, unsustainable: African resistance and a dip in the price of rubber combined with international condemnation – even by the standards of the day events in the Congo were seen as shameful – to bring about a major shift in the way the territory was governed. In 1908, Leopold was compelled to hand over responsibility to the Belgian government, which permitted private companies to continue to operate but which also managed to bring the worst of the abuses to an end.

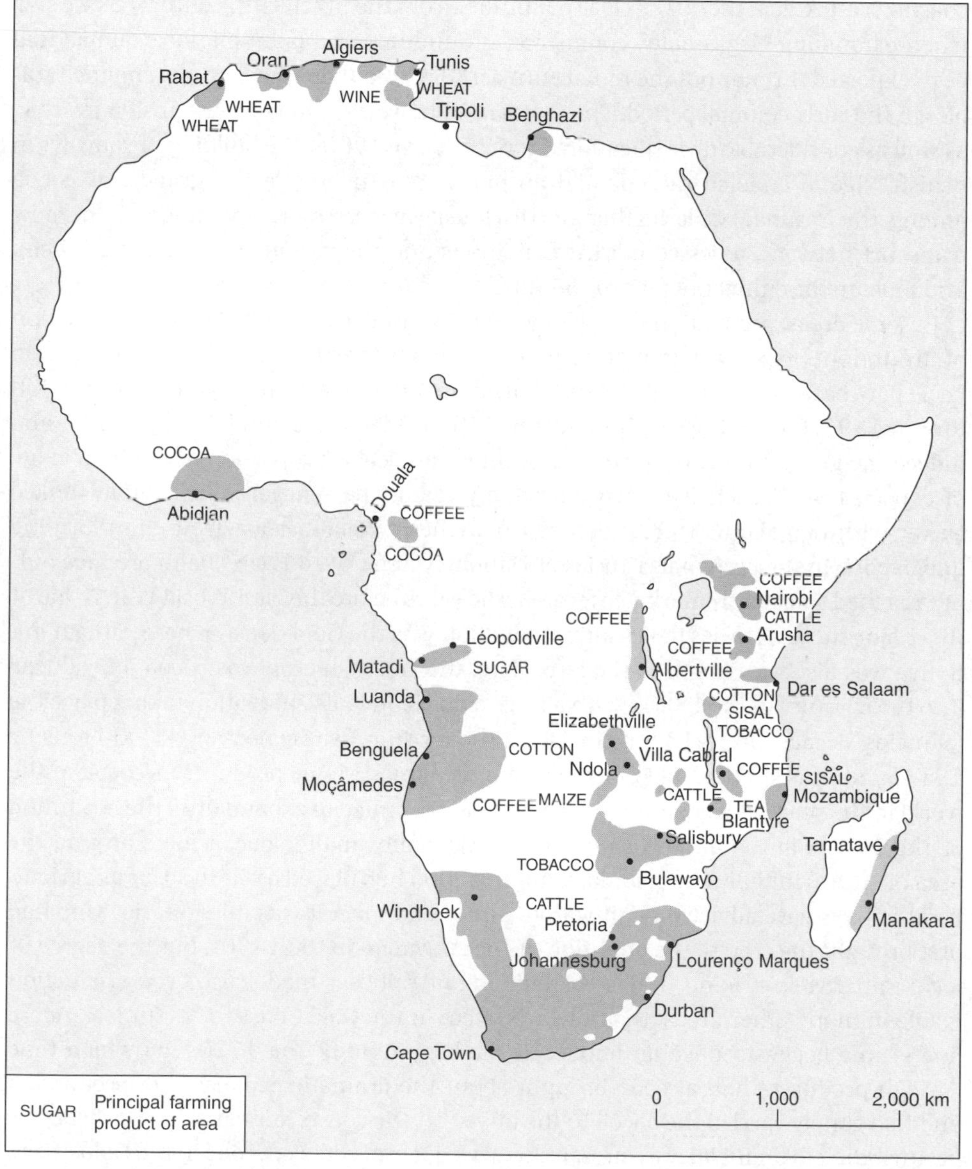

Colonial economics (1): areas of European farming. Source: From B. Davidson, *Modern Africa: A Social and Political History*, 3rd ed. (London and New York: Longman, 1994), p. 15, Map 2. © 1994 by Basil Davidson. Reproduced with permission of Taylor and Francis.

Elsewhere, there were instances of the same kind of plundering and forced labor as in the Congo, notably in Côte d'Ivoire, Cameroon, and Mozambique. But more generally across the tropical belt, production was largely left to African peasant producers, whose efficiency was widely acknowledged – at least in the early years of colonial rule – and in British and French West Africa, farmers were encouraged to produce cash crops for export.[13] Successful export production was usually the result of a combination of factors, including African initiative, external demand, official encouragement, the monetarization of tax systems (farmers needed to acquire cash to pay their taxes), and the creation of transport infrastructures, including railways and roads. In many parts of coastal West Africa, there was clear continuity from the nineteenth century: as we saw when examining "legitimate" commerce, groundnuts and palm oil, for example had been exported throughout the nineteenth century, and these same crops remained staples in the early colonial period. There was now, however, a massive expansion in scale, as well as considerable diversification. From the early 1900s, the building of railways in British Nigeria enabled the colonial authorities to encourage the growth of cocoa among the Yoruba, while further north Hausa farmers took advantage of the new transport network, assessed market conditions and the various options before them, and took up the cultivation of groundnuts.[14]

In some areas, production quickly reached remarkable levels. In Senegal, production of groundnuts expanded dramatically in the years before the First World War, again in large part because of the railway that linked the interior with the coast. From 50,000 tons in 1897, the territory was producing 240,000 tons of groundnuts by 1913 – and indeed the groundnut continued to account for a sizeable proportion of the total value of exports from French West Africa for many years. The Senegal railway finally linked Dakar with Bamako in 1923, opening up further possibilities for groundnut farming and export. In the French territories of Dahomey and Côte d'Ivoire, palm produce output reached similarly remarkable levels in the years before the First World War.[15] One of the major success stories in peasant production was the Gold Coast, where African initiative was also very much to the fore. Here, the key cash crop was cocoa, introduced into the territory in the 1880s, with a huge expansion in its cultivation taking place the following decade. From 13 tons in 1892, the territory was exporting 40,000 tons by 1914, and thus did the Gold Coast become the largest single producer of cocoa in the world in the space of a generation. Production continued to expand until the beginning of the 1970s, in the hands of millions of Akwapim smallholder farmers around the area of Accra. Initially, the colonial administration had played a role in so far as agricultural officers gave advice on cultivation, although in fact it was missionaries who had first brought the crop to the attention of the Akwapim in the 1880s, but the degree of local initiative is striking. While the building of railways made cash-crop production viable in many other areas, the railway system in the Gold Coast – the Kumasi–Accra line – only began to have an impact at the beginning of the 1920s, by which time African producers had already brought about the dramatic expansion in production and had simply carried the cocoa to the buyers at the coast. Nor can economic success be attributed to financial pressures, as tax was not especially onerous in the Gold Coast, at least compared to other territories. It is clearly the case that the presence of European trading companies was instrumental in the growth of the cocoa business, but Africans, rather than Europeans, were the entrepreneurs, the former bringing the cocoa to the latter. The Akwapim were not novices to the export trade, having sold wild rubber and palm oil to European traders in the course of the nineteenth century, but as prices for these commodities dipped in the last years of the century, the Akwapim were open to new ideas, and on the lookout for new markets and products. As with all cash-crop producers, they had to balance the cultivation of crops for export with that of food crops, and apportion land accordingly, a pressure which was ever-present (and particularly severe during periods of global downturn, as we shall see). Their selection of cocoa indicated long-term economic vision. Moreover, cocoa required large areas of land, and bush clearance would involve considerable labor, while the cocoa tree itself can take up to fifteen years to mature. Cocoa cultivation, therefore, represented an investment for the future. The Akwapim were confronted with a further challenge in that the area was densely populated, and thus a number of pioneer farmers moved westwards into the less-populated Akim territory, joining together to purchase land from the Akim. Initially, making use of the labor of women and junior members of the household, and perhaps also slaves, the Akwapim then attracted local labor to clear the area of vegetation, and eventually hired porters to carry the cocoa to the coast. In the Akwapim, then, we can see something of a class of capitalist farmers emerging.[16]

In the Gold Coast, as in other parts of Atlantic Africa, there was a certain continuity from the precolonial to the colonial eras; the production of cocoa at least in part reflected long experience of the export trade, and it can thus be argued that in this context, the colonial state was relatively unimportant in bringing about socioeconomic change. In eastern Africa, however, there was profound discontinuity, and the late nineteenth and early twentieth centuries witnessed socioeconomic transformation. This was because in eastern Africa commercial agriculture was ill-developed by the late nineteenth century, at least in terms of global export, if not at the very local level; exceptions included Zanzibar, a major exporter of cloves and other spices, and a handful of other localities near the coast or in the immediate hinterland. Soon, however, the commercial frontier advanced into the interior. The Chagga around Mount Kilimanjaro, for example became prodigious producers of coffee.[17] Uganda demonstrates the dramatic transition very well, and here profound economic change originated in the kingdom of Buganda, whose highly centralized and hierarchical political system offers a striking contrast with the decentralized and egalitarian Akwapim in the Gold Coast. In the second half of the nineteenth century, Buganda's export economy was based on slaves and ivory, the purchasers of which were Arab traders, yet this trade was inimical to long-term economic development, and during the 1880s and 1890s it was in terminal decline. Within a few years, however, Uganda had become a major producer of cotton, and unlike in the Gold Coast, the colonial state can be seen to have been instrumental in bringing about change. The Uganda Railway was clearly crucial, making cash-crop production viable in the Lake Victoria area; without it, no commercial agriculture would have been possible. From 1902, moreover, the "cotton gospel" was spread by the British Cotton Growing Association, active in many parts of the British Empire, which identified Uganda as an ideal area for such production. In 1904, in the face of such official encouragement, the Ganda chiefly class embraced cotton, but the fact that it did so also reflected certain social and cultural values in Buganda itself. Ganda society was highly competitive, and in many respects was a meritocracy, with individuals encouraged to win access to the center of power – in the nineteenth century the royal court – by seizing whatever opportunity came their way. The cotton project offered such an opportunity. The chiefs involved, moreover, were predominantly members of the Protestant elite, who believed themselves to belong to a new political order; they were innovative, energetic, and had embraced the notion of the close links between Christianity and commercial development. Such chiefs played a crucial role in traveling to rural areas and encouraging the adoption of cotton, and peasant farmers responded positively, not least because the value of the tenant's land increased considerably once cotton was planted. By the First World War, cotton production in southern Uganda had expanded dramatically and represented another cash-crop success story; moreover, soil fertility and a moist climate meant that southern Uganda enjoyed the rare security of a regular food supply (the banana being the staple food crop) alongside a lucrative cash crop.[18]

Cotton was also one of the staples of the French-administered western and central African savannah, as well as parts of the forest, where officials "encouraged" its production by forcing local chiefs to deliver a certain quantity to market every year. Indeed, in some areas, the introduction of cotton was associated with a particularly oppressive colonial approach, as in German East Africa in the early 1900s, and in French Central Africa (present-day Central African Republic) from the mid-1920s, where cotton production was based on forced labor and artificially low prices. Nonetheless – or, perhaps, as a result – cotton became the mainstay of the colonial economy across large areas of French western and equatorial Africa.[19] Cotton was king in Egypt, too, where the British in the late nineteenth century set about redesigning and rebuilding an extensive irrigation system, including the deepening of canals and the construction of dams. Above all the British consul general, Lord Cromer, believed that cataracts on the Nile would generate the income needed to develop not only the Egyptian economy, but that of Sudan, too, where further economic possibilities were opened up in the wake of the defeat of the Mahdist state in 1898. Irrigation in Egypt brought about a huge expansion of cultivated land, although there were negative consequences in terms of soil exhaustion. As agricultural yields increased, however, the British were also concerned to develop Egyptian industry, and processing plants for cotton, sugar, and tobacco produced a certain amount of revenue for the European financiers who allied themselves with government in these activities.[20] Further south, in Sudan, the partnership of private and public initiative was critical in the development of a massive irrigation scheme in the Gezira area, where cotton was again envisaged as the major crop. While the British government encouraged the scheme, the Sudan Plantations Syndicate provided much of the finance, and while in theory land remained under Sudanese control, in reality the government dictated the terms by which land could be held by individual tenants.[21] Cotton in Gezira was a great success, becoming the engine of the Sudanese economy and contrasting with the commercial exclusion of the vast region of southern Sudan; as with many other territories, however, the reliance on a single crop rendered Sudan vulnerable to shifts in the global market, as demonstrated dramatically in the years of the Great Depression.

White Settlement

In those territories where production was not in the hands of African farmers, communities of white settlers were positioned at the center of colonial economies. In the settler zone – as in the industrial zone, as we see below – Africans were politically marginalized, and fulfilled the role of cheap wage labor feeding economic systems over which, again, they had little control, at least until they discovered that they did indeed have a certain amount of muscle. In a number of territories – for example Uganda, which had initially been earmarked as an area for possible European settlement – African peasant farmers succeeded in keeping white farmers at bay because the latter could not compete with the highly efficient, small-scale productive units of the former, but elsewhere – Kenya, or Southern Rhodesia – white settlement was systematically encouraged, and indeed subsidized by colonial government. These territories had very different paths of economic, social, and political development.[22]

In Kenya, the implications of white settlement were profound. Again, the Mombasa–Kisumu railway was crucial, as it shifted the center of political gravity from the coast to the highlands, and facilitated the emergence of a distinctive community around a railway junction that would in time become the sprawling metropolis of Nairobi. Initially, built at the British taxpayer' expense, the early colonial administration sought to create a viable economy in the territory to recoup the costs; in this respect, it was faced with two principal concerns. First, there was the issue of Kenya's geography. Much of the territory was arid savannah, with low rainfall and a sparse, dispersed population. The exception was the southern zone, the Rift Valley and surrounding highlands, which had a healthy, temperate climate and good rainfall, and which was quickly identified as an attractive area for European settlement. Second, in terms of the sociopolitical organization of the peoples of the area, there was a stark contrast between Kenya and neighboring Uganda. Buganda, as we have seen, had a centralized monarchical system which had been "opened" to Christian influence; Ganda chiefs played a crucial role in the development of cash-crop farming, acting as the agents of commercial agriculture. But the Kenyan interior was sparsely populated by mostly "stateless" groups, and thus there were no natural intermediaries with whom business could be done and who might act as the agents of change; moreover, the bulk of the territory's indigenous population, including the Maasai, the Kikuyu, and the Luo, was more pastoralist than that of, say, neighboring Uganda; Kenyan economies were characterized by the keeping of livestock alongside a comparatively small agricultural base. Early administrators thus saw little prospect of peasant agriculture developing, and from 1903, the administration encouraged settler farming by providing financial incentives. Initially piecemeal and haphazard, nonetheless by the time of the First World War a small but significant settler community had emerged; they were a motley bunch, including Afrikaners ironically seeking a new life away from aggressive British imperialism in South Africa, and British aristocrats who staked out huge areas of land, and who enjoyed both political influence and financial backing. There were big-game hunters, too, an assorted mix of adventurers and itinerants, and together they would make up one of the most eclectic, dynamic European communities in colonial Africa.[23]

The early settlers purchased land from the Kikuyu, the predominant group in the area, but increasingly the government expropriated Kikuyu land and parceled it out to the settlers. It was the best land, too, huge tracts of what would in time become known as the "white highlands," set aside for European use and cleared of their African inhabitants. Here was the fundamental difference between the settler colony and other forms of territory: Africans would be both politically and economically marginalized, notwithstanding the fact that the settler economy relied on their labor. Pressures of tax compelled Africans into the labor market, but forced labor was increasingly common, beginning before 1914 and expanding in the 1920s. There was resistance, but it was brutally crushed, and as the Kikuyu and others found themselves dispossessed, the settlers were given an increasingly powerful voice in the administration of the territory, though never as much as their counterparts further south, in Southern Rhodesia.

A system of reserves developed, with African land located, predictably, in areas characterized by poor soil and far from the main markets. At the same time, however, a system of "squatters" emerged: white settlers often expropriated more land than they could actually farm, and so African squatters were encouraged to settle on plantations and cultivate their own crops, in return for which they would work a certain number of days per year for the white landowner. Thousands of squatters found this preferable to life on the reserves, and provided a source of cheap labor for European farmers. During the early years of the colony, the government was involved in propping up the settler economy with financial and other assistance. There was a thriving agricultural department for white farmers, providing seeds, equipment, and advice; banks provided start-up loans, and the administration offered cheap transportation rates on the railway. Crucially, moreover, African farmers were excluded by law from the export trade; prohibited from growing coffee, for example, Africans could only compete on the domestic market, notably in terms of growing foodstuffs for expanding Nairobi. In fact, it would be many years before the settler economy became broadly profitable, and it developed along two distinct lines. On the one hand, there was the small-scale family farm, where maize was grown for the local market and some livestock kept; seldom doing more than subsisting, these kinds of units were essentially parasitic, requiring subsidies from the state, and indeed African smallholder farmers were much more efficient, a fact not lost on many colonial officials. However, these small-scale units were largely irrelevant to the Kenyan economy, the wealth of which rested on the large-scale plantations which were capital-rich and independent of government support; these were involved in commercial agriculture, growing coffee or tea for export.[24]

Elsewhere, dreams of gold – a "second rand" – in Southern Rhodesia were swiftly disappointed. There was gold, but nothing on the scale of that found further south; in Rhodesia, it was located in a series of small reefs, unlike in South Africa, as we see below, where it was concentrated in a single area. There was thus little chance of consolidating the industry, and in the years following the arrival of Rhodes' pioneer column and the suppression of the Shona–Ndebele uprising, the territory was flooded with white farmers who combined small-scale and localized gold-mining with some cultivation and keeping of livestock. As in Kenya, Africans were compelled into a wage labor market, and as in Kenya, land settlement was harsh for the African population. Southern

Rhodesia was long seen as the poor relative of booming South Africa, but its settlers were able to match those of the latter in terms of political ambition and fierce independent-mindedness. White power was gradually consolidated until in 1923, the territory achieved self-governing status, under the watchful eye of a governor appointed by London, awarding the settlers a degree of political autonomy which their Kenyan counterparts could only envy. In 1930, the Land Apportionment Act squeezed the bulk of the African population into 7.5 million acres of reserve land, while the settlers took 49 million acres of the best land. The implications for the future political and socioeconomic development of the territory were enormous.[25]

In terms of scale, Algeria was second only to South Africa – to which we turn below – as a territory of white settlement. The first settlers – colons, or pieds noirs – had begun to arrive in the 1830s: from around 25,000 at the end of that decade, the white population exceeded half a million in the 1890s. They were largely concentrated along the Mediterranean coast, and comprised mostly poor peasants, especially from southern France, who saw migration as a chance to escape poverty at home and seize new opportunities; they owned small plots of land and generally struggled to expand beyond subsistence level. There were also substantial Italian and Spanish populations. Increasingly, the urban centers – notably Algiers and Oran – attracted settlers, including those who had abandoned their unprofitable farms, and from here the colon community began to exercise political muscle. They secured direct representation in the Paris assembly and established a considerable degree of control over the internal affairs of Algeria. Their political identity was expressed in the concept of Algérie Française, portraying the territory as a part of France overseas, and in so doing they asserted racial and cultural superiority over the Arab and Berber populations. Through the early twentieth century, the colons would repeatedly and doggedly reject any suggestion from Paris that certain categories of the indigenous population might be enfranchised or granted other rights of citizenship; in the process, Algeria would loom increasingly large in French domestic and foreign policy.[26]

Industry

Across southern Africa, and in the Union of South Africa in particular, mining economies shaped the nature of political administrations, while migrant labor systems linked together the Union, Northern and Southern Rhodesia, Nyasaland, and even southern Congo. Northern Rhodesia was largely, like Nyasaland, an exporter of labor in the first two decades of the twentieth century, but in the 1920s, it became one of the world's largest producers of copper, and Southern Rhodesia, as we have seen, was a settler economy based on farming and small-scale gold-mining. By the First World War, however, South Africa was producing 40 percent of the world's gold, while Johannesburg had a population of 250,000, making it the largest urban center south of the Sahara. Large-scale diamond-and gold-mining operations were dominated by huge companies, their equally huge profits made possible by a combination of European capital and cheap African labor.[27] Indeed, it was the need to ensure a steady supply of the latter which shaped social and economic policy in South Africa through the twentieth century, and around which much racial ideology was formed, although racialism in the territory had its roots in the nineteenth century and earlier, as we saw in Chapter 4.

During the brief downturn in the fortunes of the gold industry – the years either side of the second Boer war – African labor proved difficult to recruit, and alternative strategies were required. Companies turned to the international labor market, and between 1903 and 1907 some 60,000 Chinese workers were brought in, and paid markedly low wages, i.e. on average one-third of that paid to their white counterparts. The latter felt threatened, and demanded – and succeeded in having granted – a series of "color bars" which specified that certain jobs could only be filled by whites. In 1907, the Chinese were sent home; the gold-mining industry began to recover, and unemployment and tax demands drove Africans back to the mines. But the color bars remained in place. At the same time, a major cross-border labor recruitment system developed. The Witwatersrand Native Labor Agency, for example, operated across the region, recruiting labor from impoverished rural areas in particular, mostly from Northern Rhodesia and Nyasaland. Migrant labor served the mining industry for many years: Nyasas, Barotse, Swazi, Sotho, and Tswana moved back and forth across the region, the wages they earned in the course of their short-term contracts being returned to their rural homelands, at least in the early years of the system. Both conditions of service and the compound system developed to house workers were usually horrendous. The southern and central African labor force was run on highly militarized lines, with workers housed in compounds and hired – for the first few years, at any rate – on short-term contracts with a view to preventing the emergence of a wider "national" or working-class consciousness, although as we see in a later chapter, this was unsuccessful in the longer term. Migrant laborers came without families and were thus paid lower wages as single men; they were subject to a brutal system of rules and ordinances, a legal structure backing mine-owners which aimed at absolute social control and economic growth. The breaking of a contract, for example, was regarded as tantamount to military desertion, with punishment meted out accordingly. In areas where "voluntary" recruitment remained slow, a system of forced labor was created, known as *chibaro*.[28]

In the 1920s mining for copper on a large scale began in Northern Rhodesia, and the "copper belt" attracted companies pursuing many of the same policies found further south. Migrant labor formed the bulk of the workforce, maintained on low wages and short-term contracts; skilled jobs were reserved for European workers. Conditions were marginally better in the copper mines of neighboring Katanga province, in southern Congo, where Africans were offered longer-term contracts, provided with a basic education, and trained in, and allowed access to, more skilled positions. Workers were initially brought in from Northern Rhodesia, but by the 1930s, most came from elsewhere in the Congo, and from Rwanda and Burundi.[29] Overall, a regional economy developed, as brutal and exploitative as it was dynamic, and the bedrock of which was an itinerant, underpaid, and politically oppressed African labor force. In time, migrant labor gave way to more settled proletariats and more coherent and organized protest would result. But immense damage was done to rural economies, as both short-term migration and long-term urbanization drained communities of some of their most able-bodied members.

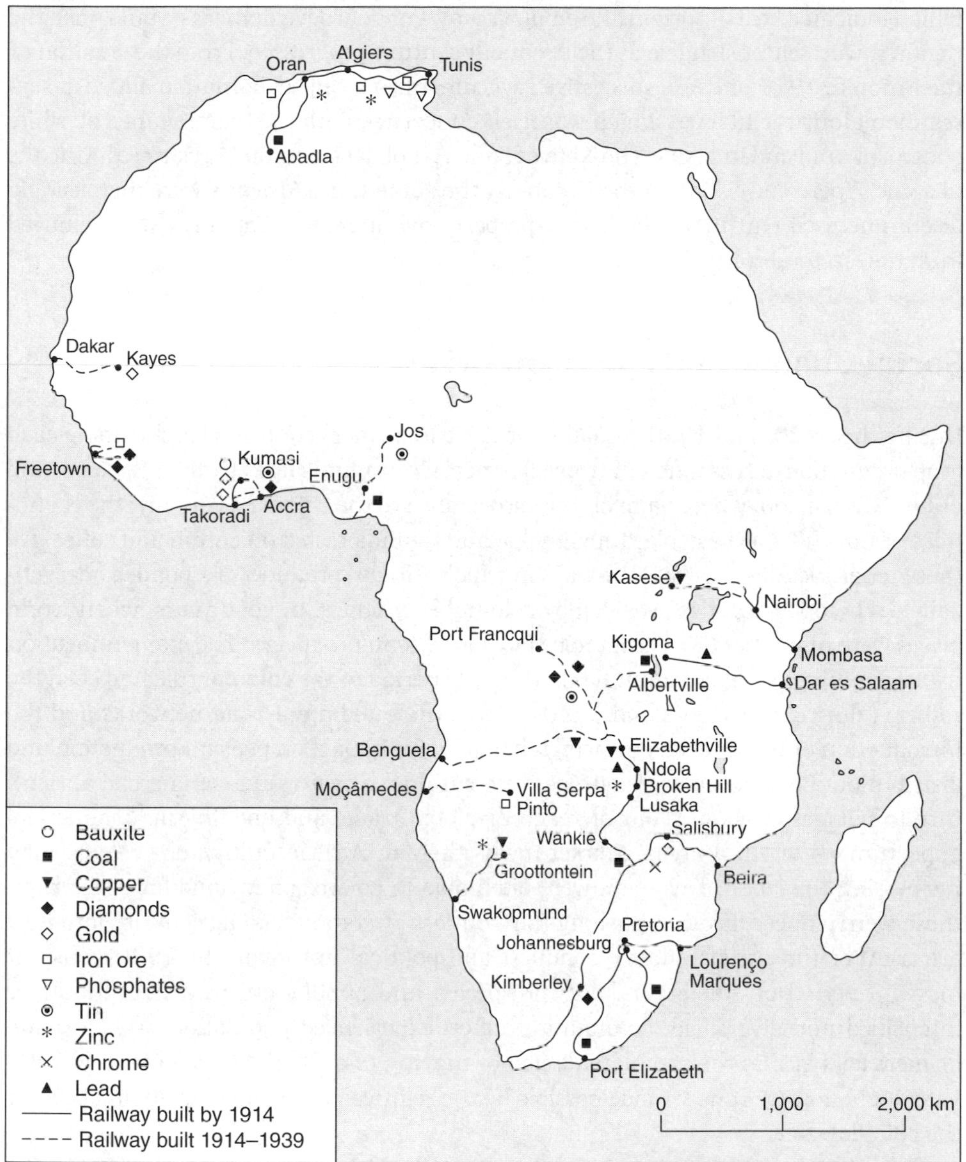

Colonial economics (2): mineral exploitation and railways. Source: From B. Davidson, *Modern Africa: A Social and Political History*, 3rd ed. (London and New York: Longman, 1994), p. 49, Map 5. © 1994 by Basil Davidson. Reproduced with permission of Taylor and Francis.

The combination of a sizeable white minority and the emergence of an industrial mining system in South Africa led to the alienation of land from the early 1900s onward. Africans were increasingly confined to designated "reserve" territories and could only legally travel to areas of white settlement or to the cities by carrying a pass which indicated "tribal" origin and employment. Political developments would push the region toward bitter struggle as the twentieth century progressed. From the creation of the Union in 1910 onward, successive governments developed legislation aimed at segregation along racial lines, which was itself concerned with the maintenance of white control of land and industry. The Natives Land Act of 1913, notably, restricted Africans to some 7 percent of land in the Union. At the same time, Africans were increasingly disenfranchised, with the last of them – a property-owning elite in Cape Province – removed from the electoral roll in 1936.[30]

Social Change and Emergent Crisis

During the 1920s and 1930s, small-scale African farmers continued to dominate cash crop production across much of tropical Africa. Groundnuts flowed out of Senegal, and out of Nigeria, too, where palm oil was also central to the colonial economy; the economies of Côte d'Ivoire, Angola, Tanganyika, and Uganda rested on cotton and coffee. All these territories demonstrate the ways in which African producers responded energetically to the opportunities provided by colonial economics. In good years, when world prices were high, there was profit to be had for African producers. The main innovation transforming peasant communities in the early period of the colonial rule had been the railway; during the 1920s and 1930s, it was the building of road networks and the introduction of motor transport which had a major impact on peasant production and distribution. Lorries penetrated deeper into rural areas, carrying commercial agriculture to villages previously out of reach of global trade, and opening up commercial opportunities in rural areas. Market towns thrived. African cultivators, mostly men harnessing the labor of women, were often able to colonize new land for cash crops; these were pioneer farmers, pushing the frontiers of commercial agriculture into new areas. After the era of military conquest and political upheaval, the 1920s was, for many, a period of stability, relative prosperity, and population growth. Agriculture intensified and diversified, communities often experienced population pressure, and farmers fell back on the precolonial habit of moving to new land to colonize and cultivate, a phenomenon now made possible by the relative peace and security imposed by the colonial state.

The migration of communities, the expansion of commercial agriculture, the advance of entrepreneurs in search of new opportunities: all this created much social change and indeed social unrest. One of the key themes for West Africa in the late nineteenth and early twentieth centuries, for example, was the migration of people from the interior to the coast in search of work. New communities were being formed: these were in part "peasant," with family groups farming their own land using their own labor, producing for domestic consumption, and in part "capitalist," sometimes employing wage labor in agriculture, producing for the external market, and reinvesting profits. A commercial hierarchy developed, with small groups of powerful and successful African entrepreneurs dominating production, for example in the Gold Coast and Nigeria. Full-blown capitalism was hindered in most areas, however – as it may have been in the nineteenth century, too – because of a combination of several factors. Even the poorer groups in society usually had access to some land, and thus a degree of economic independence, while wage laborers could usually demand payment of a proportion of crops cultivated, or a portion of land for themselves, as was the case in Côte d'Ivoire. In the Gold Coast, cocoa production expanded rapidly during the 1920s, based largely on the share-cropping system which was both popular and deep-rooted: individuals or family groups would come to the cocoa-producing area, and the resident community would permit them to grow cocoa privately on its land in exchange for a share of the produce, usually a third. Thus did production grow, but thus, too, was a fully "capitalist" system prevented.[31]

Europeans – whether colonial officials or traders – were generally hostile to increasingly powerful and wealthy African entrepreneurs. There was a constant concern, doubtless in part rooted in the experience of the late nineteenth century, that the latter might develop too much market strength, and colonial administrations preferred to deal with the "traditional" authority supposedly invested in the indirect-rule chiefs. This was perhaps clearest across British West Africa, but it was a strategy employed, too, by the French and the Belgians. Colonial authorities were wary of the rise of new economic elites which would increasingly dabble in politics: they were the products of the colonial system, and had emerged in response to the socioeconomic environment created by colonial rule, but they were increasingly in a position to challenge that very system. As far as colonial planners were concerned, these groups needed to be curtailed and restrained within the parameters of "traditional" authority. Importantly, moreover, conflict would develop, on the one hand, between new elites and older chiefs, as the former increasingly rejected the authority of the latter, and on the other, between peasant farmers more broadly and indirect-rule chiefs.

That would come later, but the fragility of the economic system was already clear enough. In the early decades of the twentieth century, Africans displayed the same economic vitality and creativity as they had in the nineteenth century – and in the right circumstances, profit and "progress," however the latter is defined, were eminently achievable. But optimists who in the 1920s pointed happily to Africans' steady economic development – as defined in the imperial manifestos of the late nineteenth century – failed to appreciate long-term instability. Indeed, a myopic presentism would increasingly come to dominate external analyses of African economic performance as the twentieth century progressed. Africans had few means at their disposal, whether economic or political, to fundamentally influence the parameters of the system – in particular, the vagaries of the market, and the political decisions affecting the operation of the market itself. Moreover, Africa's main exports were agricultural and forest products, as well as minerals, as had been the case since the early nineteenth century in some areas, which severely limited the potential for sustainable "development," according to the broadest definition of that term. Indeed, in some parts of West Africa, the "legitimate commerce" of the nineteenth century essentially continued unaltered through much of the colonial era – with all that this demonstrated in terms of the dynamism of the African engagement with the global economy but also with all that it implied about the essential inequity of that economy.

A somewhat different set of stresses were present in white settler colonies, and Kenya illustrates the point. Here, the combination of land alienation and population growth created problems for such groups as the Kikuyu and the Maasai. Through the 1920s and 1930s, Africans experienced intense land pressure, squeezed into increasingly overcrowded reserves. Under the "squatter" arrangement, there had been some land available for temporary settlement, but throughout the 1920s, as Europeans themselves grew in number, settlers brought more land under cultivation and demanded more labor from their squatters. The colonial administration was increasingly committed to the creation of an African labor force: it was ever more common for squatters to be expected to work six months of the year for white landowners. Global depression brought some relief for Africans: as demand for cash crops fell in the early 1930s, many settlers faced ruin, and a number drifted home, abandoning land and homesteads and allowing Africans to creep back onto farms, cultivating for themselves and local markets. Excluded from commercial agriculture, they were – unlike peasant farmers in Uganda, or Tanganyika, or Gold Coast – relatively unaffected by the global slump. However, the respite did not last long. By the mid-1940s, international demand was again on the rise, and with it, the arrival of an expanded community of white settlers. This time, the aim was the abolition of the squatter system and the creation of a permanent wage labor force, and the result, by the end of the decade, was a looming social crisis: ever larger numbers of Africans were forced off European land into the reserves, or else drifted into the cities in search of work, whether Nairobi in the highlands or Mombasa at the coast. The landless poor – lacking in skills and access to them, working as laborers either on white farms or in the swelling urban centers – constituted a huge chunk of the populace, increasingly politicized, radicalized, and open to revolutionary political ideas. They were ripe for mobilization, and began to congregate around any cause that held out the promise of destruction of the extant political and social system.[32] These were the underlying roots of the Mau Mau revolt, to which we will return in a later chapter.

The mounting tension, however, was not simply that between African and European. There was also significant differentiation and socioeconomic stratification within Kikuyu society, and these divisions have been as important a dynamic in the shaping of modern Kenya's history as the presence of a European settler community. Since the First World War, the bulk of Kikuyu had striven to survive within new socioeconomic circumstances by producing a surplus for the domestic market. Yet widespread land shortage, overcrowding in the reserves, and huge demand for labor had compelled most people into a subsistence economy, with only a fortunate minority able to exploit the opportunities offered by the domestic economy by cultivating surpluses in the reserves and carving out for themselves a relatively advantageous position in the colonial system. Many of these "pioneer farmers" were mission-educated and were members of chiefly lineages dating to the nineteenth century, or had become chiefs under British tutelage. With access to land; labor, and modest capital, they had economic advantages not shared by most Kikuyu, and were able to exploit the internal market created by the expansion of Nairobi, successfully competing with smallholder European farms in the supplying of foodstuffs to the urban center. The political implications were far-reaching, as a growing gulf emerged between a comparatively comfortable minority and the vast majority lacking access to land and control over their own labor. In the course of the 1930s, members of the elite became pillars of the colonial order, with a stake in the system, seeking not to represent the landless and marginalized majority, but to protect their own interests against the power of the settler state. By the end of the 1940s, these various strains within Kenyan African politics would compound the mounting social crisis among the urban poor and rural landless. On the eve of Mau Mau, the latter looked to radical, populist leaders for solutions, notably Jomo Kenyatta, who used the rhetoric of radical populism but who in reality counted among the elite, and who was scarcely interested in the destruction of the existing order. Increasingly, the Kikuyu elite would find itself the target of popular hostility, and indeed later of Mau Mau violence; prosperous Kikuyu were as stark a representation of what was wrong with the system as European settlers themselves.[33]

Hearts and Minds

In principle, the education of the African was at the heart of the civilizing mission; yet there was much variation in education policy across the continent, and much uncertainty about what role education was actually to play in Africa's development. There was considerable disagreement between colonial administrations and the missionaries who did most of the educating. In very broad terms, however, colonial education policy reflected the ascendancy of the concept of "association" over the "assimilationist" ideas of the earlier nineteenth century, which had envisaged the incorporation of educated Africans into European culture and civilization. Thus would create a class of "black Englishmen" and "black Frenchmen." Instead, in line with the thinking behind indirect rule, for example, education should be made relevant to Africans' own cultural points of reference and background; the "Africanization" of schooling would mostly involve the education of "natives" within certain parameters, and, for most of them, only up to a certain level. Even within these constraints, however, only small minorities were exposed to education – and this was mostly at the primary school level – which for many years remained in the hands of evangelical Christian orders, in the case of sub-Saharan Africa, and Muslim instructors in the north. Boys were more likely to attend school than girls, but the vast majority of Africans lacked access to schools of any kind. The French and the Portuguese were marginally more interested in training up an assimilate elite than the British, and these were supposed to be the beneficiaries and upholders of the colonial order. Some were indeed both.[34]

In some areas, the potential existed for competition between Christian and Islamic learning. While British authorities sought to restrict missionary activities in Muslim areas in order to prevent conflict, however, the French frequently sought to undermine Islam by closing Quranic schools. Islamic learning had a long history across Saharan and northern Africa, but with the advent of colonial rule in Egypt and the Maghreb, European education systems were established across the region which produced a new class of North Africans steeped in European language and culture. From the 1880s,

Tunisian students were fluent in French and graduates actively lobbied for an expansion of the colonial education system; their counterparts in Algeria were comparatively minute in number, with the imported French system functioning primarily for settlers. In Libya, Italian education vied with a Sanusiyya system which promoted Islamic culture and anticolonial resistance. The British made sure that the Egyptian colonial administration would only accept graduates of schools on the European model, and a class of Egyptians which was European in its outlook and which eschewed much Islamic culture soon emerged. In Egypt, notably, girls as well as boys – albeit middle class – had access to education.[35]

It is impossible to divorce most colonial education south of the Sahara from Christian proselytizing; most Africans who converted to Christianity after about 1900 did so as a result of schooling. Christian missions proliferated in the late nineteenth and early twentieth centuries: the Church Missionary Society, the Wesleyan Missionary Society, the London Missionary Society, the Baptist Missionary Society, the American Bible Society, to name some of the largest, were all involved in the establishment of schools. These schools may have been unevenly spread and may have served the interests of a narrow elite – the children of chiefs, for example – but they had a profound impact on those who sat in their classrooms. Their lives were usually irrevocably changed as a result; in addition to the inculcation of Christian belief, children were made aware of the civilizing properties of the colonial state, to which they were taught absolute loyalty, were made literate and numerate, and sometimes were exposed to vocational training. According to some historians, mission schools were the clearest manifestations of cultural imperialism; for others, they might be seen as ultimately advancing the cause of African development and modernization.[36] Either way, while missionary orders themselves might sometimes enjoy the patronage of colonial authorities, they were not infrequently in conflict with them. Education was not particularly high on the agenda of colonial administrations and was seen as purely functional: colonial bureaucracies needed a number of literate Africans who could write and speak in European languages, who could work as translators, assistants, and clerks, while the system depended on trained people performing a range of lower-ranking jobs. But beyond this, no great value was placed on education as a force for social transformation – indeed, this was the last thing that colonial governments wanted to encourage.

For this reason, there were comparatively few institutions of higher education in colonial Africa. Where they did exist – for example Cairo University, Gordon Memorial College in Khartoum, Makerere College in Kampala, the Lovedale Institute in South Africa, Yaba Higher College in Lagos – their curricula were designed to produce an administrative elite capable of filling bureaucratic roles. In time, however, and certainly by the 1930s and 1940s, the colonial state became rather more involved in education, subsidizing schools, and taking a greater interest in curriculum development. The French sought to render education more relevant to "African conditions," for example, by extending it into rural areas. In the late 1940s and early 1950s, new colleges were founded in a number of British territories, for example at Kumasi in the Gold Coast, Ibadan in Nigeria, Nairobi in Kenya, and Salisbury in Southern Rhodesia. In some respects, this reflected a more general tendency toward greater interventionism and in particular a concern to control the kind of elites that were being produced, as well as the patterns of social change that they symbolized. Arguably, however, in taking so little interest in universal education for much of the colonial era, European powers rendered the task of creating viable modern nation states virtually impossible; illiteracy, notably, was one of the single most important factors behind the failure of participatory politics in the postcolonial era. Moreover, the elitist nature of colonial education produced class tensions and opened up further divisions within African societies. Nonetheless, it is also the case that members of the new educated elite had been made aware of European constitutional and legal history, and of such concepts and principles as "democracy" and "civil rights"; they were also perfectly conscious of the fact that these had been denied to Africans themselves, and thus education sowed the seeds of political discontent. African self-awareness, elite though it was, represented a paradox at the heart of the "civilizing mission" which would lead ultimately to the destruction of the colonial order – something which Europeans themselves had doubtless long feared.

More broadly in terms of social change and continuity, family life and the status of women remained remarkably unaffected by colonial rule across swathes of sub-Saharan Africa. While burgeoning towns offered some degree of "escape" from male control, even in these settings beer-brewing and prostitution were the most common fates for women who had left their rural homes. Elsewhere, while the cash-crop economy brought commercial opportunities for both men and women, most of these went to men; women engaged in some casual labor, but their roles were often confined to domestic work, such as cultivating food crops, and rearing children, especially in areas where the men were involved in labor migration. Polygamy proved resistant to colonial rule in many areas, for the same reason it had been prevalent in the precolonial era: it awarded men control over female labor. Christian marriage made few inroads, owing largely to the prohibitive doctrines of European churches. Yet there was considerable regional variation. While polygamy remained common in western Africa as late as the middle of the twentieth century, it declined dramatically across Eastern and Central Africa, as well as north of the Sahara. Moreover, women in West Africa participated in trade more vigorously than their counterparts elsewhere, a role which dated to the nineteenth century.[37]

Nonetheless, while basic family structures proved remarkably resilient through the colonial period – nineteenth-century Africans would have recognized the polygamy, the strategic thinking that underpinned most marriages, and the use of bridewealth in the twentieth – there were also shifts in family relationships which would have important consequences for longer-term sociopolitical development. Wealthier parents may have had power over their sons in terms of inheritance, but the young also found new outlets for their social and political energies and talents. Youth had always been a vital dynamic in the shaping of African state and society; in the colonial period, young men would become involved in the cultural and political organizations discussed later in the book, and had access to education and – in the form of labor migration – economic opportunities which opened up worlds very different from those of their parents.[38] This brought about intergenerational conflict in many societies, as did competition for wives – a core dynamic of African social history – and brought about a gradual reconceptualization of family and kin, authority, power, and the meaning of community, on the part of a new generation. In sum, much as family networks had been disrupted by commercial change in nineteenth-century Tanzania, for example, young men – though to a much lesser extent young women – rejected or at least modified the world of their parents, or adapted the latter to suit the changing sociopolitical circumstances of the age. This would be further accelerated with rapid urbanization.

Environment and Medicine

Just as economic change was unfolding in the late nineteenth and early twentieth centuries, so the environmental impact of contact with the wider world was dramatic. By no means, fairly obviously, was the whole continent affected in the same way, but the themes of environmental and ecological change highlight some of the most important facets of the colonial experience at large, and in particular, are crucial to understanding the concept of the "ambiguity" of colonial rule. Between the middle of the nineteenth century and the 1920s, swathes of eastern and central Africa experienced environmental crisis, involving heightened levels of disease, depopulation, and demographic decline, the result of both man-made and natural causes. To place this in context, it is important to return briefly to a theme outlined at the beginning of the book, namely the ongoing struggle on the part of Africans to "colonize" the continent, to tame and domesticate often harsh environments, and to carve rich and complex civilizations out of landscapes and ecological systems frequently hostile to human settlement. Arguably one of Africans' greatest contributions in the grand sweep of human history, this struggle dated back centuries, indeed millennia, and in many areas was not yet complete in the second half of the nineteenth century, notably in parts of eastern and central Africa. Here, African cultivators and herdsmen were confronted with a series of challenges, including poor, thin soils and slight, variable rainfall; the constant threat posed by wild game which caused damage to crops; and a range of diseases such as malaria and trypanosomiasis, or more popularly "sleeping sickness," the latter spread by the bush- and woodland-dwelling tsetse fly, which is also carried by wild animals. Sleeping sickness was fatal to livestock, while there was also a human variation, which devastated communities until well into the twentieth century, as we shall see. Nonetheless, it is broadly true that, barring periodic crises, states and societies across the region had achieved a degree of mastery over their environments by the nineteenth century: agricultural skills had been developed as the result of intimate knowledge of the land and its capacity, and some measure of control over and immunity from local disease environments had been achieved. It was a delicate balance between man and environment, however, and in many areas, it had broken down by the early twentieth century, largely – though not exclusively – because of the expansion of the tsetse-fly zone.[39]

Across eastern Africa, a wave of crises disturbed the balance from the middle of the nineteenth century onward. The first came in the wake of the political insecurity of the slave trade, during which the region witnessed the movement of armies in search of captives, and a rise in criminality, which in turn produced new patterns of settlement.

Formerly, people had tended to live in scattered settlements, a pattern which had kept bush and thus sleeping sickness at bay over a wide area, but heightened levels of insecurity led people to abandon dispersed habitats and come together in larger communities for protection. This made sense in terms of self-defense in the age of Mirambo and Nyungu-ya-Mawe, but it was disastrous for fragile human control of the environment, for as people withdrew from particular areas, bush rejuvenated, wild game crept forward and the tsetse-fly frontier advanced. The consequent sleeping-sickness epidemic – both animal and human forms of the disease – devastated swathes of eastern and central Africa. In some of the worst-affected areas, for example around the northern shore of Lake Victoria, it killed some 200,000 people in the late nineteenth and early twentieth centuries. Across equatorial Africa, it may have killed up to 90 percent of the population. It erupted in lower Congo in the 1890s, too, spreading upriver and reaching Lake Tanganyika by 1901. The disease then spread south, reaching the area of present-day Zambia by 1907 and having similarly disastrous effects.[40]

Sleeping sickness was soon compounded at the end of the nineteenth century by another destructive wave of cattle disease, in the form of the deadly rinderpest which arrived in the Horn of Africa at the end of the 1880s – probably introduced through infected cattle brought by the Italians – and which then swept south, reaching the area of Tanzania, Kenya, Malawi, and Zambia by the early 1890s; it had appeared at the Cape by 1897.[41] A new disease to the continent, it was catastrophic, killing up to 90 percent of cattle in some areas of eastern and central Africa, and especially destructive among pastoral communities such as the Maasai of Kenya and Tanzania. The initial impact of rinderpest was offset to a very small degree by the fact that it also killed tsetse-carrying wild game, and thus went some way to halting or at least slowing the advance of the fly, but game recovered more quickly than did domesticated livestock, and was soon once more on the increase, and with it the tsetse fly. This clearly greatly exacerbated the effects of the original rinderpest, and the timing of both sleeping sickness and rinderpest was calamitous, coinciding with the aggressive incursions of Europeans and undermining the African capacity for resistance in many areas.[42]

These epidemics were bad enough, but more was to come, the direct result of colonial encroachment. Diseases came with soldiers, traders, missionaries, and of course, with migrating population groups, displaced by sleeping sickness, rinderpest, and European invasion itself. Sub-Saharan Africa was somewhat less affected – and Africa north of the desert less still – by imported disease at the point of European invasion than other parts of the world on the receiving end of Western expansion, notably Central America or Australia. The latter had been much more "isolated" from Eurasia prior to the arrival of white men and their germs; Africa, however, had had centuries of global contact prior to the Scramble, and therefore coastal communities, at least, had developed a degree of immunity from European bacteria. Nonetheless, widespread exposure to new diseases attended colonialism, which brought with it new strains of smallpox, for example. There was also a plague of jiggers, the sand flea introduced from Latin America which buries itself in the skin, particularly of the feet, and causes great suffering and often loss of limbs. While rarely fatal, it was nonetheless painfully demobilizing, destroying labor patterns and undermining local economic systems as it swept from the Atlantic to the Indian Ocean coasts. In addition to smallpox and jiggers, there were also epidemics of cholera, yellow fever, and meningitis. While some believed – understandably – that Europeans had introduced these diseases deliberately, others saw in these catastrophes, the abandonment of communities by their gods; others again blamed sexually transmitted diseases in particular on Arab traders. In Uganda, for example, Arabs were widely held responsible for having introduced new and virulent strains of syphilis, with which a great many Ganda were said to be infected in the early years of the twentieth century. There was, of course, endemic syphilis, but in the second half of the nineteenth century, a new venereal disease in the form of gonorrhea appeared across equatorial Africa, causing infertility particularly in women; this was certainly one of the major factors behind low birth-rates in the region during the early twentieth century.[43]

The imposition of colonial rule had other adverse effects on the environment. Colonial warfare during the 1880s and 1890s, and the bitter campaigns waged to suppress anti-colonial uprisings, resulted in widespread destruction in many areas. In German East Africa, up to a third of the population of the affected area may have died as a result of the war fought to crush the Maji Maji rebellion, while female fertility was affected in the long term as the result of scorched-earth tactics and famine, as revealed in research undertaken during the 1930s.[44] Famine and environmental ruin were frequently the outcome of colonial campaigns; the process of "pacification" often involved the wholesale destruction of villages and arable land, driving communities from their natural economic habitats. The Italian conquest of Libya, lasting twenty years, may have resulted in the deaths of up to a third of the population; the devastation of the German suppression of the Herero revolt in South West Africa in 1904 is evidenced by the fact that of an estimated population of 80,000, only some 16,000 survived, according to a 1908 census.[45]

Environmental breakdown frequently manifested itself in famine, and famine itself was often seen as evidence in European eyes of the "lazy native," and as the outcome of backwardness and ignorance – as it was, too, in Russia and Ireland during the nineteenth century. The era of the partition coincided with a widespread failure of rains across the savannah belt in the 1880s and 1890s, and in many regions, it was not until the 1920s that rainfall levels began to recover. In the late 1880s and early 1890s, there were major famines in Ethiopia – known locally as "Awful Day" – and Sudan. The "Great Famine," as the Kikuyu called it, in parts of eastern Africa lasted between 1898 and 1900, and killed thousands, and catastrophic food shortages struck Transvaal in 1896.[46] Famine, then, was the result of climatic change, as well as of the devastation wrought by disease; it was also the consequence of the breakdown of indigenous economic systems, itself often brought about directly by colonial policy. Demands for labor and the payment of tax, as we have seen, frequently compelled people to move in search of work, undermining the economic capacities of homelands; in areas already hit by famine, "food for work" was sometimes held out as a means of getting hold of cheap labor. And there were the commercial pressures, too: farmers were often compelled to sell more surplus than they would normally have done, and to place greater emphasis on cash crops than subsistence foods. In parts of the western savannah in 1913–14, the combination of drought, tax, cash crops, and labor migration proved deadly, and persistent famine across French Equatorial Africa between 1918 and 1926 was largely the result of a combination of demands for tax and labor.[47] It was ironic, then, that Europeans themselves viewed as part of the "civilizing mission" the need to save "primitive races" from the ravages of disease and famine. As Rudyard Kipling put it,

> Take up the White Man's Burden,
> The savage wars of peace –
> Fill full the mouth of Famine,
> And bid the sickness cease.[48]

Hunger and disease had become colonial stereotypes, conditions associated with non-European peoples; early European misunderstanding of disease and famine would haunt the continent for several decades, and indeed perhaps continues in some respects to distort Western understanding of the African political, economic, and cultural environment. If colonialism could be justified through the stereotypes surrounding famine and disease, then – as we see in a later chapter – the provision of modern food aid can be equally political, even "ideological," in intent.

In other ways, too, colonial policy had detrimental consequences for the African ability to manage their own environments. Prohibitions on hunting meant that Africans were unable to control the damage inflicted by wild game on crops and homesteads. In their concern to control wider communities, colonial authorities sought to create more concentrated centers of population, particularly once they recognized that Africans often dispersed in order to avoid demands for tax and labor. Authorities sought to create villages of a certain size, for example, and again, as in the nineteenth century, this brought about the abandonment of areas which then reverted to bush, and further outbreaks of sleeping sickness in formerly cultivated land. New centers of population themselves were breeding grounds for bacteria: rates of tuberculosis among mine workers living in crowded compounds in southern Africa were higher than among soldiers in the trenches of the Western Front between 1914 and 1918. Much of this also needs to be considered in conjunction with the phenomenon of labor migration itself, which frequently weakened rural communities – although, of course, the prolonged absence of young men also brought about the empowerment of women in many such communities. But the rural poverty which has become characteristic of Africa in recent decades has its roots, to a considerable extent, in the early colonial period.

These phenomena were compounded across eastern and central Africa by the ravages of the First World War: scorched-earth tactics, famine, and Spanish influenza hit communities already reeling from the crises described above. Overall, across swathes of sub-Saharan Africa, it is probable that population levels dropped between the 1890s and the 1920s, at which point they stabilized and began to recover. Reliable demographic data is difficult if not impossible to come by for the early colonial period – still less for the second half of the nineteenth century – but widely accepted "guestimates" are that, for example the population of the Belgian Congo fell by between 30 and 50 percent between 1880 and 1920, through a combination of war, sleeping sickness and other diseases, and famine. A similar figure can probably be applied to French Equatorial

Africa, which was particularly badly hit by declining female fertility during the first half of the twentieth century. Other areas which probably experienced net population loss include the northern and western Great Lakes region, western Ethiopia and southern Sudan, and northern Angola.[49]

Medicine is also relevant in this context. Before the middle of the nineteenth century, again, swathes of Africa – certainly between the tropics of Cancer and Capricorn – had been inaccessible to Europeans because of climate and the disease environment. The West African coast, for example, had long been known as the "White Man's Grave" because of malaria, and the survival rate of Europeans residing there for long periods had been extremely low. But advances in medicine changed this quite dramatically, and in particular, the development of quinine prophylaxis reduced death-rates significantly, increasing considerably the length of time Europeans could remain in equatorial zones, the distances they could travel, and the activities they could undertake. But medicine took on even greater significance under colonial rule, and very effectively demonstrates the ambiguity of the imperial mission. Among many claims made in support of European colonialism – particularly in the 1950s and 1960s, when historians were prone to drawing up "balance sheets" for empire – was that it brought about greatly improved health for swathes of the non-European world. Health care, in other words, was an unalloyed "positive" for colonial systems, according to this interpretation: colonialism eradicated certain diseases, brought about better public health and sanitation, especially in urban settings, built clinics and hospitals, and made basic medicines widely available. In reality, as ever, things are not quite as straightforward as this standpoint suggests. Colonialism also *brought* contagious disease, altered ecologies (in many areas devastatingly so), changed patterns of susceptibility and immunity, and forced the movement of populations from healthy to unhealthy environments; above all, perhaps, colonial authorities used the medical expertise at their disposal only selectively in the curing of disease.[50]

By the middle of the nineteenth century, advances in European medical knowledge meant that the health practices of peoples beyond Europe were regarded as fatalistic and superstitious; *their* approaches to the human body were barbaric, in contrast to Europeans, who were imbued with science and reason. At the same time, European stereotypes reinforced anxieties about "the tropics": while diseases in the temperate zone were safe and curable, those of the tropics were dangerous and incurable, as well as containing not a few which were wholly unfamiliar. Tropical Africa was seen as an intrinsically disease-stricken environment. Diseases that had been largely conquered in Europe – notably cholera, malaria, plague, smallpox – were increasingly evident to Europeans in Africa, as well as in Asia, and this in itself seemed to reinforce the notion of those zones of the world as impossibly backward. The illnesses and infections of Africa reminded Europeans of their own Middle Ages. By the late nineteenth century, consequently, Africa and Asia had become, in a sense, laboratories for medical investigation; they were frontiers of medical science, where disease could be studied in a form no longer possible in Europe. Medicine in this way became a potent manifestation of European domination and inherent superiority, while access to medicine was something to be prized and protected; African peoples could be made into "objects" of medical study and scientific research more broadly, and accordingly a form of control could be imposed on Africans which could no longer be applied in Europe itself.

Medicine was power. The wider utility of medicine allowed colonialism to demonstrate apparent benevolence as well as superiority. Missionary doctors – the most common healthcare practitioners in the early decades of colonial rule – cured illness as a means to gaining access to souls. Europeans could contrast their knowledge with the "magic" of local medicine-men, thus again both underpinning the supposedly inherent superiority of Western civilization and justifying European authority.[51] Indigenous health care was often driven underground, or to the margins of communities, although it survived and – in some areas – proved remarkably robust and adaptive. Still, as with economic systems more broadly, medical knowledge served as a powerful tool of both cultural and political hegemony. Nowhere was the power of medicine more clearly demonstrated than in the massive campaigns often launched for the eradication of a particular disease, as the British did in Uganda against sleeping sickness. These campaigns were indeed often successful, but they were attended by draconian legislation, and were enormous exercises in state intervention and social manipulation. Medicine meant that the colonial state could assume an unprecedented right over the health and thus the bodies of its subjects.

Early colonial medicine had focused on the health of colonial soldiers and officials, but increasingly Africans' bodies were a matter of concern, especially those in contact with Europeans, or upon which the colonial state depended: administrative employees, mine-workers, laborers, and prostitutes. At the same time, there was an increasing focus on sanitation, which called for social engineering solutions; disease and high mortality among Africans were attributed to unhealthy living and working conditions, overcrowding, poor diet. Concerted efforts were made to "clean up" the urban environment in these respects, while "germ theory" also inspired the creation of separate residential quarters for whites and "natives" in many cities – particularly convenient in those territories underpinned by aggressive racial ideologies, for example segregationist and apartheid South Africa, or Eritrea under the Italians in the 1930s. Cities, indeed, were breeding grounds for social tensions as well as bacteria, especially as populations grew. Overall, however, during the interwar years – after the hiatus of the First World War – there were significant reductions in mortality rates, as sanitation was improved and general public health provision was expanded.

As sleeping sickness increased, colonial authorities – for example in Nyasaland and Tanganyika – moved people out of affected areas *en masse*; these large open areas would eventually become the game parks so important to the modern-day tourist industry. This was a process of cumulative crisis which underlined the ambiguity of colonial rule. The encroachment of colonial rule and, ultimately, global capitalism undoubtedly worsened environmental crises and involved the introduction of disease; yet colonial regimes were later able to reverse the process through commercial agriculture, reclaiming bush, controlling game, and pushing the tsetse fly back into retreat. European rule also introduced medicine that could treat diseases of long-standing, as well as tackling those which had been carried into Africa by Europeans themselves. Colonial rule involved the building of transport networks which could – in theory, at any rate – get aid to famine-stricken communities more quickly than at any time in the past. While in many parts of the continent, Africans found their ability to self-manage impaired by the very nature of the colonial system, that same system also provided Africans with new commercial, and in time also political, opportunities. Ultimately, of course, Africans survived the crises of the late nineteenth and early twentieth centuries, although clearly some communities recovered rather more quickly than others, and it might be argued that other communities have yet to fully recover. It is clear, however, that from the 1920s and 1930s onward, the continent's population was on an upward curve, as reproductive fertility increased and rainfall stabilized. Africans recovered both despite, and because of, the so-called *pax colonia*.

Notes

1 Lugard, *Dual Mandate*, 7.
2 Richard J. Reid, *A History of Modern Uganda* (Cambridge, 2017), 223.
3 Lugard, *Dual Mandate*, 17.
4 Myron Echenberg, *Colonial Conscripts: the Tirailleurs Sénégalais in French West Africa, 1857-1960* (London, 1991); Michelle R. Moyd, *Violent Intermediaries: African Soldiers, Conquest, and Everyday Colonialism in German East Africa* (Athens, OH, 2014); D. Killingray & D. Omissi (eds.), *Guardians of Empire: The Armed Forces of the Colonial Powers, c.1700–1964* (Manchester, 1999); T. Parsons, *The African Rank-and-File: social implications of colonial military service in the King's African Rifles,1902–1964 (Oxford, 2000)*; James Lunt, *Imperial Sunset: Frontier Soldiering in the Twentieth Century* (London, 1981).
5 Lunt, *Imperial Sunset*, 171–313; also Anthony Clayton & David Killingray, *Khaki and Blue: Military and Police in British Colonial Africa* (Athens OH, 1989).
6 Echenberg, *Colonial Conscripts*, chap. 3.
7 Adam Hothschild, *King Leopold's Ghost: A Story of Greed, Terror, and Heroism in Colonial Africa* (London, 1998).
8 Heather Streets, *Martial Races: The Military, Race, and Masculinity in British Imperial Culture, 1857–1914* (Manchester, 2004).
9 The issue is explored in Suzanne Miers & Richard Roberts (eds.), *The End of Slavery in Africa* (Madison WI, 1988), and in a follow-up volume, Suzanne Miers & Martin Klein (eds.), *Slavery and Colonial Rule in Africa* (London, 1999).
10 Susan Pedersen, "Back to the League of Nations," *American Historical Review*, 112:4 (2007).
11 Austen, *African Economic History*, 123–5; also J. Forbes Munro, "Monopolists and speculators: British investment in West African rubber, 1905–1914," *Journal of African History*, 22:2 (1981) and J. Forbes Munro, "British rubber companies in East Africa before the First World War," *Journal of African History*, 24:3 (1983).
12 Joseph Conrad, *Heart of Darkness* (London, 1899); Hothschild, *King Leopold's Ghost*.
13 John Tosh, "The cash crop revolution in tropical Africa: an agricultural reappraisal," *African Affairs*, 79 (1980). For a contemporary assessment, see A. McPhee, *The Economic Revolution in British West Africa* (London, 1926).
14 Jan S. Hogendorn, "Economic initiative and African cash farming: pre-colonial origins and early colonial developments," in Peter Duignan & L.H. Gann (eds.), *Colonialism in Africa 1870–1960. Vol 4: The Economics of Colonialism* (Cambridge, 1975); Austen, *African Economic History*, 124–9.

15 See for example Jean Suret-Canale, *French Colonialism in Tropical Africa* (London, 1964), 199–204 and *passim*.

16 Polly Hill, *The Migrant Cocoa Farmers of Southern Ghana: A Study in Rural Capitalism* (Cambridge, 1963); and see also by Gareth Austin, "The emergence of capitalist relations in south Asante cocoa-farming, c.1916–1933," *Journal of African History*, 28:2 (1987), and his major book on the topic, *Land, Labour and Capital in Ghana: from slavery to free labour in Asante, 1807–1956* (Rochester NY, 2005).

17 M.A. Ogutu, "The cultivation of coffee among the Chagga of Tanzania, 1919–1939," *Agricultural History*, 46:2 (1972).

18 Torbjorn Engdahl, *The Exchange of Cotton: Ugandan peasants, colonial market regulations, and the organisation of the international cotton trade, 1904–1918* (Uppsala, 1999).

19 See for example T. Bassett, "The development of cotton in Northern Ivory Coast, 1910–1965," *Journal of African History*, 29:2 (1988).

20 R.L. Tignor, *Egypt: A Short History* (Princeton 2011), chap. 10.

21 T. Barnett, *The Gezira Scheme: An Illusion of Development* (London, 1977).

22 Paul Mosley, *The Settler Economies: Studies in the Economic History of Kenya and Southern Rhodesia* (Cambridge, 1983).

23 Brett Shadle, *The Souls of White Folk: White Settlers in Kenya, 1900s–1920s* (Manchester, 2015).

24 Colin Leys, *Underdevelopment in Kenya: The Political Economy of Neo-colonialism 1964–1971* (London, 1975), 28–40.

25 R. Palmer, *Land and Racial Domination in Rhodesia* (London, 1977); I. Phimister, *An Economic and Social History of Zimbabwe, 1890–1948: Capital Accumulation and Class Struggle* (London, 1988).

26 Benjamin Stora, "The "Southern World" of the *Pied Noirs*: references to and representations of Europeans in colonial Algeria," in C. Elkins & Susan Pedersen (eds.), *Settler Colonialism in the Twentieth Century: Projects, Practices, Legacies* (New York & London, 2005). Also James McDougall, *History and the Culture of Nationalism in Algeria* (Cambridge, 2006), chap. 2; Adria K. Lawrence, *Imperial Rule and the Politics of Nationalism: Anti-colonial Protest in the French Empire* (Cambridge, 2013), 73–90.

27 For a solid introduction, see T.R.H. Davenport, *South Africa: A Modern History* (London, 1991). Also: F. Wilson, *Labour in the South African Gold Mines, 1911–1969* (London, 1972); F.A. Johnstone, *Class, Race and Gold* (London, 1976); S. Jones & A. Muller, *The South African Economy, 1910–1990* (Basingstoke, 1992).

28 Alan Jeeves, *Migrant Labour in South Africa's Mining Economy: The Struggle for the Gold Mines' Labour Supply, 1890–1920* (Kingston & Montreal, 1985); Charles Van Onselen, *Chibaro: African Mine Labour in Southern Rhodesia 1900–1933* (London, 1976).

29 Lawrence J. *Butler, Copper Empire: Mining and the Colonial State in Northern Rhodesia, c.1930–1964* (Basingstoke, 2007); B. Jewsiewicki, "Belgian Africa," in Roberts (ed.), *Cambridge History*, Vol. 5, 473ff.

30 Harvey Feinberg, "The 1913 Natives Land Act in South Africa: politics, race, and segregation in the early twentieth century," *International Journal of African Historical Studies*, 26:1 (1993); Davenport, *South Africa: A Modern History*, 280–4.

31 Hopkins, *Economic History*, chaps. 5–7; and see also A.I. Nwabughuogu, "From wealthy entrepreneurs to petty traders: the decline of African middlemen in Eastern Nigeria, 1900–1950," *Journal of African History*, 23:3 (1982).

32 Frank Furedi, "The African crowd in Nairobi: popular movements and elite politics," *Journal of African History*, 14:2 (1973); Dave Hyde, "The Nairobi General Strike [1950]: from protest

to insurgency," in Andrew Burton (ed.), *The Urban Experience in Eastern Africa, c.1750–2000* (Nairobi, 2002).

33 Bruce Berman & John Lonsdale, *Unhappy Valley: conflict in Kenya & Africa. Book Two: Violence and Ethnicity* (Oxford, 1992).

34 See for example Carol Summers, "Education and literacy," in Parker & Reid (eds.), *Handbook of Modern African History*; P. Gifford & T.C. Weiskel, "African education in a colonial context: French and British styles," in P. Gifford & W.R. Louis (eds.), *France and Britain in Africa: Imperial Rivalry and Colonial Rule* (New Haven CT, 1971); P. Foster, *Education and Social Change in Ghana* (London, 1965); S. Sivonen, *White-Collar or Hoe Handle? African Education Under British Colonial Policy, 1920–1945* (Helsinki, 1995). For two landmark contemporary reports by the Phelps-Stokes Fund, see Thomas Jesse Jones, *Education in Africa: a study of West, South, and Equatorial Africa* (New York, 1922), and Thomas Jesse Jones, *Education in East Africa: A Study of East, Central, and South Africa* (New York, 1925).

35 See for example L. Anderson, *The State and Social Transformation in Tunisia and Libya, 1830–1980* (Princeton, 1986); M.H. Kerr, "Egypt," in James Coleman (ed.), *Education and Political Development* (Princeton, 1965).

36 Adrian Hastings, *The Church in Africa, 1450–1950* (Oxford, 1994).

37 For a useful overview, see Barbara Cooper, "Women and gender," in Parker & Reid (eds.), *Handbook of Modern African History*. See also: Jean Allman, Susan Geiger, & Nakanyike Musisi (eds.), *Women in African Colonial Histories* (Bloomington IN, 2002); Andrea Cornwall, *Readings in Gender in Africa* (Bloomington IN, 2005); Nancy Hafkin & Edna Bay (eds.), *Women in Africa: Studies in Social and Economic Change* (Stanford CA, 1976); Nancy Rose Hunt, Tessie P. Liu, & Jean Quataert (eds.), *Gendered Colonialisms in African History* (Oxford, 1997).

38 Nicolas Argenti & Deborah Durham, "Youth," in Parker & Reid (eds.), *Handbook of Modern African History*. See also Andrew Burton & Helene Charton-Bigot (eds.), *Generations Past: Youth in East African History* (Athens OH, 2010); and Richard Waller, "Rebellious youth in Colonial Africa," *Journal of African History*, 47:1 (2006).

39 For a regional study, see H. Kjekshus, *Ecology Control and Economic Development in East African History: the case of Tanganyika, 1850–1950* (London 1995).

40 For example, see Michael Worboys, "The comparative history of sleeping sickness in East and Central Africa, 1900–1914," *History of Science*, 32:1 (1994); Maryinez Lyons, *The Colonial Disease: a social history of sleeping sickness in northern Zaire, 1900–1940* (Cambridge, 1992).

41 Charles Van Onselen, "Reactions to rinderpest in southern Africa, 1896–97," *Journal of African History*, 13:3 (1972).

42 J. Ford, *The Role of the Trypanosomiases in African Ecology: a study of the tsetse fly problem* (London, 1971).

43 Shane Doyle, *Before HIV: Sexuality, Fertility and Mortality in East Africa, 1900–1980*, (Oxford, 2013); M. Tuck, "Syphilis, Sexuality, and Social Control: a history of venereal disease in colonial Uganda," PhD thesis, Northwestern University, 1997.

44 A.T. Culwick & G.M. Culwick, "A study of population in Ulanga, Tanganyika Territory," *Sociological Review*, 30 (1938).

45 Olusoga & Erichsen, *The Kaiser's Holocaust*, 230.

46 Richard Pankhurst & Douglas Johnson, "The great drought and famine of 1888–92 in northeast Africa," in Douglas Johnson & David Anderson (eds.), *The Ecology of Survival: Case Studies from North East African History* (London, 1988); and for a wide-ranging, innovative survey of the context, see John Iliffe, *The African Poor: A History* (Cambridge, 1987).

47 Catherine Coquery-Vidrovitch, "Population et démographie en Afrique Equatoriale Française dans le premier tiers du XXe siècle," in Christopher Fyfe & David McMaster (eds.), *African Historical Demography* (Edinburgh, 1977).

48 Rudyard Kipling, "The White Man's Burden" (1899), in Boehmer (ed.), *Empire Writing*, 273.

49 Bruce Fetter (ed.), *Demography from Scanty Evidence: Central Africa in the Colonial Era* (Boulder CO, 1990). The study of historical demography in Africa remains a contentious subject. See for example Karl Ittmann, Dennis Cordell, & Gregory Maddox (eds.), *The Demographics of Empire: The Colonial Order and the Creation of Knowledge* (Athens OH, 2010).

50 David Arnold (ed.), *Imperial Medicine and Indigenous Societies* (New York, 1988); and see also S. Feierman & J.M. Hanzen (ed.), *The Social Basis of Health and Healing in Africa* (Berkeley CA, 1992).

51 In the Ugandan context, for example, see Mackay, *Pioneer Missionary*, and A.R. Cook, *Uganda Memories 1897–1940* (Kampala, 1945).

12 Hard Times

Protest, Identity, and Depression

Making Tribes

To define "identity" is never a straightforward task: historians, political scientists, and anthropologists continue to debate the concept in the African context.[1] Two broad observations can be made at the outset, however. The first is that identity is continually shifting: it changes over time, inexorably if sometimes imperceptibly, and at times quite dramatically. Identity changes according to shifting circumstances, and the roots of particular identities, as well as self-image itself, are perceived differently through time. Second, "identity" is rarely a singular phenomenon: usually, we should refer to *identities*, namely a series of overlapping and interlocking self-images and levels of identification with a place, or a group of people, or a particular historical experience. Precolonial Africans had long had several identities simultaneously: they belonged to lineages, clans, villages, chiefdoms, language groups. One particular identity might be emphasized above others at a given point in time, or according to circumstances; but ultimately identities overlapped and interlocked in a highly complex sociopolitical and cultural order. Both observations hold true in Africa from the early nineteenth century: some identities developed, or were strengthened, as a result of the colonial experience, while others were, in some form or another, rooted in the nineteenth century and earlier. There has been a great deal of scholarly attention paid to the transformative power of colonial rule in this respect – to the idea, in other words, that the experience of colonial rule led in different ways to the creation of so many new ethnic identities, where previously Africans had lived in amorphous or at least highly fluid groupings.[2] The needs of colonial administration, meanwhile, likewise involved the invention of ethnic units – or "tribes," in contemporary European parlance. However, we need to be extremely careful

A History of Modern Africa: 1800 to the Present, Third Edition. Richard J. Reid.

in this regard. There can be little doubt that the impact of conquest, the establishment of colonial rule, and the political and socioeconomic changes thus set in motion meant that identities and affinities were thrown into flux. Africans developed multiple identities, related to locality, province, "tribe," and, increasingly, profession. Later, new identities would emerge in terms of wider colonial territory, as nationalism took root, as well as a sense of "African-ness." However, in a host of cases, group cohesion – rooted in shared culture, language, economy, territory, "tradition" – long predated colonial rule and stretched continuously over several centuries, into the deep past. As with all such communities, reevaluations and reinventions were constant; identities were continually in motion – and at certain times, these patterns of change were more intense than at others. In the nineteenth century – an era of profound and often violent upheaval – a range of new groups came into being as a result of creative economic, political, and military flux. It was a markedly formative epoch, ongoing at the time of the European partition, in which the changes wrought by colonial rule constituted the latest stage. Again, European administrative systems were frequently coopted into long-term African processes. In other words, it was the dynamism of Africa's "long" nineteenth century, not – or not simply – the colonial impact, which drove much of the creativity of the era under examination.

The "tribe," meanwhile, was in large part a European invention, the idea behind the concept being that Africans did not live in anything as sophisticated as "nation-states," for example. Colonial states strove to develop "tribes" as rigid categories for Africans, particularly – though not exclusively – through indirect rule. In many cases, such tribal identities became formalized; peoples were classified accordingly, and often the groupings which resulted were given territorially demarcated areas in which to live. The colonial state required fixed, delineated identities for administrative purposes. Often, too, particular characteristics and personalities were attributed to them, a practice which was common in the nineteenth century: pastoral or agricultural, subservient or dominant, warlike or peace-loving, intelligent or docile, and so on. Yet the African agency in this process was usually paramount; certainly, "tribalism" in various forms would harden as the twentieth century progressed. Africans themselves found that it was advantageous to invest in the tribal idea, as it strengthened the "group" and enabled it to compete more vigorously within the colonial system. Tribal solidarity was a source of potential political and economic muscle, while elites had an interest in strengthening tribal identities as a means to gaining access to resources and political power. In other words, the building of the "tribe" represented what we can call a "coalition of interests": just as the state desired the invention of tribal units through which to govern, so Africans built tribes to belong to and created identities which could be shared within defined groups.[3] This was assisted by the fact that in the first decades of the twentieth century, Africans were essentially local in their outlook, and localism increasingly took the form of tribalism.

Yet there was nothing intrinsically novel about this process; it was as old as human society itself. It is also the case that many of the "new" affiliations themselves were only amendments to, or extensions or enhancements of, extant groupings. Many "tribal" identities –Yoruba, Fulani, Zulu, Ganda, and Asante – did indeed have their roots, in different ways, in the precolonial past. They may not have been "tribes" in the manner devised by the colonial state, but they imposed themselves on colonial systems and manipulated the needs of those systems. Clearly, it was often the case that ethnic groupings became rather more rigidified entities in the colonial context – and some of these, again, had their roots in the relatively recent past, in the turbulence of the nineteenth century. The Fulani, for example, had been a vast, amorphous group scattered across the West African savannah in the nineteenth century. In the process of their definition as a "tribe" in the early twentieth century – by the British, the French, and the Germans, as of course they straddled the borders of Nigeria, Cameroon, and Niger – the term "Fulani" came to include various smaller ethnicities which had never considered themselves as such, or which had only relatively recent been conquered by them. At the beginning of the nineteenth century, the Zulu had been a tiny subgroup, but on the back of their state-building revolution, they came to incorporate a host of other groups which in time came to describe themselves as "Zulu." A sense of "being Zulu" intensified during the twentieth century, in large part as a response to the repression of white-dominated South Africa. The case of the Nyamwezi is rather more curious: the term itself did not exist in any meaningful sense before the nineteenth century, being used to describe the peoples of the interior (the "people of the new moon") from the viewpoint of the East African coast. As trade expanded, the so-called "Nyamwezi" became prodigious traders, and in time came to describe themselves as "Nyamwezi," thus giving rise to a new ethnic identity which again was formalized with the establishment of colonial rule. The Germans established a system of headmen through which to govern this large new "tribe," and the British inherited the system in the 1920s. There were other examples of expansion in "tribal scale." The Yoruba in their modern sense – in the nineteenth century the term referred to the old Oyo Empire – came into existence in the course of the nineteenth century largely as a result of the violent upheavals of the age but also through the work undertaken by missionaries to translate the Bible into a common vernacular; thus did people "become" Yoruba through shared language. The Akan of the Gold Coast was a convenient "large-group" unit from the early 1900s, but in reality the Akan comprised several peoples – Akim, Fante, and Asante – with their roots in the deeper past who would not have recognized the appellation "Akan" just a few decades earlier.[4]

Along with such enlarged scale and hardened boundaries came the forceful and opportunistic articulation of myths and pasts to justify "tribal" consciousness and identity. Colonial administrators and "tribal" elites sometimes collaborated in this process: thus in Uganda, the British came to see Buganda, with its increasingly Anglicized, Christian political establishment, as the historically dominant power in the region and the preferred vehicle for "development" in the protectorate. The Ganda used their favored position under British tutelage to extend their influence across central and southern Uganda by the 1920s and 1930s, reaching into areas which had never before been under Buganda's sway. The Ganda ruling elite regarded themselves as being in the vanguard of the civilizing mission. Notably, the Ganda had a clear advantage over their historic rivals, the Nyoro: where the Ganda had worked with the British, the Nyoro fought them, and there thus developed the colonial stereotype of the Ganda as intelligent and progressive, while the Nyoro were backward and undeveloped. Under the terms of the Uganda Agreement in 1900, Buganda had won an extension of their precolonial territory at the expense of Bunyoro, and the "lost counties" issue was a matter of deep resentment in Bunyoro throughout the colonial period.[5] In southern Nigeria in 1912, Lugard's administration attempted to recreate the eighteenth-century Oyo Empire, setting up king and court to rule over a large area based on a somewhat spurious reading of the past.[6] It was the process of reinvention in Rwanda, however, which produced the most tragic long-term consequences. Here, precolonial relations between the majority agricultural Hutu and the cattle-owning Tutsi were complex and fluid; there was indeed not only rivalry between them but also a great deal of intermarriage and economic and cultural interdependency. On the eve of colonial rule, they spoke the same language and shared much in the way of culture and religion; differences were largely related to class, and these divisions widened during the colonial period, as German and Belgian administrations sought to bolster the perceived social and political dominance of the Tutsi over the Hutu. From the early 1900s, myths of historic hegemony and superiority were created around the Tutsi – both by colonial administrators and by the Tutsi themselves – based on everything from physical stature (height and bearing), to economic specialty (the dignity of pastoralism), to racial provenance (the Tutsi were the carriers of civilization from the north). A singular, hierarchical Tutsi monarchy, which had not existed in this form before 1900, was created through which to administer the Hutu majority.[7]

The assertion of "historical truth" to underpin a new status quo was not new; nor was this simply a matter of "invention," but rather of selection and repositioning. Even so, in the cases of the Ganda, the Tutsi, and the Yoruba, for example, the early twentieth century witnessed the writing of "tribal histories" by supposedly "traditional" authorities, the formalization of "tribal customs" for which claims of great antiquity and inviolability were made, and the transcription of local languages into standardized forms. Identities which had been fluid, pragmatic, and continually evolving in the precolonial era now became rigid and codified, and the written word was used to produce the impression of permanence. This contributed to the hardening of "tribal" identities, and facilitated the emergence of hegemonic narratives, often at the expense of historical complexity and of smaller groups who were now subsumed within larger identities, or at least marginalized. Much of this was the work of intellectuals who promoted the development of larger rather than smaller identities and who lobbied for "tribal unity," as among the Somali, for example. But it was not solely an intellectual exercise. In other spheres of life, socioeconomic circumstances fostered such identities: as the historian John Lonsdale has pithily suggested, "modern tribes were often born on the way to work."[8] Certainly, migration and labor recruitment promoted wider identities and novel forms of group consciousness.

Emergent Protest in the Islamic World

As we have seen in earlier contexts, Islamic resistance to changing political realities in the Mediterranean, and ultimately to European hegemony across northern Africa, was deeply rooted, and drew on historical precedent. In the late nineteenth and early twentieth centuries, Islamic reformism took new forms, as Muslim leaders sought to develop innovative ways of both combating European rule and creating identities capable of doing so; these were, moreover, modern nationalisms in the making. Broadly, such movements were often "Islamist" in that they sought to establish *shari'a* law within the modern secular nation state. In Egypt, Islamism was particularly associated with the Salafiyya, an intellectual movement within which the leading figures were Jamal al-Din al-Afghani, Muhammad 'Abduh, and Rashid Rida. The Salafiyya placed great emphasis on the creation of a polity governed by the Quran and the Sunna – the code of behavior and custom laid down by the Prophet himself – and in so doing sought to revitalize Islam and more effectively resist Western imperialism. Yet in contrast to the Islamic revivalist movements of the eighteenth and earlier nineteenth centuries, the Salafiyya did not reject outright European models, principally in the shape of the modern nation state; rather, the movement can be seen as an attempt to bridge the gulf between Islamic reformism and European "modernity," by promoting the wider participation of the entire community in political processes, the pursuit of science and reason over blind superstition and belief in "tradition," and acting within the framework of an Egyptian nation-state. Al-Afghani was the chief exponent of this approach, and he saw in modernizing Islam the potential for the rebirth of autonomous Muslim nations. His disciple Muhammad 'Abduh differed only in the greater emphasis he placed on spiritual revival, for while al-Afghani saw the dilemma confronting Muslims as fundamentally a political one, 'Abduh perceived it in religious terms.[9]

Either way, in the 1880s and 1890s, the Salafiyya created the impetus for political revival in Egypt in the wake of the defeat of Urabi Pasha, much as the "Young Turks" would do in the former Ottoman state. The movement's ideas would arouse a new generation of political activists, and the Salafiyya was the inspiration behind the formation of the Muslim Brotherhood in 1928. The Brotherhood embraced the message of Islamic reform and asserted that the Quran should become the "constitution" for an Egyptian nation-state, but its aim was deeply political, namely to awaken the patriotism of the Egyptian people in the struggle against European political and cultural hegemony. Gradualist and moderate, the Brotherhood nonetheless rejected all Western cultural influences, which they perceived as having infiltrated Egypt's ruling elite. It would grow in strength and popularity, claiming a million members in the 1940s, and would form alliances with later nationalist movements in Egypt.[10] The Salafiyya would also be influential in Algeria, where its ideas were promoted by the Association of Ulama, and where it rejected both "collaboration" with colonial authorities and the heterodoxy of the sufi orders. But the importance of the latter in Algeria dated to the nineteenth century, and by the 1930s and 1940s some – including the Rahmaniyya – were closely involved with emergent nationalist parties. Conflict between the sufi orders and the Salafiyya would repeatedly undermine nationalists' attempts to achieve a broad united front in their struggle against the French.[11]

As in centuries past, Cairo was at the heart of Islamic scholarship and political thought in the early decades of the twentieth century; elsewhere, armed resistance against European rule continued in the interwar years, as in Libya, where the Sanusiyya held out against the Italians until the early 1930s. Only through violent repression, the use of concentration camps for the nomadic population, and the capture and execution of key leaders were Sanusiyya brought under some semblance of control. 'Abd al-Karim led similarly dogged resistance in Morocco in the 1920s. Elsewhere in the Maghreb, however, a combination of Islamic reformism, modernization, and nationalism would, as in Egypt, lead to political movements aimed at the building of new Muslim as well as national identities. In Tunisia and Algeria, protest would become sharper and more cogent in the interwar years; we return to this later.

Salvation and Resistance: The African Church

One of the earliest expressions of protest – for a time almost invisible to the European eye – was linked to the growth of Christianity across swathes of sub-Saharan Africa. The failure of armed resistance in those areas which had attempted it between the 1870s and the First World War had resulted in the destruction or at least severe compromising of African political authority; this in turn often meant the undermining of spiritual authority, too, as in nineteenth-century state and society political and religious power had been closely intertwined. This process of destruction and reconstruction helped facilitate the spread of Christianity, conversion to which frequently represented a quest for new answers to some old questions, and an attendant rejection of nineteenth-century forms of authority and many of the values associated with it. Increasingly, however, the newly converted rejected the European domination of the Church and sought to recreate a form of worship which was not so closely tied to European culture and institutions of colonial authority. The so-called "Ethiopian church" movement – after the use of the term "Ethiopia" to describe Africa in the Bible – was especially strong in central and southern Africa, where a number of independent churches were founded in the years immediately before and after the First World War. They embraced the Bible as a revolutionary handbook, which spoke of justice and equality, and which perhaps above all contained the extraordinarily potent notion of a "second coming," a concept easily interpreted as denoting the imminent destruction of colonial rule and the ending of white oppression. Many of these churches may be regarded as representing early expressions of quasi- (or perhaps proto-) nationalist protest, and were certainly in the vanguard of anticolonial resistance wherever they sprang up.[12]

Africanized Christianity was frequently radicalized Christianity, imbued with political messages that were born of the trauma of conquest and the social and economic change which followed it. At first, some churches defied European convention by embracing polygamy, as the African Church Organisation did when it broke from the Anglican Church in 1901. In many areas, African women felt stifled by monogamous Victorian wedlock, not least in economic terms, and thus were drawn to such churches for reasons that went beyond the purely spiritual. Later, religious movements became more overtly political. The Watchtower movement across central–southern Africa in some respects took its inspiration from the Jehovah's Witness movement, predicting the end of colonial rule and the attendant salvation of the "chosen people." In Nyasaland, for example, Elliot Kamwana, from 1908, preached how the second coming of Christ would bring about

Africa's liberation. Kamwana was arrested and exiled, but the Watchtower movement grew in strength, particularly in Nyasaland and the neighboring Rhodesias.[13] The geographical spread of Watchtower was no coincidence, for it was across this region that the migrant labor system which fed the southern African mining economy was bringing about considerable social upheaval and creating new pools of protest identity. Later, again in Nyasaland, the preacher John Chilembwe founded his own church, and in 1915, led a full-blown rebellion, sparked by the ravages caused by prolonged combat with the Germans, and a series of perceived colonial injustices more broadly. Chilembwe was killed attempting to escape as the British closed in, but his martyrdom would inspire a later generation of Malawian nationalists.[14] Like many others in this period, he was an early symbol of anticolonial resistance, as was Simon Kimbangu in the Belgian Congo, who in 1921 proclaimed himself a prophet, established his own church, and preached that God would soon deliver the people from colonial oppression. "Kimbanguism" continued to flourish even after the arrest of its charismatic founder: its adherents periodically defied the colonial state by refusing to pay tax, or grow cash crops, and the movement was particularly powerful during times of rural hardship. Drought, for example, pushed new members into the movement's ranks, as the poor and the dispossessed sought spiritual succor in the face of disaster, man-made or otherwise, and oppression.[15]

The independent church movement continued to grow, and by the 1930s, with the onset of the Depression, there was increasing dissatisfaction with mission education and the ideologies which underpinned it. In South Africa, for example, Zionist churches, with white roots in the late nineteenth century, grew during the interwar years and integrated elements of indigenous faith into Christian belief, shaping the latter to more effectively meet African needs; Zionists, notably, did not reject polygamy, and indeed provided prominent roles for women.[16] The mission school could no longer provide answers to Africans' questions, especially during times of such economic hardship, and the messages which emanated from proselytizing education – the image of the "white Christ," the apparent selectivity which attended salvation and equality, the unconditional loyalty which should be offered to the colonial state via the Church – were increasingly inapposite to Africans' own experiences. Thus was the expansion of independent churches in the 1930s directly linked to socioeconomic distress, such as that founded in 1934 in Southern Rhodesia by a group of unemployed men. Powerful political messages were often contained within spiritual rhetoric. The Watchtower movement, again, organized Southern African mineworkers and was instrumental in the creation of some measure of "worker consciousness." Workers were actively recruited into the movement, which offered spiritual solutions to the grim conditions of compound life, and were told that with the second coming they would be saved as "the elect."[17]

Class and Tribe: The Industrial Complex

Watchtower found ready recruits among the burgeoning ranks of the industrial labor force. Economic change brought about new patterns of resistance in other ways, too, most dramatically in South Africa, where the need to control labor and to contain

Africans in reserves had given rise to the invidious and oppressive system of passes. Here, some of the earliest organized protest outside Islamic North Africa appeared in the years immediately before and after the First World War. To some degree, this was confined to political elite: in 1912, the South African Native National Congress was founded by members of that elite, becoming the African National Congress (ANC) in 1923. Its broader appeal was limited at this stage; nonetheless, the organization laid the foundations for wider political action, notably in its cooperation with Indian and "Coloured" ("mixed race" in segregationist legislation) groups. But already there were other manifestations of popular protest. In 1919, there were massive anti-pass-law demonstrations in South Africa, indicating the possibilities for mass participation in political action, while the following year some 40,000 mineworkers went on strike. It was this kind of muscle that facilitated the foundation of the Industrial and Commercial Workers' Union (ICU) in 1919, an organization which boasted 100,000 members by the mid-1920s. Structural problems and internal rifts brought about the Union's collapse by the end of the decade, but once again, it had demonstrated the potential for mass action, and at least suggested the existence of a growing worker consciousness.[18]

Worker consciousness developed slowly, and, according to a standard view, three broad phases are discernible in its emergence. The period between the 1890s and the 1920s was one of "informal protest"; that between the 1920s and 1940s was characterized by the protest of the "semiproletarians," and from the 1940s, we see the emergence of fully fledged trade unions and a recognizable working class, aware of its collective strength and with a measure of group cohesion. This is somewhat formulaic, of course, and patterns of change in certain areas do not necessarily fit the model, but it is nonetheless a useful guide. For the early period, there is little evidence of widespread or collective worker action: there were no trade unions, no leaders capable of mobilizing workers, and – with the notable exception of the 1920 strike in South Africa – no major strikes. Yet unions and strikes are not necessary in identifying some form of worker consciousness, as workers themselves often registered protest informally: confronted with a brutal and exploitative system, they developed complex intelligence networks, which first and foremost sought to *understand* that system, and thereafter they learnt how to work against the new economic order from within. Desertion was one option, albeit somewhat extreme; more commonly, passes were forged, machinery was sabotaged when supervisors' backs were turned, work rates were slowed. Shared experiences facilitated the growth of communal identity, demonstrable in the development of informal systems of communication and mutual protection.[19]

Toward the end of the 1920s, and certainly in the 1930s, collective consciousness began to translate into strike action. In large part, this was also connected to the emergence of a settled "proletariat" capable of cohesive and organized activity, as temporary migration gave way to more permanent residency in industrial areas. The strike at Shamva mine in Southern Rhodesia in 1927, for example, was organized by Nyasa workers who had been settled there for several years, and who were now able to put their understanding of the system, its functioning and management, to good use. But the worker population needed to be geographically concentrated, too: the problem in Southern Rhodesia was that mines were scattered over a wide area, making large-scale action involving several mines problematic. However, in the Northern Rhodesian copper belt, where mines were closer together, workers were able to organize more widely and pass information more easily from one mine to the next. Major strikes took place on the copper belt in 1935 and in 1940, the latter being particularly painful for the British, coming as it did while the RAF was trying to see off the Luftwaffe. The miners knew little about the Battle of Britain, but they did know that the British seemed to need copper, and the concessions they won on that occasion indicated to them that, if organized, they did indeed have considerable economic muscle. Importantly, these strikes were not organized by trade unions – these would only emerge later – but by a range of innovative and dynamic associations developed within the mine and the compound. Watchtower, again, was often important in mobilizing workers, as were cultural associations such as the Mbeni dance societies, organized in the first instance to provide entertainment and as an outlet for repressed energy. Miners divided themselves into competing teams, and adopted uniforms and titles which mocked the authorities; the overall effect was the creation of a sense of worker solidarity, and it was members of the Mbeni who acted as intermediaries during the copper belt strikes, for example. Women as well as men, moreover, were involved as dancers and organizers.[20]

Crucially, however, ethnic rivalry was fostered by increasing competition for access to resources, in the job market, and in the increasingly territory-wide economy. Group solidarity – providing a sense of belonging and of protection – necessarily involved categorizing and caricaturing others, and thus the colonial economic environment also encouraged "tribal" tensions. Migrant labor, again, had initially supplied the mining economy, involving men hired on short-term contracts from rural areas, working for three or six months before returning home. These men have been characterized as "urban tribesmen," raiding the industrial urban economy for cash wages that were then used back in the "tribal" homeland. Increasingly, however, from 1920s onward, longer-term contracts and the settling of workers with their families in the mining areas laid the foundations of an urban working class. Johannesburg, built on gold, is the most notable example, but across the continent cities sprang up through the 1920s and 1930s, swelled by people migrating from the countryside in search of work. Lagos, Leopoldville, Nairobi, and Salisbury, all grew steadily, and indeed such rural–urban migration is perhaps the single most important theme in Africa's modern social history. Urban identities were never straightforward: early immigrants were temporary residents, with their roots still in the village; they often recreated aspects of "tribal" and rural culture while in towns. "Tribalism" retained a powerful hold, perhaps *especially* in towns, as it was often here that the competition for resources was greatest. Nonetheless, towns also became cultural melting pots, cosmopolitan environments in which ethnic groups rubbed against one another; intermarriage, shared experience, and the exchange of ideas, languages, and customs, produced distinctively "urban cultures." In the urban setting, new conventions and modes of living developed. A gendered lens reveals the manner in which towns opened up new forms of behavior: women, for example, often found in the town an escape from the patriarchal authority of the homestead and the village, and a degree of economic freedom from male control.[21]

The 1930s witnessed a collapse in wages across the continent, too; wage labor suffered in the mining economy, on white-owned plantations, and in the urban centers to which Africans increasingly drifted in search of work. South Africa saw, for the first time, significant levels of African unemployment, largely unknown since the rapid expansion of the industrial economy at the end of the nineteenth century. The impact of declining wages was to some extent offset by a corresponding fall in the cost of living, but this was hardly significant in real terms. In reality, the 1930s was a period of genuine hardship for millions of Africans and large numbers of poor whites, and the fall in living standards was not reversed until the second half of the 1940s. Furthermore, a rise in inflation in many territories affected urban wage labor in particular, and again wages did not increase in real terms until the late 1940s. The white working class also suffered during this period, and indeed the rise of white militancy was seen to pose a very real threat to the South African state's careful management of class and race in the early decades of the twentieth century. In particular, the commercialization of farming as a result of the "mineral revolution" from the end of the nineteenth century had seen tens of thousands of poor whites driven from their land and, often, into the cities in search of work. While these migrants comprised an increasingly militant underclass whose members had to compete with Africans in the job market – hence the color bars described in an earlier chapter – those whites who remained on their land in rural areas existed in considerable hardship, despite the subsidies handed out by the state to keep them politically reliable. Poor white farmers were not producers of lucrative cash crops, like their counterparts north of the Limpopo or in Kenya, but struggled to supply maize to the burgeoning cities, and lived lives not much different from those of their nineteenth-century frontier forebears.[22] The poor white population, both urban and rural, would constitute a threat to South Africa's delicate sociopolitical balance in the 1930s and 1940s; it was their support which ever-more-radicalized Afrikaner nationalist leaders would seek to mobilize.

Cash Crops, Rural Crises, and Peasant Protest

Commercial agriculture did not necessarily mean rural prosperity, as the changed circumstances of the 1930s demonstrate. Africans had to balance subsistence farming with export crops, while the import of European manufactured cloths and other commodities gradually undermined Africa's own economic development. Peasant farmers had no control over the prices they were paid for their exports, nor over the prices they were compelled to pay for imports. The European commercial oligopoly kept African producers in a potential poverty trap: they suffered from international price rises, and overall, between the wars, they paid ever more for their imports and were paid ever less for what they produced.[23] This situation was especially acute during the 1930s, when, in order to meet demands for tax and to compensate for falling prices, Africans had to use up ever larger areas of land for the cultivation of cash crops, often at the expense of subsistence food crops. The result could be soil exhaustion and even famine, such as that which broke out in Niger in 1931. The depression manifested itself in various ways across rural Africa. Prices offered for exports collapsed as the international terms of trade turned sharply against peasant producers – as they also did against white settlers.

Rural protest differed from that found in the industrial areas.[24] In good years, for example for much of the 1920s, many did well enough from the cash-crop economy, but the fundamentally unfair nature of the international economic system quickly gave rise to political consciousness, which manifested itself in a range of new forms of protest. By the end of the 1920s, a handful of European companies had come to dominate the West African import–export trade, including the enormous United Africa Company. African producers were soon on the defensive, establishing farmers' associations at a local level to protect their interests. In 1929, in Nigeria, Igbo women rioted and attacked the offices of the trading companies in protest at the decline in the prices paid for exports; this was the "Women's War," and it resulted in dozens of deaths.[25] In the Gold Coast, the cocoa "hold-up" was one method of protesting at the power of the commercial oligopoly, which was held responsible for price fluctuations. Action took the form of farmers refusing to sell their cocoa until the price on offer was increased. It was unsuccessful: companies were able to ignore local concerns and simply buy from other sources, while farmers themselves, of course, ultimately needed to eat and pay taxes.[26] The situation in the Gold Coast also revealed the tensions building up within the indirect rule system. So-called "traditional" chiefs, in the pay of and answerable to the colonial administration, were frequently reluctant to support cocoa hold-ups and farmers' associations, as they could not afford to embarrass the large companies so important to the functioning of the system. Over time, chiefs and peasants would find their differences irreconcilable, and their needs incompatible; a younger, Western-educated generation of political activists would later attempt to create popular movements based on farming communities, and would come to perceive indirect rule chiefs as obstacles to the achievement of independence and modernization.[27]

Politicized peasant consciousness is also evident in Uganda, where cotton production had spread across the south of the country between the early 1900s and the 1920s. Here, tenant farmers were increasingly resentful of a chiefly class of absentee landlords that charged them high rents, and indeed in 1927 the colonial authorities stepped in to place a ceiling on the rents which chiefs could impose on their tenants.[28] In addition, however, cotton producers were becoming ever more aggrieved at marketing arrangements, which favored Indian merchants and a small number of large companies which were lined up behind them. Indeed, in Kenya as well as in Uganda there was a burgeoning Asian business community which fulfilled the same role as European buyers in West Africa, and Ugandan farmers were increasingly resentful of their exclusion from the marketing of cotton. In the course of the 1930s, populist groups appeared of an almost trade union nature, lobbying for closer monitoring of tenant–landlord relations and for greater power in the marketplace. This kind of economic grievance laid the foundations for later political protest; meanwhile, the Indian community remained economically powerful until Idi Amin imposed his brutal "solution" to the "problem" by expelling Ugandan Asians from the country in the early 1970s. Political activity in Uganda was also provoked during the interwar years by talk of an East African federation, linking

African view of the colonial order: Congolese wood carving from the 1920s. Source: Reproduced with permission of Werner Forman Archive/Musée Royal de l'Afrique Centrale, Tervuren.

Uganda, Kenya, and Tanganyika; specifically, there was fear among Ugandans that their territory might become another Kenya.[29]

The global depression heightened levels of disillusionment and served to focus protest much more sharply, as peasant farmers recognized the injustices – and indeed the cruel vagaries – of the colonial economy. "Self-help" associations sprang up across the continent, with economic, religious, and ideological motivations; small-scale artisan movements were set up, involving craftsmen refusing wage employment. These kinds of associations served to articulate anticolonial grievances at the very local level, and thus, singly, they were little more than irritations to colonial administrations. But as a wider phenomenon, they were representative of a crisis of confidence in the colonial order. This crisis was not manifest in any mass, coherent movement, but in widespread disillusion and resentment expressed through a host of different economic, cultural, and religious associations.

The reaction of the colonial state in many territories was greater concern for government intervention, especially in terms of the rural economy and the marketing sector. As the 1930s drew to a close, faith in the market to provide a basic standard of living had given way to a belief that colonial government should become more closely involved in the marketing of exports, attempting to alleviate the impact of price fluctuations and thus social distress; this would, it was hoped, offset social unrest and political protest. In particular, as prices for exports continued to fall, colonial administrations feared that peasant farmers would opt out of the market altogether, threatening not only the export economy but the tax revenue system, too; in this way, the effects of the global depression were seen to threaten the entire fabric of the colonial system. This new concern was manifest in the establishment of marketing boards with a view to fixing the prices paid to farmers, and taking responsibility for the marketing of exports. At the same time, there was a move toward state intervention in production itself, again notably in the rural sphere; colonial agricultural departments identified what were perceived to be certain inefficiencies in peasant farming techniques, and were increasingly concerned by the threat of environmental disaster in certain areas.[30] A growing population in the midst of economic and social hardship led to overgrazing and overcultivation, while the unsustainable pressures on soil could produce the kind of food shortage witnessed in Niger in 1931. Governments began to intervene more directly to both protect the soil and maximize production, either attempting to improve local farming techniques with a view to increasing output; or making plans to marginalize African producers and encourage white settlement backed up by large-scale capital with a view to introducing plantation-farming systems on the North American model. From the end of the 1930s, such aggressive interventionism would stoke up bitter rural resentment for the future. There were political implications, too, as the colonial state increasingly bypassed the indirect rule chiefs, thus gradually eroding the authority of a system which was already seen as irrelevant by Africans in many walks of life.

Other Voices

There were many other ways in which African grievances were expressed in the early decades of the twentieth century. While one view of African arts in the colonial period is that European rule brought about cultural degeneration – and destroyed the "authenticity" of local artistic endeavor – another is that in fact African artistic forms proved both resilient and adaptive (and indeed influential, as in Picasso's work, for example). By the 1930s, African artists and craftsmen were gently mocking the European and the systems of governance which held him aloft, notably in sculpture; indeed, as with imported religion, the Africanization of artistic styles widely perceived as European itself represented a form of resistance, or at least the expression of cultural buoyancy.[31] Newspapers were crucial in some areas, notably in South Africa, where some of the earliest of these appeared, in the 1900s. An "African voice" was soon heard in West Africa, too, where by the interwar years newspapers were an increasingly important forum for debate and anticolonial opinion. Lack of literacy restricted circulation to an educated elite, although by the Second World War it was not uncommon for village meetings to take place around the reading aloud of a newspaper by one of the literate people in the community. This new educated elite was increasingly aware of the injustice of colonial society and economy, and increasingly restless about its exclusion from the system. Before the early 1940s, however, few thought in terms of outright independence and the wholesale destruction of the system, but rather reform within the system; this would only change during the Second World War itself.

External influences were also being brought to bear on the creation of wider African identities, rooted in the common experiences of colonialism and racism. The pan-African movement was expanding in North America and the Caribbean during the 1920s and 1930s. Marcus Garvey, who never actually set foot on the African continent himself, was nonetheless an increasingly influential figure, founding the Universal Negro Improvement Association, and preaching a message of "Africa for the Africans" and the expulsion of Europeans. "Garveyism," eccentric though it was in some respects, had a profound appeal to young African nationalists in the 1940s and 1950s, heightening anticolonial aspirations and instilling the kind of "African pride" which was expressed through the concept of *négritude* in Francophone Africa. *Négritude*, a prominent exponent of which was Senegalese poet and later first president Leopold Senghor, encouraged a sense of black self-respect, representing a celebration of *Africanité* and the antiquity of African culture and civilization.[32]

Wider territorial identities, articulated by new educated elites, also emerged in the interwar years, vying with – if not taking the place of – more locally rooted associations. Political debate among urban elites thrived in French West Africa in the 1920s and 1930s, and indeed the authorities became concerned about the possibility of mobilizing rural support. One of the key figures in the interwar years was the political activist – and one-time communist – Tiemoko Garan Kouyate, whose writings focused on the rise of the proletariat as well as of African nationalism. He belonged to a new class of educated agitators across French western and equatorial Africa, men – as men they invariably were – who busied themselves producing newspapers, organizing early trade unions, and corresponding with figures such as Garvey, and also with George Padmore, the Trinidadian activist who became head of the African section of the Comintern in 1927. They thus had far-flung linkages, and sources of inspiration. A similar class of the politically aware was emerging in Lusophone Africa, too, and here, again, *négritude* was a popular unifying theme. Yet African politicians in this period were not necessarily inveterate opponents of the colonial system. When Blaise Diagne was elected to the French assembly from Senegal in 1914, he was able to mobilize the support of the rural poor, but, after an initial clash with French commercial concerns in the territory, Diagne positioned himself as an ally of the French, reconciled to and indeed imbued with the ethos of the new order, and a public defender of a number of colonial policies during the First World War, including conscription. In the late 1920s, Andre Matswa's Société amicale des originaires de l'Afrique equatoriale française, based in the French Congo, were strident in their demands for French citizenship, and the rights and exemptions which came with it. Nonetheless, their activism was as much a matter of concern to the authorities as any other kind, and by the early 1930s the local administration had moved against both Matswa and his society. Alongside this range of political activity was sporadic urban unrest: a dock-workers' strike at Conakry in Guinea in 1919; rioting in Porto Novo in 1923, and major disturbances in Lome a decade later; strike action by railway workers, in 1925 and again in 1938.[33]

Urban idyll: Freetown, Sierra Leone, c.1960. Source: Interfoto/Alamy Stock Photo.

In British West Africa, political vision was expanding, and political activity becoming ever more "supra-tribal," at least in rhetoric. A commercial and professional elite formed the National Congress of British West Africa, with branches in Nigeria, the Gold Coast, Sierra Leone, and the Gambia. The Congress secured the concession of having representatives elected to territorial legislatures through the 1920s, particularly in the coastal towns where a new politicized class was fast reaching maturity in terms of lobbying power and message. The Congress also spawned other organizations which reflected expanded political vision, such as the West African Students' Union, which fostered radical debate and introduced young West African students in London to pan-African ideas. The leaders of these new movements were now thinking regionally, largely because it was believed that no single colony could challenge the British; hence the influence of pan-Africanism, which advocated a unity of purpose across territories, and which was associated in particular with such figures as the Nigerian Nnamdi Azikiwe.[34] In any case, many argued, strictly territorial political activity was illogical, as individual colonies themselves were wholly artificial; the British themselves, indeed, were largely unconcerned about the growth of "nationalism" in their tropical African colonies, regarding the latter as mere geographical units.

Nonetheless, territorial movements did begin to emerge, positioning their political arguments within the framework of territorial nationalism. Thus Herbert Macauley founded the Nigerian National Democratic Party, while in 1936 the Nigerian Youth Movement broke away from the latter under the leadership of younger men critical of Macauley himself. The Youth Movement called for "complete autonomy within the British empire" – notably *not* total independence *from* the British Empire – and advocated the creation of a united nation of Nigeria. It won considerable support during its brief lifespan, but omens soon materialized of what was to come for African nationalist politics across the continent. In 1941, the movement was split asunder following inter-ethnic rivalry between the Yoruba and the Igbo, each of which suspected the other of wishing to dominate it.[35] The question of whether "nationalist" leaders would be able to overcome this kind of "tribal" division, or indeed if they even possessed the political will to do so, would haunt nationalist politics from the late 1930s onward. The situation in Uganda through the 1920s and 1930s was not dissimilar: here, anticolonial protest was as often directed at the dominant position of the Ganda as it was at the British themselves. The ongoing controversy surrounding Buganda, and its head, the kabaka, did not bode well for the future of Ugandan nationalism, or for Ugandan national unity, while some of the most strident "ethnic nationalism" was to be found inside Buganda itself; the Ganda promoted themselves as a separate entity, deserving of separate consideration.[36]

Moreover, these new movements – fractured though they may have been – signified the increasing importance of the young in political developments. Empowered by either education, or economic migration, or both, African youth were involved in political associations, in new Christian organizations, in cultural movements and unions – and in so doing were often posing a challenge to their parents' generation. Many continued to be dependent upon their parents, and deferential to their parents' traditions; most obviously, it was necessary for fathers to pay their sons' bridewealth. But many were also in the vanguard of change and were at the forefront of forging new identities and new forms of resistance. In this way, too, would the young also become the backbone of a number of later nationalist parties across the continent. Unable to exercise violence, at least in the sense that their ancestors had up to the late nineteenth century – a key aspect of the loss of sovereignty which colonialism involved – young men developed new strategies for protest and resistance, and the identities needed to bring these to life. But they also, in many places, inherited the conflicts of earlier generations, which would later resurface with the achievement of independence.

By the time of the Second World War, then, Africans had embraced an array of identities, and had begun to develop new ones – including, in spatial terms, the local, the "tribal," the national, and the supranational, and in socioeconomic terms, the rural, the transient urban, and the proletarian. All of these involved conflict in various forms, including that between old and new elites, and that between "tribal" groupings. Ethnic chauvinism and generational competition were at the centre of new political debates and forms of self-expression. Such conflict would have a profound impact on the development of African nationalism; suffice it to say here that nationalism, and the broadly defined anticolonial struggle, cannot be understood without taking into account clashes of identity, and competing manifestations of group consciousness.

Notes

1 For example, Richard Waller, "Ethnicity and Identity," in Parker & Reid (eds.), *Oxford Handbook of Modern African History*.
2 The issue is dealt with in Crawford Young, *The African Colonial State in Comparative Perspective* (New Haven & London, 1994), and in Jeffrey Herbst, *States and Power in Africa: Comparative Lessons in Authority and Control* (Princeton, 2000).
3 Iliffe, *Modern History of Tanganyika*, 324.
4 There is a considerable literature on this. As an introductory sample, see R.G. Abrahams, *The Peoples of Greater Unyamwezi, Tanzania* (London, 1967); J.D.Y. Peel, *Religious Encounter and the Making of the Yoruba* (Bloomington & Indianapolis, 2000). See also H. Chimhundu, "Early missionaries and the ethnolinguistic factor during the "invention of tribalism" in Zimbabwe," *Journal of African History*, 33:1 (1992).
5 Colonial Office (UK), *Uganda: Report of a Commission of Privy Counsellors on a Dispute between Buganda and Bunyoro* (London, 1962).
6 J.A. Atanda, *The New Oyo Empire: Indirect Rule and Change in Western Nigeria, 1894–1934* (London, 1973).
7 Jean-Pierre Chrétien, *The Great Lakes of Africa: Two Thousand Years of History* (New York, 2003), esp. chap. 4.
8 Lonsdale, "The European scramble and conquest," 758.
9 Lapidus, *History of Islamic Societies*, 516–18.
10 C.D. Smith, *Islam and the Search for Social Order in Modern Egypt* (Albany NY, 1983).
11 A. Nouschi, *La Naissance du nationalisme algérien* (Paris, 1962); A. Merad, *Le Reformisme musulman en Algérie de 1925 a 1940* (The Hague, 1967).
12 F.B. Welbourn, *East African Rebels: A Study of Some Independent Churches* (London, 1961); David Maxwell, "Historicising Christian Independency: the southern African Pentecostal movement, c.1908–1960," *Journal of African History*, 40:2 (1999). See also Joel Cabrita, *Text and Authority in the South African Nazaretha Church* (Cambridge, 2014).
13 John McCracken, *A History of Malawi, 1859–1966* (Woodbridge, 2012), 112, 123–4.
14 Shepperson & Price, *Independent African*.
15 M.L. Martin, *Kimbangu* (Oxford, 1975).
16 N.A. Etherington, "The historical sociology of independent churches in South East Africa," *Journal of Religion in Africa*, 10:2 (1979).
17 J.R. Hooker, "Witnesses and Watchtower in the Rhodesias and Nyasaland," *Journal of African History*, 6:1 (1965); K.E. Fields, *Revival and Rebellion in Colonial Central Africa* (Princeton, 1985).
18 Davenport, *South Africa*, 238–9, 270–3.
19 For example, see A.P. Cheater, "Contradictions in "modelling" consciousness: Zimbabwean proletarians in the making," *Journal of Southern African Studies*, 14:2 (1988); R. Palmer, "Working conditions and worker responses on Nyasaland tea estates, 1930–1953," *Journal of African History*, 27:1 (1986).
20 T.O. Ranger, *Dance and Society in Eastern Africa, 1890–1970* (London, 1975); I. Henderson, "Early African leadership: the Copperbelt disturbances of 1935 and 1940," *Journal of Southern African History*, 2 (1975); C. Perrings, "Consciousness, conflict and proletarianisation: an assessment of the 1939 mineworkers strike on the Northern Rhodesian Copperbelt," *Journal of Southern African Studies*, 4:1 (1977).
21 See for example Christine Obbo, *African Women: their Struggle for Economic Independence* (London, 1980).

22 John Iliffe, *The African Poor: A History* (Cambridge, 1987), chap. 8.

23 For a wide-ranging set of studies, see Ian Brown (ed.), *The Economies of Africa and Asia in the Inter-War Depression* (London, 1989).

24 See Susan M. Martin, *Palm Oil and Protest: An Economic History of the Ngwa Region, Southeastern Nigeria, 1800–1980* (Cambridge, 1988); and D. Meredith, "Government and the decline of the Nigerian palm-oil export industry, 1919–1939," *Journal of African History*, 25:3 (1984).

25 Marc Matera, Misty L. Bastian, & Susan Kingsley Kent, *The Women's War of 1929: Gender and Violence in Colonial Nigeria* (Basingstoke, 2012).

26 J. Milburn, "The 1938 Gold Coast cocoa crisis," *African Historical Studies*, 3 (1970).

27 For an alternative view of indirect-rule chiefs, however, see Michael Crowder, "Tshekedi Khama and opposition to the British administration of the Bechuanaland Protectorate, 1926–36," *Journal of African History*, 26:2 (1985).

28 D.A. Low, *Buganda in Modern History* (London, 1971), 89; C.P. Youe, "Peasants, planters and cotton capitalists: the 'dual economy' of Uganda," *Canadian Journal of African Studies*, 12:2 (1978).

29 See "East African Federation Proposals: memorandum on the proposed federation of the British East African dependencies…," 29 October 1927, in D.A. Low (ed.), *The Mind of Buganda: Documents of the Modern History of an African Kingdom* (London, 1971).

30 For example, David Anderson, *Eroding the Commons: The Politics of Ecology in Baringo, Kenya, 1890–1963* (Oxford, 2002).

31 Sidney Littlefield Kasfir, "Visual Cultures," in Parker & Reid (eds.), *Handbook of Modern African History*.

32 Leopold Senghor, "Negritude and African Socialism," in P.H. Coetzee & A.P.J. Roux (eds.), *The African Philosophy Reader* (London, 1998).

33 Jonathan Derrick, *Africa's 'Agitators': Militant Anti-colonialism in Africa and the West, 1918–1939* (London, 2008).

34 Philip Garigue, "The West African Students' Union: a study in culture contact," *Africa*, 23:1 (1953).

35 Toyin Falola & Matthew Heaton, *A History of Nigeria* (Cambridge, 2008), chap. 6. See also A.G. Hopkins, "Economic aspects of political movements in Nigeria and the Gold Coast, 1918–1939," *Journal of African History*, 7:1 (1966).

36 For example, E.M.K. Mulira, *Troubled Uganda* (London, 1950).

13 Battles Home and Away

Africa in Global War (Again)

The War in the Continent

As in the 1914–18 conflict, the Second World War saw African colonies drawn into what was primarily a European conflict, and once again, throughout the war the continent was a crucial source of men and materials for the colonial powers involved – chiefly Britain, France, and Italy.[1] The British depended on their African territories particularly heavily, recruiting men from both West and East Africa, and coming to rely on the various colonies' agricultural produce and industrial sectors. At the same time, Egypt was of vital importance to the success of British geopolitical strategy, owing once more to the artery that was the Suez Canal. Egyptian nationalism, accordingly, was a constant source of anxiety in London, and even while German tanks rumbled into the Western Desert along the coast road in 1942, British armored vehicles surrounded government buildings in Cairo – not to protect them, but to keep an eye on the movements within. Egyptian nationalists were resentful of the renewed British military presence, and their loyalty was wholly contingent upon events.[2] Elsewhere, Britain could generally rely on the loyalty – or at least grudging acquiescence – of its African subjects. South Africa was the partial exception: here, according to the Statute of Westminster of 1931, there was no constitutional obligation to become involved in the war with Germany, and indeed a significant minority within the Afrikaner political establishment lobbied for neutrality, or at least nonbelligerence. There was even tacit sympathy for some of the tenets of Nazism. But there was, in the Union, enough of a sense of imperial loyalty and of the moral and cultural obligations of Dominion status to carry the day, and the government, under Smuts, secured support for a declaration of war in parliament – just. As he had during the Great War, Smuts became an important member of the Allied command, as well as a valued *confidante* of Churchill himself, and spent much of the war outside South Africa.[3]

France was in a rather different position. The armistice with Germany in June 1940 placed the French African Empire in an ambiguous and dangerous position; they appeared to be at the mercy of the Germans, while Churchill himself was perfectly willing to contemplate an attack on Francophone territory if necessary. Initially, territorial governors had little choice but to offer their loyalty to Vichy, but the colonies at length declared for de Gaulle's Free French movement, beginning with the "peripheral" territories which were followed (albeit somewhat more reluctantly) by Senegal and Algeria. In so doing, they provided vital strategic and material support for the war effort, particularly in the context of the Mediterranean and Middle Eastern theaters of operation.[4] As for Italy, the only Axis power with territory in Africa, it made extensive use – as it always had – of troops recruited in Eritrea, from which it had invaded Ethiopia in 1935; from his new "East African Empire," comprising Eritrea, Ethiopia, and Italian Somaliland, Mussolini eyed Sudan and Kenya, and from Libya Italian forces invaded Egypt, an adventure which handed the British their first morale-boosting victories in late 1940. Italian aggression in East and North Africa, indeed, was short-lived: much to Hitler's disgust, Italian armies were defeated relatively swiftly in northeast Africa, for example, in 1941–2.[5]

For Africans, indeed – and also for African-Americans in North America and the Caribbean – the Second World War had in many ways begun in 1935 with the Italian invasion of Ethiopia from colonial Eritrea, neither the first nor the last time that that particular frontier zone would be the cause of regional instability. With the partial exception of Liberia – partial, as Liberia was in many respects an American vassal state – Ethiopia was the only African state which could in any sense be described as "independent" north or south of the Sahara, but it was now the target of Mussolini's expansionist ambitions. It had long been one of the core aims of the Fascist state to build a "new Roman empire," and it would spring in part from Eritrea, driven by the quest for revenge for the defeat of the Italians in the hills around Adwa by Menelik in 1896. This was a stain on Italy's honor which it was Mussolini's destiny to eradicate, and accordingly, through the early 1930s, he was simply looking for an excuse to unleash vengeance on the Ethiopians. Notably, he sought international support prior to 1935 by arguing that Ethiopia was an anachronism, a savage and unstable state whose sovereignty was an affront to the civilized world. It practiced slavery and was no more worthy of international recognition than any other African people – thus its destiny must lie in Italian hands, as an Italian protectorate. Some, in London and Paris and elsewhere, were privately loath to disagree; yet Mussolini's public language made the British and French governments uncomfortable, redolent as it was of the aggressive imperialism of an earlier era. Il Duce's speeches seemed to belong to the 1880s, not the 1930s, and ironically it was Italian imperialism, rather more than the empire of Haile Selassie, which seemed curiously anachronistic.[6] And, after all, Ethiopia – like it or not, and many had their doubts – was now a full sovereign member of the League of Nations.

Nonetheless, in an era when even small European states might be sacrificed for the sake of wider security, Ethiopia could expect little support from the League of Nations, and in any case Britain and France had secretly, and somewhat ignominiously, already accepted the Italian subjugation of Ethiopia. Claiming an unprovoked attack by the Ethiopians at some watering holes close to the Somali border, Italy invaded in October 1935. This would be no repeat of 1896: the disparity between Italian and Ethiopian military technology and organization was now vast, and Italian armored columns, backed by aircraft and the occasional (and illegal) use of poison gas, swept all before them. Haile Selassie's army was much depleted, equipped with much the same weaponry as Menelik's had been forty years earlier, and was no match for a modern European army, despite some desperate heroism. By early 1936, the Ethiopian army was all but smashed, and Mussolini's forces entered Addis Ababa. Haile Selassie had already fled into exile, his hopes of British and French assistance dashed; besides some half-hearted sanctions, London and Paris were not prepared to alienate Italy over this relatively minor "crisis." The emperor spoke to the General Assembly of the League in Geneva, warning that it might be Ethiopia today, but it would be Europe tomorrow, and from thence he went to England, where he would remain until much larger events over which he had no control restored him to his throne. In fact, the Italians could never really claim to be in control of Ethiopia in its entirety; guerrilla activity on the part of the "Patriots" continued for the duration of the Fascist occupation, and swathes of the country remained beyond Italian jurisdiction.[7]

Abroad, Ethiopia became a *cause celèbre* – liberal opinion in Britain was outraged, for example, and a dedicated group of intellectual Ethiophiles gathered around the displaced emperor in his hour of need – while within the African-American community and inside Africa itself, Ethiopia became the focus of "pan-African" protest and nascent nationalism, respectively. Ethiopia, the embodiment of free and ancient "black" civilization, had long been a source of inspiration to early African nationalists and African-American political activists alike. Among the latter, it had inspired the Rastafarian movement in the Caribbean, named after Ras ("prince") Tafari, as Haile Selassie was known prior to his accession to the imperial throne. Passionate Afro-romanticists, the Rastafarians perceived Haile Selassie as the "Lion of Judah," of biblical genealogy – the emperor belonged to the so-called Solomonic line, claiming descent from King Solomon himself – and wove wonderful myths around this great, ancient, and "true" African civilization. Menelik's defense (indeed affirmation) of Ethiopia's independence during the European partition only served to underpin its status as Africa's only "great power." Now, the Italian invasion was regarded as an outrageous violation, a holy sacrilege, and a generation of African-Americans and African nationalists looked increasingly to Ethiopia as the symbol of their struggle against colonialism and racism, and as the ultimate source of "black pride," or *négritude*.[8]

They did not have to wait long for Ethiopia's "liberation," such as it was. In early 1941, Allied forces – the British using troops from West Africa, reinforced by French and Belgian colonial units from central and equatorial Africa – advanced into both Italian Eritrea and Ethiopia, and the Italians generally put up scant resistance, the bloody battle of Keren, northwest of Asmara in Eritrea, being a notable exception. By May 1941, Ethiopia and Eritrea had both been "liberated," and Haile Selassie restored to power, although this was compromised somewhat by the presence of British military and political "advisors." In Eritrea itself, the British, resource-starved and short of men, set up a tenuous administration – the British Military Administration – which relied heavily on Italian personnel to carry out the day-to-day running of the colony, now nonetheless classified as "occupied enemy territory." In the early 1940s, indeed, it was the continued prominence of former members of the Fascist administration which so aroused Eritrean indignation, and prompted at least some Eritreans to look south to Ethiopia as the champion of their final "liberation" from foreign domination. Haile Selassie and the Amhara political establishment, as we shall see, were only too happy to fulfill the role, and within months of the Italian defeat the Ethiopians were beginning to lobby for the supposed "return" of Eritrea to the "motherland." Other Eritreans, however, eschewed any suggestion of union with Ethiopia, and their own lobby would intensify in the years to come. The political battle would be bitter and would soon become a violent one.[9]

The only other theater of actual combat on the continent was along a coastal strip a few miles wide facing the Mediterranean. The Italians had invaded Egypt from Libya in the late summer of 1940, but had soon been pushed onto the defensive by a comparatively small British force that proceeded to advance into Libya itself. The situation was only transformed with the arrival of the German Afrika Korps, which – notwithstanding some further ebbing and flowing of the front line – was soon driving into Egypt toward the Suez Canal, apparently unstoppably. Egyptian nationalists grew restless, and anti-British sentiment heightened; Cairo was tense. However, when the British halted the Germans at El Alamein in October 1942, the tide turned, and Suez was safe for the British Empire – for now. In fact the threat from Egyptian nationalism was to prove rather more durable than that offered by Field Marshal Rommel. As British and Australian forces now drove the Germans back into Libya and toward Tunisia, at the other end of the Mediterranean a US army landed in Morocco and Algeria to end the uneasy political ambiguity there brought about by the Vichy arrangement. Allied forces, closing in from west and east, met in Tunisia and expelled the last Axis troops from Africa in May 1943.

African soldiers also served beyond the continent itself. Troops from the Francophone and Anglophone zones served in Italy between 1943 and 1945; and the British made extensive use of African regiments in Burma, the "forgotten war." By the end of the war, there were over 370,000 Africans serving in the British armed forces. Many had become politically conscious through their wartime experience, and had developed heightened awareness of the colonial system and the world in which it functioned. Some, professional soldiers proud of the regimental colors and "traditions," would be demobilized and retire peacefully back into their communities. But others would have a major influence over those communities, where they might be drawn to – or even become the agents of – radical politics, and the instigators of political protest, in the postwar period. Returning war veterans had a much broader view of the world and a more informed view of Europe. As in the 1914–18 conflict, only on a much larger scale, Africans had served alongside Europeans of various classes, though their interaction with working-class whites must have been a particularly novel experience; they had killed Europeans, and seen European weakness and failure at close quarters. The myth of European supremacy – moral or otherwise – was finally exploded, and it was this shift in African perceptions of their colonial masters which was to prove of enormous and lasting significance.[10]

For the empire? West African troops in action in Burma, c.1943. Imperial War Museum Q 53630. Source: Reproduced with permission of AP Images.

Military tradition: officer and men of the Kings African Rifles, Uganda. Source: Courtesy of the Council of the National Army Museum, London.

Shifts in Politics and Society

American, French, and British flags may have fluttered between Cairo and Casablanca during the closing years of the war; but the future of Anglo-Franco-American hegemony across North Africa was far from certain, as nationalists of various hues in Morocco, Algeria, Tunisia, Libya, and Egypt made plans to use the political capital they had accumulated through support – tacit or otherwise – of the Allies' prosecution of the war. Significantly, in some cases, older North African elites would find themselves under threat from a younger generation of nationalists, associated as the former were with "collaboration" with Europe, an ongoing political and indeed spiritual antagonism which had its roots in the nineteenth century. Moroccans expected the granting of full sovereignty upon the achievement of the Allied victory – they were reportedly promised this by Roosevelt himself, and the Sultan, Sidi Mohammad, had remained loyal throughout the war – but after the war the French suppressed the new nationalist party, Istiqlal (Independence). The Sultan himself became a key figure in the nationalist struggle through the late 1940s. In neighboring Algeria, the nationalist cause which had been gaining momentum in the interwar years was given a further spur with the US invasion in 1943. In that year, a number of French-educated nationalists, including the key figure Ferhat Abbas, drew up a "Manifesto of the Algerian People" which called for political and economic reform. With de Gaulle promising full citizenship for the Algerian elite, Abbas founded the Amis du Manifesté et de la Liberté (AML) which demanded, among other things, the establishment of a republic to be federated with France. The movement was, however, attacked on two fronts: by the settlers, and by more radical political elements which regarded Abbas as too moderate, including the Parti du Peuple Algérien (PPN) under Ahmed Messali. Violent protest in 1945 was met with a brutal response, and Abbas was briefly detained, as was Messali; when they were released the following year, they founded rival parties, and the French permitted a quota of Algerian representatives to be returned to the constituent assembly. But as the 1940s progressed, nationalists were repeatedly frustrated by the French government's continued support for the white settler community, and indeed by the rigging of elections. The Tunisian nationalist leader Habib ibn Ali Bourguiba had been loyal to the Free French cause during the war, but when the monarch Moncef Bey began agitating for political reform, he was swiftly exiled and replaced by a more "reconciled" figure. Nonetheless, the nationalist Neo-Destour party was increasingly popular, and in the years after the war, Bourguiba spent a great deal of time abroad, garnering support for Tunisian independence.[11]

The situation was somewhat more complicated in Libya, which was technically occupied enemy territory; here, the fate of the former Italian colony was to be decided by the four victorious powers – Britain, France, the United States, and the Soviet Union – but it would be delayed for several years, until a peace treaty could be signed with the Italians themselves. Certainly, at least initially, independence was not considered an option. The British had benefited during the war from the support of the Sanusi leader Sayyid Mohammed Idris, and had developed a certain interest in the nurturing and protection of Cyrenaica province; Cyrenaica's status contrasted to some extent with that of Tripolitania, which had long been more socioeconomically "developed" under the Italians, but which itself was deeply divided internally. Most of the Italian settlers in Libya were also in Tripolitania, moreover.[12] In Egypt, however, nationalists were rather better organized, and certainly more vocal. In 1939, the British had converted Egypt into their main base for operations in the Middle East and the eastern Mediterranean, which they were entitled to do under the terms of a 1936 treaty. They were able to control the king, but had to keep an eye on a succession of premiers who were alternately faintly pro-Axis or studiously neutral. By the 1940s, the Muslim Brotherhood had made the transition from religious reform movement to stridently nationalist party, and it was joined by a communist party and the Young Egypt Party, founded by Ahmed Hussein – though neither of these proved particularly successful in building broader bases of support. Most Egyptians had been ambivalent, at best, about British military successes against the Germans during the war; but socioeconomic hardships (including rampant inflation and food shortages), and the high-handed British action in stationing tanks around the royal palace had exacerbated not only anti-British feeling but also hostility toward the apparently ineffectual and irresolute monarchy of King Faruq, and toward the Wafd. In the years after the war, strikes and protests became common, and in the late 1940s, Egyptian politics were increasingly explosive; throughout, however, the British were concerned first and foremost to protect their strategic and financial investment in the Suez Canal.[13]

South of the Sahara, the support of the French territories for Charles de Gaulle had been critical in providing troops, as well as strategically valuable land and air supply routes across the continent. The contribution thus made provided African nationalists with increased leverage. As the war unfolded, de Gaulle found that there were demands to be met and promises to be made: in 1944, at Brazzaville, the Free French leader was compelled to offer a "new deal" of political reform in the colonies once the war was won, a package of concessions necessitated by their military and economic contributions.[14] Yet this package was also a tacit recognition of how important the African colonies were likely to be in France's postwar recovery. Attempted appeasement of nationalist leaders was frequently aimed at the stabilization and retention of the colonies; France, like Britain, could not contemplate surrendering its colonies, and thus the promise of reform was tactical. While there was no talk of political independence, there *was* talk of the incorporation of Africans into higher administrative positions; the possibility of a measure of self-government was dangled in front of nationalist politicians. The political concessions thus offered can be seen to have laid the foundations for an eventual transfer of power and decolonization, but this was by no means the intention of such reform at the time.

War brought socioeconomic hardships – inflation, disruption of trade, and depressed prices for exports – which compounded those experienced during the 1930s. Yet African workers also recognized their own economic muscle, and by the early 1940s were using strike action and nascent trade unionism to considerable effect, particularly in the mining economies of southern and central Africa. When Northern Rhodesian copper miners went on strike in 1940, Britain was fighting for its life against the Luftwaffe; in an industry so vital to their survival, the British had no choice but to offer concessions to the strikers in terms of pay and working conditions.[15] Indeed, it was the potential for social unrest and a recognition – originating before the war – of the fragility of the social fabric that produced a rather more cautious approach on the part of colonial authorities than had been seen during the First World War. In both British and French Africa, the Second World War came at a time of concern for the nature of the colonial order, characterized by anxieties over growing African protest, and thus did the war witness more sophisticated methods of "persuasion" of Africans in the great struggle against fascism. The British employed propaganda to this end: films, radio broadcasts, newspapers, and pamphlets were aimed at "encouraging" and "persuading" Africans to cooperate with colonial authorities, to volunteer for service, to "do their bit." It was an approach which necessitated the projection of the colonial state as fundamentally "good," and the ideologies against which the British and French were fighting as "evil," and to some extent it reflected the perceived need to justify and explain colonialism to Africans to an unprecedented degree. Naked force was no longer acceptable; blind faith and obedience on the part of African subjects could no longer be taken for granted.[16]

The African voice was increasingly difficult to ignore, or indeed to appease. Criticisms of colonial rule became ever more trenchant, and public, and came through newsletters and the kinds of local associations noted in an earlier chapter. African newsletters in particular spread dramatically through the 1940s, and reached an ever wider audience, even if the debate contained therein was often transmitted orally. Africans were becoming politicized to an unprecedented degree, aware of the issues of the day and of their own role in the European war. They were also conscious of colonial hypocrisy. Many dwelt upon the supposed difference between fascism in Europe and colonial rule in Africa, particularly following the Atlantic Charter in August 1941, details of which were widely reported in local newspapers and via the news broadcasts of the Allies themselves. The Charter was the work of Churchill and Roosevelt, and proclaimed the fundamental right of all peoples to self-determination and protection against aggression and persecution. It caused quite a stir in African educated circles; did this not also apply to them? No, said the British prime minister, who felt compelled to make the point that the peoples of the British Empire were already being adequately looked after. But the damage had been done, as political activists across the continent now sensed the weakness of the colonial system and the moral bankruptcy of the philosophies which underpinned it. Nor was President Roosevelt particularly convinced by Churchill's robust defense either: anti-imperial by political instinct, Roosevelt began to pressure his British ally to set a postwar timetable for decolonization, or at least the transition to some degree of self-government.[17]

As the war drew to a close, a group of young, educated Africans was emerging, many of them living or having been educated abroad – in both Europe and the United States – galvanized by their experience both of the war itself and of having observed colonialism from beyond the continent. Many of them were also dedicated pan-Africanists, which would have profound implications for the shape of the postcolonial continent. These young men – as men they invariably were – were the first generation of African nationalists, and would later constitute the continent's first wave of independent leaders. At the fifth Pan-African Congress, held in Manchester, England, in 1945, they no longer talked in terms of merely modifying the system, or of submitting polite petitions to their colonial masters. The central theme of the congress was the unconditional dismantling of the colonial empires, even if detailed plans and strategies were not yet developed. The demand was total independence.[18]

Yet if this was one significant outcome of wartime experience, then the revival and strengthening of colonial states was another. For the remaining principal colonial powers – Britain, France, Portugal, and Belgium – their African territories were more important to them than ever. Interventionist policies were pursued with renewed vigor in the years after 1945. As we saw in an earlier chapter, the belief in an essentially laissez-faire economy had been predominant until the early 1930s, when the ravages of the Depression persuaded the British and French in particular that greater levels of state management were necessary; the Second World War made it clear that such interventionist programs must continue, and indeed intensify. The African contribution to Europe's postwar economic recovery was deemed vital, and thus European governments needed to become more closely involved in managing colonial economies themselves, for example in terms of the expansion of crop production.[19] This amounted, in the British zone at least, to what has been described as a "second colonial occupation," stretching from about 1945 until the early 1950s.[20] Thus were postwar battle-lines drawn: just as African nationalist protest became a force to be reckoned with, colonial governments became more determined than ever to invest in, develop, and above all defend their African possessions. How long the struggle would last, and how it would conclude, were unknowns as the Germans and then the Japanese surrendered; but it certainly *was* clear that the war itself had unleashed potent forces for change.

Notes

1 A sample survey of the literature would include: "World War II and Africa," special issue of the *Journal of African History*, 26:4 (1985); R. Rathbone & D. Killingray (eds.), *Africa and the Second World War* (London, 1986); K. Jeffrey, "The Second World War," in J. Brown & W.R. Louis (eds.), *The Oxford History of the British Empire, Vol 4: The Twentieth Century* (Oxford, 1999); Judith A. Byfield, Carolyn A. Brown, Timothy Parsons, & Ahmad Alawad Sikainga (eds.), *Africa and World War II* (Cambridge, 2015).

2 Jeffrey, "The Second World War," 318.

3 J.C. Smuts. *Jan Christian Smuts* (London, 1952), 393–487.

4 Suret-Canale, *French Colonialism*, 463–77.

5 A.J. Barker, *Eritrea 1941* (London, 1966).

6 Esmonde M. Robertson, *Mussolini as Empire-Builder: Europe and Africa, 1932–36* (London, 1977).

7 Anthony Mockler, *Haile Selassie's War: the Italian-Ethiopian Campaign, 1935–1941* (New York, 1984). See also a range of fascinating, and very different, contemporary sources: Evelyn Waugh, *Waugh in Abyssinia* (London, 1936); Edward Ullendorff (tr. & ed.), *The Autobiography of Emperor Haile Selassie I: 'My Life and Ethiopia's Progress', 1892–1937* (London, 1976), chaps. 34–50; Andrew Hilton, *The Ethiopian Patriots: Forgotten Voices of the Italo-Abyssinian War, 1935–41* (Stroud, 2007).

8 John Sorenson, *Imagining Ethiopia: Struggles for History and Identity in the Horn of Africa* (New Brunswick NJ, 1993), 26–7.

9 Redie Bereketeab, *Eritrea: The Making of a Nation, 1890–1941* (Trenton NJ, 2007), chap. 5. For an intelligent contemporary British assessment, see G.K.N. Trevaskis, *Eritrea: A Colony in Transition, 1941–52* (London, 1960).

10 David Killingray, *Fighting for Britain: African soldiers in the Second World War* (Woodbridge, 2010); Waruhiu Itote (General China), *'Mau Mau' General* (Nairobi, 1967), chaps. 1 & 3.

11 For example, Lawrence, *Imperial Rule*, chaps. 4 & 5.

12 John Wright, *A History of Libya* (London, 2012), chap. 16.

13 Artemis Cooper, *Cairo in the War, 1939–45* (London, 1989); Afaf Lutfi Al-Sayyid Marsot, *A Short History of Modern Egypt* (Cambridge, 1985), chap. 5.

14 Suret-Canale, *French Colonialism*, 484–7.

15 Andrew Roberts, *A History of Zambia* (New York, 1976), 186, 193, 203.

16 Wendell P. Holbrook, "British propaganda and the mobilisation of the Gold Coast war effort, 1939–1945," *Journal of African History*, 26:4 (1985); but see also David Killingray, "Military and labour recruitment in the Gold Coast during the Second World War," *Journal of African History*, 23:1 (1982).

17 R.D. Pearce, *The Turning Point in Africa: British Colonial Policy, 1938–1948* (London, 1982); David Reynolds, *Britannia Overruled: British Policy and World Power in the 20th Century* (Harlow, 2000).

18 Hakim Adi & Marika Sherwood, *The 1945 Manchester Pan-African Congress Revisited* (London, 1995).

19 I. Spencer, "Settler dominance, agricultural production, and the Second World War in Kenya," *Journal of African History*, 21:4 (1980); D. Meredith, "The Colonial Office, British business interests, and the reform of cocoa marketing in West Africa, 1937–1945," *Journal of African History*, 29:2 (1988).

20 D.A. Low & J.M. Lonsdale, "Introduction: towards the new order, 1945–1963," in D.A. Low & Alison Smith (eds.), *History of East Africa, Vol. III* (Oxford, 1976), 12–16.

Part V The Dissolution of Empire

In the period between 1945 and 1970, the "colonial moment" came to an end across most of Africa and did not last much longer even in those areas which proved rather more resistant to change. In some places, indeed, the experience of colonial rule had lasted little more than a couple of generations; the consequences may on certain levels have been profound, but in other respects what followed was a reversion to an earlier, nineteenth-century, pattern of relations between Africa and Europe. This may or may not have been the ultimate objective of colonial administrators, depending on how much we believe there to have been a "grand plan" in Rome, London, Paris, Lisbon, or Brussels; but the speed with which colonial rule itself came to an end was certainly not anticipated. The empires created in the 1890s and 1900s were meant to last rather longer than they did; in the end, they were overcome by both unforeseen, external events, and the organic pressures manifest in African protest and the power of militant African identity – whether violent or otherwise.

Individual dates are usually arbitrary, in so far as they are used to indicate "turning points" or "watersheds"; but 1945 did indeed herald a new era, and the onset of a new world order in which the imperialisms of the late nineteenth century would be increasingly obsolete. The 1940s, indeed, was a decade of profound change for colonial states and African nationalists alike. Among the former, Britain and France now sought to exploit their territories rather more efficiently (it was believed) than had been the case previously. For African nationalists, there were both opportunities to be seized and obstacles to be overcome in the building of mass movements and political parties, and in the creation of forces for change. As the Pan-African Congress met in Manchester in 1945 and demanded an unconditional end to colonial rule, colonial strategists devised ways of securing their territories for the foreseeable future. For Portugal and Belgium,

A History of Modern Africa: 1800 to the Present, Third Edition. Richard J. Reid.

this meant a refusal to move much beyond limited political concessions, and a conviction that their African colonies were essential to their economic and geopolitical survival in the post-war era. Britain and France also perceived their colonies as essential to post-war recovery, and in the late 1940s and early 1950s developed policies aimed at their commercial development; at the same time, this would be accompanied by the gradual incorporation of Africans into administrative structures to appease nationalists. In the course of the 1950s, however, successive governments in London and Paris recognized both the power of nationalist movements and the fact that they might be able to exercise continued economic (and indeed cultural) influence without the trouble of political administration. In the metropolitan mind, thus, African sovereignty was often seen as the happy coalescence of various interests – even if the actual process was invariably messier in reality.

Belgium and Portugal would ultimately lose control of events, as violence erupted in Mozambique, Angola, and Guinea-Bissau, and chaos threatened to consume Congo. But the British and French would also be shaken by violence, in Kenya and Algeria, respectively. Events in those territories – driven as they were in large part by the presence of large European settler minorities – ultimately persuaded London and Paris of the dangers, and the inimicality, of violent confrontation with rebels and nationalists. The French conceded defeat to the Algerian rebels directly, while the British crushed the Mau Mau insurgents before handing power to a moderate elite not directly involved in the revolt. Elsewhere, there were largely peaceable, if at times Byzantine, negotiations with African politicians across much of sub-Saharan Anglophone and Francophone Africa, which led to a constitutional transfer of power in those zones. Late-nineteenth-century imperial high-handedness had a final throw in Egypt in 1956 when British and French troops invaded the Suez Canal zone in response to Nasser's nationalization of the Canal Company; but final throw it certainly was, as in the face of international condemnation, Britain and France were forced into a sharp and humiliating retreat. The age of empire, indeed, seemed to be finished as 1957 dawned; but white settler regimes became entrenched, oblivious to any "winds of change" that might have been blowing elsewhere, and governments in South Africa and Rhodesia, for example, presented particularly difficult obstacles for nationalists fighting for "internal" decolonization. Settlers created political and cultural frameworks within which the likelihood of violence increased dramatically.

But what of African protest itself? It was manifest in different ways in different places before the 1940s, although there were broadly similar trajectories and forms of action. But now, nationalists had to develop political parties through which to channel such protest, and to develop wider territorial consciousness. The elections organized by colonial authorities in many territories provided a platform on which such parties could posit national agendas. Nonetheless, the conflicts which emerged between various groupings – ethnic, regional, and religious – were frequently continuations of nineteenth-century struggles, sharpened in most cases by the experience of colonial rule which added new elements to the competition, not least in the provision of a "national" space within which such competition was now to be played out. The divisions between Africans which were obstacles to "national" identities were also opportunities in the

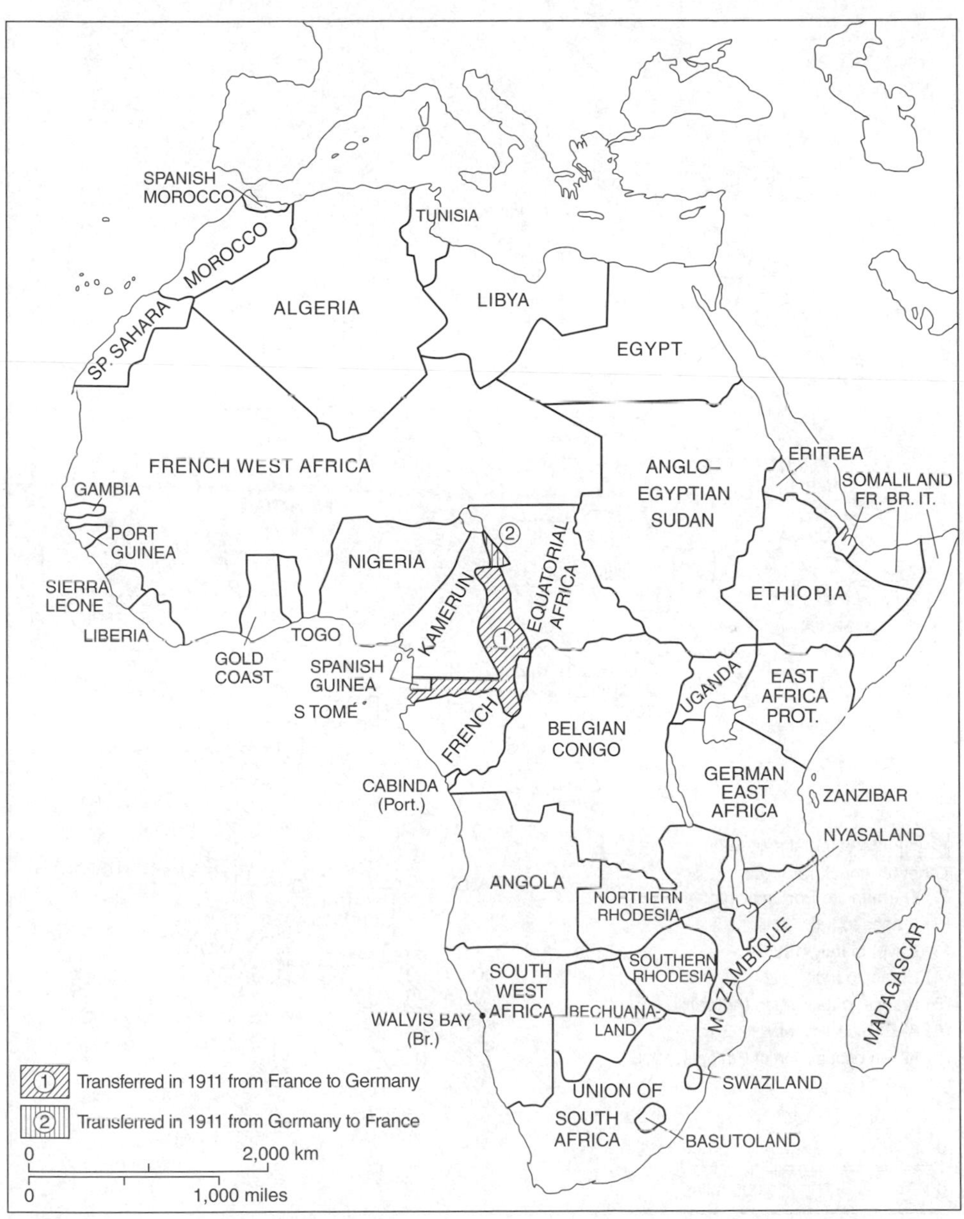

Political boundaries (1): 1914. Source: From A. D. Roberts (ed.), *Cambridge History of Africa. Vol. 7: 1905–40* (Cambridge, 1986), Map 1. © 1986 by Cambridge University Press. Reprinted with permission from Cambridge University Press.

struggle for the future, as subnational groupings competed for the political and material resources of the nation to come.

Across much of tropical Africa, genuinely nationalist movements were novel in the immediate postwar years; only in northern Africa, and in the Union of South Africa, were the roots of nationalism rather deeper. In Algeria, Tunisia, and Egypt,

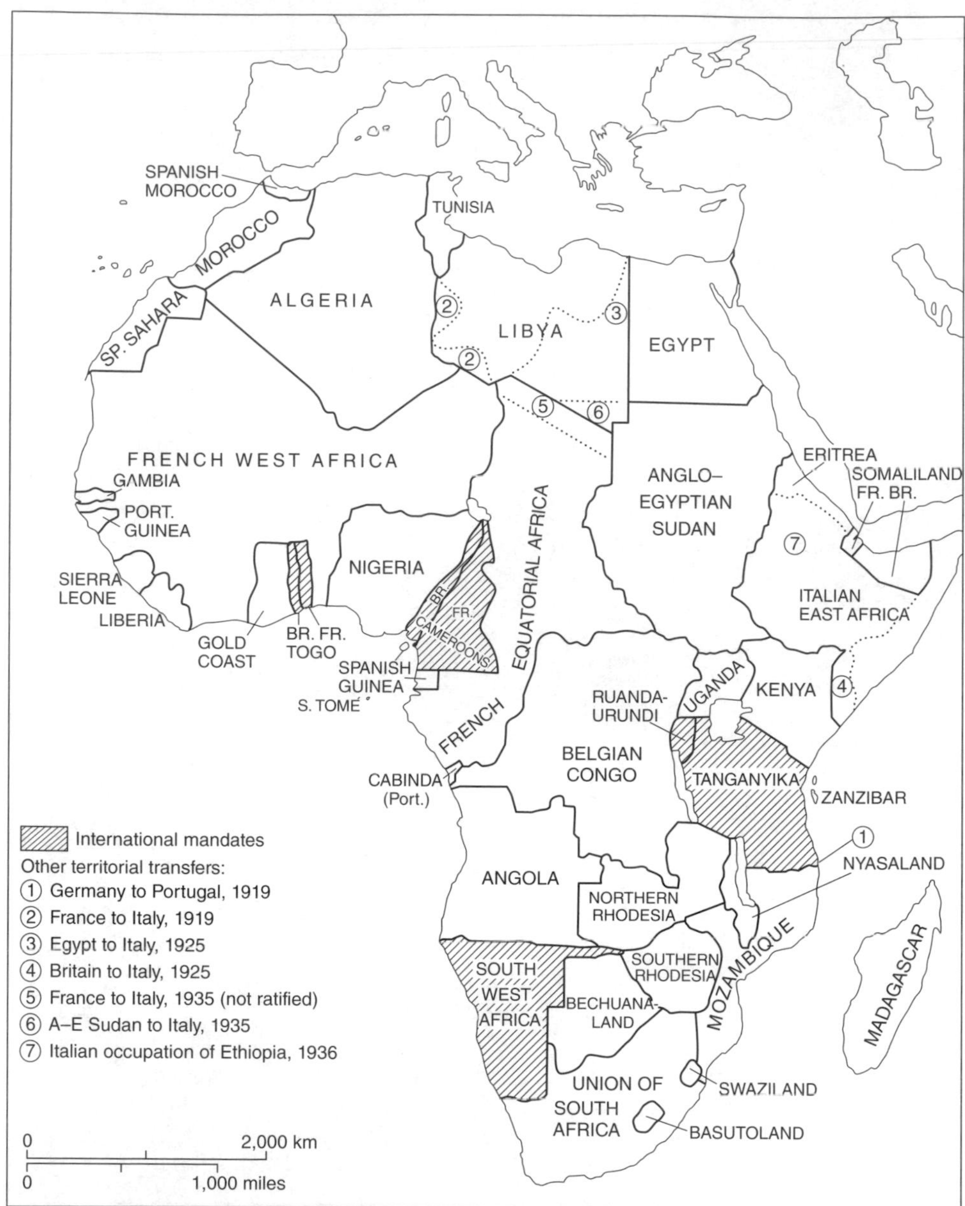

Political boundaries (2): 1939. Source: From A. D. Roberts (ed.), *Cambridge History of Africa*. Vol. 7: *1905–40* (Cambridge, 1986), Map 2 © 1986 by Cambridge University Press. Reprinted with permission from Cambridge University Press.

political activists drew on a range of precedents and inspirations, including Islamist thought, European nationalism, and Arab identity; in South Africa, an educated elite set a precedent for the wider region in founding the South African Native National Congress as a vehicle for political lobbying. Of course the forms taken by political movements were very much influenced by the challenges they had to overcome. In the Gold Coast, or Senegal, or Tanzania, it was a matter of image-making and careful combination of negotiation and veiled threat when it came to dealing with retreating colonial authorities. In Uganda or Nigeria, nationalists of different hues spent as much time in the 1950s squabbling with each other about the future of their territories as they did combating the evils of colonialism. In these instances, colonial officials became brokers of deals and negotiators. The achievements of the generation that would lead much of Africa to independence were many, not least in terms of political creativity, but so were the problems confronting them. They were not necessarily the builders of stable and durable political orders, such was the nature of decolonization – which was, arguably, as rushed and unplanned as had been the original partition of the continent. The two biggest problems confronting nationalist leaders were, firstly, that they were operating in unfamiliar territory, a uniquely twentieth-century landscape into which they had been thrust by colonial rule; and secondly that a great many tensions and divisions represented unfinished business from the precolonial era, and the nineteenth century in particular. Their problems were new, and they were old.

There were further challenges for those politicians attempting to negotiate with colonial regimes which clearly did not take such negotiations seriously – except in the sense that they were aimed at maintaining the status quo. The result, in the course of the 1950s and 1960s, was the eruption of armed struggle in South Africa, Rhodesia, Algeria, Mozambique, and Angola; the politics of these nationalist movements became the politics of violence, and the violence that ensued shaped these territories and their peoples in the most fundamental of ways. For guerrillas, the challenge was not only the overthrow of intransigent racialism and, in some cases at least, foreign capital; it was also the construction of new order out of bloody sacrifice, the creation of life out of death among shattered communities.

In the end, Africa became independent – politically, at least – through both compromise and conflict, negotiation and violence; sometimes, it was both simultaneously, in other cases, it was one or the other. Nationalists might claim victory over colonial masters, and the fulfillment of the people's destiny; they could hardly do otherwise. Governments in the metropole might claim that missions had been completed and that the transfer of power to African governments was simply the last stage in the discharge of the imperial mandate. Neither position was sustainable. While nationalist movements might occasionally have subdued colonial militaries by sheer force of arms, such triumphs rarely represented the total destruction of extant political systems, and rarely did they represent the will of entire populations. More commonly "nationalist victories" were in fact negotiated settlements, and no less remarkable for all that. While outgoing colonial authorities may occasionally have left behind "friendly" regimes, with governments run by people themselves educated within the system, ideologically and culturally "reconciled," they also left behind social and political structures noteworthy only for their inequity and instability, and which were unsustainable over the longer term. Again, however, it is important to emphasize that this was not *merely* a matter of the failures of decolonization, although these were manifold; also in evidence is the resurgence of various nineteenth-century dynamics in African political culture and economic development – notably the struggle to win access to scarce political and material resources, a struggle often characterized by violent upheaval, the forging of new communities and the consolidation of old ones. Ultimately, for both former colonial rulers and new African governments, decolonization only represented the latest stage in ongoing political, economic, and indeed cultural struggles which are in some ways unresolved.

14 The Beached Whale

Colonial Strategies in the Postwar World

In September 1939, as Britain and France went to war with Germany, colonial rule had seemed impregnable. There had, of course, been challenges to colonial authority before the war: political movements that appeared to foreshadow the emergence of modern nationalism; rural protest on the part of cash-crop farmers; urban workers' organizations and strike action, and even the beginnings of trade unionism; Islamic and Christian movements which rejected, for different reasons, the assumptions on which colonial rule was based; and overall a louder and more aggressive African voice emerging through a range of media, from artisans' self-help associations to newspapers. Yet there had been little that threatened to completely overthrow the colonial system, despite some of the deeper anxieties harbored by far-flung colonial officials. No European power, moreover, had given any serious thought to retreating from its African Empire, except in the most abstract of ways and only in the most long-term of timeframes. Nonetheless, within twenty years, all of this had changed. As the 1950s drew to a close, profound political change had taken place; Britain and France had already initiated irreversible programs of decolonization, and Belgium was teetering on the brink. Only Portugal, as well as such white settler regimes as Southern Rhodesia and South Africa, remained intransigent, with devastating consequences. Just as Europe had scrambled *into* Africa, it would scramble *out* of it, in more or less the same period of time. And just as with the partition of the continent in the late nineteenth century, processes of decolonization would be driven by both external factors – those pertaining to European domestic or foreign policy considerations – and internal dynamics, namely the activities of African political movements and changing realities which they brought about on the ground.

A History of Modern Africa: 1800 to the Present, Third Edition. Richard J. Reid.

But it is important, as ever, not to abuse hindsight, for even in 1945 this seemed a long way off. The immediate postwar era would indeed be critical in shaping the nature of Africa's eventual decolonization and of the political movements that would lead various territories to independence. Widespread disillusionment, the myriad of associations and organizations that had emerged around anticolonial grievances, and the heightened political consciousness fostered by the experiences of the 1930s and the Second World War itself, would crystallize in the years after 1945, and facilitate the development of broader-based and better-organized political parties mounting a more serious and coordinated challenge to the colonial system. At the same time, however, colonial administrations, to greater or lesser degrees, developed new strategies and policies, or built on existing ones, which were generally aimed above all at the stabilization of colonial empires and the maximizing of the material benefits to be derived from them.

Postwar Africa and the International Climate

The world was dramatically different in 1945 from what it had been six years earlier. The international political climate had changed, and Africa's position must be understood in the light of several factors – although, as we shall see, each of these must be qualified and placed in perspective. First, events in parts of Asia had been significant in some respects for Africa and for the non-European world more broadly. The advances achieved by Indian nationalist movements immediately after the war, for example, appeared to point toward an empire in retreat, and served as an inspiration to African movements, both north and south of the Sahara. During the war itself, the example set by Japan had been important, too. Japan had been seen by many – at least initially – as the model of a successful non-European, anticolonial state, emerging to dynamically challenge Western imperialism. It had humbled the Dutch, the British, and the French across southern and Southeast Asia through the early 1940s; Japanese forces, with astonishing ease, had captured Singapore, the center of British imperialism in Southeast Asia, and had even threatened India. (African troops, indeed, had seen this at first hand in the jungles of Burma, as we have noted.) Japan, therefore, had been something of an inspiration and was perhaps comparable to Ethiopia in this respect. Yet this needs to be qualified: clearly, Japanese influence had been more strongly felt in Asia and the Pacific than in Africa, while its reputation as a "liberating" anticolonial power was largely destroyed through its own behavior toward the populations of the territory it occupied.[1]

The emergence of the United States as a truly global power also had an enormous impact, as indeed will become apparent through the remaining portion of this book. During the war years, the personal politics of President Roosevelt had been particularly important; his deeply felt antipathy toward European imperialism was partly the result of his own background, and partly the result of his conviction that it had contributed to two world wars. Roosevelt's influence in British political circles was profound, even on the arch-imperialist Churchill, who was only too aware of Britain's wartime dependence on the United States. Roosevelt used this relationship to push for a timetable for decolonization, or at least the introduction of reforms that would lead to more "humane" and representative government. Nonetheless, after 1945, anti-imperialism dropped down the US foreign policy agenda somewhat: following Roosevelt's death and the defeat of the Axis powers, the US under Truman and later Eisenhower was less concerned with the dismantling of the European empires than with the exigencies of the Cold War. Of prime concern was that the so-called "Third World" – Africa, Asia, Latin America – should be protected from communism, which, it was believed, preyed on the vulnerable and the destitute. Just as Europe itself was to be given aid through the Marshall Plan, so European imperialism might be interpreted as offering protection to primitive, ill-developed peoples prone to the predations of the radical Left. The US continued to espouse an anticolonial doctrine, but its antipathy to communism was much stronger, and it was willing to intervene in support of colonial regimes threatened by communist insurrection: military aid, for example was provided to the Portuguese fascist regime fighting Marxist guerrillas in Angola and Mozambique in the 1960s.[2]

The United States was not the only "new" player on the global stage, for the Soviet Union also came of age in many respects in the late 1940s. From the outset of the Cold War, the USSR presented itself as anticolonial to its very core. Just as the Americans might point to an anti-imperial genealogy dating to the late eighteenth century, the Soviet Union founded its own doctrine on Lenin's (somewhat derivative) argument that imperialism was the highest form of capitalism, and espoused the liberation of oppressed peoples around the world.[3] Again, however, it is important not to predate the Soviet impact on Africa, which was minimal in the early stages of decolonization. Only after Stalin's death, and Khruschev's renewed interest in taking the struggle to other corners of the globe, did the USSR become significant in this respect. Certainly by the 1960s, Moscow was prepared to give diplomatic and military support to African movements seeking independence or to governments in need of "protection" from Western aggression. The Soviet Union, crucially, would come to represent an ideological alternative and offered the possibility of acquiring military hardware.

Economic Policies and Visions, c. 1945–50

In 1945, Europe was economically exhausted. In this new bipolar world, Europe had finally lost the preeminence it had enjoyed for some four centuries, and was economically as well as politically marginalized by the power of the United States and the Soviet Union. It was a situation which placed European colonial powers in a new relationship *vis-à-vis* their African territories: in the postwar period, colonial territories were more important than ever in economic terms. The British, for example, arguably came to rely more heavily on their African colonies than ever before; and thus there was, again, something of a "second colonial occupation," which involved efforts to open up new areas for trade, investment, and production, and to exploit with renewed vigor areas which were now perceived as having lain undeveloped and fallow for too long. Large areas of eastern and central Africa, notably, were regarded as newly important sources of raw materials vital to resource-starved Britain. Importantly, moreover, they were outside "dollar control," and thus vital to British recovery, if this was not to be completely dependent on the United States, to which London was already heavily indebted. Nonetheless, it needs to be noted that, in the longer term, the relative economic weakness of colonial regimes did not necessarily mean their collapse; indeed, the opposite is broadly true. Portugal, the weakest of all the colonial empires in economic terms, lasted the longest – until the 1970s – and it was precisely because of such economic disadvantages that Lisbon clung to its overseas empire, a vital commercial and industrial crutch, with grim determination. By contrast, Britain, which recovered relatively quickly and which in the 1950s was the strongest of the European colonial powers, decolonized fastest; and again, it was precisely because of British economic buoyancy and political influence that it could afford to decolonize, while retaining postcolonial influence.[4]

The immediate postwar period witnessed increased interventionism on the part of the colonial state, a policy dating to the 1930s but now pursued with new urgency. As demand for African goods in Europe increased, governments became more closely involved, for example in the expansion of crop production after 1945, commonly through state-run marketing boards. In British West Africa, the West African Produce Marketing Board sought to manage and maximize production and bring about ever greater economic stability; a similar procedure was enacted for Uganda. From the mid-1940s, substantial government funds were made available – for the first time, in some areas – for colonial development. In the French colonies, the postwar recovery took rather longer: the war had collapsed levels of foreign trade, and the French economy itself was devastated. But even here, by the end of the 1940s, marketing boards had been established to take advantage of the agricultural boom, with profits being diverted into development projects. Even in supposedly independent Liberia, the Firestone rubber company invested in huge plantations, an early example of modern African sovereignty compromised by foreign commercial concerns.[5] The process of investment and development was assisted by the fact that international terms of trade switched back in favor of the African producer, to some extent, for the first time since the onset of the global depression; a rise in prices for certain export crops meant a postwar boom for some. At the same time, however, some attention was also given to the introduction of capital-intensive schemes, a new kind of colonial economy in which African farmers would be largely marginalized in favor of the large-scale importation of mechanized equipment and settler experts. One of the more notable instances of this was the groundnut scheme in Tanganyika, where the idea was developed of creating huge plantations, on the lines of North American prairie-style farming, which would involve using more machinery, clearing larger areas of land, and employing more Europeans than Africans. Groundnuts in Tanganyika would herald the beginning of a new era of cooperation between capital and the state.

It was a large-scale and expensive disaster. In Tanganyika, it was swiftly discovered that the ground was too dry and the soil too thin for this kind of agriculture, while the machinery proved vulnerable in such a climate. The collapse of the scheme provoked political outrage in Britain – particularly following the advance publicity it had received – and cost the taxpayer millions of pounds.[6] In the fallout in the early 1950s, there was growing skepticism concerning the suitability of such capital-intensive schemes to Africa. There was similar disillusionment in French Sudan, where large-scale investment in dams on the Niger was made with a view to creating an extensive area of irrigated land for the production of cotton. The project in fact dated to the 1930s, but was expanded considerably after the Second World War. The results, however, fell far short of expectations: local farmers used the land to grow sugar and rice for the domestic market, and cotton production never reached significant levels in the area.[7]

At the same time, African producers were aware that marketing boards did not benefit them. Across the continent, such boards ensured the stability of prices for cash crops that were fixed regardless of the state of the global economy; they were aimed at avoiding the socioeconomic problems of the 1930s. This meant – in theory – that in good years, when the value of exports was higher than the price given to farmers, the marketing board could accumulate a surplus which would then be distributed to producers in bad years, when prices were low. In effect, however, the controls thus imposed meant that Africans were only ever paid a small percentage of the value of their labor, and while governments were able to build up a surplus in good years, this surplus was not used for its intended purpose but instead was often channeled into grand schemes for further capital development. Such boards, moreover, proved disastrous for the long-term economic development of those territories in which they operated, establishing state-controlled marketing systems which built up funds for governments but which depressed profits paid out to farmers. In later years, independent governments retained marketing systems and often used the foreign earnings thus acquired for political ends.

Interventionist policies were pursued in other spheres, too, notably with a view to altering peasant economies and improving productivity, policies which came to be deeply resented by African farmers. Again, ideas about "development" dated to the interwar years, but were pursued with new vigor in the late 1940s. Schemes were put in place to prevent soil erosion, for example forcing farmers to dig trenches on their plots during the rainy season in order to prevent the loss of topsoil. An arduous task, it provoked hostility in rural communities. Crop rotation was enforced, as was cattle-culling, the latter in communities believed to have "too many" cattle; to many this was further evidence of Europeans' misunderstanding of the cultural as well as the economic value of livestock. All these policies were perceived as intrusive and insensitive and served to politicize peasants across the continent, creating a groundswell of anticolonial grievance into which nationalist leaders sought to tap from the late 1940s onward.

The same can be said of the Portuguese colonies, where increasing numbers of white working-class settlers, lacking in skills and capital, were arriving in the years following the Second World War. The colonies were seen as extensions of Portugal itself; the French saw Algeria in the same way. For Salazar's government in Lisbon, colonies were important outlets for surplus population – indeed it is notable that Fascist Italy had envisaged a similar role for Eritrea and Ethiopia – as well as markets and sources of raw materials, very much in the tradition of the late nineteenth century. Portugal's fascist system was exported to Angola, Mozambique, and Guinea-Bissau; opposition was not tolerated, nor was reform contemplated.[8] So it was, too, in Belgian Congo, which experienced something of an economic boom during and immediately after the Second

World War. Congolese copper, rubber, gold, and tin had buoyed the Allied forces during the war – as had Congolese uranium, vital to the bombs dropped on Hiroshima and Nagasaki – and these industries continued to expand after it. Such economic stimulation was to the benefit of an emergent African middle class within the territory, but above all Congo was key to Belgium's postwar economic recovery.[9] Economically much weaker *vis-à-vis* much of Western Europe, Portugal and Belgium had fewer options; while Britain and France could ultimately fall back on economic *influence* in Africa, Portugal, even more than Belgium, relied more completely on its colonies in economic terms, and feared that decolonization, even reform, would expose Lusophone Africa to Anglo-French interference. For Lisbon, economic control equaled political control; for Britain and France, economic control could be maintained without political control. The contrast between their respective colonial visions was that between the late nineteenth century and the mid-twentieth.

Political Plans, c. 1945–50

There were also changes in European political thinking about the colonies, at least in part reflecting shifts in European domestic politics; the experience of the war itself had, in a broad sense, made mainstream governments more socially conscious and politically sensitive. In Britain, for example the Labour government of Clement Attlee represented a rejection of many of the social and political values of the 1920s and 1930s; its view of the empire, in certain important ways, was not that of prewar governments. Nonetheless, changes in thinking about the colonies had their roots in the depression years of the 1930s, to some extent; the socioeconomic traumas of that decade had forced a reassessment of the nature of colonial rule. The postwar rethink was also a reflection of promises made *during* the war concerning reform and of the political debts incurred to the colonies in the course of the fighting, as in the case of the French in the wake of Brazzaville. Throughout the war, similarly, the British Colonial Office had sought to justify colonialism through educational and health reform, and by promoting economic development. This intensified after 1945.[10]

From about 1947, then, the British government was emphasizing the need to move away from indirect rule, in place since the 1890s, and toward the incorporation of the emergent educated elite, which had been knocking on the door of the political establishment since the 1930s. The French, too, began to consider the gradual transfer of power and responsibility to Africans, although they envisaged a somewhat different pattern of relations between metropole and eventual former colony, characterized by much stronger links – essentially those of patron (France) and client (former colony) – and therefore a more qualified degree of "autonomy" rather than unconditional independence.[11] Political thought was rather different, too, when it came to territories of white settlement. For the British, this meant Kenya and Southern Rhodesia, both with small but politically and economically important white minorities; for the French, it meant Algeria, regarded as quite distinct from any sub-Saharan territory (l'Afrique noire). In London, the Colonial Office, in thinking about the long-term development of its various colonies, envisaged the creation of special powers for white settlers, guaranteeing for them a privileged position and continuing economic dominance. It was certainly *not* imagined that the "transfer of power" in Kenya, for example, would mean a system of "one man, one vote" – the ultimate aspiration of African nationalist politicians – which would mean the destruction of white minorities. Rather, at best, there would be some degree of power-sharing between African and European (and indeed, where appropriate, Asian) communities, with Europeans possessed of a final veto. The practical application of such a policy would prove rather more complex than originally envisaged, in Algeria, in Kenya, and in Southern Rhodesia.[12]

Yet what did "decolonization" actually mean in London and Paris? Those involved in planning in the late 1940s were in little doubt that former colonies would remain under broad metropolitan influence; the idea of some final severing of ties was unthinkable, for both European and African. Indeed, it needs to be borne in mind more generally that only a very gradual transfer of power was being advocated at this stage, even though as it happened the process would be remarkably swift. Changes in political thinking were taking place at a time when the colonies had become more important in economic terms; and while on one level this might appear contradictory, in fact these political and economic considerations formed part of the same process, namely securing the colonies – rendering them economically more profitable and politically more stable – in the longer term. Again, the same objective applied to the Portuguese and the Belgians, except that neither Lisbon nor Brussels envisaged anything more than the most superficial of political reform. Local elites might be further co-opted into legislative bodies, but no significant widening of the franchise was contemplated, still less independence or even local autonomy. Their intransigence would render their respective territories more violently unstable than most in the longer term. Italy found itself in a rather different position. As a defeated power, it had lost its African empire of Libya, Somaliland, Eritrea, and – a rather more temporary acquisition – Ethiopia. The latter had been restored, more or less, to its former sovereign status; the status of the other territories was to be considered by the victorious Allies, and eventually by the UN, in the years after the war. There were some in Italy who lobbied for some degree of influence, at least, over the former colonial territories. It was not to be: Italy's colonial moment was over, except among the Somalis, over whom Italy was granted a ten-year trusteeship which ended with Somali independence in 1960. Eritrea was federated with Ethiopia. Libya, under the UN, was granted independence in 1951 under the Sanusi monarchy of King Idris, although for much of the 1950s and 1960s it was heavily dependent on British and American economic support.

Ultimately, the British and the French, in their different ways, envisaged that peaceful, legal, constitutional change would facilitate the rise of moderate, educated, pliable African leaders who were prepared to compromise and who would protect the interests of the outgoing colonial power. Civil society as well as political system would mirror that of the metropole, however badly colonial authorities themselves prepared their charges for such earnest emulation, as we shall see. There was no room for extremists or radicals, and certainly not – in the context of the ever colder Cold War – communists. Indeed the exigencies of the Cold War cannot be overlooked: hardening ideological polarity formed the international backdrop to thinking about the future of the colonies, and would come to encroach on African political processes, aggressively in many cases. In the late 1940s, this can perhaps be most clearly discerned in the Horn of Africa, where Ethiopia successfully positioned itself as a champion of Western interests against communism (and, later, militant Islam); as a result, under American pressure, the former Italian colony of Eritrea would be denied an early chance at independence and as a federated part of Ethiopia would be the site of a huge US military base (for a time the largest outside the United States itself) until the 1970s.[13] In general, however, it is clear that despite the desire of colonial regimes to carefully manage any transfer of power within particular territories, African nationalism now became a force for change, often forcing the pace of such change in those territories not dominated by white minorities, and posing a potentially violent challenge in those territories which were.

Notes

1 See for example Li Narangoa & Robert Cribb (eds.), *Imperial Japan and National Identities in Asia, 1895–1945* (London, 2003).
2 Arthur Gavshon, *Crisis in Africa: Battleground of East and West* (London, 1981), 19.
3 V.I. Lenin, *Imperialism: The Highest Stage of Capitalism* (New York, 1939; orig. pub. 1916) was derived in large part from J.A. Hobson, *Imperialism: A Study* (London, 1938; orig. pub. 1902).
4 Pearce, *Turning Point*; R.F. Holland, *European Decolonisation 1918–1981: An Introductory Survey* (London, 1985).
5 Hopkins, *Economic History of West Africa*, 212, 267–88; for a broad survey, see D.K. Fieldhouse, *The West and the Third World: Trade, Colonialism, Dependence and Development* (Malden MA, 1999).
6 Alan Wood, *The Groundnut Affair* (London, 1950).
7 Manning, *Francophone Sub-Saharan Africa*, 114–15.
8 See Patrick Chabal *et al.*, *A History of Postcolonial Lusophone Africa* (Bloomington IN, 2002).
9 Holland, *European Decolonisation*, 175–90; Manning, *Francophone Sub-Saharan Africa*, 114–15.
10 Ronald Hyam, *Britain's Declining Empire: The Road to Decolonisation, 1918–1968* (Cambridge, 2006), chap. 2. These developments are also documented in Hailey, *African Survey* (1957 edition).
11 Frederick Cooper, *Citizenship between Empire and Nation: Remaking France and French Africa, 1945–1960* (Princeton, 2014).
12 Caroline Elkins, "Race, Citizenship, and Governance: settler tyranny and the end of empire," in Elkins & Pedersen (eds.), *Settler Colonialism*.
13 Okbazghi Yohannes, *Eritrea: A Pawn in World Politics* (Gainesville FL, 1991), chap. 7.

15 Conceiving and Producing Nations

"Nationalism" and "nation" are often problematic terms in the African context.[1] Most African territories had to make the difficult and often violent transition from colonial administrative unit to nation-state, and – given the speed with which decolonization would eventually take place – were expected to do so in a remarkably short space of time. In reality, in many cases, it is possible to argue that the transition is not yet complete. In the colonial era, it is not always easy to identify the point at which anti-colonial protest became "nationalism"; indeed, very often the former has been mistaken for the latter, and sometimes avowedly "nationalist" movements were actually largely concerned to protect the interests of a particular region, or group, and as much with the shape of the territory *after* the departure of the colonial authority as with the expulsion of the latter. The search for African "nationalism," therefore – in the sense of shared consciousness within colonial boundaries – is sometimes a red herring: too often, it involves European models of territorial nationalism as measurements, whereas in fact the vast bulk of colonial territories were wholly artificial, mere geographical units lacking ethnic and linguistic logic as well as deeper historical roots. "Nationalism" in the African context frequently meant heightened struggles between emergent or preexisting groups – whether ethnic, religious, regional, or socioeconomic – and while some of those rivalries had been engendered or sharpened by colonial rule, others were of much longer standing. Notably, a range of polities – whether states or looser ethnic and cultural associations – which had been dominant in the nineteenth century often pursued their own "nationalist" agendas, and sought either ascendancy within the broader territory-wide anticolonial struggle, or even autonomy from it. Nonetheless, it is clear that many of the manifestations of anticolonial hostility noted in previous chapters – political associations, trade unionism, militant Christianity and Islam, *négritude*,

A History of Modern Africa: 1800 to the Present, Third Edition. Richard J. Reid.

pan-Africanism – represented a groundswell of protest that might be harnessed by politicians with recognizably nationalist aspirations seeking to mobilize much wider constituencies across colonial territories. In the period following the Second World War, a new generation of African leaders needed to do just that in order to build viable nationalist movements capable of forcing the pace of decolonization and, thereafter, of forging viable nation states.

The Widening Horizons of Belonging

"Africa" – like "Europe" or "Asia" – is an abstract notion, formed largely in the Western imagination, through Western travel-writing, art, and literature, and political and cultural discourse.[2] The notion of "Africa" was given "physical" form, as it were, at the end of the nineteenth century through the partition, with all its intellectual implications, and we are still living with the consequences of that imposition, because on several levels what Africa is today has its roots in that era. Yet we need to consider briefly the concept of the evolution of an "African identity." "Africa" was continually made and remade in the European imagination – for example in the course of the nineteenth century – and subsequently, it was "invented," in practical terms, through "conquest," whereupon the continent became something mapped, known, and governed. As we have seen, however, this was no one-way relationship. Africans themselves formed their own perceptions and understandings of what Europe represented, and responded accordingly, on their own terms and according to their own cultural and political points of reference. Indeed, in many circumstances, they were able to impose their own visions on Europeans, however unaware the latter may have been of this. Yet more than this, Africa was being invented by and for Africans themselves from the early twentieth century onward. Africans shaped new political realities and developed a clearer appreciation of who they were being governed by, a sharper sense of how they were "seen" by Europe.[3] In time, African exposure to Western political concepts would lead to the embracing of these novel political ideas and forms, including – at length – "the nation" and "nationalism," rooted in a wider sense of place, as weapons with which to combat European hegemony. All the while, of course, this involved a process of Africanization, for imported ideas – as with most other types of import – were rendered meaningful to indigenous communities through customization and, often, subversion. It was a constructive process and a destructive one.

Thus, we are dealing with what we might term the "organic" growth of an internal African identity. But there was also a process of external invention, most clearly manifest in the emergence of the pan-African movement outside the continent itself. The conquest of Africa had ignited the imagination not only of Europeans themselves but also of African-Americans who began to seek this ancestral identity in much clearer terms. At the first Pan-African Congress in 1900, only a handful of delegates were actually African, indicating the degree to which a North American "African consciousness" was already so deeply rooted in both the United States and the Caribbean. The pan-African movement, which would spawn great intellectuals and eccentrics in equal measure in the first half of the twentieth century, defined itself against perceived historic white dominance, brutality, and injustice; thus, the early concerns of pan-Africanism were the racism of the white man's world, the evils of slavery, and the colonial experience itself, identified as the ultimate manifestation of exploitation and oppression.[4]

"Africa," in sum, came to be embraced by those inside and outside the continent; a geographical, political, and cultural "reality" was accepted and developed. Initially, of course – as we have seen in earlier chapters – many adapted to, worked within, and benefited from the colonial system. In the 1920s, for example, there was indeed a belief in the rectitude and appropriateness of the "civilizing mission" among certain groups in society. But equally there would develop "traditions" and patterns of resistance within the system, and ultimately against it. A process, again, of Africanization had begun and would on one level culminate in the emergence of nationalist identities; in so doing, Africans would take certain ideas – whether European, or African, or amalgams of both traditions – such as liberalism, socialism, even the central tenets of the Christian faith, in addition to the Islamic faith which had long been embraced by millions of Africans, and make them subversive, and turn them to the building of new political and cultural communities. The process continues apace.

Tensions and Transitions: From Political Consciousness to Political Parties

The key obstacle to the growth of organic African nationalisms that encompassed the new territorial spaces created by colonialism was the fact that there existed numerous and much more powerful identities – language, culture, ethnicity, kingdom, and, latterly, class – which militated against it.[5] Nonetheless, recognizably "nationalist" movements had begun to appear before the Second World War. Sub-Saharan Africa was slower in this respect than North Africa, where elites – some of them rooted in the precolonial period – had a clearer sense of their territories. Egyptian nationalism in its modern sense, for example, dates to at least the 1870s and 1880s: Egyptian modernizers had visions of creating a nation state along European lines, while others who rejected insidious Western influence fused the concept of territorial identity with Islamic revivalism. Yet in Egypt there also existed an organic national identity, which celebrated the territory's antiquity, its historic and cultural achievements and coherence, and into which early twentieth-century activists were able to tap. (Only Ethiopia, perhaps, was comparable in this respect, and even then a rather greater degree of myth-making was required.) In Egypt, the leading nationalist party by the 1920s was the Wafd; its rejection of the 1922 declaration by which Britain unilaterally granted Egypt sovereign status was based partly on the fact that London reserved control over defense, foreign relations, and Sudan. But the Wafd also set its face against the liberal constitutionalism that now replaced direct imperial administration, and this brought it into conflict with the monarchists throughout the interwar years. The Wafd under Sa'ad Zaghlul sought to build alliances against the king, Fuad, challenging his constitutional powers; but it did so through parliamentary battles, and soon after the Wafd gained control of parliament in the 1929 election, the king suspended constitutional government, sparking further political conflict through the early 1930s. Only with the death of Fuad in 1936 and the succession of Faruq was parliament restored, whereupon the Wafd once again won a majority of seats. In that same year, an Anglo-Egyptian treaty reduced British influence in the territory, although the issues of the Suez Canal and Sudan remained.

In Egypt, parliament had become the major arena for nationalist politics, despite monarchist attempts (with British backing) to argue for the advantages of authoritarianism for the sake of national unity and stability. During the Second World War, the Wafd's credibility was undermined through its association with the ineffectualness of parliament in the face of the monarchy's irresolution and the British military presence in Cairo. In its place, the Muslim Brotherhood became the major vehicle for popular political protest, alongside the Young Egypt Party. Socioeconomic hardship fuelled nationalism in the years following the war, and it was with the support of the Brotherhood that in 1952 a military *coup d'état*, led by Colonel Abdel Nasser, removed the deeply unpopular and corrupt monarchy of Faruq and set in motion a series of social, economic, and political reforms.[6] Egyptian nationalism came of age in the 1950s, although confrontations were still pending with the British over both Sudan and the Suez Canal. Elsewhere in North Africa, too, the forces of change were gaining momentum. The vigor of Moroccan protest, led by the sultan Sidi Muhammad, as well as the increasingly violent struggle in the Spanish portion of the territory, compelled the French to withdraw by 1956. Tunisian nationalism reached irresistible proportions in the same decade, although in the early 1950s Neo-Destour was paralyzed by factional fighting between the relatively moderate Bourguiba and the more radical Ben Yusuf, while the French briefly attempted to crush protest and strong-arm Tunisian politicians into a more conciliatory stance. Bourguiba's faction won through and achieved full independence under Neo-Destour in 1956.[7]

North African nationalism found cogency through older patterns of Islamic protest and political thought and was facilitated by more easily accessible historical and territorial identities; increasingly, too, North African nations in the making could appeal to an emergent pan-Arabism which reached beyond the continent itself, into the Middle East. Nationalists further south found greater obstacles in their paths in these respects. The oldest sub-Saharan movement that was discernibly "nationalist" was at the other end of the continent, in South Africa, where the South African Native National Congress was formed in 1912; it became the African National Congress (ANC) in 1923.[8] In an earlier context, we noted the formation in 1920 of the National Congress of British West Africa by professional and commercial elites, with branches in Nigeria, the Gold Coast, Sierra Leone, and the Gambia; soon afterwards, the Nigerian National Democratic Party, under Herbert Macauley, demonstrated the possibilities for territory-wide action and the mobilization of popular support. The short-lived Nigerian Youth Movement – short-lived because of ethnic tensions within the organization – organized itself in the late 1930s on a platform of territorial unity.[9] Still, territorial political action was relatively rare before the Second World War. It was possible in smaller territories that bore some resemblance to precolonial states, such as in Rwanda and Burundi – although these were also characterized by deep ethnic cleavages – or in

Basutoland (Lesotho). In Tanganyika, it was facilitated by the widespread use of Swahili, linguistic unity providing opportunities for territory-wide political action. Here, the Tanganyikan African Association was founded in 1929 with branches established throughout the territory.[10]

Rare though territorial nationalism may have been, movements and leaders with visions of "the nation" were emerging by the time of the Second World War and immediately afterward; moreover, the experience of the war itself pushed nationalism forward, notably on the back of socioeconomic hardship and heightened political awareness of the wider world. Western education, however restricted, fostered new political elites who now sought to recreate in Africa the nation state of Europe and North America. They also had to bridge the gap between themselves and the broader populace: the crucial task confronting such leaders was to harness popular urban and rural unrest and create a broad political platform.[11] Many nationalist parties sought to broaden their social bases, too: women found roles in such parties, as organizers and activists, and campaigned for "liberation" and social reform on a range of issues. The promise of gender equality was not always fulfilled after independence; but women were energetic champions of nationalist and reformist agendas in liberation struggles across the continent.[12] Critically, in the longer term, nationalism needed to be something rather more than mere opposition to European colonialism in order to unite a range of groups within a given territory; nationalism could not merely be a *negative* force – articulating only what it was against – but also a *positive* force, uniting and creating a common identity for the peoples within a given territory. It usually failed to be, ultimately; but the experience of colonialism itself, to some degree, fostered a sense of common identity, and the challenge for nationalist leaders was to develop this, if they were to build truly popular, broad-based movements capable of challenging European empires.

An important stimulus for nationalism was the organization of local elections by the colonial state, for example across British and French West Africa. Fighting elections meant that political parties needed to be formed that had more clearly defined *national* programs; such movements needed to persuade people at the local level that nationalist parties would protect their interests at the wider territorial level. When the Syndicat Agricole Africain was founded in Cote d'Ivoire in 1944 by cocoa and coffee farmers, its primary aim was to have forced labor abolished. The following year, parliamentary elections saw the Syndicat mobilize popular support for its leader, Felix Houphouet-Boigny, who was duly elected to the Assembly in Paris, where he succeeded in securing the abolition of the hated *corvée*. While in Paris, he allied himself with a group of West African representatives, and together they formed a new party, the Rassemblement Democratique Africain (RDA), which constituted the major nationalist bloc pushing for radical reform of the French African empire. Similarly, in Senegal, the extension of the franchise enabled the poet and activist Léopold Senghor to form a nationalist party with the bulk of its support in the rural areas; Senghor proceeded to launch an assault on the urban monopoly on political process and discourse. Major reforms to the administration of French West Africa between 1945 and 1951, meanwhile, made for an intricate electoral system and a complex series of elections. Between the mid-1940s and the mid-1950s, Francophone West African voters participated in several ballots, electing delegates to the National Assembly in Paris, the Assembly of the French Union (established by the new constitution of 1946), the Grand Councils now sitting in Brazzaville and Dakar, and the (more local) territorial assemblies. This was in addition to several referenda and two new constitutions. It remained to be seen, however, whether this veritable avalanche of polls would give rise to a culture of participatory and accountable – not just electoral – politics.[13]

The Belgian approach contrasted sharply with the French. Belgium had at first sought to prevent any significant reform movements and to isolate nationalists from developments elsewhere in the continent. In the immediate postwar period, there were no meaningful changes to the manner in which Congo or Ruanda-Urundi was governed, and a firm lid was kept on dissent. The same pressures for change evident elsewhere were mounting in the Belgian territories, too, however. Local elections in 1957–8 were designed largely to placate demands for reform; in fact, they encouraged the rapid emergence of an array of nationalist parties, including the broad movement under the charismatic and ideologically driven Patrice Lumumba, who in many respects appeared to be the only Congolese interested in creating a truly nationwide organization. Political rallies in 1958 and 1959 led to rioting, and violence spread through the territory. The Belgians for all practical purposes began to lose control of Congo as a result: elections had been delayed too long, and Belgium had left it too late to manage the transition to its advantage, or even in a reasonably orderly fashion.[14]

In the Gold Coast – supposedly a "model colony," where, cocoa hold-ups notwithstanding, serious trouble had been relatively rare – nationalist leaders likewise sought to tap into growing popular unrest in both the towns and the countryside. The territory had become radicalized over time. There was resentment among cocoa farmers at the West African Produce Marketing Board which controlled the price paid to them for their produce. In 1946–7, when the authorities ordered the destruction of some 2.5 million trees following the outbreak of swollen shoot disease, it was seen as further evidence of an insensitive, brutal system determined to intervene at the local level. In the towns, a postwar depression saw shortages of certain imported goods for which high prices were charged and on which restrictions were imposed; Europeans were favored, predictably. While prices rose faster than wages, there was also unemployment in the urban centers, which served to politicize an unlikely alliance of young school-leavers and returning ex-servicemen, the latter in particular resentful of the fact that there were few rewards for their wartime loyalty. Discontent across a broad social spectrum – merchants, farmers, school-leavers, and war veterans – was manifest in many ways. A popular boycott of European companies in 1948 forced the latter to lower prices and ease restrictions. At the same time, ex-servicemen marched on government buildings in major towns; through the late 1940s riots took place during which the offices of European commercial and industrial concerns were attacked. Taken together, these events seemed to herald a new era of radical politics, and although compared to some other territories the disturbances were actually relatively small scale, the British were sufficiently taken aback to reconsider their dealings with nationalist politicians.

The new constitutions of 1942 and 1946 in the Gold Coast allowed for direct elections to a legislative council, through which a limited number of Africans could become involved in the internal political affairs of the territory. Crucially, as in French West Africa, such elections provided the opportunity for the organization of political parties, and thus in 1947, the United Gold Coast Convention (UGCC) was founded under J. B. Danquah, who belonged – as did most of the leadership – to a small, professional, middle-class elite. Moderate and unwilling to break the law, the UGCC was the kind of political party favored by the British, who appreciated Danquah's tactic of using eloquent argument to persuade the colonial government of the need for reform. But for another group of angry, restless young activists, it was not a tactic that held much appeal. In 1947, the young pan-Africanist radical Kwame Nkrumah returned from the United States, where he had spent several years, to take up his post with the UGCC. But amid the rioting and the rising social tensions, he quickly grew disillusioned with Danquah's party, from which he split in 1949 to form the Convention People's Party (CPP). In part inspired by the example of Gandhi in India, the CPP advocated the politics of "positive action": it was nonviolent, and sought to avoid military confrontation, but it *was* willing to break the law, organizing strikes and boycotts. The British lost patience with the movement, and in 1950, Nkrumah was arrested, along with several other prominent leaders.[15]

Kwame Nkrumah, first leader of independent Ghana. Source: akg-images/ullstein bild.

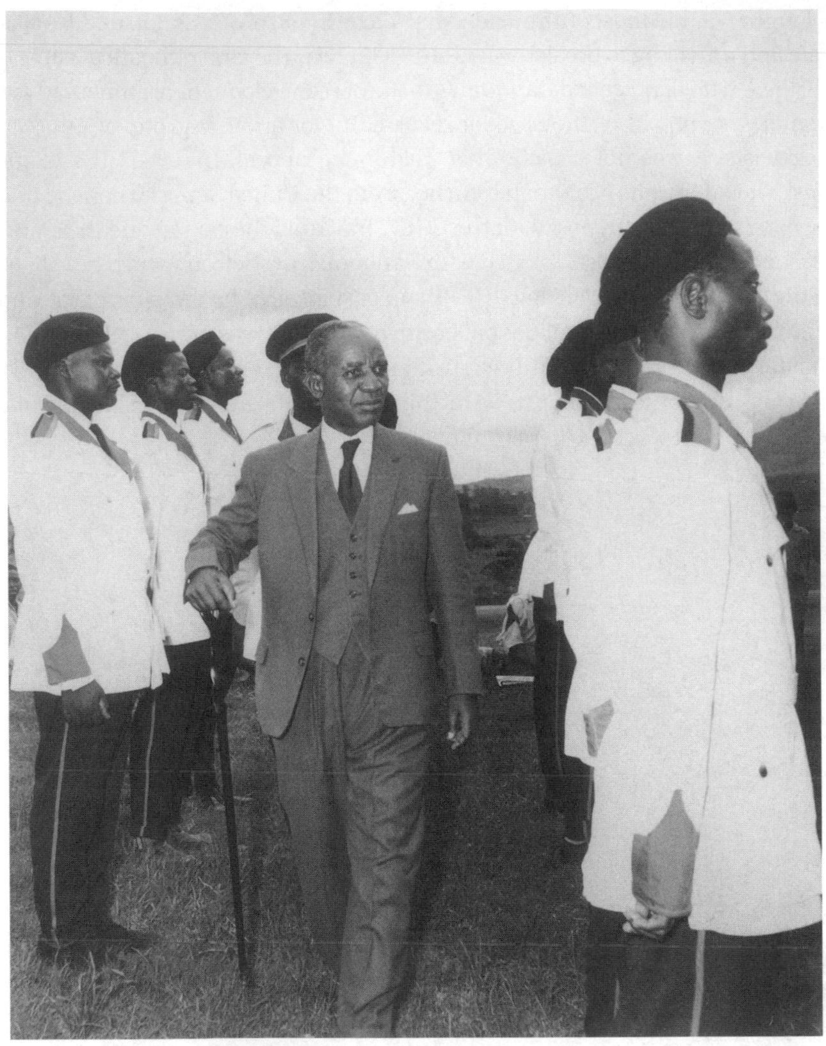

Hastings Banda, first leader of independent Malawi. Source: Central Press/Getty Images.

In fact the CPP served as a model for a number of political parties across the continent. Yet the Gold Coast was also an example of simmering regional tension, between a largely Christian and Europeanized south, and a Muslim north where trans-Saharan links were at least as important as those with the Atlantic world. Such problems were even more entrenched in Nigeria, a larger territory with a larger and more deeply divided population. North and south had actually been governed autonomously until 1946; the north was predominantly Muslim, with historic links to North Africa, while the south was heavily Christian, with a long history of interaction with Europe. In the south, there was an intense rivalry between the two largest ethnic groupings, the Yoruba in the southwest and the Igbo in the southeast; within the north, there were tensions centered on the dominant role of "aristocratic" elements in the social order.

The Nigerian Youth Movement failed to create a united platform, but the movement's stated objectives did set a precedent, and from 1944, nationalist aspirations were expressed through the National Council of Nigeria and the Cameroons (NCNC). One of the most important founder members was the newspaper editor Nnamdi Azikiwe – an earlier exponent of broader regional political activity – who now sought to make the NCNC a truly nationwide organization. He was thwarted in this, however, by the fact that the movement' main base of support was among the Igbo, and the NCNC failed to unite Nigerians under its nationalist banner. By the beginning of the 1950s, fear of Igbo domination in elections organized by the British had led to the formation of rival movements, chiefly the Northern People's Congress, mostly drawn from the Hausa and Fulani in the north, and the Yoruba Action Group.[16]

Nationalism was likewise undermined by internal disunity in French West Africa, where, although the RDA purported to represent Africans from all over the region, territorial and sectional tensions soon undermined unity. In 1948, for example, the Senegalese broke away under Senghor to form the Bloc Democratique Sénégalais (BDS). In particular, wealthier territories such as Côte d'Ivoire and Gabon were wary of having to subsidize the poorer regions further north in the future. Subsequently, arguments among nationalist leaders focused largely on what course of action to follow regarding eventual decolonization and the approach to be taken in negotiations with the French.[17] Divisions were evident in Uganda, too, where resentment was directed at the special status of the kingdom of Buganda. The Ganda had long enjoyed privileges over the other peoples of the territory, stemming from the assistance they had rendered the British in the initial establishment of colonial rule. When in 1953 the kabaka, head of Buganda, protested vigorously at the British plan to incorporate the kingdom fully into Uganda, the colonial authorities deported him; the incident only served to further inflame Ganda ethno-nationalism. Indeed, the British were prepared to make concessions to Buganda in the longer term: under the 1961 constitution, the kingdom was granted internal self-government, separate from central government. More broadly, there were also geographical divisions: northerners were suspicious of educated nationalists who were mostly southern Christians. Within the south of the country itself, Protestants vied with Catholics for access to political power, a competition which also dated to the late nineteenth century. The struggle for independence, therefore, was as much a competition between various groups about the distribution of power after decolonization as a struggle against the British themselves, and the main parties reflected this. The Uganda National Congress, formed in 1952 (it became the Uganda People's Congress in 1960), drew mostly on a combination of northern and Protestant support, while the Democratic Party, established in 1956, was supported largely by southern Catholics. In the wake of the 1953 crisis, the Ganda formed a party of their own, the Kabaka Yekka ("King Alone") movement.[18]

In some territories, the absence of a handful of large, hegemonic ethnic groupings or consolidated precolonial state structures competing in the political marketplace to the detriment of smaller groups facilitated a more cohesive national identity.[19] Such a scenario is discernible in Tanganyika, where the African Association had been operating since 1929, but it was only in the early 1950s that the organization came into its own, mobilizing those Africans who had been forced to make way for white settlers, in the district of Meru, for example – a policy linked to the renewed economic interest in the territory noted in the last chapter. Fear of white settlement was one of a number of local issues that sparked widespread political activity and drove the nationalist movement in its early stages. The African Association dynamically went about building a popular base, and it led to the establishment in 1954 of the Tanganyika African National Union (TANU) under the leadership of the charismatic Julius Nyerere. Like Nkrumah, Nyerere had spent a number of years abroad, and indeed had been inspired by the activities of Nkrumah and the CPP in the Gold Coast. Through the mid-1950s, Nyerere continued to broaden TANU's appeal and develop its organizational structure, transforming it into a genuinely nationwide movement. TANU utilized popular rural unrest that stemmed from both fear of white settlement and the brutal interventionism of colonial government into African agricultural practices. Rioting erupted in 1955 in response to enforced terracing, for example, and again like Nkrumah, Nyerere skillfully used veiled threats of violence to further nationalist aims. Importantly, TANU's success was greatly assisted by the territory's relative linguistic unity. Swahili had become established in the region with the expansion of long-distance trade in the nineteenth century, and had been further developed as a "national language" under colonial rule for the purposes of education and administration; now, TANU was able to foster some sense of national unity through the use of Swahili, and was further helped by the relative lack of divisive ethnic politics of the kind so problematic in Nigeria and Uganda.[20]

Irresistible Force and Immovable Object: Nationalists and Settlers

Nationalists in territories of white settlement were confronted with an altogether different challenge, quite aside from that associated with the creation of cohesive political programs. Unlike many of their counterparts described above, who "simply" had to negotiate with colonial administrations that were essentially detached from the territories over which they claimed jurisdiction, they had to deal with entrenched white minorities that had no intention either of physically retreating, or of sharing power with the African majority. In Kenya, Southern Rhodesia, South Africa, and Algeria, African nationalists clashed with intransigent settler governments, and violence usually resulted. In Kenya, the growing social crisis brought about by land alienation – leading to an increasingly radicalized underclass in both the reserves and the urban centers – provided an opportunity for nationalist politicians, despite the fact they had almost as little in common with the rural and urban poor as did white Kenyans. Popular discontent, as in Tanganyika, was further fuelled by interventionist agricultural policies aimed primarily at the prevention of soil erosion, which was attributed to inefficient African techniques. A series of measures was introduced – terracing, dam construction, and contour planning – to prevent environmental degradation. As elsewhere, this caused deep resentment in the course of the 1940s and early 1950s, and hostility was directed at the colonial administration, the white settler community, and the more prosperous Kikuyu. Meanwhile, those who drifted to Nairobi in search of work and to escape overcrowded reserves joined the swelling ranks of casual laborers, the criminalized and politicized urban poor. It was in this explosive atmosphere that the Mau Mau uprising would erupt, beginning with sporadic rural bloodshed at the end of the 1940s, followed by more serious and sustained violence through 1951 and 1952.

The Kikuyu middle class was itself alarmed at the white settlers' increasing control over agricultural policy and planning. In 1947, the Kenya African Union (KAU) was established under the presidency of Jomo Kenyatta, quickly expanding into a broad-based movement: led by well-off moderates, it also attracted the poorer and more radical elements in African society who used the KAU as an umbrella organization while contemplating more violent means to achieve their objectives. The cause of Kenyan African nationalism was also advanced through trade unions in Nairobi and Mombasa, where they became critical foci of political unrest. Meanwhile, Kenyatta himself had returned to Kenya to lead the KAU after many years abroad, including a time studying in London. His was an ambivalent position, for although he represented the moderate wing of African nationalism, his public messages were couched in the language of violence. As Mau Mau escalated, he was imprisoned and the KAU banned, yet Kenyatta himself had little to do with the mounting violence across the so-called "White Highlands." By the early 1950s, nationalism had indeed emerged as a powerful force, but the Kikuyu themselves were deeply divided between moderates – like Kenyatta – who wished to see "legitimate" and peaceful change, and the leaders of the landless poor who were willing to use violence to achieve their stated objectives of "land and freedom."[21]

Settlers in Kenya had some power, but those in Southern Rhodesia had rather more, with self-government since 1923. Until 1953 a series of white governments, to some extent taking their cue from South Africa, pursued political, social, and economic segregation; in 1953, the territory became part of the Central African Federation, which also included Northern Rhodesia and Nyasaland, both of which had rather less significant numbers of European settlers. The aim of the Federation – the total amalgamation of the economic resources of the region, not least the copper belt of Northern Rhodesia, under white control – was hardly lost on African nationalists who bitterly opposed it, seeing in the project their complete exclusion from political and economic power for the foreseeable future. Organized protest was already well developed in Southern Rhodesia: the late 1940s had witnessed the emergence of workers' movements, for example, instrumental in the organization of a crippling general strike in 1948. Labor protest was therefore in the vanguard of the political struggle; at the same time, this period also saw the heightening of a radical peasant consciousness in rural areas, the result of a massive expansion in white farming from the late 1940s onward. As in Kenya, popular nationalism was fanned by loss of land, and leaders sought to utilize discontent: in 1957, the African National Congress was founded under the trade union leader Joshua Nkomo, becoming the Zimbabwe African People's Union (ZAPU) in 1962. As the settler government became ever more entrenched, however, splits appeared in the African nationalist camp. Nkomo was reluctant to countenance more strident tactics, and in 1963, a group of prominent ZAPU figures – including Ndabaningi Sithole and Robert

Mugabe – broke away to form the Zimbabwe African National Union (ZANU). In part, this split reflected ethnic divisions, as Nkomo's support came mostly from among the Ndebele, while ZANU was rooted in the Shona population. ZANU was willing to consider an altogether more aggressive approach, but it was only after the white government in Salisbury declared independence from Britain unilaterally in 1965 that it embraced violence, launching the first guerrilla attacks the following year.[22]

Elsewhere, the presence of white settlers likewise pushed territories inexorably toward violence. In Portuguese Angola, Mozambique, and Guinea-Bissau, nationalist leaders were compelled toward violent confrontation, faced with administrative intransigence and increasingly racist policy. In Angola, the Movimento Popular de Libertaçäo de Angola (MPLA), founded in 1956, was able in the early 1960s to take advantage of a widespread peasant uprising that had erupted in response to forced labor and cotton cultivation, practices which had been long since abandoned in the Anglophone and Francophone colonies. The MPLA took the struggle to the urban centers, embarking on a war which would last for years to come. In Mozambique, FRELIMO – Frente de Libertaçäo de Mocambique, formed in 1962 – was an alliance of various movements, and likewise launched a war of liberation which would be as prolonged as it was destructive.[23] Yet there would be no bloodier war of national liberation than in Algeria, where white settlers were as entrenched as anywhere south of the Sahara. Within France, the notion prevailed that Algeria was not a "colonial" territory but a province of France, an extension of the motherland overseas, and thus indelibly linked to the French state and domestic economy. Schemes in Algeria for constitutional reform were half-hearted and continually sabotaged by the colonial authorities through the 1950s. Ultimately such schemes were seen by Algerian nationalists as headed precisely nowhere, and even constitutionally minded politicians became sufficiently disillusioned to turn to violence to achieve their goals. In the early 1950s, the influence of leaders such as Messali – by now exiled in France – and Abbas was waning; already, in 1948, a group of younger nationalists from Messali's Mouvement pour le Triomphe des Libertés Democratiques had formed the Organization Secrète and were contemplating armed struggle against the apparently intransigent settler regime and its metropolitan backer. It collapsed in the early 1950s, but a handful went on to found the Comité Revolutionnaire de l'Unité et de l'Action in 1954, and this group, in alliance with others, became the Front de Libération Nationale (FLN). It was the FLN that launched the war for Algerian independence in earnest in November 1954, a war which was to be fought on two fronts: inside Algeria, guerrilla tactics would be used against the French army, while outside the country, the FLN would engage in international diplomacy in order to win support for the Algerian cause. The FLN would take its case to the UN, court the growing nonaligned movement, and appeal to its North African and Middle Eastern brothers through the prism of pan-Arab nationalism.[24]

Still, it was perhaps in South Africa that nationalists had furthest to travel, against a capital-backed, ideologically motivated white minority which had governed the Union as an imperial dominion since 1910. The legislation that had created the Union represented a historic compromise between two competing white communities, namely British settlers and Afrikaners, or Boers, of Dutch descent; at root, however, the white population as a whole sought to defend its privileged position in political and economic terms. Between the First World War and the 1940s, a succession of governments had developed legislation aimed at racial segregation. All mainstream white political parties, and other influential lobbies such as Anglican missionaries, embraced the idea of segregation. For some, notably more extreme Afrikaners, it was a crucial means to controlling and exploiting the African labor force, while at the same time underpinning intrinsic white supremacy. For others, segregation was key to "black development," and a means to actually "protecting" indigenous peoples (as well as whites themselves) from the dangers of racial intermixing, and from exposure to economic, cultural, and political "modernity." Whatever the vision, however, it was a received wisdom that segregation was a "good thing," economically and morally important.[25]

The expansion of the South African economy, particularly during and immediately after the Second World War, provided new employment opportunities for the rapidly expanding African population, and thousands migrated to cities in search of work. Such rural–urban migration, in addition to African population growth, prompted the Afrikaner National Party – since the early 1900s in the vanguard of extreme racial politics – to play on white fears, and set up a future scenario in which blacks, unless properly controlled, would swamp the urban areas and overwhelm the industrial economy. White political debate in the late 1940s centered on economic and demographic change, and fear of the "black peril" persuaded a large enough proportion of the white population, in the 1948 general election, to vote for the National Party, under the leadership of D. F. Malan. The party had campaigned on a platform of *apartheid* – an Afrikaans term meaning "separateness" – which essentially involved taking previous segregationist policy into a new, more extreme phase; and with a healthy majority it now formed a government, and would remain in power until 1994.[26]

We observed earlier that there were various other forms of protest, both formal and informal, which developed over time, and very largely in the workplace, but it would be some years before "nationalism" *per se* would become a force for change. The industrial economy, and more especially the militaristic organization of the African labor force, militated against the emergence of a wider African identity, and certainly hindered the growth of a "nationalist" one. In its early years the African National Congress (ANC) represented only very narrow interests, primarily those of middle-class moderates, a small group of African professionals who preferred the petition to street protest. Down to the 1940s, the ANC was by no means a radical movement, eschewing "illegal" activity and pursuing cautious tactics; largely ineffectual, it could do little to prevent the development of segregationist legislation. Nevertheless, the ANC's activities laid the foundations for more widespread political action, particularly in terms of its cooperation with the large Indian and "Coloured" (mixed race) political movements. It demonstrated the potential for larger-scale and more potent political protest. At the same time, trade unionism – for example the Industrial and Commercial Workers' Union (ICU) in the 1920s – indicated the potential power of a worker consciousness, which white political and business leaders had sought to prevent through the militaristic organization of the labor force. Segregation was designed to reinforce "tribal" identities, with a view to keeping the African population divided. Prior to 1948, a system of segregation had been designed to confine Africans to certain economic spheres, living areas, social activities; the government of the National Party built on this system and elevated segregation to the level of state ideology. The basic aim of apartheid in its early stages was to restrict Africans to the already-crowded reserves, out of "white" areas, unless of course they were in white employment. Ultimately, one of the grand aims of apartheid – indeed one of the more ludicrous and tragic manifestations of the policy – was the movement of all Africans not employed in the mining economy to self-governing republics on the fringes of white society, racially "purifying" South Africa. In time, and particularly from the 1960s, reserves that had been designated for African habitation would become autonomous "Homelands," or Bantustans, a disingenuous kind of "decolonization" aimed at the solution of the "native problem." They were characterized by corruption, violence, and misgovernment.

Apartheid depended on the systematic classification of people into distinct racial categories. The Population Registration Act of 1950 divided the population broadly into white and nonwhite; the latter were subdivided into "Coloured," Indians, and "Bantu," or African. (The term "Bantu" was thus abused, as it was solely a linguistic term.) The Bantu category was further divided into "tribal" groupings, for example Zulu, Xhosa, Sotho. This core piece of legislation was closely linked to the Group Areas Act, also in 1950, which specified where particular "tribes" could live, in an attempt to segregate and divide the "native" population; the aim was to undermine a sense of African unity and hinder the growth of nationalist feeling. Further laws restricted movement and provided directives regarding social activity, segregating public places, public transport, and education, and outlawing sexual relations between the white and black "races." In many respects, the system was economic in objective, aimed at maintaining the African population as a subordinate, largely unskilled working class. African trade unions were banned, facilitating the payment of low wages. Moreover, the Bantu Education Act of 1953 placed Africans in designated government schools whose curricula emphasized racial distinctions and provided education only in basic skills. One of the most detested pillars of the apartheid system, it facilitated social control and constituted an exercise in social engineering.

Crucially, however, a fortunate elite was able to pass through the system and would be in a position to organize and lead popular protest. In the 1950s, African nationalist leaders, faced with a newly aggressive regime, recognized the need for more vigorous resistance. Public demonstrations erupted across South Africa against the new legislation, while the traditionally moderate and cautious ANC was rejuvenated under a new generation of young, gifted leaders, such as Nelson Mandela, Oliver Tambo, and Walter Sisulu. In 1952–3, for example, a "defiance campaign" involved widespread protest against the pass laws, and resulted in mass arrests. By the mid-1950s, the various "nonwhite" groups had joined together and were calling for a democratic, nonracial South Africa; the alliance was fragile, given the potential for hostility between Africans and Asians, most dramatically manifest in the Zulu riots against Indians in Durban in 1949. Indeed, there were also tensions within the ANC leadership, some of whom resented the influence of non-Africans, notably white liberals and those involved in the communist movement. By the end of the 1950s, a breakaway section had formed the Pan-Africanist

Congress (PAC), but the nationalist struggle was gaining momentum, and the conflict would become increasingly bitter.[27]

A Time of Contrasts

Taking stock, it is clear that the period of the late 1940s and 1950s was one of contrasts. It was a period of heightened internal conflict and competition, as ethnic, cultural, and regional groupings consolidated and sought to dominate the nationalist struggle in their respective territories. Some of these frontiers of political combat dated to the nineteenth century: Uganda exemplifies the process, where a specifically Ganda nationalism was pitted against coalitions of others, representing, in essence, a continuation of nineteenth-century rivalries. In Nigeria, too, an axis of competition and indeed outright violence had operated between the Hausa–Fulani north and the coastal forest-dwellers since at least the early nineteenth century. In almost all cases, such rivalries morphed into new forms of competition for control of the political space to be inherited from colonial regimes: the 1950s witnessed local actors seeking to co-opt exogenous political infrastructures to best advantage, and in so doing often creating – or seeking to create – new or enhanced pools of ethnic or regional identity, as across French West Africa. These increasingly bitter rivalries, and the cynical alliances they often prompted, boded ill for the future, at least at the level of individual territories' internal affairs.

At the same time, however, the 1950s was an era of extraordinary optimism and vitality: for ideas about pan-Africanism and the continent's intrinsic unity – however vague such notions often were – and for the African struggle more generally, characterized by an increasingly assertive self-confidence. This was reflected in the intellectual and artistic renaissance of the era. It was during these years that "African history" as a distinct and recognized scholarly discipline was born, among both a small but expanding group of Western scholars and a dedicated corps of African academics. The latter were usually the products of Western universities: when the Nigerian Kenneth O. Dike was awarded a PhD by King's College London in 1950, he was the first to achieve the distinction using oral traditions as the basis for historical research.[28] Yet these academics went on – as Dike did in Ibadan – to lead African university history departments as pioneers in what would prove to be a golden age, if a brief one, for African historical scholarship.[29] In the arts, African achievement was increasingly recognized: African painting and sculpture moved, if tentatively, beyond the plains of "tribal artifact" and into the uplands of intrinsic aesthetic value, even if the tastes of the European market for work in wood or bronze continued to influence output in the most fundamental of ways. In literature, too, the 1950s was a fertile time: both Camara Laye's *L'Enfant noir* (1954) and Chinua Achebe's *Things Fall Apart* (1956), in French Guinea and British Nigeria, respectively, dealt with romanticized notions of a lost or threatened precolonial past in the face of colonial modernity, and represented new strains of cultural resistance to ideas about Western hegemony.[30]

In many respects, there would never be a time like it again. In the twilight of colonial rule, many things seemed possible, even as the dirt of political struggle gathered in the engines of change. But there were many obstacles to be overcome, and elsewhere on the continent, Africans faced even greater and more complex struggles. The time of Dike's doctorate and Achebe's first novel was also the time of hardening race laws in South Africa and violent, increasingly chaotic, insurgency in Lusophone Africa and in Belgian Congo; it was also the era of brutal wars in Algeria and Kenya. As the 1950s passed on, a combination of evolving internal conflict and botched decolonization across the continent would facilitate the resurgence of the militarized cultures of governance and ferocious competition for resources – material and political – which had characterized Africa's nineteenth century. Precolonial dynamics would once again come to the fore.

Notes

1 For standard introductions which place Africa in a wider context, see Ernst Gellner, *Nations and Nationalism* (Oxford, 1983); Eric Hobsbawm, *Nations and Nationalism Since 1780: Myth, Programme, Reality* (Cambridge, 1992); Anthony D. Smith, *State and Nation in the Third World: the Western State and African Nationalism* (New York, 1983).
2 See footnote 21 in Chapter 1, for example.
3 A. Adu Boahen, *African Perspectives on Colonialism* (Baltimore & London, 1987).
4 Imanuel Geiss, *The Pan-African Movement: A History of pan-Africanism in America, Europe and Africa* (New York, 1974).
5 Thomas Hodgkin, *Nationalism in Colonial Africa* (New York, 1957); J.S. Coleman & C.G. Rosberg (eds.), *Political Parties and National Integration in Tropical Africa* (London, 1964); Basil Davidson, *The Black Man's Burden: Africa and the Curse of the Nation-state* (New York, 1992).
6 For a contemporary view, see Joachim Joesten, *Nasser: The Rise to Power* (London, 1960); also J.J. Terry, *The Wafd* (London, 1982).
7 Perkins, *History of Modern Tunisia*, chap. 4.
8 Peter Limb, *The ANC's Early Years: Nation, Class and Place in South Africa before 1940* (Pretoria, 2010): P. Walshe, *The Rise of African Nationalism in South Africa: the African National Congress, 1912–1952* (Berkeley CA, 1971).
9 Robert Sklar, *Nigerian Political Parties: Power in an Emergent African Nation* (Princeton, 1963), 48–55.
10 Iliffe, *Modern History of Tanganyika*, chap. 13.
11 John Lonsdale, "The emergence of African nations," in Ranger (ed.), *Emerging Themes*; John Lonsdale, "Some origins of nationalism in East Africa," *Journal of African History*, 9:1 (1968); Ian Henderson, "The origins of nationalism in East and Central Africa: the Zambian case," *Journal of African History*, 11:4 (1970). For an innovative examination of some of these themes, see also Frederick Cooper, "'Our Strike': equality, anticolonial politics, and the 1947–48 railway strike in French West Africa," *Journal of African History*, 37:1 (1996). For a more recent reassessment, see Miles Larmer & Baz Lecocq, 'Historicising nationalism in Africa', *Nations and Nationalism*, 24:4 (2018).
12 See Susan Geiger, "Women and African nationalism," *Journal of Women's History*, 2:1 (1990).
13 Tony Chafer, "Education and Political Socialisation of a National-Colonial Political Elite in French West Africa, 1936–1947," *Journal of Imperial and Commonwealth History*, 35:3 (2007); James E. Genova, *Colonial Ambivalence, Cultural Authenticity, and the Limitations of Mimicry in French-Ruled West Africa 1914–1956* (New York, 2004); Cooper, *Citizenship between Empire and Nation.*

14 Rene Lemarchand, *Political Awakening in the Belgian Congo* (Berkeley CA, 1964).
15 D. Austin, *Politics in Ghana, 1946–1960* (London, 1970).
16 J.S. Coleman, *Nigeria: Background to Nationalism* (London, 1971); and see Nnamdi Azikiwe, *Zik: A Selection from the Speeches of Nnamdi Azikiwe* (Cambridge, 1961).
17 Cooper, *Citizenship between Empire and Nation.*
18 D.A. Low, *Buganda in Modern History* (London, 1971).
19 This is one of the themes in Mahmood Mamdani, *Citizen and Subject: Contemporary Africa and the Legacy of Late Colonialism* (Princeton NJ, 1996).
20 See Nyerere's own account, and interpretations, in *Freedom and Unity (Uhuru na Umoja): A Selection from Writings and Speeches, 1952–1965* (London, 1967).
21 Bruce Berman & John Lonsdale, *Unhappy Valley: Conflict in Kenya & Africa. Book Two: Violence and Ethnicity* (Oxford, 1992).
22 Jocelyn Alexander, JoAnn McGregor, and Terence Ranger, *Violence and Memory: One Hundred Years in the 'Dark Forests' of Matabeleland* (Oxford, 2000), chap. 5.
23 Anthony Clayton, *Frontiersmen: Warfare in Africa since 1950* (London, 1999), 42–51.
24 Alistair Horne, *A Savage War of Peace: Algeria 1954–1962* (London, 1977).
25 Saul Dubow, *Racial Segregation and the Origins of Apartheid in South Africa, 1919–1936* (Basingstoke, 1989).
26 See for example Dan O'Meara, *Volkskapitalisme: Class, Capital and Ideology in the Development of Afrikaner Nationalism, 1934–1948* (New York, 1983).
27 Nelson Mandela, *Long Walk to Freedom: The Autobiography of Nelson Mandela* (London, 1995), Parts 3 & 4; Elinor Sisulu, *Walter & Albertina Sisulu: In Our Lifetime* (London, 2003), Part 2; Tom Lodge, *Black Politics in South Africa since 1945* (London, 1983); S. Marks & S. Trapido (eds.), *The Politics of Race, Class & Nationalism in Twentieth-Century South Africa* (Harlow, 1987).
28 This work would later be published as *Trade and Politics in the Niger Delta, 1830–1885: An Introduction to the Economic and Political History of Nigeria* (Oxford, 1956).
29 Ranger, *Emerging Themes*; Toyin Falola, *Nationalism and African Intellectuals* (Rochester NY, 2001); Toyin Falola & Saheed Aderinto, *Nigeria, Nationalism, and Writing History* (Rochester NY, 2010).
30 Dan Izevbaye, "West African literature in English: beginnings to the mid-seventies," and Mildred Mortimer, "African literature in French: sub-Saharan Africa during the colonial period," in F. Abiola Irele & Simon Gikandi (eds.), *The Cambridge History of African and Caribbean Literature*, Vol. 2 (Cambridge, 2004).

16 Compromising Conflict

Routes to Independence

Between 1945 and the early 1950s, there was considerable diversity among European colonial powers, in terms of economic standing, political influence, and – connected to both – ideological and legal relationships between metropolitan powers and colonial territories. This meant that across the continent Africans were confronted with a range of experiences, both obstacles and opportunities, in the years following the war. This diversity explains the complexity of process by which different territories achieved "liberation." At one end of the spectrum was the peaceful, constitutional political party, working within the system to achieve independence in conjunction with outgoing colonial authorities – a scenario found in many Anglophone and Francophone territories; at the other was the armed guerrilla movement, compelled to adopt violence as a means to bringing colonial rule to an end, as in the Portuguese territories. The years following the Second World War, therefore, were crucial in determining the nature of African anticolonial movements, nationalist parties, and liberation ideologies.

Debate and Debacle: "Constitutional" Transfers of Power

We begin with "peaceful" transfers of power, so-called in relative terms only, clustered as these were between the mid-1950s and mid-1960s. But it is important to note from the outset that the specter of violence haunted – indeed drove forward – many a supposedly "calm" and "nonviolent" decolonization process. We return to armed insurgency a little later, but the sound of armed conflict raging elsewhere frequently filled the silences in between negotiations concerning orderly handovers of authority. For the French, notably, the war in Algeria (1954–62) cast a long shadow, forming the grim backdrop to dealings in the sub-Saharan colonies. The perceived threat of the kind of violence witnessed in Algeria was a major influence over metropolitan decision-making south of the Sahara. After 1945, Paris envisaged that – by whatever route – the colonies would broadly remain part of a "Greater France," and indeed, the basic concept was for a time supported in principle by a Francophone African elite that had become assimilated into French culture. Disillusion stemmed from the realization that French West Africans were *not* to be accorded full citizenship. Following legislative reforms in the mid-1940s, moreover, the western and equatorial colonies were permitted to send representatives to the French National Assembly, but with less than 3 percent of the seats, Africans were chronically underrepresented. One response to this among some nationalist leaders was to form two separate federal blocs – western and equatorial – which would give the colonies collective political and economic muscle in negotiations with France. Others opposed the idea, however, notably Ivorian nationalists who believed that the cash-crop wealth of their territory would be used to subsidize poorer territories in the region.[1]

Spurred by the violence in Algeria, the French introduced further reforms in the mid-1950s, leading to internal self-government in 1956; metropolitan government, however, retained control over the military, foreign affairs, and economic planning. As the situation in Algeria worsened, President de Gaulle – concerned to remove any potential for conflict – offered the colonies a straight choice in 1958 between maintaining the link with France, which promised economic benefits, or complete independence, involving a severance of all "aid" and protection from the mother country. At this stage, most

The cost of violence: funeral of the victims of the Philippeville massacres in Algeria, 1955. Source: © Charles Courriere/Paris Match/Scoop.

African leaders voted for maintaining the metropolitan connection, while hoping for further reform in the future; only Guinea, under Sekou Touré, elected for uncompromised sovereignty. De Gaulle now sought to demonstrate just how dependent the colonies were on France by making an example of Guinea. All economic assistance was cancelled; French personnel were withdrawn, and equipment removed. Guinea was to be crippled; yet it survived, thanks largely to assistance from the Soviet Union and newly independent Ghana.[2] Indeed, soon nationalists across Francophone Africa were following Guinea's example, pressing for independence doubtless with an eye on the speed of events in British West Africa. After ensuring continuing economic ties between France and the African colonies, de Gaulle acquiesced, and in 1960 – often referred to as "the Year of Africa" – the French colonies of western and equatorial Africa became independent. In the end, as was the case across much of British West Africa, decolonization had been achieved through a continual dialogue between metropolitan center and nationalist movements, giving rise to compromise and the recognition of mutual interests. Only in Cameroon was there serious trouble. Here, communist agitation led to the formation of a French-backed moderate coalition in 1956, which in turn sparked a leftist insurrection; the uprising continued for several years, even after Cameroon achieved independence in 1960, and was only crushed with considerable bloodshed by an army commanded by French officers.[3]

There was trouble, too, in Rwanda, where the run-up to independence was dominated by growing tensions between Tutsi and Hutu. A Hutu uprising against the Tutsi monarchy in 1959 involved a great deal of bloodshed and was only brought under control by the Belgian authorities which now sought to manage the transition to majority Hutu rule. In local elections held in 1960, Parmehutu, the principal Hutu political party, swept the board, and the following year the Tutsi monarchy was abolished; Parmehutu took Rwanda to independence in 1962, although ethnic tensions continued in the years to come.[4] Indeed, it was the apparent threat that the Tutsi were aiming to seize power again that sparked the horrific massacre of both Tutsi and their perceived Hutu "friends" in 1994. In neighboring Burundi, the Tutsi retained power from independence until 1993.

Britain, too, sought to remain in control of events by dealing with the nationalists themselves, though strategies differed according to circumstances.[5] In response to escalating social problems and political challenges in the Gold Coast at the end of the 1940s, the British set up a commission of enquiry – the Coussey Commission – to discover what had gone wrong in their supposedly "model colony." In its report, the Commission advocated more representation for African politicians and further constitutional reform; at the same time, it remained the hope of the administration that these reforms would facilitate the integration of the moderate political elite, represented by UGCC leader J. B. Danquah. Accordingly, there was a deliberate attempt to discredit CPP leader Kwame Nkrumah, who was arrested and detained in 1950. He was depicted as the "wild man of the Left," a dangerous radical, while Danquah was actively promoted as the safe pair of hands, the future of African politics in the Gold Coast. But in the elections held in 1951, things did not go as the British had planned: Nkrumah and the CPP won a sweeping victory, and achieved the crucial political breakthrough. The authorities quickly

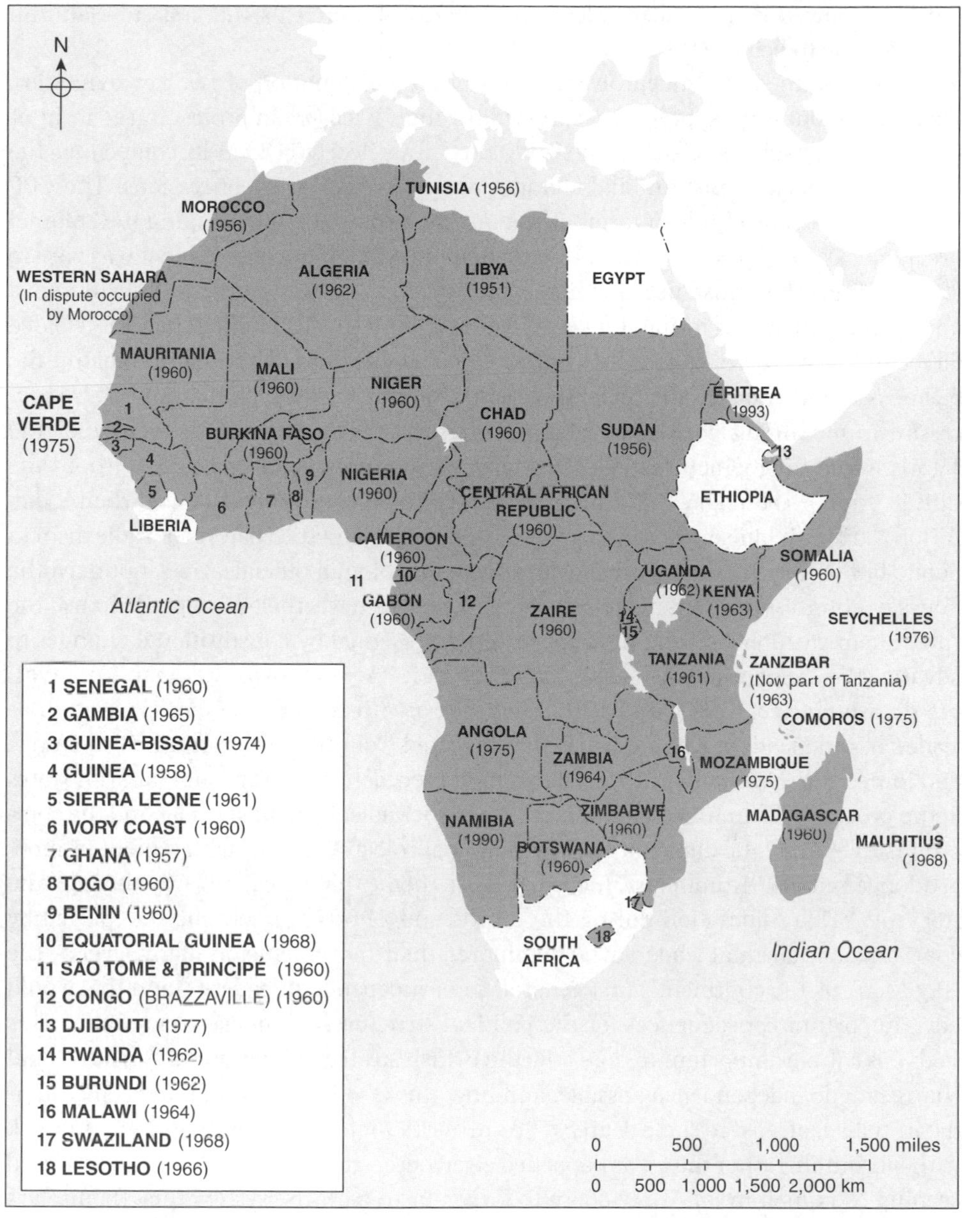

Decolonization. Source: From G. Arnold, *Africa: A Modern History* (London: Atlantic Books, 2005), p. xxii. © 2005 by Guy Arnold. Reprinted with permission from Atlantic Books Ltd and the author.

decided that there was little option but to release Nkrumah and attempt to work with the CPP. Initially leader of government business, Nkrumah gently forced the pace of decolonization, in so doing using the good working relationship he developed with the governor, though he combined diplomacy with an ability to make political capital out of the supposed risk of massive internal disorder. Internal self-government in 1954 was quickly followed by full independence in 1957. "Ghana" was the first sub-Saharan African state to achieve this.[6]

Ghana became independent as the result of a concatenation of two key dynamics. Popular nationalism, apparently expressed through widespread protest in the form of rioting, demonstrations, strikes, and boycotts, was clearly critical in compelling the British to consider constitutional changes and the offering of concessions. The CPP itself played a central role in terms of the tactics employed in challenging the colonial order, advocating "positive action," but eschewing outright violence, and it was wise to do so, witness the British use of extreme force against the Mau Mau rebellion in Kenya and against guerrillas in the jungles of Malaya, both in the 1950s. The CPP avoided direct military confrontation but applied considerable political pressure, making the business of government difficult for the colonial administration. The party was also successful in mobilizing popular support in order to win elections in the course of the 1950s, something which the UGCC, by comparison, notably failed to do. Without the CPP, in sum, it is unlikely that Ghana would have achieved independence when it did. As for Nkrumah himself, he was a great orator, employing the rhetoric of radicalism in public but tempering this in private dealings with colonial officials. He denounced the Coussey Commission from his prison cell, but he was nevertheless prepared to use the subsequent elections, seizing the opportunities presented by constitutional changes to advance the cause of independence under the CPP. Nkrumah was willing to work with the British between 1951 and 1957, and did so with remarkable facility; indeed, as leader of independent Ghana, he swiftly retreated from his earlier anti-British stance and joined the Commonwealth, establishing a precedent for future sub-Saharan states in the process. Nkrumah was a combination of the radical, populist leader and the compromising, pragmatic diplomat, and his personal role in Ghana's achievement of independence was clearly immense. Indeed, this is a theme that threads its way through the story of Africa's liberation during the 1950s and 1960s, namely the role played by charismatic individual leaders who dominated their movements on many levels – the "Big Men" of the continent's first generation of independent leaders – and this would have important consequences for the political structures of independent states. This said, it is equally important to note how the British strategy of continual constitutional change made independence possible, and how this also helped Britain to keep hold of the initiative, at least to some degree. The authorities took the decision in 1951 to work with Nkrumah, rather than – as happened elsewhere – rejecting the election results and keeping Nkrumah in jail. They chose to forge ahead with the system they themselves had set up and work with the individuals who had benefited from it, no matter how disagreeable (at least initially) those individuals might have been to them.

So it was too in Tanganyika, where Julius Nyerere spent the late 1950s and early 1960s building up the trust of the colonial administration, while establishing the Tanganyika African National Union (TANU) as a territory-wide organization with some of the most effective grassroots mobilization anywhere in the continent. The transfer of power was at first characterized by the creation of a multiracial constitution that increased representation for Africans to some degree, but which basically provided an inordinately powerful voice for the minority European and Asian communities; the policy was influenced by developments in neighboring Kenya. But Nyerere skillfully managed to persuade a number of white settlers' representatives to support TANU, and the movement won a majority in the assembly elections of 1958. Independence for Tanganyika was granted in 1961.[7] The British held on to Zanzibar until 1963, but within weeks of being given independence, the island underwent a violent revolution that saw the "Arab" government overthrown by African rebels. It was an explosion of vengeful hostility which in many ways had its roots in racial tensions dating to the nineteenth century.[8] In early 1964, Nyerere oversaw the amalgamation of Tanganyika and Zanzibar into the republic of Tanzania, but Zanzibar would experience low-level political turbulence for decades to come, centered largely on the nature of its relationship with the mainland.

In other territories, decolonization so often verged on debacle. In Ghana, the CPP was able at least to uphold the *image* of national unity; only after independence did cracks appear in the edifice. But in Uganda, such cracks were only too clear in the years prior to the lowering of the British flag and the raising of its Ugandan replacement. The Uganda People's Congress (northern, Protestant), the Democratic Party (Catholic), and the Kabaka Yekka, or "The King Alone," movement (Ganda) competed with one another in the countdown to independence, and major differences remained unresolved. A short-term alliance, in part brokered by the British, between the UPC and Kabaka Yekka took the territory to independence in 1962, under the premiership of the northerner Milton Obote. The following year, the special status of Buganda was underlined when the kabaka was installed as executive president of the new state. But Obote's own support increased after independence, to the point where he considered the Ganda alliance unnecessary and indeed damaging to his plans. The new constitution he pushed through in 1966 involved his own elevation to the position of executive president, whereupon he ordered the army to attack the kabaka's palace; the Ganda monarch fled into exile, and Buganda's special status was abolished.[9] Nonetheless, Obote had only papered over the cracks, as the tensions and divisions of Ugandan society persisted, and indeed would have tragic consequences. Such deep sociopolitical cleavages were also evident in Nigeria, where the decolonization process was slowed by the inability of the Northern People's Congress, the Yoruba Action Group, and the National Council of Nigeria and the Cameroons to agree on a constitution. The basic choices facing Nigerian nationalists were a single, unified state under a highly centralized government; a federation of largely self-governing states within the territory of Nigeria; and the complete division of the territory into three or more separate sovereign states. In reality, the last of these was scarcely an option in Britain's mind; a dangerous precedent would be set in terms of the dismemberment of colonial territories, something that would be recognized later by the Organization of African Unity. But the crucial challenge was to overcome the tensions that existed between the Muslim north and the Christian south – northerners feared domination by "Europeanized" southerners who might be favored in a postcolonial constitutional arrangement – and those between Yoruba and Igbo within the southern zone. "Tribalism" haunted Nigeria's decolonization, but ultimately the federal system was opted for, and in 1960, Nigeria became independent with Sir Abubakar Tafawa Balewa as prime minister. Tensions were rife in the 1960s: the north dominated the first federal parliament, while all three regions – north, southwest, and southeast – had considerable autonomy, leading to a situation in which majority groups in each region dominated over sizeable local minorities.[10]

Most of French and British tropical Africa became independent with a minimum of actual violence; the same was not true of Kenya, where mounting social problems had created an incendiary political climate by the beginning of the 1950s. Here, the decolonization process may be seen as taking place in three stages. The period c. 1945–52 was one of emergent crisis, leading to the declaration of a state of emergency. The main period of Mau Mau violence was between 1952 and 1956, and while the rebellion was crushed, it forced Britain to reconsider its position, and that of the settlers. Subsequently, from the mid-1950s through to the early 1960s – including the lifting of the state of emergency in 1959 – Kenya experienced reconstruction and the dismantling of the settler polity, a process culminating in the granting of independence.

Unlike across West Africa, where constitutional change had taken place in favor of African representatives, in Kenya white settlers were seen as central to the territory's political and economic future in the late 1940s and early 1950s; the compromise reached after 1947 involved the establishment of multiracial councils that brought together African moderates and settlers, although the latter were guaranteed the necessary majority. It was against this background of limited constitutional reform that the first acts of rural violence occurred in the late 1940s. By the early 1950s, such violence had spread, with assassinations of prosperous Kikuyu as well as white settlers. The Mau Mau fighters themselves were mostly Kikuyu, with some Emba and Meru, bound together by the taking of oaths, and were drawn from former squatters and the urban poor. They operated in the forests and hills of southern-central Kenya. The origins of the term "Mau Mau" itself are unclear; the fighters themselves never actually used it, and it may have derived from a European mispronunciation of the Kikuyu word *uma* ("out") – "*uma uma*," "out, out," referring to the settlers – or *muma*, meaning "oath." In 1952, the British declared a state of emergency, arrested the KAU leadership, including Jomo Kenyatta, and brought in the army. Villages were targeted across the region; indiscriminate search-and-arrest tactics resulted in the placement of thousands of Kikuyu in detention camps. The ruthlessness and violence of the British response to the insurrection served to drive many young men into the ranks of Mau Mau; at the same time, the British employed Kikuyu "loyalists" to serve as a "home guard," and organized countergangs to fight Mau Mau.[11] The war was one of the most violent and indeed reprehensible anywhere in Britain's shrinking empire in the postwar era, and by the time the uprising had effectively been suppressed in 1955–6, Kenya had changed forever.

Vastly superior British firepower had undoubtedly played its part in the defeat of Mau Mau, but the uprising also failed because it was unable to establish a broader and more popular base. In many respects, it remained isolated in the Kenyan highlands, hindered by the absence of a coherent ideology and a distinct lack of popular appeal, both inside and beyond Kenya itself. Unlike the FLN in Algeria, for example, which spread its appeal beyond the territory and tapped into strident Arab nationalism across North Africa and the Middle East, Mau Mau made no diplomatic contacts beyond Kenya, and thus in some respects, the world saw the revolt through British eyes, as tribal, bloodthirsty, and

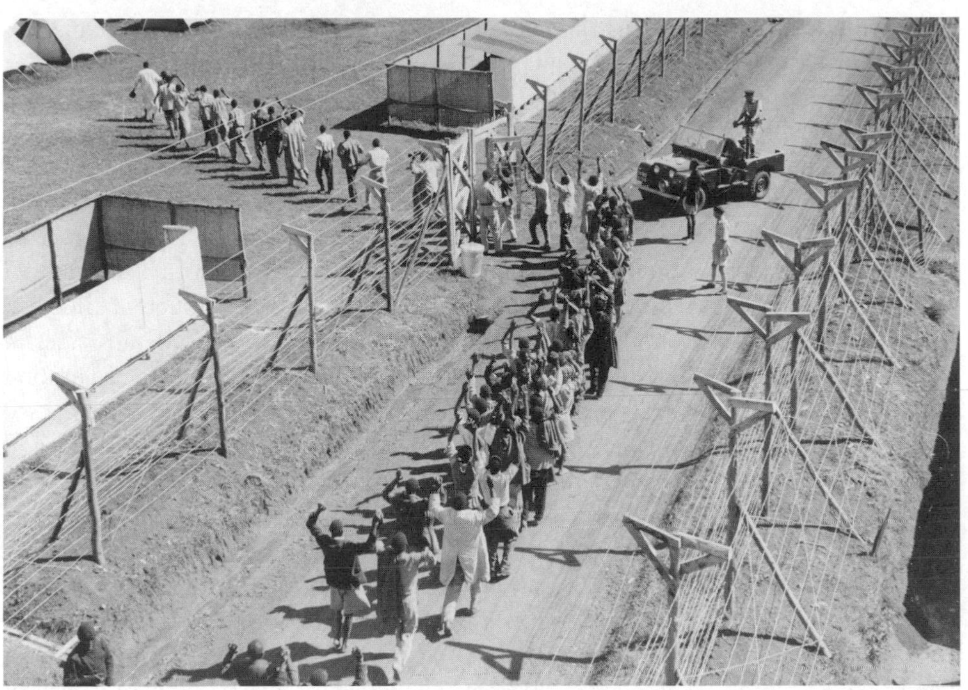

Response to insurgency in Kenya. Source: Popperfoto/Getty Images.

atavistic, with no clear program beyond its primitive, awful oaths and targeting of innocent civilians. And yet it had a significance far beyond the period of the actual fighting, bringing about a fundamental shift in British attitudes toward the colony and its future. During the mid-1950s, colonial officials began to question the wisdom of keeping the settler community at the heart of Kenyan politics and economy, particularly those who sought a clearer understanding of the revolt and its social roots. During the fighting, Mau Mau had been regarded, essentially, as a disease; now, many argued that it was in fact a symptom of social displacement on a massive scale, and that therefore mere military action could not be a final solution, because the problems at the root of the uprising would eventually re-emerge.[12] By 1955, it was accepted that socioeconomic change was needed in order to preserve security, and as a result "reconstruction" was begun, involving the consolidation of African landholdings, particularly in terms of the guaranteeing of property rights. A new land settlement scheme for the Kikuyu was initiated at considerable expense. However, the British did not address the biggest problem at the root of the Mau Mau uprising, namely the existence of the landless poor. In the resettlement scheme, many Kenyans lost out, particularly former Mau Mau detainees, to the benefit of those identified as "loyal." In the short term, reconstruction seemed to work: agricultural productivity increased, and a prosperous African peasantry, whose value was now recognized, was bolstered. Yet the discontent of the landless, again, had not been addressed. At the same time, resentment over European control of the best land in the "White Highlands" persisted, as did settler domination of the export economy;

eventually, the colonial administration loosened restrictions and allowed Africans into the lucrative export market in what amounted to an assault on the settler economy.[13]

As the 1950s closed, a split emerged in the settler community. Many continued to refuse to deal with Africans, and sought the maintenance of the privilege to which after several generations they had become accustomed, but the New Kenya Group, including a number of business managers and plantation owners, indicated themselves willing to make economic and political concessions, and strove to prevent the re-emergence of Mau Mau. Change was thus set in motion, and constitutional reforms that moved toward the abolition of white privilege were introduced. Moreover, much of this took place against the background of a British government enquiry into the atrocities at Hola Camp during the uprising. At Hola, following the administration's declaration that Mau Mau was actually a pathological illness, detainees were treated with marked brutality, including brainwashing and forced labor with the aim of cleansing body and mind of the "disease." Many detainees had refused to work and had been subjected to physical abuse, some of them being beaten to death.[14] As details of Hola emerged in the late 1950s, during Prime Minister Harold Macmillan's administration in Britain, there was widespread outrage and condemnation of the use of such violence in attempting to solve colonial "problems." Indeed, events in Kenya led many to question empire itself; Macmillan himself was now skeptical about the economic advantages of colonies, while colonial rule was now, in his view, something of a political embarrassment and an electoral liability at home. It would be hyperbole to suggest that Mau Mau ultimately brought the British Empire to its knees, but there can be little doubt that the violence of the 1950s, not least Britain's own brutal response to deep-rooted social problems – and coming as this did in the wake of the disaster at Suez – compelled many to question the morality and indeed the very existence of the imperial mission.

Multiracialism was abandoned in favor of African majority rule. With the lifting of the state of emergency, nationalist parties were re-established, including the Kenya African Democratic Union (KADU) and the Kenya African National Union (KANU). On his release from prison, Kenyatta became president of KANU, and following elections, took Kenya to independence in 1963.[15] In the final months of colonial rule, the British set up the Land Purchase Scheme, whereby they purchased over a million acres of land from departing European farmers with the aim of redistributing it among African farmers: in essence, it was intended to assist the incoming government by giving it something to offer the landless poor. At the same time, however, a "willing buyer – willing seller" scheme was established through which land might be acquired by Africans with the money to do so. The beneficiaries of this scheme, clearly, were not the landless poor, but those Africans who were already well-established and prosperous landowners. The outgoing British were determined to see the maintenance of property rights through the creation of a stable middle class: only this, it was argued, would ensure social order and security.[16] In the process of creating an independent African government, then, Britain was also transferring power to a middle class willing and able to safeguard British interests. It is possible to suggest that, in some respects, this was not so much decolonization as a new form of indirect rule, and something similar might be described for former French western and equatorial Africa. Certainly, such political realities created in the early 1960s would lead to accusations against former imperial powers of "neocolonialism" in the years to come.[17]

Ultimately, such transfers of power – while conducted in an orderly fashion, at least on the face of things, and awarded due constitutional pomp – were deeply flawed. The late-colonial state had not produced the kind of civil society that was needed to safeguard political stability or provide appropriate checks and balances. The colonial "modernization" project was in the end a botched job, not least in terms of education, which until the last years of colonial rule had been open to only a minority of Africans: it meant a citizenry-in-waiting among which illiteracy rates remained high, where both the willingness and the ability to hold leaders to account was lacking, and which was thus vulnerable from the outset to manipulation and exploitation by ruthless or unsteady elites. Even those elite groups themselves, emerging as a governing class, were frequently ill-equipped for the task at hand, the product of rushed training programs in advance – and only just – of independence. The political volatility which resulted, however, was not simply the corollary of colonial failure and ill-conceived decolonization. Alongside these short-term factors were the longer-term dynamics of state-formation, and the political and economic conflict this invariably involved, dating back to the nineteenth century. The failings of the late colonial state compounded these, to be sure, but the "new era" of independence witnessed the reassertion of long-term, distinctively African, dynamics.

Violence: Growth, Form, and Impact

Decolonization in many areas, then, involved a relatively peaceful transfer of power, even in a territory such as Kenya where a period of violence propelled the process forward. In these colonies, the very nature of that process – constitutional and legal – meant that compromises were reached which often shaped future political relations; the economic and indeed cultural influences of the former colonial power continued after independence was achieved. It was true to some degree in Kenya, and in Ghana; in the former French zone, too, there was heavy investment by the former metropolitan power in the commercial sector and also in particular leaders themselves. The European "involvement" often involved a substantial military presence, too. This has been described by some as "neocolonialism," to which we will return in a later chapter; suffice to note here that peaceful decolonization often had a significant bearing on the kinds of nation states that former colonies became.

Some territories, however, achieved independence through violence.[18] Algeria experienced a bloody conflict between 1954 and 1962 that resulted in the deaths of several hundred thousand people, settlers as well as Algerians; when de Gaulle finally ordered a withdrawal, the bulk of the settler population departed too. The Lusophone colonies also fought liberation wars between the early 1960s and the mid-1970s; Mozambique, Angola, and Guinea-Bissau finally became independent in 1974, following the *coup d'état* in Portugal itself. Indeed, civil war continued in these newly sovereign states for many years after, indelibly and tragically intertwined with the machinations of the Cold War.

Civil war rumbled on for several decades in Sudan, where a profound north–south divide was only the most dramatic manifestation of this enormous territory's spatial illogic. In Southern Rhodesia – simply "Rhodesia" after 1965 – a liberation war for "internal" decolonization against white minority rule was waged from 1966, only ending in 1979–80 with the establishment of African majority rule. And so it was, too, in South Africa, where a bitter political and military struggle unfolded against the apartheid regime from the early 1960s until the beginning of the 1990s. There are many other examples across the continent, for example Eritrea, where guerrillas fought for thirty years against Ethiopian rule between the early 1960s (Ethiopia abolished the federation and forcibly incorporated Eritrea into the empire in 1962) and 1991, and Namibia, where rebels battled against South African occupation until achieving victory in 1990. Such conflicts differed considerably in origins and form; there was great variation in the means employed in the waging of liberation struggle, in the social character of the armed movements themselves, and in the impact of violence on society and polity more broadly, both during and after actual conflict. It is an open question, perhaps, whether the nation states which were born of violence were in certain respects "more independent" than those which had emerged from peaceful compromise; quite possibly, it is ultimately a meaningless proposition. But there can be little doubt that the process of violent decolonization differed dramatically from that involving ordered, constitutional transfers of power. For those communities touched by it, death had a significance which went beyond mere politics. The long-term context of this also needs reiterating, for this period witnessed the reappearance of an evolving culture of violence in political affairs, rooted in the upheavals of the nineteenth century. Again, although the short-term cause of armed conflict during the 1950s and 1960s was badly managed decolonization, such conflict also needs to be understood in the context of long-term militarization of African polity and society: in many ways the "wars of liberation" of the mid-twentieth century represented the latest manifestation of Africa's nineteenth-century military revolution.

North African territories became independent in a variety of ways, but mostly peacefully, or at least without large-scale bloodshed. Egypt had achieved sovereignty in stages, from the 1922 declaration, and the 1936 Anglo-Egyptian treaty, but it was not until Nasser's *coup* in 1952, and his subsequent showdown with the British and French over Suez in 1956–7, that Egyptian national sovereignty could be said to have been confirmed. Nationalist pressure had forced the French from Tunisia and Morocco, by largely peaceful means. Matters were dramatically different in Algeria, however. The war there escalated through the early 1950s, and it entered a bitter new phase in 1956 with the planting of bombs in Algiers by the FLN, while in that same year the French government doubled the size of its army in the country, now amounting to some half a million men. The FLN organized itself successfully abroad, initially through the energetic efforts of Ahmed Ben Bella, who had escaped from prison and oversaw a steady of supply of arms to the movement. The FLN also had important allies abroad, not least Nasser's Egypt. Fighting in Algiers was bitter through 1956–7; it was followed by both failed negotiations between Paris and the FLN, and abortive attempts by the French settlers to take matters into their own hands by seizing control of colonial government. In the late 1950s, de Gaulle's offensives against the FLN, while hugely destructive and undertaken at immense cost in both money and lives, were ultimately unsuccessful, while within France itself there was increasing public criticism of the war. By 1960, when the UN formally recognized Algeria's right to self-determination, it seemed that the days of French rule were numbered. There would be several more false dawns – in the form of failed negotiations and further atrocities – before in July 1962 the French finally withdrew and Algerian independence was recognized. Up to a million *colons* departed with the administration, but the 10,000 *colon* casualties paled in significance compared to the million or more Algerians who had died in the course of one of Africa's bloodiest liberation wars.[19]

The Portuguese response to a popular uprising in Angola in the early 1960s was characteristically brutal; moreover, the liberation struggle itself was shaped by foreign intervention. While Portugal initially received support from the United States, the avowedly Marxist MPLA was bolstered by Soviet assistance; at the same time, other movements soon emerged in the bush with external support, including *Uniao Nacional para a Independencia Total de Angola* (UNITA), backed by South Africa as a more friendly alternative to the MPLA, and the FNLA, supported by the United States once it was decided that counter-insurgency through a rival movement was a more effective means of shaping events in Angola than backing the Portuguese themselves. The result was that when Angola finally achieved independence, it was racked by civil war; the Soviet-backed MPLA secured partial "victory" in early 1976, but UNITA remained undefeated in the southeast of the country. External meddling clearly exacerbated conflict, but the various parties were also organized according to ethnic affinity, and thus represented a set of ongoing endogenous antagonisms. The MPLA had sought a wide base of support, but it was primarily a Mbundu movement, while UNITA's support was mainly Ovimbundu, and indeed its southern orientation was at least partly a response to the domination of the FNLA by northerners. In Mozambique, FRELIMO succeeded in achieving a greater degree of unity, taking the territory to independence through socialist revolution, although in later years, the emergence of an opposition movement, RENAMO, led to a bloody civil war. RENAMO was backed by South Africa, among others, and the conflict plunged the country into desperate straits.[20]

So often violence was splintered and divisive and exposed the awful fragility of the colonial creations of the late nineteenth century. Nowhere was this clearer than in Belgian Congo. Fearing a total collapse of law and order, and "another Algeria" – Algeria again being the horrifying standard by which many colonial regimes measured the state of their own colonies – the Belgians effectively fled in 1960, following several years of mounting unrest. Chaos ensued. Nationalists themselves were taken by surprise, and political parties proliferated in the months that followed, many of them steeped in the ethnic regionalism which now threatened to destroy Congo before its sovereignty had even begun. Patrice Lumumba initially attempted to hold together a national coalition, but the state was collapsing around him, with the army in mutiny and the copper-rich Katanga province seceding in the south. Inter-ethnic violence was intense in the district of Kasai. Again, foreign interests fuelled civil war, with the Americans, the Russians, the Chinese, even the Belgians themselves, becoming involved either covertly or overtly, and so Congo presented the UN with its first – but by no means its last – major African adventure (indeed the operation cost the life of the secretary-general, Dag Hammarskjöld, whose plane crashed in September 1961 in Zambia during a round of negotiations). A UN peacekeeping force had brought Katanga under control by 1962; but in the meantime, Lumumba had been kidnapped and murdered, possibly with the knowledge, and certainly to the relief, of the Americans, who feared Lumumba's leftist leanings and charisma. Instead, it was now the US-backed Congolese army commander, General Joseph Mobutu, who took control, finally securing power in 1965. With the army reformed, Mobutu re-established centralized, and extraordinarily violent, government, and successfully molded himself into one of the West's most important Cold War allies in Africa. Mobutu later renamed the country "Zaire," and himself "Mobutu Sese Seko," in a somewhat bizarre exercise in Africanization, and the country became – as it had been under Leopold in the early 1900s – a byword for rampant corruption and chronic misgovernment, the clearest manifestation of everything that was "wrong with Africa." Yet Mobutu himself continued to enjoy the support of the West until the end of the Cold War.[21]

As Congo underwent these traumas, a little further south, in British Central Africa, another crisis was unfolding which would, as in the Lusophone zone, bring about a period of prolonged conflict. Britain had long been uneasy about the Central African Federation, fearing a repeat of the situation in South Africa and settler entrenchment; the British, after all, had only recently "resolved" the situation in Kenya, and British policy generally was no longer to bolster settler regimes, but to facilitate the transition to African majority rule. A few years earlier, Harold Macmillan had warned the South African parliament – vainly – that a "wind of change" was sweeping across the continent, and now the Rhodesias and Nyasaland were not to be exempt. Any hopes the British may have had that the Federation would involve the gradual political incorporation of Africans were proving unfounded, as the federal government had already indicated that it had no intention of sharing power, an attitude reflecting the dominance of Southern Rhodesia in the partnership. In 1963–4, the federation collapsed, the result of forceful British intervention and mounting African opposition, the latter led by such charismatic figures as Hastings Banda in Nyasaland and Kenneth Kaunda in Northern Rhodesia. In two of the territories involved, the transfer of power was relatively straightforward, with Northern Rhodesia awarded independence as Zambia, under Kaunda's United Nations Independence Party, and Nyasaland as Malawi, under Banda's Malawi Congress Party.[22] But the problem of Southern Rhodesia, with its increasingly intransigent white minority, remained.

From the early 1960s, the dominant settler political party in the colony was the Rhodesia Front, an increasingly extremist movement in the mold of the Afrikaner National Party in South Africa, which differed from the more moderate settler parties of the 1950s in the hard line it adopted toward the question of "race" and in its unshakeable belief in white privilege. The Front reached beyond big business, representing white farmers and the white urban working class, an expanding sector in settler society that was more fearful of African majority rule because they had the most to lose from it. Thus they represented the extreme right wing of the settler community, bitterly opposed to compromise and constitutional change, and indeed increasingly suspicious of and hostile to the British themselves, whom they suspected of wishing to sacrifice them on the altar of "black nationalism." Rhodesia Front leader Ian Smith became internal

Nelson Mandela and associates at the Treason Trial, South Africa, 1956. Source: Drum Social Histories/Baileys African History Archive/africanpictures.net.

prime minister in 1964, and the following year, refusing to be pressured by Britain into negotiation over the country's future, Smith's government issued its Unilateral Declaration of Independence (UDI). The "Rhodesia question" loomed large in the foreign policy of successive British governments from Harold Wilson to Margaret Thatcher, which were hampered in their dealings with Smith by the political sensitivity which would be involved in using force to bring Rhodesia to heel; white Rhodesians were, after all, "kith and kin." It was never a realistic strategy.[23]

In Congo peacekeepers had been deployed; now, the UN imposed sanctions on Rhodesia in an attempt to bring down the "illegal" Smith regime. For a time, however, the result was the reverse of that which had been intended; the Rhodesian economy was stimulated as Smith successfully sought regional commercial and strategic partners in the form of the Portuguese regimes in Angola and Mozambique, and South Africa, a key ally. The first few years of UDI actually witnessed rising living standards, for Africans as well as whites, and this meant that from 1966, when ZANU guerrillas first clashed with the security forces, ZANU struggled initially to win popular support, particularly in the rural areas. The movement was unable to persuade many of the need for armed struggle at a time of relative economic prosperity. The nationalist cause, meanwhile, was also hampered by divisions between ZANU and ZAPU, and the latter, indeed, would only make a significant contribution to the armed struggle in the second half of the 1970s. As elsewhere, these cleavages were ethnic as well as ideological and tactical: ZANU's roots were among the Shona, while ZAPU drew support primarily from the Ndebele. Such "tribalism" was used by apologists for the settler state as evidence of the bloody instability that awaited a majority-rule Rhodesia in the future.

Military prospects improved, however, in the early 1970s. As a guerrilla movement, ZANU grew in stature and experience, becoming better organized militarily and politically. As it became professionalized, so it was better able to develop motivational ideologies, using a combination of coercion, cajoling, and the rhetoric of "people's war" to reach deeper into rural communities in search of recruits and succor.[24] Moreover, ZANU developed close cooperation with FRELIMO in neighboring Mozambique, with ZANU rebels able to use FRELIMO bases across the border as provisioning and recuperation posts from 1972. FRELIMO's victory in 1974–5 brought about increased material and moral support for ZANU. Meanwhile, following the defiant "boom years" of the late 1960s, the Rhodesian economy was now experiencing a sharp downward turn, the result of the isolation imposed on it: lack of export markets produced widespread unemployment and poverty, particularly among Africans, many of whom were propelled into the guerrillas' ranks. White farmers, no longer able to sell their tobacco abroad, forced their way into the internal maize market, pushing Africans further to the fringes of the domestic economy. Conditions on African reserves worsened dramatically, and ZANU was able to cultivate a much broader base of support than previously. By the mid-1970s, even South Africa, previously a patron, was becoming less friendly, no longer convinced that this was a war which Smith could win (in stark contrast to its own, of course); and accordingly Pretoria began to pressure Smith to enter into negotiations with ZANU. Britain and the United States, deeply suspicious of the radical Mugabe, likewise sought to engineer the rise of a moderate African government, but they failed in their attempts to establish a compromise "joint government" bringing together the Rhodesia Front and an African contingent under the moderate Abel Muzorewa. In 1980, with the settlers militarily beaten and the guerrillas in control of most of the country outside the main cities, Smith was forced to accept majority rule; in the subsequent election, Robert Mugabe was swept to power as leader of the renamed Zimbabwe, although major internal tensions – notably around land distribution and ethnicity – still had to be resolved. Within twenty years, Mugabe would embark on a disastrous attempt to address the issue of land by evicting white farmers from theirs.[25]

From Suez to Sharpeville, and Beyond: The End of High Imperialism

Nasser's government in Egypt was determined to eradicate all Western influences that compromised the nation's sovereignty, and the inevitable clash centered on the Suez Canal, which – since its inception in 1869 – had been an affront to Egyptian nationalists. In late 1954, in fact, the British had agreed to evacuate their forces from the Suez zone. But a little over two years later, the Canal was at the center of an international standoff which marked a political shift of remarkable proportions. Several factors prompted the British and French governments to send forces into Suez, aided by Israel. Nasser had come to be seen as a threat to British interests across the Middle East, especially from the point of view of a Conservative government in London that sought to reassert its imperial authority. The French were likewise keen to humiliate Nasser following his support for the FLN in Algeria. Ostensibly, however, the Anglo-French invasion was motivated by Nasser's decision to nationalize the Suez Canal Company, an act which was itself prompted by the cancellation of funds for a hydroelectric dam south of Aswan by the British, the Americans, and the World Bank. The invasion was an unmitigated disaster. It was condemned around the world, most conspicuously by the US government, and stunned politicians in London and Paris were cowed into abandoning the operation. The Israelis quickly followed suit. British Prime Minister Anthony Eden resigned soon after, ostensibly because of ill health. Nasser's triumph was a victory for pan-Arabism, in particular, but Africans could celebrate his accomplishment too, for it seemed to symbolize the ascendancy of the new postcolonial state over the old imperial powers. Within a few years, Britain and France were in full retreat from the continent. Not since Adwa in 1896 had a European power been so roundly humiliated on African soil, and the ramifications appeared as profound.[26]

While Suez marked a watershed in terms of Europe's imperial era, at the other end of the continent, in South Africa, another struggle was unfolding, even more bitter and as important as Suez in denoting a new era in African liberation war. As decolonization swept across the continent during the 1950s, the apartheid regime was hardening, repression was heightening, and African political activists, in both the ANC and the PAC, pushed ever further down the road of violent protest. The turning point in the early anti-apartheid struggle came in 1960, in Sharpeville, where police opened fire on a crowd of unarmed demonstrators. Most were shot in the back as they fled. In the wake of the massacre, as South Africa was internationally condemned, the government banned the ANC and the PAC and pushed the struggle underground. At the same time, several newly independent African and Asian states attempted to have UN sanctions imposed, but such proposals were repeatedly vetoed by Britain and the United States – indeed they would do so down to the 1980s – indicating the extent of their economic interests in South Africa, although the official reason was that sanctions would only "hurt the African population." (Rhodesia, however, was a somewhat softer target.) Defiant and indignant, South Africa withdrew from the British Commonwealth in 1961 and declared itself a republic, as the anti-apartheid struggle entered a new phase: the

ANC now founded a military wing, Umkhonto we Sizwe (Spear of the Nation), while many of its leadership went into exile, organizing support abroad very effectively. The ANC suffered a major setback in 1963, however, when several key leaders, including Mandela, were captured; Mandela put up an inspired defense at his trial, but he and several others were eventually sentenced to life imprisonment.[27]

This was a blow to the ANC. But by the 1970s, resistance was diversifying and becoming more widespread, particularly in terms of worker protest. The Black Consciousness (BC) movement also emerged, aimed at the rediscovery of African self-respect. One of BC's iconic young leaders was Steve Biko. The anti-apartheid struggle generally was given a boost in the mid-1970s with the collapse of the Portuguese empire; ANC guerrillas now had bases in Mozambique, as well as in Zambia, and in the ZANU-held areas of Rhodesia. South African security forces intensified their attacks on ANC across the region, and heightened repression within the country. Their response was invariably brutal: in 1976, the police fired on a peaceful march of 15,000 schoolchildren protesting at the inferior level of black education, in Soweto, a poor Johannesburg suburb. It sparked a huge wave of violent revolt across the country, in what was tantamount to a civil war in some areas; thousands were arrested, and many were killed and wounded in clashes with the police. Biko, for example died in police custody and became one of the most important martyrs of the struggle. The conflagration continued through the late 1970s and into the 1980s, with certain areas in a state of perpetual unrest. Meanwhile, the political

Anarchy in the Congo, 1960: Patrice Lumumba is arrested by Mobutu's soldiers. Source: © Bettmann/CORBIS.

and armed struggle itself had splintered, with the ANC in conflict with the BC, and black suburbs carved up among rival gangs seeking to take advantage of the political and social chaos, and developing their own, often idiosyncratic, interpretations of "the revolution."

Indeed it was such chaos, and the ever-greater threat of complete social collapse, that compelled the government to consider certain limited reforms. In 1984, a new constitution gave superficial parliamentary representation to Indians and "Coloureds," but it was all very half-hearted, and the African majority remained politically marginalized and under-represented. Popular boycotts of white businesses and government schools in the mid-1980s forced the government to establish "townships," African residential areas administered by African-run councils. But these were swiftly discredited, descending into violent chaos under frequently corrupt local leaders lacking any support among the urban poor and the politically conscious, and indeed many townships soon became ungovernable. In response, in 1985 President P. W. Botha declared a state of emergency and clamped down on protest, as well as international reportage of such protest; mass arrests and state-sanctioned killings reached shocking new levels. International condemnation increased, and even countries that had previously remained quiet over apartheid, or at least tempered their criticisms of it, for economic and ideological reasons (notably the British and US governments), could no longer justify such an attitude. The Afrikaner community at large, and the National Party in particular, had lost credibility, even though many Afrikaner leaders continued to deny the fact. But it was a situation out of control, and which required urgent action. In 1989, F. W. de Klerk became president, and initiated a dramatic reassessment of apartheid. Though formerly known as a hardliner, de Klerk was essentially pragmatic, and took the bold step of cancelling both the Population Registration and Group Areas acts; in early 1990 bans on the ANC and the PAC were lifted, and Mandela was released. Apartheid was essentially finished. These dramatic developments were followed by intense negotiations regarding the future of the country, against a background of rising violence between rival groups in the townships, between protesters and security forces, between the ANC and a number of rival groups. Right-wing Afrikaners threatened revolt, while the newly reformed Inkatha Freedom Party, the movement of the Natal Zulu under Mangosuthu Buthelezi, attempted to undermine ANC support in that region.[28]

Bad as it was, the situation might have been altogether worse had Mandela himself not adopted such a magnanimous stance toward the dying regime, and taken with such apparent ease to the role of elder statesman around whom so many South Africans could unite. Protracted negotiations led in 1994 to the first free and nonracial elections in South Africa's modern history; Mandela became president, and the ANC was swept to power. Profound inequity and high levels of violence hindered social and political development, and threatened major problems for the future; yet Mandela's vision of the "rainbow nation," and the ANC's generally pragmatic and competent administration, were crucial in bringing about a stability which was remarkable given the events of the preceding decades. There was no civil war, as many had predicted, nor was there the anticipated backlash against white South Africans. Indeed the Truth and Reconciliation

Commission was later set up with a view to healing the deep wounds inflicted by apartheid – though opinion was divided on what the TRC achieved.[29] Above all, however, expectations among the majority of South Africans about what might be achieved by the ANC government were extraordinarily, and understandably, high, and would be disappointed in the short term at least.

Notes

1 Manning, *Francophone Sub-Saharan Africa*, 139–40; Cooper, *Citizenship Between Empire and Nation*, passim.

2 Elizabeth Schmidt, *Mobilising the Masses: Gender, Ethnicity and Class in the Nationalist Movement in Guinea, 1939–1958* (Portsmouth NH, 2005); Mairi MacDonald, "A vocation for independence: Guinean nationalism in the 1950s," in Tony Chafer & Alexander Keese (eds.), *Francophone Africa at Fifty* (Manchester, 2013).

3 Stephen L. Weigert, *Traditional Religion and Guerrilla Warfare in Modern Africa* (London, 1996), 36–48.

4 For a contemporary snapshot, see A.L. Latham-Koenig, "Ruanda-Urundi on the threshold of independence," *The World Today*, 18:7 (1962).

5 Wm Roger Louis, "The dissolution of the British empire," in J. Brown & Wm Roger Louis (eds.), *The Oxford History of the British Empire, Vol 4: The Twentieth Century* (Oxford, 1999).

6 Basil Davidson, *Black Star: A View of the Life and Times of Kwame Nkrumah* (London, 1973); Austin, *Politics in Ghana*; and Nkrumah's own account, *Ghana: The Autobiography of Kwame Nkrumah* (New York, 1957). See also Richard Rathbone, *Nkrumah and the Chiefs: The Politics of Chieftaincy in Ghana 1951–1960* (Oxford, 2000); R. Crook, "Decolonisation, the colonial state, and chieftaincy in the Gold Coast," *African Affairs*, 85:338 (1986); Jean Allman, "The Youngmen and the Porcupine: class, nationalism, and Asante's struggle for self-determination, 1954–57," *Journal of African History*, 31:2 (1990).

7 Iliffe, *Modern History of Tanganyika*, chaps. 14–16; see also Susan Geiger, *TANU Women: Gender and Culture in the Making of Tanganyikan Nationalism, 1955–1965* (Portsmouth, NH, 1997), and James R. Brennan, *Taifa: Making Nation and Race in Urban Tanzania* (Athens OH, 2012), esp. chaps. 4 & 5.

8 Michael F. Lofchic, *Zanzibar: Background To Revolution* (Princeton, 1965); Jonathon Glassman, *War of Words, War of Stones: Racial Thought and Violence in Colonial Zanzibar* (Indiana IL, 2011).

9 For the kabaka's own account, see The Kabaka of Buganda, *The Desecration of My Kingdom* (London, 1967). See also Gardner Thompson, *Governing Uganda* (Kampala, 2003).

10 Coleman, *Nigeria*; Toyin Falola & Matthew Heaton, *A History of Nigeria* (Cambridge, 2008), chap. 6.

11 Dan Branch, "The enemy within: loyalists and the war against Mau Mau in Kenya," *Journal of African History*, 48:2 (2007); Huw Bennett, *Fighting the Mau Mau: The British Army and Counterinsurgency in the Kenya Emergency* (Cambridge, 2012). See also a Kenyan perspective in Itote, *Mau Mau General*.

12 John Lonsdale, "Mau Maus of the Mind: making Mau Mau and remaking Kenya," *Journal of African History*, 31:3 (1990); Dane Kennedy, "Constructing the colonial myth of Mau Mau,"

International Journal of African Historical Studies, 25:2 (1992). For a contemporary psychiatric assessment, see J.C. Carothers, *The Psychology of Mau Mau* (Nairobi, 1954).

13 The situation on the eve of independence is brilliantly captured in Ngugi wa Thiong'o's novel, *A Grain of Wheat* (Nairobi, 1967). See also Dan Branch, *Defeating Mau Mau, Creating Kenya: Counterinsurgency, Civil War, and Decolonisation* (Cambridge, 2009).

14 David Anderson, *Histories of the Hanged: Britain's Dirty War in Kenya and the End of Empire* (London, 2005); Caroline Elkins, *Britain's Gulag: The Brutal End of Empire in Kenya* (London, 2005).

15 See his own account of these momentous events in Jomo Kenyatta, *Suffering Without Bitterness: The Founding of the Kenya Nation* (Nairobi, 1968).

16 Gary Wasserman, "Continuity and counter-insurgency: the role of land reform in decolonising Kenya, 1962–70," *Canadian Journal of African Studies*, 7:1 (1973).

17 The classic statement is Kwame Nkrumah, *Neo-Colonialism: The Last Stage of Imperialism* (London, 1965); see also Colin Leys, *Underdevelopment in Kenya: The Political Economy of Neo-colonialism, 1964–1971* (London, 1975).

18 Frantz Fanon, *The Wretched of the Earth* (New York, 1963), is concerned with Algeria, but swiftly acquired a much wider status as the classic statement on anticolonial violence. See Clayton, *Frontiersmen*, for a basic overview.

19 Horne, *Savage War*; D. Ling, *The Passing of French Algeria* (London, 1966); D. Ottoway & M. Ottoway, *Algeria: The Politics of a Socialist Revolution* (Berkeley CA, 1970).

20 A. Isaacman, *Mozambique: From Colonialism to Revolution, 1900–1982* (Boulder CO, 1983); D. Birmingham, *Frontline Nationalism in Angola and Mozambique* (London, 1992).

21 Georges Nzongola-Ntalaja, *The Congo from Leopold to Kabila: A People's History* (London & New York, 2002), chaps. 2 & 3. For contemporary analysis, see: Catherine Hoskyns, *The Congo since Independence: January 1960–December 1961* (London, 1965); René Lemarchand, *Political Awakening in the Congo: The Politics of Fragmentation* (Los Angeles, 1965); Crawford Young, *Politics in the Congo: Decolonisation and Independence* (Princeton, 1965).

22 Patrick Keatley, *The Politics of Partnership: The Federation of Rhodesia and Nyasaland* (London, 1963); and see Kenneth Kaunda's own account in *Zambia Shall Be Free: An Autobiography* (London, 1962).

23 Robert C. Good, *U.D.I.; The International Politics of the Rhodesian Rebellion* (London, 1973).

24 Norma Kriger, *Zimbabwe's Guerrilla War: Peasant Voices* (Cambridge, 1991).

25 For a fascinating snapshot from the moment of independence, see W.H. Morris-Jones (ed.), *From Rhodesia to Zimbabwe: Behind And Beyond Lancaster House* (London, 1980).

26 Barry Turner, *Suez 1956: The Inside Story of the First Oil War* (London, 2006); Wm Roger Louis, *Ends of British Imperialism: the Scramble for Empire, Suez, and Decolonisation* (London, 2006).

27 Saul Dubow, "Were there political alternatives in the wake of the Sharpeville-Langa violence in South Africa, 1960?," *Journal of African History*, 56:1 (2015).

28 R. Price, *The Apartheid State in Crisis: Political Transformation in South Africa, 1975–1990* (Cambridge, 1991); Tom Lodge, "Resistance and Reform, 1973–1994," in Robert Ross, Anne Kelk Mager, & Bill Nasson (eds.), *The Cambridge History of South Africa, Vol 2: 1885–1994* (Cambridge, 2011).

29 This is evident, for example, in the play by Jane Taylor and William Kentridge, *Ubu and the Truth Commission*, first performed in Johannesburg in 1997.

Part VI Legacies, New Beginnings, and Unfinished Business

The end of colonial rule brought some new issues, and continuations and variations of some old ones. African states carried the legacy of foreign rule, in many spheres of life – in politics, in economics, in terms of cultures and social structures. Patterns of social, commercial, and political relations which had receded, or been driven underground, with the onset of colonial rule now re-emerged, and there can be little doubt that many of the issues and challenges confronting Africans in the contemporary age are precolonial in origin. In particular, the effects of political transformations across the continent and the militarization of polity and society during the nineteenth century now came to the fore once again. The violent upheaval of that era had to some extent been in abeyance since the imposition of the colonial *pax*, which had itself been made possible through African agency; but political enmities – and in some places outright armed conflict – resurfaced in earnest in the 1950s and 1960s, as groups old and new sought to build competitive and indeed hegemonic communities within the arena of the nation-state. Many of the economic dynamics confronting Africa's new nations were likewise rooted in the nineteenth century, which had witnessed the consolidation of a global economic system over which Africans had little direct influence. There was demand for what Africans grew, or dug up – and even this was often under outside control; but virtually none for what they *made*, while opportunities for profit were wholly contingent on developments elsewhere. Unquestionably, these emerging problems were greatly exacerbated by the colonial experience. There might be new beginnings for some as new nations were born, and certainly much nationalist rhetoric focused on the notion of rebirth; but more often than not the trajectories of these new nations would be complicated by their problematic inheritances, from both the deep and the more recent past.

A History of Modern Africa: 1800 to the Present, Third Edition. Richard J. Reid.

In the first instance, of course, Africa had to contend with a challenging set of global circumstances. The ideological polarity of the Cold War was of little concern to millions of Africans, even though many of their governments were content enough to take advantage of it; but the Cold War was crippling in many respects, exacerbating or creating conflicts, many of which rumbled on for years, and led the West to justify support for some of the most odious regimes the planet has ever witnessed. To some extent, the intrusions of the Cold War further complicated extant long-term problems. Economic underdevelopment was rooted in the inequities inherent in nineteenth-century "legitimate commerce," and to a very real degree, even earlier, in the Atlantic slave-trading system; and further underdevelopment was the result of colonial economics. While African governing elites have not always made the best choices in terms of policy directions, they have been greatly constrained by the fragile and unbalanced systems they inherited, and by the unfavorable commercial relationship with the wider world in which they have been snared. Similarly, in political terms, the legacy of the nineteenth century, an era of violent creativity, was one of aggressive entrepreneurialism and social mobility, and heightened competition for control of people, goods, and ideas between expansionist center and armed frontier. Europe harnessed this turmoil at the end of the nineteenth century; and in its turn, colonialism bequeathed Africa systems based on militarism and violence, latent or explicit, as well as on oppression and unaccountability. African rulers soon developed their own updated variations on these themes: patronage and personal rule predominated, in ways which simultaneously drew upon precolonial experience and also, in some cases, warped precolonial paradigms. In recent years, there have been more concerted, and more violent, challenges to the oppressive regimes which, with rare exceptions, defined the continent's political culture in the decades following decolonization. In that sense, there is reason to hope that communities and individuals will find ways to secure greater access to resources and power, and not necessarily at others' expense. Old systems have collapsed, or continue to morph into new forms, whether under sheer popular pressure or under a hail of small-arms fire. Electoral processes have proliferated, and political consciousness has grown, as has intolerance of oppression; when such consciousness comes armed, however, the result can be bloody indeed. Armed struggle and popular agitation can certainly effect change, of various kinds; but likewise politicization can be manifest in the explosion of angry prejudice, as in Rwanda. Meanwhile, genuine democracy makes only halting progress across the continent, political reform is often superficial, and authoritarianism has proven remarkably resilient, and also comes in new guises – not least in the form of organizations of "popular" or "revolutionary" or "democratic" liberation which dominate the political space, as in South Africa, Namibia, Mozambique, and Ethiopia.

In one sense, the relationship between Africa and the world beyond continues to develop, with noticeable shifts in attitude since the early 1990s; yet in other respects, it is possible to discern a great deal of continuity throughout the period examined in this volume. The continent is still objectified by governments and other "interested" bodies and agencies across the "developed" world, and on a planet with no shortage of "troubled regions" Africa is regarded as the clearest representation of what happens when human affairs go awry. Africa, as it was when the slave-trade abolitionists were making their case in the late eighteenth and early nineteenth centuries, or when Livingstone and other missionaries despaired at the state of human society on the continent in the age of high imperialism, is a condition to be addressed, though not necessarily understood; it is there to be "improved," "saved." Arguably, the late twentieth century witnessed a return to some of the values and approaches of the late eighteenth. Increasingly "ethical" Western intervention has been aimed at economic restructuring – the latest manifestation of the struggle to "modernize" the continent in economic terms ongoing since the early nineteenth century – while in the context of political change there has been a concern to spread the doctrines of liberalism (elections and human rights) rather more effectively than was the case in the mid-twentieth century. Even so, since the terrorist attacks on New York on September 11, 2001, the United States and others have lent support to "friendly regimes" considered to be on the right side of the struggle against violent Islamism, regardless of – indeed often thanks to – those regimes' tight control over political dissent, as in Ethiopia, or Uganda. As long as they do so, they risk being profoundly damaged by the fallout when such regimes are overthrown from within, as events in Egypt – where Mubarak was another long-term Western ally – demonstrated.

In the early twenty-first century, progress has been made toward the resolution of some conflicts – Darfur, or Cote d'Ivoire – while others persist, and new ones have emerged. The long-running civil war in Sudan was brought to a close with the secession of South Sudan, which became Africa's newest nation in 2011, though within two years it descended into civil war. Nearby, an uneasy "no war, no peace" situation persisted between Eritrea and Ethiopia until a peace deal in 2018, though it remains to be seen whether the deep-seated tensions which sparked the conflict in the first place can be fully resolved. In Somalia, African Union troops have made some progress against the Islamist insurgency of al-Shabaab, but violence persists in Mogadishu and across the country, and Somalia remains some way from anything approaching normative definitions of stability. Meanwhile, why the basically functioning state of Somaliland remains formally unrecognized by the international community while South Sudan was granted sovereignty is an open question. It certainly functions rather more effectively than Libya, which collapsed into civil war in the wake of Qaddafi's overthrow in 2011, and where rival factions struggle over control of territory and oil. Among Libya's factions are Islamist fighters, and similar groups have also been active in northern Mali and Niger, while the Islamist Boko Haram insurgency in northern Nigeria continues to grow in scale and impact. Eastern Congo, long a frontier of violence, remains explosive, owing in no small part to the intrusions of neighbors, chiefly Uganda and Rwanda. And for every place like Darfur or South Sudan, on which has been lavished attention and facilitators and funding in the search for ceasefires, there is a territory like Western Sahara, largely forgotten by the world, where the Sahrawi people struggle for recognition against Moroccan occupation.

It is not always easy to identify why one war is targeted as worthy of attention by the wider world, while others rumble on largely unnoticed; why one warlord is indulged but another is ignored or vilified; why one odious regime is roundly condemned but another carries on the daily business of oppression and scarcely registers in either newspapers or the memos of foreign affairs departments overseas. Such selectivity will prove difficult to overcome and will lead inevitably to accusations of hypocrisy toward the UN, western governments, and NGOs alike. More generally, the long-term historical significance of war in Africa – representing the ongoing struggle for control of human and material resources, and social and cultural cohesion – is routinely misunderstood, or ignored.

Conflict is an inevitable part of human affairs; but across Africa, violence has been greatly exacerbated by the persistent problems of drought, debt, and underdevelopment – although of course the relationship between conflict and such problems can also operate in the opposite direction. African governments remain saddled with debts which have escalated since the 1960s, and their room for maneuver has been severely curtailed in terms of the development of social and economic infrastructure. Foreign aid, as a rule, while ever more inventive, can never be anything other than a stopgap measure, and indeed in some circumstances it might be seen as counterproductive. Above all, much conflict has been driven by lack of access to basic resources, and it is axiomatic to suggest that economic development – as well as understanding of historical context – will be essential if resolution is to be achieved within and between communities and states across the continent.

Africans have been engaged in much unfinished business in recent years, and this will continue into the foreseeable future. Of course historians are also now dealing with unfinished business, and it is this which makes our task all the more difficult, if not impossible. Historians should not deal in futures; that is for others, no matter how much historical research may itself point toward possible future developments and provide prognoses in terms of the future patterns of human relations. There has been enough in the way of events and trends since the 1990s to satisfy both optimists and pessimists regarding "the state of Africa" in our own era. The ambiguity is perhaps best symbolized by the events of 1994, the year which witnessed the democratic overthrow of one of the continent's most oppressive and racist regimes and the birth of the "rainbow nation" in South Africa, but which also witnessed the horrific genocide in Rwanda, involving the killing of close to a million people in little more than a dozen weeks. Indeed the events of 1994 offer a salutary lesson in how it is dangerous to search for "turning points" and "new beginnings" at the expense of identifying gradual shifts. In 2005, governments from the "developed" world made much noise about debt cancellation and new directions in assisting Africa; at the time of writing, little of practical value has been done, although token gestures (and speeches) abound. At the same time, this is the era of "Africa Rising," which has seen extraordinary GDP growth rates across swathes of the continent fuelled in part by inward investment from China, India, and the Gulf States and a sharp upturn in exports of raw materials from Africa. Yet in other respects this looks like a "new scramble" for the continent, in which avaricious foreigners are involved in the large-scale extraction of Africa's natural wealth. African elites have benefited politically and financially, but the rich-poor divide remains profound and is growing in many countries.

Africa-watchers will be familiar with the "new initiatives" that come along every few years – around debt relief, literacy, and disease – driven alternately by governments,

NGOs, or a small but increasingly active group of Western philanthropists (or "philanthrocapitalists," to use a current term). Such initiatives occasionally do some good, without doubt, but they often disguise deeper issues, such as the dynamics of Africa's historical development, and the very nature of the historical relationship between Africa and the rest of the world. Given the essential superficiality of the "developed" world's approach to and understanding of Africa's past, it seems clear that, to use another recent cliché, solutions to current crises lie with Africans, and no-one else. Greater confidence is needed, perhaps, to realize this in tangible ways. The problem with failing to historicize Africa in the early twenty-first century is that it can lead to rather gloomy prognoses which are themselves founded on somewhat shallow interpretations of the available evidence. A long-term approach is essential to understanding Africa's political, social, and economic development. As this book has hopefully demonstrated, the history of Africa over the past two centuries is characterized by an extraordinary dynamism and creativity on the part of its peoples, and this alone is enough to suggest that further innovation and development – driven by Africans themselves – is not simply possible but inevitable. There will be destruction as well as construction along the way; but the story continues.

17 Unsafe Foundations

Challenges of Independence

Building the Nation (1): Economy and Society

Arguably, the most tangible manifestation of Africa's problematic inheritances has been the economic condition of much of the continent since the 1960s. Economics, indeed, lie at the root of many of Africa's modern political and social crises, whether in terms of a lack of resources, or – rather more commonly – an imbalance in the distribution of and access to those resources. It remains broadly true that poverty and underdevelopment feed the fires of civil unrest, contribute ineffably to the failure of democratic politics and civil society, and exacerbate ethnic tensions. Independent Africa was left with the burdens of the cash crop economy, namely the creation by colonial states of systems of production that were organized around a handful of key commodities and geared toward the export of those commodities rather than internal consumption and the development of an internal market. Accordingly, African states have struggled with unfavorable international terms of trade and have had to cope with their inability to control prices. Colonialism, at its core, was not concerned with developing African internal economic infrastructures, or with facilitating productive self-sufficiency; rather, the main aim was to create colonial territories that could pay for themselves through export profits and through tax levied on commerce and peasant production. By the 1950s, the continent's capacity to produce food for its own consumption was diminishing, while cash crop production for overseas markets continued to increase. A rural poverty trap had resulted in many areas, particularly where export production was undermining subsistence farming. African producers also suffered continually from heavy taxation, which scarcely eased off following the attainment of independence, and were burdened by agricultural marketing boards, introduced by colonial governments in the 1930s and 1940s, and

A History of Modern Africa: 1800 to the Present, Third Edition. Richard J. Reid.

retained by independent states.[1] Such boards, as noted earlier, paid fixed low prices to farmers whose produce was sold abroad at much higher prices; the difference, according to colonial theory, was to be used for internal development, but in fact amounted to government revenue. It was a pattern that had appeared in Ghana in the late 1950s and which would be repeated elsewhere across the continent. This was underdevelopment in essence: peasant producers were part of an international marketing system – and a crucial part at that – but were marginalized within it, and received none of the benefits associated with it. Moreover, the transport and communications infrastructure was inadequate for Africa's internal development and had been designed to facilitate colonial exploitation of agricultural produce and raw materials: the entire system was geared toward export, as it had been in its nineteenth-century incarnation. Roads and railways linked areas of production with the coast, and in a pattern of economic relations that as we have seen dated to the early nineteenth century, African economies fed external consumption, and external economic growth, through the export of "primary produce" – from slaves, ivory, and palm oil in the nineteenth century, to cotton, cocoa, and gold in the twentieth.[2]

And yet, in the 1950s and 1960s, there had been a reasonable expectation of considerable economic growth among newly independent governments and foreign observers alike. In large part, this was suggested by the economic boom after the Second World War: world prices for a number of cash crops had been high since the mid-1940s, and while African peasants may have been "poor" in relative (i.e. European) terms, they were by no means the world's poorest. The indigenous West African commercial class, for example, was rather more prosperous in about 1950 than its South Asian equivalent. In addition to a booming rural economy, there had also been a postwar expansion in mining across the continent; this had the most stable foundation in southern Africa, but in many other territories, oil and gas and a range of other minerals were being successfully exploited from the late 1940s onward. This in turn fed growth in the manufacturing sector, and in the 1950s, in some territories at least there were signs that industrial "take-off" might be possible.

By the 1970s, however, the continent was in economic crisis. Some of the reasons for this veritable collapse were not, in fact, directly related to policy decisions by governments, which were frequently unable to control events. The rapid population growth experienced across much of the continent from the 1950s onwards placed enormous strains on existing resources and socioeconomic infrastructures; governments found their ability to invest economic surpluses in development programs which could keep up with such growth severely curtailed. In this sense, African demography over the past half-century is deserving of closer study: the impact of demographic change on economic development, on the provision of adequate social infrastructure and social services – health care, education, land distribution – and ultimately on levels of both urban and rural poverty has been enormous. This was an internal change unforeseen by African politicians and which was perhaps unforeseeable. But in external terms, too, the continent was the victim of changes in the global market, exposing a vulnerability which again had its roots in the colonial era and probably earlier. States dependent on a small handful of key exports were especially susceptible to shifts in global demand and

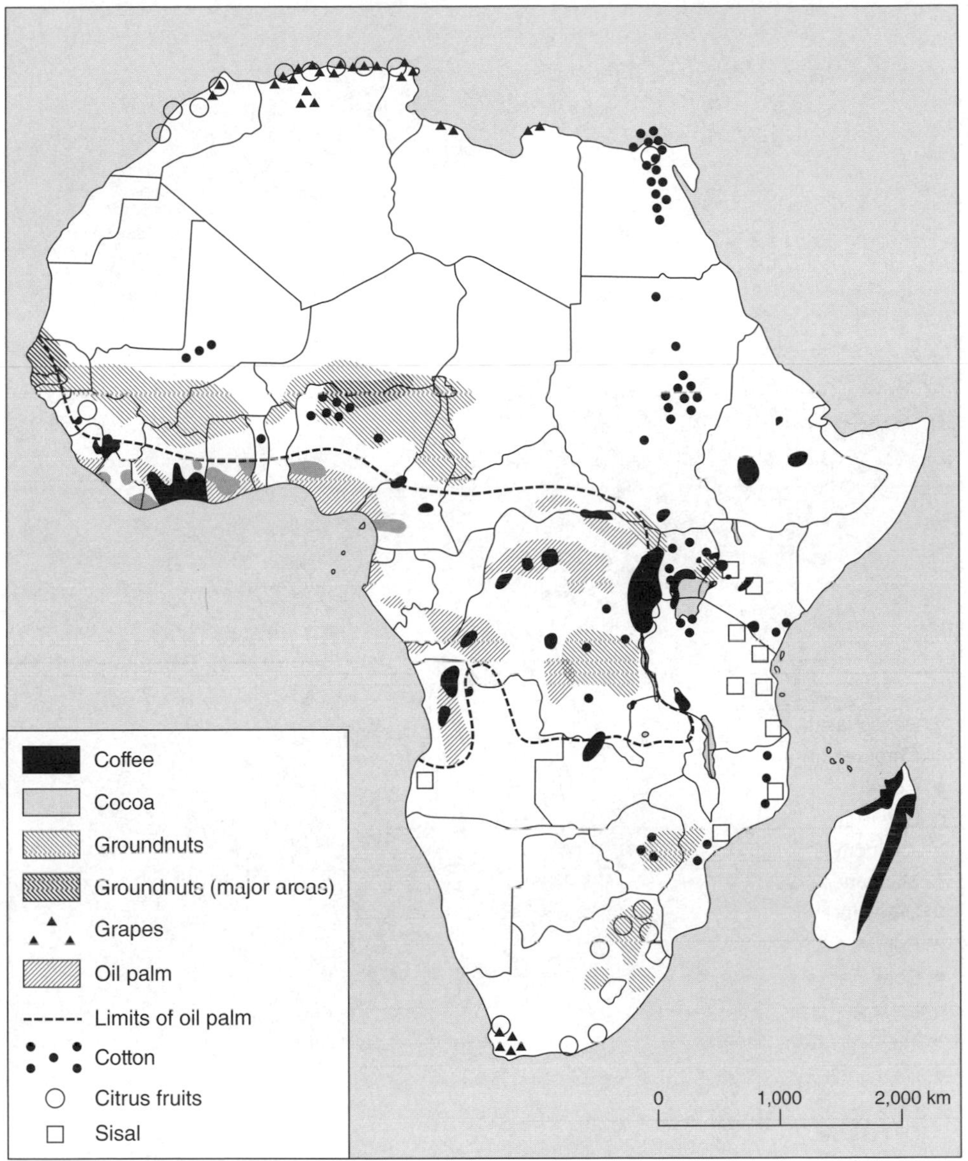

Postcolonial cash-crop economies. Source: From B. Davidson, *Modern Africa: A Social and Political History*, 3rd ed. (London and New York: Longman, 1994), p. 222, Map 10. © 1994 by Basil Davidson. Reproduced with permission of Taylor and Francis.

pricing. During the 1970s, for example prices for agricultural exports collapsed and remained low through much of the 1980s, only beginning to recover in the early 1990s. States reliant on cash crops were badly hit. Likewise, the collapse in the global market for certain industrial products devastated countries dependent since the colonial era on one or two commodities. The dramatic fall in copper prices between the mid-1970s and the mid-1980s ravaged the economies of copper-producers such as

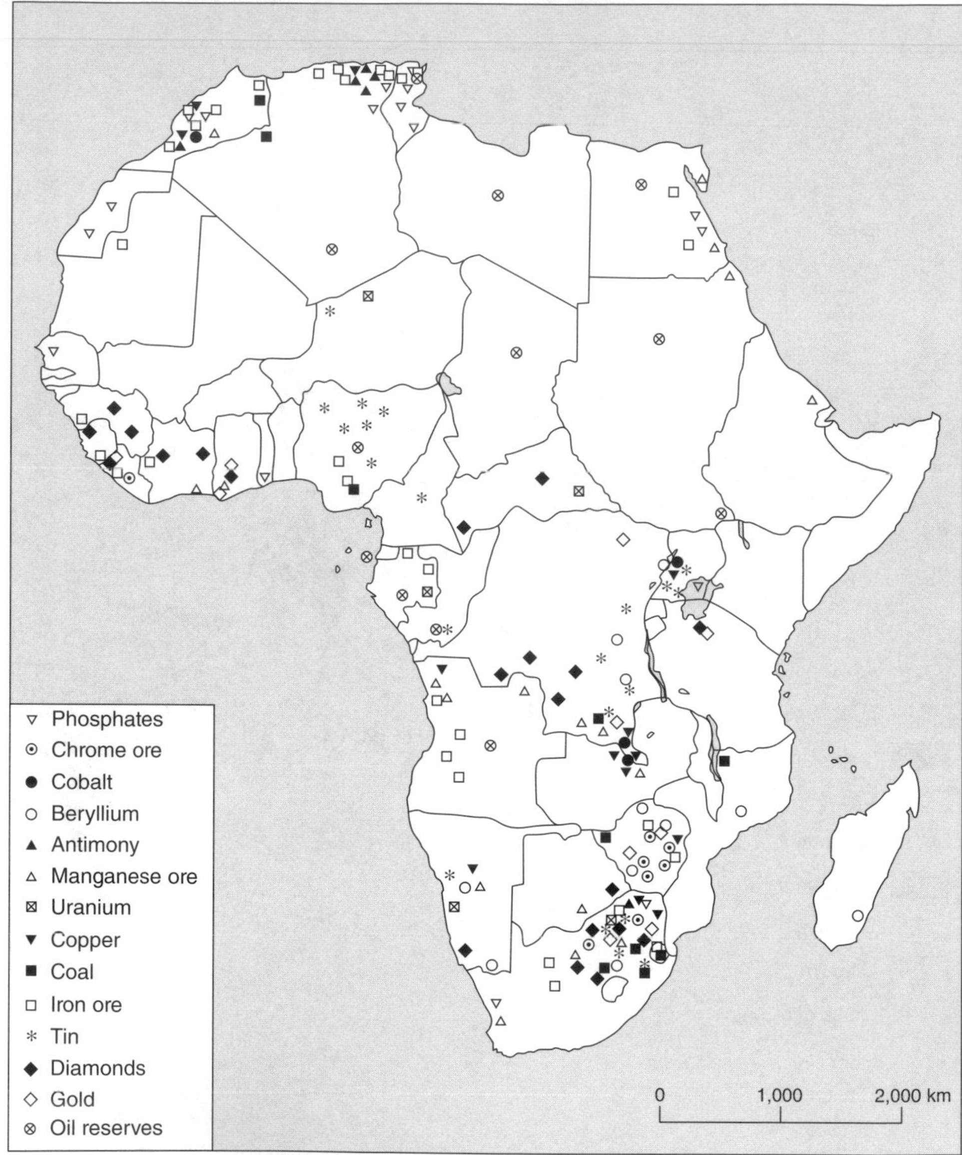

Postcolonial mineral exploitation. Source: From B. Davidson, *Modern Africa: A Social and Political History*, 3rd ed. (London and New York: Longman, 1994), p. 235, Map 11. © 1994 by Basil Davidson. Reproduced with permission of Taylor and Francis.

Zaire and Zambia.[3] African leaders may well have often been short-sighted, or complacent, in failing to diversify their economies and thus protect them from such chronic global fluctuations; many also failed to buoy up domestic food production as insurance against the social misery which would result when global markets for exports collapsed. Yet it was nonetheless a colonial legacy that so many countries were thus reliant on a limited range of exports, an inheritance of precariousness exacerbated by the absence

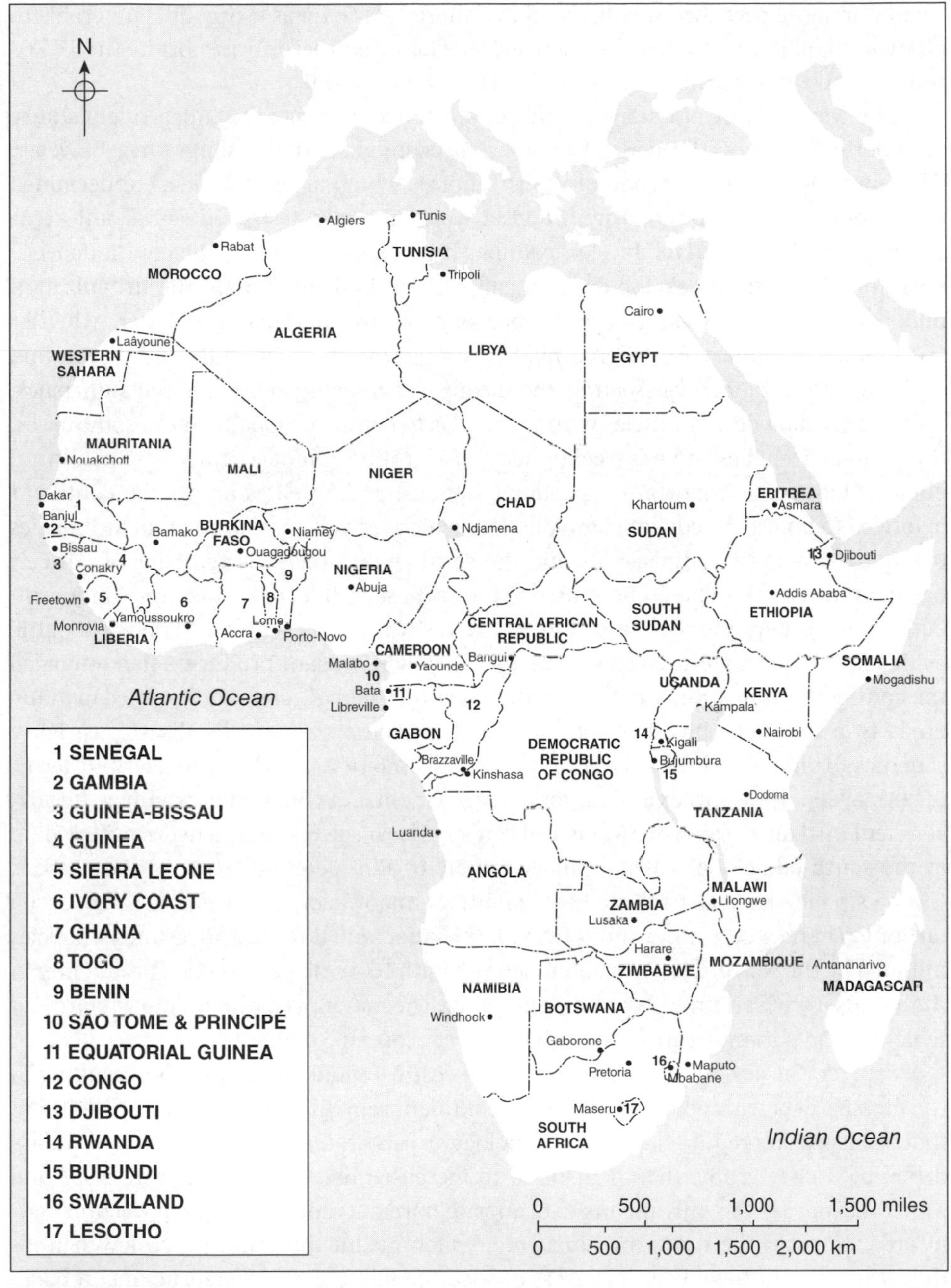

Modern African nation-states.

of a strong domestic market. Similar crises were provoked by rising prices for imports: when the price of oil spiraled upward in the early and mid-1970s, African importers with no alternative sources were devastated, and it is no coincidence that it was at this point that transport systems and in particular road networks began to deteriorate rapidly, in large part through disuse. Sub-Saharan Africa was especially vulnerable to changes in oil prices, as there was a heavier reliance on motor transport by the 1970s than on any other means of transport, such as water or rail.

These were broadly phenomena and circumstances inherited by independent states, or otherwise outside the control of their governments. At the same time, however, African politicians made economic policy choices which at the very least undermined the potential for economic growth and at worst actually destroyed significant areas of commercial activity. Notably, for example, it was believed at the outset of independence that in order to develop economically, Africa had to emulate the urbanization and industrialization patterns of Europe and North America. The latter, whether subliminally or otherwise, offered models of "progress" and wealth and power, and rapid industrialization was seen as the means to achieving economic self-sufficiency, and as providing new countries with the means to compete globally. Yet in some cases, the strategy went beyond mere economic considerations; in part, it was also a cultural choice. With some important exceptions, nation-building elites across the continent belonged to an urban, educated middle class which tended – as did colonial authorities before them – to regard peasants and the rural environment as symbolic of Africa's backwardness; rural life represented Africa's past, while peasants were ignorant, conservative, unproductive, and inherently resistant to "progress." There was little evidence for such a view, given the manner in which peasant producers had managed the continent's transition into the twentieth-century global economy; yet it led in many areas to a failure to invest in agriculture. The policy was usually disastrous. Early schemes for industrialization were often wildly ambitious, and ill-conceived in terms of both available resources and national requirements. In Ghana, for example, the government instigated expensive industrial "prestige" projects, notably a hydroelectric dam at the south end of Lake Volta, guided largely by European advisors. In the process, Ghana's policy-makers neglected the country's major economic asset, namely cocoa farming. There were few new initiatives for the latter, and little new investment; policies initiated by the Nkrumah government led at length to a collapse in cocoa production in the 1970s, by which time Nkrumah himself had been removed by a military *coup d'état* which was in part motivated by misgivings over economic policy.[4]

Moreover, the pursuit of these policies was costly in financial terms, too, resulting in the massive debt with which much of the continent remains saddled to the present-day. Industrial projects required foreign technology, expertise, and loans, leading to spiraling debts; by a cruel irony, this in turn led to increased dependency on cash crops and mineral exports – the only means to acquiring hard currency for many governments – in order to repay the debts thus incurred, which meant there were even fewer funds than there might have been to invest in socioeconomic development against a background of population growth.[5] Overall, this meant systemic poverty, and indeed ever-worsening terms of trade for African states. By the end of the 1970s, many African economies had buckled. The term "neocolonialism," in popular currency through the 1960s and 1970s, described the West's continuing economic control over politically independent Africa, and was a phenomenon against which the members of the Organisation of African Unity (OAU) were keen to caution. Yet many of these same members had seen themselves ensnared by these very circumstances. Neocolonial relationships could be identified everywhere, but they were perhaps clearest in the former French colonies, where France had invested heavily in mining projects and thus exercised considerable control over the economies and finances of several supposedly sovereign states. In fact, however, there was nothing particularly "neo" about "neocolonialism": it was, rather, a reversion to an earlier, nineteenth-century, economic relationship, and in many respects was a continuation of the colonial economy – in the essentials, if without the political encumbrances.[6]

It was partly to offset such foreign dependency that other states sought "indigenous" ways forward, often using ideology to justify their own economic visions. If Nkrumah was guilty of neglecting and undermining the agricultural sector, Julius Nyerere in Tanzania was at the other end of the spectrum, although the result was not, in fact, dissimilar. In order to prevent both foreign cash – which Nyerere argued would not assist Tanzania's development in the long term – and the evils of capitalist differentiation, the Tanzanian government pursued a socialist agenda, in so doing creating village collectives that were meant to increase productivity and aid the provision of social and economic infrastructure.[7] The strategy was presented as an African solution to African problems, a shining example of Africans helping themselves. Yet such villagization was often forced, with entire communities moved at gunpoint, and ultimately the policy was a disaster, as were similar schemes in Ethiopia and Mozambique. Productivity collapsed through the 1970s, and in fact rapid urbanization ensued in Tanzania as disenchanted peasants drifted to the cities in search of work and better prospects.

The 1970s and 1980s also witnessed environmental and climatic catastrophe which exacerbated economic crisis in a number of states. Persistent drought across the Sahel belt from the early 1970s and into the 1980s affected states from Mauritania and Mali in the west to Sudan and Ethiopia in the east. Drought and resultant famine compounded the effects of civil war in Sudan and Mozambique, and of both internal conflict and forced-villagization policies in Mengistu's Ethiopia in the early and mid-1980s.[8] Overall, indeed, it was agrarian decline which lay at the heart of Africa's economic crisis by the 1980s: several states had come to rely on foreign aid and were net importers of food. Governments maintained the mechanisms they had inherited from colonial states, such as the marketing boards that depressed prices paid to producers. Indeed, a major inheritance from the colonial era more generally was huge state involvement in the economy, which was centrally managed to a remarkable degree, while the public sector in most African states was likewise enormous. There was continued population growth, but it was unevenly distributed: in many areas, for example, the population was growing dramatically faster than the availability of arable farmland. Population pressure and the scarcity of good land led to heightened conflict and social tension. Farming communities, particularly those affected by drought, often expanded into pastureland or into unhealthy areas in a desperate attempt to produce sufficient food.[9] At the same time, urban growth was rapid, as many young Africans saw few reasons to remain in rural areas, where land was scarce and a decent living an increasingly unlikely prospect, and moved to cities. This continues at the time of writing, and it has tended to compound rural crisis, as urban migration has drawn labor away from agriculture.

Cities themselves were ill-prepared for this rapid influx of people, and in general, the pattern has been the creation of sprawling slums surrounding former colonial centers, a marked increase in unemployment, and an attendant increase in criminality, or at least the development of so-called "black economies." Lagos, Addis Ababa, Nairobi, and Dar es Salaam all provide examples of these processes.[10]

Urban growth, of course, also facilitated new forms of protest and mobilization. It is worth keeping in mind that much early anticolonial protest had been economic in origin: protesting peasants and urban workers, driven by a range of economic grievances, had been in the vanguard of political resistance from the 1920s onward. There has been, in other words, a rich tradition of political protest among the economically marginalized and oppressed through the twentieth and early twenty-first centuries. The expectations of what would be gained at independence were high, and they were not long in being disappointed. While cognizant of colonial inheritances, millions of Africans also perceived gross mismanagement, corruption, and incompetence among their governing elites, and many would come to embrace more vigorous and often violent challenges to the state. Economic grievances, as in the colonial era, fuelled insurrection: economic failure was at the root of popular unrest in a number of countries, from South Africa in the 1970s and 1980s, when industrial workers were at the forefront of anti-apartheid protest, to Tunisia in 2010–11, when a popular revolt was sparked by the self-immolation of Mohamed Bouazizi, whose desperate act resonated with a population weary of mass unemployment, inflation, and corruption.[11]

In many respects, then, Africa's economic independence was stillborn; the achievement of political sovereignty was not attended by economic sovereignty. Rather, dependency and commercial subordination characterized much of the continent's economic history in the immediate postwar period, the outcome of both crippling colonial legacies and indigenous failings. It was also the corollary of a rather longer-term set of dynamics, for in the course of the nineteenth century – and arguably even earlier – Africa was locked into an essentially extractive, even predatory, economic system of which colonial rule was a recent manifestation. Indeed, postcolonial failures led to the imposition of a new orthodoxy, for in the 1980s and 1990s African governments, under pressure from the IMF and the World Bank, were compelled to accept the necessity of wholesale economic reform. This usually took the form of so-called "SAPs" – structural adjustment programs – which involved rolling back the state and rendering extant state institutions more efficient, and loosening central controls on trade, currency, and the internal market.[12] One of the earliest examples was Ghana, where in 1983, Jerry Rawlings' military government imposed rigorous economic controls under the guidance of the IMF.[13] The impact of this restructuring, and its aftermath, is something to which we return in the final chapter.

Building the Nation (2): Polity

The various political challenges confronted by new nation states – problems of internal unity and stability, the failure of democracy and accountability, and, as examined later in more detail, the preeminence of the military in politics and governance – are closely interconnected. Again, a central theme here concerns the colonial legacy, namely the degree to which the problems faced by newly independent African states can be understood as stemming from the colonial experience. In terms of the methods of control and administration, the colonial state established patterns of local competition and domination – often through ethnicity or "tribalism," region, or religion – and precedents for unaccountability and the use or threat of force, all of which were utilized by independent governments. At the same time, the patterns and processes of decolonization also had a profound influence on the nature of the independent state that emerged in the course of the twentieth century. Thus, in territories such as Nigeria and Uganda, chronic internal problems came to the fore during the transfer of power in the 1950s and saw the opening up of huge cleavages between political elites and across society more broadly. Arguments during decolonization were as much about the balance of power and the nature of the state *after* the achievement of independence as they were about how best to achieve "national liberation." But again, there were deeper dynamics at work, and to interpret these internal strains as solely the direct product of colonial misrule is both to attribute to the "colonial moment" rather more significance than it warrants, and to neglect the formative developments of the nineteenth century. Much of the ferocious competition for control of the political space in the mid-twentieth century was a continuation of evolving struggles in the nineteenth. Rivalries between key groups in a range of territories – in Gold Coast, Nigeria, Côte d'Ivoire, Congo, Uganda, Kenya – can be dated to the nineteenth century, traced through much of the colonial period, and identified as resurgent and newly politicized in the middle decades of the twentieth. The nineteenth century had been an era of rapid, turbulent political change, as new polities coalesced and older ones reformed (and armed) themselves: this transformative process continued into the twentieth. In the 1950s and 1960s, the emergence of "Big Men" – charismatic leaders at the head of increasingly dominant and sophisticated political parties – was the perpetuation, in new formats and according to new political circumstances, of nineteenth-century political and military entrepreneurialism, of adventurers attracting people through their ability to distribute (or promise) political and material largesse. Outgoing colonial powers, whether wittingly or not, often contributed significantly to these internal tensions, conflicts, and disunities.

Clearly, then, discussions of the colonial legacy should not be reduced to the level of attributing blame for everything that has "gone wrong" in independent Africa to European rule, as this does not permit a nuanced understanding of modern Africa's peculiar challenges, as well as achievements. In the 1950s and 1960s, when "African history" was born as an academic discipline, scholars, observers, and politicians alike often attempted to condense the argument into a kind of "pros and cons" diagram for colonial rule. While some constructed academic defenses of colonialism, arguing that on balance colonial rule had done more "good" for Africa than "bad," others – somewhat more radically – sought to destroy what they saw as the myths of colonialism and to highlight the brutality, destructiveness, and racial and cultural arrogance inherent in the system.[14] In the 1970s, as the continent descended into political chaos and economic catastrophe, as the civil war, the famine, and the *coup d'état* came, for many, to define Africa itself, there were plenty of doomsayers waiting in the wings to point out how "good" colonial rule had actually been for this benighted continent, and how the thinking of the late nineteenth century – that Africans were incapable of governing themselves – had been sound after all. For many others, however, Africa's problems were attributable to the colonial legacy, and it was precisely because of colonial misrule that the continent found itself in such dire straits within a few years of independence. Clearly, balance is required, and it has never been more important than at the time of writing to assess the nature of the legacy and of patterns of governance since independence. It is indeed clear that to a considerable extent the roots of ongoing crisis can be located in the colonial era, but there is also enough evidence of corruption, willful mismanagement, and incompetence among African ruling elites to suggest that there have been serious indigenous failures. Meanwhile, patterns of dramatic change in the course of the previous century have too often come to be ignored by those seeking to apportion immediate "blame."

Above all, the lowering of colonial flags across the continent in the middle decades of the twentieth century, while in some ways marking watersheds in the modern history of Africa, did not actually represent a "break" from the past, or a "new beginning," in terms of those territories' internal histories. Rather, it is possible to discern clear continuity in terms of political power struggles, ethnic, regional, and religious tensions, and the distribution of and access to resources. Among the more fundamental political problems facing African states was the issue of the artificiality of the territories themselves. Across the continent, between the 1880s and the 1900s, artificial boundaries were created for colonies which paid no heed to precolonial statehood, society, or ethnicity. Borders sliced through communities and population groups bound together by history, culture, language, trade. By the same token, peoples were squeezed into territories created for European convenience, and these peoples were, upon independence, expected to transform mere geographical units into viable, functioning nation states on the European model, and to invest their political, economic, and intellectual energy in them. The European nation state itself, defined and redefined in its modern form between the seventeenth and the nineteenth centuries, had come into being through enormous political upheaval, violence, and revolution. Much blood had been shed between the Atlantic and the Ural Mountains before some degree of stability in national form had been achieved. Africans were expected to do the same virtually "overnight," for territories which in most cases were little more than a couple of generations old, and with little preparation, and seen in this context, the violence which has attended African political processes since independence was entirely predictable.[15]

Directly linked to this was the question of national unity, something with which we have dealt in looking at the emergence of African "nationalism" itself. While anticolonialism may have been a unifying factor prior to independence – and even this should be carefully qualified, as we have seen – the problem remained of how to create a genuine sense of "nationhood." It remained the single largest political problem for the new generation of would-be builders of nations. Half a century or so of colonial rule, and the development of somewhat more cosmopolitan urban identities, had scarcely altered the fact that, across the continent, Africans tended to be loyal to, or identify with, their ethnic group, or even a sub-group within it, their district or immediate locality, rather than the "nation." The idea of being "Nigerian," or

"Congolese" – at least in the first instance – remained distant in the 1960s. There were exceptions, of course, albeit sometimes partial. In countries with a charismatic leader at the head of a single, dominant political party, and characterized by a relative absence of "tribal" politics, such as Tanzania under Nyerere or Senegal under Senghor, some degree of genuinely "national" identity can be identified. Senegal enjoyed a unity provided by language and Islamic faith, and democracy expanded from the early 1980s (after Senghor himself had retired from public life). In North Africa, political and religious elites were able to foster modern national identities by stressing the essential historicity of their territories as well as Islamic unity, for example in Egypt. But more commonly across the continent, political parties tended to be regionally, ethnically, or religiously based, and their leaders more concerned with the promotion of sectional interests than those of the "nation" as a whole. As in other spheres, Ghana set an early precedent in this respect: by the late 1950s, a significant proportion of the electorate was voting against the CPP, particularly in the predominantly Muslim north which resented the party's centralizing ethos and the ethnic and regional imbalance within it. Such parties, while they might become nationally preeminent through the political maneuvers of the decolonization process, were unable – and often unwilling – to build broader national bases and to reach out beyond their natural constituencies. National disunity, therefore, was frequently top-down, as movements in the vanguard of political change failed to represent the wider national community. The result was ethnic and regional favoritism, with particular groups and places elevated at the expense of others, and in the emergence of pools of resentment, opposition, and frequently active hostility to the state which was perceived as having been "captured" and monopolized by a particular party. Such hostility often involved outright violence, civil conflict, or even – though this was relatively rare – provincial secession, as in Nigeria and Congo. Irredentism was even rarer, but it existed among the Somalis of Ethiopia, for example. These struggles had profound implications for the plurality of independent nation-states: the state was a prize to be fought over among competing groups, and consequently dominated by the winner to the exclusion of all others, not a neutral, apolitical entity in which all citizens had an equal and legal share.[16]

The same was also true – perhaps even more so – of territories which experienced armed struggle. Guerrilla movements were just as susceptible to ethnic or regional imbalances, and again, this had enormous implications for postwar state and society.[17] In such instances, a sense of exclusivity among war veterans and former brothers-in-arms undermined the potential for political pluralism. Victorious guerrilla leaders often felt that they and they alone had won the right – through bloodshed and sacrifice – to shape and dominate the state which had been so violently seized. Often such political intransigence was even more strident than in states which had achieved independence through peaceful, "constitutional" means; military arrogance and ideological dogma – the latter often "socialist," broadly defined – engendered a culture of political self-righteousness. This in turn bred financial corruption, ethnic chauvinism, and rampant nepotism, all of which have been in evidence in Zimbabwe, for example, and to some extent in Eritrea.

Independent governments were also supposed to inherit certain types of political system. In most territories, "foreign models" in the shape of Western-style parliamentary systems were imposed which were wholly unfamiliar to those now appointed to run them. The parliamentary model thus bestowed – based on the legislatures set up by outgoing colonial powers, and aping the House of Commons in Britain, or the National Assembly in France – was the peculiar outcome of several centuries of political and social change in Europe. It was scarcely appropriate in a continent with vast variation in terms of political history and culture; and again Africans themselves had very little experience of how such systems actually worked in practice. Colonial rule had been founded and sustained through military conquest and the subsequent use, or threat, of force, and thus in the most general sense African leaders inherited a tradition not of pluralistic, democratic, inclusive debate, but of – de facto – dictatorship, political oppression, and implicit or explicit military rule.[18] Opposition had been suppressed, or at very least carefully controlled; only in the 1940s had there been, in certain territories, the limited incorporation of an educated elite into administrative structures and the beginnings of African representation on legislative councils. In most territories – and in this sense there is a contrast to be made with British India, for example – there was neither an experienced political class nor a civil service in place to sustain parliamentary systems. Only north of the Sahara, for example in Egypt or Tunisia, had there been indigenous attempts to emulate the Western parliamentary model, dating to the nineteenth century; in sub-Saharan Africa, the only systems of similar antiquity were to be found in settler societies, such as South Africa. The colonial legacy, therefore, was one of exclusion, suppression, and hegemony in political processes.

The outcome of all these combined and interrelated problems was chronic instability. This instability often manifested itself in violent regionalism – the persecution by central government of particular provinces – or, less commonly as we have noted, in attempts at outright secession. The province of Katanga attempted to break away from Congo between 1960 and 1962; in Nigeria, the war of 1967–70 involved the secession of the Igbo province in the southeast of the country as the republic of "Biafra," and Sudan, though perhaps less clear-cut as an example, witnessed an intermittent north–south conflict between the 1950s and the 2000s.[19] The irony, indeed, was that despite the artificiality of African boundaries and of nation states themselves, and despite what appeared to be the chronic impracticality of such nations, African governments were terrified of secession and eschewed any suggestion of altering borders. In founding the OAU, the offspring of pan-Africanism in the earlier twentieth century, in 1963, member-states wrote into the charter an article emphasizing the absolute sanctity and immutability of colonial boundaries. Some leaders had very good domestic reasons for this: in Ethiopia, for example, Haile Selassie was confronted with serious provincial unrest in the north (Eritrea) and in the east (the Somalis of the Ogaden), both of which were "secessionist" in Ethiopian terms; and the emperor therefore was keen to see his own borders guaranteed by fellow heads of state.[20] More generally, it was recognized that to open up boundaries for negotiation – for example adjusting them according to notions of precolonial ethnicity – would be to invite a veritable bloodbath, and certainly a generation or more of political chaos. The OAU decided that, unsatisfactory though the colonial inheritance might be in this respect, African nations had to work with what they had been given, and that there was no other model which could possibly be employed.

African leaders, moreover, quickly came to reject multiparty parliamentary systems as unworkable in the African context. A number of Western observers came to similar conclusions, arguing that the continent was not sufficiently politically mature to maintain such a system, and that "strong leadership" – often a rather disingenuous euphemism for bloody dictatorship – was needed in the first instance to guide the continent toward stability. Botswana, with relative ethnic homogeneity and an economic stability based on diamonds, was something of an exception in that it enjoyed regular democratic elections[21]; but one-party states had become the norm by the beginning of the 1970s. It is true that these were not necessarily to be equated with absolute autocracy: there were examples of one-party states, for example Tanzania and Zambia, in which limited local democracy thrived, a healthily critical press existed, and political leaders could to some extent be held accountable. TANU in Tanzania, for example, was sufficiently broad-based and involved in the grassroots of rural society to engender a sense of both unity and participation, and certainly to prevent violent insurrection (although Zanzibar would become a thornier problem over time). Yet such cases were relatively unusual. More commonly, single-party states led to an abuse of power and the establishment of oppressive, vice-ridden, and nepotistic authoritarianisms, and to governments which could only be removed by force. In this context, as we see in more detail later, it was the army that came increasingly to intervene in politics to remove what were seen as incompetent civilian governments, at a time when African armies were perceived as pristine and driven by higher motives, beyond the grubby business of civilian politics. This was particularly true in the absence of deeply rooted civil society across the continent, namely the lack of other institutions and public bodies able to offer checks and balances against the power of politicians.

The endemic insecurity of postcolonial political systems resulted in leaders literally hoarding power, monopolizing it for kin, or for provincial or ethnic or religious buddies, intolerant of opposition, and intrinsically hostile to pluralism. "Big men," again, dominated politics, answerable to neither "the people" nor legal systems; leaders developed webs of patronages around themselves, and monopolized both legislative and executive power. The list of such rulers between the 1960s and the 1980s is a long one indeed, but would include Zaire under Mobutu, Uganda under Idi Amin, the Central African Republic under Jean-Bedel Bokassa (who renamed it the Central African Empire), Kenya under Jomo Kenyatta, and subsequently Daniel arap Moi, Ghana under Jerry Rawlings, Malawi under Hastings Banda. Many of these enjoyed foreign support of one kind or another: Idi Amin and Jean-Bedel Bokassa, for example, were, initially at least, looked on favorably as stable regimes by Britain and France, respectively. Amin was seen as an attractive alternative to the left-leaning Milton Obote, whom he overthrew in 1971.[22] In Malawi, Banda sought to apply strident Presbyterianism – in which he had been steeped while living as a medical doctor in Scotland – to all walks of social, cultural, and political life.[23] In some cases, as we have seen, ideology and sociopolitical "revolution" was used to justify political autocracy, and dictatorship for the greater good, notably in

Ethiopia, which witnessed the overthrow of the *ancien régime* of Haile Selassie in 1974 and the onset of a supposedly Marxist revolution under Mengistu Haile Mariam. Mengistu, known somewhat dubiously as the "black Stalin," presided over a reign of political terror and instigated some of the most brutal policies of social engineering on the continent; in so doing, his regime (known as the Derg, Amharic for "committee") exacerbated internal revolt, including that in Eritrea, and the effects of the worst drought in the region for a century.[24]

From the 1980s, and in particular with the end of the Cold War, there was an expansion of what can be broadly termed "people power," and the emergence of more vigorous challenges against the kind of dictatorship with which Africa had become synonymous since independence. In broad terms, people became more politically conscious and less tolerant of state-level abuses, while the autocratic states themselves were weakened by economic catastrophe and less able to exercise absolute control. It was also the case, as we will see, that armed insurgents had easier access to the modern weaponry necessary to confront political systems. Yet the situation was ambiguous, for while in some ways international political, humanitarian, and economic pressure increased on "old" authoritarianisms from the 1990s onward, many such systems proved to be both adaptable and robust. Meanwhile, key international actors (the US, the UK, France) either continued to support them, tacitly or otherwise, as providing "regional stability"; or, as in the case of China, wished merely to do business with them without any of the demands for political reform characteristic of the West's approach to African "development."

Political Stability and Islam

Throughout this book, the antiquity of Islam across Africa has been emphasized. Over several centuries, the spread of Islam – in the Maghreb, across the West African savannah, in the Nile Valley and the Horn – involved both conflict and cooperation with other spiritual systems, whether local religions and Orthodox (Coptic) Christianity, or, latterly, European and American Christianity. Muslims had long been merchants, peaceably plying both their trade and their faith along a myriad of commercial highways which linked a vast array of states and societies; in this way had Islam (outside the Ethiopian highlands, at least) been accepted gradually by royal courts, absorbed into urban environments, and, even more slowly, spread among rural populations. Yet Muslims were also leaders of violent politico-religious revolutions and builders of states, as was appropriate for those adhering to a faith in which no distinction was made between the realms of politics and spirituality. In the eighteenth and nineteenth centuries in West Africa, for example, jihad was frequently deemed necessary to bring about a revived and purified Islam and to create polities which more closely resembled Muhammad's community in Medina. In Sudan in the 1880s, as elsewhere across the Islamic world, Mahdism sought to reconstruct the pristine *umma* or Islamic community which would herald the beginning of a new global spiritual order. And from the late nineteenth century onward – in Egypt, for example – there would exist Muslim brotherhoods which

Power in the postcolonial state: President Mobutu of Zaire (Congo), 1984. Source: © AFP/Getty Images.

grappled with the dilemma of renewing Islam alongside the need to embrace the modern nation state, and which struggled to contain or influence secularizing government. In this sense, there was a long history of Muslims being both part of the state apparatus, and railing against that apparatus once it was seen to have failed or drifted away from the righteous path.

These patterns continued into the postcolonial era. Debates, and sometimes violent confrontation, centered on the application of Islam and its role in government have persisted within independent states since the 1950s and 1960s. Strident Islamism has generally been less common in sub-Saharan Africa – the precolonial history of jihad in certain areas notwithstanding – than in the north, however. In sub-Saharan Africa, Islamists in the postcolonial era have been concerned with the rights of Muslims in countries in which populations are more or less evenly split between Muslim and

Christian. An example of this is Nigeria, where *shari'a* law is applied in the north, but where more broadly, the postcolonial political arena has often been dominated by debates about the access to power and resources enjoyed by Muslims and Christians, respectively. It is also the case that Islam in sub-Saharan Africa has generally remained highly localized, with Islam itself adapted to local circumstances, and Muslim communities concerned with local issues and identities. Traditional sufism also predominates across West and East Africa, and sufi orders – eclectic, unorthodox, influenced by local practices and norms – were so often identified as the enemy of those seeking the restoration of "pure," orthodox Islam. There are also ethnic divisions between Muslims across sub-Saharan Africa, and these cleavages have so far militated against the growth of a militant pan-Islamic identity down to the present-day, although we return to this in the final chapter.

This said, in other territories, where Muslims are a minority, they have been able to organize themselves into effective political lobbyists and even political parties, fighting against what they have seen as Christian or moderate Islamic domination of government. This was perhaps most dramatically demonstrated in Kenya, where something like 10 percent of the population is Muslim. Here, with relative political liberalization in the early 1990s, Muslims in the north and in the coastal areas organized themselves around the common grievance that they had been economically marginalized under KANU, and that other groups (largely non-Muslim) had benefited at their expense.[25] Politicized Islamic opposition of a similar kind emerged in Tanzania, also around the issue of economic exclusion.[26] Yet here, notwithstanding the (largely political) tension surrounding the status and rights of Zanzibar, where the vast majority of the population is Muslim, Tanzania continues to enjoy relative religious harmony, in some respects the legacy of solidarity bequeathed by Julius Nyerere.

The confrontation between state and faith was rather sharper across parts of West Africa, where Muslim opposition was often mobilized in response to government repression. Similarly, in North Africa, the push for the application of *shari'a* law and a demand for the restoration of orthodox Islam – as well as a concomitant refusal to countenance a separation between politics and religion – often brought Islamist groups into conflict with governments which adopted a more secular or moderate line. While in Morocco and Tunisia, for example, Islamists generally accepted electoral means by which to fight their political and spiritual battles, in Egypt and Algeria there were Islamist groups which advocated violent struggle in order to bring about change. In Morocco, King Hassan II, who through the 1970s and 1980s ruled with a heavy hand and enjoyed a certain friendship with Washington, found his authority repeatedly challenged by Islamists who argued that monarchy had no place in Islam. Nonetheless, Hassan was widely regarded by the West – and by Israel – as a steadying influence in a country otherwise prone to extremist-induced anarchy.[27] In Tunisia, while the modernizing and largely secular President Bourguiba permitted the Palestine Liberation Organisation a base from the early 1980s, he sought to suppress Islamic activism inside his own borders, and attempted to steer a course which incorporated both Islamic and European traditions. He remained in power for more than thirty years before being displaced by an army coup in 1988.[28] Despite the upheaval of 2011, when a popular uprising overthrew the Ben Ali regime and sparked the so-called "Arab spring" across North Africa and the Middle East, Tunisia has generally managed to contain Islamism, notwithstanding the terrorist incidents which have become a serious challenge almost everywhere in the region.

In Egypt, however, radical Islamists have long posed a more sustained threat, for they saw as an affront the secularizing, mixed-economy policies of Nasser's successors, Anwar Sadat and Hosni Mubarak. It was in part Sadat's conclusion of a peace accord with Israel which prompted Egypt's expulsion from the Arab League, and his assassination in 1981 at the hands of Islamists in the army. Subsequently, Mubarak was confronted with a rising threat from the Muslim Brotherhood which abhorred his liberalism, encouragement of secularism, and attempts to control spiraling birth rates. Moreover, the movement considered Mubarak's regime rather too democratic, a label which might be disputed by some of his political opponents. Acts of violence on the part of Islamists have proliferated since the 1980s. With Mubarak's overthrow in early 2011 came a renewed opportunity for members of the Muslim Brotherhood, as well as a range of Islamic activists and scholars, to become involved in the constitution-making process in particular, and in the remaking of Egypt more generally. Mohamed Morsi, with the support of the Muslim Brotherhood, served briefly as president in the immediate aftermath of the 2011 uprising, but concerns in some quarters about his vision for Egypt as an Islamic democracy, and popular protests against the influence of the Muslim Brotherhood, led to his removal from office by military coup d'etat in July 2013. Since then, General Abdel Fattah el-Sisi has run the country in an increasingly authoritarian manner.[29] Meanwhile in Algeria, the Islamic Salvation Front – inspired by the Muslim Brotherhood in Egypt and indeed with offices and contacts in Cairo – came to challenge the moderate regime of the FLN, leading to the eruption of bloody civil war in the early 1990s. The death toll in that decade was high, and only Abdelaziz Bouteflika's emergence with army backing in 1999 promised an end to the violence.[30]

Under Colonel Muammar Qaddafi, who overthrew the aging, pro-Western Sanusi monarch King Idris in 1969, Libya represented a remarkable social, political, and religious experiment. The success of the project was always debatable, but Qaddafi's political genius has rarely been in doubt. He used Islam as a unifying force for the Libyan people, but sought to combine religious fervor with strident nationalism as a means of rejecting the failed ideologies of both East and West. In that sense at least he owed much to his neighbor Nasser, but he went on to develop a redistributive socialism that abhorred atheism and was rooted in the Quran itself. Qaddafi used so-called "Quranic socialism" to curtail severely the power of old elites, but the "revolution" – administered by inefficient committees responsible for absolute centralized control – was a disaster, bringing the Libyan economy to its knees by the end of the 1980s. Capable of reinvention, Qaddafi abandoned it and restored a measure of private enterprise, tempered by considerable political authoritarianism. Oil revenue helped in the country's recovery, too. Demonized in the West, and by the United States in particular, Qaddafi harbored something of an obsession with Arab unity, and he pursued various forms of union with Egypt, Tunisia, and Sudan, for example, without success. He reinvented himself again, however, as a pan-Africanist of sorts, and in the 1990s became rather more involved in affairs south of the Sahara. Yet greater challenges – from among his own long-suffering population – lay ahead for the charismatic Libyan "brother leader," as he styled himself. A bloody uprising that began in eastern Libya in early 2011 eventually overwhelmed the hollowed-out state, and Qaddafi himself met an ignominious and brutal end. Since then, Libya has scarcely functioned as a unified state, and a civil war between Islamist and more moderate groups continues to rage over the future of a country which will long struggle with Qaddafi's legacy.[31]

In Sudan, on the other hand, the north–south divide was exacerbated by the existence of an aggressive, Arabizing Islam in the north which has attempted to impose itself on the south, with disastrous consequences; here, civil war raged from 1955 until 1972, and it erupted once again in 1983. The struggle intensified in the wake of the National Islamic Front's seizure of power in Khartoum in 1989, and by the time the bitter civil war had ended in 2002 some 1.5 million people were estimated to have died.[32] A similar north–south cleavage in neighboring Chad – Christians in the south, Arabs and Muslims in the north – led to a devastating civil war there between the mid-1960s and the mid-1980s. Tensions between these two demographic and religious blocs erupted once more into open civil war between 2005 and 2010, when incumbent President Idriss Deby was aided in part by French support and in part by the disorganization of the rebels ranged against him.[33] Sudanese Islamism attracted the unwelcome attention of the United States, which saw the Sudan of President Bashir as a destabilizing influence on the region and an exporter of terrorism. But such Islamism has also been eyed nervously by a number of states within the region, not least Ethiopia and Eritrea, both of which, governed by Christians both before and after the revolutionary shifts of the early 1990s, had their own reasons to be concerned about sizable Muslim populations. But while Christian and Muslim have often achieved peaceful coexistence in both countries, tensions are rarely far from the surface, and there are histories of conflict in the religious arena. In Eritrea, for example it was the Muslim population of the western lowlands that dominated the struggle for liberation in its early years, in the form of the Eritrean Liberation Front (ELF), and which looked to the Arab world – emulating the FLN in Algeria to some extent – for succor. In later years, the largely Christian Eritrean People's Liberation Front (EPLF) commandeered the nationalist struggle, following a civil war which saw the ousting of the ELF from the field of combat.[34] At first the aggressively secular EPLF succeeded in maintaining a largely harmonious relationship between Christian and Muslim in Eritrea, but in recent years, tensions have unquestionably increased, mostly around indefinite national service and the brutal intrusion of the state into Muslim life. In Ethiopia, similarly, there have been clashes between Muslims and security forces in recent years.[35]

The early decades of the twenty-first century have witnessed new, or resurgent, strains of radical Islam in the Horn and across West Africa. Somalia witnessed the rise of al-Shabaab, an Islamist insurgency implacably opposed to the UN-backed consensus on the administration of that war-wracked state.[36] The collapse of Qaddafi's regime in Libya gave new impetus to Islamist movements across the Sahel: in the case of Mali, for example Tuareg mercenaries who had been fighting for Qaddafi returned, heavily armed, to lend their firepower to an Islamist rebellion in northern Mali in 2012. Their advances were halted following French military intervention, but the challenge persists. And it does in Nigeria, too, where the movement known as Boko Haram has terrorized the north with what seems at times like impunity for a number of years.[37] These kinds of movements proliferate, and whether motivated by true belief or mobilized by the dispossessed and the marginalized as a means to restitution, they represent a violent and growing challenge to the political order.

Crowded House: Africa and the Cold War

Processes of decolonization, and many of the political and economic developments across the continent during the first decades of independence, must be understood against the background of an international order defined by the Cold War. We need to step back for a moment and examine Africa in this broader global context, and the ways in which the politics and conflicts of the Cold War affected, and were represented in, the continent. In this sense, Africa shares with certain other parts of the non-European world – Southeast Asia and Central America foremost among them – the experience of being the location of many a "proxy conflict" between the superpowers. Africa was a Cold War "periphery" which nonetheless witnessed the opening of a number of ideological and strategic frontlines; it became the focus of attention for both US and Soviet global strategists, and African governments and political movements alike sought to utilize Cold War rivalries, and themselves became the victims of such rivalry.[38]

In some respects, Africa had caught the attention of revolutionary Marxists long before the Cold War "proper"; Lenin, after all, had regarded imperialism as the "highest stage" of capitalism, and also its weakest link in that it was colonialism which would engender a death struggle between the capitalist-imperialist nations, culminating in their mutual destruction. Thus, through the early activities of the Comintern in the 1920s, the young Soviet Union had encouraged non-European Marxist revolutionary movements as a means to bringing about global revolution, though its attention was drawn more to Asia than to Africa at this stage. Under Stalin, however, Soviet foreign policy became rather more isolationist, and Stalin himself largely ignored the Comintern; the tendency to overlook the potential of communist-inspired *anti-colonial* protest and, later, nationalism remained characteristic of Soviet policy until Stalin's death in 1953. This was true despite the fact that the USSR espoused anti-imperialism, and claimed to support the rights of oppressed colonial peoples to national self-determination. While at the very least the Soviet Union represented, to emergent African protest movements, an alternative ideological reference point to Western Europe, in fact communism had only a very limited impact on African politics much before the late 1940s. South of the Sahara, only in South Africa, which had one of the continent's earliest communist parties, thriving in the interwar years, and to a lesser degree in the urban mining areas of southern-central Africa, did communist ideas have much influence. They also had some impact in northern Africa, for example in Egypt in the 1920s.[39] From the mid-1950s onward, however, the Soviet Union, first under Nikita Khruschev and thereafter under Leonid Brezhnev, became much more active in the African continent – as it also did in

Asia and Latin America – in terms of promoting, encouraging, and sometimes lending material assistance to communist or leftist movements. Physical intervention became increasingly common through the 1960s and 1970s. The United States, as well as former colonial powers, would respond in kind.

The Cold War had an impact on Africa in a variety of ways. First, and somewhat ironically, the Cold War in its early stages actually provided a justification for the strengthening and retention of African empires, rather than their dissolution – ironic, that is, in view of the US's stated antipathy to European colonialism, and in view of the supposed revolutionary anti-imperialism of the world's new superpower, the Soviet Union. In the new world order after 1945, Britain, for example – with American support, tacit or otherwise – portrayed the empire as a global bulwark against the spread of communism; a strong, ideologically friendly imperial bloc was the best defense against Soviet expansionism, argued the British government, and hasty decolonization would expose swathes of the globe to the Soviet threat. By the same token, Britain's reinvigorated interest in its African colonies after 1945 – the "second colonial occupation" – involved the investment of funds which were presented, on one level, in much the same way as was the Marshall Plan in Western Europe. These were aimed at the stabilization of colonies in order to protect Africans from the predations of communism, which was, it was believed, the product of poverty and misery.

At the same time, however, African nationalist leaders quickly became conscious of the political ramifications of the Cold War and of the tactical and strategic opportunities presented by the East–West struggle. Some leaders were genuinely drawn, in the course of the 1950s, to the opportunities offered by communist ideology for mass mobilization and revolutionary political action, and naturally leaned to the Left in building nationalist movements. Others cleverly used the language of popular revolution to evoke the omnipresent threat of mass violence. In the Gold Coast, for example Kwame Nkrumah combined the two. He found inspiration in leftist ideology, but was also conscious of the impracticality of "mass revolution"; nonetheless, this did not prevent him from employing the language of the Left with a view to popular mobilization, and he did so convincingly enough to be branded a dangerous radical by the British. As leader of independent Ghana, Nkrumah demonstrated a willingness to remain "close" to Britain, joining the Commonwealth, but he also cultivated relations with the Soviet Union, from whom he received material aid in the late 1950s. In the same period, following the complex negotiations between France and its sub-Saharan colonies regarding decolonization, Guinea chose outright independence, and only survived through the timely arrival of Soviet support, the French having attempted to humble its former territory by withdrawing all assistance.[40]

It was perhaps in North Africa, however, that the Soviet Union first made its presence felt to considerable effect. Moscow offered patronage and material assistance to such nationalist figures as Ahmed Ben Bella, prominent organizer for the FLN outside Algeria until his capture, and Gamal Abdel Nasser in Egypt. For a generation of African nationalists, the Algerian war was a rallying point, and for many a source of alienation from the West. Soviet support for the FLN apparently emphasized a great gulf between West and East in their respective attitudes toward the cause of self-determination across

Africa. The Soviet Union was also swift to support Nasser's nationalization of the Suez Canal, and condemn the Anglo-French action at Suez in 1956 – never mind that the United States was equally indignant at the high-handed imperialism of London and Paris. The "friendship" between Nasser and Khruschev was never more than skin-deep, the former having no significant leanings toward socialism – and indeed Nasser's successor, Anwar Sadat, would later expel Soviet military advisors – but they shared much in the way of anti-imperialist and more specifically anti-Western rhetoric.[41] As in the case of Algeria, Moscow appeared so much more sympathetic toward African nationalism than any government in the West.

There were also independent governments which espoused and attempted to implement what can broadly be termed "African socialism," involving a rejection of both Western finance and Western values in terms of social, economic, and political development. "Socialism," indeed, was held to be organically African, based on a romanticized notion of certain cultural values, notably the supposed communalism of some ill-defined past era. In Tanzania in the 1960s and 1970s, Nyerere pursued "villagization" as a means to socialist self-sufficiency, with largely disastrous results; at the same time, however, he also cultivated a friendship with the Chinese, who funded the building of a railway linking Tanzania and Zambia. In Ethiopia, under the Marxist military dictatorship of Mengistu Haile Mariam from the mid-1970s, foreign policy veered away from the United States – for a long time its natural ally – and toward the Soviet Union, while at the same time pushing through an aggressive socialist program which involved,

New alliances: Kwame Nkrumah of Ghana and Gamal Abdul Nasser of Egypt. Source: Stan Wayman/Time and Life Pictures/Getty Images.

among other things, the relocation of entire communities.[42] These were leaders who sought, to greater or lesser degrees, foreign assistance and support via particular ideological standpoints. By the same token, there were others who allied themselves firmly with the West, and who assiduously cultivated the support of the British, the Americans, the French; the latter, in turn, were prepared to turn so many blind eyes to human rights abuses, however flagrant, in exchange for economic concessions and military bases. In Zaire, Mobutu Sese Seko, despite presiding over chronic corruption and mismanagement, received Western support from the mid-1960s through to the early 1990s; Kenya, likewise, remained a firm British ally throughout the Cold War, despite its authoritarianism and institutionalized vice.[43]

The Cold War also made itself felt in civil conflicts and armed struggles across the continent. Immediately after the Second World War, the British and French had depicted their empires as necessary bulwarks against communist infiltration. From the mid-1950s, however, with decolonization under way, the Soviet Union began to take a much greater interest in the continent, perceiving it as a useful "second front." From the 1960s, both the United States and its allies on the one hand, and the USSR and its European satellites, or China, on the other, became actively involved in a number of conflicts. Indeed, there was scarcely a war on the continent which was not in one way or another bound up in the politics of the Cold War, especially once President Kennedy had launched his strategy of counterinsurgency in "Third World" conflicts in the early 1960s. The withdrawal of Belgium from Congo, for example, led to internal anarchy, and a number of powers became involved. The CIA took an active part in the elevation of Mobutu as the archetypal pro-Western strongman, creating a superpower rivalry across central Africa that took on a particular urgency following the global energy crisis

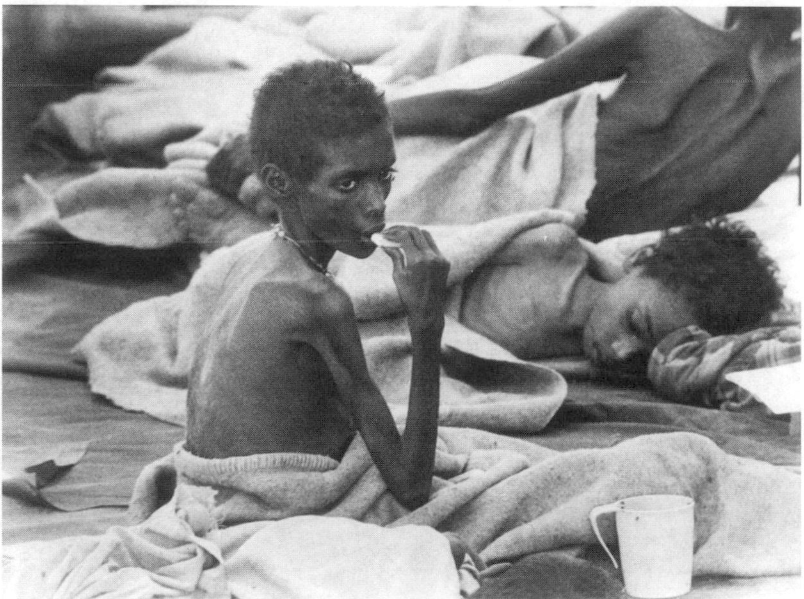

Victims: famine in northern Ethiopia, mid-1980s. Source: Finn Frandsen/AFP/Getty Images.

in 1973. Congo/Zaire offered considerable rewards in terms of its natural resources.[44] Likewise, Angola and Mozambique witnessed the emergence of rival guerrilla movements backed by one external power or other; South Africa, regarding itself as the region's superpower, also became involved in these conflicts, largely because it was directly affected by events in the Portuguese empire. The South Africans were notoriously cagey about their global alignment, but they received much of their military hardware from the West and did broadly adopt an anti-communist stance, particularly when it came to the leftist leanings of the ANC.[45] Guerrilla and rebel movements across Africa were frequently drawn to socialist programs, whether genuinely motivated by the principles involved, or attracted by the military support on offer through alignment with Moscow. It is also the case that socialism – at least as interpreted by armed ideologues – facilitated greater degrees of political control within movements and among wider populations than might otherwise have been the case. More generally, Cold War intervention prolonged, intensified, and in many cases further complicated internal conflicts.

A snapshot of Africa in the early 1970s reveals a continent broadly split between the two global camps, notwithstanding the periodic efforts by some governments to develop a "nonaligned" movement with a number of Asian states, while some states had a foot in both camps. The United States had security assistance agreements with Kenya, Zaire, Ghana, Liberia, and Senegal; it also had a long-running military relationship with Ethiopia until the mid-1970s. Britain had military missions in several West African countries, and training and supply agreements with most of its former colonies, Tanzania excepted. France likewise had defense and cooperation pacts with the Central African Republic, Gabon, Niger, Burkina Faso (Upper Volta in the early 1970s), Côte d'Ivoire, Senegal, Cameroon, and Djibouti. The Soviet Union gave assistance to Guinea, Mali, Nigeria, and Uganda, and by the end of the 1970s, Moscow also had "treaties of friendship," which involved the provision of military assistance, with newly Marxist Ethiopia, Angola, and Mozambique. China had military aid arrangements with Cameroon, Guinea, Mali, and Tanzania; Cuba had similar military agreements with Congo-Brazzaville, Guinea, Angola, Mozambique, and Ethiopia. Much of this amounted to an intense arms race, with a range of weaponry being channeled directly or indirectly to favored governments.[46]

Overall, the Cold War blinded external powers to the problems confronted by nascent African nation states. The exigencies of global strategic and ideological competition meant that authoritarianism, and in many cases brutal and bloody dictatorship, was not merely accepted as a fact of African political life but even encouraged – by both blocs – and actively supported through an array of aid and assistance. The political retardation of African states suited the requirements of foreign powers between the end of the 1950s and the beginning of the1990s, and many of the political and humanitarian disasters of the era were at the very least indirectly exacerbated by foreign intervention. Nonetheless, a situation which is open to abuse still requires people to abuse it, and the Cold War enabled a number of African leaders to exploit foreign support for their own ends, cultivating it assiduously in order to buoy up bankrupt regimes and using it in the suppression of domestic opposition. A handful of governments borrowed the language of Marxist revolution and implemented programs of social and economic change which were as much, if not more, about the achievement of total political control as about "solving problems." Likewise, guerrilla movements, with varying degrees of sincerity, utilized socialist rhetoric to mobilize populations and wage "people's wars." At any rate, the end of the Cold War in 1989–90 resulted in the withdrawal of foreign support from regimes that had long been discredited in the eyes of their own citizens. Yet the degree to which the Cold War can be seen as having somehow "hijacked" or otherwise distorted Africa's own paths of political and economic development, and fanned the flames of conflict where such conflict would otherwise have been avoided or resolved, depends to some extent on our assessment of developments across the continent over the last three decades.

Notes

1 R.H. Bates, *Markets and States in Tropical Africa: The Political Basis of Agricultural Policies* (Berkeley CA, 2005; 1st ed., 1981).

2 I. Roxborough, *Theories of Underdevelopment* (London, 1979); D.K. Fieldhouse, *Black Africa 1945-1980: Economic Decolonisation and Arrested Development* (London, 1986); G. Kitching, *Development and Underdevelopment in Historical Perspective: Populism, Nationalism, and Industrialisation* (London, 1989).

3 Fieldhouse, *The West and the Third World*, 289–98.

4 Stephan F. Miescher, "Nkrumah's Baby: the Akosombo Dam and the Dream of Development in Ghana, 1952-1966," *Water History*, 6:4 (2014).

5 Trevor W. Parfitt & Stephen P. Riley, *The African Debt Crisis* (London & New York, 1989).

6 Nkrumah, *Neo-Colonialism*; Alex Thomson, *An Introduction to African Politics* (New York, 2000), 179–81.

7 Julius K. Nyerere, *'Ujamaa': The Basis of African Socialism* (Dar es Salaam, 1962); A. Coulson (ed.), *African Socialism in Practice: The Tanzanian Experience* (Nottingham, 1979).

8 See for example Michael Mortimore, *Adapting to Drought: Farmers, Famines and Desertification in West Africa* (Cambridge, 1989).

9 The classic study is Ester Boserup, *The Conditions of Agricultural Growth: The Economics of Agrarian Change under Population Pressure* (London, 1965).

10 Bill Freund, *The African City: A History* (Cambridge & New York, 2007), chap. 5.

11 Robert F. Worth, "How a single match can ignite a revolution," *New York Times*, 21 January 2011.

12 Christopher Clapham, *Africa and the International System: The Politics of State Survival* (Cambridge, 1996), 169–81.

13 Kwadwo Konadu-Agyemang, "The Best of Times and the Worst of Times: Structural Adjustment Programs and Uneven Development in Africa: the case of Ghana," *The Professional Geographer*, 52:3 (2000).

14 Dane Kennedy, *The Imperial History Wars: Debating the British Empire* (London, 2018) provides some fascinating context.

15 Davidson, *The Black Man's Burden*.

16 Hodgkin, *Nationalism in Colonial Africa*; J.-F. Bayart, *The State in Africa* (London, 1993); Coleman, *Nationalism and Development in Africa*; Clapham, *Africa and the International System*, passim. For more recent studies of nation and citizenship, see for example James R. Brennan,

Taifa: Making Nation and Race in Urban Tanzania (Athens OH, 2012); and Emma Hunter (ed.), *Citizenship, Belonging, and Political Community in Africa: Dialogues between Past and Present* (Athens OH, 2016). For the North African context, see J.P. Entelis (ed.), *Islam, Democracy and the State in North Africa* (Bloomington IN, 1997).

17 Clapham (ed.), *African Guerrillas*.

18 Mamdani, *Citizen and Subject*.

19 P. Anber, "Modernisation and disintegration: Nigeria and the Ibos," *Journal of Modern African Studies*, 5:2 (1967); Frederick Forsyth, *The Making of an African Legend: The Biafra Story* (London, 1977); Michael Gould, *The Biafran War: The Struggle for Modern Nigeria* (London, 2013); Douglas Johnson, *The Root Causes of Sudan's Civil Wars* (Oxford, 2003).

20 John H. Spencer, *Ethiopia at Bay: A Personal Account of the Haile Selassie Years* (Algonac MI, 1984), 307–8.

21 Patrick P. Molutsi & John D. Holm, "Developing Democracy When Civil Society is Weak: the case of Botswana," *African Affairs*, 89:356 (1990).

22 Henry Kyemba, *State of Blood: The Inside Story of Idi Amin's Reign of Fear* (London, 1977), 238.

23 McCracken, *History of Malawi*, chap. 16.

24 Andargachew Tiruneh, *The Ethiopian Revolution, 1974-1987: A Transformation from an Aristocratic to a Totalitarian Autocracy* (Cambridge, 1993); C. Clapham, *Transformation and Continuity in Revolutionary Ethiopia* (Cambridge, 1988).

25 Donal B. Cruise O'Brien, "Coping with the Christians: the Muslim predicament in Kenya," in Holger Bernt Hansen & Michael Twaddle (eds.), *Religion and Politics in East Africa: The Period Since Independence* (Oxford, 1995).

26 Bruce E. Heilman & Paul J. Kaiser, "Religion, identity and politics in Tanzania," *Third World Quarterly*, 23:4 (2002).

27 Miller, *History of Modern Morocco*, chap. 7.

28 Perkins, *History of Modern Tunisia*, chaps. 5 & 6.

29 Neil Ketchley, *Egypt in a Time of Revolution: Contentious Politics and the Arab Spring* (Cambridge, 2017).

30 International Crisis Group, *Islamism, Violence, and Reform in Algeria: Turning the Page*, Report No. 29, 30 July 2004.

31 See Qaddafi's own political musings – often bizarre – in *The Green Book* (London, 1976). Also Ulf Laessing, *Understanding Libya since Gaddafi* (London, 2018).

32 Johnson, *Root Causes*; for an accessible overview, see Robert O. Collins, *A History of Modern Sudan* (Cambridge, 2008).

33 International Crisis Group, *Chad: Powder Keg in the East*. Report No. 149, 15 April 2009.

34 Gaim Kibreab, *Critical Reflections on the Eritrean War of Independence: Social Capital, Associational Life, Religion, Ethnicity, and Sowing Seeds of Dictatorship* (Trenton NJ, 2008).

35 International Crisis Group, *Ethiopia: Governing the Faithful*, Briefing No. 117, 22 February 2016.

36 Stig Jarle Hansen, *Al-Shabaab in Somalia: The History and Ideology of a Militant Islamist Group, 2005-2012* (Oxford, 2013); see also Alex de Waal (ed.), *Islamism and its Enemies in the Horn of Africa* (London, 2004).

37 Alexander Thurston, *Boko Haram: The History of an African Jihadist Movement* (Princeton & Oxford, 2018).

38 J. Mayall, *Africa: the Cold War and After* (London, 1971); A. Gavshon, *Crisis in Africa: Battleground of East and West* (London, 1981); B.D. Porter, *The USSR in Third World Conflicts: Soviet Arms and Diplomacy in Local Wars, 1945-1980* (Cambridge, 1984); Z. Laidi,

The Superpowers and Africa: the constraints of a rivalry, 1960-1990 (Chicago, 1990); P.J. Schraeder, *United States Foreign Policy Toward Africa: Incrementalism, Crisis, and Change* (Cambridge, 1994); Elizabeth Schmidt, *Foreign Intervention in Africa: From the Cold War to the War on Terror* (Cambridge, 2013).

39 See for example Irina Filatova & Apollon Davidson, *The Hidden Thread: Russia and South Africa in the Soviet Era* (Roggebaai, 2013), esp. chap. 4.

40 Mairi MacDonald, "A vocation for independence: Guinean nationalism in the 1950s," in Tony Chafer & Alexander Keese (eds.), *Francophone Africa at Fifty* (Manchester, 2013).

41 Karen Dawisha, *Soviet Foreign Policy Towards Egypt* (London & Basingstoke, 1979), chap. 2.

42 Martin Bailey, "Tanzania and China," *African Affairs*, 74:294 (1975); M. Ottaway & D. Ottaway, *Afrocommunism* (New York, 1986); M. Ottaway, *Soviet and American Influence in the Horn of Africa* (New York, 1982).

43 Gavshon, *Crisis in Africa*, 174; Samuel M. Makinda, "From quiet diplomacy to Cold War politics: Kenya's foreign policy," *Third World Quarterly*, 5:2 (1983).

44 Gavshon, *Crisis in Africa*, 180.

45 See for example John Daniel, "Racism, the Cold War and South Africa's regional security strategies, 1948-1990," in Sue Onslow (ed.), *Cold War in Southern Africa: White Power, Black Liberation* (Abingdon, 2009).

46 Schmidt, *Foreign Intervention*, and Gavshon, *Crisis in Africa*, both passim.

18 Violence and the Militarization of Political Culture

The Military in African Politics

Political instability and economic fragility facilitated military intervention across much of Africa within a few years of independence. One of the most striking features of postcolonial Africa's trajectory has been the proliferation of violent conflict, and what can be termed the militarization – and the "securitization" – of political culture. In many respects, this was indeed the outcome of a particular set of postcolonial dynamics, but it needs to be reiterated here that the process had deep roots and can be traced to the violent upheaval of the nineteenth century, when warfare became increasingly significant as an extension of political and economic strategy, and as states and societies – both old and new – became increasingly militarized. In certain ways, the colonial period involved the *demilitarization* of African polity and society – most obviously, in the sense that Africans could not bear arms beyond that in the service of the colonial state. But this was a temporary arrangement, and involved the creation of internal pressures that would come to the surface during, and after, processes of decolonization. Indeed, the enduring legacies of colonialism in this context are the perception of Africa's supposedly "tribal" violence as fundamentally illegitimate, and as an expression of the continent's innate savagery. This is an idea that can also be traced to the nineteenth century, and the establishment of new territorial parameters – what has been termed the "curse of the nation state" – within which heightened conflict might unfold. Some of the conflict which appeared in the middle decades of the twentieth century can be seen as a continuation of nineteenth-century war; some of it is more clearly the specific corollary of colonial conditions, notably in terms of particularly recalcitrant regimes that resisted meaningful decolonization, as in Lusophone Africa, or in the white settler states. In

A History of Modern Africa: 1800 to the Present, Third Edition. Richard J. Reid.

other scenarios, army officers quickly became involved in politics, and government came to be in the hands of the military – and indeed, later, of guerrilla forces. But each of these dimensions needs to be understood as part of an ongoing, long-term process of militarization in African political culture across the two centuries covered in this book.

In considering the failure of democracy in Africa – and assuming for the moment that that political concept has universal applicability – political scientists and other observers tended to point toward the absence of those institutions and behaviors that constitute civil society, for example the separation of legislative and executive bodies, and of party and state; an impartial civil service and apolitical bureaucracy; and an independent judiciary.[1] Retreating colonial authorities often tried to create civil society, but it was all too superficial, and much too late, and it was certainly not supported by two crucial props, namely African faith and African experience. However, the one stable and genuinely apolitical institution appeared to be the army, which quickly came to fill the vacuum left by failing civilian elites. By the early 1970s, a remarkable number of African states had succumbed to military rule, and the intervention of the army had become a defining characteristic of African politics. The military *coup d'état*, of course, is by no means unique to Africa, and indeed, it has perhaps been more closely associated with Latin America; nor is it unknown in modern European history. But over the last half-century or more, Africa has become noted for its politicized military. There have been more than seventy successful military seizures of power since 1957, the year of Ghana's independence, and many other attempts that have been thwarted. Some countries were more vulnerable than others, owing to a particularly powerful and ambitious military establishment, particularly deep ethnic or regional fissures, and an especially undeveloped culture of participatory politics: West Africa, for example has a remarkable record, particularly Nigeria, Ghana, Sierra Leone, and the republic of Dahomey (modern-day Benin). In the 1960s, Dahomey suffered four different coups, and between 1963 and 1969 had twelve governments and six constitutions. The *coup d'état* that perhaps reverberated most loudly around the world was that in Ghana, in 1966, which removed Kwame Nkrumah, one of the fathers of African nationalism and a continental icon. At the time of writing, only a handful of Africa's fifty-four nations has not had their governments overthrown at some point by the army, among them Tanzania and Kenya – and even Kenya experienced an attempted army takeover in 1982. More recent examples of those to succumb are Côte d'Ivoire – particularly noteworthy as the country had enjoyed several decades of relatively stable civilian government – Togo, Niger, Guinea, Mauritania, Zimbabwe and Sudan.[2]

Three broad themes need to be outlined in relation to the historical role of the military in Africa. First, it is important to remind ourselves of the importance of armies and militarism in nineteenth-century state and society. In Western Europe, over time, the army had come to be seen as essentially apolitical, professional (to varying degrees), and wholly removed from the business of policy-making and government, but in most precolonial African societies, the military and politics were closely intertwined, even indistinguishable. Political leaders were very often soldiers, or needed to be perceived as such, even if it was not actually true; politics and command of armies went hand-in-hand, and successful rulers often had to have proved themselves in battle, or have had faithful lieutenants develop stories about their heroism and valor. The nineteenth century witnessed the increasing professionalization of African armies, one of the central features of the continent's military transformation: witness the regiments created in Bunyoro and Buganda, Yoruba "war boys," and Ethiopia's expanding military apparatus, as well as the age-based regimentation evident among the Zulu, or the Maasai, or certain branches of Oromo. Otherwise, in most African societies, armies were more akin to part-time militias, called up according to circumstances, but the key point is that in both scenarios, armies were often "private" rather than "public" forces in so far as they followed particular local leaders, clan heads, or wealthy individuals. The notion of an army standing above politics, existing only for the protection of "the state," was largely alien, and the colonial experience of a professional, separate military structure was wholly novel for most Africans – even though, as we see below, colonial armies paradoxically *were* the means to internal control, and thus had the potential to become rapidly politicized. In any case, such colonial professionalism was swiftly subverted and co-opted into emerging African military forms: in other words, there was already a long tradition of military involvement in politics in Africa dating back at least to the nineteenth century. For our purposes, this was particularly clear in the second half of the nineteenth century, when control of or access to firearms was increasingly important in shaping centers of political power, and the very nature of that power. This situation would be mirrored, to some extent, in the later twentieth century, when governments found themselves struggling against the power of those with access to guns.

The other two themes relate to the cultures and ethos engendered in the army through the colonial experience. The armies that existed in African states upon independence had developed directly out of colonial forces, and thus had their roots in the armies of conquest used from the 1890s and early 1900s onward. They, therefore, had histories of conquest of, and control over, Africans themselves, and this military element had of course been one of the pillars of the colonial state itself. Further, and directly related to this, African armies had a history of internal or domestic usage and were generally employed for internal control only; with the notable exception of the two world wars, these armies had not been concerned with "external" affairs, such as territorial defense, for example and this meant that African soldiers were much more predisposed to intervention in politics. This said, it remains broadly true – ironically, given the history described above – that upon independence African armies were indeed regarded as professional, detached, disciplined; many retained European officers through the 1960s, in advisory and training capacities during transitional periods. Through the 1960s and 1970s, as armies moved with increasing frequency against what were perceived as inefficient and corrupt civilian regimes, military coups were often welcomed, at least initially. Armies, building on existing reputations for professionalism, projected themselves as guardians of state and citizenry, free of corruption and unsullied by politics. In fact, the culture of the coup constituted a *reassertion* of African military power at the heart of these new polities.

Be that as it may, military commanders were seen as saviors, salvaging order from political chaos, and providing the "strong leadership" so critical to fragile and explosive states. During 1964 and 1965 in Congo, for example, General Mobutu was hailed as a hero by many as he restored the power of central government against a backdrop of ethnic violence and rebellion. Indeed, his achievements were all the greater, considering that a couple of years earlier the army itself had split into several rival components. Between 1967 and 1970, it was the Nigerian army under General Gowon that held the country together in the face of the Biafra revolt, itself led by a group of Igbo army officers. Nigeria remained under military rule until 1979 as the army steadied the ship of state and prepared for the transition back to civilian rule; this was short-lived, however, with the next civilian phase characterized by rampant corruption. The army was back in charge again in 1983. In Nigeria, as in Ghana, which also experienced military interventions in the 1960s and 1970s, coups offered much-needed relief from grasping civilian politicians, and army officers often appeared rather more determined to tackle basic economic and social problems. In Ghana, there was a popularly held belief that army rule – in this case under Flight Lt. Jerry Rawlings – was only needed to prepare the way for a return to more stable and pluralistic civilian government.[3]

Generally, however, it did not take long for such pristine imagery to evaporate. Armies seized control for a variety of reasons, and not only to remove corrupt civilian politicians for the greater good. Soldiers became involved in disputes surrounding national policy; perhaps more commonly they were motivated by specifically military grievances, most obviously those stemming from pay and conditions. They were as much affected by ethnic tensions as any political party; and sometimes it was the sheer personal ambition of their commanders which drew armies into government. In many colonies, armies had been recruited from among "marginal" ethnic groups in society; such minorities, overwhelmingly rural, living on the edges of the colonial state, were regarded as less sophisticated and thus more naturally obedient. They were often as alien as Europeans themselves in the eyes of the bulk of the population, and frequently they were identified as "martial" peoples, as we saw in an earlier chapter. These recruits themselves viewed military service as a means to advancement, social status, and relative security. The ethnic balance of the armies thus inherited by independent states had important political consequences: armies with a prevalence of one group or other saw intervention in politics as a means of advancing narrowly defined ethnic or provincial interests. A good example of this is Uganda, where Idi Amin, a northerner of the comparatively tiny Kakwa group, ruthlessly persecuted other minorities, including those represented in his army, perceiving them as sources of potential opposition.[4]

Uganda also illustrates the kind of extraordinarily brutal military tyranny that often emerged following army takeovers; the Central African Republic under Jean-Bedel Bokassa is another example. In the 1970s, such rulers became virtual caricatures of the corrupt, power-mad, and quite possibly insane African military dictator as developed beyond the continent itself. Bokassa's extraordinary vanity, and his tragi-comic delusions of grandeur, led him to rename his landlocked equatorial state the Central African Empire, and he had himself (naturally) crowned emperor in a ceremony replete with Napoleonic references. The French approved, indeed, and the president, Valéry Giscard d'Estaing, enjoyed a close relationship with Bokassa. It was of mutual benefit:

Bokassa received military and financial backing, the French got uranium.[5] In an echo of the effects produced by nineteenth-century travelogues, Western audiences were titillated by tales of cannibalism (Bokassa supposedly ate political opponents), sexual depravity (in the case of Princess Elizabeth of Toro, Idi Amin's one-time foreign minister), and the ruthless murder of cabinet ministers (*de rigueur* for both Amin and Bokassa).[6] Unquestionably, their brutality, and the violence they meted out to opponents actual and suspected was real enough; but these represented extremes, more the exception than the rule. More commonly, military regimes were no more corrupt or incompetent or brutal than the civilians they had replaced. Legislatures were carefully controlled, judicial independence was undermined, and powers of arrest and detention were greatly widened. However, terrible mayhem and bloodshed often attended the collapse of such regimes, and followed in their wake. Armies which were seen to have abused power, and which had consequently lost their "moral right" to rule, often themselves provoked extreme violence, as was the case in Liberia from the early 1980s, where army-led brutality following the 1980 coup sparked civil war and ultimately the very collapse of society itself. Longstanding military regimes, moreover, often kept a firm lid on rising social, political, or ethnic tensions; once such regimes disintegrated or were overthrown, virtual anarchy might erupt, as happened in Somalia in the early 1990s following the ousting of Siad Barre.[7]

The propensity of the armed forces to intervene in politics persists, especially in West Africa. There has been a slight shift in attitude – at least formally – across the continent, for while the General Assembly of the Organisation of African Unity was replete with uniforms, its successor, the African Union (AU), is less tolerant of army takeovers, routinely condemning them when they happen and seeking sanctions against the offending regime. Nevertheless, there remains a significant military presence in the AU, for soldiers still represent states – as in the case of Mauritania, for example – and in a number of other places soldiers wield vast amounts of power within government, as in Togo and Guinea Bissau. More generally, of course, the army's attitude toward the incumbent regime is the difference between whether a particular wave of popular protest will succeed, or whether it will be violently suppressed – as events in Tunisia, Egypt, and most recently Sudan (where the army in essence withdrew its support for presidential incumbents) demonstrated. This has also been clear in Zimbabwe, where the army's role in persuading Robert Mugabe to step down in 2017 was decisive. However, many of the soldiers who now gather at AU Heads of State meetings are not conventional officers in the mold of the old postcolonial military establishment, but represent, rather, another long-term development in African political culture, namely the militarization of the bush, leading in many instances to government by guerrilla.

The Politics and Cultures of Insurgency

In recent years, the militarization of politics has taken on new forms, with further implications for the development of political stability at the time of writing. Very broadly, the political soldiers of the 1960s and 1970s were the direct descendants of the indigenous agents of colonial rule. Officers had almost always seen colonial service, and straddled the transition of African militaries from colonial forces to national armies. Fundamentally, they had in common with their European predecessors the all-important monopoly on physical force; they had almost complete control over available weaponry in a given territory, and, for a time at least, had as powerful a monopoly on moral rectitude. The army barracks of the 1960s and 1970s were the sole repositories of the moral and the physical order. Increasingly, however, professional armies of colonial heritage found themselves challenged by well-armed guerrilla forces which in some respects constituted a "second wave" of military intervention in African politics.[8] The military state has found itself under attack from the military anti-state, or the military state-in-waiting, the latter purporting to represent the oppressed masses, and aiming not simply at the capture of the extant system but its complete destruction, and subsequent rebuilding – or at least this is what the rhetoric of such movements promised. In part, in the 1970s and 1980s, this reflected the influences and intrusions of the Cold War, most dramatically manifest in the massive influx into the continent of automatic weapons, and in particular the increasingly ubiquitous AK-47. Such weaponry enabled populist groups to challenge the state to much greater effect than previously; and since the Cold War, indeed, the flood of small arms into Africa has, if anything, increased, as former Eastern Bloc countries search for new markets in the "Third World" on which to dump their surplus manufactures. Marginal and disaffected groups which in the 1960s resisted the state using Second World War rifles, even spears in the remoter rural areas, had access in the 1980s to machine-guns and rocket-launchers. The monopoly on military might, maintained since the 1890s and guarded jealously by, successively, colonial regimes and postcolonial governments was gone.

This had already been signposted by the late anti-colonial insurgencies of the 1960s and 1970s, in Angola, Mozambique, Guinea Bissau, Rhodesia, and insurgencies proliferated during these years. These were guerrilla movements which sought to seize, first, the firepower necessary to challenge the state; secondly, the moral high ground, in terms of popular ideological revolution; and third, political power itself.[9] In southern Sudan, a revolt against northern rule fizzled into life between the late 1950s and early 1960s – and despite an eleven-year hiatus between 1972 and 1983, this particular war would still earn the dubious distinction of being Africa's longest. Elsewhere in the region, Eritreans fought a prolonged war for independence against Ethiopian occupation from 1961 until victory under the Eritrean People's Liberation Front (EPLF) in 1991, although not before the armed struggle itself had undergone some bitter internal twists, including an intermittent civil war during the 1970s. Civil war – essentially conflict between rival insurgencies – was a common feature of armed struggle, notably in the Lusophone territories, as we have seen. In Ethiopia alone, numerous armed movements emerged between the 1960s and the 1980s, fighting successive regimes – as well as, often, one another – over the future of the polity. Leaving aside the Eritreans, who wanted independence from Ethiopia and little to do (they said) with Ethiopia itself, there were insurgencies in Tigray, among the Oromo, in the Somali Ogaden, and along the Sudanese borderlands. It was a coalition of some of these various forces – the Ethiopian People's Revolutionary Democratic Front (EPRDF) – which finally toppled the Marxist dictatorship in 1991, in alliance with the EPLF to the north. Elsewhere, the South West African People's Organization (SWAPO) fought South African occupation in Namibia from the mid-1960s, only winning independence as apartheid collapsed in 1990. In Zimbabwe, meanwhile, the "patriotic front" forces – comprising both Mugabe's ZANU and, rather later, Nkomo's ZAPU – maneuvered themselves into a position from which they could challenge for political power through prolonged military action against white minority rule, and then achieved actual power through electoral success in 1980. Other highly successful movements–successful, that is, in maintaining internal political cohesion and marching on the center to seize power – emerged later: in Uganda, notably, the National Resistance Army (NRA), led by Yoweri Museveni, fought Milton Obote's regime through the early 1980s (Obote having returned to power in 1980) before capturing Kampala in 1986. The Rwandan Patriotic Front (RPF) advanced steadily from the north of Rwanda through the early 1990s, and seized power amidst genocidal mayhem in 1994.[10]

The Horn of Africa provides a particularly useful illustration of how "liberation war" often erupted along old fault lines – much of the violence of the later twentieth century can be traced to the nineteenth – and also of how such conflict might unfold in labyrinthine ways, against the backdrop of the Cold War. Under Emperor Haile Selassie, Ethiopia had presented itself as a staunch ally of the West, anti-communist and defender against Islam. This was indeed of great benefit to Washington, in particular, considering Ethiopia's key geographical position on the Red Sea, straddling both Africa itself and the Middle East. In the 1950s, the United States established a series of military agreements with Haile Selassie (the grateful emperor even sent a contingent of Ethiopian troops to fight in Korea), and, through the UN, engineered the award to Ethiopia of the former Italian colony of Eritrea in exchange for the development of a military base at Kagnew, in the Eritrean capital Asmara. For many years, Kagnew station was the single largest US base outside the United States itself, housing thousands of personnel at its height; it was developed as a listening post for the Indian Ocean, northern Africa, and the Middle East. This mutually beneficial arrangement came under attack, however, when in 1974 the ageing Haile Selassie was overthrown by a Marxist junta. Through the mid-1970s, Ethiopia increasingly aligned itself with Moscow, and the Americans pulled out. The Soviet Union, formerly a patron of neighboring Somalia, itself episodically at war with Ethiopia, switched its allegiance and poured enormous amounts of military aid into Ethiopia, including "advisors" and hardware. In 1977, Ethiopia was sufficiently emboldened to go to war with Siad Barre's Somalia in what was a reprise of the 1964 conflict between the two countries.[11]

The main purpose of this equipment, however, was to crush the growing insurgency in Eritrea and Tigray. The main northern guerrilla movements themselves – the EPLF in Eritrea, which had grown out of the original Eritrean Liberation Front in the early 1970s, and the Tigray People' Liberation Front (TPLF), founded in 1975 – developed Marxist programs; but assistance from Moscow was clearly not forthcoming, while the Americans were now content to watch events from a distance. The TPLF looked for alternative role models, and fixed its gaze on Albania as an example of nonaligned Marxism in action – and indeed of total Stalinist control. The Eritreans, for their part, had a history of sending guerrillas for training to China, and also, in an earlier phase of the armed struggle in the 1960s, to Syria; but through the 1970s, the EPLF developed a strategy of isolationism, rejecting the USSR as "imperialist," and indeed pouring contempt on any African movement which was identified as being led by "lackeys" of foreign interests. The EPLF, by 1976–7, had been remarkably close to victory, having captured most of the territory outside the major cities, but Soviet intervention on the Ethiopian side dramatically tipped the scales against the Eritreans, who were now forced to withdraw to the far north of the country in the face of a series of overwhelming assaults. The EPLF would tone down its Marxism over time – it was a markedly pragmatic movement, both militarily and politically – and developed its own highly motivational blend of social reformism and nationalism. Through the 1980s, the movement fought with growing success against the full weight of the Ethiopian and Soviet military machines, capturing equipment and using it against the enemy. By the late 1980s, with *glasnost* and *perestroika* in motion, Soviet premier Mikhail Gorbachev was already warning the Ethiopian government that military aid was to be scaled down dramatically. The EPLF had been remarkably successful on its own, but there can be little doubt that Soviet withdrawal weakened Ethiopia, and in 1991, Eritrea won its independence, and an alliance of armed rebels, including Eritreans and Tigrayans, overthrew the Marxist regime in Addis Ababa.[12]

If the Horn demonstrates the ways in which the Cold War intersected with local wars, in the first half of the 1990s the prevalence of conflict in post-Cold War Africa was already evident. In Rwanda, longstanding ethnic tensions between Tutsi and Hutu erupted in 1994, resulting in the deaths of some 800,000 Tutsi and so-called "moderate" Hutu. There was similar fragility in neighboring Burundi, where strains between Tutsi and Hutu persist, following an anti-Hutu pogrom in 1988 and the coming to power of the Hutu as the result of elections held in 1993. This great central African war spilled over into Congo, as Ugandan and Rwanda forces aided the overthrow of Mobutu but soon fell out over objectives; eastern Congo would quickly become a morass of identities, fault lines, and violent entrepreneurialism. The region of eastern DRC and the Great Lakes was caught between two fires – the Rwandan genocide and the collapse of the state in Congo itself – and witnessed the proliferation of warlords and militia groups which often had the covert backing of neighboring states, chiefly Uganda and Rwanda. It has become one of the most violent zones in Africa, the scene of multiple external interventions largely motivated by a concern to secure access to resources. The DRC was, in the words of one scholar, "Africa's world war."[13]

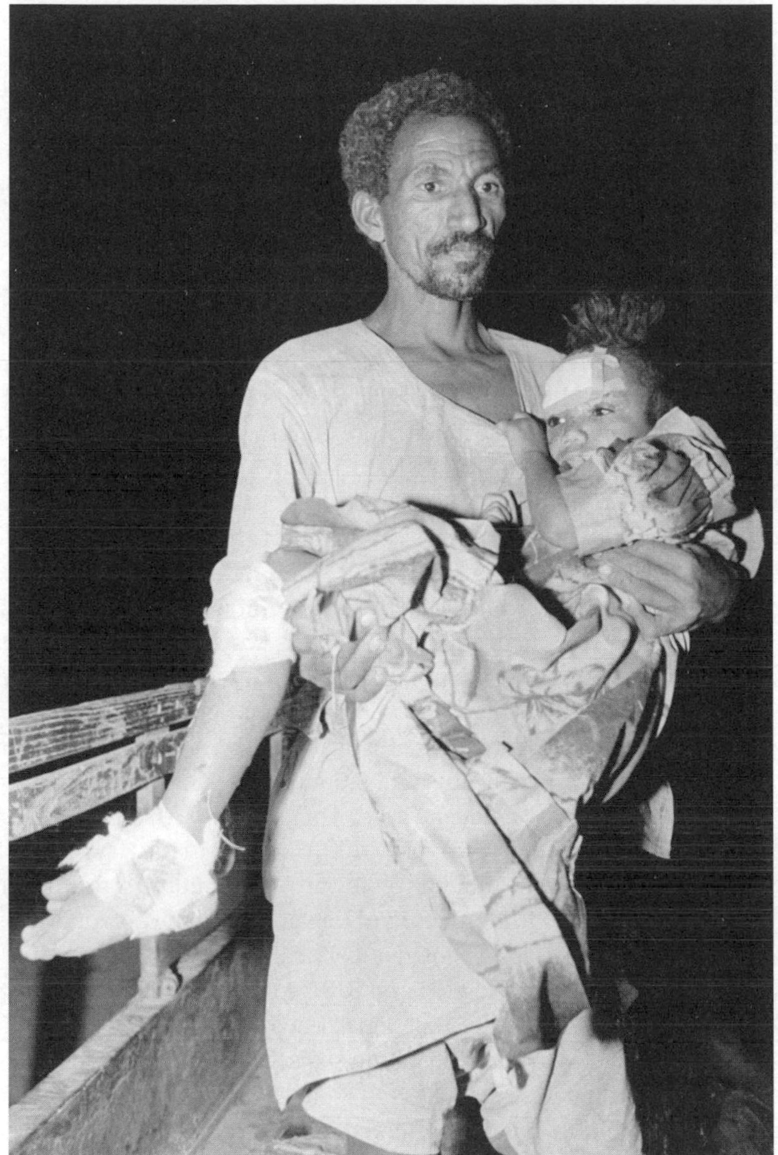

Victims: a father brings his wounded daughter to an EPLF hospital, Eritrea, early 1980s. Source: Photo by Mike Goldwater.

Meanwhile, Somalia's implosion in the late 1980s and early 1990s opened up a new vortex of instability across the region, and a US-led intervention – "Operation Restore Hope" – ended in disaster. It would be a long time before anyone else, Ethiopia excepted, would attempt direct involvement in the increasingly complex affairs of Somalia.[14] State collapse in Sierra Leone and Liberia involved the proliferation of warlords which in the

West African context meant leaders of ragged bands of disaffected and traumatized young men, exchanging precious minerals for arms. They were the economic and political failings of the modern African state writ large, and they inflicted enormous suffering on defenseless populations.[15] The Ugandan army had its own version to deal with in the north of the country, where the Lord's Resistance Army brutalized local people in the name of an idiosyncratic amalgamation of Old Testament and indigenous spiritualism.[16] While many outsiders despaired at the spread of this "new barbarism"[17] – inexplicable to those who had seen a new era of global stability heralded with the ending of the Cold War – many of the forms and tactics did indeed bear some resemblance to the violence of the nineteenth century. Much conflict in the early twenty-first century had a distinctly indigenous character, no longer directed (or at least nowhere near as much) by outside interests as it had been during the Cold War; and the foreign policies of a number of African governments became much more militarized and adventuring than they ever were during the Cold War. We return to this below.

Meanwhile, a range of politically and militarily sophisticated insurgencies had seized power across the continent between the second half of the 1970s and the first half of the 1990s. All of them remain in power, in some shape or form, and often largely unreconstructed, at the time of writing. Whether these movements of "popular armed struggle" – essentially made up of military amateurs who have proved themselves so successful in turning themselves into professional armies – are any more attracted to pluralism and inclusiveness is still, at the very least, an open question, although the initial signs are not especially promising. In Uganda, for example the hangover of a bloody postcolonial history has meant the National Resistance Movement's absolute domination of the political space: under a system of "nonparty" politics, Museveni won a series of elections from the mid-1990s onwards which were characterized by increasing levels of intimidation and intolerance toward opposition groups. Similarly, in Rwanda, the Tutsi-dominated RPF, under Paul Kagame, used the horror of genocide in 1994 to justify its subsequent closing down of political debate. In Mozambique, years of catastrophic civil war between FRELIMO and RENAMO were brought to an end in the mid-1990s with elections, since when the fragile peace has held, but while Mozambique has been widely regarded as one of the region's success stories, the fact remains that FRELIMO is hegemonic, much as the ANC is in South Africa, and the EPRDF remains in Ethiopia. ZANU-PF's political control has come under strain in recent years, and for a time, it was compelled to share power with the opposition, the Movement for Democratic Change, but with Mugabe's (reluctant) departure from office, and his replacement by ZANU-PF veteran Emmerson Mnangagwa the liberation front continues to dominate.[18] In all these cases, elections have been held, however flawed, but not in Eritrea, where since the early 1990s, the EPLF has created a highly authoritarian state, and one of the AU's most unabashedly militarized (and unpopular) members. Nonetheless, across the board, societies "liberated" by force of arms have become, albeit in different ways, more militarized and tightly controlled as a result of guerrillas becoming governments, and as a result of former fighters professionalizing and institutionalizing their military outfits. As we noted above, these are movements which feel that they and they alone have won the right to political control. Moreover, such movements are also often imbued

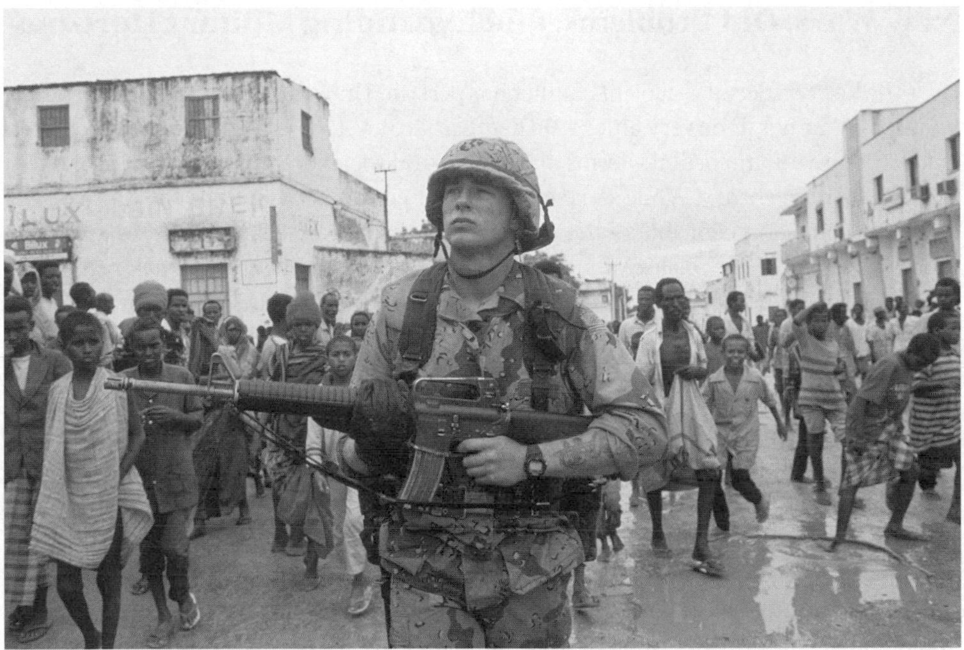

Humanitarianism or neo-imperialism? A US soldier in Mogadishu, Somalia, 1992. Source: © Peter Turnley/CORBIS.

with a sense of political mission and righteousness, buoyed by the memory and celebration of the blood sacrifice – which in some respects has rendered them even more politically entrenched than their predecessors. It remains to be seen whether such movements can in the longer term demobilize themselves and extend power to those who were not originally or directly involved in the armed struggle. Yet this is not simply a question of whether guerrillas can become democrats, though this is complex enough; it is also a question of whether long-term, indigenous processes of militarization, dating to the nineteenth century, might come to incorporate comparatively recent ideas about "democratic rights," however imperfectly such ideas are actually applied.

In some cases – Somalia, Liberia, and to an extent Sierra Leone – armed uprising led to bloody anarchy, as armed groups were not so much ideologically driven revolutionaries as disaffected, brutalized, and nihilistic youth. In fact, in both Liberia and Sierra Leone, the use of the old-fashioned machete was terrifyingly effective alongside the AK-47, and during the Rwandan genocide of 1994, it was the machete, not the AK-47, which was the iconic tool of the slaughter.[19] But the crucial point here is the empowerment of extremist factions in political as well as military terms. Since the early 1990s, these forms of particularly brutal and "privatized" violence have come to characterize much so-called "low-level" African conflict, whether in the West African bush, in the lowland plains of Somalia, or in the forests abutting the Great Lakes region.

New Wars, Old Problems, and Expanding Military Horizons

Over the last two decades, violent conflict has persisted in some areas, and started afresh in others. War has done very little to aid democratic development, although it does often lead to creative – and brutal – forms of political and social organization, just as it did in the nineteenth century. While some of this violence can be seen to be the more or less direct outcome of recent shifts – the ending of longstanding dictatorships, notably, and therefore an explosive release of pressures – much of it can be traced back rather further than the immediate postcolonial era. At the same time, while some of the wars may be "new," the problems invariably are not: these still include political, ethnic, and cultural oppression, economic marginalization, and straightforward greed, or at least restless ambition. The truth – although it is, in some quarters, an uncomfortable one – is that parts of Africa in the late twentieth and early twenty-first centuries have been evocative of the nineteenth century, with its warlords and militia and struggles for both material and political power in the context of rapid global change.[20]

The early years of the twenty-first century witnessed ongoing conflict in Angola, in Congo, and in Somalia, which virtually ceased to exist and which was divided between clan warlords and the Union of Islamic Courts, until the US–Ethiopian intervention noted above put the latter to flight. This in turn sparked the Islamist insurgency of al-Shabaab, which continues at the time of writing, although it has been pegged back to some extent. Ethiopia and Eritrea, meanwhile, used Somalia to continue their own war by proxy, while the Eritreans supported the ongoing low-level Oromo insurgency in southern Ethiopia. At the same time, conflict in the western Sudanese province of Darfur involved a range of rebel movements fighting for autonomy and rights against forces backed by Khartoum. Khartoum-sponsored violence against the local population was frequently characterized as genocidal, and the war quickly spilled over into neighboring Chad. The conflict has abated somewhat, but Sudan's President Bashir is still wanted by the International Criminal Court for crimes against humanity in Darfur. The North–South civil war in Sudan was brought to an end in 2005 by a peace accord after several years of delicate negotiation, and South Sudan became an independent state in 2011. But December 2013 saw the eruption of a civil war *within* South Sudan, and while in some ways, the violence unfolded along ethnic lines – the Dinka of President Kiir against Nuer opposition led by Riek Machar – it was messier than that simple formulation would suggest. In the meantime, Sierra Leone and Liberia began a process of recovery after many years of some of the most horrendous violence yet witnessed on the continent; indeed Liberia had the singular honor of electing, in 2006, Africa's first female head of state in Ellen Johnson Sirleaf. One of the ghosts she had to exorcise, Charles Taylor, former rebel leader and president, was tried for, and found guilty of, war crimes in The Hague.

The impotence – indeed, often, indifference – of the United Nations in these situations has at times been only too painfully clear, although in the wake of the Rwandan genocide, the UN was prepared to devote more manpower and resources to a range of conflicts on the continent. Peacekeepers were deployed in Congo, and along the border between Eritrea and Ethiopia, and the UN set up a war crimes tribunal in Arusha,

Tanzania, to bring the perpetrators of the Rwandan genocide to justice. Increasingly, however, diplomatic pressure and sanctions are the more usual responses to wayward regimes and violent protagonists. Where "boots on the ground" have been deployed, UN forces have been supplemented, and sometimes supplanted, by observers and troops from the African Union – as in Somalia, and DRC. Otherwise, armed international intervention with a view to imposing peace has been highly selective. In the 1990s, US president George Bush Sr.'s mission to Somalia and UK Prime Minister Tony Blar's armed interjection in Sierra Leone were driven by a "liberal interventionism" of which many late-nineteenth-century lobbyists would have approved, but elsewhere, in recent years, there have relatively fewer takers – notably in Somalia, where the Islamist insurgency continues. Apart from the ever-interested Ethiopians (and Eritreans, for different reasons), the international mission there is in the hands of the AU, which is itself represented by a few thousand Ugandans, Burundians, and Kenyans, although an international naval presence was assembled to combat Somali piracy, itself an extension of economic problems on land. Other recent examples include French interventions in Niger and Cote d'Ivoire. The decision by several NATO powers to launch air strikes on Libya in 2011 had some applauding muscular humanitarianism, but others immediately suspected a baser motive – oil – and saw Western neo-imperialism in action, if a rather half-hearted kind. Nevertheless, a rather more constant intervention is that of the foreign arms-dealer. Since the 1990s, swathes of the continent have been awash with cheap weaponry and equipment, the debris of ideological conflict; and there was plenty more to be purchased cheaply from Russia and the former Soviet bloc countries desperate to sell their state assets. War in the Horn, for example, was waged largely using small arms, tanks, artillery, and anti-aircraft guns purchased from arms manufacturers in Eastern Europe. Regardless of the rights and wrongs of humanitarian intervention, whether armed or diplomatic, it seems safe to say that there will always be military hardware available to those willing and able to fight supposedly new wars over some rather old problems.

The ethos of insularity that has characterized the African military for much of the twentieth century is changing. War in postcolonial Africa has largely been "internal" – in other words, we can broadly define it as "civil war" – and inter-state conflict has been relatively rare. Among the largest have been those between Ethiopia and Somalia over the issue of the former's Somali-populated Ogaden province, first in 1963–4, and again in 1977–8. These conflicts were striking in terms of both scale, and the acute discomfort they caused the OAU, which was understandably anxious about wars erupting across colonial-era boundaries. Ethiopia – the permanent home, of course, of the OAU, as well as it successor the AU – won the backing of the organization, Somalia failing to gain the all-important international recognition of its cause. In 1979, it was a Tanzanian army (together with some Ugandan émigrés) that invaded Uganda (in response to Idi Amin's own frontier aggression) and that was instrumental in the overthrow of Amin himself. There was also conflict between Algeria and Morocco over the question of Western Sahara, the former Spanish territory which the Moroccans invaded, but where the Algerians supported the armed resistance movement, Polisario.[21]

These are among the small number of examples of cross-border conflict prior to the 1990s. But the incidence of foreign military adventurism, proxy war, and inter-state conflict increased between the 1990s and 2010s.[22] This raises the question of the extent to which war in Africa had once more become, as it was in the nineteenth century and as it has been in Europe for several centuries, an extension of national policy. Angola and Congo became inter-African free-for-alls during the 1990s, involving several regional powers violently protecting their interests; they were concerned both to gain political leverage over favorable regimes, and to win access to the mineral wealth in both of these vast, troubled, but resource-rich countries. The Ethiopian–Eritrean war between 1998 and 2000 was the largest of its kind in the world at that time, involving mass mobilization of men and national resources, and a series of conventional ground offensives with air support against elaborate systems of trenches. The war – waged over the issue of borders, partly, but more importantly over identity and regional hegemony – was fought to a standstill in mid-2000, after which relations between the belligerents remained tense for a number of years, while the conflict spilled into proxy wars elsewhere in the region.[23] A peace deal was finally signed in 2018. Meanwhile, the stationing of West African peacekeeping troops in the region's trouble-spots, such as Sierra Leone, likewise represented a new phenomenon, as did the deployment of African Union soldiers in some of the volatile places across the continent. In recent years, African peacekeepers have been dispatched to the Ethiopia–Eritrea border, Darfur, and Somalia, while the AU has also sought to broker a peace deal in South Sudan – another conflict involving the armed intervention of neighbors, including Uganda.[24] The tangible efficacy of the AU's Peace and Security Committee might be a matter of debate, but the PSC's existence alone is representative of a rather more vigorous culture of interventionism than was evident in the OAU. "Peacekeeping" has become big business, in political terms, in the first few years of the new millennium.

Peacekeeping missions may be novel, but foreign adventurism is not a new phenomenon in African politics. In the precolonial era, inter-state war was commonly motivated by political and economic considerations, while military intervention in neighboring states and societies was a common tactic aimed at the creation of friendly regimes and the extension or invention of kinships and dynasties. But in recent years, it appears to be taking innovative and more dangerous forms, particularly since, with the end of the Cold War, African governments have been able to take greater responsibility for and control over foreign policy. Proxy war proliferates, as regional actors covertly or less subtly lend support to armed insurgencies inside neighboring territory – Rwandans and Ugandans in Congo, Chadians and Eritreans in Darfur, Eritreans in Somalia, which has led to the imposition of sanctions on Eritrea, despite the latter's fierce rebuttal of the accusation. In other words, these are not hermetically sealed, self-contained conflicts, but regional wars involving a range of regional actors.

At the same time, the seemingly inexorable escalation of the transnational terrorist threat posed by violent Islamism – evidenced in Nigeria, Somalia, Kenya, Niger, and elsewhere – has meant the alignment of local regimes' security agendas with those of Western partners, notably the United States. Armies across the continent have benefited – in terms of funding, training, and hardware – from external partnerships keen to see particular incumbent regimes remain in power for fear of less palatable alternatives. The historically close relationship between military and political establishments may well manifest itself in new ways, as armies look beyond national frontiers and become instruments as much of foreign policy as of internal control.

Notes

1 For an exploration of these issues, see Crawford Young, *The African Colonial State in Comparative Perspective* (New Haven & London, 1994); and Mamdani, *Citizen and Subject*.

2 J.M. Lee, *African Armies and Civil Order* (London, 1969); W.F. Gutteridge, *Military Regimes in Africa* (London, 1975); Samuel Decalo, *Coups and Army Rule in Africa: Motivations and Constraints* (New Haven & London, 1990).

3 Decalo, *Coups*, chap. 2; Falola & Heaton, *History of Nigeria*, chaps. 7 & 8; Emmanuel Hansen & Paul Collins, "The Army, the State, and the "Rawlings Revolution" in Ghana," *African Affairs*, 79: 314 (1980).

4 Kyemba, *State of Blood*, 46–7.

5 The relationship is explored in Brian Titley, *Dark Age: The Political Odyssey of Emperor Bokassa* (Montreal & Kingston, 1997), chap. 5.

6 For Uganda, in addition to Kyemba, *State of Blood*, see also Princess Elizabeth of Toro, *African Princess: The Story of Princess Elizabeth of Toro* (London, 1983).

7 Clapham, *Africa and the International System*, 52, 156–7; Lewis, *Modern History of the Somali*, chap. 11.

8 For an excellent overview, see William Reno, *Warfare in Independent Africa* (Cambridge, 2011).

9 Clapham, *African Guerrillas*; but see also a survey of somewhat differently configured and motivated movements in Morten Boas & Kevin C. Dunn (eds.), *African Guerrillas: Raging Against the Machine* (Boulder CO, 2007).

10 The literature dealing with these various instances is vast, but a sample would include: Johnson, *Root Causes*; David Pool, *From Guerrillas to Government: the Eritrean People's Liberation Front* (Oxford, 2001); Richard J. Reid, *Frontiers of Violence in Northeast Africa: Genealogies of Conflict Since 1800* (Oxford, 2011), chap. 7; Gebru Tareke, *The Ethiopian Revolution: War in the Horn of Africa* (New Haven & London, 2009); P. Ngoga, "Uganda: the National Resistance Army," in Clapham, *African Guerrillas*; Gerard Prunier, *The Rwanda Crisis: History of a Genocide* (London, 1996).

11 Gebru Tareke, "The Ethiopia-Somalia war of 1977 revisited," *International Journal of African Historical Studies*, 33:3 (2000); Lewis, *Modern History of the Somali*, 231–48.

12 Pool, *From Guerrillas to Government*; Dan Connell, *Against All Odds: A Chronicle of the Eritrean Revolution* (Lawrenceville NJ, 1997).

13 Gerard Prunier, *Africa's World War: Congo, the Rwandan Genocide, and the Making of a Continental Catastrophe* (Oxford, 2009). See also F. Reyntjens, *The Great African War: Congo and Regional Geopolitics, 1996-2006* (Cambridge, 2009).

14 Hussein M. Adam, "Somali civil wars", in Taisier M. Ali & Robert O. Matthews (eds.), *Civil Wars in Africa: Roots and Resolution* (Montreal & Kingston, 1999).

15 Paul Richards, *Fighting for the Rain Forest: War, Youth and Resources in Sierra Leone* (Oxford, 1996); Stephen Ellis, *The Mask of Anarchy: The Destruction of Liberia and the Religious Dimension of an African Civil War* (London, 1999).

16 T. Allen & K. Vlassenroot (eds.), *The LRA: Myth and Reality* (London, 2010).

17 R.D. Kaplan, "The coming anarchy," *Atlantic Monthly*, February 1994.

18 See for example the case studies in Ali & Matthews (eds.), *Civil Wars in Africa*, Part One.

19 Philip Gourevitch, *We Wish To Inform You That Tomorrow We Will Be Killed With Our Families: stories from Rwanda* (London, 1998).

20 For a range of perspectives, see: R.H. Bates, *When Things Fell Apart: State Failure in Late-century Africa* (Cambridge, 2008); P. Collier, *The Bottom Billion: Why the Poorest Countries are Failing and What Can Be Done about It* (Oxford, 2008); C. Cramer, *Civil War is Not a Stupid Thing* (London, 2006); Reno, *Warfare in Independent Africa*; and Paul D. Williams, *War and Conflict in Africa* (Cambridge, 2016).

21 Peter Woodward, *The Horn of Africa: Politics and International Relations* (London, 2003), 126–30; T. Avirgan & M. Honey, *War in Uganda: The Legacy of Idi Amin* (Westport CONN & London, 1982); Alice Wilson, *Sovereignty in Exile: A Saharan Liberation Movement Governs* (Philadelphia, 2016).

22 Williams, *War and Conflict*, passim.

23 Tekeste Negash & Kjetil Tronvoll, *Brothers at War: Making Sense of the Eritrean-Ethiopian war* (Oxford, 2000); Sally Healy & Martin Plaut, *Ethiopia and Eritrea: Allergic to Persuasion* (London, 2007); Richard Reid (ed.), *Eritrea's External Relations: Understanding Its Regional Role and Foreign Policy* (London, 2009).

24 International Crisis Group, *South Sudan: Keeping Faith with the IGAD Peace Process*. Africa Report No. 228, 27 July 2015. For a range of case studies and theoretical approaches, see Patrick Chabal, Ulf Engel & Anna-Maria Gentili (eds.), *Is Violence Inevitable in Africa? Theories of conflict and approaches to conflict prevention* (Leiden, 2005); and Alfred Nhema & Paul Tiyambe Zeleza (eds.), *The Resolution of African Conflicts: The Management of Conflict Resolution & Post-conflict Reconstruction* (Addis Ababa & Oxford, 2008).

19 Rectification, Redemption, and Reality

Issues and Trends in Contemporary Africa

Africa and the Contemporary World

An understanding of contemporary Africa – that is to say, the continent over the last two decades or so – must begin with an appreciation of the intersection between "old" and "new" dynamics. In many respects, the roots of the continent's current trajectory – certainly in political and economic terms, the central foci of this book – can be traced back many decades, and current conditions must be understood as the outcome of cumulative processes. At the same time, however, certain comparatively novel dynamics can be discerned – not least in terms of shifts in international politics – although vigilance is always required: closer inspection often reveals the "new" to be, in fact, a reversion to, or a modification of, rather older patterns or attitudes. In a very broad sense, and in different ways, the end of the Cold War had a major impact on Africa, and the "developed world" subsequently came to view the continent a little differently following the collapse of the Soviet Union. On the face of it, in the 1990s and 2000s, the West became more concerned with human rights, political structures, "good governance" and democracy, and sound economic and commercial systems and practices. The contemporary era has been one of crises and solutions, with a range of actors – including African governments themselves – seeking to manage modernity, and identifying solutions to the challenges of political instability, debt and underdevelopment. Working through nongovernmental organizations (NGOs) and charity and aid-giving bodies, through the World Bank and the International Monetary Fund, the West became, if anything, more interventionist in certain spheres than previously. They seemed more prepared to apply pressure to African governments to change their political and economic practices, and more enthusiastic about engaging with Africa in terms

A History of Modern Africa: 1800 to the Present, Third Edition. Richard J. Reid.

of economic "modernization" – in fact a "struggle" that dates to the early nineteenth century – and the social and political well-being of Africans themselves. Yet over the last decade or so, African economies themselves have witnessed extraordinary growth, fuelled in large part by the industrial and financials interventions of relatively "new" players such as China and India. This has given rise to what some have termed the "new scramble for Africa" – this time purely for resources rather than actual territory – and it has enabled some African states to be selective and strategic about how to engage with their old partners, and former imperial powers, in the West.[1]

As for African governments, they have found themselves under greater scrutiny from their own peoples, arguably, than at any time since the achievement of independence, and it is broadly accepted that something akin to a "second wave of liberation" swept the continent in the 1990s and 2000s.[2] The number of "political dinosaurs" – the term applied to that generation of nationalist politician in the "first wave" of liberation – has dwindled somewhat, partly the result of simple biology, but partly because they have been unable to withstand popular opposition and indeed, in some case, sociopolitical collapse. In recent years, for example, two of the very last of that generation – Muammar Qaddafi in Libya and Robert Mugabe in Zimbabwe – have been removed from power, Mugabe in rather more civilized fashion than Qaddafi. The central point is that there are ever fewer countries in Africa which have not seen off older rulers, and undergone some kind of electoral process or at least limited democratization. The sudden dispatch of Presidents Ben Ali and Mubarak in Tunisia and Egypt respectively, following mass

Protesters gather at Tahrir Square in Cairo April 1, 2011. Thousands of demonstrators gathered in Tahrir Square calling for the demands of the revolution that toppled Egypt's former president Hosni Mubarak from power to be met. Source: Reuters/Mohamed Abd El Ghany.

demonstrations in early 2011 reminded us that permanence is an illusion – Eritrea and Uganda be warned – and that when change comes after decades of stasis, incumbents may not be allowed a dignified exit. And yet, authoritarian or semi-authoritarian regimes do not simply survive, they continue to flourish, sometimes in new ways. Some, indeed – such as Uganda and Ethiopia – enjoy the support of Western backers, overtly or otherwise.

Nonetheless, the relationship between the West and Africa has in some ways become more complex over the last two decades: *realpolitik* may not change, but moral politics has come much more to the fore in the West's dealings with the continent. The Western shift in attitude can be seen to have originated in a number of ways. Partly, it arose from feelings of guilt, which has become, in often subtle ways, an important influence on policy-making and popular perceptions of the African continent. Guilt, of course, is frequently media-driven, in that it has become more difficult to be unaware of human catastrophe than it was, say, thirty years ago. Considerable reportage attended the famine in eastern Nigeria in the late 1960s during the Biafra war, for example, and the Ethiopian famine of 1973; but the Ethiopian famine of the mid-1980s became almost iconic in terms of the world's "understanding" of Africa. Unprecedented television coverage of starving millions prompted an equally unprecedented public campaign to collect funds, and in many ways left a profound sense of responsibility among many beyond the continent itself. Since then, there has been a much more concerted effort within the "donor community" to prevent famine, catch it early and fast, and more generally to assist in development programs through which Africans can enjoy the same securities and rights as all other citizens of the world. In other words, the rich world has a duty to make sure that the poor world does not starve.

Guilt also follows from inertia in the face of political disaster. During the Rwandan genocide of 1994, around 1 million Tutsi and moderate Hutu were killed in the space of three months – between April and July – while the world, including the UN, which had a small presence there but which was unable or unwilling to act, stood back and watched. In fact the UN had some sound intelligence beforehand regarding the ethnic tensions which were then mounting.[3] In the aftermath, as the recriminations began, the "developed world" was again grasped by a sense of remorseful culpability.[4] The world, it was increasingly believed – on both sides of the political spectrum, although sometimes for different reasons – must become more closely involved in Africa. As the exigencies of the Cold War vanished, the considerable debris scattered across the globe came into view – in Africa, Southeast Asia, and Central America. To the Left, at least, it was a shameful sight, and it was now believed that the disasters of the immediate post-colonial generation had been something in which everyone must take a share of the blame.

Yet in many ways such shifts in attitude came about, above all, because with the end of the Cold War, the continent was no longer an ideological or strategic battleground in quite the way it had been. If the period from the 1960s to the 1980s had been the age of militant anti-communism and counterinsurgency in the West, the 1990s was supposed to be the age of democratization and humanitarian relief. But initially, it was a process of change which came about as much as anything by default.

As the Soviet Union collapsed and its involvement in a number of African states – Ethiopia and Angola, for example – accordingly vanished, so the West withdrew its support from those "bulwark" anti-communist dictatorships which had now outlived their purpose, for example Mobutu in Zaire.[5] Now, instead, pressure could be placed on leaders to change their ways, hold elections, open up their economic systems to free trade and foreign investment, and in so doing roll back the state. Democratization, economic development, and the alleviation of poverty were all interlinked, it was argued, and therefore Western interventionism must be multilayered. The deal laid before African regimes was that acceptance of structural adjustment programs involving both political and economic liberalization would be rewarded with massive inward investment and World Bank funds for development projects. New efforts would be made to stimulate agricultural and industrial production and to reduce the continent's dependence on foreign imports by utilizing local raw materials and labor. Of course, this putatively "new" economic orthodoxy – interventionism with a view to "modernization" – was not in fact so new, and could be traced to the early nineteenth century and the abolition of the slave trade, as we have seen. Nonetheless, the perceived success of a number of countries in this respect inspired US president Bill Clinton, on a landmark tour of sub-Saharan Africa in 1998, to talk of an "African renaissance," although he was in fact borrowing the notion from South African Deputy President Thabo Mbeki, who was in turn drawing inspiration from Cheikh Anta Diop in the 1950s.[6] Either way, the concept referenced a new era of good governance and economic growth, and a newfound confidence in the future – captured in the enormous (and somewhat controversial) monument constructed in Dakar, Senegal, between 2006 and 2010.

Clearly, while the Cold War had involved a particular ideological struggle, the last twenty years or so has witnessed the resurgence of a rather older agenda, dusted off and repackaged. Africa is once again a condition to be addressed; an enormous industry, employing a lot of people both inside and outside the continent – a diplomatic/humanitarian/developmental complex, as it were – is now geared toward the "fixing" of Africa. Solution-oriented agendas, meanwhile, are invariably strikingly ahistorical, containing little or no hint of historical consciousness, which means that there is little apparent awareness of Africa's trajectory over the longer term, although it does mean that key external actors can easily reinvent themselves every so often. It is also worth noting that the "Africa Rising" narrative has since supplanted the "African Renaissance," underscored by some extraordinary GDP growth rates across the continent. This has complicated somewhat Western development agendas, and in turn has encouraged a kind of ahistorical, presentist framework for understanding modern Africa, as rapid economic growth tends to do.

Meanwhile, changes in global politics have meant subtle shifts in approaches to African states in recent years. The attacks on American embassies in Nairobi and Dar-es-Salaam in 1998, and on the United States directly on September 11, 2001, produced those changes. Various Western states, including the United States, demonstrated a readiness to overlook certain shortcomings on the part of African states in exchange for support of the so-called War on Terror, as it was known under the Bush administration. Just as the struggle against global communism induced a certain blindness to the less pleasant aspects of African governments' internal affairs, so the war on Islamic extremism has engendered a pragmatism of approach in attracting global allies. Support is routinely offered to authoritarian or "hybrid" (semi- or quasi-democratic) regimes in exchange for military cooperation. Numerous African governments have their own concerns about Islamic extremism, and have seen their security forces' capacity bolstered by the United States or European partners – inevitably with implications for domestic politics, not least in the strengthening of incumbent regimes. This is demonstrably true in Uganda, and in Ethiopia: in the latter case, the United States has long supported Ethiopia's armed involvement in Somalia – where a US intervention in the early 1990s failed so spectacularly – notably after 2006–7, when US–Ethiopian cooperation led to the overthrow of Islamic authority in much of the country and an effort to destroy the al-Qaeda cells there. That intervention spurred the emergence of the Islamist militia al-Shabaab, affiliated with al-Qaeda,[7] but as noted in Chapter 17 this is part of a wider phenomenon, with similar movements gathering momentum in Nigeria, Libya, and Mali. Of course, the degree to which the West is genuinely *interested* in what happens in Africa should never be taken for granted, and certainly not exaggerated. Africa, or at least large swathes of it, remains low on most countries' foreign policy agendas, even if the War on Terror has recently heightened concern that parts of the continent may be breeding grounds for terrorists and economic migrants alike.

Democracy and Authoritarianism: Trends in Governance

Much of the political change which took place in the 1990s and 2000s was forced from within, the result of either increasingly aggressive popular protest or "vanguard" movements claiming to represent the broad populace. A particular interpretation of Africa's political history in recent years holds that democracy has made advances – trembling, uncertain, but advances nonetheless.[8] In a number of countries, opposition parties have become both well-established and protected by law, and their activities regarded as legitimate by those in office. Civil liberties have likewise become more entrenched across the continent. The right to freedom of speech, of worship, and of faith, the existence of an independent, critical media, protection from arbitrary arrest and the right to fair trial: all of these are increasingly in evidence in Africa since the end of the 1980s. The OAU may have adopted the African Charter of Human and People's Rights as long ago as 1981, but it is only in recent years that such a professed concern for these rights has had any practical implications. This change must also be seen in global perspective: similar processes of democratization were witnessed in Latin America and in Eastern Europe from the early 1990s, and these zones offered inspiration across Africa to political activists increasingly weary and intolerant of regimes which had been in place since decolonization. Among the earliest examples of Africa's so-called "second wave of independence" in action was Benin, long under the Marxist dictatorship of Mathieu Kerekou who conceded electoral defeat in 1991 – yet in a remarkable turn of events which seemed to reinforce new-found Beninese democracy, elections in 1996 saw Kerekou returned to power, and his former rival Nicephore Soglo serving under him as prime minister. In Mali, a popular uprising overthrew the military dictatorship of Moussa Traore, and elections followed; indeed in the course of the 1990s democracy and a culture of constructive debate became well-established in Mali, despite its overwhelming poverty. The path to stable democracy has proved somewhat rockier in Zambia, where, after founding president Kenneth Kaunda oversaw the transition to multipartyism in the early 1990s, his successor Frederick Chiluba resorted to familiar authoritarian tactics to ensure his own position and the neutering of opposition. Yet Chiluba went quietly at the end of his term in 2002, and was in fact later investigated on corruption charges, of which he was acquitted.[9] Meanwhile, Botswana boasts a rather longer democratic pedigree. Here, since independence in 1966, there have been several robustly contested elections, followed by the peaceful retirements of several incumbents. Botswana is usually paraded as one of Africa's success stories in terms of democratic culture, not to mention its markedly low level of corruption.[10] In Ghana, multiparty politics had been restored in 1992, and here an exceptionally close election result in 2008 – which would have prompted violent protestations in neighboring Côte d'Ivoire, or in Nigeria – nonetheless led to the incumbent, John Kufuor, making way for John Atta Mills, who had won only half a percent more of the vote. The fact that this legitimate transfer of power took place on the eve of an oil bonanza made it all the more remarkable, and seemed to confirm Ghana's "arrival" as the region's stable democracy.[11]

Elsewhere, the promise of democratization was held out by an array of armed fronts which represented – or so it was believed – what might be termed "bush democracy," the march of the armed frontier in the name of popular liberation. Notably, several of the sources of Clinton's inspiration in 1998 – Meles Zenawi of Ethiopia, Isaias Afeworki of Eritrea, Yoweri Museveni of Uganda, Paul Kagame of Rwanda – were former guerrilla fighters. Increasingly well-armed and well-organized challenges to the state were taking place across the continent, and the outside world had to take account of these changes. In the Horn, guerrillas undoubtedly benefited from the collapse of the Soviet Union, but more importantly, they had fought themselves into a politically powerful position over many years and were able to drive home that advantage once Moscow sounded the retreat. Events in Ethiopia demonstrate this very well. By 1990, the Mengistu regime was faced with the enormous military success of the Tigrayan and Eritrean guerrilla forces in the north. Mengistu's benefactor, the Soviet Union, was pulling out, and the United States intervened at the last minute, facilitating Mengistu's flight from Ethiopia in 1991 (he was given sanctuary in Zimbabwe) and trying to use their influence to prevent Eritrea from declaring their independence from Ethiopia, despite the military success of the EPLF. The Eritrean response to the Americans was polite but firm: sovereignty had been won, and no amount of diplomatic pressure could alter the new military and political reality on the ground. In the meantime, the Ethiopian People's Revolutionary Democratic Front (EPRDF) seized control in Addis Ababa, purporting to represent all Ethiopians – not least the dispossessed and marginalized millions who had long been on the receiving end of Amhara imperialism. In the early 1990s, therefore, Ethiopia and Eritrea boasted new management – self-confident, apparently politically aware, and possessed of considerable energy.[12]

Similar patterns can be identified elsewhere. In South Africa, increasing foreign pressure had undoubtedly weakened the apartheid state, but it was popular internal revolt and the sociopolitical chaos that that had engendered which forced de Klerk to release Mandela, legalize the ANC, and set in motion the political changes which led to the first truly democratic election in the country's history. In Uganda, the National Resistance Army coalition under Museveni had seized power in 1986 after many years in "the bush," and embarked on a process of political and economic change.[13] "People power," or various manifestations of it, was making itself felt across the continent, as popular opposition erupted against the "dinosaurs" of the postcolonial era. Siad Barre of Somalia and Mobutu in Zaire were kicked out, although in these cases the results gave rather less cause for celebration. Somalia was torn apart by clan violence within months of Siad Barre's being ousted in 1991; it has scarcely functioned as a sovereign polity since then, though progress has been made and a national government, now based in Mogadishu rather than Nairobi, has started on the long road to reconstruction.[14] Zaire – which would soon become known as Democratic Republic of Congo (DRC) – likewise descended into violent mayhem both during, and immediately following, Mobutu's overthrow in 1997, although DRC survived as a (basically) functioning polity. The leader of the rebellion in the east of the country that brought about Mobutu's downfall, Laurent Kabila, did not last long – he was assassinated in 2001 – but his son and successor as president, Joseph Kabila, has remained in power since, although he is under pressure to step down at the time of writing.

In the case of Kenya, enormous internal pressure finally witnessed the departure of Daniel arap Moi in 2003 and the election of Mwai Kibaki, the irony being that Kibaki himself belonged to a generation not so much younger than Moi's. Yet within a few years, Kibaki himself was confronted by widespread protest, allegations of corruption, and ethnic violence. Following disputed elections in 2007, in which Kibaki claimed victory, violence erupted as Kalenjin and Luo groups attacked Kikuyu (Kibaki's own ethnic group) living outside their home areas. Hundreds died before a power-sharing coalition was put in place involving key opposition leaders. Kibaki did not contest the next election in 2013, which was won by Uhuru Kenyatta – son of Kenya's first president – but the validity of which was again challenged by opposition groups, led by Raila Odinga (also the son of a key independence-era figure). Odinga again ran for the presidency in 2017, and again, Kenyatta was declared the winner – at least temporarily, as the Supreme Court this time ordered a re-run of the election. Kenyatta won that, too, though in large part because of apparent voter apathy and the opposition's decision to boycott the poll. But in early 2018, Odinga and Kenyatta announced their determination to put their differences aside and work together in the national interest. Elections in Kenya have become tense, dramatic affairs, but the violence of 2007–8 has not been repeated; Kenya has in some ways come to be seen as a test-case for the strength (or otherwise) of African democracy, and as such, there would seem to be cause for cautious optimism, at least at the time of writing.[15] And then there was Nigeria, which experienced something of a democratic revival after the army relinquished its hold on power in 1998–9. The winner of the 1999 election – the first in sixteen years – was Olusegun Obasanjo, the former military ruler born again as a democrat and, indeed, a Christian.[16] The optimistic interpretation was that Nigeria – in spite of electoral violence, harassment of opponents, and lack of faith in the political process on the part of opposition parties – was nonetheless moving, haltingly, toward an acknowledgment of basic democratic rights. It was a rocky path – corruption and political bad faith became the hallmarks of those following Obasanjo as president, Umaru Yar'Adua (2007–10) and Goodluck Jonathan (2010–15) – though the election in 2015 of Muhammadu Buhari, former military strongman who had briefly led Nigeria in the mid-1980s, on an anti-corruption ticket seemed to indicate some progress.

As in Kenya, Nigeria continues to be crippled by corruption and electoral malpractice, but, as in Kenya, people *have* been able to vote, and human rights abuses are scrutinized to an unprecedented degree, both within and from outside. Of course, altogether less sanguine interpretations of Africa's recent political history are also possible. To begin with, do occasional elections, or even established electoral cycles, signify a deep-rooted democratic culture? The answer, it seems, is no, or at least not necessarily, and indeed elections – much trumpeted, and (pending their conduct, of course) producing approving noises from international observers – can be serious distractions from the real business of assessing the nature and direction of political culture, in particular accountability and plurality. Nigerian elections, for example, continue to be manipulated by those with access to the most cash, are concerned with deals and trade-offs between rivals, and are routinely marred by violence. In Côte d'Ivoire, elections in 2010 were supposed to be the crowning achievement of a fragile peace process after several years of civil war, but the incumbent and apparent loser, Laurent Gbagbo, simply refused to leave office – although he was compelled to, in the end, following French and UN support for opposition forces. Experiments in power-sharing in Kenya and Zimbabwe proved to be destabilizing and unworkable, and provided examples, perhaps, of what happens when outside pressure forces incompatible parties together in the desperate pursuit of "stability"; the greatest crime, it seems, is to be seen to be doing nothing.

Meanwhile, events in North Africa between 2010 and 2012 certainly demonstrated the power of mass protest, now facilitated in part by social media. Aging and arthritic dynastic systems in Tunisia and Egypt were overthrown by popular action, albeit in both cases because security forces were essentially sympathetic to the protestors' cause. Here, and across North Africa, a young population – unemployed, impoverished, and, often, overeducated – felt able to flex its considerable muscle like never before. Sheer desperation, and weariness with extraordinarily remote political elites, forced them onto the streets. But the gains of those heady months are not yet easily identifiable – least of all in Egypt, where authoritarianism has once again taken hold; or indeed in Libya, where Qaddafi's ouster revealed a deeply and violently divided country.[17]

Irresistible momentum: Nelson Mandela and F. W. de Klerk of South Africa. Source: RASHID LOMBARD/AFP/Getty Images.

We dealt in the previous chapter with the militarization of political culture, and noted how so far the democratic record of former guerrilla movements is not especially impressive – though they have often proven themselves to be both dexterous and resilient. In Ethiopia, ostensibly one of the more stable parliamentary democracies on the continent, the EPRDF government has long demonstrated a deep-rooted intolerance of genuine opposition, not least that associated with particular ethnicities in the center and south of the country.[18] Following the 2005 elections, notably, which were strongly contested by opposition parties – indeed the latter won a number of seats, and captured Addis Ababa itself – opposition groups were violently suppressed, and demonstrations on the streets were likewise brutally crushed. Key leaders were either arrested or fled into exile.[19] The opposition remained in disarray for many years: in 2010, the EPRDF swept the board in carefully controlled polls, winning an improbable 99 percent of seats. Even Meles Zenawi's admirers and supporters – the United States and the United Kingdom, especially – expressed discomfort at the incredible result, but accepted it in the final analysis. Leadership succession has been handled smoothly and peacefully – from Meles, following his death in 2012, to Hailemariam Desalegn, and from the latter to Abiy Ahmed in 2018 – but these were largely internal EPRDF matters, and reflected power struggles and compromises within the movement. Only after 2016–17 was there evidence that mounting popular unrest might force change – as when Hailemariam resigned following months of protests, and his successor Abiy Ahmed began to instigate some degree of political reform. In Uganda, successive elections were increasingly robustly contested, but Museveni still won comfortably, not least because the NRM had access to vast financial resources for campaigning and persuasion.[20] In Rwanda, Paul Kagame's RPF government tolerates no dissent from the government position, the specter of genocide lurking behind the rhetoric around the need for national unity.[21] Zimbabweans who in 2018 hoped for progressive change through the ballot box following the removal of Mugabe the previous year were disappointed, at least in the short term: the army clamped down hard on post-election protests by opposition supporters, and seemed determined to maintain ZANU-PF in power. In Sudan, a tense standoff continues at the time of writing between protestors and the military in the wake of Omar al-Bashir's ouster. Eritrea, however, is perhaps in a different league altogether. Here, a relatively liberal constitution was ratified by a nascent national assembly in the mid-1990s but never enacted. There have been no elections in Eritrea since independence in 1993, and in recent years political freedoms have been severely curtailed, while enormous political power and patronage is concentrated in the President's Office.[22]

The continent has been a patchwork of success and failure between the 1990s and the 2010s; much recent change has been ambiguous at best. That ambiguity is perhaps best encapsulated by South Africa, regarded by many as the great beacon for the rest of Africa in the 1990s. Mandela himself was lauded on a global stage, and for good reason: his message of reconciliation and magnanimity, and his vision of the multiracial and multicultural "rainbow nation," played a huge role in stabilizing the country in what were critical years after the mid-1990s. Yet the image of Mandela, aging as he was when he assumed the presidency, in many respects disguised the deep-rooted problems in South Africa, including the rampant poverty of the vast majority of black South Africans, the endemic violence in many of the cities – Johannesburg vied with Nairobi and Lagos as among the supposedly most violent urban centers in the world – and the chronic AIDS problem, toward which, at times, Mandela's successor Thabo Mbeki adopted an unhelpful stance. Considering the euphoria of 1994, the ANC was destined to disappoint popular expectations. While the worst excesses of white colonialism had been endured, the awful legacy of the vast inequity in economic and social opportunity persisted: the majority of South Africans remained mired in overwhelming poverty, from which its new leaders would be increasingly removed. During the presidencies of Thabo Mbeki (1999–2008) and Jacob Zuma (2009–2018), that gulf was ever more in evidence, and allegations of corruption and incompetence dogged the ANC. Internationally, South Africa was recognized as a genuine "middle power" in terms of economic capacity, and outside observers were wont to point to South Africa's "leadership potential" across the continent as a whole. Closer to home, however, the ANC's legitimacy was increasingly tested, and questioned.

More broadly, there is the question of the degree to which human rights and democracy can be considered "universal," and the extent to which they represent yet another Western invention superimposed upon a wholly different set of cultural and political systems. It might be seen as ironic, for example, that while colonial states failed to bequeath to their African subjects any kind of democratic legacy, the "developed" world has in recent years lamented the absence of democratic structures and respect for human rights in Africa. Perhaps, in fact, the individualism which underpins human rights in the West is "traditionally" lacking in African cultures – diverse though the latter are – and the wider community has historically been more important. This may be true, to some extent at least, of Islamic North Africa; in Islam, emphasis is placed on collective rather than individual rights, and therefore Western notions of rights and freedoms are arguably incompatible with the collective duties and responsibilities of the *umma*, the Islamic community. The best that can be said about the idea when applied south of the Sahara, however, is that it is a dangerous generalization: there is no single precolonial "African political culture," and systems characterized by "communalism," accountability, and popular participation in politics sat alongside those defined by despotic authority and the vertical exercise of violent power. Moreover, it might be assumed that in historically underpopulated regions, the importance of individual status and "contentment" within the extant order meant that "human rights" (loosely defined) were rather more organic across much of Africa than they were in areas where control of land was more significant. Of course, it might also work in reverse: low population density meant that state structures could only develop through violent authoritarianism. What is certainly true, nonetheless, is that in the late twentieth and early twenty-first centuries millions of Africans themselves embraced the concepts of "human rights" and democratic individualism with great vigor, spurred, at least in part, by the political failures of the postcolonial state. They were also connected – for better and for worse, and it is indeed both – via a range of social media and rapidly evolving communications technology to a putatively "global" community keenly aware of democratic entitlement. The mobilization of political protest has become both easier, and faster.

It is difficult to generalize, then, about what recent developments amount to. On one level, they need to be considered as only partly a matter of postcolonial struggle, and rather more the extension of a process of ongoing political reform dating to the nineteenth century – however incompatible that process may be, at times, with Western notions of what constitutes "progress." In more contemporary terms, however, one broad theme which seems applicable to much of the continent in the 1990s and 2000s is that of greater accountability among Africa's leaders, and governments having to act more responsibly and being unable to ride rough-shod over their peoples, or at least not to the same extent as has been the case in the deeper past. There has also been greater political consciousness among Africans themselves, for, although illiteracy and indeed abject poverty continue to restrict full participation in political processes, they are more than ever aware of their rights as citizens and of the opportunities which have been denied them.

Body and Mind

It is axiomatic that education has been at the root of many of Africa's recent challenges and is the key to its overcoming these challenges in the future. The provision of health care, too, remains a critical issue. In fact, after independence many African governments invested heavily in education as a means to national development, with primary school enrolment expanding dramatically between the 1960s and the early 2000s; there have been concerted efforts to expand the number of girls in school in particular, at least at primary level.[23] Yet success rates have been extremely variable across the continent, particularly in terms of literacy levels. In recent years, there have also been problems in terms of aging infrastructure, declining levels of government expenditure and quality of instruction; regional imbalances remain, with urban areas or those close to them, as ever, privileged over more remote rural districts. The gender gap is significant: rural girls are the most disadvantaged of national populations, and female illiteracy remains much higher than for boys. Sub-Saharan adult illiteracy generally is higher than for any other region in the world. There can be little doubt that the economic crisis with which Africa has struggled since the 1970s has led, in many places, to a remarkable drop in state funding for education, and this is as true of higher as it is of primary and secondary education. While university admissions have increased steadily, neither funding levels nor improvements in basic infrastructure have kept pace. For academic staff, too, the day-to-day issue of simply making ends meet has meant a steep decline in the research output of African universities, after the initial boom that many experienced in the 1960s. One way of offsetting a more general decline has been the expansion in "private" schools and universities since the 1990s, evident in a number of sub-Saharan capitals, although these have tended to privilege the already affluent.[24] North of the Sahara, governments have also invested heavily in schooling and universities, often with a view to replacing European models and cultures with curricula which underpin Islamic, Arabic-speaking identities. Yet here, too, there have been gender biases – families will endeavor to educate their sons at the expense of their daughters – while the economic pressures experienced south of the Sahara have likewise hindered state expenditure on education from primary through to tertiary north of the desert. Literacy levels remain low across North Africa. Nonetheless, the tradition of Islamic learning has offered a viable alternative, with primary schools opened by Muslim charities, and branches of Muslim education developing within universities. Often, these have proved effective in politicizing and radicalizing a new generation of North Africans, encouraging opposition both to Western culture and perceived hegemony, and to postcolonial governments seen to have failed to fulfill the expectations of independence. Indeed, a critical mass of relatively well-educated, but underemployed young people was one of the factors behind the uprisings across North Africa in 2011–12.

Education is, of course, a political weapon more broadly, and even a small increase in the proportion of the population which is literate can mean an increase in the number of people in a position to read newspapers, access the Internet – now a potent forum for political expression – and engage in political discourse more generally. Literacy in itself is not a precondition for political consciousness, but it certainly empowers, facilitating heightened aspirations and increasing the capacity for more cogent challenges to oppressive regimes. It is for this reason, indeed, that women – outside elites, at least – have gained much less in the way of access to political power and influence from independence than men. The attempts by some movements and governments to control education – often, ironically, under the banner of "raising political awareness," which usually means engendering support for particular ideological worldviews – indicate the degree to which ruling elites recognize the power of learning and indeed of scholarship. Universities such as Makerere in Uganda were long hotbeds of political debate and dissent; financial hardship and a desire to simply "get on" has increasingly undermined students' willingness to engage in (and their capacity for) political protest, but the activism evident among students in Addis Ababa, for example, as well as the Ethiopian government's response to it, demonstrates the power which they still have. Political activism is also the outcome, again, of widespread unemployment among graduates, notably in North Africa but elsewhere too.

Another prerequisite for social and economic growth is a population that is healthy, as well as one that is educated. We observed at the beginning of the book that Africa's history has been shaped to a very real degree by a uniquely harsh disease environment. Many of the same devastating diseases with which Africans struggled in 1800 hinder African development in the early twenty-first century: malaria and sleeping sickness remain prevalent, for example, while HIV/AIDS has become the latest affliction in a continent which also has to contend with other global maladies such as cholera and tuberculosis. In fact it is malaria, endemic in most regions of Africa, which remains the most crippling of these; even when it does not kill, it is severely debilitating, and literally sucks the lifeblood out of rural communities in particular, where economic capacity is devastated. Sleeping sickness, as we have seen in other contexts, has had a similar impact, despite programs during the colonial era and up to the 1960s to bring the disease under control, which were met with a certain amount of success in some areas. But by the 1990s and 2000s, there was evidence that sleeping sickness, spread in forest and woodland by the tsetse fly, was advancing again, and – as with malaria – has proved catastrophic in terms of rural communities, especially those dependent on the keeping of livestock.

Many of these diseases are indigenous to Africa and are products of various environments, such as the ubiquity of malaria-carrying mosquitoes in tropical climates, and the continued prevalence of these diseases is a reflection of the inability of states since independence to provide adequate and sustained healthcare to significant swathes of their populations. As with education, available budgets for health-care shrank in the late twentieth century, and facilities deteriorated, provision remains uneven, and trained personnel are in short supply – or, increasingly, have left the continent for better-paid jobs in the United States or Europe. Most African governments continue to focus on curative medicine rather than on public health and prevention more broadly. The donor community, often through NGOs, has been able to assist to some extent, and outside agencies – notably under the aegis of the World Health Organization – have played an ever greater role in attempts to eradicate certain diseases, by providing medicines and professional expertise. Yet diseases are also the result of abject poverty, of malnutrition, bad sanitation (particularly in cities), and contaminated water supply. Cholera, for example, of which epidemics remain common in Africa, is the product of dirty water or contaminated food, and its outbreak has been most common in the slum areas of cities. Again, economic failure can be seen to have been at the root of diseases which have disappeared from many other parts of the world.[25]

More than two-thirds of the world's cases of HIV/AIDS are in Africa, where around 35 million people have been infected since the early 1980s, when the first cases were identified. Of those, some 15 million people have died as a result of AIDS, a significant number – around 3 million – of whom have been children. AIDS orphans proliferate, and the death toll is expected to continue for the foreseeable future, particularly across Eastern and Southern Africa, which are the regions worst affected by the epidemic. The devastation caused by HIV/AIDS in human terms, and in terms of socioeconomic stability, is clear. The reasons for the epidemic are numerous. Again, poverty and migration are explanatory factors – in particular, people whose immune systems are weakened by HIV have become susceptible to tuberculosis – as is the high incidence of a range of sexually transmitted diseases, including syphilis. But the main mode of transmission has been through heterosexual intercourse, and it is certainly sexual behavior which has been the chief target of governments and NGOs involved in attempting to control the epidemic. In this context, some countries have enjoyed considerable success in terms of public awareness and, ultimately, in reducing HIV infection rates. Uganda is one such case; Senegal has also achieved some success. These countries have been overtaken by a cluster of nations in southern Africa – Namibia, Zimbabwe, Botswana, Swaziland, South Africa – in terms of high and/or climbing infection rates. In South Africa, the government has been markedly less efficient in dealing with the problem, in part because of a reluctance to admit its scale, and similar tardiness has been evident in Kenya in the recent past. The absence of adequate drugs to control the disease has long been the biggest obstacle to states' capacity to tackle the crisis, although definite progress has been made: in the last decade, the number of people receiving anti-retroviral treatment has increased dramatically, and the number of AIDS deaths has declined. Yet the true impact of HIV/AIDS across swathes of Africa may only become clear after many years.[26]

Life expectancy, sanitation, and health care, therefore, all lag behind in Africa compared to other zones of the world. But there are important gender and regional differences. North Africans enjoy better health provision than is found in most countries south of the Sahara; southern Africans suffer from lower life expectancy than people in the western, central, and eastern regions, stemming from a uniquely challenging set of socioeconomic circumstances rooted in the late nineteenth and twentieth centuries. Owing to the burdens of social roles and poverty, women and children remain the most vulnerable to sickness across the continent; and in rural areas, access to health care remains much more limited than in urban centers. At the same time, however, sustained action can produce results, especially when foreign assistance works in conjunction with local government programs. The availability of basic medicines and the establishment of immunization schemes, notably, have meant that infant mortality rates in sub-Saharan Africa have dropped dramatically since the 1960s, and that life expectancy has risen by several years. It is clear that even small investments in public health, whether at the local or the national level, can have a major impact.

Contemporary Economics: Assessing "Development" and "Growth"

Economic challenges remain among the most pressing for the continent in the early twenty-first century, and in many respects contemporary economic issues can be seen as extensions of those discussed throughout the book – not least Africa's commercial relations with the wider world, the management and maximization of available resources, the quest for mastery over nature. On these various fronts, Africa has experienced both significant change and marked continuity over the past two decades. The key narrative of the last decade or so has focused on "Africa Rising" – a narrative based largely on impressive annual GDP growth rates, and the foreign investment in the extractive industries and in infrastructure which has fuelled those growth rates. At the same time, for some, the "Africa Rising" trope is a somewhat sanguine interpretation of what is essentially a "new scramble" for the continent's resources, and there is no question that in terms of the economic "opening up" of Africa, we have been here before. Moreover, there is a significant difference between "growth" and "development," and this is something with which successive African governments (and their external partners) have wrestled for several decades.[27]

In many ways, of course, these developments have as their prelude the structural adjustment programmes of the 1980s and 1990s.[28] The core aims of these reforms, in keeping with the neoliberal agenda of the contemporary age, included addressing the problem of the swollen, inefficient, and unproductive public sector, and making the economic environment in Africa much more conducive to foreign investment. In other words, the state's involvement in the economy needed to be scaled back dramatically, and there needed to be large-scale privatisation. Over the medium term, the approach could be seen to be successful, at least according to certain measures: inward investment increased significantly, and GDP began to grow dramatically, albeit from a low baseline. Between 1980 and 2000, sub-Saharan Africa's GDP growth rate stood at an annual average of 2.4 percent; between the early 2000s and the early 2010s, it jumped to 5.7 percent. Some of the world's fastest growing economies were in Africa, including Angola, Nigeria, Ethiopia, Chad, Mozambique, and Rwanda. Such impressive growth was indeed linked to rapid privatization which attracted loans and investment from relatively "new" external actors, chiefly China, but also India and the Gulf States, who began to challenge the economic hegemony of the West for the first time in the modern era. China's seemingly insatiable desire for raw materials, in particular, drove much of Africa's growth.[29] Across the continent, infrastructure developed apace, cities grew, and there emerged a new urban middle class on the back of neoliberal economics.

So far, so good. However, there have been a number of more problematic consequences. Inward investment tended to follow natural resources: oil, most obviously (for example Angola, Nigeria, Gabon), precious metals and minerals (Congo, and many others), uranium (Niger, Gabon), bauxite (Guinea), iron (Liberia, Mauritania), and phosphates (Togo). This industrial surge was in some ways a positive development, considering that most nations had resorted to a heavy dependence on their agricultural sectors in the course of the 1970s and 1980s after the initial failure of early industrial projects. At that point only a handful states possessed relatively advanced industrial infrastructures, including Egypt, Botswana, and South Africa. But once again the most dynamic African economies were now developing around particular raw materials, with political as well as economic implications. In "oilocracies," for example, increasingly entrenched political elites were able to manage, and benefit directly from, the rush in foreign investment, which gave incumbent regimes resources to bolster their political bases while also funding comparatively lavish lifestyles. This has given rise to the notion of "state capitalism," in which economies are only quasi-privatized and are essentially under the control of political elites connected to the ruling party and its subsidiaries. In this hybrid "open-closed" economic system, the only real beneficiaries are the well-connected, and this in turn has given rise to rampant corruption, as in Uganda. Meanwhile, while there *were* tangible infrastructural benefits for Africa – new roads and port facilities, most obviously – it was clear that much of this economic boom was driven, as in the late nineteenth century, by the extraction of raw materials which were ultimately for the benefit for more developed economies overseas. Therefore, this looked, to some, like a "new scramble" for Africa – though this time without any of the moral and few of the political imperatives, for Africa's new trading partners, notably China and Qatar, do not attach the political conditions to economic engagement which Western partners historically have. At the same time, while a relatively prosperous middle class was everywhere in evidence, the reality was a growing chasm between haves and have-nots, and increasing levels of socio-economic inequity. It is worth remembering that structural adjustment involved a dramatic reduction in state expenditure in areas such as health and education.[30]

Such economic growth was also sustained by borrowing, and it is important to note that economic development has often been held back by the large external debt burdens with which most African countries are saddled. The debt crisis that had its roots in the period soon after independence has proved economically crippling across Africa. It has been a cumulative crisis, beginning with risky loans to fund ill-starred projects in the 1960s and 1970s, and leading to African governments taking out new loans whose sole purpose was to service old ones. Terms of trade grew ever less favourable, and prices for exports fell steadily in the first years of independence, which meant that African states lacked the revenue-raising power to finance themselves through mounting economic crisis. Africa's total debt in 1970 – to Western governments and banks as well as to the World Bank and the IMF – was $9 billion. By 1997, this had spiralled to $321 billion. Arrears had grown year by year; high interest rates meant that enormous chunks of debt went unpaid, compounded old debts, and led to states diverting ever larger proportions of GDP away from domestic spending to service the interest on loans. A growing campaign to cancel Africa's debt became the latest in a series of very public lobbies – beginning with the movement to abolish the slave trade in the late eighteenth century – aimed at the rejuvenation or salvation of a supposedly benighted continent. In 1996, even the World Bank and the IMF proposed debt relief (although not always full cancellation) for some of the world's poorest nations, the bulk of them in Africa. Following the 2005 meeting of G8 finance ministers at Gleneagles, it was announced that a number of countries classified as both "poor" and "indebted" would be eligible for debt relief – on condition that they could demonstrate progress on fighting corruption and implementing further structural adjustment programs. In some ways, it was a largely meaningless initiative, as many countries which had their debts written off were not actually paying them in any case. Still, it was an important development in its own way.[31]

However, in the wake of the global financial crisis of 2008, there was a boom in lending to low- and lower-middle income countries as lenders in the West sought to get around quantitative easing and low interest rates at home by charging higher interest rates to developing countries. The result has been a massive increase in the amounts of debt owned by African governments, and debt-to-GDP ratios have once again risen to worrying levels, often above 40 percent of GDP. This has escalated concerns at the time of writing that many African nations, even at the moment of impressive growth rates, are facing a potentially catastrophic debt crisis.

The problem of debt, of course, contains its own momentum, as new loans and aid packages are often required to cover the domestic financial shortfall. Western aid has long been necessary to African governments to pay for social services and infrastructure; it also gave the donor community unprecedented influence over the economic – and, by extension, political – strategies of otherwise sovereign states. Of course, the West had long used loans for political purposes: during the Cold War, funds had been channelled into the treasuries of governments regarded as Western allies in the global struggle against communism, including dictatorships in Nigeria and Zaire-Congo, while apartheid South Africa had also been able to rely on financial support from Western backers. Over the past twenty years or so, the donor community has been able to use aid to shape domestic policy; money has come with conditions attached, as we have seen, in the form of structural adjustment and liberalization. At the same time, across the continent, the nongovernmental organization (NGO) has been in the frontline of attempts to address poverty, work with the oppressed and marginalized, provide emergency relief in disaster areas, and empower communities through technical training and assistance. NGOs – in many areas, the most potent and visible manifestation of the "donor community" – have proliferated in recent years, and range from international to small-scale groups, professional, research-based or religious; a great many of these receive substantial proportions of their budgets from Western governments or the European Union. Many NGOs are in fact grassroots and indigenous organizations, often working in conjunction with external funding and technical bodies. A list of some of the better-known organizations would include Oxfam, Save the Children, CARE, the Salvation Army, Catholic Relief Services, and World Vision; the Red Cross and Médécins Sans Frontières are involved specifically in the provision of humanitarian assistance. The United Nations itself is perhaps the biggest player in the relief and aid industry, notably via the activities of UNICEF (concerned with children) and UNHCR (refugees). Many of these work in war zones or in areas recently traumatized by conflict, and whatever our assessment of their long-term value – or indeed the moral and cultural implications of their work – in the immediate term many represent the difference between life and death for countless communities. In turn, based on their field experience, NGOs are in a position to shape government policy and set development agendas at home. Their recent prominence at least in part stems from the economic orthodoxy that has seen a reduction in state-level activity: NGOs can fill gaps left by ineffective state provision, while the voluntary sector has been favored by Western governments eager to see their money spent more "efficiently."[32]

Debates about the efficacy and indeed rectitude of NGO work continue.[33] For some, they make a real difference in terms of empowerment and popular participation. Impressive grassroots work has been done across East Africa, for example. Their critics accuse them of, alternately, cynicism or naivety, and are skeptical about the claims made for deep-rooted, lasting change. NGOs have also been caught up in the politics of conflict – American food aid to southern Sudanese rebels was distributed via several Christian NGOs, as well as USAID, for example – while others have been seen as undermining African governments themselves and unwittingly or otherwise hindering the ability of the latter to act. Certainly, African states have sometimes had troubled relationships with NGOs, and nowhere more so than in Eritrea, where the government accuses them of profligacy, undermining national sovereignty, and duplicating the work it is already doing.

Nonetheless, millions of Africans continue to be exposed to the vagaries of climate and environment, a realm in which NGOs often do their most vital work. Democracy may have been fragile, but no more so than both food supply and climate in parts of the continent over the past half-century. Famine has been a recurrent problem, and indeed has become an enduring image of modern Africa to the outside world. By the 1970s many African states had become net importers of basic staples. In recent years, for example, the region of sub-Saharan Africa has seen greater population growth than any other part of the non-Western world, and yet it has also experienced the slowest growth in food production. In terms of famine causation, three broad categories of explanation can be identified. First, climate is clearly important: drought, flood, or other forms of unseasonal weather have all affected the supply of food. Rainfall was chronically low, for example, across the Sahel belt during the 1970s and 1980s. Beyond such natural phenomena, however, human agency becomes critical. The second explanation is that concerned with overpopulation – in its simplest, and classic, form, "too many people, not enough food." Most closely associated with early-nineteenth-century economist and demographer Thomas Malthus,[34] the thesis has been critiqued in recent years, but remains important in certain environmental circles; environmentalists have argued that too many people in a given area can be the cause of the declining fertility of the soil, and that the Sahel famines of the 1970s and 1980s, for example were caused by human communities having exceeded the carrying capacity of fragile lands. The third argument is more overtly political: it has been asserted that political decisions about food distribution, prices, and market regulation are factors in the occurrence of famine, and have a great impact on its severity. The explanation centers on the idea of "entitlement" and "access," namely the various ways in which people have the right and the ability to produce or purchase food. Entitlement varies according to social status, for example as well as geographical location; and in many famine situations, there is little or no decline in the actual volume of food available, but rather changes in access to it.[35]

Each of these explanations can be applied to Africa at different times in different places. It is also clear that war has been both the cause and the result of famine: it is no coincidence that many areas of armed conflict in recent years have also been those suffering drought or food shortage. Critics also identified the unresponsiveness of African governments, and what were interpreted as political decisions regarding the distribution of wealth, as well as urban-centric policies which denied resources to rural areas. Other factors include the lack of an adequate transport and communications infrastructure, and a dependence on cash crops for foreign exchange and a consequent neglect of subsistence food crops, both of which can be understood, at least partially, in terms of a colonial legacy. Nonetheless, during the colonial era, famine was a cause for concern for authorities: famines raised the threat of social disorder, but they also raised moral questions around the humanitarian aspects of colonial government. They also cost money. These were all good reasons for avoiding famine, and thus colonial administrations – in Asia as well as in Africa – sought to regulate economies through rigorous central planning and control, attempting to regulate the movement of foodstuffs, and encouraged the cultivation of drought-resistant "relief crops". This, combined with the authorities' willingness and ability to intervene when food shortage loomed, meant that, on balance, the colonial world was probably less prone to famine than it had been, though there are exceptions, mostly during wartime.[36]

Yet famine in postcolonial Africa has been connected with other factors. The movement of people has been hugely significant in the last few decades, for example. Forced migration as the result of prolonged conflict has greatly weakened the agrarian base of many regions, and persecution and violence have led to the mass movement of people in South Sudan, Ethiopia, and Congo. Refugee camps of staggering proportions have sprung up in troubled regions, some of these acquiring a permanence which bodes ill for the economic recovery of those areas. By the same token, there is something of a vicious circle in the movement of people from stricken countryside to urban center, and cities have become swollen with migrants whose departure from their homelands has further exacerbated rural decline. Again, the economic weakness of many African states is linked to a dependence upon the export earnings from a relatively narrow range of commodities; many of these commodities are agricultural, vulnerable to climatic changes as well as political upheaval. The "dual vulnerability" of a narrow export economy, and a dependence upon markets located, and economic decisions taken, in the "developed world," has diminished African states' room for maneuver. This is also linked to neoliberal economics, and Zimbabwe offers a salutary case study. For a number of years during the 1980s, the Zimbabwean government kept stores of grain as a reserve against famine, providing the country with basic food security, and enabling it to regulate the price of grain on the local market by adjusting supply, mostly with a view to keeping the price low. But the structural adjustment programs in place since the early 1990s – supported by the governments of the "developed world," the World Bank, and the IMF – argued for the ending of all policies in the so-called "Third World" which restricted market forces. The storage of grain in Zimbabwe was an example of the overmighty state in Africa, and was criticized as artificially suppressing the market, denying the farmer a fair price for his grain. Further, it was argued that the Zimbabwean government would earn useful foreign exchange by selling its grain stores on the open market, reflecting the basic belief that foreign reserves were preferable to grain stores. If famine threatened, the government could then use its foreign currency to purchase the required grain on the international market. Much of this was fine in theory. But in practice, it actually heightened Zimbabwe's vulnerability to famine, witness the situation in the 1990s as the country experienced a mounting crisis of food supply. The extent of a shortfall in food supply following inadequate rains does not become clear until people begin to move from the countryside into the urban centers in search of food aid, and with no grain reserves to release onto the market, the government was obliged to import food, a process which takes time. In the meantime, as the problem worsened, the government had to petition aid agencies for emergency relief, and the response was not always as fast as it might be.[37]

Even so, in recent years, individual African states have sought to put measures in place to offset the threat of famine. Ethiopia developed a system of early warnings; in Niger, measures for famine prevention – supported by Chinese funding – included the cultivation of crops such as rice which could be harvested, stored, and distributed in bad years. Often greater emphasis has been placed on localized, grassroots production; this has been the case in recent years in Ghana and Malawi, for example.

Overall, in economic terms, Africa is at a juncture which is both exciting and challenging. GDP growth has been impressive of late, but it has not necessarily meant "development," and even measuring economic performance is not straightforward.[38] "Growth" in general benefits many of the same kinds of elites – the entrepreneurial adventurers, whether political, economic, or military, of Africa's modern history – as it did in the nineteenth century. More broadly, however, poverty remains rife, and most African countries occupy the space which one economist has described as the "bottom billion"[39]. For millions of Africans, education remains a privilege and not a right, proper health care remains elusive, and access to capital a matter of birth. In each context, women are especially vulnerable. At the same time, the public treatment of Africa's manifold challenges in the West is often emotional and simplistic, especially in an age of fatigue around humanitarian crises. Politicians, like the missionaries of the nineteenth century, too often treat "Africa" as a concept, as a condition to be addressed, and as a screen onto which they can project the fundamental benevolence of Western liberalism and civilisation. Ultimately, the challenge, now as in the nineteenth century, lies in the distribution and reinvestment of the proceeds of commerce, especially as Africa's population grows in the decades ahead. Debates will continue over how growth can best be translated into development, and, hopefully, an important part of those debates will be a more sophisticated treatment of Africa's economic trajectory from a historical perspective.

Notes

1 For example, Padraig Carmody, *The New Scramble for Africa* (Cambridge, 2011).

2 For a range of perspectives on this, see for example S.M. Makinda, "Democracy and multiparty politics in Africa," *Journal of Modern African Studies*, 34: 4 (1996); C. Monga, "Civil society and democratisation in Francophone Africa," *Journal of Modern African Studies*, 33:3 (1995); C. Young, "The end of the post-colonial state in Africa? Reflections on changing African political dynamics," *African Affairs*, 103: 410 (2004); J.-F. Bayart, S. Ellis & B. Hibou, *The Criminalisation of the State in Africa* (Oxford, 1999).

3 Romeo Dallaire, *Shake Hands With the Devil: The Failure of Humanity in Rwanda* (London, 2004); Linda Melvern & Paul Williams, "Briannia waived the rules: the Major government and the 1994 Rwandan genocide," *African Affairs*, 103: 410 (2004).

4 William Shawcross, *Deliver Us From Evil: Warlords and Peacekeepers in a World of Endless Conflict* (London, 2000).

5 D. Volman, "Africa and the new world order," *Journal of Modern African Studies*, 31:1 (1993).

6 Cheikh Anta Diop, *Towards the African Renaissance: Essays on African culture and development, 1946-1960* (London, 1996); Washington A. J. Okumu, *The African Renaissance: History, Significance, and Strategy* (Trenton NJ, 2002).

7 Ken Menkhaus, "Somalia and Somaliland: terrorism, political Islam, and state collapse," in Rotberg (ed.), *Battling Terrorism*; Ken Menkhaus, "The crisis in Somalia: tragedy in five acts," *African Affairs*, 106:424 (2007).

8 Nic Cheeseman, *Democracy in Africa: Successes, Failures, and the Struggle for Political Reform* (Cambridge, 2015).

9 For a survey of democratic progress (or otherwise), see Leonardo A. Villalon & Peter VonDoepp (eds.), *The Fate of Africa's Democratic Experiments: Elites and Institutions* (Bloomington & Indianapolis, 2005).

10 For a more guarded analysis, see Kenneth Good, "Enduring elite democracy in Botswana," *Democratization*, 6:1 (1999).

11 Lindsay Whitfield, ""Change for a better Ghana": party competition, institutionalisation, and alternation in Ghana's 2008 elections," *African Affairs*, 108:433 (2009).

12 Woodward, *Horn of Africa*, chaps. 4 & 5.

13 A. Omara-Utunnu, "The struggle for democracy in Uganda," *Journal of Modern African Studies*, 30:3 (1992).

14 Mary Harper, *Getting Somalia Wrong? Faith, War and Hope in a Shattered State* (London, 2012).

15 For analysis of the events of 2007–8, see Nic Cheeseman & Dan Branch (eds.), "Special Issue: Election Fever: Kenya's Crisis," *Journal of Eastern African Studies*, 2:2 (2008).

16 John Iliffe, *Obasanjo, Nigeria, and the World* (Woodbridge, 2011); see also J. Ihonvbere, "Are things falling apart? The military and the crisis of democratisation in Nigeria," *Journal of Modern African Studies*, 34:2 (1996).

17 There is now a burgeoning body of literature on the "Arab Spring," as it was popularly labelled by Western media: see for example Robert F. Worth, *A Rage for Order: the Middle East in Turmoil, from Tahrir Square to ISIS* (New York, 2016); and Mark L. Haas & David W. Lesch (eds.), *The Arab Spring: The Hope and Reality of the Uprisings* (New York & London, 2018).

18 Jon Abbink & Tobias Hagmann (eds.), "Special Issue: Ethiopia's Revolutionary Democracy, 1991–2011," *Journal of Eastern African Studies*, 5:4 (2011).

19 J. Abbink, "Discomfiture of democracy? The 2005 election crisis in Ethiopia and its aftermath," *African Affairs*, 105:419 (2006).

20 Aili Mari Tripp, *Museveni's Uganda: Paradoxes of Power in a Hybrid Regime* (Boulder CO, 2010); Rita Abrahamsen & Gerald Bareebe, "Uganda's 2016 elections: not even faking it anymore," *African Affairs*, 115:461 (2016).

21 Filip Reyntjens, "Post-1994 politics in Rwanda: problematizing 'liberation' and 'democratization'," *Third World Quarterly*, 27:6 (2006).

22 Gaim Kibreab, *Eritrea: A Dream Deferred* (Woodbridge, 2009).

23 For background and context, see for example The World Bank, *Education in Sub-Saharan Africa* (Washington, 1988).

24 For a discussion in the Ugandan context, see Mahmood Mamdani, *Scholars in the Marketplace: The Dilemmas of Neo-liberal Reform at Makerere University, 1989–2005* (Kampala, 2007).

25 P. Gibbon, "The World Bank and African poverty, 1973–1991," *Journal of Modern African Studies*, 30:2 (1992).

26 T. Barnett & P. Blaikie, *AIDS in Africa* (London, 1992); J. Iliffe, *The African AIDS Epidemic: A History* (Oxford, 2006).

27 Ian Taylor, *Africa Rising? BRICS – Diversifying Dependency* (Woodbridge, 2014); Carmody, *New Scramble*.

28 For early assessments, see T.M. Shaw, "Reformism, revisionism and radicalism in African political economy during the 1990s," *Journal of Modern African Studies*, 29:2 (1991); J.B. Riddell, "Things fall apart again: structural adjustment programmes in sub-Saharan Africa," *Journal of Modern African Studies*, 30:1 (1992); D. Plank, "Aid, debt, and the end of sovereignty: Mozambique and its donors," *Journal of Modern African Studies*, 31:3 (1993).

29 Chris Alden, *China in Africa* (New York, 2007); Howard W. French, *China's Second Continent: How A Million Migrants are Building A New Empire in Africa* (New York, 2014).

30 See for example Graham Harrison, *Neoliberal Africa: The Impact of Global Social Engineering* (London & New York, 2010).

31 Trevor W. Parfitt & Stephen P. Riley, *The African Debt Crisis* (London, 2010); Mark R. Thomas & Marcelo M. Giugale, "African debt and debt relief," in Celestin Monga & Justin Yifu Lin (eds.), *The Oxford Handbook of Africa and Economics: Vol 2: Policies and Practices* (Oxford, 2015).

32 Robert Pinkney, *NGOs, Africa, and the Global Order* (London, 2009); Jennifer N. Brass, *Allies or Adversaries: NGOs and the State in Africa* (Cambridge, 2016).

33 Hans Holmen, *Snakes in Paradise: NGOs and the Aid Industry in Africa* (Boulder CO, 2009).

34 T.R. Malthus, *An Essay on the Principle of Population* (Oxford, 1993; 1st pub. 1798).

35 Amartya Sen, *Poverty and Famines: An Essay on Entitlement and Deprivation* (Oxford, 1981).

36 David Arnold, *Famine: Social Crisis and Historical Change* (Oxford, 1988); J. Dreze & A. Sen (eds.), *The Political Economy of Hunger*, 3 vols. (Oxford, 1990–91).

37 For a wide-ranging critique of the approach to food shortage, see Alex de Waal, *Famine Crimes: Politics and the Disaster Relief Industry in Africa* (London, 1997); see also Michael Lofchie, "Political and economic origins of African hunger," *Journal of Modern African Studies*, 13:4 (1975).

38 Morten Jerven, *Poor Numbers: How We are Misled by African Development Statistics and What to do About It* (Ithaca & London, 2013).

39 Collier, *The Bottom Billion*.

Further Reading

General Histories, and Regional and Thematic Surveys

Abun-Nasr, J. (1971). *A History of the Maghrib*. Cambridge.

Ajayi, J.F.A. and Crowder, M. (eds.) (1985–7). *History of West Africa*, vol. 2. Harlow.

Anderson, D.M. and Rathbone, R. (eds.) (2000). *Africa's Urban Past*. Oxford.

Austen, R. (1987). *African Economic History: Internal Development and External Dependency*. London.

Barber, K. (2006). *Africa's Hidden Histories: Everyday Literacy and Making the Self*. Bloomington & Indianapolis.

Bayart, J.-F. (1993). *The State in Africa*. London.

Birmingham, D. and Martin, P. (eds.) (1983). *History of Central Africa*, vol. 2. London.

Boehmer, E. (ed.) (1998). *Empire Writing: An Anthology of Colonial Literature 1870–1918*. Oxford.

Chabal, P. and Daloz, J.-P. (1999). *Africa Works: Disorder as Political Instrument*. Oxford.

Clapham, C. (1996). *Africa and the International System: The Politics of State Survival*. Cambridge.

Clapham, C. (ed.) (1998). *African Guerrillas*. Oxford.

Clayton, A. (1999). *Frontiersmen: Warfare in Africa since 1950*. London.

Cooper, F. (2002). *Africa Since 1940: The Past of the Present*. Cambridge.

Curtin, P.D. (1964). *The Image of Africa: British Ideas and Action 1780–1850*, vol. 2. Madison, WI.

Curtin, P., Feierman, S., Thompson, L., and Vansina, J. (1978). *African History*. London and New York.

Davidson, B. (1992). *The Black Man's Burden: Africa and the Curse of the Nation-State*. London.

Decalo, S. (1990). *Coups and Army Rule in Africa: Motivations and Constraints*. New Haven, CT.

Ellis, S. and Ter Haar, G. (2004). *Worlds of Power: Religious Thought and Political Practice in Africa*. London.

Falola, T. and Jennings, C. (eds.) (2002). *Africanizing Knowledge: African Studies Across the Disciplines*. New Brunswick, NJ.

Fisher, A.G.B. and Fisher, H.J. (1970). *Slavery and Muslim Society in Africa: The Institution in Saharan and Sudanic Africa, and the Trans-Saharan Trade*. London.

Fleish, A. and Stephens, R. (eds.) (2016). *Doing Conceptual History in Africa*. New York & Oxford.

A History of Modern Africa: 1800 to the Present, Third Edition. Richard J. Reid.

Freund, B. (2007). *The African City: A History*. Cambridge.

Gann, L.H. and Duignan, P. (eds.) (1969–75). *Colonialism in Africa, 1870–1960*, vol. 1–2, 4–5. Cambridge and London.

Gifford, P. and Louis, W.R. (eds.) (1982). *The Transfer of Power in Africa: Decolonisation, 1940–1960*. London.

Goody, J. (1971). *Technology, Tradition and the State in Africa*. London.

Gray, R. and Birmingham, D. (eds.) (1970). *Pre-Colonial African Trade*. London.

Gutteridge, W. (1975). *Military Regimes in Africa*. London.

Hamilton, C., Mbenga, B.K., and Ross, R. (eds.) (2010). *The Cambridge History of South Africa: Vol 1, from Early Times to 1885*. Cambridge.

Hargreaves, J.D. (1996). *Decolonisation in Africa*. London.

Harlow, V. and Chilver, E.M. (eds.) (1965). *History of East Africa*, vol. II. Oxford.

Hastings, A. (1994). *The Church in Africa, 1450–1950*. Oxford.

Herbst, J. (2000). *States and Power in Africa: Comparative Lessons in Authority and Control*. Princeton, NJ.

Holland, R.F. (1985). *European Decolonization, 1918–1981: An Introductory Survey*. Basingstoke.

Hopkins, A.G. (1973). *An Economic History of West Africa*. Harlow.

Iliffe, J. (1983). *The Emergence of African Capitalism*. London.

Iliffe, J. (1987). *The African Poor: A History*. Cambridge.

Iliffe, J. (2007). *Africans: The History of a Continent*. Cambridge.

Isichei, E. (1997). *A History of African Societies to 1870*. Cambridge.

Ki-Zerbo, J., Mokhtar, G., Hrbek, I. et al. (1981–93). *UNESCO General History of Africa*, vol. 8. London.

Kopytoff, I. (ed.) (1987). *The African Frontier: The Reproduction of Traditional African Societies*. Bloomington & Indianapolis.

Laroui, A. (1970). *The History of the Maghrib*. Princeton NJ.

Levtzion, N. and Pouwels, R. (eds.) (2000). *The History of Islam in Africa*. Oxford.

Lovejoy, P. (2012). *Transformations in Slavery: A History of Slavery in Africa*. Cambridge: 1st pub. 1983.

Low, D.A. and Smith, A. (eds.) (1976). *History of East Africa*, vol. 3. Oxford.

Magali, M. (1984). *North Africa 1800–1900: A Survey from the Nile Valley to the Atlantic*. London and New York.

Manning, P. (1998). *Francophone Sub-Saharan Africa, 1880–1995*. Cambridge.

Munro, J.F. (1976). *Africa and the International Economy 1800–1960: An Introduction to the Economic History of Africa South of the Sahara*. London.

Nugent, P. (2004). *Africa since Independence: A Comparative History*. Basingstoke.

Oliver, R. and Fage, J. (1962). *A Short History of Africa*. London.

Oliver, R. and Fage, J. (eds.) (1975–86). *Cambridge History of Africa*, vol. 8. Cambridge.

Oliver, R. and Mathew, G. (eds.) (1963). *History of East Africa*, vol. I. Oxford.

Parker, J. and Rathbone, R. (2007). *African History: A Very Short Introduction*. Oxford.

Parker, J. and Reid, R.J. (eds.) (2013). *The Oxford Handbook of Modern African History*. Oxford.

Peterson, D. and Macola, G. (eds.) (2009). *Recasting the Past: History Writing and Political Work in Modern Africa*. Athens OH.

Philips, J.E. (ed.) (2005). *Writing African History*. Rochester NY.

Ranger, T.O. (ed.) (1968). *Emerging Themes of African History*. Nairobi.

Reid, R.J. (2012). *Warfare in African History*. New York.

Reno, W. (2011). *Warfare in Independent Africa*. New York.

Robinson, D. (2004). *Muslim Societies in African History*. Cambridge.
Ross, R., Mager, A.K., and Nasson, B. (eds.) (2011). *The Cambridge History of South Africa: Vol 2, 1885-1994*. Cambridge.
Taylor, I. and Williams, P. (2004). *Africa in International Politics: External Involvement on the Continent*. London & New York.
Thompson, L. and Wilson, M. (eds.) (1969–71). *The Oxford History of South Africa*, vol. 2. Oxford.
Trimingham, J.S. (1980). *The Influence of Islam upon Africa*. London.
Valensi, L. (1977). *On the Eve of Colonialism: North Africa before the French Conquest*. London.

Index

References to Notes are indicated by the page number followed by 'n' and the Note number.

08/01/2022